D0538639

HOLT

American Government

CONTENT REVIEWERS

Andrew DiNitto, Ph.D
State University of New York—Empire State College and Fulton-Montgomery Community College
American government

Scott Hays, Ph.D.
Southern Illinois University at Carbondale
State government, political behavior

Eloise Malone, Ph.D.
United States Naval Academy
American government

Paula D. McClain, Ph.D.
University of Virginia
American government, public policy

Robert Miewald, Ph.D.
University of Nebraska—Lincoln
Public administration, executive branch

Edward G. Moore, Ph.D.
University of Texas at Brownsville
American government

Dario Moreno, Ph.D.
Florida International University
Comparative politics, civil rights

David Nichols, Ph.D.
Montclair State University
Executive branch, constitutional law

Mary Alice Nye, Ph.D.
University of North Texas
U.S. political system, legislative and executive branches

Mitchell Rice, Ph.D.
Texas A&M University
American government, public administration

EDUCATIONAL CONTRIBUTOR

Denny Schillings
Homewood-Flossmoor High School
Flossmoor, Illinois

EDUCATIONAL REVIEWERS

Rusty Benson
Ponca City High School
Ponca City, Oklahoma

Randy Boal
La Canada High School
La Canada, California

Mackie Brown
Stephens County High School
Toccoa, Georgia

Gayla Harris
Redlands Senior High School
Redlands, California

Randy McClendon
Enid High School
Enid, Oklahoma

Patricia Runeari
Oswego High School
Oswego, New York

FIELD TEST TEACHERS

Mackie Brown
Stephens County High School
Toccoa, Georgia

Kimberly Kennedy Calahan
McAllen High School
McAllen, Texas

Richard Carlson
Monte Vista High School
Spring Valley, California

James M. Freeman
Dowagiac Union High School
Dowagiac, Michigan

Robert J. Holub
Western Albemarle High School
Crozet, Virginia

Janet Landfried
Redlands Senior High School
Redlands, California

Randy McClendon
Enid Senior High School
Enid, Oklahoma

Claudia Turner
Prattville High School
Prattville, Alabama

Sue Wallace
Redlands Senior High School
Redlands, California

HOLT

American Government

S TEVEN K ELMAN

HOLT, RINEHART AND **WINSTON**
Harcourt Brace & Company

Austin • New York • Orlando • Atlanta • San Francisco • Boston • Dallas • Toronto • London

About the Author

Steven Kelman is Weatherhead Professor of Public Management at Harvard University, John F. Kennedy School of Government. He received a bachelor's degree *summa cum laude* from Harvard College and received his doctoral degree in government from Harvard University.

Kelman's research has focused on the behavior and management of government agencies, on environmental policies, and on comparative government. He has written four books on these topics, as well as numerous articles and essays.

Kelman has served two periods of government service, including one as Associate Director for Management Planning in the Bureau of Consumer Protection of the Federal Trade Commission. He has also served on the Board of Editors of the *Journal of Public Administration Research and Theory,* the Editorial Board of *The American Prospect,* and the Scientific Advisory Board of the Volvo Research Foundation. In 1995 he was elected a Fellow of the National Academy of Public Administration.

Executive Editor

Sue Miller

Managing Editor

Jim Eckel

Editorial Staff

Diana Holman Walker, Senior Editor
Holly Hammett Norman, Project Editor
Anne Cannon, Associate Editor
Anthony Pozeck, Editor
Tracy C. Wilson, Editor
Kevin N. Christensen, Associate Editor
Bob Fullilove, Editor
Larry A. Cook, Assistant Editor

Nancy Katapodis Hicks, Copy Editor
Joseph S. Schofield IV, Copy Editor
Carmen Saegert, Administrative Assistant

Editorial Permissions

Jan Harrington

Book Design

Diane Motz, Art Director
Candace Moore

Image Services

Greg Geisler, Art Director
Elaine Tate
Linda Richey

Photo Research

Peggy Cooper, Photo Research Manager
Bob McClellan
Terry Janecek

Cover Design

The Quarasan Group, Inc.

New Media Design

Carey Smith, Design Manager

New Media

Randy Merriman, Vice President, New Media
Ken Whiteside, Senior Technology Projects Editor

Production

Gene Rumann, Production Manager
Rosa Mayo Degollado, Production Coordinator
Leanna Ford, Production Assistant

Media Production

Kim Anderson
Belinda Barboza
Nancy Hargis

Manufacturing

Jenine Street

Copyright © 1999 by Holt, Rinehart and Winston

All rights reserved. No part of this publication may be reproduced or transmitted in any form or by any means, electronic or mechanical, including photocopy, recording, or any information storage and retrieval system, without permission in writing from the publisher.

Requests for permission to make copies of any part of the work should be mailed to the following address: Permissions Department, Holt, Rinehart and Winston, 1120 South Capital of Texas Highway, Austin, Texas 78746-6487.

For acknowledgments, see page 617, which is an extension of the copyright page.

Printed in the United States of America

ISBN 0-03-050583-6

4 5 6 7 8 9 032 00 99

HOLT

American Government

CONTENTS

UNIT 1

⋯⋯▶ Foundations of Government xxxviii

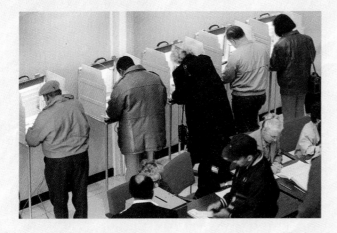

Chapter 3

THE U.S. CONSTITUTION 46

Chapter 4

FEDERALISM 66

The Granger Collection, New York

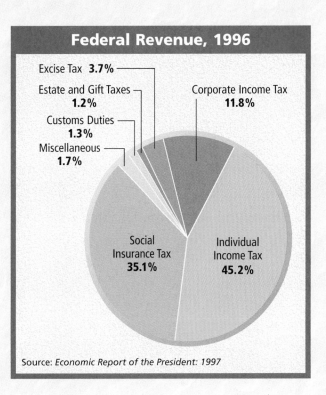

Federal Revenue, 1996

Excise Tax **3.7%**

Estate and Gift Taxes **1.2%**

Customs Duties **1.3%**

Miscellaneous **1.7%**

Corporate Income Tax **11.8%**

Social Insurance Tax **35.1%**

Individual Income Tax **45.2%**

Source: *Economic Report of the President: 1997*

UNIT 4

......➤ The Judicial Branch 246

Chapter 12

THE U.S.
LEGAL SYSTEM   270

UNIT 5

Rights and Responsibilities 294

Chapter 13

FUNDAMENTAL FREEDOMS 296

Chapter 14

ASSURING INDIVIDUAL
RIGHTS   318

UNIT 6

The U.S. Political System 364

Chapter 16

PUBLIC OPINION 366

UNIT 7

⋯⋯▸ State and Local Government 458

Chapter 20

STATE GOVERNMENT 460

Chapter 21

LOCAL GOVERNMENT 480

Features

Case Studies

Careers in Government

Comparing Governments

Citizenship in Action

Linking Government to Other Curricula

Charts and Graphs

Consumer Price Indexes, 1986–1996

Source: *Bureau of Labor Statistics, U.S. Department of Labor*

Maps

Reference

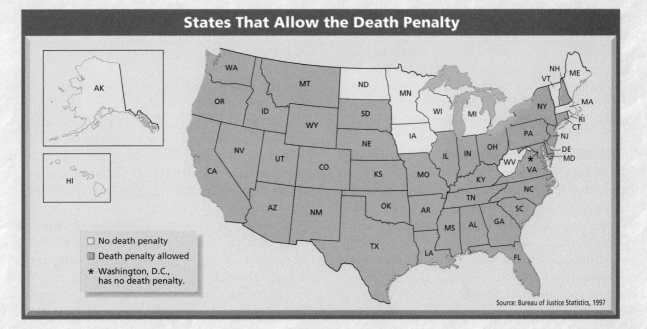

States That Allow the Death Penalty

☐ No death penalty
▨ Death penalty allowed
★ Washington, D.C., has no death penalty.

Source: Bureau of Justice Statistics, 1997

THEMES IN AMERICAN GOVERNMENT

Holt American Government examines the way in which government in the United States is organized and the impact that many aspects of government have on the lives of citizens. From this study of government emerges a series of themes: Political Foundations, Principles of Democracy, Constitutional Government, Political Processes, World Affairs, Citizenship, and Public Good. These themes provide a basis for defining and analyzing the U.S. political system and its effectiveness in fulfilling the needs of the public.

Political Foundations In understanding how the U.S. political system is structured, it is important to understand the connection between historical events and the framing of the Constitution. Many factors influenced the values and beliefs of the framers of the Constitution. These values and beliefs have an enduring influence through the key documents on which the U.S. political system is based.

Principles of Democracy Democratic systems of government are established to serve all of the people and to protect such democratic values as individual liberty, political representation, freedom of speech, and freedom of religion. Throughout the nation's history, changing political, economic, and social conditions have, in turn, led Americans to new interpretations of these basic democratic values. Furthermore, because of the overlapping nature of these principles, citizens, legislators, and the courts have struggled with the issue of how best to legislate for the protection of these rights. Government plays an important role in attempting to resolve conflicts over these principles.

Constitutional Government A constitution establishes regulations that strive to benefit all people in a society and to ensure that government promotes the good of society as a whole rather than that of a few individuals. In order to prevent one person or group from becoming too powerful, a constitution outlines the division of powers and responsibilities among several branches of government. A constitution also limits the power of the government and the people so that all can live in an orderly, secure environment, where basic freedoms and liberties are protected.

Political Processes The needs and desires of the citizens of the United States change. The political system must be flexible enough to meet the country's changing needs. Institutions such as political parties, elections, and public and private associations allow citizens to monitor and influence laws and the officials who write the laws.

World Affairs Thousands of governments exist around the world. The world, however, has no political system to establish relationships and to regulate interactions between countries. Throughout history, governments have used a variety of different methods to build relationships and to solve conflicts. With the development of technology that makes long-distance communication easier, international relations have become an essential role of government. Governments must choose how best to maintain foreign relationships.

Citizenship Citizens play a vital role in democratic systems of government. They are members of a self-governing community that depends upon the participation of the public to provide security and necessary services. Citizens are responsible for ensuring that government serves its purpose of protecting the fundamental rights of all people and promoting the shared good of the public.

Public Good Democratic government systems are organized to serve the needs of the people of the nation as a whole. What is good for one person or a small group may not serve the interests of the entire nation. Promoting the public good, however, also requires that government protect the rights of the minority and thus balance the needs of all people.

Sometimes, however, government does not promote the good of the people as a whole. Inefficiency, corruption, poor organization, lack of money, and changes in the needs of the people are all elements that contribute to governments' inability do what is best for the country as a whole.

Throughout *Holt American Government*, you are asked to think critically about the events and issues that have both shaped the U.S. political system and affected its place in the global community. Critical thinking is the reasoned judgment of information and ideas. People who think critically study information to determine its accuracy. They evaluate arguments and analyze conclusions before accepting their validity. Critical thinkers are able to recognize and define problems and develop strategies for resolving them.

The development of critical thinking skills is essential to effective citizenship. Such skills empower you to exercise your civic rights and responsibilities. For example, critical thinking skills enable you to judge the messages of candidates for political office and to evaluate news reports.

Helping you develop critical thinking skills is an important tool of *Holt American Government*. Using the following 14 critical thinking skills will help you better understand the forces behind political development. Additional skills strategies can be found in the Skills Handbook, which begins on page xxiv.

U.S. presidential campaign buttons.

1 **Recognizing point of view** involves identifying the factors that color the outlook of a person or group. Someone's point of view includes beliefs and attitudes that are shaped by factors such as age, sex, religion, race, and economic status. This critical thinking skill helps us examine why people see things as they do and reinforces the realization that people's views may change over time, or with a change in circumstances. A point of view that is highly personal or based on unreasoned judgment is said to be *biased*.

2 **Comparing and contrasting** involves examining events, situations, or points of view for their similarities and differences. *Comparing* focuses on both similarities and differences. Contrasting focuses only on differences. For example, by comparing democratic and nondemocratic political systems you might note that although both systems maintain different power structures, they are each established to keep order in society. By contrasting, you might note that in a democratic system the citizens are the ultimate authority in determining how the government is run. In a nondemocratic system, royal or military leaders may hold all governing power.

3 **Identifying cause and effect** is part of interpreting the relationships between political events. A *cause* is any action that leads to an event; the outcome of that action is an *effect*. Important events may have multiple causes and effects. For instance, a lack of unity among the states, combined with the need for a national defense, led political leaders to draft the Articles of Confederation. In turn, weaknesses in the Articles caused political leaders to plan for a revision, which led to the writing of the Constitution,

William Gropper's Senate Hearing *is a dramatic example of U.S. political art.*

which in turn led to a federal system of government. (For a more detailed discussion of Identifying Cause and Effect, see page xxv.)

4 **Analyzing** is the process of breaking something down into its parts and examining the relationships among them. By analyzing the parts, you can better understand the whole. For example, to analyze the U.S. judicial system, you might list all the levels of courts, as well as the responsibilities of each type of court.

5 **Assessing consequences** means studying an action, event, or trend to predict or determine its long-term effects and to judge its desirability. *Consequences* are effects that are indirect or unintended. They may appear long after the event that led to them. One could, for example, assess the consequences of the Supreme Court's ruling in *Marbury* v. *Madison*.

6 **Distinguishing fact from opinion** means separating the facts about something from what people say about it. A *fact* can be proved or observed; an *opinion*, on the other hand, is a personal belief or conclusion. Thus, in an argument, opinions do not carry as much weight as facts, although some opinions can be supported by facts. One often hears facts and opinions mixed in conversations—in advertising, political debate,

and television news programs. (For a more detailed discussion of Distinguishing Fact from Opinion, see page xxvi.)

7 **Identifying values** involves recognizing the core beliefs held by a person or group. *Values* are more deeply held than opinions and are less likely to change. Values commonly concern matters of right and wrong and may be viewed as desirable in and of themselves. In U.S. society, for example, individual freedom is highly valued, and many laws have been established to protect individual freedoms.

8 **Hypothesizing** is forming a possible explanation for an event, a situation, or a problem. A *hypothesis* is not a proven fact. Rather, it is an educated guess based on available evidence and tested against new evidence. A political scientist, for example, may hypothesize about the motives behind an interest group's financial donation to a political candidate's campaign. The political scientist would gather evidence supporting his or her hypothesis and challenge any other explanations of the group's motives.

9 **Synthesizing** involves combining information and ideas from several sources to gain a new understanding of a topic or an event.

Much of the narrative writing in this textbook is based on synthesis. *Holt American Government* pulls data together from many sources into a picture of the development of political systems in our country and others. Synthesizing the events of the Constitutional Convention, for example, might involve studying letters and journals, newspaper articles written in 1787, and legal documents, including the Constitution.

10 Problem solving is the process of reviewing a situation, determining its troublesome elements, and then making recommendations for improving or correcting them. Before generating a solution, however, the problem must be identified and stated. For instance, in seeking a solution to the problems caused by government overspending, you might state the issue in terms of the relationship between a large national debt and rising taxes. You would then propose and evaluate possible courses of action, select the one you think is best, and give the reasons for your choice.

11 Evaluating involves assessing the significance or overall importance of something, such as the success of a foreign policy or the influence of a president on society. You should base your judgment on standards that others will understand and are likely to think are important. To evaluate trade relations after the adoption of the North American Free Trade Agreement (NAFTA), for example, you might examine attitudes toward the condition of the U.S., Canadian, and Mexican economies. You also would assess the improvement, or lack of substantive improvement, in the economies of and political relationships among these countries.

12 Taking a stand means identifying an issue, deciding what you think about it, and persuasively expressing your position on it. Your stand should be based on specific information. In taking a stand, even on a controversial issue such as gun control, state your position clearly and give reasons to support it.

13 Studying contemporary issues and problems involves identifying a current topic frequently discussed in the media, reading several sources of information on the topic, and evaluating that information. Finding space for all the trash people create, for example, is a contemporary problem with which you may be familiar. You might feel the effects of it through recycling programs in your community or school. By studying this issue, you will be able to understand the cause of excess waste and evaluate solutions others have developed to ease the problem.

14 Applying a model involves depicting something in its ideal state and evaluating how well a specific example matches the ideal. A model of an ideal democratic system, for example, might be applied to the political system of Mexico. By evaluating how well each element of Mexico's political system matches each element of your model, you can determine whether Mexico has a democratic system of government or how closely it matches an ideal system.

Newspapers are an excellent source of information about contemporary issues in government and politics.

*G*overnment is entwined in almost every aspect of our daily lives. To grasp this relationship, you will need to understand the forces that shape government. The skills covered in this handbook will enable you to analyze government systems and policies. The handbook will also introduce you to key sources of government information, which can be presented in a variety of forms. Your understanding and appreciation of government will grow as your study skills improve. Your study of government will also provide you with opportunities to sharpen your research, writing, and test-taking abilities.

1 IDENTIFYING THE MAIN IDEA

In the study of government, significant events and concepts sometimes get lost among surrounding issues. A key to understanding any complex issue is the ability to identify its central elements. This book is designed to help you focus on the most important concepts in government. The objectives at the beginning of each section are intended to guide your reading, and the chapter summary reinforces the main ideas presented.

How to Identify the Main Idea

Read introductory material. Read the title and the introduction, if there is one, which may point out the material's main ideas.

Have questions in mind. Formulate questions that you think might be answered by the material. Having such questions in mind will focus your reading.

Note the outline of ideas. Pay attention to any headings or subheadings, which may provide a basic outline of the major ideas.

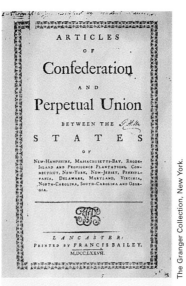

Identifying the main idea is critical to understanding the meaning of documents such as the Articles of Confederation.

The Granger Collection, New York.

Distinguish supporting details. As you read, distinguish sentences providing additional details from the general statements they support. A trail of facts, for instance, may lead to a conclusion that expresses a main idea.

Applying Your Skill

Read the paragraph below, from the Chapter 13 subsection titled "Balancing Rights and Interests to Promote the Public Good" to identify its main idea.

❝Although the Constitution guarantees civil liberties, it does not guarantee absolute freedom to do as one wishes. The freedom to assemble with others in pursuit of a goal, for example, does not give people the freedom to riot or to destroy property, which would violate other people's right to safety and protection of their property. Recognizing the responsibilities that come with freedom is part of being a good citizen.❞

As the lead sentence indicates, the paragraph focuses on limits to the personal freedoms guaranteed in the Constitution. Details are included to illustrate this concept—for example, the fact that the constitutional freedom of a group of people to assemble does not give them the right to riot, to harm others or their property, or to violate other people's right to safety. The main idea—that people who are good citizens generally respect the rights of others while exercising their constitutional freedoms—is most clearly stated in the concluding sentence—recognizing the responsibilities that come with freedom is part of being a citizen.

Practicing Your Skill

Read the first paragraph of the subsection "Assembly and Private Property" on page 313 of Chapter 13, and answer the following questions.

1. What is the paragraph's main idea? How does the writer support that idea?
2. What is the relationship between the main ideas in this paragraph and the one excerpted on the previous page? Combine the main ideas of both paragraphs into one statement that summarizes both of them.

2 IDENTIFYING CAUSE AND EFFECT

Identifying and understanding cause-and-effect relationships is fundamental to interpreting government concepts. A *cause* is any action that leads to an event; the outcome of that action is an *effect*. To investigate both why an event took place and what happened as a result of it, political scientists ask questions such as What is the immediate activity that triggered the event? and What is the event? Your task is simpler than political scientists': to trace what he or she has already determined or theorized about the web of actions and results.

How to Identify Cause and Effect

Look for clues. Certain words and phrases are immediate clues to the existence of a cause-and-effect relationship.

Identify the relationship. Read carefully to identify how events are related. Writers do not always directly state the link between cause and effect. Sometimes a reader has to infer the cause or the effect.

Check for complex connections. Beyond the superficial, or immediate, cause and effect, check for other, more complex connections. Note, for example, whether (1) there were additional causes leading to a given effect; (2) a cause had multiple effects; and (3) the effects in turn caused any additional effects.

Applying Your Skill

The diagram below presents a cause-and-effect relationship in the problems surrounding U.S. and Soviet actions during the Cuban missile crisis. Note how an effect becomes a cause.

Cause and Effect Clues

CAUSE	EFFECT
as a result of	aftermath
because	as a consequence
brought about	depended on
inspired	gave rise to
led to	originated from
provoked	outcome
produced	outgrowth
spurred	proceeded from
the reason	resulting in

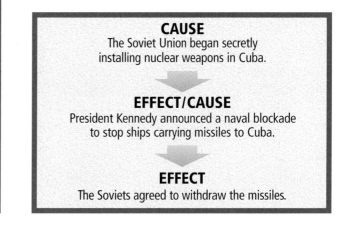

CAUSE
The Soviet Union began secretly installing nuclear weapons in Cuba.

EFFECT/CAUSE
President Kennedy announced a naval blockade to stop ships carrying missiles to Cuba.

EFFECT
The Soviets agreed to withdraw the missiles.

Practicing Your Skill

From your knowledge of the U.S. government, choose a political process that you believe to be shaped by cause-and-effect relationships. Draw a chart showing the relationships between the actions and the outcomes. Then write a paragraph explaining the connections.

❸ DISTINGUISHING FACT FROM OPINION

The ability to distinguish facts from opinions is essential in judging the soundness of an argument or the reliability of a political analysis. A fact can be proved or observed; an opinion, on the other hand, is a personal belief or conclusion. Thus, in an argument, opinions do not carry as much weight as facts, although some opinions can be supported by facts. One often hears facts and opinions mixed in everyday conversation as well as in advertising, political debate, and government policy statements.

How to Distinguish Fact from Opinion

Identify the facts. Begin by asking yourself whether the statement at hand can be verified. Determine whether it can be checked for accuracy in a source such as an almanac or encyclopedia. If so, it is probably factual. If not, it probably contains an opinion.

Identify the opinions. Look for clues that signal statements of opinion—for example, phrases such as *I think* or *I believe*. Comparative words like *greatest* or *more important* and value-laden words like *extremely* or *ridiculous* imply a judgment, and thus an opinion.

Applying Your Skill

Assessments of a document like the Constitution often mix fact and opinion. For example, read the following description of the Constitution, taken from a speech by Franklin D. Roosevelt:

❝ Our Constitution is so simple and practical that it is possible always to meet extraordinary needs by changes in emphasis and arrangement without loss of essential form.

That is why our constitutional system has proved itself the most superbly enduring political mechanism the modern world has produced. It has met every stress of vast expansion of territory, of foreign wars, of bitter internal strife, of world relations. ❞

Roosevelt's assessment—that the U.S. Constitution is nearly perfect and superior to other devices for organizing a government system—is an opinion. Note Roosevelt's use of value-laden words and phrasing: *so simple, practical, possible always, extraordinary, most superbly, met every stress*.

Practicing Your Skill

Read the campaign advertisement and answer the questions below.

1. Can any of the statements in the advertisement be proved true?
2. What word does this advertisement use to describe the type of tax increases that Smart has voted against?
3. Does the advertisement provide any facts about Smart's voting record?

Teresa Smart
for U.S. Senate

According to recent studies, the public considers experience and a consistent voting record to be the most important qualifications of a senator.

- Smart has served in the U.S. Senate for eight years.
- Smart has voted against all legislation that calls for unreasonable tax increases.
- Smart voted in favor of 20 bills to increase funding for public education.

Elect Teresa Smart
She Is the Voice of Experience

4 BUILDING VOCABULARY

Studying government may challenge your reading comprehension as you encounter many new words. However, you can master new words and expand your vocabulary. Following the steps outlined below will assist you in this endeavor.

How to Build Vocabulary

Identify unusual words. As you read, be aware of words that you cannot pronounce or define. Keep a list of these words. Words that are somewhat familiar are the easiest to learn.

Study context clues. Study the sentence and paragraph where you find each new term. This *context*, or setting, may give you clues to the word's meaning. The word may be defined by either an example or another more familiar word that has the same or similar meaning.

Use the dictionary. Use a dictionary to help you pronounce and define the words on your list.

Review new vocabulary. Look for ways to use the new words—in homework assignments, conversation, or classroom discussions. The best way to master a new word is to use it.

Practicing Your Skill

1. What is context? How can it provide clues to a word's meaning?
2. As you read a chapter, list any unusual words that you find. Write down what you think each word means, and then check the definitions you wrote against those in a dictionary.
3. Use each of the words in your list at least one time. Try to think of ways in which you can use each word in everyday conversation.

5 CONDUCTING RESEARCH

To complete research papers or special projects, you may need to use resources beyond this textbook. For example, you may want to research specific subjects or business organizations not discussed here, or to learn additional information about a certain topic. Doing such research typically involves using the resources available in a library.

How to Find Information

To find a particular book, you need to know how libraries organize their materials. Books of fiction are alphabetized according to the last name of the author. To classify nonfiction books, libraries use the Dewey decimal system and the Library of Congress system. Both systems assign each book a *call number* that indicates where it is shelved.

To find a particular book's call number, look in the library's card catalog. The catalog lists books by author, title, and subject. If you know the author or title of the book, finding it is an easy task. If you do not know this information, or if you just want to find any book about a general subject, look under an applicable subject heading. Many libraries have computerized card catalogs. These catalogs generally contain the same information as a traditional card catalog, but

---

The general theory of employment, interest, and money
    by John Maynard Keynes.
    San Diego : Harcourt, Brace, Jovanovich, 1964 [1991 printing]
    xii, 403 p. : ill. ; 21 cm.
    Originally published: 1953.
    "A Harvest/HBJ book."
    Includes bibliographical references and index.
Subjects:
    Economics.
    Money.
    Monetary policy.
    Interest.
Search for other works by:
    Keynes, John Maynard, 1883-1946.

Language	Call Number	LCCN	Dewey Decimal	ISBN/ISSN
English (eng)	HB99.7 .K378 1964	91006533 //r91	330.15/6	0156347113 : $8.95

take up less space and are easier to update and to access.

Librarians can assist you in using the card catalog and direct you to a book's location. They also can suggest additional resources. Many libraries now rely on computerized resources and have access to the Internet. Specialized CD-ROMs such as the *Holt Researcher CD-ROM: Economy and Government* also provide access to statistics and other government information.

Many research projects require the use of library resources.

How to Use Resources

In a library's reference section, you will find encyclopedias, specialized dictionaries, atlases, almanacs, and indexes to recent material in magazines and newspapers. Encyclopedias often will be the most readily available resource. Encyclopedias include economic, political, and geographical data on individual nations, states, and cities, as well as biographical sketches of important historical figures. Entries in these books often include cross-references to related articles.

To find up-to-date facts about a subject, you can use almanacs, yearbooks, and periodical indexes. References like *The World Almanac and Book of Facts* include government information and a variety of statistics. Encyclopedia yearbooks keep up with recent, significant developments not fully covered in encyclopedia articles.

Periodical indexes, such as the *Readers' Guide to Periodical Literature*, can help you locate current articles published in magazines. *The New York Times Index* catalogs the articles published in the *Times,* the U.S. daily newspaper with perhaps the most in-depth coverage of U.S. and world events.

Practicing Your Skill

1. In what two ways are nonfiction books classified?
2. What kinds of references contain information about government?
3. Where would you look to find the most recent coverage of a political or social issue?

⑥ ANALYZING PRIMARY SOURCES

There are many sources of firsthand government information, including editorials, policy statements, and legal documents. All of these are primary sources. Newspaper reports and editorial cartoons also are considered to be primary sources, although they are generally written after the fact. Because they permit a close-up look at the past—a chance to get inside people's minds—primary sources are valuable historical tools.

Secondary sources are descriptions or interpretations of events written after the events have

occurred by persons who did not participate in the events they describe. Government books such as *Holt American Government,* biographies, encyclopedias, and other reference works are examples of secondary sources.

How to Analyze Primary Sources

Study the material carefully. Consider the nature of the material. Is it verbal or visual? Is it based on firsthand information or on the accounts of others? Note the major ideas and supporting details.

Consider the audience. Ask yourself: For whom was this message originally intended? Whether a message was intended, for instance, for the general public or for a specific, private audience may have shaped its style or content.

Check for bias. Watch for words or phrases that present a one-sided view of a person or situation.

When possible, compare sources. Study more than one source on a topic. Comparing sources gives you a more complete, balanced account.

Practicing Your Skill

1. What distinguishes secondary sources from primary sources?
2. What advantage do primary sources have over secondary sources?
3. Of the following, identify which are primary sources and which are secondary sources: a newspaper, a biography, an editorial cartoon, a deed to property, a snapshot of a family vacation, a magazine article about the government system of Brazil. Think about the distinctions between primary and secondary sources. How might some of these sources prove to be both primary and secondary sources?

 WRITING ABOUT GOVERNMENT

The Section Reviews and Chapter Reviews in *Holt American Government* present several writing opportunities. Following the guidelines below will improve your writing about government as well as other subjects.

How to Write with a Purpose

Always keep your purpose for writing in mind. That purpose might be to analyze, evaluate, synthesize, inform, persuade, hypothesize, or take a stand. As you begin your assignment, your purpose will determine the most appropriate approach to take, and when you are finished, it will help you evaluate your success.

Each purpose for writing requires its own form, tone, and content. The point of view you are adopting will shape what you write, as will your intended audience—whoever will be reading what you write.

Some writing assignments in *Holt American Government* ask you to write in a specific manner. For example, you might be required to create a brochure, a newspaper editorial, or an advertisement.

★ A **brochure** is a booklet containing descriptive, educational, or advertising material. Its purpose is to inform people or to promote an idea, a product, a service, or an event.

★ A newspaper **editorial** is a public statement of an opinion or a viewpoint. It takes a stand on an issue and gives reasons for that stand.

★ An **advertisement** is an announcement to promote a product or an event. Effective ads are direct and to the point, and use memorable language, such as jingles and slogans, to highlight important features.

How to Write a Paper or an Essay

Each writing opportunity will have specific directions about what and how to write. Regardless of the particular topic you choose, you should follow certain basic steps.

There are five major stages to writing a paper or essay: prewriting, creating an outline, writing a first draft, evaluating and revising the draft, and proofreading and producing the final paper. Each stage can be further divided into more-specific steps and tasks. The guidelines outlined below can help improve your writing abilities.

Prewriting

Choose a topic. Select a topic for your paper. Take care to narrow your subject so that you will be able to develop and support a clear argument.

Identify your purpose for writing the essay or paper. Read the directions for the assignment carefully to identify the purpose for your writing. Keep that purpose in mind as you plan and write your paper.

Determine your audience. When writing for a specific audience, choose the tone and style that will best communicate your message.

Collect information. Write down your ideas and the information you already know about your topic, and do additional research if necessary. Your writing will be more effective if you have many details at hand.

Create an outline. Make a plan before you begin writing your first draft. Organize themes, main ideas, and supporting details into an outline.

Creating an Outline

Order your material. Decide what you want to emphasize. Order your material with that in mind. Determine what type of information belongs in an introduction, what belongs in the body of your paper, and what to leave for the conclusion.

```
                The President's Roles
I. Chief Executive
    A. Head of the executive branch
    B. Responsible for carrying out the nation's laws
II. Commander in Chief
    A. Head of the U.S. armed forces
        1. Commands all military officers
        2. Not responsible for leading troops into
           battle
    B. Has final say in wartime decisions
III. Chief Agenda Setter
    A. Delivers several messages a year to Congress
    B. Delivers a State of the Union Address annually
    C. Sends Congress a budget plan
        1. Recommends how Congress should raise
           money
        2. Recommends how money should be spent
IV. Representative of the Nation
    A. Lobbies Congress on behalf of all Americans
    B. Gives support during times of crisis
```

Identify main ideas. Identify the main ideas to be highlighted in each section. Make these the main headings of your outline.

List supporting details. Determine the important details or facts that support each main idea. Rank and list them as subheadings, using additional levels of subheadings as necessary. Never break a category into subheadings unless there are at least two: no *A*s without *B*s, no *1*s without *2*s.

Put your outline to use. Structure your paper or essay according to your outline. Each main heading, for instance, might form the basis for a topic sentence to begin a paragraph. Subheadings would then make up the content of the paragraph. In a more lengthy paper, each subheading might be the main idea of a paragraph.

Writing the Draft

In your first draft, remember to use your outline as a guide. Each paragraph should express one main idea or set of related ideas, with details added for support. Be careful to show the relationships between ideas and to use proper *transitions*—sentences that build connections between paragraphs.

Evaluating and Revising the Draft

Review and edit. Revise and reorganize the draft as needed. Improve sentences by adding appropriate adjectives and adverbs. Omit words, sentences, or paragraphs that are unnecessary or unrelated to the main idea.

Evaluate your writing style. Make your writing clearer by varying the sentence length and rephrasing awkward sentences. Replace inexact wording with more precise word choices.

Proofreading and Publishing

Proofread carefully. Check for proper spelling, punctuation, and grammar. Then prepare a neat and clean final version. Appearance is important. It can affect the way your writing is perceived and understood.

Practicing Your Skill

1. What factor—more than any other—should affect how and what you write? Why?
2. Why is it important to consider the audience for your writing?
3. What is involved in the evaluating and revising of a first draft?
4. How can you make your writing clearer? In what ways might varying sentence length improve the quality of writing in your paper or essay?

8 LEARNING FROM VISUALS

Visuals are graphic images that can provide information about culture and society. These clues are available in a broad range of formats, including photographs, paintings, television, Web sites, and political cartoons. Visual images record diverse data. To extract this data, you must carefully examine the details in the image.

How to Study Visuals

Identify the subject. Look at the content of the picture. What is the main focus? For example, is it a group of people, a building, or a particular event? Who is the intended audience? What do you think the creator of the image is trying to convey? Read the title or captions or listen to the dialogue to pick up clues to its subject matter.

Examine the details. Gather subtle information from the image. Are there clues about time or place? Look at details such as clothing style, architecture, and the arrangement of the image's components to further evaluate its effect and meaning.

Identify the tone. Most people think that visuals present only facts. A visual image, however, also exposes feelings about a subject. What do the images reveal about people's feelings? How do you feel when you look at the picture? Does it make you laugh or feel sad or angry? Try to identify what specific elements in the image evoke your response.

Put the data to use. Combine the information you gather from the visual images and written or spoken words to analyze a particular subject.

Practicing Your Skill

1. What is the subject of the cartoon on this page?
2. What are the clues that help you identify the place and the person illustrated in the cartoon?
3. What is the cartoonist's opinion of U.S. foreign policy? Do you agree with this opinion? Why or why not?

Images such as political cartoons provide valuable clues about U.S. culture and society's perception of government.

⑨ UNDERSTANDING MEASUREMENT CONCEPTS AND METHODS

Measurements can give us information about the magnitude, amount, or size of a particular item. Measurements usually are presented in the form of numbers. Finding the information you need from these numbers, however, may be difficult unless you know what you hope to find. Understanding measurement methods and learning to read the results is key to learning about government and many other subjects.

Many measurements in *Holt American Government* are *statistics*. These are facts presented in the form of numbers and are typically arranged to show applicable information about a subject. Statistics often are presented in the form of *percentages* or *ratios*.

Measurements can provide a wide variety of information. For instance, you might read measurements that tell you how many people in your state agree with higher speed limits or what the rate of inflation was over the past year.

How to Read Measurements

Look for clues. Use the information presented with measurements to help you understand their significance. If the measurements appear in a chart or graph, read the title or labels to find clues. If the numbers appear in the text, read the paragraph surrounding them to gain more information.

Identify form. In what form is the measurement? Is it expressed as a percentage? a ratio?

Evaluate the method and purpose of the measurement. How was the data collected—through a poll, government census, or price analysis? Why was this information collected, and who will use it?

Put the data to use. Use the information in the measurements to build a mental picture of the data or group described. Draw conclusions from the information presented.

Practicing Your Skill

1. What is the subject of the first graph? the second graph?
2. Why do you think the data is presented in the form of percentages?

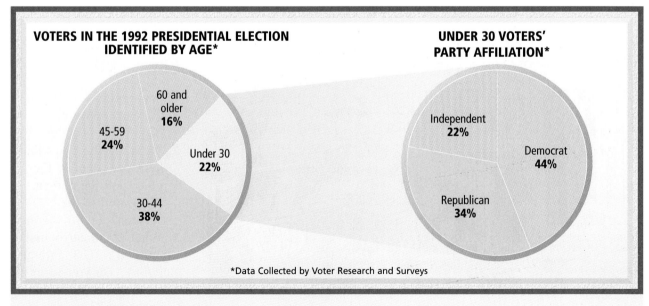

VOTERS IN THE 1992 PRESIDENTIAL ELECTION IDENTIFIED BY AGE*

- 60 and older **16%**
- 45-59 **24%**
- Under 30 **22%**
- 30-44 **38%**

UNDER 30 VOTERS' PARTY AFFILIATION*

- Independent **22%**
- Democrat **44%**
- Republican **34%**

*Data Collected by Voter Research and Surveys

Understanding measurements, such as this graphic illustration of statistics, is key to learning facts about government.

3. Which age group made up the smallest percentage of voters? Which political party made up the largest percentage of voters?

4. How was the data collected? What groups, organizations, and individuals would be interested in using this data?

🔟 UNDERSTANDING CHARTS AND GRAPHS

Charts and graphs are means of organizing and presenting information visually. They categorize and display data in a variety of ways, depending on their subject. Several types of charts and graphs are used in this textbook.

Charts

Charts commonly used in government include tables, flowcharts, and organizational charts. A *table* lists and categorizes information. A *flowchart* shows a sequence of events or the steps in a process. Cause-and-effect relationships are often shown by flowcharts. An *organizational chart* displays the structure of an organization, indicating the ranking or function of its internal positions or departments and the relationships among them. For example, see the Federal Court System chart to the right.

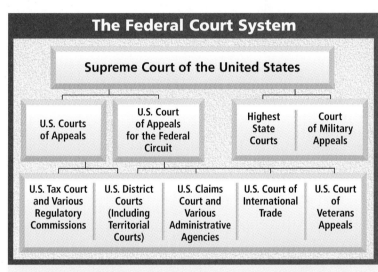

The Federal Court System

Supreme Court of the United States

- U.S. Courts of Appeals
- U.S. Court of Appeals for the Federal Circuit
- Highest State Courts
- Court of Military Appeals

- U.S. Tax Court and Various Regulatory Commissions
- U.S. District Courts (Including Territorial Courts)
- U.S. Claims Court and Various Administrative Agencies
- U.S. Court of International Trade
- U.S. Court of Veterans Appeals

Organizational charts show the relationship among different components of an organization.

How to Read a Chart

Read the title. Read the title to identify the focus or purpose of the chart.

Study the chart's elements. Read the chart's headings, subheadings, and labels to identify the categories used and the specific data given for each one.

Analyze the details. When reading quantities, note any increases or decreases in amounts. When reading dates, note intervals of time. When viewing an organizational chart, follow directional arrows or lines.

Put the data to use. Form generalizations or draw conclusions based on the data.

Graphs

There are several types of graphs, each of which is well-suited for a particular purpose. A *bar graph* displays amounts or quantities in a way that makes comparisons easy—for example, see the Biggest Recipients of U.S. Foreign Aid, 1993 bar graph on the next page. A *line graph* plots information by dots connected with a line. This line is sometimes called a *curve*. A line graph such as the one on the next page—Net Budget Receipts, 1990–1995—shows changes or trends over time. A *pie graph,* or *circle graph,* displays proportions by showing sections of a whole as if they were slices of a pie.

How to Read a Graph

Read the title. Read the title to identify the subject and purpose of the graph. Note the kind of graph it is, remembering what each kind is designed to emphasize.

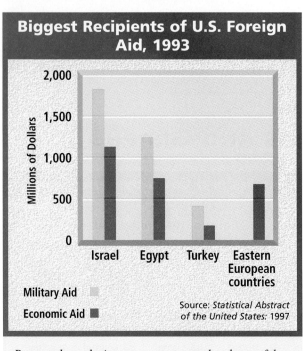

Bar graphs make it easy to compare related sets of data.

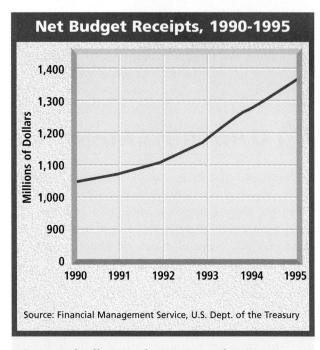

Line graphs illustrate changes or trends over time.

Study the labels. To identify the type of information presented in the graph, read the label for each axis. The *horizontal axis* runs from left to right, generally at the bottom of the graph, while the *vertical axis* runs up and down, generally along the left-hand side. In addition, note the intervals of any dates or amounts that are listed. Study the labels for each axis in the Biggest Recipeients of U.S. Foreign Aid, 1993 chart on this page.

Analyze the data. Note increases or decreases in quantities. Look for trends, relationships, and changes in the data.

Put the data to use. Use the results of your analysis to form generalizations and to draw conclusions about the subject matter of the chart or graph.

Practicing Your Skill

Use the Net Budget Receipts, 1990–1995 line graph on this page to answer the following questions:

1. Describe the type of data illustrated and the intervals used for the horizontal axis and the vertical axis.
2. What generalizations or conclusions can you draw from the information in this graph?

11 READING MAPS

The study of government and geography often are related. Government describes the political institutions and laws that regulate a group of people. Geography describes how physical environments affect human events and how people influence the environment around them. Geographers have developed five themes—human-environment interaction, location, place, region, and movement—to organize this information.

Geographic information for all five themes can be presented in text or represented visually in maps. Maps convey a wealth of varied information through colors, lines, symbols, and labels. To read and interpret maps, you must be able to understand their language and symbols.

Types of Maps

A map is an illustration drawn to scale of all or part of the earth's surface. Types of maps include physical maps, political maps, and special-purpose maps. *Physical maps* illustrate the natural landscape of an area. Physical maps often use shading to show relief—the rises and falls in the surface of the land—and colors to show elevation, or height above sea level.

Political maps illustrate political units such as states and nations by employing color variations, lines to mark boundaries, dots for major cities, and stars, or stars within circles, for capitals. Political maps show information such as territorial changes or military alliances. The Hazardous Waste Sites in the United States, 1996 map on this page is a political map.

Special-purpose maps present specific information such as explorers' routes, the outcome of an election, regional economic activity, or population density. The U.S. Boundaries, 1853 map on page xxxvi is a special-purpose map.

Many maps combine various features of the types of maps listed above. For example, a map may combine information from a political and a special-purpose map by showing boundaries between nations as well as trade routes from one region to another region.

Map Features

Most maps have a number of features in common. Familiarity with these basic elements makes reading any map easier.

Titles, legends, and labels. A map's *title* tells you what the map is about, what area is shown, and frequently the time period represented. The *legend,* or key, explains any special symbols, colors, or shading used on the map. *Labels* designate political and geographic place-names as well as physical features like mountain ranges, oceans, and rivers.

The global grid. The *absolute location* of any place on the earth is given in terms of *latitude* (degrees north or south of the equator) and *longitude* (degrees east or west of the prime meridian). The symbol for a degree is °. Degrees are divided into 60 equal parts called minutes, which are represented by the symbol '. The *global grid* is created by the intersection of lines of latitude *(parallels)* and lines of longitude *(meridians)*. Lines of latitude and longitude may sometimes be indicated by tick marks near the edge of the map or by lines across an entire map. Many maps also have *locator maps,* which show the subject area's location in relation to a larger area, such as a continent or hemisphere.

Maps present geographic information in a visual form.

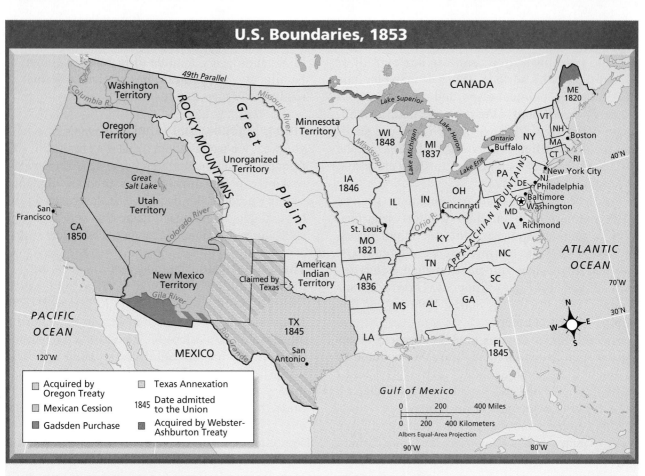

U.S. Boundaries, 1853

Special-purpose maps illustrate a particular topic and may include features of physical and political maps.

Directions and distances. Most maps in this textbook have a *compass rose,* or *directional indicator.* The compass rose indicates the four cardinal points—N for north, S for south, E for east, and W for west. You can also determine intermediate directions—northeast, southeast, southwest, and northwest—using the compass rose. These directions are helpful in describing the relative location of a place. (If a map has no compass rose, assume that north is at the top, east is to the right, and so on.)

Many maps include a *scale,* showing both miles and kilometers, to help you relate distances on the map to actual distances on the earth's surface. You can use the scale to find the true distance between any two points on the map.

How to Read a Map

Determine the focus of the map. Read the map's title and labels to determine the map's focus—its subject and the geographic area it represents.

Study the map legend. Read the legend and become familiar with any special symbols, lines, colors, and shadings used in the map.

Check directions and distances. Use the directional indicator and scale as needed to determine direction, location, and distance.

Check the grid lines. Refer to lines of latitude and longitude, or to a locator map, to fix the locations in relation to a larger area.

Study the map. Study the map's basic features and details, keeping its purpose in mind. If it is a special-purpose map, study the specific information being presented.

Practicing Your Skill

For each of the maps in this lesson, answer the questions on the next page.

1. What is the special focus of each map in this lesson?
2. How is a map helpful in presenting this information?

3. What standard symbols, if any, are used in the map?
4. What do the color variations and different lines indicate?

12 TAKING A TEST

When it comes to taking a test, for government or any other subject, nothing can take the place of preparation. A good night's sleep added to consistent study habits give you a much better chance for success than hours of late-night, last-minute cramming. By preparing well, you will be better able to ignore distractions during the test.

But keeping your mind focused on the test and free from distractions is not all you can do to improve your test scores. Mastering some basic test-taking skills also can help. Keeping up with daily reading assignments and taking careful notes as you read can turn preparing for a test into a mere matter of review. Reviewing material that you already know takes less time—and causes less stress—than trying to learn something new under pressure.

You will face several basic types of questions on government tests—for example, fill-in-the-blank, short answer, multiple choice, matching, and essay. In answering multiple-choice questions, eliminate any answers that you know are wrong, in order to narrow your field of choice. When completing a matching exercise, first go through the entire list, matching only those items whose connection is clear. Then study any that remain.

Read essay questions carefully so that you know exactly what you are being asked to write. Make an outline of the main ideas and supporting details that you plan to include in your essay. Keep your answer clear and brief, but cover all necessary points.

How to Take a Test

Prepare beforehand. This all-important step involves more than just studying and reviewing the material prior to the test. It also means being physically rested and mentally focused on the day of the test.

Follow directions. Read all instructions carefully. Listen closely if the directions are oral rather than written.

Preview the test. Skim through the entire test to determine how much time you have for each section. Try to anticipate which areas will be the most difficult for you.

Concentrate on the test. Do not watch the clock, but be aware of the time. If you do not know an answer, move on to the next question.

Review your answers. If you have time, retu to questions that you skipped or were unsure and work on them. Review your essays to and correct any mistakes in spelling, punct or grammar.

Practicing Your Skill

1. How can you improve your chances o multiple-choice questions?
2. Why is it important to skim through entire test before you begin?
3. Name three things that can help you taking a test.

Good preparation is essential for successful test-taking.

UNIT
1

PUBLIC POLICY LAB

Do students have guaranteed
rights while they are attending
school? Find out by reading this
unit and taking the Public Policy
Lab challenge on pages 86–89.

FOUNDATIONS OF GOVERNMENT

ROLE OF GOVERNMENT

W hat prevents someone from placing a garbage dump next to your house or apartment? What makes sure you have the proper training to drive a car and determines when you can get your license? What ensures that the hamburger you buy at a local restaurant has been cooked safely? Who makes rules about whether or not school officials can search your locker?

The answer to these questions is government. You might think that government does not affect your every-day life or that it affects you only in negative ways. For example, some people complain about the taxes they have to pay. However, government actions, including collecting taxes, are intended to serve a vital purpose—promoting the well-being of a country's people. This chapter takes a close look at the role of government and how it affects the lives of the people it governs.

Government Notebook

In your Government Notebook, write a paragraph about the purpose of government. What role does government play in your life?

GOVERNMENT AND THE PUBLIC GOOD

Political Dictionary

government
state
citizen
sovereignty
law
public policy
legitimacy
social contract
natural right
politics
value
public good

Objectives

★ What is government, and why is it important?
★ How have some philosophers described the nature and purpose of the state?
★ What functions does government perform?
★ How does government serve the public good?

Imagine what things would be like if there were no traffic rules. For example, what if no one had to stop at a stop sign? Consider a busy highway with no posted speed limits or warnings for drivers to obey. Driving a car under these conditions would be very dangerous.

Government—an institution with the power to make and enforce rules for a group of people—posts the signs that help make roads safer for travelers. Setting traffic rules—as well as enforcing those rules—is just one way government works to make people's lives safer and more secure. In the words of English philosopher Thomas Hobbes (1588–1679), life without such security would be "nasty, brutish, and short."

What Is Government?

Signs of government at work are everywhere: a postal service logo on a mailbox, a badge worn by a police officer, a flag flying in front of a school. Government also appears in less obvious ways: a bridge over a highway, a curfew for young people, an older citizen's visit to the doctor's office.

Government, however, is more than just a collection of these symbols and services. As you have just read, it also establishes the rules and regulations that govern everyday life. Of course, other institutions also establish rules. Religions, social clubs, and professional associations, for example, set rules for their members. It is government, however, that has the authority to set rules for all the people living in a political unit, or **state**.

This absolute authority that a government has over its **citizens**, or members of a state, is called **sovereignty**. The United States, France, Egypt, Japan, Russia, Mexico, China, Indonesia, and Nigeria are examples of the nearly 200 sovereign states in the world.

How do the governments of these and other sovereign states establish rules for their societies? They do so by making law. **Law** is a set of rules, made and enforced by government, that is binding on society. There are laws covering everything

POLITICAL FOUNDATIONS *City snowplows clear the streets during a blizzard in New York City.* **What signs of government do you see every day in your community?**

from punishment for crimes such as murder and theft to littering and programs for building highways, granting college loans, and providing job training. Laws also govern the ways in which such rules are enforced, such as by determining the amount a person can be fined for breaking a rule.

Most societies have thousands of laws. These are part of **public policies**, or the plans and decisions that a government makes in a particular area of public concern. A government makes public policies on a broad range of issues. The public policy on traffic safety, for example, includes laws that set speed limits, require the use of seat belts, and establish rules for issuing driver's licenses. Regardless of their focus, all laws and policies have two things in common—they deal with a public problem and they are enforceable.

Origins of Government

Scholars have long debated the origins of the state and government. In the past, philosophers argued that rulers—typically kings and queens—receive their authority to govern from God. The rightful authority any government has over its citizens is known as **legitimacy**.

In the 1600s Thomas Hobbes argued that people create the state by entering into a **social contract**. Under this contract, the people give up their individual sovereignty to the state. In exchange, the state provides peace and order.

English philosopher John Locke (1632–1704) developed his own ideas about the social contract. Locke argued that the contract creates a limited government that relies entirely on the consent of the governed. In other words, the government has legitimacy because the people, not God or anyone else, give it authority to govern.

Locke also believed that government's proper job is to secure people's natural rights. **Natural rights** are those that people have simply because they are human beings. The U.S. Declaration of Independence lists some of these natural rights: life, liberty, and the pursuit of happiness. Locke argued that the people may throw out governments that do not secure these rights. In *Of Civil Government,* from *Two Treatises on Government,* Locke stated,

❝ Whosoever in authority exceeds the power given him by the law . . . may be opposed as any other man who by force invades the right of another. ❞

Functions of Government

A government should secure citizens' natural rights and fulfill its part of the social contract by performing a variety of functions. In the United States you can see government working toward these goals all around you: the police officer walking a beat, the soldier coming home on leave, the health inspector checking a restaurant, officials debating ideas at a public meeting. These actions are examples of the critical functions of government: to maintain order, provide services, resolve conflicts, and promote society's shared values. How many of these functions a government actually serves varies from country to country.

Maintaining Order Government maintains order in society by enforcing laws that protect

PUBLIC GOOD *To enforce laws that prohibit littering, the government fines those who do not properly dispose of their trash.* **In what other ways does government fulfill its part of the social contract?**

Political Scientist

Answer the following questions.

TRUE or FALSE

- ■ I enjoy watching political debates on television.
- ■ I keep up with current events and political issues.
- ■ During an election year, I try to stay informed about the candidates.
- ■ I have my own opinions when it comes to our government.

Like most people, you probably think of scientists as specialists who study the life sciences, such as biology. Some scientists, however, are social scientists. The role of a social scientist is to study the structure of a society and the activities of its members.

A social scientist who studies the structure and role of government is called a political scientist. Political scientists explore how government and political institutions function. They answer questions about government as well as seek solutions to its problems. They also offer theories on how to make government function better. For example, a political scientist might study a presidential campaign and election, analyzing the election's outcome and the public's response. He or she then might present the findings in a report or article. Such an election analysis might be useful in future elections, or it might help gauge the nation's attitudes toward government and politics in general.

Many political scientists teach at universities. **How do you become a political scientist?**

Most political scientists are employed as teachers or researchers at universities. Many others work in government agencies, conducting research and analyzing data. Still others work as members of "think tanks" for corporations and private institutes to research and study political issues and problems.

How do you become a political scientist? Education is key. Most jobs for political scientists require an advanced college degree. A budding political scientist must also have a keen interest in government and the political process. Review your answers to the True/False questions above. Perhaps you are already on your way.

the safety and security of people and property. For example, police officers help protect society from those who murder, steal from, or harm other people.

In addition, government works to protect people from unfair or harmful business practices. It establishes laws that promote respect for individual rights in the workplace and in society. For example, government attempts to ensure that employers do not discriminate against workers because of race, ethnic origin, gender, or religion. Government also protects and promotes businesses through such means as regulating commerce and protecting national industries. This protection allows businesses to perform functions essential to the community—building houses, transporting people, and creating new jobs, for example.

Government also maintains order by protecting the country from foreign invasion. National security is important for all governments because it helps protect citizens' lives, rights, and property.

Providing Services Government provides many needed services that people cannot easily provide on their own. It builds roads that carry people and goods. It inspects and approves food and medicines to make sure they are safe. Government also delivers mail across the country, provides assistance to the needy, and builds schools.

Some people argue that other institutions, such as private businesses, could provide many of these services. In fact, private industry and other institutions do provide some important services. For example, people can send packages using a private delivery company instead of using the U.S. postal service. Private charities, churches, and other volunteer organizations also provide assistance to needy people. In general, however, government provides important services that private industry alone would not make available to all citizens. Because most government services do address issues of widespread concern, the benefits are shared by everyone.

Resolving Conflict Government helps resolve conflict by bringing people together to reach common goals through compromise. A compromise is a resolution of conflict in which each side gives up some of what it wants.

Government brings about compromise through **politics**, the process by which people participating in government express opinions about what government should do (or not do). Government then makes decisions according to those opinions.

The court system—part of government—has the authority to enforce the decisions reached in these compromises. Courts also act as a neutral party working to peacefully resolve disputes between people.

Promoting Values Maintaining order, providing services, and resolving conflict help government fulfill a fourth function—promoting common values. **Values** are basic principles by which people act and live their lives. These values include safety and willingness to compromise. Society in the United States also values equality of opportunity, respect for individual rights, a good education, health care for older people and the needy, and personal responsibility. Because people find it difficult to promote common values by themselves, government helps out by passing laws and setting policies.

PUBLIC GOOD *As in other countries, people in the United States value quality health care for older people.* **How does government promote the values of U.S. citizens?**

The Public Good

These functions of government all share a fundamental purpose: to serve the public good. The **public good** is another term for the public interest or the well-being of society as a whole. Good government tries to pursue policies that serve the public interest.

How do governments determine what policies serve the public good? After all, people disagree about which public policies are best. Should government spend money on public schools, or should it provide grants to parents who want to send their children to private schools? Should

PUBLIC GOOD *Passengers in San Luis Obispo, California, board a federally funded Amtrak train.* **What other types of services does government provide?**

government spend money building more roads, or should it increase funding for public transportation? Deciding which of these options makes good public policy is a vital responsibility of government.

One way to determine if a policy serves the public good is to ask if it reflects the narrow interests of a few or the broad concerns of many. Policies that fulfill only narrow interests usually do not serve the public good, while policies that

address a wide range of concerns tend to promote the public good.

Throughout this textbook you will have the opportunity to consider whether various government policies serve the public good. You will investigate not only the structure and workings of government but also the results of government policies. Thus, you will not only study how government works, you also will have the opportunity to decide whether it works well.

SECTION 1 — REVIEW

1. Define the following terms: government, state, citizen, sovereignty, law, public policy, legitimacy, social contract, natural right, politics, value, public good.

2. What is the purpose of the rules you must follow in school or in a club of which you are a member? How is the purpose of those rules similar to the purpose of rules established by government?

3. How did Thomas Hobbes view the relationship between the people and the state? How did John Locke view government's responsibility to the people?

4. Describe the basic functions of government. What common values does the U.S. government promote?

5. **Thinking and Writing Critically**
   Suggest some government policies that you believe promote the public good. What is it about these policies that makes them serve the public good? Do you think the public good is served when government leaves some decisions completely to individuals? Explain your answers.

6. **Applying** **PUBLIC GOOD**
   Establishing policies that protect and preserve the environment is just one of the services government provides. Conduct an Internet search to find out more about government agencies that are set up to enforce these policies. Write a paragraph describing one of these agencies and its function.

FORMS OF GOVERNMENT

Political Dictionary

monarchy	authoritarian
constitutional	totalitarian
monarchy	unitary system
republic	federal system
democracy	confederal system
dictatorship	presidential system
autocracy	parliamentary
oligarchy	system

Objectives

★ In what ways are monarchies, republics, and dictatorships different from one another?

★ What are the features of unitary, federal, and confederal systems?

★ What are the major differences between presidential and parliamentary forms of government?

Many kinds of government exist around the world. The form of government in the United States, for example, differs from those in South Korea, the United Kingdom, and Saudi Arabia. Governments differ in their sources of authority and in how power is shared among and within their national, regional, and local levels.

Sources of Authority

Whatever form a government takes, a key consideration is the source of the government's power. How does the government receive its authority to rule? The answer to this question is crucial—the basis of a government's power determines whether narrow interests or the public good is served.

Monarchies In some countries, the head of state is a hereditary position. In most of these countries,

which are called **monarchies**, the head of state is a king or a queen. Until the early part of the 1900s, most countries were ruled by monarchs. Today around 40 countries have monarchs.

Many of these countries are **constitutional monarchies** in which the monarch is primarily a ceremonial head of state. The real power lies in another part of government. Constitutional monarchies include the United Kingdom, Japan, Norway, Sweden, Denmark, and the Netherlands. Monarchs have substantial power in only a few countries, such as Saudi Arabia, Bahrain, and Kuwait.

Republics Most countries today are republics. In its true form, a **republic** is a country in which the government's authority comes only from the people. The government in a republic is made up of representatives elected by the people. How the people are represented differs, but all true republics base their governments on some form of representation. The United States is a republic, as are France, Mexico, Argentina, South Africa, and India. Constitutional monarchies also have representative systems of government.

The terms *republic* and *democracy* often are used interchangeably. **Democracy** comes from two Greek words that together mean "rule by the people." Democracy recognizes the authority of citizens to control their government—by voting, expressing their views, and forming or joining

CONSTITUTIONAL GOVERNMENT *Here, Queen Elizabeth of Great Britain leaves Buckingham Palace in a parade.* **What is the role of a king or queen in a constitutional monarchy?**

Governments

Japan's Constitutional Monarchy

After Japan's defeat in World War II, its military-dominated government was abolished. Under the terms of the war's peace treaty, Japan was required to establish a peaceful government. In 1947 a new constitution was enacted, creating a system of government based on a European civil law system and heavily influenced by the British and the U.S. systems of government.

For this reason, there are several similarities among the governments of Japan, the United States, and Great Britain. For example, Japan's executive head of government is an elected prime minister, who is chosen by the Japanese legislature, the Diet. Like the U.S. Congress, the Diet is elected by the people. It is made up of two houses—a 511-member House of Representatives and a 252-member House of Councillors.

Japan is organized into 47 prefectures, which are similar to states or provinces. Like the elected governors of the United States, an elected governor administers each of Japan's prefectures.

Unlike the United States, however, Japan is a constitutional monarchy. Like Great Britain, which has a king or queen, Japan has a ceremonial head of state, the emperor. The reigning emperor is a symbol of the nation and holds no executive power.

the monarch—one person—holds all the power.) If a small group of people holds the power, the government is an **oligarchy**, which means "rule by few."

Dictatorships' authority may rest on a combination of their leaders' political power, military power, wealth, and/or social position. Dictators achieve and maintain power through force. Some dictators claim they truly represent the will of the people. In truth, however, dictatorships are **authoritarian** because rulers answer only to themselves, not to the people.

Sometimes dictatorships are so extreme that they become totalitarian. **Totalitarian** rulers

Sources of Authority

MONARCHY
- Head of state is a hereditary position.

Constitutional Monarchy
- King or queen is only the ceremonial head of state.
- Real power lies in another branch of government.

REPUBLIC (DEMOCRATIC)

BALLOT
- People are the source of authority.
- Government is made up of representatives elected by the people.

DICTATORSHIP
- Political and/or military power, wealth and/or social position are the source of leaders' authority.
- Power is achieved and maintained through force.

One of the differences between types of government systems is the source of authority. **What is the source of authority in the U.S. government?**

political groups. Constitutional monarchies may also have a democratic form of government.

Dictatorships Some countries that call themselves republics have governments over which the people have little, if any, control. In some cases, government officials are not elected by the people. In others, elections are unfair or manipulated by those in control. These countries are not truly republics. They are dictatorships.

Power in a **dictatorship** is concentrated in the hands of a single person or a small group of people. If a single person holds the power, the government is an **autocracy**, which means "rule by one." (Note that a monarchy can be autocratic if

seek complete control over all aspects of citizens' lives, including political, religious, social, cultural, and even personal activities. There are several totalitarian states in the world today, including Burma (Myanmar) in South Asia.

Totalitarian governments use a variety of methods to control a society. Such governments often employ vast security networks and secret police to control citizens' actions. In addition, they try to influence people's beliefs through controlling the everyday aspects of life such as what news organizations report and what schools teach. Free speech is outlawed, and political organizations that oppose the government are banned. Opponents of the government are imprisoned and sometimes killed.

Power Among Levels of Government

Governments also differ in how power is distributed among the national, regional, and local levels. Ways of distributing power fall into three types of systems: unitary, federal, and confederal.

Unitary Systems In a **unitary system**, all legal power is held by the national, or central, government. Local governments, such as those for provinces and cities, have no independent powers and are simply local representatives of the national government. Their job is to carry out decisions made by the national government. The United Kingdom, Israel, and Japan are examples of unitary systems.

Federal Systems Some countries have **federal systems** in which powers are divided among national, state, and local governments. In this system, some powers belong only to the national government, others only to state and local governments, and still others are shared by all three. The United States has a federal system of government, as do Germany, India, Australia, and Malaysia.

Confederal Systems In a **confederal system**, independent states join together to accomplish common goals. There may be no central government, but the members of the confederation may set up an organization to carry out agreed-upon policies.

The United States was a confederation from 1781 to 1789. In 1789 the Articles of Confederation were replaced with the U.S. Constitution and a federal system of government. Today, Russia and the United Arab Emirates are examples of confederations. The European Union (EU) is a confederation of nations made up of 15 European countries that joined together to promote economic and political cooperation.

Power Within Levels of Government

Just as power may be distributed among levels of government, power within a single level of government also may be divided. In other words, different powers are given to the different branches of a government. The relationship between the

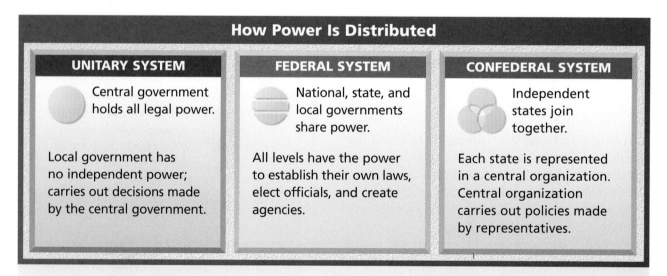

How Power Is Distributed

UNITARY SYSTEM	FEDERAL SYSTEM	CONFEDERAL SYSTEM
Central government holds all legal power.	National, state, and local governments share power.	Independent states join together.
Local government has no independent power; carries out decisions made by the central government.	All levels have the power to establish their own laws, elect officials, and create agencies.	Each state is represented in a central organization. Central organization carries out policies made by representatives.

Power among levels of government may be classified according to three types of systems. **How is power distributed in the U.S. government?**

branches of government may take two basic forms: presidential systems and parliamentary systems.

Presidential Systems

The legislative branch, which makes the law, and the executive branch, which carries out the law, are separate and independent of each other in a **presidential system** of government. The executive branch usually is headed by a president, who is chosen independently of the legislature. This chief executive serves a set term in office and has powers separate from those of the legislature. Members of the executive branch cannot be members of the legislative branch. In addition to serving as head of the executive branch, the president also represents the country as head of state.

The United States has a presidential system of government. Each branch of government acts as a check on the others' powers. In some presidential systems, however, one branch of government may have much more power than the other(s). In France, for example, the president can dissolve part of the national legislature and call new elections.

Parliamentary Systems

The chief executive, often called a prime minister or premier, is chosen by the parliament, or legislature, in a **parliamentary system** of government. The prime minister or premier and other officials appointed from the parliament make up the executive. If the

PRINCIPLES OF DEMOCRACY *Egypt has a parliamentary system of government. The head of state, President Hosni Mubarak, was elected by the national legislature.* **How is the head of state chosen in a presidential system?**

executive loses the parliament's support, a new government must be formed or a new legislative election held.

In parliamentary systems the chief executive of the government and the head of state are separate offices. In some parliamentary systems, such as in the United Kingdom, the head of state is a monarch. In others, such as in Israel, the head of state is a president.

SECTION 2 — REVIEW

1. Define the following terms: monarchy, constitutional monarchy, republic, democracy, dictatorship, autocracy, oligarchy, authoritarian, totalitarian, unitary system, federal system, confederal system, presidential system, parliamentary system.

2. What is the source of authority in a monarchy? in a democratic republic? in a dictatorship?

3. How does a confederal system differ from federal and unitary systems?

4. Does the United States have a presidential or a parliamentary system of government? Support your answer by listing the features of each system.

5. **Thinking and Writing Critically**
Some dictatorships are called "benevolent dictatorships" because the rulers appear to want to do good things for the people. Such rulers might be less harsh or oppressive than other dictators. Do you think these types of dictatorships are ever beneficial, or are they by nature always harmful? Why?

6. **Applying** POLITICAL FOUNDATIONS
Conduct an Internet search to learn more about parliamentary systems of government. Choose one country with a parliamentary system and briefly describe its national government. Include a simple chart that shows the government's organization.

FOUNDATIONS OF DEMOCRACY

Political Dictionary

anarchy
majority rule
minority rights
direct democracy
representative democracy

Objectives

★ What are the major principles of democracy?
★ What is the difference between direct democracy and representative democracy?

During the 1900s, democracy has been the one form of government that has not seen a decline. Totalitarian dictatorships in Nazi Germany and Italy were defeated in World War II, and few countries today are ruled by absolute monarchs. Dictatorships that ruled Russia, as well as many countries in Eastern Europe and the rest of the world, have been replaced for the most part by democratic governments. Some authoritarian and totalitarian dictatorships still exist, but many countries have turned to democracy.

Why does democracy endure? Does it provide things that other forms of government do not?

Benefits of Democracy

In its ideal form, democracy is based on five broad principles that foster its success. It should

★ give people the opportunity to make choices,
★ recognize the dignity and worth of each person,
★ promote respect for the law,
★ protect the rights of the minority, and
★ produce policies that promote the public good.

Allowing Choice Imagine a restaurant in which the waiter selects your dinner for you. Even if you enjoy the food, you might feel you have missed something by having the waiter choose your meal. After all, deciding what to eat is a valued exercise of choice for most people. Many people want the same right to choose when it comes to more important matters, such as who governs their community and country. Most people want their government's decisions to reflect citizens' wishes.

In democracies, people have the opportunity to make their own choices. Some people have argued that ordinary people are not wise enough to govern themselves. Even though people sometimes make mistakes, the opportunity to choose is important because it allows people to take responsibility for their lives.

People living in a democratic society make their own choices in free and fair elections. For example, voters in the United States elect a president every four years and representatives every two years. Voters also freely choose their state and local leaders and representatives.

Ideally, people in a democracy also have the right to make their own choices regarding other areas of their lives. No one can be forced to join or reject a particular religion or to worship in a particular way. People are free to declare their opinions publicly, to decide what kind of jobs they

PRINCIPLES OF DEMOCRACY *Democracies give people the opportunity to choose their own jobs. Citizens of the United States are free to choose jobs that suit their interests and abilities.* ***What other benefits does a democracy provide?***

Citizenship in Action

Teenage Volunteers Lend a Helping Hand

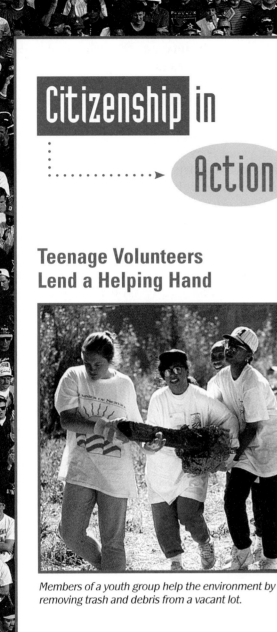

Members of a youth group help the environment by removing trash and debris from a vacant lot.

The spirit of volunteerism in the United States—neighbors helping neighbors—is as old as the nation itself. In the early 1800s, for example, volunteer societies established by Christian groups supported educational activities and other concerns.

Today many of the nation's volunteers are young people. According to Denny Barnett of Volunteers of America, one of the country's oldest human-service agencies, people "are . . . getting involved at an earlier age." A recent study showed that more than 60 percent of kids between the ages of 12 and 17 volunteer an average of more than three hours per week to a special cause.

No matter where you live or what your talents are, there is a nearby organization, group, or individual in need who could benefit from your efforts. For some volunteers, a favorite cause, such as the environment, is the best motivator for becoming involved. For example, in St. Louis a group of young people called the Earth Defenders scours vacant lots and other dumping sites, collecting and recycling thousands of pounds of discarded household items. The Earth Defenders clean these sites frequently, because within days of a cleanup project the lots are covered with trash again. Although the Earth Defenders may tire of picking up the trash, they are rewarded with the knowledge that their efforts have greatly benefited the environment.

Through their hard work and dedication, the Earth Defenders have converted six vacant lots into habitats for wildlife. The group also has been able to support its efforts with money raised through recycling, wise investment, and other activities. The members donate some of what they raise to other environmental causes, such as the National Wildlife Federation.

Involvement brings many rewards, not only to the community but to the volunteer as well. "I can say volunteering has helped me grow as a person," a young New Jersey volunteer said. In 1996 a report from the National Association of Secondary School Principals recommended that high school students receive academic credit for community service. Some people have even suggested that volunteer work be required for high school graduation.

Like Anne in Florida who helped the American Red Cross deliver aid to hurricane victims, or Ramiro in San Francisco who organized the planting of a vegetable garden to aid a homeless shelter, you too can make a difference by volunteering your time. Start small—visit a nursing home, help clean up a beach or park, run a race for your favorite cause, or campaign for a political candidate. These are some of the many ways that you can put your citizenship into action.

What Do You Think?

1. Why do you think many of the country's young people volunteer their time to a special cause?
2. Do you think that high school students should receive academic credit for their volunteer work? Why or why not?

would like to have, to pursue higher education or not, to live where they like, and to associate with others as they please.

The right to make one's own choices also carries responsibilities. One of the most important responsibilities is learning about candidates and issues in order to make educated voting decisions. People also have a responsibility to respect the rights and freedoms of others.

Ideally, participation in government teaches people to adopt a broader point of view and consider more than just their own concerns. By applying these lessons to the tasks of self-government, people will hopefully make decisions that promote the public good. Besides, in a democracy, government decisions will require the agreement of others. Political arguments that reflect only the self-interests of a small group generally will not succeed unless they appeal to the interests of people outside the group.

Thus, an organization whose goals ignore the needs and wants of others will probably have a hard time getting votes for its proposals. For example, a group that backs a policy of allowing developers to build houses in the Grand Canyon would probably not gain much support. People who enjoy the beauty of the canyon would oppose such development.

Recognizing Individual Worth By allowing all citizens to participate in governing, democracy promotes the value of every human being. In a democracy, the views of each person—regardless of wealth, race, gender, or position in life—should be considered and valued.

Ideally, democracy promotes equality by giving all citizens the chance to participate fully in society. Equality of opportunity, however, does not mean equality of results. Rather, in a democracy all people are allowed equal opportunity to take risks and to succeed or fail on their own merits. Democracy thus allows people to take personal responsibility for their successes and failures.

Promoting Respect for Law If citizens participate in government, they generally are more likely to respect its laws than if the laws are simply forced upon them. How can citizens participate in making the laws that govern them? In the United States, citizens can speak at city council and other local government meetings. They can write to their representatives. You can participate in making rules that govern you by attending meetings of the student council and the school board, for instance.

Ideally, democracy also gives people the right to challenge the fairness of a law. A citizen who happens to disagree with a law may organize other citizens to try to change it. All people in a democracy, however, have a responsibility to obey the laws that are established by government. If citizens ignored laws they did not like, or if government simply did not establish laws to maintain order in society, the result would be **anarchy**—a state of political disorder resulting from the absence of rules or government.

Protecting Minority Rights
Most decisions in a democracy are made by majority rule.

CITIZENSHIP *The Internet is an excellent resource for keeping informed about political candidates and issues.* **What are some other ways that citizens can remain informed about their government?**

Majority rule occurs when decisions are based on the desire of more than half of the membership of a group. One of the ways that citizens in a democracy express what they want from government is by voting. Decisions are then based on the desires of the voters.

In its ideal form, democracy also protects the rights of the minority. **Minority rights** are political rights that cannot be abolished in a democracy even though they are held by less than half of the population. These rights include freedom to attend a particular place of worship even if most people attend another. In addition, all citizens have the right to express their opinions even if their views are not popular.

Those in the majority have a responsibility to respect the views of the minority, even if they do not agree with them. Democracy encourages a respect for individual worth that makes it more likely that this responsibility will be recognized.

Promoting the Public Good If all citizens participate in government, decisions likely will better promote the public good than if decisions are left to just a few people. Why? Remember that the public good is best served through policies that address a wide variety of society's concerns rather than just a few. Because democracy allows citizens to participate in the political processes that lead to decisions, more ideas and points of view are considered. Democracy thus serves the public good because it allows citizens to make informed decisions about which public policies are best for them.

Forms of Democracy

Although all democracies are based on these principles, not all democracies work the same way. There are two types of democracy: direct and representative.

Direct Democracy Systems in which laws may be made directly by all citizens are called **direct democracies**. Town hall meetings held in some parts of the United States, in which citizens of a town gather to vote on community matters, are an example of direct democracy.

You might be part of a direct democracy. Are you a member of a club? Perhaps you and all the other students in your school voted on the theme for a dance or the destination for a field trip. If so, you have participated in a direct democracy.

POLITICAL FOUNDATIONS *The Acropolis is a hilltop in Athens, Greece, upon which Athenians built their main religious and government buildings during the 400s B.C.* **How is the political system of ancient Greece reflected in the U.S. political system?**

CASE STUDY

The Greek Polis

POLITICAL FOUNDATIONS The roots of direct democracy reach back for centuries to ancient Greece. Ancient Greece had a well-developed political system that, by the 700s B.C., was centered around the polis. The polis, commonly translated as "city-state," was made up of a town or city and its surrounding countryside. Athens and Sparta were among the most important of the ancient Greek city-states.

The polis typically was ruled by an oligarchy of wealthy citizens. However, all citizens, which included only free (nonenslaved) males, were expected to participate actively in the government of the polis.

By the 500s B.C. some city-states had begun to move away from rule by oligarchies. Despite the fact that free males were still the only group to be considered citizens, important democratic changes began to take place.

Athenian direct democracy reached its height in the 400s B.C. All Athenian citizens formed the popular assembly. A Council of Five Hundred, chosen by a drawing from among all citizens, ran the daily business of government. The assembly, however, in which all citizens had the right to vote, had the real power to decide domestic and foreign matters.

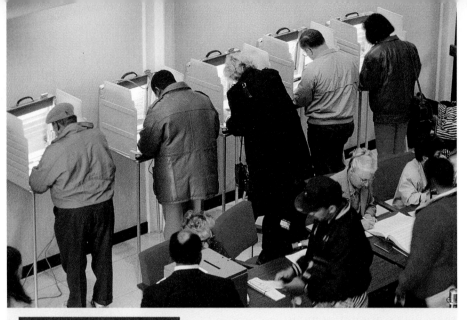

PRINCIPLES OF DEMOCRACY *In a representative democracy, people elect leaders to make public policies. Here, citizens vote in a presidential election.* **Who makes public policies in a direct democracy?**

Representative Democracy It is not always practical for public policies to be made directly by the people. This is particularly true in countries with millions—or, as in the case of the United States, hundreds of millions—of citizens. Most people agree that direct voting on every single law would be difficult if not impossible. Thus, in **representative democracies** such as the United States, the people elect representatives to conduct the business of government for them.

Unlike in dictatorships and other authoritarian forms of government, in representative democracies, government officials answer to the voters. If voters believe that government officials have not acted to promote the public good, they may vote those officials out of office and replace them with other representatives.

SECTION 3 — REVIEW

1. Define the following terms: anarchy, majority rule, minority rights, direct democracy, representative democracy.

2. What five broad principles does democracy promote? Give an example of how each democratic principle affects you personally.

3. How does democracy protect the rights of the minority?

4. How are town hall meetings examples of direct democracy? How is the national government of the United States an example of representative democracy?

5. **Thinking and Writing Critically**
   In what ways do you think modern technology might make direct democracy more practical in the United States? Provide some examples that support your answer.

6. **Applying CITIZENSHIP**
   One way for you to participate in government is to write to your legislators about issues that concern you. Think about some of the issues of concern to your community or to your school. How do these issues affect you? Write a brief letter explaining your concerns to your congressmember.

CHAPTER 1 — SUMMARY

SECTION 1 Government is an institution with the power to make and enforce rules and regulations for a group of people. These rules apply to everyone who lives within the political unit, or state, over which the government has authority. The authority that a government has over the members of a state is called sovereignty. The rules that sovereign states establish for their societies are called laws. The collection of laws and policies that a government makes is referred to as public policy.

Some philosophers have said that rulers—typically kings and queens—receive their authority to govern from God. Others have said that government receives its power from the people it governs and that government should protect the natural rights of citizens. This authority or power is called legitimacy.

Government performs a variety of functions. Included in these are maintaining social order, providing services to people who cannot easily provide for themselves, working to resolve conflict through compromise, and promoting common values shared by society. Good government also works for policies that serve the public good, or public interest.

SECTION 2 Governments differ in their sources of authority and in how power is shared among and within national, regional, and local levels. Forms of government include monarchies, democratic republics, and dictatorships. Monarchs achieve their positions by birth. In democratic republics, authority comes from the people. In dictatorships, one person or a small group of people relies on a combination of political power, military power, wealth, and/or social position to rule.

A government may be a unitary, federal, or confederal system. The power of the central government in relation to other levels of government differs in each system. In a unitary system, the national, or central, government holds all legal power. In a federal system, powers are divided among national, state, and local governments. In a confederal system, independent states join together to accomplish common goals.

Just as power may be distributed among levels of government, power within a single level of government also may be divided. The relationship between the branches of government may take one of two basic forms: presidential systems and parliamentary systems. In a presidential system, the legislative branch, which makes the law, and the executive branch, which carries out the law, are independent of each other. The executive branch is usually headed by a president, who is chosen independently of the legislature. In a parliamentary system, the chief executive, often called a prime minister or premier, is chosen by the parliament, or legislature.

SECTION 3 The five principles of democracy give people the opportunity to make choices, recognize the worth of each person, promote respect for the law, protect minority rights, and make policies that serve the public good.

There are two types of democracy: direct and representative. In a direct democracy, all citizens may directly make laws. In a representative democracy, the people elect representatives to conduct the government's business.

✎ Government Notebook

Review what you wrote in your Government Notebook at the beginning of this chapter about the purpose of government. Now that you have studied the chapter, how would you revise your answer? How well do you think government in the United States carries out its functions? Record your answers in your Notebook.

REVIEW

REVIEWING CONCEPTS

1. How is government authority distributed in unitary, federal, and confederal systems?

2. What are the major functions of government? Which do you consider most important? Why?

3. Why is it important that democracy gives people the opportunity to make choices? Does equality of opportunity mean the same thing as equality of results? Why or why not?

4. What is the difference between direct democracy and representative democracy?

5. How do monarchies and dictatorships differ from democratic republics? Do monarchs of all countries have the same authority? Explain your answer.

THINKING AND WRITING CRITICALLY

1. **POLITICAL FOUNDATIONS** Read the U.S. Declaration of Independence on page 562 of this textbook. In what ways does the Declaration of Independence reflect John Locke's argument of a social contract between government and the people? Provide specific examples from the Declaration to support your position.

2. **POLITICAL PROCESSES** Recall the differences between presidential and parliamentary systems. In which system does the legislative branch choose the chief executive of government? How is the chief executive (the president) chosen in the United States? Do you think the influence of voters is stronger in one system compared to the other? Explain your answer.

3. **CITIZENSHIP** Recall the discussion in Section 1 of the functions of government. What role do you think citizens should play in helping government fulfill each of its functions?

4. **PUBLIC GOOD** In your own words, explain what the term *public good* means. How do you think government can promote the public good?

CITIZENSHIP IN YOUR COMMUNITY

Many communities have citizens' organizations that try to influence government decisions on particular issues. Such organizations include people concerned about senior citizens' issues, the environment, and taxes. Interview a member of one such group about the group's history, purpose, and activities. Use the information you collect to create a brochure about the group. You might want to use images of the group's activities to highlight the brochure's important points.

INDIVIDUAL PORTFOLIO PROJECT

Imagine that you have been appointed U.S. ambassador to a country whose people only recently have overthrown an authoritarian government. You have been invited to give a speech to representatives of the country who are trying to set up a new government. The country has had little experience with democracy, having been ruled for most of its history by dictators. Your job is to describe the benefits and challenges of democracy, using the United States as an example. To prepare your speech, you should consider several questions. Why has democracy worked so well in the United States? What will democracy provide the country's citizens that authoritarian governments did not? What will be required of citizens to make democracy work in their country? Your speech should last about five minutes.

PRACTICING SKILLS: CONDUCTING RESEARCH

To conduct research, you need to use multiple sources. To learn more about dictatorships, start with your textbook. Look up the definition in the Glossary and write it down on a sheet of paper. Then use the Index to find other chapters that discuss this topic. Take notes on the information you find.

To find more information about dictatorships, visit your school or public library. You may want to use the card catalog to find sources containing specific information. Continue taking notes while you work. After you have gathered enough information, write a two- to three-paragraph report defining *dictatorship* and describing how this system of government differs from a democracy.

THE INTERNET: LEARNING ONLINE

Can the Internet help promote democracy? Conduct an Internet search for government discussion groups. You might start with search words such as *government* and *democracy.* What topics are being discussed? Are individuals expressing their opinions, working with others, or calling for action? Write a paragraph explaining why you think the Internet either expands democracy or has no effect on it. Below your paragraph, include a list of each discussion group you visited in your search.

ANALYZING PRIMARY SOURCES

LEVIATHAN

English philosopher Thomas Hobbes (1588–1679) developed theories on the necessity and purpose of government. In *Leviathan* (1651), he describes a world without government (the "condition" mentioned below). Read the excerpt from *Leviathan* and answer the questions that follow.

❝ *In such condition there is no place for industry, because the fruit thereof is uncertain; and consequently no culture of the earth; no navigation nor use of the commodities that may be imported by sea; no commodious [comfortable] building; no instruments of moving and removing such things as require much force; no knowledge of the face of the earth; no account of time; no arts; no letters [literature]; no society; and, which is worst of all, continual fear and danger of violent death; and the life of man solitary, poor, nasty, brutish, and short. . . .*

To this war of every man against every man, this also is consequent [following as a result]: that nothing can be unjust. The notions of right and wrong, justice and injustice, have there no place. Where there is no common power, there is no law: where no law, no injustice. Force and fraud are in war the two cardinal [main] virtues. Justice and injustice are none of the faculties [abilities] neither of the body, nor mind. . . . They are qualities that relate to men in society, not in solitude. It is consequent also to the same condition that there be no propriety [proper way of doing things], no dominion [rule], no mine and thine distinct; but only that to be every man's, that he can get, and for so long, as he can keep it. And thus much for the ill condition which man by mere nature is actually placed in, though with a possibility to come out of it consisting partly in the passions, partly in his reason.

The passions that incline men to peace are fear of death, desire of such things as are necessary to commodious living, and a hope by their industry to obtain them. And reason suggesteth convenient articles of peace, upon which men may be drawn to agreement. ❞

1. According to Hobbes, what does organized society provide? How do these provisions benefit the people in the society?

2. What passions "incline men to peace"?

3. Would a world without government be as Hobbes describes it? Explain.

CHAPTER 2

ORIGINS OF U.S. GOVERNMENT

You are part of one of the most important experiments in the world—the U.S. government. You may not think of your country as an experiment in popular government, but that is exactly how many other nations and peoples view the United States. This means that others have looked to the United States to see if government formed by the people—by citizens such as yourself—can keep a country united.

As you can imagine, the task of forging one nation out of 13 independent states was no small achievement. When the framers of the Constitution transformed a loose confederation of colonies into a federal union, they created a new form of government that has survived, and succeeded, for more than 200 years.

Government Notebook

In your Government Notebook, create a list of the rights and freedoms you have as a U.S. citizen. Where do you think these rights and freedoms originated?

SECTION 1

EARLY INFLUENCES

Political Dictionary

constitution
Magna Carta
rule of law
bicameral
Petition of Right
English Bill of Rights
charter

Objectives

★ What political ideals did English colonists bring with them to North America?
★ What major documents limited the power of English monarchs?
★ How were the ideals of limited and representative government evident in colonial governments?

When English colonists came to North America, they brought with them more than just tools needed to survive, such as hoes and axes for building homes and farms. They also brought the tools for creating a government—important ideals that had formed the basis of government in England.

An English Heritage

The ideals the English colonists brought to North America can still be found in British government today. Although Great Britain does not have a written **constitution**—a basic set of laws and principles establishing the nation's government—it has laws, historical documents, and judicial decisions dating back hundreds of years.

Two important British ideals strongly influenced the colonists in North America: limited government and representative government. These ideals helped shape government in the colonies—and later in the United States—in a way that serves the public good.

Limited Government Before the 1200s there were few limits on government in England. For example, monarchs could tax people or seize property at will, as well as give land to people who were loyal to them.

Consider what it would be like if student-body presidents had such power. They might reserve part of the gym for use only by their close friends. They might even decide to charge students a fee to pay for student government.

Of course, student-body presidents do not have such power. A president must act within the rules set by the school administration and an elected student council. In short, these forces limit what student government can do without the consent of the governed—the students.

The English nobles—the weathy landowners who enjoyed certain social and legal privileges—were no happier with their monarch's unlimited power than you would be with an all-powerful student-body president. In 1215 these nobles forced King John to sign **Magna Carta**, or "Great Charter." This

The Granger Collection, New York

POLITICAL FOUNDATIONS *This engraving created in the 1800s shows King John signing Magna Carta in 1215.* **How did Magna Carta help to limit the monarch's power?**

document limited the monarchy's power by helping establish the **rule of law**, under which government leaders, even monarchs, must act according to set laws. For example, monarchs could no longer levy taxes without the nobles' approval. The charter also gave people accused of crimes the right to a trial by their peers, or equals. This right prevented a monarch from imprisoning people or taking away their property on his or her sole authority. Although Magna Carta was meant only for the nobility, in time its protections applied to all English citizens.

By requiring English monarchs to consider how their decisions would affect the people they governed, Magna Carta laid the foundation for government that promotes the public good. As noted in Chapter 1, government promotes the public good when it reflects the interests of society as a whole instead of the narrow interests of the few or of one individual, such as a monarch.

Representative Government The English ideal of representative government is even older than the ideal of limited government. Representative government has its roots in a council of nobles and high religious officials that advised monarchs even before the signing of Magna Carta. This council gradually grew in importance. Eventually, representatives of local towns and villages became part of the council.

Over time the advisory council evolved into a **bicameral**, or two-chamber, legislature called Parliament. Nobles composed the upper house, or the House of Lords. The lower house, or the House of Commons, included lesser officials and local representatives. As representatives of the people, members of Parliament worked to limit the power of English monarchs. Two important documents—the Petition of Right and the English Bill of Rights—helped Parliament do this.

PRINCIPLES OF DEMOCRACY *England's bicameral Parliament is illustrated in these drawings of the House of Lords (left) and the House of Commons (right). **Which house was made up of lesser officials and local representatives?***

Parliament forced Charles I to sign the **Petition of Right** in 1628. Like Magna Carta, the Petition of Right limited the ability of the monarch to act on his or her sole authority. The Petition of Right said that monarchs could not imprison people illegally, force citizens to house soldiers in their homes, or establish military rule during times of peace. It also required monarchs to obtain Parliament's approval, rather than simply the nobles' approval, before levying taxes.

Like Magna Carta, the Petition of Right was crucial to the development of government that promotes the public good. In forcing Charles to sign the Petition of Right, a representative body had placed restrictions on the monarch's power. It gave the people, through their representatives, a voice in government and made sure that the many opinions in a society would be heard.

The Petition of Right was part of an extended conflict between Charles and Parliament. That conflict eventually erupted into a civil war in which the army of Parliament defeated Charles's supporters. Charles was beheaded in 1649, and England did not have another king until 1660, when Charles II assumed the throne. James II, Charles's brother, succeeded him in 1685.

Parliamentary leaders who disagreed with James and his policies forced him from the throne by encouraging William of Orange, the husband of James's daughter, Mary, to invade England. In the Glorious Revolution of 1688, William arrived with his troops, and James fled the country. Parliament then asked William and Mary to serve as king and queen of England. Before they took the throne, however, Parliament forced them to accept the English Bill of Rights.

The **English Bill of Rights** clearly established that the monarchy could not rule without consent of Parliament. The document included many protections, such as the right to petition the king without fear of punishment and free parliamentary elections. It also forbade the monarch from maintaining an army without parliamentary consent and said that Parliament should operate without royal interference.

Along with Magna Carta and the Petition of Right, the English Bill of Rights helped protect citizens' rights from government violation. The government could not violate or deny these rights and could rule only with the consent of the people it governed. This idea remains fundamental to ensuring that government serves and protects the public's best interests.

Colonial Development

By the time the Petition of Right and the English Bill of Rights were passed, English colonists had begun to settle parts of North America. The first permanent English colony was established at Jamestown, Virginia, in 1607. The organization of Jamestown and of later settlements clearly showed the influence of the basic principles of English government.

Charters The Jamestown colony was the first of several permanent colonies established by charter. A **charter** was an agreement whereby the English monarch gave settlers the right to establish a colony.

The efforts to limit government in the colonies were evident in most charters. The Massachusetts charter, for example, guaranteed elections.

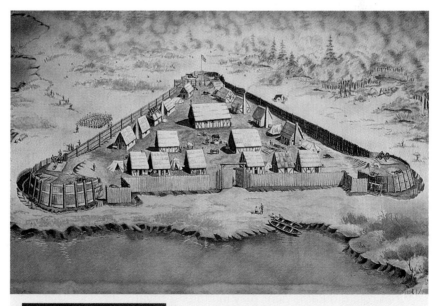

POLITICAL FOUNDATIONS *This painting of Jamestown, Virginia, by Francis Dayton illustrates the first permanent English colony in North America.* **What was the purpose of charters during English colonization?**

PRINCIPLES OF DEMOCRACY *This portrait of the trustees of Georgia, the ruling body of the colony of Georgia, is believed to have been painted in the 1700s.* ***How did colonial governments reflect the ideals of limited and representative government?***

Officers were chosen from among the male settlers who were given the charter. The charter also gave these men the power and authority to establish an assembly that would make laws, elect officers, and govern the colony.

Governments With the addition of Georgia in 1733, the number of colonies grew to 13. Each colony had a system that reflected the ideals of limited and representative government. For example, each colony's governor served as the government's executive. Some governors were appointed and others were elected. Most governors, however, were

advised by a council, which also served as the highest court in the colony and, in some cases, had as much power as the governor. The councils generally were made up of 12 male property owners who acted as advisers to the governor. In some colonies the council served as the upper house of the colony's assembly. Most colonies also had an assembly made up of the colonists' elected representatives. These councils and representative assemblies served to limit the governors' power.

There were three types of colonies—royal, proprietary, and corporate. Royal colonies—the most common type—belonged directly to the crown. Virginia was a royal colony. Proprietary colonies were those whose territory was granted by the king to an individual (or small group of individuals), called a proprietor, and put under the proprietor's personal control. Pennsylvania and Maryland were proprietary colonies. Corporate colonies were founded without any authorization from the English government. Although England controlled military affairs and trade in the corporate colonies, the Crown exercised such control on an irregular basis. Connecticut and Rhode Island were corporate colonies.

SECTION 1 — REVIEW

1. Define the following terms: constitution, Magna Carta, rule of law, bicameral, Petition of Right, English Bill of Rights, charter.

2. Describe the political ideals the colonists brought from England to North America.

3. In what ways are Magna Carta, the Petition of Right, and the English Bill of Rights related? What role did Parliament play in limiting royal power in England?

4. How was the power of colonial governors limited?

5. **Thinking and Writing Critically**
The English people worked to limit what they believed was the unjust exercise of authority over them. They were not, however, trying to eliminate all authority over their lives. Why should authority, when it is exercised fairly, be respected? Why is it important?

6. **Applying POLITICAL FOUNDATIONS**
Conduct an Internet search for the English Bill of Rights. List the fundamental freedoms that it guaranteed. Which freedoms do you think are more important?

INDEPENDENCE

Political Dictionary

New England
   Confederation
Albany Plan of Union
Stamp Act
tyranny
boycott
delegate
unicameral

Objectives

★ What were two early attempts at unity among the colonies?
★ What British policies pushed the colonies to cooperate with one another?
★ What were some of the ideals that influenced the writing of the Declaration of Independence?
★ How were the governments of the newly independent states similar?

When the first English colonists arrived in North America, they found that the land presented them with dangers as well as opportunities. These common dangers pushed the 13 colonies toward unity. Although early attempts at unity failed, the British government's actions eventually united the colonists in a common cause: independence.

Searching for Unity

Uniting the 13 colonies was a difficult task that presented several obstacles. What were the sources of differences among the colonies?

Obstacles One obstacle to colonial unity stemmed from the colonists' having come to North America for different reasons. Early colonists who settled in Virginia, for example, were sent by a company that wanted to make money from the region's natural resources. In contrast, the Puritans

of the Massachusetts Bay Colony came to establish an ideal society in which they could freely practice their religion. The colony of Georgia, meanwhile, was created as a refuge for debtors who would otherwise have been put in jail. It also attracted people fleeing from religious persecution.

Varying economies and geography also led to differences among the colonies. The New England colonies developed fishing, lumber, and crafts industries. In contrast, South Carolina's colonists grew crops that thrived in a warm, moist climate. (See "Linking Government and Geography," page 27.)

Attempts at Unity Despite their differences, the English colonists did face some of the same dangers, such as the possibility of conflict with neighboring American Indians and non-English colonists. The need for defense produced two important, though unsuccessful, attempts at unity.

The first attempt was the **New England Confederation** of 1643. The colonies in this confederation agreed to work together to defend against attacks by American Indians or by settlers of nearby Dutch colonies. The confederation had few powers, however. The objection of just one colony could keep the confederation from taking

The Metropolitan Museum of Art, Bequest of Jacob Rupert, 1939 (39.65.53)

POLITICAL FOUNDATIONS *The bronze statue* The Puritan, *made by American artist Augustus Saint-Gaudens in the 1800s, symbolically portrays Puritan life.* **Why did many Puritans leave England to live in North America?**

action. As a result, disagreements often prevented cooperation. The lack of cooperation, as well as an easing of the threat of attack by unfriendly neighbors, led to the end of the confederation in 1684.

Conflict between Britain and France brought a new effort at unity 70 years later. France controlled a part of present-day Canada and other land to the west of the British colonies. To plan for a defense against possible attacks by the French and their American Indian allies, the British government called a meeting of colonial representatives in 1754. Representatives of seven British colonies met with the Iroquois in Albany, New York, to form an alliance and develop a plan of action.

At the meeting, colonial representatives adopted the **Albany Plan of Union**, proposed by Benjamin Franklin. The plan called for a council of colony representatives that could levy taxes and raise an army. The council also would regulate trade with American Indians. The individual colonial and British governments rejected the plan, however, so it was never put into effect.

An Ocean Apart

Although the need for common defense did not unify the colonies, other developments brought the colonies closer together. At the same time, however, these developments strained the relationship between the colonies and Great Britain.

Political Distance Most of the colonies shared a growing political distance from Britain. The colonists had long been allowed to handle many of their internal affairs. In the more than 150 years since the first permanent settlement was established, elected assemblies in the colonies had gradually increased their authority.

In turn, the power of governors and their advisory councils began to weaken. Governors often felt more pressure from local colonial interests than from the far-away British government. In addition, the governors' salaries were controlled by the elected colonial assemblies.

British Policies The political distance between the colonies and Great Britain widened further after 1760, when the British throne passed to George III. There was a growing attitude among members of Parliament that the colonies had become too independent. The real spark to tensions, however, was the Seven Years' War, a global struggle that involved several European countries, including Great Britian.

The Seven Years' War had plunged Britain deep into debt. Because part of the conflict—known as the French and Indian War—was fought on North American soil, the British government believed the colonists should help pay off the debt. Many members of Parliament also thought that it was time for the colonists to help pay for their own future defense against hostile forces.

To help raise money, the government under George III began to enforce a number of trade restrictions and taxes. In 1765, for example, Parliament passed the **Stamp Act**, which required colonists to pay a tax on many paper goods. A tax stamp on a newspaper, contract, or deck of playing cards showed that the tax had been paid.

In addition to raising money, the Stamp Act and other policies also served to protect British businesses. By forcing colonists to pay taxes on goods purchased from other countries, the government gave British businesses an advantage—the taxes made non-British foreign goods more expensive than those from Britain. The high prices caused by the policies angered colonial businesspeople who made money by importing non-British goods to sell in the colonies.

POLITICAL FOUNDATIONS *Benjamin Franklin, shown in this portrait painted by Joseph Wright, proposed the Albany Plan of Union.* **What did the plan propose?**

Linking Government and History

Geographic Differences Among the Colonies

Before the colonists declared their independence from Great Britain, few common ties unified the American colonies. The colonies had been founded at different times and for different reasons. In addition, geographic factors such as climate and soil quality caused the northern, middle, and southern colonies to develop economies that were distinct from one another. These factors also created political divisions among colonies, particularly the northern and southern colonies.

In the northern colonies, short growing seasons; thin, rocky soil; and frigid, hostile winters made farming difficult. Land was divided into small farms owned by individual families. Each of these farms usually produced only enough crops to feed the family that operated it. Poor agricultural conditions led many New Englanders to find work in other occupations. Many colonists fished full-time to earn their living, which helped spur economic growth in coastal port cities.

The settlement of the middle colonies was similar to that of the northern colonies, with land divided into individual family farms. However, the region's geography—rich soil, good water resources, and a moderate climate—made agriculture more profitable in this region. Farmers were able to raise crops for export to domestic and foreign markets.

In contrast, the warm, wet climate and an extended growing season of the southern colonies allowed southern planters to raise more crops in a year than farmers in the middle and northern colonies. Property in this region was divided into large plantations that produced export crops. Plantations were often built along large rivers and had their own docks, so ships could load crops and head directly for major trade destinations. This reduced the need for coastal port cities in the South.

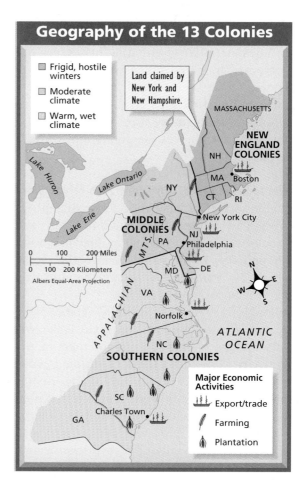

Early colonists produced a variety of goods and services. Each region's geographic features helped to shape its economy.

Although the northern, middle, and southern colonists lived in different geographic regions, they all faced the challenges of settling and clearing land. Transporting goods to colonial markets also was difficult for farmers and planters throughout the colonies.

Eventually, the colonies achieved the unity needed to launch a new nation. Common goals, such as the desire for independence from Great Britain, forced them to unite in spite of geographic and economic differences.

What Do You Think?

1. Do you think that citizens of the United States still identify with the geographic regions in which they live? Give examples to support your answer.

2. How has technology eliminated some of the physical barriers among the colonies?

Colonial Reaction

Many colonists were outraged. They not only saw the policies as unfair to colonial businesses but also objected to being taxed when the British Parliament had no colonial representatives. Colonists argued that such taxation without representation was **tyranny**—absolute rule by a government that ignores the rights and welfare of the people.

Protests In October 1765, representatives from nine colonies met in New York at the Stamp Act Congress. They wrote a Declaration of Rights and Grievances to protest the Stamp Act and other British policies. Colonists also boycotted some British goods. A **boycott** is an agreement to stop buying or using a good or service.

Although Parliament eventually repealed the Stamp Act, it passed additional taxes and laws. Protests against such actions continued in the colonies. In 1770 these tensions erupted when British soldiers fired into a crowd of angry colonial protesters in Boston. Five people were killed in what became known as the Boston Massacre.

In 1772 colonial activist Samuel Adams formed a group in Boston to help with the growing colonial resistance. The group developed as part of a network of patriotic groups called the Committees of Correspondence, which had been established in 1763. The network allowed colonists to communicate with each other about British policies.

In 1773 violence again broke out when Adams and other angry colonists, dressed as American Indians, boarded ships in Boston Harbor and dumped British tea overboard. This event, known as the Boston Tea Party, was a protest against a decision by Parliament to give a company outside of North America all rights to the tea trade in the colonies.

In response to the Boston Tea Party, the British government passed another set of laws in 1774. Called the Intolerable Acts by the colonists, the new laws tightened British control over the colonies even further and inspired the colonists to greater action.

Continental Congresses In 1774 delegates from all the colonies except Georgia met in Philadelphia at the First Continental Congress. A **delegate** is someone who officially represents the interests of other people or of a government. The Congress protested British policies and sent George III the Declaration and Resolves of the First Continental Congress. It also called for a boycott of British goods until British colonial policies were changed. The delegates planned for a second congress to meet the following May if need arose.

Officials in the British government responded by passing even stricter measures to tighten control over the colonies. The growing tensions finally led to battles between British troops and Massachusetts colonial militia at Lexington and Concord, on April 19, 1775.

Less than a month after the battles at Lexington and Concord, the Second Continental

PRINCIPLES OF DEMOCRACY *The Boston Massacre of 1770 is portrayed in this engraving of a painting by Alonzo Chappel.* **How did the British government spark the rebellion that erupted into the Boston Massacre?**

Comparing → Governments

Canada's Independence from Great Britain

When America's 13 colonies declared their independence from Great Britain in 1776, a new, completely independent nation was born. In 1867 Canada also gained independence from Britain. However, by signing the British North America Act, Canada did not make a complete break with Great Britain. Instead, the new Dominion of Canada became a self-governing nation with control over only its domestic policies. Great Britain continued to govern Canada's foreign affairs until 1931. Eventually, Canada gained complete independence with the passing of the Constitution Act in 1982.

Today Canada is a federation with a parliamentary democracy. It is a member of the Commonwealth of Nations, an association of nations and territories that were once part of the former British Empire. The Canadian prime minister is the nation's leader, while the British monarch functions as Canada's symbolic head of government. The national parliament features a 104-member Senate and a 295-member House of Commons. Each of Canada's 10 provinces—which are similar to U.S. states—and 2 territories has a parliament headed by a provincial prime minister.

Congress met in Philadelphia. Again, representatives from 12 of the 13 colonies attended. This time, however, they met to discuss a plan of action, for the war had already begun. The road to independence lay ahead.

Declaration of Independence

By June 1776 nearly all delegates to the Second Continental Congress favored independence. They appointed several people to a committee to write a document explaining why they believed that independence was necessary. The Second Continental Congress adopted the Declaration of Independence on July 4, 1776. (See pages 562–64.)

The Declaration of Independence was written by a committee of five men: John Adams, Benjamin Franklin, Thomas Jefferson, Robert Livingston, and Roger Sherman. Jefferson, however, wrote most of the document.

Jefferson wrote about the "unalienable rights" of human beings—rights that cannot be taken away—including "life, liberty, and the pursuit of happiness." Recalling the arguments of philosopher John Locke, Jefferson also wrote that governments receive "their just powers from the consent of the governed." When a government fails to protect citizens' natural rights, the people have the right "to alter or to abolish it, and to institute new government." The Declaration also criticized George III's refusal to support actions that were "wholesome and necessary for the public good."

In many ways the Declaration of Independence mapped out the kind of government that Jefferson and his fellow delegates wanted for the colonies.

POLITICAL FOUNDATIONS *This painting by American artist Jean Leon Gerome Ferris shows Thomas Jefferson, John Adams, and Benjamin Franklin drafting the Declaration of Independence.* **How did the Declaration of Independence outline the basic rights and liberties of citizens?**

Such a government was one that would include protections for basic rights and liberties. It also was one that would rely on the consent of the governed for authority and consider their broader interests. In short, this government would be more likely than other forms of government to act in ways that promote the public good.

State Governments

The individual governments of the colonies changed with independence. In early 1776, even before independence, some colonies had adopted new constitutions. Following the Declaration of Independence, the other colonies also adopted new constitutions. The new constitutions were similar in a number of ways.

Structure Not surprisingly, the constitutions reflected a desire for limited government. Legislatures elected by the people dominated the state governments, and legislative elections were held each year in all but one state. Colonists' belief in the importance of regular elections could be seen in a statement by John Adams: "When annual elections end, there slavery [of the people] begins."

All the legislatures were bicameral with the exception of Pennsylvania's **unicameral**, or one-chamber, legislature. (In their first constitutions,

Georgia and Vermont also had unicameral legislatures. Later, they adopted bicameral legislatures, as did Pennsylvania.) Most new state constitutions gave few powers to the states' governors, because people associated a strong executive with the abuses of monarchy. They feared that a strong executive might eventually destroy representative government. Nine of the constitutions even limited a governor's term to one year.

Rights The new state constitutions also showed the influence of earlier efforts to protect individual rights. For example, most constitutions listed the rights that belonged to the people. Many of these rights were the same as those outlined in the English Bill of Rights and in colonial charters.

In addition, some states expanded voting rights. Although the colonial assemblies were elected bodies, not everyone had been able to vote in the elections. Depending on the colony, as much as 50 percent of free males could not vote, because many of the colonies had property qualifications for voting. In the new state constitutions, some of these restrictions were removed or lessened. By 1790 five states allowed all adult white male taxpayers to vote. Restrictions based on race and gender generally prohibited most American Indians, free and enslaved blacks, and women from voting, however.

SECTION 2 — REVIEW

1. Define the following terms: New England Confederation, Albany Plan of Union, Stamp Act, tyranny, boycott, delegate, unicameral.

2. What were the purposes of the New England Confederation and the Albany Plan of Union? Why were they unsuccessful?

3. How did British colonial policy change after 1760? How did colonists react?

4. Why did the authors of the Declaration of Independence believe that British colonial policies violated the ideals of limited and representative government?

5. Why did early state governments have weak governors?

6. **Thinking and Writing Critically**
   How do you think history might have been different had the Albany Plan of Union been approved by the British and colonial governments? Do you think that America still would have become an independent nation?

7. **Applying** POLITICAL FOUNDATIONS
   The Stamp Act of 1765 created conflict between the colonists and the British government. Conduct an Internet search for other acts established by the British government to tax the colonists. Name one of these acts and briefly describe the products it taxed. Does the site you found describe colonial reaction to the act?

THE FIRST NATIONAL GOVERNMENT

Political Dictionary

Articles of
  Confederation
ratification
Northwest Ordinance

Objectives

★ What were the powers of the national government under the Articles of Confederation?

★ How did limits on its power weaken the national government under the Articles?

★ How did the states continue to struggle with unity after independence?

★ How did Shays's Rebellion highlight the need for a stronger national government?

Most of the fighting in the Revolutionary War ended with a U.S. victory at the Battle of Yorktown in 1781. A new challenge now lay before the 13 independent states—that of forming a new government. In the same year the war ended, the states created a confederation, or what they called a "league of friendship." The weaknesses of this confederation, however, made unity among the states difficult and created pressure for a stronger national government.

Articles of Confederation

The Second Continental Congress had held the 13 states together during the war. It had run the affairs of the new nation during much of the fighting and had appointed George Washington as commander in chief of the army in 1775. The Congress also had negotiated treaties with foreign powers, created a national currency, borrowed money, and established

a postal service. There was, however, no constitution or other legal document giving Congress the authority to take these actions.

To remedy this, in 1777 the Second Continental Congress created a document to form a single national government. This document, the **Articles of Confederation**, loosely tied together the 13 independent states and gave a new national Congress the authority to act that the Second Continental Congress had lacked. Before it could go into effect, however, the Articles required the **ratification**, or formal approval, of all 13 states. Maryland, the last state to ratify the Articles, did so in 1781.

Many leaders in the former British colonies wanted a loose confederation of states. They feared that creating a strong national government would threaten the power of the states and the freedoms of the people. Therefore, the Articles of Confederation limited the powers of the national government.

Powers The powers of the new government lay in a unicameral legislature: the Congress. Delegates to the Congress were chosen by each state's legislature. Each state delegation had one vote. Majority approval was required to pass most decisions, while nine votes were necessary to make major decisions, such as whether to wage war or to sign a particular treaty. Any amendment to the Articles required the approval

POLITICAL FOUNDATIONS *The Articles of Confederation were ratified by the colonies in 1781.*
Why did many leaders want the loose confederation of states that was created under the Articles?

of all 13 states. There was no national executive or judicial branch.

Only Congress, not the individual states, had the power to declare war and to conduct foreign policy. Congress appointed Benjamin Franklin and John Adams as U.S. representatives to France, for example. The Articles also gave Congress the authority to borrow money, establish military forces, settle arguments between states, and manage relations with American Indians.

CASE STUDY

The Northwest Ordinance

 **POLITICAL FOUNDATIONS** The Articles of Confederation also gave Congress the power to admit new states to the Union. This power proved to be critical to the future of the United States.

Through a peace agreement signed after the Revolutionary War, the United States acquired

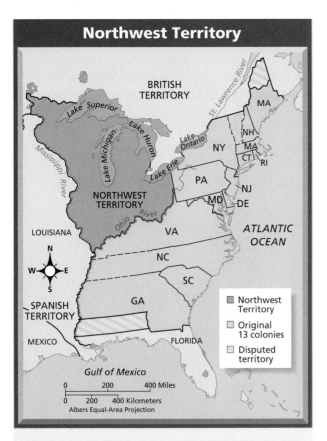

Northwest Territory

Legend:
- Northwest Territory
- Original 13 colonies
- Disputed territory

*The Northwest Ordinance was passed by Congress in 1787 to manage the development of the newly acquired Northwest Territory. **What were some of the main points of the Northwest Ordinance?***

from Great Britain a large area between the 13 states and the Mississippi River. To manage development of this area, Congress passed the **Northwest Ordinance** of 1787, which set procedures for granting statehood to territories within the region.

The ordinance was one of the most important bills passed by the national government under the Articles of Confederation. Of particular importance was its ban on slavery within the Northwest Territory. The ordinance also served as the model for admitting all other states to the Union. It allowed new states to join the Union as equal partners with the original 13 states. This condition showed the desire of the country's leaders to prevent new states from being unfairly ruled by the original states. They did not want to replace British tyranny with a new tyranny of the original 13 states.

In addition to its rules on statehood, the ordinance included a bill of rights for the territories. These rights guaranteed representative government, religious freedom, and trial by jury, among other freedoms. These rights ensured that new states would have governments whose authority came from the consent of the people.

Limits on Power The Articles gave Congress several powers. To keep the national government from becoming stronger than the states, however, those powers were limited. For example, the exclusion of a president and an executive branch meant that there were no officials to carry out Congress's laws.

Congress also had no power to tax. It could ask member states for voluntary contributions, but it could not require that they pay. This meant that it was difficult to raise money for a national army or to repay money that the country had borrowed. In addition, Congress could not prevent the states from issuing their own money.

Furthermore, Congress had no power to regulate trade among states or with foreign countries. The states therefore could tax products coming from other states. For example, Virginia passed a tax law stating that any ship at its ports that failed

Limits on the Power of the National Government Under the Articles of Confederation (1781)

- No president or executive branch
- No national court system
- No officials to enforce laws
- No power to tax
- No power to regulate trade
- No power to establish national armed forces (each state raised its own troops under the direction of Congress)
- Major laws required approval of 9 out of 13 states to pass

The Articles of Confederation, ratified in 1781, limited the power of the national government. **How did these limits create obstacles for the national government?**

differences to unite against Great Britain, these cultural, economic, and geographic obstacles resurfaced after the war.

Cultural Differences Although many citizens of the new nation had a common language and ancestry, their beliefs—particularly religious ones—and ways of life often varied from state to state. Domination by a particular religious group varied from colony to colony. For example, while the Baptist Church was strongest in Rhode Island and North Carolina, the Presbyterian Church had the most members in New Jersey and Delaware. In addition, although around 48 percent of the colonists were from England, settlers had also come from Germany, France, and Sweden. Cultural differences raised concerns about a union that tied states too closely together. Many people feared that a strong unified government might force some groups to give up their beliefs.

Economic Differences Important economic differences from colonial years also were evident in the new nation. States feared that the economic interests of certain regions would win unfair advantages under a strong national government.

Slavery was a divisive economic as well as cultural issue. Southern plantation owners used slaves to work their fields. Many people, particularly in the states where slavery was illegal, opposed this practice. They believed that slavery violated the principles on which the nation was founded, especially the need to protect the natural rights of all

to pay duty could have its cargo legally seized. This law was intended to keep Maryland, Pennsylvania, and Massachusetts businesses from competing with those in Virginia. Such barriers to trade created major obstacles to economic development in the young country.

The absence of a national court system also added to the weakness of the national government. The lack of national courts meant that the government was forced to rely on state courts to enforce national laws. In addition, Congress had no powers to force states to obey the laws it passed.

Efforts to strengthen Congress's powers to deal with important problems often failed because amendments to the Articles required the approval of all the states. In other words, just one state could block approval of an amendment.

Obstacles to Unity Resurface

The weaknesses of the Articles made unity among the states difficult. As noted in Section 2, differences among the colonies had been obstacles to unity before the Revolutionary War. Although the colonies had temporarily put aside many of their

POLITICAL FOUNDATIONS *This painting from the 1700s shows slaves bringing indigo in from the fields. Colonists had conflicting views on the practice of slavery.* **What principle did many people believe slavery violated?**

human beings. Southern states thus feared that their economic livelihood would suffer under a strong national government that opposed slavery.

Geographic Isolation The size of the new nation also made it difficult to form ties among the states. Transportation between northern and southern states was not easy or quick. (See "Linking Government and Geography," page 27.)

Pressure for Stronger Government

The relative independence of the various states posed many problems for the young nation. Some states refused to pay taxes to the national government, obey laws passed by Congress, and respect terms of foreign treaties. In fact, some states negotiated directly with foreign powers. Some states even formed their own armed services. These problems led many people to believe that a strong national government posed far less of a threat to the public good than did a weak government that could not unify the country or enforce the law.

In September 1786, representatives from Virginia organized a convention in Annapolis, Maryland, to try to resolve some of the differences among the states. Only five states—Delaware, New Jersey, New York, Pennsylvania, and Virginia—attended the Annapolis Convention, but the delegates determined that a future meeting should be called to consider changes to the Articles. The convention called for all of the states to send representatives to Philadelphia in May 1787.

An armed rebellion in Massachusetts later in 1786 was further proof that a stronger national government was needed to maintain order and to protect and promote the public good of citizens in all states. The incident involved groups of armed farmers trying to prevent the state from seizing the property of people who could not pay their debts. (The Revolutionary War and economic problems afterward had left many farmers burdened by heavy debt.) The fighting came to be known as Shays's Rebellion, named after its leader, Daniel Shays. The rebellion eventually was put down by force, but it caused some people, including George Washington, to express frustration that the new nation could win a difficult war but could not keep order in peacetime.

As a result, by early 1787 several states had already chosen delegates for the May meeting. Shays's Rebellion also had forced the national Congress to officially recognize the need for a meeting among the states. Officials declared, however, that the meeting in Philadelphia was "for the sole and express purpose of revising the Articles of Confederation." No mention was made of writing a new constitution.

SECTION 3 —REVIEW

1. Define the following terms: Articles of Confederation, ratification, Northwest Ordinance.

2. What powers did the Articles of Confederation give the national government?

3. How did the states limit the powers of the national government under the Articles?

4. How did cultural, economic, and geographic problems make unity among the states difficult after the Revolutionary War?

5. What was Shays's Rebellion? How did it highlight weaknesses of the national government under the Articles?

6. **Thinking and Writing Critically**
What do you think would have happened if the Northwest Ordinance had not required that new states be admitted to the Union as equals to the original states? What might it be like today if the original 13 states had more say in how the national government makes decisions than the other states?

7. **Applying** POLITICAL FOUNDATIONS
Conduct an Internet search to find information about colonial settlements in North America. List the reason each was founded, if available. Where was each located? Does the site list resources of each colony?

THE CONSTITUTIONAL CONVENTION

Political Dictionary

Virginia Plan
New Jersey Plan
Great Compromise

Objectives

★ Who were the delegates to the Constitutional Convention?
★ What major competing plans of government did the convention delegates debate?
★ What were some of the compromises reached by the delegates?

On May 25, 1787, delegates met in Philadelphia to consider establishing a stronger national government for the 13 states. As the delegates arrived in the city, Philadelphia newspapers trumpeted their arrival, printing their names and political honors. Many in the city were proud that Philadelphia had been chosen as the site for the meeting, instead of New York City, where Congress met.

At the time, the delegates' home states did not attribute as much significance to the Convention as people would later. For example, the states provided limited financial support. Many delegates ran into debt at the boardinghouses where they were staying. At one difficult point during the Convention, a delegate suggested that his colleagues begin each day with a prayer. Another delegate responded that the Convention lacked the money to pay a minister.

Nonetheless, the Convention proceeded through the hottest Philadelphia summer in 30 years. The windows were kept closed, shutting out swarms of flies and shutting in the Convention's discussions.

Delegates worked in secrecy, hoping to ensure free and open debate without interference from outsiders.

The delegates worked for four months, considering different plans of government. Who were these delegates? How did they finally piece together a plan for a new, stronger national government?

The Delegates

The delegates to the Constitutional Convention included many of the country's most distinguished leaders and political thinkers. Of the 55 delegates, 8 had signed the Declaration of Independence, 7 had been in the First Continental Congress, and 7 had been state governors. Most were wealthy and college-educated. Many would go on to become officials in the national government.

Among the best-known delegates were George Washington, Benjamin Franklin, and Alexander Hamilton. Washington was unanimously named chairman of the convention. His participation added a great deal of distinction to the gathering. Franklin was a respected scientist and philosopher. Hamilton had fought in the Revolution and served as a delegate in the Continental Congress.

Some other well-known leaders were absent. Thomas Jefferson was in Europe as a U.S. representative to France. Others, such as Patrick Henry from Virginia, declined to attend the Convention.

"Let's leave out "NO TAXATION" "WITHOUT REPRESENTATION"! What congress would vote taxes without consulting the people?"

© Tribune Media Services, Inc. All rights reserved. Reprinted with permission.

CONSTITUTIONAL GOVERNMENT *The decisions made by the framers of the Constitution have had a lasting influence on the role of government in this country.* **What might have happened if some of the key limits placed on government had been left out of the Constitution?**

They were suspicious that the delegates were plotting to create a powerful central government. Henry, for one, said that he "smelt a rat."

Perhaps the most important delegate to the convention was James Madison of Virginia. Madison is sometimes called the "father of the Constitution." The notes he took during the Convention became the main record of what went on during the gathering. Madison prepared himself for the Convention by studying books about history and politics. Jefferson even sent him hundreds of books from Paris.

Rival Plans

Almost as soon as the Convention began, debate moved beyond the original goal of strengthening the Articles of Confederation to one of creating a new government. Indeed, the Convention adopted a resolution calling for a national government "to consist of a supreme legislative, executive, and judiciary." Debate centered around two competing plans for the government.

Virginia Plan Madison and his fellow Virginians proposed what became known as the **Virginia Plan**. This plan called for a strong government with a bicameral legislature, a strong executive, and a judiciary, a significant change from the Articles of Confederation. Membership in the legislature would be based on a state's population. The largest states, such as Virginia, Pennsylvania, North Carolina, Massachusetts, and Maryland, would have a greater number of representatives than the smaller states.

The people would directly elect one legislative house. States would nominate candidates for the second house. The first house would then elect members to the second house from among the state nominees.

Rival Constitutional Plans

VIRGINIA PLAN		NEW JERSEY PLAN
• Strong executive who is chosen by legislature and carries out laws made by legislature	**EXECUTIVE BRANCH**	• Weak executive controlled by legislature
• Bicameral legislature • Membership based on state's population • First house elected by the people • Second house elected by first house from among candidates nominated by states	**LEGISLATIVE BRANCH**	• Strong unicameral legislature • Each state represented equally with one vote apiece • Representatives chosen by state legislatures
• A judiciary that includes a supreme court and lower courts and is elected by legislature	**JUDICIAL BRANCH**	• A supreme court with justices named by legislature
• To levy taxes • To make national laws • To regulate trade	**POWERS OF NATIONAL GOVERNMENT**	• To levy taxes • To regulate trade

Two competing plans for a national government emerged from the Constitutional Convention. **What are the major differences in the two plans?**

RESEARCHER CD-ROM

Careers in Government

National Park Ranger

When you think of park rangers, you probably envision uniformed men and women patrolling the nation's forests, canyons, and mountainsides and protecting its natural resources. Indeed, this is the role of many park rangers across the country. The National Park System, however, also includes sites of historical importance. National parks are a key part of the effort to preserve the natural and cultural heritage of the United States.

For example, at Philadelphia's Independence National Historical Park, where "the shrines of American liberty" are preserved and showcased, park rangers guide visitors through 24 historic sites daily. The park's centerpiece and most popular attraction is Independence Hall, where the Declaration of Independence was signed in 1776 and the Constitution was written in 1787. Park

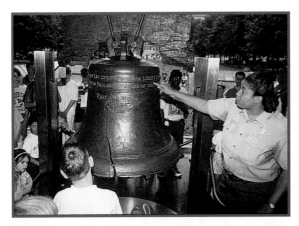

A park ranger at the Independence National Historical Park reads the inscription on the Liberty Bell to tourists.

rangers at Independence National Historical Park are responsible for providing visitors with information about the historical significance of the site as well as for keeping visitors safe and preserving the national treasures in the park.

At Independence National Historical Park, approximately 75 park rangers are employed in the area of "interpretive work." Their job is interpreting history, primarily by giving historical tours. These rangers usually bring with them an interest in U.S. history, a college degree in a field such as history, and several years of experience working as a seasonal park employee or a museum guide. Another 25 rangers are responsible for law enforcement in the park. Their job is to protect the park's resources and manage the public's use of the park.

There is a great deal of competition for park ranger jobs. Having knowledge of several different subjects—such as U.S. history, behavioral sciences, botany, geology, and forestry—is a great advantage. Park rangers employed in the area of historical interpretation must have good communication skills, because they spend much of their time providing information.

Rangers must be willing to relocate often and to work at several different parks in order to move to higher-level positions in prime locations. Entry-level positions may involve keeping the park clean, working at an information desk, giving tours, and collecting entrance fees. Higher-level jobs often require giving lectures, setting up exhibits, and managing park resources. If you think this is the career for you, the best way to start is to volunteer at a historic site in your area.

Members of both the executive and judicial branches would be chosen by the legislature. The executive would carry out the laws passed by the legislature. The judiciary would include a national court system. Both branches would check the power of the legislative branch.

The national government would have the power to levy taxes, to make laws for the whole nation, and to regulate trade. The national government could reject state laws that violated national laws.

And, in contrast to Congress under the Articles, the national government could force states to obey national laws.

New Jersey Plan Some delegates who feared that the states would lose too much power under the Virginia Plan presented a counterproposal, the **New Jersey Plan** (although not all its authors were from New Jersey). This plan also called for a national government with legislative, executive, and judicial branches. (See the chart on page 36.) Also like the Virginia Plan, the New Jersey Plan gave the national government the power to tax and the power to regulate trade across state lines.

The New Jersey Plan, however, called for the states to have a stronger role in the national government. In contrast to the Virginia Plan, the New Jersey Plan called for a unicameral legislature in which each state would be represented equally with one vote apiece. This was similar to the structure of the Congress under the Articles of Confederation. Representatives to the national legislature would be chosen by the state legislatures. There would be no house in which members were elected directly by the people.

On June 19, after only three days of debate over which of the two proposals should serve as the basis for further discussion, the delegates took a vote. Votes were by state delegation, not by individual delegates. Seven state delegations voted for the Virginia Plan, while only three voted for the New Jersey Plan. The other delegations were either split or did not vote.

The Great Compromise

Despite the strong vote for the Virginia Plan, the question of state representation in the new national legislature was not yet resolved. Small states wanted a government that gave them power equal to the large states. Success of the prospective new government depended on reaching a compromise. The delegates therefore debated the issue for another long, hot, and difficult month.

Finally, the delegates hammered out an agreement that borrowed elements from both the Virginia and New Jersey Plans. The agreement, first called the Connecticut Plan, came to be known as the **Great Compromise**. Adopted on July 16, 1787, this compromise called for a bicameral legislature. Representation in one chamber of the legislature, the House of Representatives, would be based on population. States with larger populations would have more representatives than states with smaller populations. Members would be elected directly by the people. This part of the compromise was borrowed from the Virginia Plan.

The structure of the second chamber, the Senate, was adapted from the New Jersey Plan. Each state would have two representatives in the Senate. Thus, the small states would have equal footing with the large states in one half of the legislature. Senators were to be elected by state legislatures. Both the House of Representatives and the Senate would have to approve legislation by majority votes for it to become law.

Settling Other Issues

The Great Compromise resolved the major issues dividing the Convention. The delegates then turned to other difficult issues. What emerged from their efforts has been called a "bundle of compromises."

Slavery Slavery continued to be a divisive issue. Although slavery was banned in some northern states, slaves made up a considerable part of the southern states' populations. Southern delegates wanted slaves to be counted as part of each state's population, because doing so would increase their state's representation in the new House of Representatives.

Some delegates, mostly from the North, believed that slavery was evil and violated the natural rights

CONSTITUTIONAL GOVERNMENT *The signing of the Constitution took place after almost four months of discussion and debate among the delegates.* ***What were the major issues on which delegates agreed to compromise?***

of human beings. Many of these delegates argued that because slaves had no legal rights, they should not be counted in a state's population. In addition, many of the northern delegates hoped to limit the size of the South's representation.

Although some other delegates opposed slavery, they realized that a compromise was necessary to win support of southern states for the new Constitution. In fact, some southern delegates made it clear that the resolution of the issue on whether to include slaves in a state's population would be critical in their states' decisions to join the new Union.

The delegates finally agreed to count each slave—for the purpose of determining a state's representation in Congress—as three fifths of a free person. This compromise quieted the debate over slavery—for a time. Over the next several decades, however, the issue of slavery would again challenge the young country's unity and test its citizens' belief in the natural rights of human beings.

Trade Slavery also was part of the debate over trade issues. Southerners feared that Congress would use its legislative powers to make importing slaves into the United States illegal. In addition, southern delegates wanted to prohibit Congress from passing taxes on exports. The agricultural economies of southern states depended heavily on exported goods.

The Convention compromised on the issue of slavery by deciding that Congress could not ban the importation of slaves before 1808. In addition, Congress could not tax goods that were exported to other countries.

The Presidency The delegates also were split over the issue of the nation's chief executive. Some delegates believed that the president should be elected directly by the people. Other delegates wanted the president to be chosen by the states or by the national legislature.

The delegates decided on a system in which the president would be chosen by state electors. The number of a state's electors would match the number of its representatives in both houses of Congress. Many delegates assumed that state legislatures would choose the electors, but they permitted states to choose electors by popular vote. If no presidential candidate received a majority of electoral votes from the states, the House of Representatives would choose the president.

Finalizing the Constitution

The Convention delegates finished their work on the Constitution in August 1787. On September 17, most of the delegates signed the document. Those who did not sign either had already gone home or else opposed the proposed national government. In his closing remarks to the Convention, Benjamin Franklin noted that George Washington's chair had a sun on its back. Franklin had wondered frequently whether this was a rising or a setting sun. Having seen the Convention's work, he was now convinced it was a rising sun.

SECTION 4 — REVIEW

1. Define the following terms: Virginia Plan, New Jersey Plan, Great Compromise.

2. Why was George Washington's presence important to the Constitutional Convention? What was James Madison's role in the Convention?

3. How did the Virginia Plan and the New Jersey Plan each propose to structure the new national legislature?

4. How did delegates compromise on the issues of state representation in Congress, slavery, trade, and the presidency?

5. **Thinking and Writing Critically**
In what ways did the compromises concerning slavery represent a contradiction of the ideals expressed in the Declaration of Independence?

6. **Applying POLITICAL FOUNDATIONS**
Imagine that you are one of the delegates attending the Constitutional Convention. Write a one-or two-paragraph diary entry regarding the proceedings. Describe the atmosphere of the Convention, your surroundings, and some of your fellow delegates.

SECTION 5

RATIFYING THE CONSTITUTION

Political Dictionary

Federalist
Antifederalist

Objectives

★ What were the main arguments in the debate over ratification of the Constitution?
★ What role did a bill of rights play in the debate?
★ Which key states were among the last to ratify the Constitution?

The battle to create a new government did not end with the signing of the Constitution. First, nine states had to ratify the document in special constitutional conventions, and the outcome of the ratification process was by no means certain. Both supporters and opponents of the Constitution prepared for ratification battles in each state.

Federalists and Antifederalists

Supporters of the new Constitution were called **Federalists** because they supported a stronger, federal form of government. Opponents of the Constitution were called **Antifederalists**. The Antifederalists were particularly strong in New York and Virginia. Without the support of these two key states, the battle for ratification would be more difficult.

Antifederalists Patrick Henry of Virginia was among the most famous Antifederalists. He and other Antifederalists argued that if the Constitution were ratified the national government would become too powerful. They believed that a popular government could exist only in a small territory. Popular government in a larger territory, such

as the United States, would be too difficult because of the many competing interests. A large territory with a popular government would have to be held together by force, which would restrict people's freedom. In addition, Antifederalists were concerned that a strong executive would be too similar to a monarch. Such a strong executive, they argued, would be a danger to representative government and to individual rights.

One of the Antifederalists' strongest criticisms was that the Constitution lacked something that every state constitution adopted after independence—a bill of rights that proclaimed individual rights that government could not ignore or deny. Antifederalists argued that the absence of a bill of rights from the new Constitution was dangerous. They believed that without such a bill, the document would create a powerful national government that could easily become unjust. Some also stated that adopting the Constitution without a bill of rights would cancel any previously

CONSTITUTIONAL GOVERNMENT *Patrick Henry, a famous Antifederalist from Virginia, thought the Constitution would create a national government that was too powerful.* **Why did the Antifederalists argue against a strong executive?**

The Granger Collection, New York

held laws or customs that protected individual rights. As influential Antifederalist Richard Henry Lee wrote:

> 66 There are certain rights which we have always held sacred in the United States, and recognized in all our constitutions, and which, by the adoption of the new Constitution in its present form, will be left unsecured. . . . It is to be observed that when the people shall adopt the proposed Constitution, it will be their last and supreme act; . . . and wherever this Constitution, or any part of it, shall be incompatible with their ancient customs, rights, the laws or the constitutions heretofore established in the United States, it will entirely abolish them and do them away. 99

Federalists The Federalists responded to these charges by arguing that the separate powers belonging to each branch of government would check those of the other branches. In this way, no single part of the government, such as the national legislature, could become too powerful and threaten the rights of the states or of the people.

As for a bill of rights, Federalists also argued that the Constitution limited the powers of the national government to those it listed. Any powers not listed were guaranteed to the states or to the people. For example, the Constitution did not give government the power to restrict freedom of speech. Federalists believed that the people have the right to free speech and that the Constitution did not need to specifically state this.

Ratification

Many opponents to ratification argued that the Constitution favored large states, but a small state was first to ratify it. On December 7, 1787, those attending Delaware's convention voted unanimously to ratify the Constitution. Many people in Delaware and other small states believed that the Constitution and its call for equal state representation in the Senate would adequately protect their interests against those of larger states.

Virginia and New York, however, were deeply split over ratification. Many people in each state thought that the Constitution gave the national government too much power. Virginia and New York were important because of their size, location, and population.

Patrick Henry and James Madison, both well-respected leaders, led opposite sides of the debate in Virginia. During the heated ratification process in New York, Alexander Hamilton, Madison, and John Jay wrote 85 newspaper articles supporting the Constitution. The series of articles came to be called the *Federalist Papers.* The articles appeared under the name Publius, one of the founders of the Roman Republic.

The authors hoped that the articles would persuade people to support ratification. In fact, to have more time to win over opponents, Federalists repeatedly delayed a vote in the New York convention. The strategy worked. Opposition to ratification in New York gradually weakened as other state conventions ratified the Constitution. Virginia and New York finally ratified the

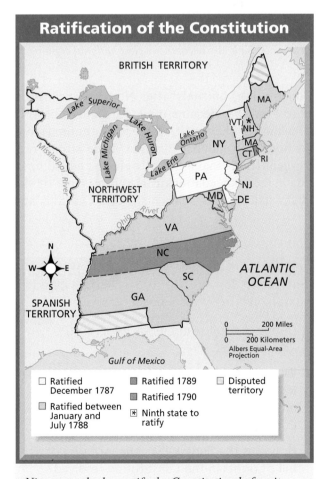

Nine states had to ratify the Constitution before it could be adopted. **Which state was the ninth to ratify the Constitution?**

The Granger Collection, New York

CONSTITUTIONAL GOVERNMENT *In this nineteenth-century engraving, New York celebrates the ratification of the Constitution with a parade. New York was an important state in the ratification of the Constitution because of its size and location.* **Which city became the first national capital?**

Virginia—which had been closely divided over whether to ratify. To secure the passage of the Constitution, the Federalists promised that in the first Congress a bill of rights would be passed that covered the concerns of the states.

North Carolina ratified the Constitution in November 1789, while Rhode Island held out until May 1790. Their actions came long after the new government had settled in at the temporary national capital of New York City. The first Congress under the new U.S. Constitution had met in New York on March 4, 1789. George Washington had been sworn in as the nation's first president on April 30, 1789.

Philadelphia held a celebration in honor of the new Constitution on July 4, 1788. A ship called the *Rising Sun*

Constitution, but only after New Hampshire on June 21, 1788, became the ninth state to do so.

Although they ratified the Constitution, conventions in a number of states made strong recommendations that a bill of rights be added to it. These recommendations came from some of the larger states—Massachusetts, North Carolina, and

fired its cannon to salute the occasion. After parading through the city, huge crowds heard convention delegate James Wilson lead 10 toasts. The crowd toasted "the people of the United States" and "the whole family of mankind." After observing the festivities, Philadelphian Dr. Benjamin Rush wrote, "'Tis done. We have become a nation."

SECTION 5 — REVIEW

1. Define the following terms: Federalist, Antifederalist.

2. Why did Antifederalists fear a strong executive in the new government? How did Federalists answer the arguments against the new Constitution?

3. How was the debate over the inclusion of a bill of rights in the Constitution resolved?

4. Locate New York and Virginia on the map on page 41. Why was their ratification of the Constitution important?

5. Thinking and Writing Critically
Delaware was the first state to ratify the Constitution. What advantages did the Constitution provide to the small states? Do you think Delaware's situation was better under the Articles of Confederation? Why or why not?

6. Applying **CONSTITUTIONAL GOVERNMENT**
Conduct an Internet search to determine the exact date each state ratified the Constitution. Draw a time line showing the order in which the states ratified the Constitution.

CHAPTER 2 — SUMMARY

SECTION 1 English settlers brought the ideals of limited and representative government with them to the 13 colonies. The ideal of limited government was established by Magna Carta, signed by King John in 1215, which limited the monarch's power and established the rule of law in England. The ideal of representative government was put forth in the bicameral legislature, called Parliament. The Petition of Right and the English Bill of Rights further limited the power. The ideals of limited and representative government were crucial to the development of colonial government and, later, those in the states.

SECTION 2 Although many people in the colonies shared these ideals, early efforts at cooperation among the colonies had limited success. There were several obstacles to unity. Colonies formed for different reasons. In addition, varying economies, climate, and geography led to differences among the colonies. The colonies did make some early attempts at unity, however, through the New England Confederation and the Albany Plan of Union. Eventually, anger over British trade and tax policies helped unite the colonies. Delegates met at the First Continental Congress to protest British policies and send King George III the Declaration and Resolves of the First Continental Congress. The British tightened control over the colonies further, and the colonies declared independence in 1776.

SECTION 3 The newly independent states' desire for a weak national government led to the Articles of Confederation. There were several weaknesses in the Articles of Confederation that caused problems for the new union, however. The national government's powers were extremely limited—there was no executive branch or national court system; there were no officials to enforce laws; and there was no power to tax, to regulate trade, or to establish national armed forces. In addi-

tion, major laws required approval of 9 out of 13 states.

The states also faced cultural, economic, and geographic differences. The beliefs and ways of life varied a great deal from state to state. In addition, the size of the nation made it difficult to form ties among the states.

The many weaknesses of the Articles, as well as the fear that the states would not stay united, led to calls for a stronger national government.

SECTION 4 Delegates from nearly all the states met in Philadelphia in 1787 to revise the Articles of Confederation. Delegates, however, moved quickly toward creating a new, stronger national government. The delegates debated two rival plans—the Virginia Plan and the New Jersey Plan. The Constitutional Convention finally adopted a compromise plan that included a bicameral legislature, a strong executive, and a judiciary.

SECTION 5 The ratification debate divided the public into two camps. Antifederalists argued that the Constitution would create a government that threatened the rights of the states and the people. Federalists countered that the Constitution would protect those rights and was necessary to hold the nation together. All the states eventually ratified the Constitution.

Government Notebook

Review the list of rights and freedoms held by U.S. citizens that you wrote in your Government Notebook at the beginning of this chapter. Now that you have studied the chapter, can you identify the origins of these rights and freedoms? Write the sources next to each item on your list.

REVIEW

REVIEWING CONCEPTS

1. How did the need for common defense and anger over British policies affect colonial cooperation?

2. Explain which key documents limited the power of the English monarchs and how they did so.

3. Compare the arguments of Federalists and Antifederalists.

4. How were colonial and state governments influenced by the ideals of limited and representative government?

5. Why was unity among the states difficult under the Articles of Confederation? How did the Constitution address the weaknesses of the Articles?

6. What role did compromise play in the Constitutional Convention?

THINKING AND WRITING CRITICALLY

1. **CONSTITUTIONAL GOVERNMENT** What do you think would have happened to the individual states had the Constitution not been ratified? Would they have stayed united? Why?

2. **PRINCIPLES OF DEMOCRACY** What kind of government do you think best protects citizens' natural rights: a stronger one similar to that under the Constitution or a weaker one similar to that under the Articles of Confederation? Explain your answer.

3. **PUBLIC GOOD** Do you think that the Great Compromise made during the Constitutional Convention promoted the public good? Explain your answer.

CITIZENSHIP IN YOUR COMMUNITY

One of the ideals on which the U.S. Constitution is based is federalism, or the distribution of power and responsibility among the federal, state, and local governments. Research how responsibilities, such as funding for public schools, are shared by your state and local governments. Create a chart showing how these responsibilities are distributed. In the first column, list the responsibilities you identified in your research. In the second, indicate which level of government assumes each responsibility. In the third, briefly explain how each responsibility affects you and other members of your community.

INDIVIDUAL PORTFOLIO PROJECT

Imagine that it is 1787 and you have been chosen to organize a debate on ratification of the Constitution. You must invite three of the key leaders at the time—such as James Madison, Thomas Jefferson, and Alexander Hamilton—to take part on each side of the issue. Prepare a debate program that lists the time of the debate, the participants, and a short biography of each. The biographies should include the participants' positions on the issue, their professions, and their life accomplishments. Make sure the program is neatly written or typed.

PRACTICING SKILLS: LEARNING FROM PICTURES

Study the details of the painting on the opposite page. Visual evidence is important to understanding both an event and its time period. Determine what the people in the painting are doing and how they are feeling. Analyze the artist's point of view by determining which details of the event are emphasized or left out.

Write a two- or three-paragraph report describing the events portrayed in the painting. Include answers to the following questions: What details reveal the mood of the people in this painting? Can you identify any of the key leaders at the Constitutional Convention? Do you think that the artist's interpretation is an accurate one? Why or why not?

THE INTERNET: LEARNING ONLINE

Conduct an Internet search for information about the Declaration of Independence, Magna Carta, and other documents that reflect the ideals of limited and representative government. You might start with search words such as *Declaration of Independence, Magna Carta, democracy,* and *bill of rights.* Web sites for major libraries, such as the Library of Congress, also provide information on these documents. Create a brochure describing how citizens could use the Internet to learn about these documents. Your brochure should include the addresses of sites you find and brief descriptions of the information available at those sites.

ANALYZING PRIMARY SOURCES

THE *FEDERALIST PAPERS*

As you have read, the *Federalist Papers* is a series of newspaper articles written by Alexander Hamilton, James Madison, and John Jay. The essays were written in defense of the Constitution to gain support for its ratification. Read the following excerpt from Madison's essay "No. 51" and answer the questions that follow.

66 *If men were angels, no government would be necessary. If angels were to govern men, neither external nor internal controls on government would be necessary. In framing a government which is to be administered by men over men, the great difficulty lies in this: you must first enable the government to control the governed; and in the next place oblige [require] it to control itself. A dependence on the people is, no doubt, the primary control on the government; but experience has taught mankind the necessity of auxiliary [additional] precautions. . . .*

The constant aim is to divide and arrange the several offices in such a manner as that each may be a check on the other. . . . But it is not possible to give to each department an equal power of self-defense. In republican government, the legislative authority necessarily predominates [has the most power]. The remedy for this inconveniency is to divide the legislature into different branches; and to render [make] them, by different modes [methods] of election and different principles of action, as little connected with each other as the nature of their common functions and their common dependence on the society will admit. 99

1. According to Madison, where does the "great difficulty" lie when a nation is constructing a government system?

2. What "auxiliary precautions" do you think should be taken to restrict government? Explain your answer.

3. According to Madison, which branch of the government necessarily has the most power in a republican government? Why?

CHAPTER 3

THE U.S. CONSTITUTION

The Constitution is the foundation on which U.S. government and society are based. It is a document that affects your life every day. It protects your freedom to write an article for the school newspaper. It also determines the scope of all laws in your community.

The Constitution has such far-reaching effects on society partly because it reflects certain basic principles of government. Two of these principles—limited and representative government—were discussed in Chapter 2. The framers of the Constitution incorporated these and other basic principles into the structures and responsibilities of the national government.

The framers also provided ways in which the Constitution could change with the times to help the country face new challenges. By doing these things, the framers not only designed a government that promotes the public good, they also crafted a system of government that has endured for more than two centuries.

Government Notebook

In your Government Notebook, write a paragraph about why you think that the plan of government provided by the U.S. Constitution has been successful for more than 200 years.

The Granger Collection, New York

BASIC PRINCIPLES

Political Dictionary

popular sovereignty
separation of powers
checks and balances
veto
judicial review
unconstitutional

Objectives

★ What are the basic principles on which the U.S. Constitution is based?
★ How does the Constitution ensure the people's authority over government?
★ How does the Constitution provide for a system of balanced government?
★ In what way does the Constitution protect the rights of the states?

The Constitution sets forth the powers that the citizens of the United States grant to the federal government. This means that the Constitution establishes rules that the U.S. government must observe. Five main principles form the basis of these rules: popular sovereignty, limited government, separation of powers, checks and balances, and federalism. These principles reflect the framers' desire to establish a national government that serves the people, prevents the concentration and abuse of power, and respects the rights of the states.

Popular Sovereignty

For a government truly to serve the people, it must be based on popular sovereignty. As noted in Chapter 1, sovereignty is the absolute authority that a government has over the citizens of that nation. **Popular sovereignty** means that the government's authority comes from the people. The principle of popular sovereignty can be found throughout the U.S. Constitution. For example, the

Preamble, or introduction, to the Constitution begins, "We the People of the United States . . . do ordain [order] and establish this Constitution for the United States of America." This passage points out that it is the people themselves who have given the Constitution its authority to create the U.S. government.

The Constitution further establishes the people's authority by setting rules for the election of government officials. No one reaches government office by virtue of his or her birth, as in a monarchy. Rather, the U.S. Constitution established a republic in which citizens elect others to represent them.

Comparing Governments

A New Constitution for South Africa

Perhaps the greatest sign that democracy was coming to apartheid-free South Africa appeared in 1995, when the government invited the people to help write a new constitution. Citizens were allowed to voice their opinions by calling a "constitutional talk-line." More than 1.7 million people called in, wrote letters, and sent messages over the Internet with their suggestions for the new constitution.

After months of debate over citizens' and lawmakers' ideas, the drafters of the constitution completed the document. The Constitutional Assembly ratified the new constitution with a 420-to-1 vote on May 8, 1996.

The constitution—described as the country's "birth certificate" by one government official—makes the Republic of South Africa a democratic nation with a federal system and a strong central government. A president holds executive power with two deputy presidents—one from the majority party and one from the largest opposition party. The new two-house Parliament features a Senate, whose 90 members are elected by the legislatures of the country's nine provinces, and a National Assembly, whose 400 members are elected by the voters.

Limited Government

A government also cannot truly serve the people if it has unlimited power. Therefore, the Constitution established a limited government. As noted in Chapter 2, the English colonists brought the ideal of limited government to North America.

The Constitution limits government by establishing guidelines for how the government may act. Section 9 of Article I, for example, lists powers that the national government does not have, such as the power to grant titles of nobility. Other parts of the Constitution keep the government from violating citizens' individual liberties, such as the freedom of speech. Each of these restrictions upholds the principle of limited government.

Separation of Powers

Although the framers wanted to give the national government the power it needed to govern, they also wanted to prevent the concentration and abuse of power. They designed the Constitution to divide the responsibilities of government among three branches. This **separation of powers** makes sure that no one branch has too much power. The framers listed the responsibilities and powers of the three branches in the first three articles of the Constitution.

Article I lists the responsibilities of the legislative branch. Congress, a bicameral legislature, makes the nation's laws. Although the House of Representatives and the Senate share responsibility for passing legislation, each chamber has its own special powers. For example, legislation to fund the government must begin in the House of Representatives. Only the Senate, however, can approve presidential appointments and treaties with foreign countries.

Article II establishes the duties of the executive branch, which is made up of the president, vice president, and various executive departments. The executive branch executes, or carries out, the laws established by the legislative branch. In addition, the president serves as the commander in chief of the nation's armed forces and has the power to direct U.S. relations with foreign countries.

Article III sets out the role of the judicial branch of government. The Constitution establishes a Supreme Court as the nation's highest court and gives Congress the authority to establish courts below the Supreme Court.

Checks and Balances

The Constitution also prevents the concentration and abuse of power by giving each branch of government the authority to check, or restrain, the powers of the other two branches. This system of **checks and balances** divides power within the government. (See the chart on page 49.)

Executive and Legislative Checks The system of checks and balances forces each branch of government to consider the opinions and actions of the other branches. This is particularly true for the executive and legislative branches. For example, if Congress does not consider the wishes of the president when it writes legislation, the president may **veto**, or reject, that legislation. This veto power often encourages congressional leaders to meet with members of the executive branch to reach an agreement about controversial legislation before it is passed. For example, congressional leaders meet regularly with the president to discuss the federal budget. In some cases, however, the negotiations on legislation are difficult.

The president's power to affect legislation is limited, however. Congress is able to override a

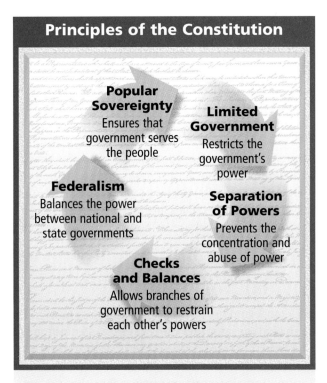

Principles of the Constitution

Popular Sovereignty
Ensures that government serves the people

Limited Government
Restricts the government's power

Federalism
Balances the power between national and state governments

Separation of Powers
Prevents the concentration and abuse of power

Checks and Balances
Allows branches of government to restrain each other's powers

The U.S. government must follow five basic principles established by the Constitution. ***Why are these principles important to a democratic system of government?***

Checks and Balances in the Federal Government

POWERS		CHECKS ON POWERS
• Passes bills into law • Can pass laws over the president's veto by a two-thirds vote of Congress • Approves appointments to top government jobs • Holds the "power of the purse"	**LEGISLATIVE BRANCH**	• President's power to veto legislation passed by Congress • Supreme Court's power to rule that laws are unconstitutional
• Approves or vetoes laws • Carries out laws • Appoints federal court judges, ambassadors, and other high-level officials • Negotiates treaties	**EXECUTIVE BRANCH**	• Congress's ability to override the president's veto by a two-thirds vote • Congress's power to approve spending by the federal government • Senate's power to approve presidential appointments to top government jobs • Senate's authority to approve all treaties • Congress's power to impeach the president
• Interprets the meaning of laws • Rules on the constitutionality of laws passed by Congress and actions taken by the executive branch	**JUDICIAL BRANCH**	• Congress's (or the states') power to propose an amendment to the Constitution if the Supreme Court rules that a law is unconstitutional • Senate's authority to refuse to approve the appointments to federal court • Congress's power to impeach a federal judge

Each branch of the federal government has its powers checked by the other branches.
What are the checks on the legislative branch?

veto if at least two thirds of the members in both houses of Congress vote to do so. Congress also checks the executive branch through its "power of the purse," for only Congress can approve spending by the federal government. Congress can, for example, limit or refuse to approve money for programs that the president wants.

Congress also has checks on other presidential powers. The Senate, for example, can reject any presidential appointments to top government jobs. In addition, the Constitution states that international treaties negotiated by the president do not become law unless approved by a two-thirds vote in the Senate. These checks on executive power mean that the president must consider the wishes of Congress when proposing legislation, making appointments, and negotiating treaties.

Judicial Review The judicial branch also has an important role in the system of checks and balances. While federal judges are nominated by the president and must be approved by the Senate, federal courts can check the powers of the legislative and executive branches through judicial review. **Judicial review** is the power of the courts to decide if laws and other government actions are valid under the U.S. Constitution.

A law or government action that is found to violate any part of the Constitution is said to be **unconstitutional**. Because the Constitution is the nation's highest law, an unconstitutional law or act is illegal and cannot be enforced by the government. (Keep in mind, however, that laws are reviewed only if their constitutionality is in question.)

Judicial review is not specifically mentioned in the Constitution. Section 2 of Article III, however, implies that the courts have such power. The principle of judicial review was firmly established by the Supreme Court in the landmark case *Marbury* v. *Madison* in 1803.

In 1801 William Marbury and others were appointed to judicial posts by the outgoing president, John Adams. The commissions, or documents, that formally gave them their posts were not delivered before Adams left office, however. Thomas Jefferson, who had defeated Adams in the presidential election, ordered Secretary of State James Madison not to deliver the commissions. Without them, the appointees could not legally take their posts.

Marbury asked the Supreme Court to order Madison to deliver the commissions. Marbury based his case on the Federal Judiciary Act of 1789, part of which stated that cases like his must be taken directly before the Supreme Court. The Court ruled, however, that the Federal Judiciary Act violated the Constitution, which specifically listed the types of cases that the Court could consider without a lower court hearing them first.

Although the ruling meant that the Supreme Court could not force Madison to deliver the commissions, it established the broader power of the courts to decide the constitutionality of congressional actions. This power of judicial review allows the courts to check the power of other branches of government.

Federalism

The Constitution is designed to protect the rights of the states by establishing a federal system of government. As noted in Chapter 1, a federal system is one in which powers are divided among national, state, and local governments. In the U.S. federalist system, some powers belong to the national government, others to state governments, and still others are shared by both. The way in which the federal system divides powers among the levels of government is more fully explained in Chapter 4.

Although the framers of the Constitution wanted to protect states' rights, they also wanted a national government that had sufficient powers to maintain order and keep the country united. They had learned that a weak government, like the one formed under the Articles of Confederation, could not force states to obey national laws.

Thus, the Constitution specifically prohibits states from exercising certain powers that belong to the national government, such as negotiating treaties, coining money, keeping troops or warships during peacetime, or engaging in war, unless the state is facing imminent danger or invasion. In addition, Article VI of the Constitution states that the power of the national government is superior to that of the state governments. This "supremacy clause" declares that the Constitution—together with U.S. laws passed under the Constitution and treaties made by the national government—is "the supreme law of the land."

SECTION 1 — REVIEW

1. Define the following terms: popular sovereignty, separation of powers, checks and balances, veto, judicial review, unconstitutional.

2. Name the basic principles on which the U.S. Constitution is based.

3. How do elections ensure popular sovereignty?

4. How does the system of checks and balances limit the power of each branch of government?

5. How did the framers of the Constitution address their concerns about balancing the powers of the state and national governments?

6. **Thinking and Writing Critically**
   How do you think the federal government would function if there were no power of judicial review? Do you think that each branch of government could ensure that the other branches always acted constitutionally?

7. **Applying** PRINCIPLES OF DEMOCRACY
   Think about some of the leaders in your school—student-council officers, team captains, and club presidents. Do any of the principles noted in this chapter, such as popular sovereignty and limited government, apply to these positions? Explain your answer.

AMENDING THE CONSTITUTION

Political Dictionary

amendment
repeal
Bill of Rights

Objectives

★ Why did the framers establish ways to amend the Constitution?
★ What are the methods for amending the Constitution?
★ What is the purpose of the Bill of Rights?

Imagine a house that was built 200 years ago. Since its construction, the house has been worked on several times. A second story, electricity, and indoor plumbing have been added. The exterior has been painted and repainted, and damaged boards have been replaced. The owners proudly say that they live in a "200-year-old house," and despite all the changes that have been made to the house, they are right. That same house has provided shelter for 200 years for generations of people.

In many ways the Constitution is like that old house. It has provided shelter for the people of the United States for more than 200 years. Also like the old house, the Constitution has changed during that time.

How and why did it change? The framers knew that they could not anticipate what challenges the government and people would face as the United States grew. Thus, just as an architect plans changes and additions to an old house, the framers developed methods for revising the Constitution.

Changes made to the Constitution are called **amendments**. All such amendments must be proposed and ratified through a formal process. The ability to amend the Constitution has allowed the government to meet new needs and challenges.

Methods of Amending the Constitution

The procedures for amending the U.S. Constitution are found in Article V of the Constitution itself. The basic premise behind these procedures is that amending the Constitution should be more difficult than passing an ordinary law. Passing an ordinary law requires a majority vote, but passing an amendment requires more than a simple majority. By making it difficult to pass a constitutional amendment, the framers helped ensure that amendments would not be frivolous and would not represent only passing interests.

The Constitution sets out two ways to propose an amendment. There also are two ways to ratify a proposed amendment.

CONSTITUTIONAL GOVERNMENT *The ratification of the Twenty-sixth Amendment in 1971 lowered the voting age from 21 to 18.* **How does the Constitution enable the government to meet the changing needs of the people?**

Proposing Amendments One way amendments may be proposed is by a vote in Congress. In fact, all amendments to the Constitution so far have been proposed by Congress. At least two thirds of both the House (290 votes) and the Senate (67 votes) must approve an amendment before it can be sent to the states for ratification.

An amendment also may be proposed by a national convention that is called by Congress at the request of at least two thirds (34) of the state legislatures. No convention has ever been called to propose an amendment, however. Many people have pointed to the wording of Article V of the Constitution as one explanation. Article V does not say whether a convention can be limited to proposing only the amendment it was called to consider. As a result, some people have worried that a convention might decide to open up the entire Constitution for revision. Then amendments that the states had no intention of considering in the first place might be proposed.

Ratifying Amendments All but one of the Constitution's amendments have been ratified by votes in state legislatures. Under this method, legislatures in at least three fourths (38) of the states must approve an amendment before it becomes part of the Constitution.

The second method for ratifying an amendment requires the approval of special conventions in at least three fourths of the states. The Twenty-first Amendment was ratified in this way. This amendment **repealed**—or reversed by legislative act— the Eighteenth Amendment, which had outlawed the production, transportation, and sale of alcoholic beverages. With its repeal, the Eighteenth Amendment was no longer a formal part of the Constitution.

C A S E   S T U D Y

The Equal Rights Amendment

CONSTITUTIONAL GOVERNMENT The struggle to ratify the Equal Rights Amendment (ERA) is a good example of just how hard it is to amend the Constitution. The ERA aimed to bar discrimination based on a person's sex. Supporters first introduced such an amendment in Congress in 1923. Finally, after increased efforts to win support for

CONSTITUTIONAL GOVERNMENT *Women in Raleigh, North Carolina, participate in a rally for the ratification of the Equal Rights Amendment.* **Why is it important for people to have the freedom to participate in political demonstrations?**

the amendment, the 1972 Congress overwhelmingly voted to send the ERA to the states. However, as with most other amendments, Congress set a deadline for ratification.

In less than a year, 30 states had ratified the ERA. At that point, it appeared that the necessary 38 states would ratify the amendment. The process, however, bogged down soon after that. Opponents criticized the ERA on a number of grounds. Many saw the amendment as an attack on traditional family values. Others believed that the Constitution and the Civil Rights Act of 1964 already guaranteed equal rights for women. (The Civil Rights Act of 1964 is more fully explained in Chapter 13.) Yet others argued that the amendment would mean difficult changes in social standards, such as requiring women to be sent into military combat.

In 1978, to give supporters more time to win approval for the amendment, Congress moved the original deadline for ratification to 1982. This effort failed, however, as only 35 states had voted to ratify the amendment by that date. In addition, 5 of the 35 states voted to rescind, or take back, their ratification.

The 27 Amendments

Because of the difficult amendment process, only 27 amendments have been added to the Constitution. The importance of these amendments cannot be overstated. They have protected individual freedoms, expanded voting and other rights, and extended the government's powers.

Protecting Individual Freedoms The first 10 amendments, the **Bill of Rights**, were designed as a protection for individual freedoms. (See the chart below.) They were adopted only two years after the Constitution went into effect. As noted in Chapter 2, many states, upon ratifying the Constitution, made strong recommendations that a bill of rights be added.

The Bill of Rights protects citizens' freedom of speech, religion, and assembly, and it guarantees a free press and the rights of people accused of crimes. In addition to protecting individual freedoms, the Bill of Rights also acknowledges the rights and powers of the states and the people. The Ninth Amendment says that people hold additional rights not specifically mentioned in the Constitution, while the Tenth Amendment says that the states and the people retain all the powers not specifically given to the national government and that the Constitution does not forbid them to have. These amendments were included in the Bill of Rights to ensure that the national government would not unjustly dominate the states and the people.

Expanding Voting and Other Rights In the more than 200 years since the Bill of Rights was ratified, other amendments have been adopted in clusters during periods of great social and political change. The Thirteenth, Fourteenth, and Fifteenth Amendments, for example, were adopted just after the Civil War. These amendments banned slavery in the United States, made African Americans U.S. citizens, and gave various rights, including the right to vote, to African American males.

In another era of social change—the first decades of the 1900s—four key amendments were passed. Two of these, the Seventeenth and Nineteenth Amendments, extended the reach of democracy by providing for the popular election of senators and by granting the vote to women.

Rights and Powers Granted by the Bill of Rights

FIRST AMENDMENT	Provides for freedom of religion, speech, press, and assembly
SECOND AMENDMENT	Asserts the need for a militia and protects the right to keep and bear arms
THIRD AMENDMENT	Prevents soldiers from taking over private homes during peacetime or war unless authorized to do so by law
FOURTH AMENDMENT	Prohibits unreasonable searches and seizures
FIFTH AMENDMENT	Protects the rights of accused persons
SIXTH AMENDMENT	Provides the right to a speedy, fair trial
SEVENTH AMENDMENT	Provides the right to a trial by a jury in civil suits
EIGHTH AMENDMENT	Prohibits excessive bail and fines, prohibits cruel and unusual punishment
NINTH AMENDMENT	Protects people's rights that are not specifically listed in the Constitution
TENTH AMENDMENT	Grants to the states and to the people powers that are not specifically listed in the Constitution

The Bill of Rights protects the basic freedoms of all U.S. citizens. **Which amendments in the Bill of Rights acknowledge the powers of the states?**

Citizenship in Action

Gregory Watson successfully campaigned for the ratification of the Twenty-seventh Amendment, which restricts the power of Congress to give itself a midterm pay raise.

Passing the Twenty-Seventh Amendment

Texan Gregory Watson accomplished what framer James Madison could not more than 200 years earlier. Largely because of Watson's efforts, the Twenty-seventh Amendment to the Constitution became law in May 1992. According to the amendment, "No law varying the compensation for the services of the Senators and Representatives, shall take effect, until an election of Representatives shall have intervened." In other words, Congress cannot give itself a pay raise in the middle of a term of office.

The amendment was introduced originally by James Madison in 1789 as part of a package of 12 amendments, 10 of which became the Bill of Rights. Maryland was the first state to ratify the amendment in 1789, and five other states soon followed. The amendment failed to be ratified by three fourths of the states, however. Because the amendment was sent to the states without a deadline, it was still considered "proposed" even though it had never been approved.

Watson believed that the passage of two centuries had not "robbed the amendment of its relevance." In 1982, when he was a student at the University of Texas in Austin, he launched a decade-long battle to ratify the dusty amendment. The project started out as a term paper and evolved into a one-man campaign.

Watson's battle began after he received a C on a research paper in which he argued in favor of ratifying the proposal that had become known as the "Madison amendment." His skeptical professor called the proposed amendment a "legal dead letter." Convinced of the amendment's timeliness despite the passage of nearly two centuries, Watson began his relentless quest to "show the American people what can be done if they just put forth a little elbow grease." Most of Watson's "elbow grease" was in the form of mail—letter after letter to legislators in the states that had not yet passed the proposed amendment.

Watson's efforts increased in 1991, when controversy arose after the U.S. Senate voted to give itself a "midnight pay raise." As many citizens shook their heads and pointed fingers at what they perceived as the greed of lawmakers, Watson became convinced that ratification of the Twenty-seventh Amendment was near.

Watson's efforts paid off on May 7, 1992, when Michigan became the thirty-eighth state—the final state needed—to pass Madison's centuries-old amendment. Justifiably proud to call his mission a success and no doubt wiser about the workings of the U.S. government, Watson stated, "You can wield (exercise) a great deal of power, and one person can still make a difference in this country."

What Do You Think?

1. Why was this amendment still relevant after more than 200 years?
2. Have you ever thought of campaigning for a change in your student or local government? What are some ways you can express your opinions about government?

Before passage of the Seventeenth Amendment, state legislatures chose senators. Women did not have the right to vote in every state until the passage of the Nineteenth Amendment.

Extending Government Powers Two other important amendments were passed during the early 1900s, both of which expanded the reach of the government. First, the Sixteenth Amendment authorized a national income tax. This tax increased the amount of money the government could collect to pay for its programs and to pay other national expenses. Then the Eighteenth Amendment made Prohibition the law of the land. This amendment expanded the national government's powers by allowing it to regulate the manufacture, sale, and transportation of "intoxicating liquors" throughout the country.

Ratification Deadlines The last amendment to the Constitution, the Twenty-seventh, was ratified by the states in 1992. (See "Citizenship in Action" on page 54.) This amendment, which was originally proposed in 1789, says that no vote to increase congressmembers' salaries may take effect until after the next regularly scheduled congressional election. The 1789 Congress had not set a deadline for ratification. Almost 200 years later, efforts were made to revive the amendment. Some people argued that the process of ratifying the Twenty-seventh Amendment had already taken too long. Since 1919, Congress usually has set deadlines—generally around seven years—for

THE FINAL CRASH
—Page in the Louisville *Courier-Journal*

CONSTITUTIONAL GOVERNMENT *This historical cartoon depicts public reaction to the Eighteenth Amendment. **According to the cartoonist, what was the response to the amendment establishing Prohibition?***

ratifying amendments. Nonetheless, supporters of the Twenty-seventh Amendment were able to secure its ratification.

SECTION 2 — REVIEW

1. Define the following terms: amendment, repeal, Bill of Rights.

2. Why is it important to be able to make changes to the U.S. Constitution?

3. Describe the methods for proposing and ratifying constitutional amendments. What do some people think might happen if a special convention were called to propose an amendment?

4. What is the purpose of the Bill of Rights? Why did its supporters consider it to be important?

5. **Thinking and Writing Critically**
   What might have been the consequences for the nation if the framers had not established ways to amend the Constitution? Provide some specific examples of what might have happened over time.

6. **Applying CONSTITUTIONAL GOVERNMENT**
   Conduct an Internet search to find out about other amendments that have been proposed but never ratified. Select one of these amendments and write a short report on it.

A FLEXIBLE DOCUMENT

Political Dictionary

executive agreement
political party
cabinet

Objectives

★ How does the Constitution give the three branches of government flexibility in using their powers?
★ How have political parties changed the way government operates?
★ How does the Constitution allow custom and tradition to help shape government?

The Constitution has been called a "living document," which means that it is flexible and allows government to adapt to changing times. One way it does this, as noted in Section 2, is through the amendment process. The Constitution, however, also has allowed government to change in less formal ways. Government actions, political parties, and custom and tradition all have helped shape government under the Constitution.

Government Actions

The judicial, legislative, and executive branches have interpreted their constitutional powers many times. This process has allowed the government to meet new circumstances.

Court Decisions As noted in Section 1, the 1803 Supreme Court case of *Marbury* v. *Madison* established the federal courts' power to determine if a law or other government action is constitutional. Because the wording is vague in some places, the courts have been able to apply the Constitution to circumstances that the eighteenth-century framers could not have anticipated.

For example, the Fourth Amendment forbids "unreasonable searches and seizures." The authors of the amendment probably never imagined how new technologies, such as telephones, might change the concepts of "searching" and "seizing." Yet the courts have interpreted the amendment to include these new technologies. For example, they have been able to forbid law enforcement officials from recording private telephone conversations—a form of searching and seizing—without following certain procedures set by law.

Congressional Legislation Like the judicial branch, Congress has a great deal of flexibility in adapting to changing times. It decides how best to carry out its responsibilities and passes legislation that responds to new situations. To do this, Congress has created structures and taken on duties that are allowed by—but not specifically mentioned in—the Constitution.

For example, Section 1 of Article III gives Congress the power to establish federal courts

CONSTITUTIONAL GOVERNMENT *John Marshall, the third chief justice of the United States, established the Supreme Court's power of judicial review.* **When and in what Supreme Court case was judicial review established?**

The Granger Collection, New York

Archivist

Perhaps you are one of the more than 1 million people who visited the National Archives in Washington, D.C., last year. The original copies of the Declaration of Independence, the U.S. Constitution, and the Bill of Rights are permanently displayed in this building, the country's storehouse for valuable historical documents.

Who is in charge of repairing, preserving, and overseeing these historical documents and other important public records? This is the job of an archivist. Archivists analyze documents, direct efforts to catalog them, and often educate researchers and government agencies about the documents, their histories, and the time periods in which they were created.

Behind the scenes at the National Archives, for example, archivists oversee the safekeeping, preservation, and display of treasured U.S. artifacts. Permanently sealed in airtight bronze-and-glass cases, the Declaration of Independence, the Constitution, and the Bill of Rights are protected

Archivists at the Library of Congress examine a manuscript to determine its condition.

from curious onlookers as well as exposure to pollutants and other damaging elements. Each night, the entire display is lowered into a "fireproof, shockproof, and bombproof" vault 22 feet beneath the floor of the exhibition hall. A special archivist, called a preservationist, gauges the documents' deterioration, or decay, with the aid of a sophisticated camera and computers.

Archivists also help make thousands of government and historical documents available to the public by compiling reference information in the form of indexes, guides, bibliographies, and microfilmed documents. Administrative duties such as preparing budgets, attending scientific and association conferences, and taking care of fund-raising activities often are part of the job as well. Because the job entails extensive research and preparation of reference materials, most archivists spend much of their time working alone with little supervision. An enthusiasm for their work, however, helps prevent most archivists from being bothered by this isolation.

A career as an archivist usually requires some experience working in a museum or library, as well as a master's degree in history or a related field. Many archivists also have an additional degree in library science.

Many people compete for archivist jobs. Numerous volunteer opportunities are available to people interested in learning more about a career in this field. A part-time or volunteer position at a local library can provide valuable experience. Museums and cultural groups in your community may train volunteers to give guided tours for their organizations. Studying history and literature is also an excellent way to prepare for a career as an archivist.

below the Supreme Court. The Constitution does not specifically say how those courts should be structured. Rather, it gives Congress the flexibility to carry out this responsibility as needed over time. In fact, as the country has grown, Congress has passed legislation expanding and changing the system of lower-level federal courts to help the court system adapt to the new needs of the population.

Congress, like the courts, also interprets vague wording in the Constitution. For example, as labor issues have become increasingly important, Congress has passed laws concerning working conditions. These laws have included workplace safety rules and minimum wages that employers must pay workers. The power to pass such laws is not specifically mentioned in the Constitution.

Because the products that workers make often travel across state lines, however, Congress has interpreted its constitutional power to control commerce among the states to include the authority to pass laws concerning working conditions.

Executive Actions The Constitution also gives the executive branch flexibility in interpreting its powers to take action. One example is the president's power to make **executive agreements**—arrangements that presidents establish with foreign governments and, unlike formal treaties, do not require Senate approval. This power has grown in ways not specifically mentioned in the Constitution.

At times, executive agreements have helped the government meet challenges that might have been more difficult to address using formal constitutional processes. In 1940, for example, President Franklin Roosevelt made an executive agreement with Great Britain to exchange old U.S. warships for the right to use British naval bases in and near North America. Roosevelt made the executive agreement because he feared that a formal treaty approving the same action would take too long. The agreement helped the United States react quickly to the challenge of improving its defense—while also helping a friend, Great Britain—during World War II.

Political Parties

Just as it does not specifically state every possible power and action of the three branches, the Constitution does not try to outline every detail of how the government should be run on a day-to-day basis. This flexibility allows officials to reorganize government to meet new challenges or react to new situations.

For example, political parties have long been an important part of U.S. elections even though they are not mentioned in the Constitution. A **political party** is an organized group that seeks to win elections and influence the activities of government. Many of the framers wanted to discourage political parties, fearing that they would divide rather than unite the nation. As is more fully explained in Chapter 18, however, political parties have played important roles in electing presidents and other government officials and in organizing the day-to-day operation of Congress. The Constitution's flexibility allowed the political system to develop in this manner.

Custom and Tradition

Finally, the Constitution allows custom and tradition to help shape government. Customs and traditions are informal, long-established ways of doing things. They are not mentioned in the Constitution, but customs and traditions strongly influence how government carries out its functions.

For example, even though the Constitution does not provide for a formal body of leaders in the executive branch, President George Washington brought the heads of the executive departments together to act as his advisers. This group of department heads is called the **cabinet**. Cabinet meetings have since become an important

CONSTITUTIONAL GOVERNMENT *President Bill Clinton and Israeli prime minister Shimon Peres signed an antiterrorism agreement on April 30, 1996. **Why is it important for the president to have the power to make executive agreements?***

POLITICAL PROCESSES *Franklin D. Roosevelt speaks to a crowd at a Bridgeport, Connecticut, train station while campaigning for a fourth term as president.* **Which amendment limits the number of terms a president can serve today?**

part of the federal government, with every president having had a cabinet to help accomplish the work of the executive branch.

Sometimes custom and tradition can bring pressure to make formal changes to the Constitution. For example, for more than 150 years no president served more than two terms in office. This custom dated back to George Washington, who did not seek re-election at the end of his second term in 1796. Franklin Roosevelt, however, was re-elected to a third presidential term in 1940 and a fourth in 1944. Many people opposed the idea of one person serving as president for so long. As a

result, Congress passed the Twenty-second Amendment, which limited presidents to two terms and thus formalized the custom that began with Washington. The amendment states that

❝No person shall be elected to the office of the President more than twice, and no person who has held the office of President, or acted as President, for more than two years of a term to which some other person was elected President shall be elected to the office of the President more than once.❞

SECTION 3 — **REVIEW**

1. Define the following terms: executive agreement, political party, cabinet.

2. How does the Constitution's wording allow the three branches of government to adapt to new circumstances? Why is it important that government be able to adapt in this way?

3. Why did many of the Constitution's framers fear political parties? How do political parties reflect the Constitution's flexibility regarding the organization of government?

4. How have custom and tradition affected how government functions?

5. **Thinking and Writing Critically**
   What are some customs and traditions in your school? Why do schools maintain them?

6. **Applying** **CONSTITUTIONAL GOVERNMENT**
   Conduct an Internet search to find the current members of the president's cabinet. Make a list of all the cabinet members and their titles.

THE CONSTITUTION AND THE PUBLIC GOOD

Political Dictionary

faction

Objectives

★ In what ways does the Constitution prevent factions from controlling the government?

★ How does the Constitution ensure that government makes laws that promote the public good?

★ Why do critics claim that the Constitution sometimes makes government less effective?

At the time of the Constitutional Convention, many delegates, such as James Madison, worried about whether popular government would be able to control the interests of **factions**—groups of people usually motivated by self-interest. A faction can consist of either a minority or a majority of the population. Majority factions, Madison argued, were more dangerous than minority factions. In a republican government, a minority faction can easily be defeated by a majority. A self-interested majority, however, can threaten the public good because a government that is run by such a group cannot be easily defeated.

Despite his concerns, Madison believed that the U.S. republic created by the Constitution could resist control by such a faction. At the same time, he argued that the Constitution provides a way to make sure that the government has sufficient authority to rule effectively and that it enacts policies that promote the public good. Was Madison right? This section explores how well the Constitution has accomplished these goals and how effective the U.S. government has been under the Constitution.

Preventing Control by Factions

Madison argued that the Constitution prevents control by factions in two ways. It takes advantage of the large size of the United States and it uses a system of checks and balances.

Size Madison was familiar with the arguments of his day that small republics were more likely to last than large republics. The citizens of small republics, it was argued, would be more likely to share interests, desires, and beliefs. Large republics, on the other hand, would have too many competing interests. Their governments would become arenas in which these interests would battle for control. The result would be tyranny by any faction that won control of government.

Madison, on the other hand, believed that having so many interests in a large republic like the United States was an *advantage.* The Constitution, with the rights and freedoms it promises, ensures that all interests have an equal chance to be represented. Madison said that with such a large number of interests competing for power, forming a faction that could completely dominate government would be difficult. In other words, a faction

POLITICAL PROCESSES *James Madison believed that the large size of the United States would give all interests an equal chance to be represented.* **Why did Madison believe that majority factions were more dangerous than minority factions?**

that did not consider other groups' interests would be unlikely to control government.

Checks and Balances Madison also argued that the Constitution prevents control by factions through a system of checks and balances. As noted in Section 1, the Constitution provides each of the branches of government with ways to check the powers of the other branches. The checks and balances system gives each branch of government what Alexander Hamilton called "constitutional arms for its own defense" against the other branches.

The framers of the Constitution believed that each branch would use its powers to check the interests of those heading the other branches. If a faction took control of one of the branches of government, for example, its power could be limited by the other branches.

Enacting Good Policies

According to Madison, the Constitution does more than just keep factions from using government for selfish, narrow interests. He also believed that the Constitution formed a republic in which it is *likely* that government will pass laws that serve the broader interests of society, or the public good.

Madison again based his beliefs on the large size of the United States. Because power under the Constitution lies with U.S. citizens, he argued that the government must pursue policies that address the interests of many people. Policies that serve only narrow, selfish interests—or that do not promote the public good—cannot win majority support in a large republic with many interests. Policies based on the principles of "justice and the general good," however, are more likely to gain enough support to become law.

You can see Madison's ideas at work in your own community. Community debates over such issues as building a new convention center often revolve around how the community as a whole will benefit. Supporters of a new convention center might say that visitors to the center will spend money in the local community, thereby generating more tax revenue. If enough voters believe this argument and value the services that tax revenue helps provide, the convention center proposal will likely win majority approval. In contrast, a proposal that benefits only the narrow interests of one group, such as local construction companies, probably would not.

POLITICAL PROCESSES *Citizens protest a government shutdown caused by political gridlock during the preparation of the federal budget in 1995 and 1996. The shutdown led to the temporary closing of many federal buildings.* **Do you think that the Constitution's design promotes gridlock? Explain your answer.**

Effective Government

More than 200 years have passed since Madison made his arguments that the Constitution would help government promote the public good. Has the government fulfilled Madison's hopes?

The fact that representative government in the United States has thrived for more than two centuries is evidence that the Constitution has worked well. It has proved successful in protecting the individual rights of U.S. citizens. Although the country still faces many challenges, it has grown stronger and more prosperous.

Some critics, however, charge that the Constitution sometimes makes it difficult for government to promote the public good and function effectively. They argue that forming a majority from among the republic's many diverse opinions in pursuit of *any* policy, even a policy that promotes the public good, is too difficult. Even when such a majority exists, the Constitution limits the majority's ability to work effectively. These critics point to two major problems that can make effective government difficult under the Constitution: gridlock and avoiding responsibility.

Gridlock Some people believe that the Constitution's design promotes gridlock, a term that usually refers to a traffic jam in which cars and other vehicles cannot move. Political gridlock occurs when the legislative process comes to a standstill because political opponents block each other's efforts.

In 1995 and 1996, for example, a Republican-led Congress and Democratic president Bill Clinton hit gridlock over the federal budget. They disagreed over tax cuts, how and when to balance the federal budget, and the funding of programs for health, education, and the environment.

After weeks of debate over the budget, Congress and the president still could not resolve their differences. Eventually, lacking funds ordinarily provided by the budget, the federal government partially shut down twice, for a total of 27 days. Thousands of federal workers—770,000 during the first shutdown and 280,000 during the second—were told not to report to work. Many people around the country began to question the government's ability to keep the nation running smoothly. They criticized both the president and Congress, saying that their disagreements should not have led to a paralysis of the government.

Avoiding Responsibility Other critics say that the Constitution makes it too easy for government leaders to avoid responsibility for failed policies and other problems. In a democracy, elected officials should be held responsible for how effective they have been during their term in office. In a system with checks and balances, however, voters often cannot decide whom to hold responsible. Because of this, one branch of government at times blames another for inaction or the wrong action.

Think about the debate over federal spending. Many people believe the federal government spends too much money or spends it the wrong way. Whom should they hold responsible for that spending? The Constitution gives Congress the responsibility of passing laws that provide funds for federal government projects. But a president may sign or veto such laws. So both Congress and the president are responsible to varying degrees for how much money the government spends, and for what purpose. This shared responsibility makes it hard to pinpoint where the blame for excessive or unnecessary spending rests and what action should be taken to avoid similar problems in the future.

Avoiding responsibility can make government less effective. Rather than make difficult but needed spending cuts, for example, some leaders might prefer to blame others for government's failure to bring spending under control. Voters, however, have the power to question the actions of their elected officials. If the president argues that Congress spends too much money or spends it irresponsibly, or if Congress charges that the president has created costly and unnecessary programs, voters can ask each side to explain why it did not take steps to block the other's actions.

After examining the issue, voters may determine that neither the president nor members of Congress are acting responsibly. The voters then can elect other people whom they believe will act more responsibly. In the end, it is the citizens in a democracy who must decide whether the government they have chosen is serving the public good and then take action accordingly.

SECTION 4 — REVIEW

1. Define the following term: faction.

2. Why did James Madison believe the Constitution would prevent government from being controlled by factions?

3. How does the Constitution take advantage of the large size of the United States to help government promote the public good?

4. How does gridlock make government less effective? How can leaders use the system of checks and balances to try to avoid taking action?

5. **Thinking and Writing Critically** Staying informed is an important part of holding leaders responsible for how well government works. How can citizens stay informed of their leaders' actions?

6. **Applying** **PRINCIPLES OF DEMOCRACY** Why might it be important for all interests to have an equal chance to be represented in government? Do you think that the diversity of interests in the United States makes the government less efficient? Explain your answer.

CHAPTER 3 — SUMMARY

SECTION 1 The framers designed the Constitution based on five principles: popular sovereignty, limited government, separation of powers, checks and balances, and federalism. Popular sovereignty means that the government's authority comes from the people. This principle can be found throughout the U.S. Constitution. The Constitution also provides for limited government by establishing guidelines for how government may act.

The Constitution divides government among three branches, thus establishing a separation of powers. The powers of these branches are listed in the first three articles of the Constitution. Dividing power among the branches also establishes a system of checks and balances, which gives each branch the authority to check, or restrain, the powers of the others. Finally, the rights of the states are protected through a federal system in which powers are divided among national, state, and local governments.

SECTION 2 The framers also created means by which the Constitution could be amended. There are two ways to propose an amendment. The first way is by a vote in Congress. The second is by a national convention that is called by Congress at the request of at least two thirds of the state legislatures, a method that has never been used.

There are also two ways to ratify amendments to the Constitution. The first is through a vote of the state legislatures. At least three fourths of the states must approve an amendment before it becomes part of the Constitution. The second method requires approval of special conventions in at least three fourths of the states.

Amending the Constitution is difficult, which has helped limit the number of constitutional amendments to just 27. The first 10 amendments, called the Bill of Rights, protect individual liberties as well as the powers of the states. Later amendments extended voting and other rights and the government's powers.

SECTION 3 Because it is a flexible document, the Constitution allows government to adapt to new circumstances. Under the Constitution, government actions, political parties, and custom and tradition have all helped government adapt to changing times. Government actions include court decisions, congressional legislation, and executive actions. Political parties play an important role in elections and in organizing the daily operations of Congress. Tradition and custom—long-established ways of doing things—strongly influence how government carries out its functions.

SECTION 4 The framers created a constitution that prevents factions from taking control of the government. They did this by establishing a system of checks and balances and by taking advantage of the great diversity of interests in the large U.S. republic. This great diversity of interests also helps government choose policies that promote the public good. Policies that serve only narrow, selfish interests are unlikely to gain majority support among so many competing interests. Although the Constitution may make government less effective at times, the freedoms and rights it guarantees ensure that government ultimately serves the public good.

Government Notebook

Review what you wrote in your **Government Notebook** at the beginning of the chapter about why you think the plan of government provided by the Constitution has been successful for more than 200 years. Now that you have finished studying this chapter, how would you revise your answer? Record your response in your Notebook.

REVIEWING CONCEPTS

1. Why is the Constitution called a "living document"? How can the Constitution be amended?

2. In what ways does the Constitution reflect the principles of popular sovereignty and limited government?

3. How does the Bill of Rights work to protect individual rights?

4. Why has the Constitution been amended only 27 times in more than 200 years?

5. Why did James Madison believe that the U.S. republic's large size would help government serve the public good?

6. How does the system of checks and balances help prevent one branch of government from becoming too powerful? In what ways does the system contribute to government that serves the public good?

7. What is the "supremacy clause"? How is it related to the principle of federalism?

THINKING AND WRITING CRITICALLY

1. **CONSTITUTIONAL GOVERNMENT** Imagine that there is a national debate in which some people would like to eliminate the system of checks and balances in order to make the U.S. government more efficient. Write a letter to the editor of your school newspaper explaining what might happen if the system were eliminated and why doing so would be harmful for the United States.

2. **CONSTITUTIONAL GOVERNMENT** How does the Constitution affect your life today? How might the way you live your life change if,

for example, there were no freedom of speech or religion?

3. **PRINCIPLES OF DEMOCRACY** Do you think that political parties are an important part of a democratic government? Do you think that political parties divide the nation, as the framers feared they might? Explain your answer.

4. **PUBLIC GOOD** How do you think the president's power to appoint federal judges promotes the public good? Do you think the interests of the people would be better protected if all government officials were elected? Explain your answer.

CITIZENSHIP IN YOUR COMMUNITY

Working with a group, research the customs and traditions in your community. Then create a brochure describing these customs and traditions for visitors to your community. The brochure should include the customs and traditions of particular neighborhoods, churches, and community groups, as well as the purposes of the customs and traditions it describes. Be sure to illustrate your brochure with pictures and other images.

COOPERATIVE PORTFOLIO PROJECT

With a group, create a handbook for student-government officers at your school. Include a description of the responsibilities and powers of each office. Make a list of the annual events and activities at your school, and indicate which grade (9, 10, 11, or 12) will be responsible for each event. Your handbook should be clearly written and easy to follow. You may want to include photographs of your student government at work.

PRACTICING SKILLS: UNDERSTANDING CHARTS AND GRAPHS

The bar graph below contains information on the votes cast by each state legislature for the ratification of the U.S. Constitution. Study the graph and answer the following questions.

1. Which states unanimously ratified the Constitution?

2. Which states accepted the Constitution by less than 60 percent? What issues do you think caused the lack of support in these states?

3. Which states ratified the Constitution by more than 70 percent?

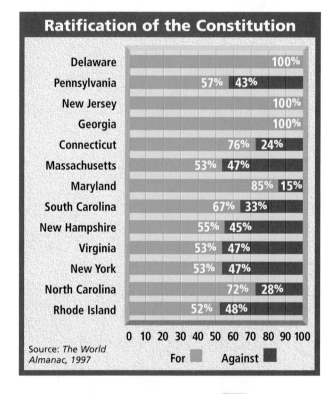

Ratification of the Constitution

State	For	Against
Delaware	100%	
Pennsylvania	57%	43%
New Jersey	100%	
Georgia	100%	
Connecticut	76%	24%
Massachusetts	53%	47%
Maryland	85%	15%
South Carolina	67%	33%
New Hampshire	55%	45%
Virginia	53%	47%
New York	53%	47%
North Carolina	72%	28%
Rhode Island	52%	48%

0 10 20 30 40 50 60 70 80 90 100

Source: *The World Almanac, 1997*

For ☐   Against ■

THE INTERNET: LEARNING ONLINE

Conduct an Internet search for Web sites containing information about the Constitution and constitutional issues. You might start with search words such as *constitution, amendment,* and *bill of rights.* Then work with a group to outline how you might create a Web site other students could use to learn more about the Constitution. What information and images would you include in your Web site? What links to other Web sites would you include?

ANALYZING PRIMARY SOURCES

MARBURY V. MADISON

The 1803 Supreme Court case *Marbury* v. *Madison* established the principle of judicial review. Read the following excerpt from the Court's majority opinion—which was written by Chief Justice John Marshall—and answer the questions that follow.

66 *The powers of the legislature are defined and limited; and that those limits may not be mistaken or forgotten, the Constitution is written. To what purpose are powers limited, and to what purpose is that limitation committed to writing, if these limits may, at any time, be passed by those intended to be restrained? The distinction between a government with limited and unlimited powers is abolished if those limits do not confine the persons on whom they are imposed. . . . It is a proposition too plain to be contested [opposed] that the Constitution controls any legislative act repugnant [disagreeable] to it. . . .*

It is, emphatically [definitely], the province and duty of the Judicial Department to say what the law is. . . . If two laws conflict with each other, the courts must decide on the operation of each. So if a law be in opposition to the Constitution, if both the law and the Constitution apply to a particular case, so that the court must either decide that case conformably to [in agreement with] the law, disregarding the Constitution, or conformably to the Constitution, disregarding the law, the court must determine which of these conflicting rules governs the case. 99

1. What would be "abolished" if the limits of the Constitution did not restrict officials?

2. Why is the judicial branch responsible for resolving conflicts between laws?

3. Do you think that the principle of judicial review established by *Marbury* v. *Madison* protects the public good? Why or why not?

CHAPTER 4

FEDERALISM

As noted in Chapter 3, one of the most important features of the Constitution is the federal system of government it established for the United States. Evidence of this system at work is all around you. Take this textbook, for example. The money to buy this book likely came from your state government or local school board. Under the U.S. federal system, it is the states and local communities, not the national government, that provide most of the money used to build schools, pay teachers, and purchase textbooks.

Knowing the way powers and responsibilities are divided among the different levels of government is key to understanding the U.S. federal system. Although this relationship has changed over time and has caused a great deal of debate, it continues to be based on the structure established by the Constitution. It is this basic structure that has helped create a federal system that promotes the public good.

 Government Notebook

What are the powers of government in the United States? In your Government Notebook, make a list of as many of these powers as you can think of, and indicate who you think holds each one: the federal government, the states, or local government.

POWERS AND RESPONSIBILITIES

Political Dictionary

expressed power
implied power
Elastic Clause
inherent power
reserved power
concurrent power

Objectives

★ Which powers does the Constitution give to the federal government, and which does it give to the states?
★ Which powers are denied to the federal government, and which are denied to the states?
★ What responsibilities do the federal and state governments have to each other?
★ What role do the courts play in the U.S. federal system?

The Constitution outlines the powers and responsibilities of both the federal government and the states. In addition, the Constitution assigns the federal courts an important role in resolving conflicts among the different levels of government.

Powers of the Federal Government

The U.S. federal government holds three types of powers: expressed, implied, and inherent. These powers generally involve matters that affect all people in the United States and that are impractical for the states to handle. Some of these powers come from the Constitution, while others are simply those that are exercised by any government of a sovereign nation.

Expressed Powers The powers that the Constitution expressly, or specifically, grants to the federal government are called **expressed powers**. For example, Article I, Section 8, lists the expressed powers of the legislative branch. These powers include issuing money, collecting national taxes, borrowing money, paying government debts, regulating trade among the states and with foreign governments, declaring war, and raising and maintaining armed forces.

Articles II and III list the expressed powers of the other two branches. Article II gives the president the power to command the armed forces and to direct relations with governments of other countries. Article III gives the judicial branch the power to decide several kinds of cases, including those concerning the Constitution, federal laws, and treaties. Federal courts also may rule on cases involving the U.S. government, certain foreign officials in the United States, and disputes among the states.

CONSTITUTIONAL GOVERNMENT *The federal government prints and issues the national currency. Here, a U.S. mint quality-control worker inspects currency-printing plates.* **Why is it more practical to have a national currency than to have each state print its own?**

Implied Powers Not all powers of the federal government are expressly listed in the Constitution. The federal government also has **implied powers**, or powers that are suggested by the expressed powers.

The source of many of Congress's implied powers is Article I, Section 8. This section gives Congress the power "to make all laws which shall be necessary and proper" to exercise its other powers. This "necessary and proper" clause has been called the **Elastic Clause**, because it allows Congress to stretch its authority in ways not specifically granted nor denied to it by the Constitution.

For example, the Sixteenth Amendment to the Constitution expressly gives Congress the power to establish and collect taxes on incomes. Using its implied powers, Congress has established the Internal Revenue Service (IRS) to do the actual tax collecting.

Inherent Powers The federal government also has **inherent powers**, or powers that naturally belong to any government of a sovereign nation. Governments of sovereign nations have used these powers throughout history. Like implied powers, inherent powers are not mentioned in the Constitution. Many of these inherent powers relate to foreign affairs, such as the making of international agreements, including acquiring new territory.

Powers of State Governments

In the U.S. federal system, some powers are reserved to the states. These **reserved powers** are not specifically mentioned in the Constitution. According to the Tenth Amendment, however, the powers that the Constitution does not give to the federal government nor specifically forbid to the states "are reserved to the states . . . or to the people."

Among the states' reserved powers are the authority to establish local governments, create public school systems, and enact criminal and civil laws. States also may pass laws promoting public health and safety, regulating business within their

POLITICAL FOUNDATIONS *The U.S. government's decision to purchase Alaska was seen as foolish by some people, who thought Alaska was just a large block of ice, as noted in the above cartoon. (See the Linking Government and Economics feature on page 77.)* **What type of power allows governments to acquire new land?**

borders, and requiring licenses to work in various professional occupations. Professionals required to have licenses may include doctors, lawyers, accountants, and even the person you pay to cut your hair.

Concurrent Powers

The federal and state governments also hold some **concurrent powers**—those that the Constitution neither grants exclusively to the federal government nor denies to the states. For example, both the federal government and the states may establish court systems, make and enforce laws, collect taxes to pay the costs of governing, and borrow and spend money.

Limits on Federal and State Powers

The Constitution also limits the powers of the different levels of government. Some powers are denied only to the federal government, some only to the states, and some to both levels of government.

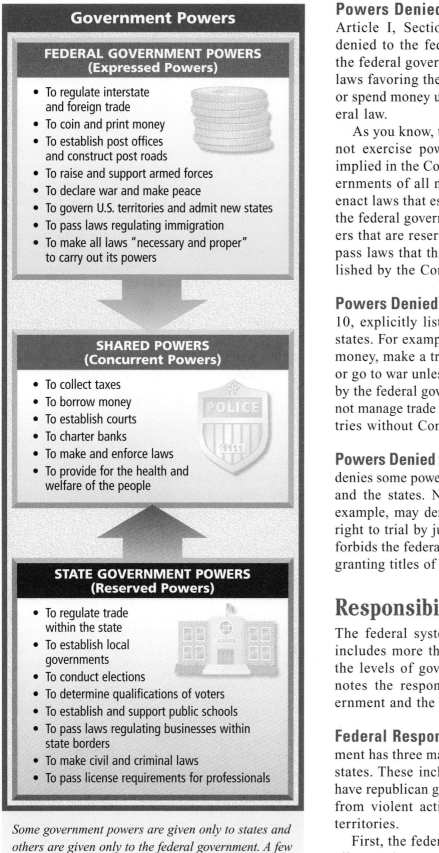

Government Powers

FEDERAL GOVERNMENT POWERS
(Expressed Powers)

- To regulate interstate and foreign trade
- To coin and print money
- To establish post offices and construct post roads
- To raise and support armed forces
- To declare war and make peace
- To govern U.S. territories and admit new states
- To pass laws regulating immigration
- To make all laws "necessary and proper" to carry out its powers

SHARED POWERS
(Concurrent Powers)

- To collect taxes
- To borrow money
- To establish courts
- To charter banks
- To make and enforce laws
- To provide for the health and welfare of the people

STATE GOVERNMENT POWERS
(Reserved Powers)

- To regulate trade within the state
- To establish local governments
- To conduct elections
- To determine qualifications of voters
- To establish and support public schools
- To pass laws regulating businesses within state borders
- To make civil and criminal laws
- To pass license requirements for professionals

*Some government powers are given only to states and others are given only to the federal government. A few powers are shared by both. **Are the powers reserved to the states specifically stated in the Constitution?***

Powers Denied to the Federal Government

Article I, Section 9, lists the powers that are denied to the federal government. For example, the federal government may not tax exports, pass laws favoring the trade of one state over another, or spend money unless authorized to do so by federal law.

As you know, the federal government also may not exercise powers that are not mentioned or implied in the Constitution or inherent to the governments of all nations. For example, it may not enact laws that establish a monarchy. In addition, the federal government may not exercise the powers that are reserved to the states, and it may not pass laws that threaten the federal system established by the Constitution.

Powers Denied to the States Article I, Section 10, explicitly lists powers that are denied to the states. For example, a state may not issue its own money, make a treaty with a foreign government, or go to war unless invaded or authorized to do so by the federal government. In addition, states cannot manage trade with other states or foreign countries without Congress's approval.

Powers Denied to Both Levels The Constitution denies some powers to both the federal government and the states. Neither level of government, for example, may deny people accused of crimes the right to trial by jury. In addition, the Constitution forbids the federal government and the states from granting titles of nobility.

Responsibilities

The federal system created by the Constitution includes more than a division of powers among the levels of government. The Constitution also notes the responsibilities that the federal government and the states have to each other.

Federal Responsibilities The federal government has three main responsibilities regarding the states. These include making sure that the states have republican governments, protecting the states from violent actions, and respecting the states' territories.

First, the federal government must ensure that all states have republican governments. Although the term *republican* is not defined in the Constitution, it has been interpreted to mean representative government. By allowing a state's representatives and senators to be seated in Congress, the federal government recognizes that a state's government is legitimate.

A second responsibility of the federal government is protecting the states from violent actions, such as foreign invasions. The framers made the federal government responsible for protecting all the states, which means that an attack against any one of the states is an attack against the United States as a whole.

Comparing ....➤ Governments

Federalism in Mexico and Germany

The United States is just one of many countries with a federal system of government. Both Mexico and Germany, for example, are federal republics operating under a centralized government.

As in the United States, the citizens in Mexico elect a president to head the federal government. Mexico's legislature consists of a 64-member Senate and a 500-member Federal Chamber of Deputies—a legislative house similar to the U.S. House of Representatives. *Distrito Federal*—a federal district similar to Washington, D.C.—houses the major federal offices. State governors, who are elected by the citizens of the country's 31 states, direct the state governments and make decisions and policies on local matters.

Germany's government is organized somewhat differently from the U.S. and Mexican governments. Its president is elected by federal and state legislators and holds a largely ceremonial position. The nation's chancellor, who is elected by the lower house of the legislature rather than by the people, is the head of the government. Like the United States and Mexico, however, Germany has a two-chamber legislature, consisting of the 68-member *Bundesrat,* or upper house, and the 656-member *Bundestag,* or lower house. In addition, citizens in each of Germany's 16 states elect members of a state legislature to govern state matters.

Although each state has the power to make and enforce laws within its boundaries, the federal government may intervene to help maintain order. In 1992, for example, federal troops helped stop violent rioting in Los Angeles. Such federal involvement has not happened often and usually has come at the request of state governors and local authorities.

In addition to protecting the states from violent actions, the federal government also helps states after natural disasters, such as earthquakes, fires, hurricanes, and floods. In 1996, for example, Congress authorized the distribution of $1.3 billion in natural disaster relief funds to states in the Northeast that had been damaged by blizzards the previous winter and to the Northwest, which had been greatly damaged by flooding.

A third responsibility of the federal government is to guard the states' territorial rights. For example, Article IV, Section 3, of the Constitution says that no new states may be formed from the territory of other states without the approval of both the states concerned and Congress.

State Responsibilities The states also have responsibilities to the federal government. They must establish, for example, the boundaries for districts from which members of the House of Representatives are elected. States also set the rules for electing members of Congress and choosing presidential electors and pay the costs of running elections—for example, printing ballots and setting up voting locations.

States also maintain National Guard units that may be called into action by the governor or the federal government during emergencies. National Guard units have even been used overseas, as in the Persian Gulf War in 1991.

The Courts and the Federal System

The framers knew that the system of government they created might lead to conflicts between the federal and state governments. They knew, for example, that states might pass laws that conflicted with those passed by the federal government. How did the framers solve this problem?

Article III of the Constitution gives the judicial branch the authority to hear cases involving the Constitution, U.S. laws, and disputes among states. Thus, the judicial branch has the authority to act as referee between the federal government and the states. In most team sports, a referee makes decisions based on rules that the participants have agreed to follow. In the federal system, the courts—and particularly the Supreme Court—make decisions based on the rules listed in the Constitution.

By agreeing to follow its rules, the states acknowledge that the Constitution is the highest authority in disputes with the federal government. As noted in Chapter 3, the framers made it clear in Article VI that the power of the federal government is superior to the power of state governments. This article of the Constitution includes the Supremacy Clause, which declares that the Constitution, federal laws, and treaties made by the federal government are "the supreme law of the land."

The Supremacy Clause guides the federal courts in solving conflicts between state and federal laws. In 1819, for example, the Supreme

PUBLIC GOOD *National Guard units provide assistance to Iowa residents after a flood in 1993.* **What type of assistance does the federal government provide to states during times of crisis?**

Court ruled in *McCulloch* v. *Maryland* that the state of Maryland could not tax the Bank of the United States. The Supreme Court ruled that if the states had the power to tax any part of the federal government, they would be superior to it, which would be unconstitutional.

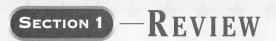

SECTION 1 — REVIEW

1. Define the following terms: expressed power, implied power, Elastic Clause, inherent power, reserved power, concurrent power.

2. Which constitutional amendment is the source of the states' reserved powers? List the states' reserved powers and the federal government's expressed powers.

3. What powers are denied to the federal government? to the states? to both?

4. What responsibilities does the federal government have to the states? What responsibilities do the states have to the federal government?

5. How do the federal courts serve as the federal system's referee?

6. **Thinking and Writing Critically**
   Why is it important that powers be divided between the federal government and the states? What do you suppose would happen if, for example, the states could negotiate their own trade agreements with foreign nations?

7. **Applying** PUBLIC GOOD
   States pass laws to promote public safety. Conduct an Internet search for recreational safety laws in your state. For example, laws may be passed to protect people while they are biking. Write a paragraph describing one of these laws, and explain whether you believe it promotes the public good.

GROWTH OF FEDERALISM

Political Dictionary

revenue sharing
grant-in-aid
categorical grant
block grant
federal mandate

Objectives

★ How has the federal government's involvement in states' affairs grown?

★ How have grants-in-aid affected the growth of federalism?

★ What role do federal mandates play in federalism?

Debates about the federal system have long been part of U.S. politics. At various times since the founding of the republic, some states have argued that they had the right to nullify, or cancel, federal laws that they opposed. In the mid-1800s, eleven southern states even claimed the right to secede from, or leave, the United States. Many of the people in these states believed that under President Abraham Lincoln's administration the government threatened southern institutions, including the system of slavery, and hence their way of life.

The Civil War defeat of the 11 southern states that seceded from the Union in 1860 and 1861 firmly established the federal government's supreme authority. In addition, the Supreme Court has ruled that the Constitution's Supremacy Clause does not allow states to reject federal laws as long as those laws are constitutional.

The debate over the power of the state and federal governments continues today. Some of the fuel for that debate has come from the ways in which the federal government has increased its involvement in states' affairs.

Increasing Federal Involvement

In the twentieth century the federal government has become increasingly involved in areas previously handled by state and local governments. In law enforcement, for example, the Federal Bureau of Investigation (FBI) often helps state and local officials solve major crimes. The federal government also helps pay to maintain the states' National Guard units.

The growth of federal involvement is particularly evident in the money that the national government has given to state and local governments. During the 1970s and early 1980s, for example, federal tax dollars were shared with state and local governments. Under this system of **revenue sharing**, states had a great deal of freedom in spending their share of federal money. Revenue sharing ended in the mid-1980s, however, under pressure to cut federal spending.

In spite of such pressure, federal aid to the states has continued and, in some ways, even grown. Today, federal grants are major sources of income for state and local governments. To receive this aid, however, states often must follow rules and requirements set by the federal government.

The Grant System

One way that the role of the federal government has grown is through grants-in-aid. **Grants-in-aid** are money or other resources that the federal government provides to pay for state and local activities. Unlike money from revenue sharing, grants-in-aid are used for specific projects and programs authorized by the federal government.

The number and value of grants-in-aid have grown a great deal during the twentieth century, but the roots of these grants reach back much further. The Land Ordinance of 1785 under the Articles of Confederation, for example, set aside land for public schools in the territories won from Great Britain during the Revolutionary War.

After the Constitution was ratified, the federal government continued to give aid to states. The Morrill Act of 1862, for example, gave grants of federally owned land to the states. The states used the money they earned from selling the land to establish colleges. Seventy state universities, including Texas A & M and Ohio State, have their origins in the Morrill Act.

Today, grants to the states support not only education but also transportation systems, housing projects, and programs for people in need. How a grant-in-aid can be used depends on its form: categorical or block.

Categorical Grants Payments by the federal government to carry out specific activities are called **categorical grants**. Categorical grant programs include those for building airports and other public facilities, unemployment compensation, fighting crime, and providing aid after natural disasters such as floods and earthquakes.

Categorical grants often base the amount of aid that a state or local government receives on certain conditions, such as population. These grants also typically require that state or local governments contribute their own funds, in an amount determined by Congress. In this way, state and local governments show their commitment to the program.

Block Grants Another form of grant-in-aid is a **block grant**. These federal funds can be used by a state or locality in a broadly defined area such as welfare, community development, health, or education. Block grant projects include developing public transportation systems, anticrime programs, and community youth activities.

State and local governments usually prefer block grants to categorical grants because, as with revenue sharing, block grants give them more freedom to decide how to spend federal money. Some critics believe, however, that this flexibility allows states to ignore the needs of those for whom the aid was intended. Supporters of block grants, on the other hand, argue that state and local governments can better determine their citizens' needs than can the federal government.

Since the 1980s, block grants have become increasingly common. Some categorical grants to support libraries, aid science education, and teach students about the metric system, for example, became a part of the broader education block grants. In 1995 and 1996 many members of

POLITICAL PROCESSES *Many state universities, including the Champaign-Urbana campus of the University of Illinois, were established as a result of federal aid provided by the Morrill Act of 1862.* **What other types of programs do grants-in-aid support?**

Congress supported proposals for turning categorical grants into block grants. Rather than determining how much money should go to every program, the federal government would allow states to decide which priorities should be pursued with available funds. Under the 1996 welfare law, for example, all federal contributions to welfare are in the form of block grants.

Federal Mandates

The federal government also has become more involved in the affairs of the states through **federal mandates**—requirements that the federal government imposes on state and local governments. The federal government passes mandates to address issues that affect people in many or all of the states. For example, some federal mandates have established protections for the environment and measures to protect the health and safety of workers.

Forms of Mandates Federal mandates come in three basic forms. One form is a law directing state or local governments to take action on a particular issue. For example, the Asbestos Hazard Emergency Response Act of 1986 required public schools to take certain steps to protect children from exposure to asbestos, a fireproof mineral that can cause health problems and that was formerly used in insulation. In buildings using this insulation, tiny asbestos fibers travel through the air, causing lung damage in people who inhale them. Supporters of the 1986 law wanted to protect children's health in the nation's public schools.

Another form of federal mandate gives states the choice between undertaking an activity themselves or having the federal government do it. For example, in 1970 the federal government passed the Clean Air Act to lower pollution levels. States were given money and were allowed to make their own rules to follow this law, on the condition that they met federal air quality levels. States that did not do so would have to accept federal enforcement of the law. State leaders often prefer to administer programs themselves because they can adapt government rules to local conditions, whereas the federal government often makes broad rules that all areas must follow.

Finally, federal mandates may come in the form of strings attached to federal aid. To receive this aid, a state or local government must follow certain requirements. For example, in 1986 Congress declared that states whose minimum age for drinking alcoholic beverages was 20 or less would lose a percentage of their federal aid for constructing and maintaining highways if they did not raise the age to 21. Establishing a legal drinking age is a state responsibility, but by the end of 1988 all states had raised the minimum legal drinking age to 21 to keep from losing full federal highway funding.

Debate over Mandates People who do not think that the federal government should issue mandates argue that federal rules violate the rights of states to handle their own affairs. For example, some people argue that environmental laws passed by Congress interfere with state and local authority. Others declare, however, that such regulation is necessary because one state's environmental pollution often affects the residents of other states.

Critics also argue that the federal government should provide the funds to pay for its mandates. For example, Congress passed a law in 1993 requiring states to adopt certain rules making it easier for people to register to vote. Supporters argued that the law would increase voter registration. Some opponents, however, argued that the law would unfairly force state governments to pay for a program that they had not created.

States have fought against unfunded mandates—and with some success. In 1995, for example, Congress passed and President Clinton signed into law a bill that required that the Congressional Budget Office (CBO) submit a report on the costs a new bill would impose on state and local governments before that bill could be considered by Congress. If the CBO determined that the legislation would require expenditures of more than $50 million, and Congress refused to provide the funds to state governments for enforcement of the new law, then that bill could not be considered by Congress unless a special "point of order" vote was taken that would allow consideration of the legislation. The debate over balancing federal and state interests, however, continues.

POLITICAL PROCESSES *Workers from the EPA clean up a toxic waste dump in Houston. Federal environmental mandates often include aid to help states follow these rules.* **Why do some people argue that the federal government should provide funds for mandates?**

C A S E   S T U D Y

Drive 55?

CONSTITUTIONAL GOVERNMENT Changing times play an important role in the establishment and repeal of federal mandates. Consider, for example, federal mandates about speed limits on the nation's highways.

In 1973 and 1974 a major rise in the price of oil caused fuel prices to skyrocket. The shock over the higher prices encouraged efforts to conserve energy. In one such effort, Congress passed a law that required any state receiving federal highway aid to lower its maximum speed limit to 55 miles per hour.

Setting speed limits is a state responsibility, but as with the federal mandate regarding a minimum drinking age, every state quickly lowered its maximum speed limit to 55 miles per hour in order to keep from losing federal funding. By the late 1980s, however, fuel prices had fallen, the fuel efficiency of cars had improved, and concern over conserving energy was less strong. Pressure from some states, notably large western states whose population centers are often far apart, led Congress in 1987 to allow states to raise the speed limit to 65 miles per hour in rural areas.

In 1995 the federal mandate on speed limits changed again. Under growing pressure to roll back

POLITICAL PROCESSES *Some states increased their maximum speed limits to 75 miles per hour after the passage of the 1995 law that allowed states to set their own speed limits.* **Why did all states lower their maximum speed limits to 55 miles per hour during the 1970s?**

federal rules, Congress passed a law allowing states to set their own speed limits on all roads. Opponents had argued that the higher speed limits would waste fuel and cause more deaths from traffic accidents. Others argued that the states could better determine safe speed limits inside their own borders. Most states set higher speed limits shortly after the law passed. The full result of these higher limits may not be known for several years.

SECTION 2 — REVIEW

1. Define the following terms: revenue sharing, grant-in-aid, categorical grant, block grant, federal mandate.

2. What are some examples of increasing federal involvement in states' affairs?

3. Describe the two kinds of grants-in-aid. Give examples of what a grant-in-aid might fund. How do these grants-in-aid reflect the federal government's increased role in states' affairs?

4. What are the forms of federal mandates?

5. How have federal mandates increased the federal government's role in states' affairs? What are some of the criticisms of this increased involvement?

6. **Thinking and Writing Critically**
In this chapter, you have read how the federal government provides grants-in-aid to the states. Have you ever received a "grant-in-aid" from someone, such as your parents, another relative, a friend, or your school? What was the grant's purpose? Were you able to use the support to complete a project or reach a goal?

7. **Applying** CONSTITUTIONAL GOVERNMENT
Some people think that the role of the federal government in states' affairs has become too large. Review the information in this section, and write a short report discussing the specific areas in which these people think the federal government has too much control. Be sure to state your own opinion.

RELATIONS AMONG THE STATES

Political Dictionary

enabling act
act of admission
civil law
criminal law
extradition
interstate compact

Objectives

★ How are states admitted to the United States?
★ In what ways do the states work together in the federal system?

Part of the federal system involves how the states deal with one another. The Constitution, however, not only establishes guidelines for state interaction, it also provides for the admission of new states. In addition, it ensures that any state, regardless of when it is admitted, has the same status and rights as all the other states.

Admitting New States

Not all states have been admitted in the same way. Of the 37 states admitted to the Union since the Constitution was ratified, 30 were admitted after often lengthy periods as U.S. territories. To become a state, a territory usually petitions, or asks, Congress to be allowed into the Union. If the petition is approved, Congress then passes an **enabling act**—legislation that directs the territory to draft a state constitution establishing a representative government.

Next, the territory elects delegates to draft a constitution. If approved by the residents of the territory, the document is submitted to Congress for approval. Once approved, Congress then passes an **act of admission**—legislation that makes the

territory a state with status equal to that of all the other states.

Some states were admitted without long periods as territories. California became a state within two years of Mexico's turning it over to the United States after losing the Mexican War. When Texas was admitted, it had been an independent republic for nine years.

Some states were formed from existing states. As noted in Section 2, a new state may not be formed from the territory of an existing state without that existing state's permission. Vermont, Kentucky, Tennessee, and Maine were formed from existing states. West Virginia also was formed from an existing state—Virginia. Because Virginia was not a state during the Civil War, however, Congress was able to admit West Virginia into the United States in 1863 without Virginia's permission.

States in the Federal System

Even though the Constitution gives states the right to manage their own affairs within their borders, it also encourages cooperation among them. How do the states cooperate with one another?

Full Faith and Credit One way that states cooperate is by recognizing one another's official acts. As Article IV, Section 1, of the Constitution states,

CONSTITUTIONAL GOVERNMENT *The Full Faith and Credit Clause in the Constitution requires states to honor other states' driver's licenses.* **What other official records must states honor?**

Government and Economics

Alaska: The Last Frontier

Soon after the United States was founded, Americans began moving west into the vast frontier lands. As Americans and new immigrants settled along the western border of the frontier, they began to push the frontier farther west. By the end of the 1800s, the nation's western frontier had disappeared. Soon, U.S. explorers began to look northward, to a territory known as Alaska, which was to become America's new frontier. Now, this frigid land is one of the United States's most sparsely populated, yet economically prosperous, states. Even today, Alaska's license plates declare it to be "The Last Frontier."

U.S. secretary of state William H. Seward negotiated the $7.2 million purchase of Alaska with Russia in 1867. Many people in the United States, viewing Alaska as a national liability rather than an asset, criticized the purchase. Skeptics demanded to know the usefulness of this frozen land. Seward, however, knew of Alaska's valuable natural resources—Russians had been trapping furs in the region's vast forests for more than 100 years. In addition, Seward believed that Alaska's geographic location made it vital to U.S. military interests. Owning Alaska would strengthen U.S. influence in the north Pacific and weaken Russia's power. Still, critics called the purchase "Seward's Folly" and made their opinions known by describing the region as "Frigidia" and "President Andrew Johnson's Polar Bear Garden."

The Alaskan Purchase, however, was soon recognized as the United States's "biggest bargain" since Thomas Jefferson's 1803 Louisiana Purchase. For less than two cents an acre, the United States gained about 600,000 square miles of resource-rich land—expanding its territory by almost 20 percent. In 1896 the Klondike Gold Rush in Alaska silenced Seward's critics forever.

Alaska's natural resources include immense mineral deposits, dense forests, and plentiful fish and wildlife, in addition to petroleum reserves that have added to the economic wealth of the state and the nation. Oil revenue generates about four fifths of the state's income. All Alaskan residents share in the wealth—just for living in the state they receive close to $1,000 per year from a state oil fund. In 1995 per capita income in Alaska exceeded $24,000 per year, among the nation's highest.

The state's largest oil reserves lie beneath the North Slope near Prudhoe Bay, on the Arctic coast. These reserves are slowly being depleted, however, spurring controversial efforts to drill in Alaska's Arctic National Wildlife Refuge, a haven for caribou. Geologists maintain that this northern coastal plain of Alaska is potentially one of the top oil-producing regions in the world. Environmentalists, however, argue that drilling in the refuge would destroy the only untouched Arctic ecosystem in the world. Although the interpretation has shifted over the years, the nickname "The Last Frontier" still applies to Alaska.

Although purchasing Alaska was initially criticized by some people, the territory was soon seen as a wise investment because of its plentiful wildlife, oil deposits, and dense forests.

What Do You Think?

1. Once Alaska's petroleum reserves in oil-rich Prudhoe Bay begin to run out, should oil companies be allowed to drill in the Arctic National Wildlife Refuge? Explain your answer.
2. Do you think that admitting Alaska into the Union was more important to the nation's economy or to its foreign policy aims? Explain your answer.

FBI Agent

When federal laws are broken in the United States, the Federal Bureau of Investigation (FBI) steps in to investigate. An agency of the U.S. Department of Justice, the FBI employs more than 10,000 agents in field offices across the country.

Approximately 280 types of crimes, such as car-jacking, kidnapping, bank robbery, the selling of military and political information to foreign countries—even failure to pay child support—fall under the FBI's jurisdiction. With so many different types of cases to investigate, the FBI must employ agents with experience in all areas of law enforcement. For example, agents with prior computer training are needed for computer fraud investigations, while agents who are fluent in a foreign language may be assigned to investigate international espionage cases.

To gather information for a case, an FBI agent must interview people, research official records, and observe suspects. Often, as in the case of the 1995 bombing of a federal office building in Oklahoma City, the FBI works with local and state law enforcement officials to capture suspects. Once enough evidence is gathered, agents make arrests. Sometimes they participate in raids—the sudden seizure of illegal operations and organizations. After a case goes to court, agents often testify about the evidence gathered during the investigation.

FBI agents examine evidence after the bombing in Atlanta, Georgia, during the 1996 Olympic Games.

How does someone become an FBI agent? The FBI employs people in many professions, including accountants, lawyers, and scientists. A college degree is required, and being able to speak one or more foreign languages is an advantage.

Potential candidates, who must be between 23 and 37 years old, go through a rigorous application process that includes written tests, interviews, a thorough background check, drug testing, and a physical examination. Those who successfully complete this process must then train for 16 weeks at the FBI Academy. During training, potential agents study academic and investigative subject matter, physical fitness, proper use of firearms, and self-defense. College students interested in a career as an FBI agent can apply to internship programs to gain an insider's look at the role of an FBI agent.

"Full faith and credit shall be given in each state to the public acts, records, and judicial proceedings of every other state." The term *public acts* refers to a state's **civil laws**—laws that govern relationships among individual parties and that define people's legal rights.

Thus, the Full Faith and Credit Clause declares that states must recognize other states' civil laws. These laws include contracts between individuals and businesses. A state also must recognize, for example, a person's legal ownership of property in another state.

States also honor the convictions, settlements, and other decisions of courts in other states. States do not have to enforce other states' **criminal laws**, which forbid certain actions and provide punishment for violations. Criminal laws cover such things as theft and murder.

Finally, the Full Faith and Credit Clause requires states to honor other states' official records, such as driver's licenses, car registrations, and wills. For example, anyone licensed to drive in Texas can legally drive in the other 49 states.

Privileges and Immunities States also cooperate with one another by respecting the rights of citizens of other states. As Article IV, Section 2, of the Constitution states, "The citizens of each state shall be entitled to all privileges and immunities of citizens in the several states." This means that a resident of one state cannot be unreasonably discriminated against by another state. Each state must offer all U.S. citizens full protection of the laws. In addition, all citizens must be allowed to pursue lawful occupations, have access to the courts, and conduct legal business with others.

A state can, however, make reasonable distinctions between its citizens and those who are residents of another state. It can require that a person become a resident of the state before being allowed to vote in local elections or serve on juries. To become a resident, a person usually must live in a state for a certain amount of time. States also may charge people who are not residents higher fees for some activities that are supported by the state's taxpayers.

Extradition A third area in which states cooperate involves people who commit a crime and try to escape the authorities by fleeing to another state. Although one state cannot enforce another state's criminal laws, Article IV, Section 2, of the Constitution provides for the extradition of people who are suspected or convicted of having committed crimes. **Extradition** is the process of sending a suspect or criminal back to the state from which he or she has fled. Criminals and suspects are usually extradited at the request of the governor of the state in which the crime was committed.

In 1987 the Supreme Court ruled that governors must honor extradition requests from other states.

CONSTITUTIONAL GOVERNMENT *Governors may request that a suspected criminal be extradited to the state where the crime was committed.* **Why might governors make such a request?**

Before that time, governors occasionally refused to extradite suspects for several reasons, such as fears that a suspect would not receive a fair trial or concerns about another state's prison conditions.

Interstate Compacts States also may make **interstate compacts**, or agreements with other states, if Congress approves. Because of the rapid economic change and growth of cities and states in the twentieth century, interstate compacts have grown in number and importance. These agreements now cover issues such as flood control, protection of natural resources, and pollution.

SECTION 3 — REVIEW

1. Define the following terms: enabling act, act of admission, civil law, criminal law, extradition, interstate compact.

2. What are the steps for becoming a state? What was unusual about the way in which West Virginia became a state?

3. Describe ways in which states cooperate with one another.

4. **Thinking and Writing Critically**
   Why is it important that the Constitution provides ways for the states to cooperate with one another? What might happen if states regularly refused to extradite people suspected or convicted of committing crimes in other states?

5. **Applying** **CONSTITUTIONAL GOVERNMENT**
   Make a list of the ways in which your school cooperates with other schools in your community or state. For example, students from your school may participate in a tutoring program at a local elementary school. What advantages do such cooperative agreements offer students in both schools?

FEDERALISM AND THE PUBLIC GOOD

Objectives

★ How does the national government in a federal system promote the public good?

★ In what ways does dividing power in a federal system help government serve the public good?

★ How has balancing federal and state interests helped to promote the public good?

A federal system of government has been vital to the growth and success of the United States. It also has kept the republic united while allowing people at state and local levels to manage their own affairs. By providing a central authority, distributing power, and balancing federal and state interests, the U.S. federal system promotes the public good.

Providing Central Authority

One way that the federal system promotes the public good is by providing a central authority: the federal government. The federal government acts on issues that are important to all of the states. Consider, for example, efforts to protect the environment. A state might hesitate to enact certain environmental protections that, although popular with the state's citizens, might lead businesses to move to states with rules that are less costly to follow. In addition, businesspeople might be frustrated by a tangle of environmental rules that differ from state to state, making it more difficult and costly for businesses to operate. Such rules might make it more difficult to operate a business effectively.

It therefore promotes the public good if the federal government adopts a national environmental policy that all states must follow. Such a policy standardizes environmental rules so that citizens and businesses can plan their actions. It also addresses the concerns of interests such as businesses, private citizens, and the states. If the policy did not address all of these concerns, it likely would not be passed.

As a central authority, the federal government also can protect the rights of all citizens, no matter where they live. A citizen in Delaware, for example, has the same constitutional rights as another citizen living in Hawaii. The federal courts can ensure that constitutional rights and federal laws are applied equally throughout all 50 states. By making sure that the rights of all citizens are protected, the federal government again promotes the public good.

Distributing Power

The federal system also promotes the public good by making sure that power is distributed among the states and not concentrated solely in the federal government. How does this distribution of power help government promote the public good?

Encouraging Alternate Solutions One way the federal system promotes the public good is by allowing the states to search for alternate strategies

CONSTITUTIONAL GOVERNMENT *In 1994 the federal government designated a portion of the Mojave Desert as a protected wilderness area.* **Why might a state be hesitant to enact strict environmental protection laws?**

in addressing common challenges. In short, the states can act as "laboratories of democracy," conducting experiments with new policies and solutions from which other states and communities can learn.

Consider the debate over how to help people in need. Some people have argued that the federal government has a responsibility to provide for people in need. Others have argued that the states should be allowed to try different ways of providing such assistance. In fact, under the welfare reform passed by Congress in 1996, states make their own rules for helping people who are poor. Supporters of the idea that more responsibility should be given to the states argue that with state governments experimenting with their own plans, more successful methods will likely be developed.

Checking Power Distributing power among the states also makes majority tyranny and an abuse of power more difficult. Should a self-interested majority somehow gain control of the federal government, the states may act in ways that check its power. One way that states can do this is by refusing to ratify constitutional amendments proposed by Congress. States' reserved powers also prevent the federal government from acting in areas over which it has no constitutional authority. It works both ways, however. As Alexander Hamilton wrote in his essay "No. 28" in the *Federalist Papers,* "The national government will at all times stand ready to check the usurpations [wrongful seizures of power] of the state governments, and these [the state governments] will have the same disposition [role] towards the [national] government." Federalism may thus be seen as an additional check and balance in the constitutional framework.

Promoting Participation Finally, distributing power in a federal system allows more decisions to be made at a local level, which means that more people can be involved in decisions that most affect their lives. For example, because the United States has a federal system, educational funding differs widely from state to state. In addition to public education, such services as fire protection, car registration, road construction, and libraries are provided by state and local government. As a matter of fact, the laws and government policies with the greatest effect on your daily life are generally state and local, not federal. By allowing decisions to be made locally and by involving more people in the decision-making process, the federal system promotes democracy and encourages government to consider citizens' concerns before making its policies. Both of these actions promote the public good.

Balancing Federal and State Interests

Creating a central authority and distributing power among the states are just two ways in which

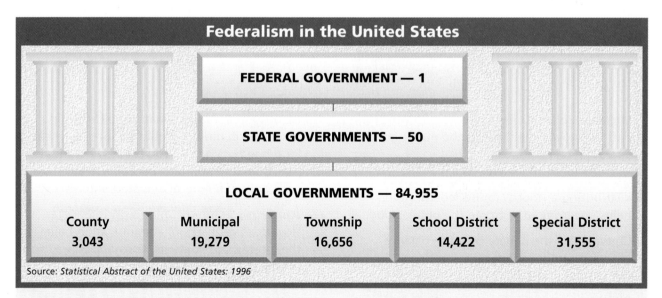

Federalism in the United States

FEDERAL GOVERNMENT — 1

STATE GOVERNMENTS — 50

LOCAL GOVERNMENTS — 84,955

County	Municipal	Township	School District	Special District
3,043	19,279	16,656	14,422	31,555

Source: *Statistical Abstract of the United States: 1996*

With thousands of different local governments, people have many opportunities to participate in the decision-making process. **How can you participate in your local government?**

a federal system of government promotes the public good. In addition, good government needs to balance federal and state interests. There is debate, however, about where to find that balance.

The development of federalism in the United States has sometimes resembled a tug-of-war between supporters and opponents of the federal government's growing influence in states' affairs. Some people have strongly protested that federal mandates, for example, violate states' rights. As noted in Section 2, supporters of states' rights pushed Congress to stop passing unfunded mandates. Some people also have argued that some federal laws, such as those meant to protect the environment, violate the rights of states and local government authorities to control their own affairs.

Others, however, have pointed to the advantages of federal action. Federal laws, for example, have succeeded in extending voting rights to all eligible U.S. citizens, even in states that have tried to restrict those rights. Federal laws protecting individual rights such as voting are the best way to ensure that all citizens are treated fairly. In addition, federal courts have worked to protect the rights of citizens in all of the states. Supporters argue that such actions are necessary to ensure that the public good is served. In the end, of course, it is the responsibility of all citizens to determine the proper balance between state and federal interests and to work to secure that balance.

Berry's World

Better downsize!

© 1993 by NEA, Inc.

BERRY'S WORLD reprinted by permission of Newspaper Enterprise Association, Inc.

CONSTITUTIONAL GOVERNMENT *Some people believe that the federal government's influence over states' affairs is too great.* **How does this cartoon illustrate the debate about the power and size of the federal government?**

SECTION 4 — REVIEW

1. List and explain some of the ways in which the national government serves the public good.

2. In what ways are the states "laboratories of democracy"? Explain other ways in which distributing authority in the federal system helps government promote the public good.

3. Characterize the debate over the balance between federal and state interests in the U.S. federal system.

4. **Thinking and Writing Critically**
   As you know, some people have argued that federal aid should come in the form of block grants. They believe that states are better able than the federal government to determine how federal money should be spent to meet local needs. What do you think? How might grants be an important part of a healthy balance between federal and state interests?

5. **Applying** **CONSTITUTIONAL GOVERNMENT**
   How does your school administration balance the interests of students, teachers, and administrators? For example, students may be allowed to select their own classes according to the guidelines set up by the faculty and administration. Do you think that student interests and faculty interests are given equal consideration? Why or why not?

CHAPTER 4 — SUMMARY

SECTION 1 The Constitution establishes a federal system by assigning powers and broad responsibilities to both the federal government and the states. The federal government has three kinds of powers: expressed, implied, and inherent. Expressed powers are those the Constitution specifically, or expressly, states. The legislative branch's expressed powers are listed in Article 1, Section 8. Those belonging to the other branches of the government can be found in Articles II and III.

The implied powers are those that are implied, or suggested, by the expressed powers. The source of many of Congress's implied powers is the Elastic Clause in Article I, Section 8. This section gives Congress the power "to make all laws which shall be necessary and proper" to exercise its other powers.

Inherent powers are those that inherently, or naturally, belong to any government of a sovereign nation. Like implied powers, inherent powers are not mentioned in the Constitution. Examples of inherent powers are the roles of the government in acquiring new territory and defending the nation during war.

The Constitution reserves some powers to the states and denies others to both levels of government. The federal court system acts as a referee when the federal government's authority conflicts with that of the states.

SECTION 2 The influence of the federal government in the affairs of the states has greatly increased over the years. One way that this has occurred is through the grant system. States receive grants-in-aid for specific projects and programs authorized by the federal government. There are two different types of grants—categorical and block.

The federal government also has become more involved in states' affairs through federal mandates. These mandates come in three basic forms. One involves directing the states to take action on a particular issue. Another form allows state or local governments to act on an issue themselves or to have the federal government do it. The third form involves an offer of aid to states that follow certain requirements.

SECTION 3 Federalism also deals with relations among the states. The Constitution ensures that all states have equal status and rights. In addition, it encourages states to cooperate with one another by requiring them to recognize official acts of other states, respect the rights of citizens from other states, and return people who have fled prosecution for crimes committed in other states. The Constitution also allows states to form interstate compacts.

SECTION 4 The federal system helps government promote the public good in several ways. It establishes a central authority that can address issues important to all states and that protects the rights of all U.S. citizens. It also distributes power among the states, allowing them to experiment with solutions to common problems, making majority tyranny more difficult, and allowing more decisions to be made at a local level. Ultimately, securing the proper balance between the power of the federal government and that of the states is the responsibility of all.

Government Notebook

Review what you wrote in your Government Notebook at the beginning of this chapter about the powers of the federal government. Now that you have studied the chapter, how would you revise your answer? Should any of the powers you listed belong to a different part of the government than it currently does? Record your answer in your Notebook.

REVIEW

REVIEWING CONCEPTS

1. What happens when the powers of the federal government conflict with the powers of the states? Which powers does the Constitution deny the states, and which does it deny the federal government?

2. What are interstate compacts? In what other ways does the Constitution encourage states to cooperate with one another?

3. In what ways does operating under a federal system help government in the United States promote the public good?

4. What are the three kinds of powers belonging to the federal government? What are some examples of reserved and concurrent powers?

5. Describe the U.S. federal system today.

6. What responsibilities do the states and the federal government have to each other?

THINKING AND WRITING CRITICALLY

1. **CONSTITUTIONAL GOVERNMENT** The concept of limited government is an important principle of the U.S. political system. In what ways does the federal system limit government?

2. **CONSTITUTIONAL GOVERNMENT** Compare the distribution of powers and responsibilities in a federal system with their distribution in your school. What advantages are there in distributing responsibilities among the elected officers of each class and the school's student government?

3. **PUBLIC GOOD** In what ways can you and other citizens help ensure that the federal system of government works to promote the public good?

CITIZENSHIP IN YOUR COMMUNITY

Working with a group, develop a list of federally funded projects and programs that affect your community. These might include specific buildings, assistance to poor and older people, or national parks in your area. To find this information, check telephone listings to locate federal offices, research local newspaper articles about federal programs, and interview citizens in your community. In addition, ask citizens you interview about the importance of these projects and programs to them. Afterward, use your list and interviews to create a short pamphlet titled "The Federal Government in [your community's name]." Illustrate your pamphlet with photographs and other images.

INDIVIDUAL PORTFOLIO PROJECT

Research one of the 37 states that was admitted to the United States after the Constitution was ratified. Then imagine that you are a newspaper reporter in that state on the day it was admitted. Write an article about the admission process, and include important facts describing the state (such as its population and the name of the capital) on the day it was admitted. Be sure to include a headline and a sketch or other image.

THE INTERNET: LEARNING ONLINE

Working with a partner, conduct an Internet search for information about federal grants. You might start with search words such as *federal grant*. What kind of information can you find on Web pages? Who created Web sites that provide information about federal grants? Use the information you collect to create a flyer that describes how to use the Internet to find out about the types of projects and programs that are funded by federal grants.

PRACTICING SKILLS: CONDUCTING RESEARCH

All levels of government have meetings that are accessible to the public. Community or town meetings often set aside time for citizens to discuss issues of importance to them. Prepare a presentation for a class "town meeting" on a policy that you would like your state to adopt. Use the resources available at your school or public library to prepare for the presentation.

Use a current events source such as the *Readers' Guide to Periodical Literature* to find journal or magazine articles on the topic. Read several articles, and take notes on background information, key people, and the success of similar laws in other states. To support your argument, look up figures and statistical data in almanacs or government reports. Conduct Internet searches for up-to-date facts and public opinions. Synthesize the information into a short argument to present to your class.

ANALYZING PRIMARY SOURCES

THE CONSTITUTION OF SOUTH CAROLINA (1895)

The federal system gives states the power to enact state constitutions. Some states have used this power to restrict the individual rights guaranteed by the U.S. Constitution. During the 1880s and 1890s, some southern states added laws to their constitutions to disfranchise, or take away the legal rights of, African Americans. These laws were meant to prevent African Americans from voting. Read the following example of disfranchisement laws taken from South Carolina's constitution, written in 1895. Then answer the questions that follow.

Article II: Right of Suffrage

66 *Sec. 4. The qualifications for suffrage shall be as follows: Residence in the State for two years, in the County for one year, in*

the polling precinct in which the elector offers to vote four months, and the payment six months before any election of any poll tax then due and payable. . . .

Up to January 1st 1898, all male persons of voting age applying for registration who can read any Section in this Constitution submitted to them by the registration officer, or understand and explain it when read to them by the registration officer, shall be entitled to register and become electors. A separate record of all persons registered before January 1st, 1898, sworn to by the registration officer, shall be filed . . . and such persons shall remain during life qualified electors unless disqualified by the other provisions of this Article. The certificate of the Clerk of Court or Secretary of State shall be sufficient evidence to establish the right of said citizen to any subsequent registration and the franchise under the limitations herein imposed. . . .

Any person who shall apply for registration after January 1st, 1898, if otherwise qualified, shall be registered: Provided, That he can both read and write any section of this Constitution submitted to him by the registration officer or can show that he owns, and has paid all taxes collectible during the previous year on property in this State assessed at three hundred dollars ($300) or more.

Managers of election shall require of every elector offering to vote at any election, before allowing him to vote, proof of the payment of all taxes, including poll tax, assessed against him and collectible during the previous year. The production of a certificate or of the receipt of the officer authorized to collect such taxes shall be conclusive proof of payment thereof. 99

1. What terms in this constitution prevented many freed slaves from voting? Explain.

2. How might the Supremacy Clause in the Constitution have played a role in later laws governing voting rights?

3. How do the limits placed on the power of state governments ensure equal opportunity for all citizens?

PUBLIC POLICY LAB

Drafting a Bill of Rights

You are a member of your school's student council. Your principal has asked the council to prepare a proposal for a bill of rights to be adopted as an amendment to your school's constitution. Next month, your principal will present the proposal at a school-board meeting open to all parents, students, and members of the community.

In the past several months, the school administration has received numerous phone calls and letters from students, parents, and community organizations concerned about the rights of students. Your principal has provided a copy of your school's constitution, a bill of rights recently adopted by another high school in your city, and two of these letters. You will find these documents on the following pages.

Review the documents, and answer the questions that accompany them in your Government Notebook. Once you have studied the documents, the council will need to work together to conduct some outside research. You may want to study articles on student rights issues and search for policies established by other high school student councils. Record the results of your research in your Government Notebook. You and other members of the council should discuss the results of your research and determine the most important issues to include in your bill of rights. Make sure your proposed bill clearly states the rights guaranteed to students. Consider reading your proposed bill of rights to the rest of the class as part of a discussion on students' rights.

Highland High School

Federal Heights, CO 80221

Office of Kate Stevenson

Memorandum

Date: February 10
To: Highland High School Student Council   *KS*
From: Principal Stevenson

I would like the Student Council to prepare a proposal for a school bill of rights to be presented in an open meeting of the Board of Education on the second Thursday of next month. If the suggested bill of rights meets the approval of the Board of Education, it will be proposed as an amendment to the school constitution at the next Student Council meeting. Study the Highland High School Constitution, taking note of the purpose of the constitution and the duties of the Student Council.

I have provided a copy of the bill of rights adopted by Eastside High School Student Council, which you may want to use as a model. I also have provided copies of two letters on student rights issues. After reviewing these documents, the council will need to conduct some outside research. The council should form small research groups, and each group should research the answer to one of the following questions:

- In the last 10 years, has the Supreme Court ruled on any cases concerning the violation of student rights? What were the rights in question? What was the Court's final ruling?
- What are some examples of negative and positive impacts of a student bill of rights at other high schools?
- What resources are needed to enforce a school bill of rights?
- What methods have other high schools used to reach a compromise between students and faculty members on issues of student rights?
- What are the safety and health issues associated with student rights?

There may be other questions that you will need to address as you conduct your research and analyze the constitution, model bill of rights, and letters. Below is a list of resources that might aid you in your research.

- relevant articles in the Readers' Guide to Periodical Literature
- interviews with school administrators or student council members at other high schools
- Internet sites on student issues

Thank you for your help. I look forward to reading your proposal.

STUDENT COUNCIL MEETING

When:
Wednesday, February 10, at 1 p.m.

Where:
Student Council Office, Room 112

We will be working on an important assignment from Principal Stevenson.

DON'T MISS THIS MEETING!

THE CONSTITUTION OF HIGHLAND HIGH SCHOOL

The Constitution of Highland High School is created in order that the elected members of the Student Council may establish better interaction among the students, faculty, and administration, as well as promote the well-being of the school and community.

Article I. Powers of the Student Council
All powers of the student government shall be vested in the Highland High School Student Council.

Article II. Membership of the Council
A. The council shall consist of no more than 40 members.
   1. The council membership shall include 10 elected representatives from each grade.
      (a) Council members from all grades except 9 shall be elected by their respective grades before May 30 of each year.
      (b) Council members from grade 9 shall be elected by their respective grade before October 31 of each year.
B. A vacancy on the Student Council shall be filled by the student who was next in line in the election results or through appointment by the faculty adviser.
C. Any Student Council member who is suspended from school will be removed from the Student Council.

Article III. Meetings of the Council
A. The Student Council shall meet after school once a week from September through May 30.
B. The Student Council shall meet once a month during the school day. This meeting shall take place on the second Wednesday of each month.
C. The president or adviser may call special meetings as needed.
D. Meetings will not commence without a quorum, or one half of the present Student Council membership plus the faculty adviser.

Article IV. Duties of the Council
The duties of the Student Council shall be:
A. To represent student opinion.
B. To discuss any concerns of the student body and to initiate action.
C. To act as a liaison between the students and faculty.
D. To promote involvement in school-sponsored activities or events.
E. To organize and promote student government elections.

Article V. Amending the Constitution
The constitution may be amended by a two-thirds vote of the entire membership of the Student Council. Any proposed amendment to the Constitution must be typed in its entirety and proposed before the Student Council in the meeting during which the vote is taken. All Student Council members will have the opportunity to present arguments for or against the proposed amendment during this meeting.

Ratified January 22, 1997

PUBLIC POLICY LAB

EASTSIDE HIGH SCHOOL
BILL OF RIGHTS

Amendment I
Students have the right to publish school newspapers, yearbooks, newsletters, and literary magazines expressing their opinions. Students have the right to express their opinions openly and participate in speech demonstrations as long as they do not commit violent acts, break laws, or disturb others.

Amendment II
Students have the right to present complaints and concerns to school officials through the Student Concerns Committee.

Amendment III
Student representatives and school administrators shall together create a code of conduct for acceptable student behavior.

Amendment IV
Students' grades shall reflect academic performance. Students' opinions or conduct in matters unrelated to established academic standards shall not be evaluated in the grading process.

Amendment V
Students shall have the right to participate in curriculum development through the student and faculty committees established by the school administration and the Student Council.

Amendment VI
School administrators may not restrict students' right to dress or appear as they choose unless it can be determined that a student's dress or appearance may present health or safety hazards.

◀ WHAT DO YOU THINK?

★ Do the rights guaranteed in this document address the needs of the students at your school? What issues or concerns are not addressed in this bill of rights?

★ Does your school have the necessary organizations and people to ensure protection of these rights?

WHAT DO YOU THINK? ▶

★ Why does Elizabeth Reynolds think that Mr. Lee's decision violated students' right to free speech?

★ Whose views does Elizabeth Reynolds think the school newspaper should represent?

★ How would an amendment protecting freedom of speech make the Highland Star more accessible to students?

Principal Kate Stevenson
Highland High School
Federal Heights, CO 80221

Dear Principal Stevenson:

I am the editor in chief of the *Highland Star*. Last month, a fellow student submitted a letter to the editor criticizing the school administration for its new policy that bans all nonschool-sponsored clubs or groups from holding meetings on school property.

Our newspaper adviser, Paul Lee, would not allow this letter to be printed in the school newspaper. He felt that because the letter criticized you and other school administrators, it should not be published. Mr. Lee does not want the newspaper to become an outlet for student complaints and criticism of school administrators.

Although I do not completely agree with what was written in this particular letter, I feel that the *Highland Star* should be accessible to all students no matter what their opinions of school faculty and administration might be. Teachers and administrators should not limit students' right to express their opinions in their own newspaper. I hope that the school administrators will consider creating some policies to protect students' right to free speech.

Sincerely,

Elizabeth Reynolds

Elizabeth Reynolds
Editor in Chief
Highland Star

Parents for Quality Education

2270 Deer Creek Drive, Suite 714 • Federal Heights, CO 80221

Principal Kate Stevenson
Highland High School
Federal Heights, CO 80221

Dear Principal Stevenson:

As an organization of concerned parents and community members, Parents for Quality Education (PQE) is disturbed by a growing problem in local junior high and high schools. We have noticed an increasing popularity in extreme and unkempt dress and hairstyles among students. PQE feels that inappropriate extremes in the dress styles of students disrupt the learning environment and can lead to disorder in the classroom.

We hope that the Highland High School administration will more carefully regulate the appearance of its students by adopting a school dress code. By establishing a dress code, the disruptive influence that inappropriate dress styles have on students will be eliminated, making the teachers' jobs easier and the school environment more conducive to learning.

Please do not hesitate to contact our organization with any comments or questions. We would be pleased to meet with members of the school administration to discuss policy changes in this area. PQE is concerned about the education of the community's youth, and we want to help make our schools the best that they can be.

Sincerely,

George Hernandez

George Hernandez
Chairman
Parents for Quality Education

▲ WHAT DO YOU THINK?

★ What policy does PQE think school administrators should adopt?

★ Would this type of policy violate students' rights?

★ What reasons does PQE give to support the proposal of this policy?

THINGS TO DO

1. Compare notes and suggestions after each council member has reviewed the documents.

2. Organize research groups and assign research questions.

3. Compile a list of student rights issues mentioned in these documents. Discuss the information you gathered in your outside research.

4. Discuss and list which rights must be included in your bill of rights proposal.

5. Prepare a neatly written or typed document containing the proposed bill of rights. Include a formal argument for your proposal based on your research.

UNIT 2

CHAPTER 5

ROLE AND POWERS OF CONGRESS

CHAPTER 6

CONGRESS AT WORK

PUBLIC POLICY LAB

Should you be able to vote at age 18 or not until age 21? Find out by reading this unit and taking the Public Policy Lab challenge on pages 136–39.

THE LEGISLATIVE BRANCH

ROLE AND POWERS OF CONGRESS

Unlike the capitals of Europe—which had grown as important cities for hundreds of years before becoming centers of government—Washington, D.C., was a planned city. It was designed in 1791 by French architect Pierre-Charles L'Enfant, with the help of Benjamin Banneker and other surveyors, under the direction of the leaders of the new American nation.

The city was located on an area of flat and marshy land carved from Maryland. When writing about his plan, L'Enfant described a hill in the area as a "pedestal waiting for a monument." On that pedestal, he placed the home of neither the president nor the Supreme Court, but that of Congress. This was a deliberate statement about the importance that the framers gave to the national legislature, which—the framers believed—would be closest to the people.

Although it has changed greatly since L'Enfant chose its location, Congress remains a vital part of the federal government. This chapter looks at the roles, houses, members, and powers of this important legislative body.

Government Notebook

In your Government Notebook, describe what characteristics and qualifications you think members of Congress should have in order to carry out their work.

ROLE OF CONGRESS

Political Dictionary

constituent
interest group
political action committee
oversight

Objectives

★ What influences how members of Congress vote?
★ What purpose do congressional investigations serve?
★ Why is it important for members of Congress to serve their constituents?

Congress—the legislative branch of the federal government—was so important to the framers of the Constitution that it was the first branch of government they discussed in the Constitution. In addition, Congress's structure and powers are outlined in much more detail than are those of the executive and judicial branches.

Congress has three key roles. Its main role is to legislate, or to make laws. However, it also oversees the performance of government agencies and provides services to the people its members represent.

Making Laws

Congress is responsible for making the nation's laws. How do members of Congress make these policy decisions? What influences how they vote?

Some of the choices that members of Congress face are easy to make. For example, suppose that a member votes for increasing Social Security benefits for older people. This decision reflects the member's personal beliefs. The member's district also has a large number of retirees that support such a policy. Interest groups representing older people have contributed a lot of money to the member's campaign fund. The leadership of the member's political party supports the legislation. Thus, the decision to support increases in Social Security benefits is easy.

Many times, however, the decisions facing members of Congress are not so easy because the forces influencing a member's vote can conflict. How do members make decisions in these more difficult situations? They must weigh the conflicting influences—in particular, their personal beliefs, constituents' interests, interest groups' concerns, and political party loyalty. The power of these influences varies from issue to issue and from member to member.

Personal Beliefs Studies show that a congressperson's personal beliefs about what promotes the public good significantly influence his or her voting decisions. Members sometimes follow their personal beliefs even when those beliefs go against the wishes of voters back home.

In 1990 many members of Congress voted against a constitutional amendment that would have banned flag burning, even though the proposed amendment had a high level of support in

PUBLIC GOOD *Representative Richard Gephardt of Missouri addresses a crowd.* **Do you think members of Congress should support local interests over general national interests?**

their districts. Some of these members believed that such an amendment would limit citizens' right of free speech. Others thought that the matter could be handled in a standard piece of legislation rather than in a constitutional amendment. In this case, the members' own views about what best serves the public outweighed any concerns about going against the wishes of voters in their district.

Constituents' Interests

Congressmembers' voting decisions also are influenced by the wishes of the people they represent. Members of Congress are elected to serve as representatives of the people. Unlike the president, who is elected by all voting U.S. citizens, members of Congress are elected by people who live in one locality (a district or a state). This means that even though Congress makes laws for the whole country, members answer only to the people of their locality.

A grasp of this situation is crucial to understanding how members of Congress behave in making laws. A member represents his or her **constituents**—the residents of his or her district or state—and must consider how policy decisions will affect them, not just the country as a whole. For example, when members from farming areas debate new agricultural policies, they must consider the effects of those policies on farmers in their districts.

The public is divided over whether members of Congress should support local interests (their district or state) over general national interests (the public good). Polls do show that most people think members should consider the public good over local interests, and many people will even criticize members for not doing so. Polls also show, however, that most people expect their congressmembers to take care of their local interests.

Interest Groups

A third force influencing congressional voting is **interest groups**—people acting together to achieve shared political goals. Interest groups provide information on issues, suggest legislation to congressmembers, and promote legislation that is favorable to their groups. They also contribute to members' campaigns through **political action committees** (PACs)—separate political branches of interest groups that are formed for the purpose of participating in politics and giving money to candidates. (The role of interest groups in the political system is more fully explained in Chapters 6 and 17.)

How do such contributions influence members' voting behavior? Some evidence shows that congressmembers who vote for a bill favored by a certain interest group have received on average far larger campaign contributions from that group than have members voting against the bill. This finding may be misleading, however. No conflict might exist between the members' personal views and those of the interest group. Besides, interest groups often contribute to a campaign to help elect someone who already is sympathetic to their goal, not because they are trying to sway that person to their point of view.

Copyright ©1984, Berke Breathed. Reprinted by permission

PRINCIPLES OF DEMOCRACY *Interest groups are sometimes criticized for using campaign contributions to try to influence congressional candidates and get them to see their group's point of view.* **Do you think that interest groups have the power to influence how a member of Congress votes on a bill?**

Careers in Government

Congressmember

Investigative hearings and debates on the floors of the House and Senate are familiar images of Congress. Much of a congressmember's work, however, takes place behind the scenes, away from the news media. Members of Congress have unpredictable schedules full of meetings and appointments. A congressmember usually works around 60 hours a week, and he or she is constantly on call for emergency meetings on pressing matters.

Members of Congress spend an average of three hours a day in the office. The rest of their time is spent meeting with constituents and interest groups, attending committee meetings, traveling to and from their home districts, and presenting, preparing, and voting on bills. An effective congressmember must have excellent communication skills, an awareness of his or her constituents' interests, and plenty of energy to maintain a fast-paced, hectic schedule.

Two of a congressmember's most important jobs, the researching and writing of bills, take place through committee meetings. The committee system allows work to be divided among members and adds to Congress's efficiency. Represen-tatives are assigned to serve on at least one committee, and senators sit on at least two. (The committee system is discussed in Chapter 6.)

Statistically, the typical member of Congress is a college-educated, white male around 52 years old. Anyone, however, can be elected to Congress, regardless of color, sex, profession, or economic status. In 1917, for example, Jeannette Rankin defied statistics to become the first congresswoman. Then in 1969, Shirley Chisholm became the first African American woman in Congress.

Members of Congress, such as Senator Olympia Snowe of Maine, work long hours attending meetings, working on legislation, and traveling to their home districts.

Many members of Congress are experienced state and local politicians. Congress, however, is made up of people from all walks of life and a diversity of experience and training. For example, Representative Steve Largent was a professional football player, and Representative Lynn Woolsey ran a consulting business for 12 years.

How do you become a member of Congress? Learning about the political process is the first step. One way to do that is by entering a congressional internship program offered through a university. Internships provide an opportunity to get an inside look at Congress in action.

Political Party Loyalty Party loyalty also affects how members of Congress vote. In fact, party loyalty on key votes in Congress has increased over the past 20 years. In 1994, for example, nearly every Republican running for the House of Representatives signed the Contract with America, a set of proposed legislative reforms. Then, in early 1995, almost every House Republican voted for most of the Contract's provisions.

Reasons for increased party loyalty include strong party leadership in Congress and in congressional election campaigns. In addition, members of the same party have increasingly shared more of the same political beliefs and values.

PRINCIPLES OF DEMOCRACY *Senator Barbara Boxer speaks to constituents at a luncheon.* **Why do you think that more people do not request help from members of Congress?**

programs. In addition, past scandals and abuses have led many citizens to become dissatisfied with the government. The public, therefore, usually supports investigations that uncover shortcomings in government agencies. Members of Congress, in turn, find that there are political incentives, such as favorable publicity, for being involved in such investigations.

Helping Constituents

Members of Congress receive more than 200 million pieces of mail each year. Much of this mail involves specific constituent requests, which can range from birthday greetings for a relative to major policy changes. Responding to such requests is an important part of a congressperson's job and is one way that members represent their constituents' interests.

One survey has revealed that roughly 17 percent of Americans report that they, or a member of their family, have at some time requested help from a member of Congress.

Individual Requests Most constituent mail involves issues such as obtaining information or expressing views about legislation, requesting help with finding a government job, or asking for assistance with government services, such as Social Security. Some mail, however, deals with more unusual, personal requests. As you can imagine, some of these requests cannot be fulfilled. For example, congressional offices have received requests to change a student's grade in a course at a state university. One constituent even requested assistance from a congressperson in moving a train track that he felt was too close to the fence in his backyard. As one observer says, there is often a

Overseeing Agencies

Congress also is responsible for overseeing the performance of government agencies. It does this through congressional **oversight**, which involves conducting investigations of agency actions and programs.

Congress oversees every aspect of agency behavior and investigates such matters as why an agency has been slow in regulating the use of a toxic chemical, if discrimination has taken place in an agency, or why an agency's new computer system is not working. Many congressional investigations involve discovering how an agency operates from day to day. Often, though, such investigations focus on abuses and scandals in government programs.

Traditionally, Congress had put little energy into congressional oversight, inspiring political scientists to label it Congress's "neglected function." Many said that members of Congress conducted so few investigations because passing new programs was more dramatic than finding out how well existing ones were working.

In the past 25 years, however, congressional investigations have increased greatly. One reason for this is that tight budgets have reduced the amount of money available for new programs, leading to greater scrutiny of both old and new

❝ Monday morning ritual wherein the congressman returns to the Washington office from a visit to the district and empties his pockets of dozens of scraps of paper, each of which contains the name and address of a constituent along with hastily scribbled notes about some difficulty the person is experiencing with a federal agency. **"**

Detecting Patterns Constituent service does more than merely help individual citizens. Congressional staffs look for changes and patterns in constituent requests. Such patterns may signal a problem with a government program or a change in constituents' general attitudes. For example, an increase in complaints about student loan applications being denied might send a signal to a congressional office that some change in the law is having an unwanted effect on students who are seeking loans. Members of Congress can use this information to change the system.

Handling Requests The majority of constituent service involves ordinary citizens with ordinary requests. These requests usually are handled by congressional staffs.

Occasionally, however, a constituent that the congressmember particularly values—a close friend, generous campaign contributor, or large employer in the locality—has a problem with a government agency. After receiving this person's request for personal assistance, the member might approach the government agency directly. Of course, government agencies respond with greater urgency to requests by members of Congress than they do to similar requests from

office staff. For this reason, members of Congress must avoid using the power of their office unethically to influence agencies on behalf of a particularly valued constituent.

CONSTITUTIONAL GOVERNMENT *Congressperson Constance Morella meets with staff in her office.* **What types of constituent requests might a congressional staff member handle?**

SECTION 1 — REVIEW

1. Define the following terms: constituent, interest group, political action committee, oversight.

2. How do constituents, interest groups, and political parties influence how members of Congress vote on legislation? What role do members' personal beliefs play?

3. On what types of issues do congressional investigations tend to focus? Why has the number of such investigations risen in recent years?

4. How do constituents' requests help members of Congress perform their jobs?

5. **Thinking and Writing Critically**
   Think about a law or regulation that affects you and that you might like to see changed, such as the length of the school year, requirements for a driver's license, or teen curfews. Compose a brief letter asking for your congressperson's assistance in dealing with this issue.

6. **Applying** **CONSTITUTIONAL GOVERNMENT**
   Congressmembers must divide their time among three key roles: making laws, overseeing the performance of government agencies, and helping constituents. If you were a member of Congress, which role would be your first priority? Why?

HOUSES AND MEMBERS OF CONGRESS

Political Dictionary

census
apportion
gerrymandering
franking privilege
immunity

Objectives

★ How do the houses of Congress differ in their structure and membership?

★ How are congressional districts drawn?

★ What is the typical profile of a U.S. congressmember?

The House of Representatives and the Senate share many responsibilities. The two houses, however, are quite different in their structures and membership.

House of Representatives

The Constitution's framers intended the House to be closer to the people than would be the Senate. Their expectation was that the House would attract ordinary citizens serving for a brief period.

Size The size of the House of Representatives is set by Congress itself, not by the Constitution. The Constitution simply states that all House seats, whatever their number, must be distributed among the states according to their population. A national **census**, or official population count, is taken every 10 years and serves as the basis for determining this distribution.

For its first meeting in 1789, the House had just 65 members. As the nation's population grew, the House added more members to represent the greater number of citizens. After the 1910 census the number of seats was raised to the current number of 435. To prevent the House from growing too large and unmanageable, this number was set as the limit. (Since 1900, four nonvoting delegates have been added to the House from the District of Columbia, Guam, the U.S. Virgin Islands, and American Samoa. In addition, Puerto Rico is represented by a resident commissioner in the House.)

Although the number of seats has ceased to grow, the nation's population has not. This means that as

Comparing Governments

Legislatures Come in All Sizes

There is no magic number when it comes to deciding the size of a country's legislature. The actual number of legislators is determined by each country's constitution, laws, or customs.

Consider the United Kingdom and Thailand, for example. Although both countries have a population of around 59 million, their legislatures vary greatly. In 1997, U.K. voters elected 651 representatives to the House of Commons, the elected chamber of the legislature. That same year, Thai voters elected 360 people to their House of Representatives. This means that there was one U.K. representative for every 91,000 people living in the United Kingdom and one Thai representative for every 164,000 Thais.

The table below compares various countries' populations and their number of elected representatives.

Country	Population	Representatives	Persons per Representative
India	952 million	545	1.7 million
South Korea	46 million	299	152,000
Venezuela	22 million	201	109,000
United Kingdom	59 million	651	91,000
Thailand	59 million	360	164,000

Source: *The World Almanac: 1997*

PRINCIPLES OF DEMOCRACY *Members of the 105th Congress gather in the House chamber for a joint session.* **Why is it impractical for the number of seats in Congress to grow as the size of the population increases?**

time passes and the population grows, members of Congress represent an increasing number of citizens. For example, the population of all the states in 1910 was roughly 91 million, so each of the 435 House members represented an average of 209,000 people. In comparison, the population of all the states in 1990 was roughly 248 million, so each member represented an average of 570,000 people.

Terms Representatives serve two-year terms. If a representative dies or resigns before the end of a term, the governor of the representative's state must call a special election to fill the seat.

Congressional Districts As noted in Chapter 2, the framers of the Constitution agreed in the Great Compromise that representation in the House would be determined by population. The larger a state's population, the greater its representation in the House. After each census, Congress uses the new population count to **apportion**, or distribute, the 435 seats among the states.

States with significant population growth may acquire seats from those that lose residents or grow less rapidly. Every state, however, is entitled to at least one representative, no matter how small its population. Over the past 20 years, the western and southern regions of the country have gained seats, largely because of the population growth of states such as California, Florida, and Texas. At the same time, the northeastern and midwestern regions have lost seats as population has decreased or growth has slowed in states such as New York and Illinois.

Once the House seats are apportioned, each state legislature usually determines the boundaries of the congressional districts in its state. Thus, the legislature of a state that holds nine seats in the House must divide the state into nine congressional districts. How such divisions are drawn has been a source of controversy since the nation's beginnings.

One Person, One Vote In the past, critics charged that the system of determining boundaries for congressional districts was unfair because districts within a state varied in population size. Because of this variation, citizens living in smaller districts had greater representation in the House than did those living in larger districts.

Residents of a district with 200,000 people, for example, would have much greater representation in the House than would residents of a district with 600,000 people. At one time, some congressional districts had eight times as many residents as other districts in the same state.

The Supreme Court addressed this issue in the 1964 case *Wesberry* v. *Sanders.* In its decision the Court established the "one-person, one-vote" principle by banning districts that had grossly unequal populations. The ruling means that each person's "vote," or representation in the House, should be equal to every other person's. This decision led to the redrawing of many districts. Although there always will be differences in population among districts, the huge variations of the past no longer exist.

Some critics still charge, however, that the system of apportioning seats *among* the states is unfair. For example, the state of Wyoming, which

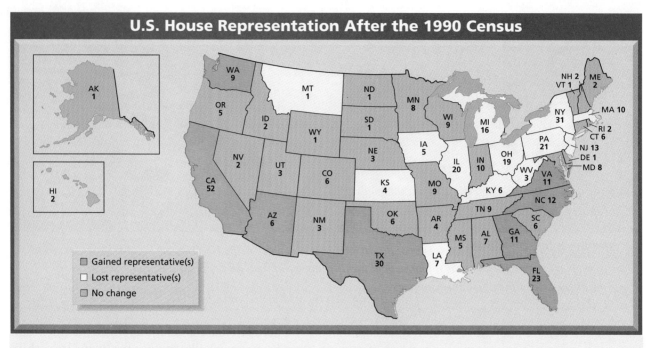

WA 9
AK 1
OR 5
ID 2
MT 1
ND 1
MN 8
WI 9
MI 16
NY 31
NH 2
VT 1
ME 2
MA 10
RI 2
CT 6
NJ 13
DE 1
MD 8
WY 1
SD 1
NE 3
IA 5
IL 20
IN 10
OH 19
PA 21
WV 3
VA 11
NV 2
UT 3
CO 6
KS 4
MO 9
KY 6
CA 52
HI 2
AZ 6
NM 3
OK 6
AR 4
TN 9
NC 12
SC 6
GA 11
MS 5
AL 7
TX 30
LA 7
FL 23

☐ Gained representative(s)
☐ Lost representative(s)
☐ No change

After each census, the seats in Congress are reapportioned among the States.
Why do some people say that the system of apportioning seats among the states is unfair?

has a population of around 480,000, has one representative. Montana, which has a population of 870,000, also has one representative. Because every state is entitled to at least one representative, regardless of population, Wyoming has the same representation in Congress as Montana. Many people say that this is unfair because Montana's member of the House is representing almost twice as many people as is Wyoming's.

Gerrymandering Another criticism of the apportionment process is that districts sometimes are drawn for political reasons. The practice of establishing district lines that favor one political party over another is called **gerrymandering**. The term dates to 1811, when Massachusetts governor Elbridge Gerry carved a district specifically to benefit the Democratic Party. Some observers noted that the oddly shaped new district looked like a salamander. Soon it became known as a "gerrymander."

Gerrymandering by political parties takes place in one of two ways. Parties may draw district lines that concentrate their strength in a number of districts. This builds a solid base for the party and ensures it will win a certain number of seats. Parties also may draw district lines that weaken the opposition party's support by splitting

it across several districts. In the 1986 case *Davis v. Bandemer,* the Supreme Court issued a decision against extreme cases of political gerrymandering, saying that if the practice existed for a long time and was truly harmful to a political minority, it violated the Constitution.

CASE STUDY

Racial Gerrymandering

PRINCIPLES OF DEMOCRACY In recent years, race often has been a central issue in debates about apportionment. Over the years, many critics have charged that some district lines were drawn to purposely keep minority candidates from winning elections. This type of discrimination was condemned in 1982 by amendments to the Voting Rights Act of 1965. The amendment forbids various unfair election practices, including gerrymandering, that discriminate against minorities. Moreover, in the 1986 case *Thornburg* v. *Gingles,* the Supreme Court ruled that it is illegal to divide areas into several districts in order to weaken the political strength of minority groups living in those areas.

In response to this decision, a number of states tried to make up for past discrimination by redrawing congressional district lines. By concentrating as many minority voters into one district as possible, these new lines made it easier for members of minority groups to be elected. The result was a number of districts that were as strangely shaped as those they replaced. These districts were challenged in court for using "racial gerrymandering" to help minorities win congressional elections. Critics charged that this was a form of discrimination against nonminority candidates.

In response, the Supreme Court ruled that there would be strict examination of any district boundaries drawn with race as a leading factor. The Court did not rule out the use of race as one consideration, however. Some House districts today continue to be challenged based on charges of racial gerrymandering, and the boundaries of some districts have been redrawn as a result of court rulings.

Qualifications
The Constitution establishes certain requirements for members of the House of Representatives. Members must be

★ at least 25 years old,
★ U.S. citizens for at least seven years, and
★ legal residents of the state they represent.

By custom, representatives also live in the district they represent, but this is not required by the Constitution.

Salary and Benefits
Representatives receive an annual salary of $133,600—an amount determined by Congress itself. Concern over the possible abuse of Congress's power to set its own compensation led to the passage of the Twenty-seventh Amendment. Ratified in 1992, this amendment states that congressional pay increases cannot take effect until after the next congressional election. As a result, a congressmember would only get the pay increase if he or she were re-elected.

Members receive many other benefits in addition to their salaries. They are provided with office space in congressional buildings near the Capitol. They receive allowances to hire office staff, to

Gerrymandering

Fourth Congressional District
Other Congressional Districts

0   25   50 Miles
0   25   50 Kilometers
Albers Equal-Area Projection

During redistricting in the early 1990s, Louisiana's Fourth Congressional District was drawn so that African Americans made up a majority of the district's population. **What major city is not within the district's boundaries?**

travel to and maintain offices in their home districts, and for stationery, newsletters, and other necessary supplies. They also have the **franking privilege**, which allows them to send official mail for free. In addition, members can take advantage of generous pensions, life insurance, special tax deductions, medical services, free parking, free health club memberships, library research facilities, and many other programs and services.

The Constitution also gives members of Congress a form of **immunity**, or legal protection. To protect their freedom of speech, members cannot be sued for anything they say while performing congressional business. They also cannot be arrested in or on their way to or from a meeting in Congress unless they are accused of a serious crime. These laws ensure that congressmembers are not unnecessarily prevented from performing their duties.

Senate

The framers of the Constitution intended for the Senate to differ from the House. They thought that the Senate should attract an older, more experienced group of people who would serve longer terms as the nation's senior leaders. These senior leaders would be somewhat more removed from the voters than representatives. Until the Seventeenth Amendment, which passed in 1913, senators were chosen by the state legislatures, not by the people.

Today the Senate does indeed have a more dignified atmosphere than the House. For example, when moving from the House to the Senate, Dan Quayle—who later became vice president—noted that there are no basketball games organized among the senators, as there are in the House. The Senate's stately atmosphere stems partly from its legacy as the more privileged body and partly from the fact that senators are older on average than are members of the House.

The difference in prominence between the two bodies also is evident in the fact that members of the House often run for the Senate later in their careers, but senators rarely go on to run for the House. Senators also are generally better known. As one congressman said, "You'd be someone who was 34 years in the House and call somebody downtown and they would say, 'What was your name, again?' . . . But when you were a senator, it was a whole different ball game."

Size The Constitution sets the Senate's size at two members from each state. The first Senate had 26 members representing the 13 original states. Today the Senate has 100 members representing the 50 states. Each senator represents his or her entire state.

Terms Senators serve six-year terms. Senatorial elections, however, are held every two years. This rotating system means that only one third of the Senate's members are up for election at one time and ensures that the Senate has continuity and experience in its membership. If a senator dies or resigns before the end of a term, the governor of the senator's state may appoint someone to fill the seat until a special election or the next regular election is held.

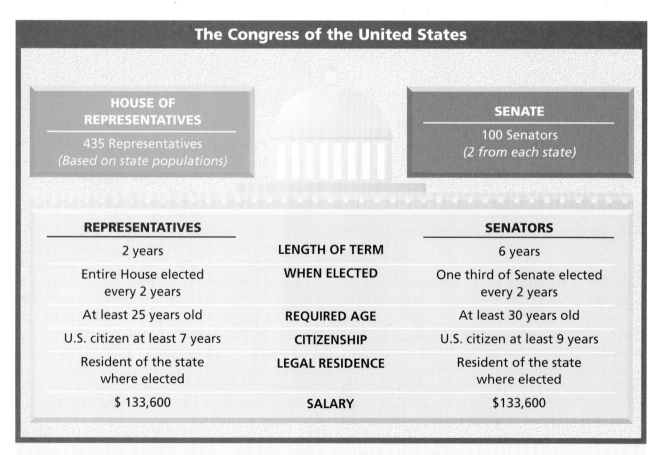

The Congress of the United States

HOUSE OF REPRESENTATIVES		SENATE
435 Representatives (Based on state populations)		100 Senators (2 from each state)

REPRESENTATIVES		SENATORS
2 years	LENGTH OF TERM	6 years
Entire House elected every 2 years	WHEN ELECTED	One third of Senate elected every 2 years
At least 25 years old	REQUIRED AGE	At least 30 years old
U.S. citizen at least 7 years	CITIZENSHIP	U.S. citizen at least 9 years
Resident of the state where elected	LEGAL RESIDENCE	Resident of the state where elected
$ 133,600	SALARY	$133,600

As you can see in this chart, the requirements for membership in the House of Representatives differ from those for membership in the Senate. **What is the salary of members of the House and the Senate?**

The Roman Senate

In writing the U.S. Constitution, the framers looked to the experiences and ideas of various peoples throughout history. The government of the ancient Roman Republic, for example, influenced how the framers structured the new U.S. government. To help keep its leaders from gaining too much power, the republic had divided authority among different members and parts of the government. Similarly, the U.S. framers assigned independent powers to three distinct branches of government.

The framers also recalled the composition of the Roman Senate. This body was composed mainly of experienced, older leaders who had held high-level government positions. In fact, the word *senate* comes from the Latin *senex*, meaning "old, old man." The framers hoped that the U.S. Senate also would be composed of older, wiser leaders.

The Roman Senate was partly an advisory body, but it also controlled public finances and set foreign policy. The Senate grew in authority throughout the years of the republic and remained a part of Roman government even after the founding of the Roman Empire.

In support of the U.S. Constitution, James Madison argued that the Senate was an important part of Roman government. Of course, Madison recognized that the Roman Republic was not a true democracy. But he saw in the Roman Senate an example of the value of mature, experienced leadership. "History informs us of no long-lived republic which had not a senate," Madison wrote.

There were, of course, differences between the Senate of ancient Rome and the Senate created by the U.S. framers. For example, Roman senators served for life. U.S. senators, on the other hand, serve only six-year terms. They can, however, be re-elected.

In addition, although there is an age requirement for the U.S. Senate, there was not for the Roman Senate. There were age requirements, however, for many other positions in Roman government. Because Romans could not be appointed to the Senate without first having held a government position, they generally were not eligible for the Senate until sometime in their thirties.

The ranks of the Roman Senate were dominated by wealthy, established families. Citizens holding jobs that the Romans considered beneath the dignity of the office—for example, gladiators and actors—were not eligible for appointment. In addition, citizens whose private businesses might have distracted them from their senatorial duties also were ineligible. Over time, however, citizens of nonestablished families were appointed to the Senate.

The number of U.S. Senate seats is 100, while during most years of the Republic, the Roman Senate had about 300 seats. The actual number varied, depending on political conditions at the time. During times of civil war or other crises, for example, many seats in the Senate might become vacant. Some Roman leaders, particularly during the empire, expanded the size of the Senate so they could appoint more of their supporters. The number of senators rose to about 2,000 in the late stages of the Roman Empire, in the A.D. 300s.

The Curia Julia *was the main meeting place of the Senate during the years of the Roman Empire. The* Curia *was built during the dictatorship of Julius Caesar (100 B.C.–44 B.C.).*

What Do You Think?

1. Should candidates running for the U.S. Senate be required to have previous government experience? Why or why not?
2. In what ways can running a private business help or hurt a government official in the performance of his or her duties?

Qualifications The Constitution also establishes certain requirements for senators. They must be

★ at least 30 years old,
★ U.S. citizens for at least nine years, and
★ legal residents of the state they represent.

Salary and Benefits Like representatives, senators receive an annual salary of $133,600. They also receive the same benefits and legal protections as House members.

Members of Congress

Who are the members of Congress? Most are businesspeople or lawyers. Almost every member of Congress has a college degree, and most have advanced degrees. Most members also are white, male, and more than 40 years old. Minority groups and women generally are not represented in Congress in proportion to their numbers in the U.S. population. For example, some 12 percent of the U.S. population was African American in 1990. In 1997, however, only 7 percent of congressmembers were African American. In addition, more than half of the population is female, and only 11 percent of all seats in Congress were held by women in 1997.

Although these groups, as well as Asian Americans and Hispanic Americans, are still underrepresented according to their numbers in the population, the disproportionately low representation of minority groups and women in Congress is gradually changing. The 1992 elections produced

PRINCIPLES OF DEMOCRACY *In 1997 Senator Ben Nighthorse Campbell was the only American Indian in Congress.* **Does the membership of Congress represent the diversity of the U.S. population?**

increases in African Americans, Hispanic Americans, and particularly in women in Congress. For example, in 1992 the number of female senators increased from two to six. One of those women was Carol Moseley-Braun, the only African American serving in the Senate. The number of women in the House increased from 28 to 47.

In addition, Ben Nighthorse Campbell was elected to the Senate in 1992—the first American Indian to serve in the Senate in 60 years. By 1997 the number of women in the House had risen to 51, and the number of women in the Senate had risen to nine. There were 21 Hispanic American and 5 Asian American representatives in Congress, and two Asian Americans, but no Hispanic Americans, in the Senate.

SECTION 2 — **REVIEW**

1. Define the following terms: census, apportion, gerrymandering, franking privilege, immunity.

2. Compare the House and the Senate, making sure to consider size, terms, and requirements for and benefits of membership.

3. Describe how congressional seats—in the House and in the Senate—are distributed among the states.

4. Describe the background of members of Congress. What changes in membership have occurred in recent years?

5. **Thinking and Writing Critically**
   Do you think the makeup of Congress—for example, age, race, sex, background—influences congressional decisions? Do you agree with the framers' vision for the makeup of the Senate? Explain your answers.

6. **Applying PRINCIPLES OF DEMOCRACY**
   Is the current system of apportionment fair? How *should* congressional districts be drawn? Be sure to consider the principles established by Supreme Court rulings on the drawing of Congressional district boundaries.

POWERS OF CONGRESS

Political Dictionary

impeach
ex post facto law
bill of attainder
writ of *habeas corpus*

Objectives

★ To what main areas of governing do Congress's expressed powers apply?
★ What special powers does Congress hold?
★ What are the implied powers of Congress?
★ What constitutional limits exist on congressional powers?

Most of the powers assumed by Congress are specifically listed in the Constitution. As you will learn, Congress has also assumed some powers that are *not* mentioned in the Constitution. The Constitution does, however, outline several specific limits on what actions Congress may take.

Expressed Powers

As noted in Chapter 4, the powers specifically granted to the federal government are called expressed powers because they are specifically expressed, or listed, in the Constitution. Expressed powers give Congress the right to make laws in five main areas: government finance, regulation of commerce, national defense, law enforcement, and national sovereignty.

The majority of these powers can be found in Article 1, Section 8, of the Constitution—for example, the power to raise and collect taxes, regulate foreign and interstate commerce, coin and print money, and provide and maintain military forces. (See the chart on this page.) Other articles within the Constitution list additional powers.

For example, Section 3 of Article 4 gives Congress the power to admit new states into the Union. Article 3, Section 3, gives it the right to determine the punishment for treason.

Special Powers

In addition to the expressed powers, the Constitution gives Congress several special powers. Some of these are held by the Senate, some by the House, and some by both.

Expressed Powers of Congress

- To lay and collect taxes, to pay the nation's debts, and to provide for the common defense and general welfare of the United States
- To borrow money
- To regulate foreign and interstate commerce
- To establish uniform rules for becoming a citizen
- To coin money and set a uniform standard of weights and measures
- To punish counterfeiters
- To establish post offices and post roads
- To make copyright and patent laws
- To establish a system of national courts
- To punish piracy and other offenses against the law of nations
- To declare war
- To raise and maintain armies
- To raise and maintain a navy
- To establish military laws
- To call up a national militia
- To organize, arm, and discipline the militia
- To govern the District of Columbia
- To make all laws that shall be necessary and proper for carrying into execution previously mentioned powers

The chart above lists some of the powers specifically granted to Congress in the Constitution. **Which expressed powers give Congress the right to make laws concerning government finances?**

Impeaching Officials Congress holds the power to formally accuse and bring federal officials to trial. The most important officials in the government, including the president, vice president, and federal judges, may be removed from office if they are found guilty of serious crimes against the nation.

The charges against an accused official must be drawn up in the House of Representatives. If a majority of representatives votes to pursue the charges, the official is **impeached**, or formally accused. The procedure of drawing up and passing the charges against the accused in the House is called impeachment.

Trials on impeachment charges are held in the Senate, with the vice president usually acting as the judge. If it is the president being impeached, however, the chief justice of the United States presides instead. In this case the vice president cannot preside because of a conflict of interest—if the president were found guilty, the vice president would become president. The members of the Senate act as the jury. If two thirds of the Senate find the official guilty, he or she can be dismissed from office.

The impeachment process has been used rarely, with only 13 federal officials having been impeached. Only one was a president—Andrew Johnson. At his impeachment trial in 1868, President Johnson was found not guilty of the charges against him by one vote. In 1974 the threat of impeachment caused President Richard M. Nixon to resign from office.

Ratifying Treaties The Senate has the power to reject any treaty, or written agreement, between the United States and other countries. A treaty that is not approved by a two-thirds vote in the Senate does not become law. This congressional right can be a powerful tool in foreign policy. Several treaties signed by U.S. presidents have never been enacted because the Senate refused to approve them.

Approving Appointments The Senate also has the right to reject all major appointments made by the president, including Supreme Court justices, ambassadors, and cabinet members. Appointments require a majority vote for approval.

Deciding Elections Congress holds the power to decide presidential elections under certain circumstances. If no candidate for president

CONSTITUTIONAL GOVERNMENT *Secretary of Health and Human Services Donna Shalala testifies before Congress.* **What major appointments by the president does Congress approve?**

receives a majority of electoral votes—ballots cast by members of the Electoral College—the House of Representatives must choose the winner from among the three candidates receiving the most votes. (The Electoral College is more fully explained in Chapter 7.) The representatives of each state collectively have one vote to cast, for a total of 50 votes. The candidate who receives a majority of the total House votes (at least 26) becomes president.

Similarly, if no candidate for vice president were to receive a majority of electoral votes, the Senate would choose the vice president. In this case, however, each senator has one vote, for a total of 100. Again, the candidate who receives a majority of the Senate votes (51) is elected.

The House has used its electoral power twice. It chose Thomas Jefferson as president in 1801 and John Quincy Adams in 1825. The Senate has used its electoral power only once—to choose Richard M. Johnson as vice president in 1837.

Implied Powers

As noted in the Expressed Powers of Congress chart on page 105, the last power listed is the most general and far-reaching. The Constitution states that Congress has the power "to make all laws which shall be necessary and proper for carrying into execution the foregoing [previously mentioned] powers" specifically granted to it. As noted in Chapter 4, the additional powers implied by this Necessary and Proper, or Elastic, Clause have allowed Congress to stretch its expressed powers. Congress has thus been able to create legislation addressing situations that have arisen long after the Constitution was written.

The debate over the Elastic Clause and Congress's implied powers has gone on almost as long as the Constitution has existed. One of the key disputes regarding this issue arose in 1819 in the Supreme Court case *McCulloch* v. *Maryland.*

The subject of the case, as noted in Chapter 4, was the Bank of the United States.

The Bank of the United States was originally established in 1791. The bank's charter ended in 1811, and a bill to establish a new charter met with opposition and was vetoed by President Madison in 1816. Eventually, however, a new charter passed, and a Second Bank of the United States began operation in 1817. The bank had been a source of controversy since the time of its creation. Many people, including Thomas Jefferson, had stated that the Constitution did not give Congress the right to set up a national bank and that its creation was a violation of states' rights. Indeed, this argument was the basis of the state of Maryland's case in *McCulloch* v. *Maryland.*

The Supreme Court, however, decided the case in Congress's favor. In a unanimous decision, the Court declared that Congress had the right to determine what was "necessary and proper" to fulfill its constitutional duties. Creating a national bank fell into this category.

Another of Congress's implied powers involves its establishment of the nation's military academies. Although not specifically given the power to do so in the Constitution, Congress set up military academies to train army, navy, air force, coast guard, and merchant marine officers. Congress justified its actions by saying that the academies are "necessary and proper" for it to carry out its constitutional right to raise and maintain an army and a navy. Thus, the Elastic Clause implies, or suggests, that Congress has the right to establish military academies.

The Elastic Clause has allowed Congress to expand its powers significantly. In fact, Congress has used this clause to justify much of the federal law passed during the 1900s. The clause aroused very little debate at the Constitutional Convention, however. The framers probably did not anticipate that Congress would use its implied powers so extensively, for the clause does not seem to grant any authority beyond that already contained in Section 8 of Article 1.

CONSTITUTIONAL GOVERNMENT *The Second Bank of the United States stands in Independence National Park in Philadelphia, Pennsylvania.* **Why was the bank a source of controversy?**

Limits on Powers

The powers of Congress are limited in several important ways. As noted in Chapter 3, the Supreme Court can use the power of judicial review to determine when Congress has reached beyond the powers granted to it by the Constitution. Any law that the Court rules unconstitutional has no force.

Another limit on Congress's powers is the Tenth Amendment to the Constitution. It declares that the states or the people shall keep all the powers not specifically granted to the national government. These powers, as noted in Chapter 4, are the reserved powers.

Article 1, Section 9, of the Constitution further restricts the powers of Congress. For example, it keeps Congress from taxing exports and from favoring the trade of a particular state. It also prevents Congress from passing an **ex post facto law**—a law that applies to an action that took place before the law was passed—or a **bill of attainder**—a law that punishes a person who has not been convicted in a court of law. In addition, Congress cannot suspend the **writ of habeas corpus**—a court order requiring police

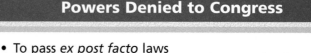

Powers Denied to Congress

- To pass *ex post facto* laws
- To pass bills of attainder
- To suspend the writ of *habeas corpus*
- To tax exports
- To pass laws violating the Constitution
- To pass laws giving a state or group of states an unfair trade advantage
- To grant titles of nobility
- To engage in spending that has not been authorized by legislation

The chart above lists the powers denied to Congress in the Constitution. **Why do you think that the framers of the Constitution denied Congress the power to grant titles of nobility?**

to bring all persons accused of a crime to court and to show sufficient reason to keep them in jail—except "when in cases of rebellion or invasion the public safety may require it." (*Ex post facto* laws, bills of attainder, and the writ of *habeas corpus* are more fully explained in Chapter 14.) See the chart on this page for additional restrictions that Article 1, Section 9 places on Congress.

SECTION 3 — REVIEW

1. Define the following terms: impeach, *ex post facto* law, bill of attainder, writ of *habeas corpus*.

2. Explain the difference between Congress's expressed powers and implied powers, and give at least two examples of each type of power. Why are implied powers important?

3. Describe the limits that the Constitution places on Congress's power, and give some examples of these limitations.

4. **Thinking and Writing Critically**
   Choose at least three powers that are denied to Congress by the Constitution, and explain in your own words what the framers intended to guard against by imposing these limits.

5. **Applying** CONSTITUTIONAL GOVERNMENT
   Imagine that you have been asked to assist in writing a new constitution for a foreign country. What limitations would you suggest placing on the country's legislative branch of government? Explain your answer.

CHAPTER 5 — SUMMARY

SECTION 1 Congress has three key roles. Its main role is to legislate, or to make laws. To decide how to vote on laws, members of Congress consider four factors: their own personal beliefs, their constituents' interests, interest groups' concerns, and political party loyalty.

Congress also oversees the performance of government agencies by conducting investigations through congressional oversight. This involves closely examining agency actions and programs. Traditionally, Congress put little energy into oversight, perhaps because passing new programs is more dramatic. Over the past 25 years, however, congressional investigations have increased greatly. The public supports such investigations because they uncover shortcomings in government agencies.

Finally, Congress provides services to its constituents. In providing these services, congressmembers and their staffs consider constituents' individual requests. They also detect patterns in requests and use them to propose corrective laws.

SECTION 2 Members of the House of Representatives and the Senate differ in their numbers, required qualifications, and terms. The House has 435 members, and the seats are distributed among the states according to population. Representatives serve two-year terms, must be at least 25 years old, U.S. citizens for at least seven years, and legal residents of the state they represent.

There are 100 senators—two from each state. Senators serve six-year terms, must be at least 30 years old, must have been U.S. citizens for at least nine years, and must be legal residents of the state they represent.

Senators and representatives receive the same benefits and protections of the law, however. House seats are apportioned among the states every 10 years according to population figures provided by the national census. State legislatures usually then set congressional district boundaries within their states.

Today's members of Congress are mostly businesspeople or lawyers. Most also are white, male, and more than 40 years old. This, however, is slowly changing, as more women and minorities are elected to Congress.

SECTION 3 Congress holds both expressed and implied powers. Its expressed powers are those specifically listed in the Constitution. Among these are those powers listed in Article 1, Section 8, such as the power to raise and collect taxes, regulate foreign and interstate commerce, coin and print money, and provide and maintain military forces.

Congress's implied powers stem from the last power listed in Article 1, Section 8—the Elastic Clause, which allows Congress to make laws that are "necessary and proper" to carry out its duties. An example of Congress's implied powers is the power to establish a national bank.

To protect the rights of citizens, the Constitution limits what actions Congress may take. For example, Congress may not pass *ex post facto* laws or bills of attainder, and it may not suspend the writ of *habeas corpus*.

Government Notebook

Review what you wrote in your Government Notebook at the beginning of this chapter about what you think are the qualifications and characteristics of a good congressperson. Now that you have studied the chapter, how would you revise your answer? Should the qualifications for congresspeople be expanded? Record your answer in your Notebook.

REVIEW

REVIEWING CONCEPTS

1. What qualifications does the Constitution set for senators and representatives?

2. What types of powers does Congress hold?

3. What powers are denied to Congress by the Constitution?

4. What are Congress's three main roles?

5. What benefits do members of Congress receive?

6. How are House congressional districts determined?

THINKING AND WRITING CRITICALLY

1. **CONSTITUTIONAL GOVERNMENT** Should members of Congress be allowed to set their own salary? Given the fact that many members serve more than one term, does the Twenty-seventh Amendment adequately prevent possible abuse of this power? Explain your answer.

2. **PRINCIPLES OF DEMOCRACY** The Constitution establishes few qualifications for members of Congress. Should there be additional qualifications, such as a set number of years of experience in state government? Write a paragraph that states and supports your opinion on this issue. Be sure to consider the need for balancing experience in governing and for maintaining a political process that is open to as many citizens as possible.

3. **CONSTITUTIONAL GOVERNMENT** Do members of Congress receive too many special benefits, or do they deserve such benefits to help compensate them for the long hours they work? Explain your answer.

4. **PUBLIC GOOD** How is the public good promoted by having congressional powers defined in the Constitution? What might happen if there were no limitations on Congress's power?

CITIZENSHIP IN YOUR COMMUNITY

Write a profile on one of your state's senators or your district's representative in Congress. Include background information, such as place of birth, education, and previous occupation, as well as information on the person's political experience: offices held, length of service in Congress, political party membership, and positions on key issues. If possible, include a photograph of your subject and any other visuals that might help complete the profile.

COOPERATIVE PORTFOLIO PROJECT

With a group, create a Serving in Congress handbook for potential congressional candidates. Your guide should inform candidates of the benefits of serving in Congress, the goals a person might fulfill by holding public office, and the terms of office and constitutional qualifications for members of both the House and Senate. Your handbook should be clearly written, well designed, and easy to follow. You might use photographs and drawings to illustrate a congressional career.

PRACTICING SKILLS: CONDUCTING RESEARCH

Research the current makeup of Congress, and create a table comparing characteristics of members of the House and the Senate. Choose at least three categories of comparison, such as sex, ethnicity, education, previous profession, and years of experience. Write an extended caption describing the table's contents.

THE INTERNET: LEARNING ONLINE

Conduct an Internet search to find information about a member of the congressional delegation from your state. For example, try to find e-mail and postal addresses, the committees on which the congressperson serves, and the location of his or her congressional district. You might want to start by searching for a page on the World Wide Web that lists members of Congress. Try using search words such as *Congress, U.S. House of Representatives,* and *U.S. Senate.* List the sources of information you find on the Web. Then write a short paragraph about the congressperson you chose.

ANALYZING PRIMARY SOURCES

WESBERRY V. *SANDERS*

As you have read, the Supreme Court established the "one-person, one-vote" principle in the 1964 case of *Wesberry* v. *Sanders* by banning congressional districts with grossly unequal populations. Read the excerpt from the Court's majority opinion, which was written by Justice Hugo L. Black, and answer the questions that follow.

❝ *We agree . . . that the 1931 Georgia apportionment grossly discriminates against voters in the Fifth Congressional District. A single Congressman represents from two to three times as many Fifth District voters as are represented by each of the congressmen from the other Georgia congressional districts. The apportionment statute thus contracts the value of some votes and expands that of others. If the Federal Constitution intends that when qualified voters elect members of Congress each vote be given as much weight as any other vote, then this statute cannot stand.*

We hold that, construed [interpreted] in its historical context, the command of Article I, Section 2, that Representatives be chosen "by the People of the several States" means that as nearly as is practicable one man's vote in a congressional election is to be worth as much as another's. . . .

To say that a vote is worth more in one district than in another would not only run counter to [contradict] our fundamental ideas of democratic government, it would cast aside the principle of a House of Representatives elected "by the People," a principle tenaciously [vigorously] fought for and established at the Constitutional Convention. . . .

It would defeat the principle solemnly embodied [represented] in the Great Compromise—equal representation in the House for equal numbers of people—for us to hold that, within the States, legislatures may draw the lines of congressional districts in such a way as to give some voters a greater voice in choosing a Congressman than others. . . .

No right is more precious in a free country than that of having a voice in the election of those who make the laws under which, as good citizens, we must live. Other rights, even the most basic, are illusory [unreal] if the right to vote is undermined [weakened]. . . . While it may not be possible to draw congressional districts with mathematical precision, that is no excuse for ignoring our Constitution's plain objective of making equal representation for equal numbers of people the fundamental goal for the House of Representatives. That is the high standard of justice and common sense which the founders set for us. ❞

1. For what reason was the apportionment system under challenge in the case?

2. On what constitutional principles did Justice Black base the Court's ruling?

3. Do you think that the Supreme Court was justified in forcing the Georgia state legislature to change its apportionment system?

CONGRESS AT WORK

Some people might praise Congress by saying that no other institution in the world operates quite like it. Others might utter these words as an insult, criticizing Congress for being slow and for operating under complicated, mazelike rules.

Still, Congress has developed a remarkable system for tackling the enormous task of making the nation's laws. To fully appreciate this system, you must begin by examining the organization of Congress as well as the legislative process. This chapter also considers the impact of Congress on the well-being of the citizens it serves.

 Government Notebook

In your Government Notebook, write a paragraph describing the process you think Congress goes through in considering and voting on legislation.

ORGANIZATION OF CONGRESS

Political Dictionary

quorum
term limits
incumbent
majority party
minority party
Speaker
floor leader
party whip
president *pro tempore*
censure
expulsion

Objectives

★ What are the terms and sessions of Congress?
★ How is congressional leadership organized?
★ What are the rules of conduct in Congress?

Making laws that govern a nation of millions of people is a great responsibility. As noted in Chapter 5, Congress operates under a set of rules that determines how to carry out this responsibility. Some of these rules are outlined in the Constitution. Others have been made by Congress itself. These rules dictate how long Congress is in session, who leads Congress, and how sessions are conducted.

Terms and Sessions

Congressional elections take place every even-numbered year in November. All of the members of the House and one third of the members of the Senate are elected in any congressional election year. Each new term of Congress begins on January 3 following the November election and lasts two years. Each Congress is numbered, from the 1st Congress in 1789 and 1790 to the 105th Congress in 1997 and 1998, and so on.

Each congressional term is divided into two 1-year sessions. Prior to the adoption of the Twentieth Amendment, which states that each new congressional term will begin on January 3, congressional terms began in December, 13 months after congressional elections had taken place. The amendment was passed to prevent congresspeople from serving an entire year as "lame ducks"— members who had not been re-elected.

After the passage of the amendment, sessions lasted from January until August or September. During the last few decades, however, Congress has remained in session almost continuously. Members take recesses, or breaks, of various lengths during the summer, before elections, and around holidays. When Congress is in session, a **quorum**, or majority of members, must be present to conduct business.

Sometimes problems that require congressional action arise while Congress is in recess. If necessary, the president can recall congressmembers to Washington for a special session. This rarely happens, however.

Term Limits

Today there are no **term limits**—legal limits on the number of terms a person can serve—for members of Congress. Term limits have been the subject of much debate in recent years, however. Those in favor of term limits criticize Congress, saying that it is an institution in which career politicians dominate the lawmaking process. These critics believe that a person who is new to Congress might be more in touch with citizens' concerns.

Political observers have noted a curious fact. Although Congress as an institution may be unpopular, voters generally are satisfied with their own representatives and senators. Therefore, **incumbents**, or officeholders, tend to have a good chance of being re-elected. This may be because of name recognition or because incumbents have had the opportunity to help constituents and to get projects and pass favorable legislation for their districts or states. They also have a record of performance in Congress that voters can evaluate. Challengers cannot be similarly evaluated because they have not been in office. Voters often remember what the incumbent has

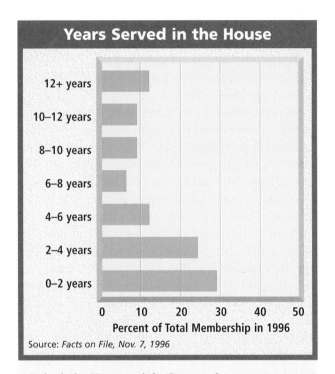

Years Served in the House

Years	
12+ years	
10–12 years	
8–10 years	
6–8 years	
4–6 years	
2–4 years	
0–2 years	

Percent of Total Membership in 1996

0 10 20 30 40 50

Source: *Facts on File, Nov. 7, 1996*

In both the House and the Senate a large percentage of congressmembers are incumbents. A fairly small percentage of incumbents, however, serves for more than 12 years. **What percentage of representatives has served more than 12 years?**

done for their state or community and view challengers as untried and inexperienced.

The Permanent Congress Since the 1950s the incumbent advantage has helped keep congressional turnover low—around 8 percent. In 1988 congressional turnover figures were particularly low—with 97 percent of the incumbents running for re-election winning their races. Such statistics fed a growing concern over lengthy periods of congressional service. Many people charged that these incumbent leaders had become entrenched in a "permanent Congress." These critics believed that Congress had become unresponsive to the people and resistant to change.

The congressional elections in 1992 marked a downturn, for a time at least, in the permanent Congress. An unusually large number of House members retired. In addition, the

number of incumbents who ran for re-election and were defeated rose from 7 in 1988 to 43 in 1992. Thus, the House saw its biggest change since 1948, with 110 representatives—more than one fourth of its membership—newly elected. In the elections of 1994 the trend continued, with 87 new members elected—35 of whom had defeated incumbents and 52 of whom had taken seats for which incumbents did not seek re-election. In 1996, however, incumbents made a much stronger showing, with around 94 percent of them gaining re-election.

Support for Term Limits Criticism of the permanent Congress has sparked a grassroots movement at the state level for term limits. In 1990 Colorado passed a law establishing term limits for its congressmembers. In 1992 thirteen more proposed laws establishing term limits made it onto state ballots, and all of them passed.

In 1995, however, the Supreme Court ruled that neither the states nor Congress may impose term limits on members of Congress without a constitutional amendment. Many citizens' groups and some legislators are working to pass an amendment for Congress similar to the Twenty-second Amendment, which limits the president to two terms.

POLITICAL PROCESSES *Grassroots movements for term limits were sparked by critics of politicians who serve in Congress for long periods.* **What are some of the criticisms of a permanent Congress?**

Effects of Term Limits

PRINCIPLES OF DEMOCRACY What effects would term limits have on the work of Congress? Critics of term limits argue that government is complicated and that it often takes several terms to understand it. Short-term members have little experience in the running of Congress and must depend more on well-informed nonelected groups, including interest groups. As a result, a Congress of only short-term members might be less likely to reach independent decisions.

Critics of term limits also argue that the chance for re-election gives politicians a reason to do a good job. A congressmember who could not run again for office would be less likely to work hard to address the concerns of voters. In addition, say critics, when voters are unhappy with the performance of an incumbent, they can remove that person from office simply by electing someone else.

Supporters of term limits reply that one or two terms is enough time to learn the job and that the current system encourages unnecessary spending. To gain re-election, they say, some representatives try to win the favor of voters by securing nonessential projects for their districts. Supporters believe that members whose terms are limited by law will do what is right rather than merely what will get them re-elected.

Congressional Leaders

Congressional leadership is organized strictly by party. In each house of Congress the political party that holds the most seats is called the **majority party**. The political party with fewer seats is called the **minority party**. Presiding officers and committee chairs always come from the majority party. Members also receive their committee assignments based on their party membership.

POLITICAL PROCESSES *House majority leader Dick Armey, Speaker of the House Newt Gingrich, and Senate majority whip Trent Lott speak to the press in 1996.* **What makes a party the majority party?**

The House operates under stronger leadership than does the Senate and is controlled by stricter rules. Having more than four times as many members as the Senate, the House requires more structure to keep it functioning smoothly.

House Leaders The most influential position in the House of Representatives is that of **Speaker**. Although the Constitution mentions the position of the Speaker, it says nothing about the powers accompanying the office. In practice, as the presiding officer of the House, the Speaker officially gives the floor to members who wish to speak. The Speaker also controls floor debates and has a powerful hand in controlling the flow of legislation. The Speaker not only assigns legislation to committees but also helps appoint committee members and other House leaders from his or her party.

The visibility of the Speaker's office has increased dramatically in the past two decades. This has been particularly true at times when one party has controlled Congress while the other party has held the presidency. In such cases the Speaker has

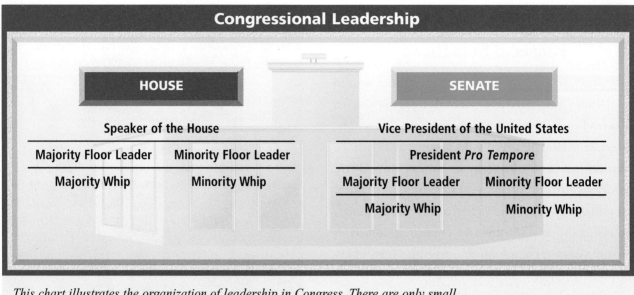

Congressional Leadership

HOUSE

Speaker of the House

Majority Floor Leader	Minority Floor Leader
Majority Whip	Minority Whip

SENATE

Vice President of the United States

President *Pro Tempore*

Majority Floor Leader	Minority Floor Leader
Majority Whip	Minority Whip

This chart illustrates the organization of leadership in Congress. There are only small differences between the organization of the leadership in the House and the Senate.
What is the vice president's role in the Senate?

emerged as a leader of the opposition to the president and his party's policies. In the mid-1990s, for example, when President Clinton and the Democratic Party held the White House and the Republicans were the majority party in Congress, Speaker Newt Gingrich became well known as a strong voice in government.

House members of each party also choose their own **floor leader**. The majority floor leader serves as an assistant to the Speaker and is the second-most-influential member of the House. The minority floor leader is the minority party's chief spokesperson. These two people are commonly referred to as the majority leader and the minority leader.

In addition, each party chooses its own **party whips**. The main function of a party whip is to monitor and influence how his or her party's members vote on legislation. Today many members are involved in each party's whip organization. For example, almost half of all House Democrats belonged to their party's whip organization during the 105th Congress. Whips act as an intelligence network for the party leadership. By discovering members' opinions on particular legislation, whips enable leaders to more efficiently drum up support for the party's official stance.

Senate Leaders The presiding officer in the Senate is the vice president of the United States.

Unlike the Speaker of the House, the vice president's only substantial role in Congress is to break tie votes. In the absence of the vice president, the **president *pro tempore*** is the formal head of the Senate. The president *pro tempore* is the person in the majority party who has been in the Senate the longest.

The general organization of the Senate parallels that of the House—and the leaders of both houses are selected in a similar manner. The most powerful Senate leader, however, is the majority leader. He or she is the main strategist for the majority party and serves as the party's chief spokesperson.

Rules of Conduct

The Constitution gives Congress the power to judge its members' qualifications. When the House or the Senate questions the constitutional qualifications of a newly elected member, it may refuse to seat the member unless its concerns are resolved. Such challenges are rarely made and may be reviewed by the Supreme Court.

Both houses also have the right to judge their members' behavior. The House and the Senate have each set strict rules of conduct for their members, including in financial matters. For example, members may not use campaign contributions for personal expenses. In addition, they must disclose their financial holdings. This helps

POLITICAL PROCESSES *Former senator David Durenberger listens to the proceedings during a Senate Ethics Committee hearing investigating charges that he improperly reported his personal finances.* **What types of punishment may congressmembers receive for violating rules of conduct?**

prevent or uncover any conflicts of interest between members' potential financial gain and the legislation they consider.

Either house may vote by a simple majority to discipline one of its members because of poor conduct. Such discipline might be in the form of a reprimand—or scolding—or it might be a stronger disciplinary measure called a **censure**.

In January 1997 the House officially reprimanded Speaker Newt Gingrich—the first formal punishment the House had ever imposed on a Speaker. Gingrich was charged with bringing discredit upon the House after it was discovered that he had used tax-exempt donations for political purposes and then submitted false information about his actions to the House Ethics Committee that was investigating him. The report submitted by the investigative subcommittee did not conclude whether Gingrich's actions were "intentional" or merely "reckless," but it did say that Gingrich had failed to seek adequate legal advice regarding the donations. In addition to the reprimand, the committee fined Gingrich $300,000. The penalty was approved by a 395-to-28 vote.

For more serious or criminal conduct, the House or the Senate may vote to expel a member. **Expulsion** requires a two-thirds vote and formally removes a member from office. Only 4 representatives and 15 senators have been expelled in the history of Congress. Of the 15 senators, 14 were expelled during the Civil War for supporting the southern states' secession. Other members, however, have resigned under threat of expulsion. Senator Bob Packwood, for example, resigned in 1995 after lengthy hearings on charges that he had engaged in sexual and official misconduct while in office.

SECTION 1 — REVIEW

1. Define the following terms: quorum, term limits, incumbent, majority party, minority party, Speaker, floor leader, party whip, president *pro tempore*, censure, expulsion.

2. When are members of Congress elected, and when do they take office? How long do their terms last?

3. Name the leadership positions in the House and in the Senate. What is the role of each? Why is leadership in the House stronger than in the Senate?

4. How does Congress oversee its members' conduct?

5. **Thinking and Writing Critically** Do you support term limits for members of Congress, or do you believe that they should be able to serve an unlimited number of terms? Why?

6. **Applying PRINCIPLES OF DEMOCRACY** As you have learned, congressional leadership is determined by party. Draw up a list of what you think are the pros and cons of this arrangement.

THE COMMITTEE SYSTEM

Political Dictionary

bill
appropriations
standing committee
subcommittee
select committee
joint committee
conference committee
seniority system

Objectives

★ What kinds of committees are there in Congress?
★ How are committee assignments made?
★ What kinds of staff help congressmembers and committees perform their work?

As you can imagine, Congress faces a huge and complex task in making the nation's laws. No member of Congress could possibly examine all proposed legislation in detail. Thus, congressional committees were formed to allow legislation to be examined by smaller bodies that are more expert in the subject than the House or the Senate as a whole. In this way, Congress can give more in-depth consideration to proposed legislation.

Each congressional committee deals with a specific area of public policy, such as defense, education, or health. Committees pore over **bills**, or proposed legislation, before they are submitted to the House or the Senate as a whole. Committees also oversee the performance of the executive branch agencies in their policy area.

Committees have existed since the first Congress. In the beginning, however, members resisted giving much power to committees. They feared that committees might develop into powerful groups that could force legislation through the rest of Congress. By the 1820s, however,

committees began to play a role similar to the one they have today.

Types of Committees

There are two basic types of committees: authorizing and appropriations. Authorizing committees establish government policies. They propose solutions to public problems, such as crime, and determine how much funding is needed to put them into effect. The actual **appropriations**—funds set aside for specific purposes—for these solutions are made by appropriations committees.

Each house has many authorizing committees but only one appropriations committee. No authorized government program can become law unless it receives funding from the appropriations committee.

Comparing Governments

British Parliament

Britain, like the United States, has a bicameral legislature, though the structure of the British Parliament is very different from that of Congress. Parliament is made up of both a lower house—the House of Commons—and an upper house—the House of Lords. The monarch holds the largely ceremonial position of chief of state. The king or queen does, however, have the power to reject legislation passed by the houses of Parliament, although no monarch has exercised this power since the early 1700s.

The 651 members of the House of Commons are elected by the people. The House of Commons is considered the primary governing body of Britain because nearly all legislation is made in this house. In addition, the House of Commons has the power to pass bills into law without the approval of the House of Lords, most of whose more than 1,200 members inherit their seats. Although the House of Lords has no veto power, it may suggest revisions to bills passed by the House of Commons.

Congressional Standing Committees

HOUSE STANDING COMMITTEES

- Agriculture
- Appropriations
- Banking and Financial Services
- Budget
- Commerce
- Economic and Educational Opportunities
- Government Reform and Oversight
- House Oversight
- International Relations
- Judiciary
- National Security
- Resources
- Rules
- Science
- Small Business
- Standards of Official Conduct
- Transportation and Infrastructure
- Veterans' Affairs
- Ways and Means

SENATE STANDING COMMITTEES

- Agriculture, Nutrition, and Forestry
- Appropriations
- Armed Services
- Banking, Housing, and Urban Affairs
- Budget
- Commerce, Science, and Transportation
- Energy and Natural Resources
- Environment and Public Works
- Finance
- Foreign Relations
- Governmental Affairs
- Indian Affairs
- Judiciary
- Labor and Human Resources
- Rules and Administration
- Small Business
- Veterans' Affairs

The chart above includes a list of House and Senate standing committees.
Why do you think that the House and Senate have many similar committees?

Congressional committees can also be divided into five other categories. These are standing committees, subcommittees, select committees, joint committees, and conference committees.

Standing Committees The permanent committees in each house of Congress are called **standing committees**. There are currently 19 standing committees in the House and 17 in the Senate. (See the chart above.) Standing committees deal with broad areas of legislation, such as trade, foreign policy, or finance.

Subcommittees Standing committees are further divided into smaller, more specialized bodies called **subcommittees**. There are about 175 subcommittees in Congress.

Traditionally, the chairs of the standing committees were able to dominate the subcommittees by appointing the subcommittee chairs. This changed, however, with reforms in the 1970s. These reforms allowed more less-experienced members to head subcommittees, which gave these members more power in the committees themselves. In addition, many new subcommittees were formed in the House. Soon, more than 50 percent of the House majority members were chairing subcommittees. In the Senate, more than 80 percent chaired subcommittees.

Select Committees Committees created to deal with special issues not covered by standing committees are known as **select committees**. These committees usually focus on investigations rather than legislation and usually are temporary. A famous select committee in the Senate investigated the Watergate case in the 1970s.

Joint Committees Committees made up of members from both the House and the Senate are called **joint committees**. These committees deal with matters that are best handled by the two houses working together. Some joint committees, such as the Joint Economic Committee, study and advise Congress in key policy areas. This is more efficient than having two committees—one in the House and one in the Senate—study broad policy issues.

Conference Committees Members of both houses of Congress also meet together in **conference committees**—temporary bodies appointed to work out a compromise between House and Senate versions of a bill passed by both houses. Conference committees are explained more fully in Section 3.

Careers in Government

Congressional Staffer

Have you ever wanted to work on Capitol Hill? The opportunity to work with lawmakers and to influence public policy attracts armies of young people seeking congressional staff jobs.

Congressional staffers generally are young, with most of them using the position as a stepping-stone to another career. Some go on to work for interest groups and government agencies. Some even run for office, occasionally winning the seat of their retiring boss.

One route to staff jobs is through summer internships. Each summer, thousands of young people take these apprentice positions, often for little or no pay. Most congressmembers hire interns only from their state or district, and most interns are college undergraduates. Students typically find summer internships with the help of a college placement office, through personal connections with the member, or through persistent letter writing.

Internship jobs usually involve clerical work, such as sorting mail, running errands, and filing papers. Interns, however, also experience the atmosphere of Congress, learn its procedures, and make contacts with staffers who can help them secure permanent jobs later.

Here, an intern works in the office of Representative Henry Bonilla. An internship can provide valuable experience for later jobs.

Competition for entry-level staff jobs is fierce. Many job-seekers move to Washington, D.C., and support themselves by working odd jobs. They submit hundreds of resumés, often going door-to-door looking for openings. Frequently, members of Congress will reward people who worked actively on their campaigns by giving them staff positions. Most people who land entry-level jobs have enthusiasm, a high energy level, good communications skills, and related job experience.

Committee Assignments

By dividing its labor into committees, Congress is better able to examine important issues and make effective decisions. At the same time, committee assignments give members a visible role for which they can claim credit in their district or state. For these reasons, committee assignments are critical to members of Congress.

Committee Chairs Given the importance of committees, committee chairs hold a great deal of power. They always belong to the majority party and traditionally were selected using the **seniority system**, or by the length of time they served on the committee in question. Today, although chairs are

not always the most senior member, seniority still plays an important role in chair assignments.

There is a case to be made for the seniority principle. Members who serve on the same committee for a long time can gain great skill in dealing with specific policy areas. The seniority principle also gives chairs considerable independence because they do not have to rely on the party leadership or on other members to keep their jobs.

As a result of the seniority system, by the 1960s some longtime congressmembers had chaired the same committees for more than 10 years. This locked out many younger members of Congress from powerful committee chair positions. Critics of the system believed that it prevented the introduction of new leadership and new ideas.

POLITICAL PROCESSES *Senator Orrin Hatch (right), chair of the Senate Judiciary Committee, speaks with Governor Michael Leavitt of Utah.* **What role does seniority play in the selection of committee chairs?**

In response, Congress in the 1970s changed the way committee chairs are selected. Today they are elected by members of the majority party. Although the most senior members still are most often elected, some younger members with fewer years of service have been made chairpersons.

In 1995 members of the 104th Congress changed the committee structure further. The Republican majority in the House cut overall committee staff by one third, limited the number of terms a person could serve as a committee chair, and eliminated three standing committees. These changes were part of a larger effort to reduce the size of government.

Committee Membership The most critical factor in determining committee membership is the members' own wishes. A member is most likely to join a committee on which he or she has asked to serve. Members ask to serve on particular committees for various reasons. Some seek special benefits for their districts or states. Members can accomplish this by influencing policy in areas important to their constituents; forest policy, for example, might be highly important to people in a logging district. A member also can help constituents by obtaining government money for projects in their locality. As one committee member said, "As far as I can see, there is really only one basic reason to be on [this] committee. . . . Most of all, I want to be able to bring home projects to my district."

Other members seek committee assignments to influence broad public policy issues of national concern, even though such assignments often give the member no particular advantages with constituents. For example, a representative might seek an appointment on the International Relations Committee even though the committee's work does not relate directly to his or her district.

The more powerful committees typically receive more applications than there are seats available. As a result, members often have to "run" for seats on committees such as the House's Appropriations, Budget, Rules, and Ways and Means Committees, and the Senate's Armed Services, Foreign Relations, Finance, and Appropriations Committees. Selections are based on the political needs of the member, how long the member has been in Congress, his or her loyalty to the party leadership, and whether or not the member's state already has representatives on the committee.

Once members have been named to a committee, they may stay as long as they wish (except for appointees to the House Budget Committee, which limits membership to six years). Many members remain on a committee to increase their seniority. The member with the most seniority often becomes the committee chair and holds great influence in directing the committee's work.

Congressional Resources

Performing all the work of Congress requires extensive resources. For this reason, congressmembers and committees have large staffs to assist them. In addition, congressional agencies conduct valuable research that helps members of Congress and their staffs do their jobs.

Personal Staff For the first 100 years of Congress, only committee chairs had staffs. The other members' offices were simply their desks on the House and Senate floors. By 1827 the House was hiring young boys as "pages," or messengers. Pages often were orphans or the children of members' friends. Members had started hiring personal staff by the 1890s.

CONSTITUTIONAL GOVERNMENT *Representative Solomon Ortiz discusses legislative issues with a member of his staff.* **In what ways do congressional staff members help Congress fulfill its responsibilities?**

Stories abound of staffers who are powerful players in making public policy. Members have even complained at times about the power of their own staffers. "Senators, I fear, are becoming annoying constitutional impediments [stumbling blocks] to the staff," a senator once said. "Someday we may just allow the staff to vote and skip the middle man."

These concerns should be kept in perspective, however. Staffers make many suggestions, but they seldom act against the wishes of their employer.

Committee Staff Committee members have staff as well. These people formally work for, and are on the payroll of, the committee. However, each member of a committee typically hires one or more committee staffers who work primarily for him or her, so they actually function much like personal staff. Because they deal with a single policy area, though, committee staffers tend to know more about the issues they work on than do personal staff.

Congressional Agencies In addition to congressional staffs, there are several agencies that help Congress carry out its work. The Library of Congress provides research facilities, and the Congressional Budget Office (CBO) helps deal with the enormous budget process each year. In addition, the General Accounting Office (GAO) watches over the spending of funds appropriated by Congress, and the Government Printing Office (GPO) prints thousands of publications that provide members and the public with information on the U.S. government.

Today the number of congressional staffers is in the thousands. These people work directly for the members and play a key role in their work. They suggest policies to members, draft bills, and negotiate with other staff about the language of proposed legislation. Before committee hearings, they write questions for members to ask witnesses.

SECTION 2 — REVIEW

1. Define the following terms: bill, appropriations, standing committee, subcommittee, select committee, joint committee, conference committee, seniority system.

2. What is an authorizing committee? an appropriations committee? How many appropriations committees are there in Congress?

3. How are committee assignments made? Why do members of Congress seek particular committee assignments?

4. Name the kinds of congressional resources. How do they help the legislative process?

5. **Thinking and Writing Critically** Does the seniority system benefit or hurt the legislative process? Explain your answer.

6. **Applying** **POLITICAL PROCESSES** Why is it important that members of Congress have many resources to help them do their jobs? What might happen if they had only one or two staff members to aid them?

HOW A BILL BECOMES A LAW

Political Dictionary

filibuster
cloture
roll-call vote
pocket veto
line-item veto

Objectives

★ How are bills referred to a committee?
★ What is the purpose of committee hearings and markup sessions?
★ What happens to a bill when it reaches the full House or Senate floor?
★ What courses of action can the president take on a bill passed by Congress?

The Constitution states that each house of Congress may set its own procedures. Thus, the House and the Senate set the specific rules for considering legislation, except for the procedures dealing with presidential vetoes, which are established in the Constitution.

The legislative process developed by the House and the Senate is slow and includes many steps. This careful process ensures that legislation is thoroughly considered before being passed or rejected. It also means that only a very small percentage of the bills introduced are passed. For example, only 610 of the 10,513 bills introduced in the 102nd Congress were passed into law.

Although citizens, interest groups, the president, and others may suggest ideas for a bill, only members of Congress may introduce legislation. A bill may be introduced first in the House or in the Senate, except for tax bills, which must begin in the House. By custom, appropriations bills also begin in the House. After being introduced, a bill generally goes through six main steps before becoming a law:

★ referral to committee,
★ hearings,
★ markup,
★ floor consideration,
★ conference committee, and
★ presidential action.

Referral to Committee

In most cases a bill that is introduced in Congress is referred to a committee, which may send it to a subcommittee for consideration. Committee consideration is crucial. A bill rarely reaches the full House or Senate floor without committee approval.

In the House, referral decisions are made by the Speaker, and in the Senate by the presiding officer. Most referrals are routine. In the Senate, for example, a bill about price supports for peanuts goes to the Agriculture, Nutrition, and Forestry Committee, and a bill about weapons development goes to the Armed Services Committee.

In cases where the referral is not so straightforward, however, the referral power gives the

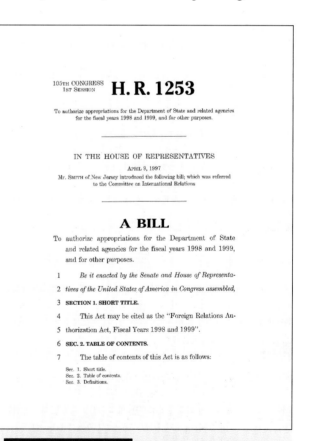

POLITICAL PROCESSES *All House and Senate bills are clearly labeled and numbered to make identification easier.* **Who is responsible for suggesting bills?**

PUBLIC GOOD *Committee hearings usually are open to the public, enabling many journalists and camera crews to attend.* **Why is it important for the public to have access to information presented in these hearings?**

majority party a powerful tool in controlling legislation. Which committee considers a bill greatly affects its fate because committees often have a consistent position on issues coming before them. For example, it makes a world of difference whether a bill dealing with the control of pesticides is referred to an agricultural or an environmental committee. The agricultural committee will tend to limit such control, while the environmental committee will tend to strengthen it. Drafters of legislation often write a bill in a way that encourages a referral to the committee most likely to favor its passage.

Hearings

Many bills have committee or subcommittee hearings, which usually are open to the public. Journalists, television camera crews, interest group representatives, and tourists crowd into hearings. Not all committee members attend, however. With busy schedules and hearing times that often conflict, all members of a subcommittee are seldom present at any but the most important hearings. Staffers often sit in for those who are absent.

Supporters and opponents of a bill testify at its hearing. Typically, testimony comes from the bill's sponsors and from federal and public officials.

Representatives of interest groups also testify. Many times, ordinary citizens who are affected by the problem the bill addresses—for example, competition from foreign products—have testified. Celebrities also have appeared. In 1994, for example, two members of the band Pearl Jam testified during a House hearing on accusations that Ticketmaster charged customers too much for concert tickets.

Committee chairs often use hearings and the accompanying media coverage to build support for, or increase opposition to, a bill. Chairs also have some freedom in deciding who testifies and in what order. Again, this freedom enables chairs to affect how committee members, the media, and the public view the bill.

Markup

In the Senate, after a subcommittee approves a bill, the exact phrasing is decided line by line at the full committee level. This process is called markup. In the House, markup typically takes place at both the subcommittee and full committee levels.

In markup sessions, crucial decisions are made about what specific features a bill will have. For example, for coal miners to qualify for government benefits, how much proof must there be that their lung disease was caused by mining? Should

Citizenship in ➔ Action

Teens Testify Before Congress

Members of the public are asked to testify in front of Congress on a regular basis. These witnesses often are experts on a particular issue before a congressional committee. Sometimes, however, young people who have taken a stand on policies that affected them are asked to present a point of view or personal story in a congressional hearing.

In 1995, for example, 17-year-old high school student Melanie Moyer wrote Representative Tom Bevill of Alabama a letter regarding her concerns about funding for the arts. As a regular performer in community theater, Melanie opposed the government's proposed funding cuts to the National Endowment for the Arts (NEA). In her letter she asked Representative Bevill to support the NEA and requested the chance to share the impact that theater had on her life. She asked for the opportunity to talk to members of Congress and

Some young people are asked to testify before congressional committees to share their view on issues that have affected their lives.

promised to be on the next plane to Washington if given the chance.

Representative Bevill accepted Melanie's offer. In March 1996, Melanie traveled to Washington, D.C., to testify before a House Appropriations subcommittee. Calling it a privilege to appear before Congress, Melanie shared with the committee the letter-writing campaign she had launched on behalf of the NEA and the supportive letters she had received in return.

Melanie Moyer is just one of many young people who have shared their views with Congress. In 1995, for example, several young people from across the country were invited to Washington to testify before the House Judiciary Committee's Subcommittee on the Constitution. At issue was the proposed Religious Equality Amendment, which would have allowed organized prayer in public schools.

One of the speakers was Jason Nauman, who had been a high school senior and student council president in 1993 when he went up against his county's school board over whether a prayer or references to religion could be included in his graduation speech. During the hearing two years later, Jason related his experience to Congress and voiced his support for the amendment. Also testifying was 13-year-old Amber Johnston-Loehner, who talked about her experiences when she sought to distribute religious material to her fifth-grade classmates in 1992.

Not everyone receives the opportunity to share his or her views with Congress. Those who do, however, often hold deep convictions and are not afraid to voice them to those in power. By sharing their views, these citizens can help formulate change in both their communities and the United States as a whole. Of course, anyone, young or old, can participate in the political process, such as by writing a letter to a congressperson on issues of concern.

What Do You Think?

1. Why are young people sometimes asked to testify before a congressional committee?
2. How did Melanie Moyer express her concern over proposed funding cuts to the National Endowment for the Arts?

employers who hire illegal immigrants be jailed or only fined? Markup is time-consuming, precise work that involves mountains of details.

Traditionally, markup sessions were held in secret. Since the 1970s, however, most have been open, though not televised. Some people suggest that the openness has increased the influence of interest groups because they can closely observe a committee's actions and possibly pressure its members. Still, markup sessions are the most likely place in Congress for genuine debate rather than speech-making and posturing for the media.

After markup, a bill must be approved by the full committee before it can move to the House or Senate floor. A bill that fails to be approved dies in committee, and no further action is taken. If a bill is approved, however, committee staff members write a committee report. This report explains the changes that the bill would bring about and presents major arguments on the bill's behalf. The report helps members who are not on the committee to make their voting decisions.

Floor Consideration

For both the House and the Senate, there are standard operating rules that guide procedures for the passage of a bill. Some rules set procedures for voting, admission to the floor, and how business is conducted. In addition, before reaching the House or Senate floor for consideration and voting, most major bills are given strict, specific floor rules that limit floor debate and the changes that can be made to a bill. Strict floor rules thus increase the influence of committees because their work cannot be changed much by the full House or Senate. In contrast, the less strict the floor rules are, the more likely it is that a committee's bill will be changed by the full House or Senate.

Floor Rules in the House   The House Rules Committee devises the set of rules that determines the conditions for debate and amendment of a House bill. Although rules can vary a great deal from bill to bill, there are traditionally three main types of rules—open, closed, and modified. An open rule allows representatives

to propose any amendments that relate to the subject of the bill at hand. A closed rule prohibits amendments altogether. A modified rule determines that some parts of the bill may be amended, but not others.

House rules are not easily changed because of tight control by the House leadership. In some cases, however, the Rules Committee may allow what is called a waiver, or an abandoning, of point of order. This waiver allows a technical violation of House standard operating procedures—such as those for voting, orders of business, and duties of officers—so that the bill will make it to the House floor more quickly.

Although the Rules Committee acts on most bills, some actually bypass the rules process altogether. For example, some minor bills go to the floor on a set day and pass with little debate. In addition, bills that are considered noncontroversial may proceed under a suspension-of-the-rules procedure, which is set by the Speaker and dictates that only 40 minutes of debate will be allowed, no amendments will be heard, and a two-thirds vote is required for passage. The Speaker may enact this procedure only if the bill calls for expenditures of less than $100 million. Yet other bills—known as "privileged" bills—may be sent to the floor at any time and do not go through the Rules Committee. These generally are major bills such as budget or appropriations bills.

POLITICAL PROCESSES   *This photo shows the electronic tally of floor votes in the House as broadcast on C–Span.* **How do committee reports help members of Congress make their voting decisions?**

POLITICAL PROCESSES *This 1965 photo shows Senate leader Everett Dirksen as he prepares materials to read in a filibuster against a bill to strike down right-to-work laws. **How can a senator use a filibuster to block legislation?***

Filibusters Sometimes it is impossible to negotiate a unanimous consent agreement. In such cases a bill may fall prey to a notorious congressional procedure known as a **filibuster**—an effort by one or more senators to hold up the final vote on a bill through delaying tactics. These tactics range from nonstop speechmaking to the offering of endless amendments. The Senate may sit for hours during a filibuster. A filibuster allows an intense minority to block the actions of the majority.

Over the years the Senate has moved to limit filibusters. In 1917 the Senate adopted a rule allowing a two-thirds, or 67-vote, majority to call for **cloture**, which stops a filibuster by setting a time limit on debate. This majority was lowered to three fifths, or 60 votes, in 1975.

Floor Rules in the Senate The Senate does not follow a strict set of rules, as in the House. Standard Senate floor rules, for example, place no limit on how much time may be spent debating a bill nor on the number and kind of amendments that may be offered.

The Senate's standard rules, however, often are set aside if the members of the Senate unanimously agree to do so. A unanimous consent agreement can change many procedures—for example, it can set the length of time a bill can be debated and determine whether amendments can be submitted, and if so, how many. Thus, if one senator objects to the Senate's standard debate rules, he or she can ask that a special rule be set for the bill.

The requirement for unanimous consent on changing a bill's particular debate rules gives senators a great deal of power. By withholding consent to the debate rule of a bill he or she dislikes, any member can tie the Senate in knots. In effect, every senator has veto power over the rules of each bill that comes to the floor. As one former representative observed, "If you just want to be unpleasant and have a temper tantrum . . . , you can have a field day in the Senate. You can break all the toys in the sandbox if that's what you want in order to get your way and you can pout with very great effect." Senate leadership must often negotiate to achieve a unanimous consent agreement.

Voting After all floor debate, congressmembers vote on the bill and any amendments made to it. Critical bills usually receive a **roll-call vote**, in which each member is called on individually to declare his or her vote.

Conference Committees

A bill that has been passed in one house is then sent to the other house for consideration. In most cases, a similar or identical bill is already being considered in the other house. The other house may pass a somewhat different bill. House and Senate versions of a bill may then be sent to a joint conference committee. As noted in Section 2, conference committees consist of both House and Senate members, who almost always come from the committees that drafted the initial versions of the bill.

Because conference committee members usually are chosen from among supporters of the bill, they have strong reasons to compromise rather than letting the bill die in conference. In addition, the bills that are sent to conference committees generally are some of the most important or controversial pieces of legislation. After differences are resolved, the committee prepares a conference report. It is rare for the House or the Senate to reject a conference committee's recommendation.

Presidential Action

A bill that has been passed by both houses is sent to the president, who may do one of four things:

★ sign the bill, which makes it law;
★ veto the bill;
★ keep the bill for 10 days without signing it. If Congress is in session during this time, the bill becomes law without the president's signature. This option is rarely used and is reserved for bills that the president dislikes but not enough to veto; or
★ **pocket veto** the bill. If the president receives a bill within 10 days of Congress's adjournment, he or she may hold the bill without signing it, and the bill does not become a law.

Vetoes are relatively rare. While Congress can pass a bill over a presidential veto, it is difficult to obtain the required two-thirds vote in both houses. Therefore, to ensure a bill's approval, Congress often works to answer presidential concerns about a bill before it is sent to the White House.

POLITICAL PROCESSES *The summary voting board is part of the electronic voting system used in the House of Representatives.* **How has technology such as the electronic voting system helped Congress speed up the voting process?**

In 1996 Congress passed, and the president approved, a bill establishing a **line-item veto**, which gives the president the additional authority to veto certain parts of a spending bill without vetoing the entire measure. Several congressmembers filed a lawsuit against the bill, saying it was unconstitutional. In June 1997 the Supreme Court ruled that the lawmakers did not have the right to file a lawsuit because the president had not yet exercised the power. The line-item veto thus remained in question.

SECTION 3 — REVIEW

1. Define the following terms: filibuster, cloture, roll-call vote, pocket veto, line-item veto.

2. How are bills assigned to a committee? How can referring a bill to a particular committee instead of another affect its fate?

3. What happens during committee hearings? Why do committees need markup sessions, and what occurs during them?

4. How are floor debate rules established in the House and in the Senate?

5. What can the president do with a bill after receiving it?

6. **Thinking and Writing Critically**
   What are the advantages and disadvantages of having committee hearings open to the public?

7. **Applying** POLITICAL PROCESSES
   As noted in this section, Congress follows particular steps in considering legislation. Why might it be important that Congress follow these steps each time a bill is introduced?

CONGRESS AND THE PUBLIC GOOD

Political Dictionary

pork-barrel spending

Objectives

★ Do special interests obstruct Congress in promoting the public good?
★ What is the main criticism of the committee system, and how does it affect the public good?
★ What role does Congress play in promoting the public good?

There is no doubt that Congress affects the well-being of the citizens it serves. The question is whether that effect is good or bad. Criticisms of Congress arose even before the 1st Congress met. One newspaper stated almost 100 years ago that "if God had made Congress, He would not boast of it." Are such criticisms justified? Or do Congress and its members work for the public good?

Influence of Special Interests

One major criticism of Congress is that it promotes special interests at the expense of the public good. In other words, congressmembers give too much weight to the narrow concerns of interest groups and of their home districts or states.

Interest Groups Critics charge that interest groups use campaign donations and other tactics to control members of Congress. As noted in Chapter 5, there is some connection between interest group support and congressmembers' voting behavior. However, this connection often stems from the fact that interest groups contribute to the campaigns of members who already share the groups' views. (The connection between

interest groups and members of Congress is explained more fully in Chapter 17.)

In fact, members often vote *against* the views of interest groups that support them. They do so because they are influenced more by their own beliefs, their constituents' views, and the position of their political party than they are by interest groups.

Home Districts Congress also has been criticized for the role that constituents' interests play in the lawmaking process. By representing their constituents, members of Congress give U.S. citizens a voice in government. Sometimes, however, members represent their constituents' interests by acquiring funds for unnecessary projects. This **pork-barrel spending** awards projects and grants, or "pork," from the government "barrel" to a member's home district or state. Projects include the construction of government buildings, roads, bridges, and other transportation projects. While these projects might be helpful to the community that receives them, they often are not the best use of taxpayers' money.

PUBLIC GOOD *Senator Jesse Helms of North Carolina meets with young people on the steps of the Capitol.* **Why is it important for Congress to listen to the concerns of the public?**

Opinions about what constitutes pork differ, however. It has been said that one person's "pork is another's good investment." For example, are there any government construction projects, such as a new highway, under way where you live? Does this seem like pork-barrel spending to you, or is it a good investment in the growth of business and jobs in your community? This may be a difficult question to answer because the response often varies depending on whom one asks.

Nonetheless, because many members work hard to bring federal money to their district or state, it is easy to find examples of what most observers would view as pork. For example, the following might qualify by most people's standards:

★ $500,000 to renovate the boyhood farm of Lawrence Welk, a television orchestra leader, so it could become a tourist attraction in Strasburg, North Dakota. The money was part of an agriculture appropriations bill.
★ $320,000 to buy the home of President William McKinley's in-laws in Canton, Ohio (McKinley's own home is no longer standing), for donation to the state of Ohio as a museum.
★ $10 million to build a ramp to Milwaukee's County Stadium parking lot.

PUBLIC GOOD *Senator Robert Byrd of West Virginia worked hard to bring the Internal Revenue Service processing center to his state.* **Why is pork-barrel spending difficult to identify?**

Others might not be so easy to identify. For example, Senator Robert Byrd of West Virginia, for many years the chair of the Senate Appropriations Committee, was particularly aggressive in seeking federal money for his state. As a result, a number of government offices moved to West Virginia, including the Federal Bureau of Investigation (FBI) Identification Center and an Internal Revenue Service (IRS) processing center. This helped bring additional money and jobs to West Virginia.

Some people defend pork-barrel spending as an appropriate way to address and represent local concerns. A problem arises, however, because not every district shares equally in such spending. Members of certain committees, such as the House Agriculture Committee and the Senate Environment and Public Works Committee, bring their constituents a much larger share of pork-barrel spending than is received by people in other areas.

What if all constituents received an equal share of pork-barrel spending? Would this promote the public good? To answer this question, you must understand how legislators pay for pork-barrel spending. Like all government spending, pork-barrel projects are paid for by taxes. Thus, if everyone's local concerns were rewarded with pork-barrel projects, high taxes would result. Pork-barrel spending, whether it is equally or unequally distributed, has a price.

The evidence suggests, however, that the granting of projects to meet district needs, like the granting of interest groups' contributions, is a problem but is not out of control. In fact, pork-barrel spending is a rather small slice of government spending, about 1 percent according to one budget expert's estimate.

Between 1980 and 1991, when measured in constant 1987 dollars, total spending on major programs that included significant elements of pork actually declined. Such spending decreased by 26 percent for water and power projects, by 14 percent for construction grants to state and local government, and by 44 percent for other project grants within government.

In addition, some people say that because many voters have demanded a decrease in pork-barrel spending, legislators are responding. During the 1994 congressional campaign, for example, instead of highlighting the federal projects they had brought home, a greater number of candidates

CITIZENSHIP *Concerned citizens in Sacramento, California, rally against pork-barrel spending.* **Why have some members of Congress campaigned against pork-barrel projects benefiting their state?**

What is the basis of this charge? As you have learned, members often serve on a committee because their constituents have a strong interest in programs in that committee's policy area. For example, a House member from a rural farming district might seek assignment to the Agriculture Committee. Critics thus charge that most committee members represent a few strong local concerns instead of the interests of the country as a whole. Many people worry that unrepresentative committees often use their powerful influence to push harmful legislation through Congress and to control congressional investigations.

There are, however, several forces that weaken committees' ability to force narrow, locally oriented policies on Congress as a whole. First, members with many different viewpoints are assigned to the key committees. As a result, committees are generally not dominated by one viewpoint. In addition, most committee assignments are based more or less proportionally on a party's representation in Congress. (The majority party controls a slightly larger percentage of committee seats than its percentage of seats in Congress as a whole.) This helps to keep committees representative.

Also, committees' recommendations are not always followed by the full House or Senate. Committee members know that they can be overruled if they stray too far from what most members and their constituents want. Finally, the opening of committee hearings to the public and to the media makes it more difficult to pass narrow legislation that does not represent the interests of the country or the wishes of a majority of congressmembers.

openly opposed pork-barrel spending in their campaigns, even for their own districts.

A number of candidates even campaigned against pork-barrel projects benefiting their own districts or states. According to one observer,

❝ People seem to feel that you're not doing them any favors by recycling their tax dollars through Washington and bringing home a few pennies. ❞

In a 1994 race, Greg Ganske, an Iowa Republican, campaigned against several projects the incumbent Democrat had brought to the district. During the campaign, Ganske said that the projects were "like shipping a nice lean Iowa pig to Washington and getting back two thin strips of bacon."

Power of the Committee System

Another criticism of Congress is that it sets up unrepresentative committees. In other words, critics believe that current congressional committees do not properly represent the concerns of Congress or the country as a whole.

Voice of the People

When judging Congress's role in promoting the public good, keep in mind that Congress is only one part of the larger system of the U.S. government. The federal government is also made up of the president, all the government agencies, and the federal courts.

CONSTITUTIONAL GOVERNMENT *Members of the House Judiciary Subcommittee on the Constitution meet to discuss committee business.* **What types of issues do you think this committee would commonly discuss?**

Indeed, the local concerns represented in Congress are checked and balanced as they should be by the executive and judicial branches. In contrast to Congress, the president and the rest of the executive branch represent the national concerns of the majority of U.S. citizens as a whole. The judicial branch defends the minority's concerns by protecting citizens' constitutional rights.

It would be inefficient and even harmful if all institutions of the national government were as locally oriented as Congress. It is essential, however, to have one branch of government that directly provides a place that represents the local concerns of the people, whether they live in the congressperson's district or are part of an interest group.

SECTION 4 — REVIEW

1. Define the following term: pork-barrel spending.

2. Why do some critics believe that interest groups and home districts keep legislators from promoting the public good? Are these criticisms justified? Explain your answer.

3. Are congressional committees unrepresentative of national concerns? Explain your answer.

4. Whom does Congress represent that no other branch of government represents? How does Congress differ from the other branches of government in this way? Why is this representation essential to promoting the public good?

5. **Thinking and Writing Critically**
Why do you think that some congressional reformers spend much of their time attacking instances of pork-barrel spending even though it accounts for only a tiny percentage of the federal budget? Should members of Congress spend more time passing legislation and performing their other duties rather than opposing pork-barrel projects? Explain your answer.

6. **Applying** **PUBLIC GOOD**
Search the Internet for information on this year's federal budget. If 1 percent of this is spent on pork, what would be the total amount of pork-barrel spending?

CHAPTER 6 — SUMMARY

SECTION 1 Congress has developed a remarkable system for facing the huge task of making the country's laws. It operates under a system of rules that determines how long it is in session, who its leaders are, and how sessions are conducted.

Each congressional term is divided into two 1-year sessions. Each session begins on January 3.

Representatives serve 2-year terms, and senators serve 6-year terms. There are no limits to the number of terms members of Congress may serve, though some people believe that the lack of term limits has led to an unresponsive Congress.

Congressional leadership is organized strictly by party. The party that holds the most seats is called the majority party. The political party with fewer seats is the minority party. Presiding officers and committee chairs always come from the majority party. The most influential person in the House is the Speaker. The presiding officer in the Senate is the vice president of the United States. In the absence of the vice president, the president *pro tempore* is the formal head of the Senate.

SECTION 2 Congressional committees are bodies that deal with a specific area of public policy, such as defense, education, or health. Committees consider proposed legislation before it moves on to the House or the Senate as a whole. Committees also oversee the performance of the executive branch agencies in their policy area.

There are two types of committees: authorizing committees and appropriations committees, and several categories of committees: standing committees, subcommittees, select committees, joint committees, and conference committees. Committee assignments are important to members of Congress because their work on congressional committees gives them a visible role to report to constituents.

To complete the large amount of work they face, members of Congress and committees need many resources. For this reason, members of Congress and their committees have large staffs and also are aided by congressional agencies.

SECTION 3 The Constitution states that each house of Congress may set its own procedures. The legislative process developed by Congress is slow and includes many steps. This process ensures that legislation is carefully considered before being passed or rejected. After a bill is introduced, there are six steps it may go through before being signed into law: referral to committee, hearings, markup, floor consideration, conference committee, and presidential action.

SECTION 4 Some critics charge that Congress serves special interests at the expense of the public good. They believe that congressmembers give too much weight to the narrow concerns of interest groups and of their home districts and states. Others say that Congress allows unrepresentative committees to decide legislation. Though it does suffer somewhat from these problems, Congress provides citizens with an essential voice in the branch of government designed to be particularly responsive to local and special interest concerns.

 Government Notebook

Review the process that you outlined in your Government Notebook at the beginning of the chapter. Now that you have studied the chapter, compare that process with the real legislative process in Congress. Is the real process much more complicated than you originally imagined? Write your answer in your Notebook.

REVIEW

REVIEWING CONCEPTS

1. Why is most of Congress's work done through committees? What types of committees are there?

2. What are the rules of conduct for members of Congress, and what official actions may Congress take against a member who breaks them?

3. How are the leaders in each house of Congress selected?

4. How are committee assignments made?

5. How long is a term of Congress? Why do some people support term limits for members of Congress?

6. What major criticisms have been made of Congress?

7. Who assists members of Congress with their work?

8. What are the six steps in the legislative process after a bill is introduced?

THINKING AND WRITING CRITICALLY

1. **PRINCIPLES OF DEMOCRACY** Although they are elected representatives of the people, members of Congress bring their own beliefs and priorities to the job. Should members vote according to their personal beliefs, or according to the wishes of their constituents? Why?

2. **POLITICAL PROCESSES** Does requiring unanimous consent on a bill's rules give individual senators too much power? Explain your answer.

3. **PRINCIPLES OF DEMOCRACY** Leaders of congressional committees always are selected from the majority party. Does this system give one party too much influence in the legislative process? Explain your answer.

4. **PUBLIC GOOD** Do you agree with the practice of allowing journalists and television camera crews to attend congressional subcommittee hearings? Do you think that media coverage of these hearings promotes the public good?

CITIZENSHIP IN YOUR COMMUNITY

As in Congress, many city and town councils create smaller committees or task forces to study particular issues, such as the need for a new transportation system, convention center, or landfill site. Research one such committee in your community. How are committee members and chairpersons appointed? Might this system of assignment affect the committee's findings? For example, you might consider whether members are selected solely by the mayor or by party affiliation. Write a report of your findings, suggesting any changes that you believe might improve the system.

INDIVIDUAL PORTFOLIO PROJECT

Imagine that you head a citizens' group that has submitted a proposal to your House representative for setting aside part of your district as a national park. Your representative has agreed to submit a bill to that effect. How can you and your fellow citizens influence the bill's progress through Congress? Write a plan of action that your group will follow to help secure the bill's passage at each step of the legislative process. You might wish to include a chart that outlines the steps.

PRACTICING SKILLS: CONDUCTING RESEARCH

Draw a flowchart of a bill's path through Congress from its introduction to presidential action. You may want to review your flowchart skills in the Skills Handbook on page xxv. The chart should be presented in a manner that makes the process easy to trace. You should use arrows to illustrate how the process begins and where it ends.

THE INTERNET: LEARNING ONLINE

Conduct an Internet search for information on the membership of Senate committees and subcommittees. You might start with search words such as *congressional committees, standing committees, Senate committees,* and *congressional subcommittees.* Create a flyer profiling the committee appointments and leadership positions held by each of your state's senators. Include a short description of each of these committees.

ANALYZING PRIMARY SOURCES

THE CONGRESSIONAL RECORD

One of the many publications printed by the General Printing Office (GPO) is the *Congressional Record.* The *Record* contains a daily accounting of the business conducted in Congress, including transcripts of members' speeches. Read the excerpt below in which Representative Earl Pomeroy speaks about the importance of balancing the budget and the difficult process of reaching a compromise on the proposed Balanced Budget Amendment. Then answer the questions that follow.

" I rise to support this budget agreement. The agreement before us represents at least procedurally the hardest thing this body ever tries to do, compromise differences, accept less than what each party wants, and tolerate aspects of the agreement each party would not include if it were simply a matter of writing its own package. Throughout the history of this place, this Chamber is mostly a matter of winner-take-all, the party of the majority passes the bills they want, and that is the end of it. In times of divided government, that often means a Presidential veto and the legislative initiative dies in the partisan standoff. Such was the fate of the balanced budget drive in the last Congress and it very well could have happened to the balanced budget effort this Congress, but the American people deserve better and the President and the leaders of Congress, both House and Senate, both majority and minority, have worked to give them better. This budget agreement accomplishes that difficult task.

Back where I come from and across the country, Americans wanted the parties to work together to iron out the most difficult problems facing this country. They wanted a balanced budget. They have to do it as individual families. Collectively they wanted to do it on behalf of the country. But they also wanted our values reflected. Those values include protecting the health care that our seniors depend upon, committing to a bright educational opportunity for our young people, and the opportunity for people at a midcareer track to go back [to school] and get the skills training they need to compete in the work force today. It means working and middle-income families find it just a little easier to make ends meet. "

1. How does the structure of the legislative branch make compromise difficult? Do you think that changes should be made to the way in which congressional legislation is passed?

2. What often happens to legislation during times when the government is divided? In what way does divided government bring this about?

3. Why do you think both parties in the House were able to reach a compromise on this issue? What values did some House members want included in the bill? Do you think the values that Pomeroy mentions reflect the public good?

Congressional Staffer for a Day

Imagine that you are part of a group of staff members who work in the office of Representative Joan Campbell. The congressmember needs your group to develop a recommendation on whether she should support a proposed amendment to the U.S. Constitution that would raise the minimum legal voting age to 21.

The issue has created a great deal of controversy, and Campbell has received a number of letters from constituents on the issue. To help you make your recommendation, your boss, the chief of staff, has given your group two of the letters and a newspaper editorial for you to review. You will find these documents and a fact sheet about the issue on the following pages.

After you review these documents, answer the questions that accompany them in your Government Notebook. Your group also will need to conduct some outside research. Record the results of your research in your Government Notebook as well.

After you have finished reviewing the documents and conducting your research, work with other group members to develop a recommendation for Campbell. Make sure the recommendation is written neatly or typed. You might want to put it in a folder or binder labeled "Confidential: Representative Joan Campbell."

In your recommendation make sure you support your decision with clear arguments based on your research and document analysis. Discuss how the letters and the editorial influenced your decision. Consider reading your recommendation to the rest of the class as part of a discussion on the factors involved in the decision-making process of a congressmember and his or her staff.

Office of U.S. Representative
Joan Campbell

STAFF MEMORANDUM

To: Staff Researchers

From: Harold Box, Chief of Staff

Representative Campbell is looking forward to hearing your recommendation on the proposed amendment to raise the minimum legal voting age to 21. Please review the fact sheet that follows. It will provide applicable background information. I also have provided two letters and a newspaper editorial on the issue.

After you read those documents, your group will need to conduct some outside research, with each member uncovering the answer to one of the following questions:

- Has the United States ever repealed an amendment? If so, explain the circumstances.
- How have amendments and other laws to extend voting rights affected voter turnout?
- What attempts have been made to increase voter turnout, particularly among young people?
- How high is voter turnout in other democratic countries? What is the minimum legal voting age in several of them?

Other research questions may cross your mind as you read the letters and the newspaper editorial. Below is a list of some sources you might find useful in doing your research. You might need to find other sources as well.

- library almanacs and encyclopedias
- *Statistical Abstract of the United States* (volumes by years)
- applicable articles listed in the *Readers' Guide to Periodical Literature*
- interviews seeking the opinions and experiences of people in the local congressional district

Good luck!

Representative Joan Campbell

CONFIDENTIAL

 **Office of U.S. Representative**
Joan Campbell

FACT SHEET

Proposed Amendment to Raise the Minimum Legal Voting Age to 21

- The Twenty-sixth Amendment was ratified in 1971. It lowered the minimum legal voting age from 21 to 18 in all federal, state, and local elections.

- Some observers have said that making people aged 18 to 20 eligible to vote has been one cause for a decline in voter turnout. About 61 percent of eligible voters cast ballots in the 1968 presidential election. Just over 55 percent voted in 1972. Turnout has been even lower since then.

- Surveys have shown that far less than half of people aged 18 to 20 even bother to register to vote. Only 38.5 percent of people in that category said they registered to vote in the 1992 presidential election. In comparison, 61 percent of all eligible voters said they registered.

- The proposed amendment would make anyone under the age of 21 ineligible to vote. Sponsors say the amendment would help ensure that eligible voters are mature enough to take their right to vote seriously.

PUBLIC POLICY LAB

CITIZENS FOR RESPONSIBLE VOTING
1111 Main Street
Chicago, IL 60607

Representative Joan Campbell
U.S. House of Representatives
The Capitol
Washington, DC 20515

Dear Representative Campbell:

As president of Citizens for Responsible Voting (CRV), I am writing to you in support of the proposed amendment to raise the minimum legal voting age back to 21. The goal of CRV is the development of educated and mature voters. We believe that your support for the amendment will help restore responsibility to the voting booth.

As you are aware, just over half of eligible voters have cast ballots in recent presidential elections. We believe the low level of voter turnout is partly because the minimum legal voting age was lowered to 18 by the Twenty-sixth Amendment.

Many of our young people today are fine, well-educated citizens. On the other hand, too many 18- to 20-year-olds do not take the time to study the election issues and candidates. In addition, many young people have not exercised their right to vote. We believe that this failure reflects a lack of the maturity that is needed to make important decisions about our government.

We believe that raising the minimum legal voting age back to 21 would give young people more time to mature and learn about our election system. When older, they will be better able to research and understand the issues and the stands taken by candidates for public office.

As you will recall, we supported your re-election last year by providing campaign volunteers and donating to your campaign fund. We did those things because of your past support for efforts to promote responsible voting. We hope you will continue to be a strong supporter of our efforts.

Sincerely,

Sheila Goldstone

Sheila Goldstone
President
Citizens for Responsible Voting

◄WHAT DO YOU THINK?

★ **What is the goal of CRV?**

★ **What does CRV believe raising the minimum legal voting age would do?**

★ **What have been CRV's connections with Representative Campbell in the past?**

WHAT DO YOU THINK?►

★ **How would the proposed amendment affect Anthony Washington?**

★ **How does Washington demonstrate that he is responsible in his role as a citizen? Does that help his argument that the amendment should be defeated? Explain.**

★ **What other reasons does Washington give to support his argument that the amendment should be defeated?**

Representative Joan Campbell
U.S. House of Representatives
The Capitol
Washington, DC 20515

Dear Representative Campbell:

I am a senior at Central High School, and I have heard that there is a proposed amendment to the Constitution that would change the minimum legal voting age back to 21. I hope you will vote against this amendment.

I have worked to register eligible voters, and I have volunteered to work on political campaigns. If the law does not change, I will vote when I turn 18.

I think raising the minimum voting age would unfairly penalize me. I know that some people my age do not vote. But no one is proposing that older people be penalized because not everyone older than 20 votes.

I will be old enough to serve my country in the military and will have other responsibilities as an adult when I turn 18. I believe I should also have the right to vote.

Please vote no on the amendment.

Sincerely,

Anthony Washington

Anthony Washington
Central High School
Chicago Ridge, IL 60415

Congress Should Reject Attempt to Raise Voting Age

Congress is considering an amendment to the U.S. Constitution that would repeal the Twenty-sixth Amendment and raise the minimum legal voting age back to 21. The amendment should be defeated because it is the wrong solution to the problems its supporters have identified.

Supporters of the amendment believe a higher minimum legal voting age would increase voter turnout. They also argue that older voters are more likely to have the maturity and sense of responsibility to educate themselves about issues and candidates for public office. Supporters of the amendment are right when they say that low voter turnout among young people is evidence that many do not take their right to vote seriously enough.

Opponents of the proposed amendment point to the Fifteenth and Nineteenth Amendments. Those amendments extended voting rights to former slaves and to women. Not all African Americans and women vote, but no one proposes repealing those important amendments.

In addition, we believe that taking away the right to vote is no way to teach maturity and responsibility. One way to become mature and responsible is by accepting the challenges that society provides. One of the biggest challenges democracy presents citizens is choosing the best people to serve in government.

Many adults under the age of 21 have accepted the challenge and responsibility of voting. They should not be penalized because others their age have chosen to ignore that same challenge.

A better solution to the problem of low voter turnout would include ways to get more voters, from the age of 18 up, to educate themselves about the issues and candidates and actually go to the polls. We should not instead be proposing laws that would prevent some people from voting. The proposed amendment should not be passed.

▲WHAT DO YOU THINK?

★ What did the Fifteenth and Nineteenth Amendments do? Are the results of these amendments applicable to the debate over raising the voting age?

★ What does the editorial writer suggest is a better solution to the problem of low voter turnout?

THINGS TO DO

1. Compare each member of your group's notes and ideas about each of the documents provided by the chief of staff.

2. Gather the research results from individual group members.

3. Discuss whether Representative Campbell should support the proposed amendment.

4. Prepare a formal report with the group's recommendation. Give the reasons for the group's decision.

UNIT
3

PUBLIC POLICY LAB

What process might you follow if you were to write a speech for the president? Find out by reading this unit and taking the Public Policy Lab challenge on pages 242–45.

THE EXECUTIVE BRANCH

THE PRESIDENCY

I f you have heard of only one address in Washington, D.C., it is likely to be 1600 Pennsylvania Avenue—the address of the White House, home and office of the president of the United States. The White House attracts more visitors each year than any other building in the country. This is not surprising, as the presidency is the major focus of attention in the U.S. political system.

Although presidents do not and cannot "run" the country single-handedly, most modern presidents have had decisive influence over U.S. foreign policy and have set much of the agenda for economic and domestic policy. This chapter looks at the many roles, qualifications, and powers of the president, as well as the presidential nomination and election processes.

Government Notebook

In your Government Notebook, list all of the presidents who have served since you entered the first grade. What do you remember about these presidents and their terms in office?

THE PRESIDENTIAL OFFICE

Political Dictionary

State of the Union
 Address
diplomacy
foreign policy
presidential succession

Objectives

★ What are the roles of the president?
★ What are the qualifications and terms of the office of the presidency?
★ What is the order of presidential succession?

Since 1789 many children in America have proudly exclaimed, "I'm going to grow up to be president." However, speaking as a present-day high school student, would you like to apply for the job? Before you answer, read on to learn about the president's roles in the U.S. government as well as the position's qualifications and terms of office.

The President's Roles

The president plays many vital roles in U.S. government. Some of these roles are outlined in the Constitution. Others have been assumed and expanded by those who have held the office.

Chief Executive Article II, Section 1, of the Constitution states that "the executive power shall be vested in [given to] a President of the United States of America." This means that as head of the executive branch, the president is responsible for executing, or carrying out, the nation's laws.

Commander in Chief Article II, Section 2, of the Constitution states that "the President shall be Commander in Chief of the army and navy of the United States." As head of the U.S. armed forces, the president commands all military officers in both wartime and peacetime. This does not mean that he or she actually leads U.S. troops into battle. The president does, however, stay in frequent contact with the nation's military leaders and has the final say in wartime decisions.

Chief Agenda Setter The Constitution requires that the president "shall from time to time give to the Congress information of [about] the state of the Union, and recommend to their [Congress's] consideration such measures as he shall judge necessary." To carry out this provision, each year the president delivers several messages to Congress. In January the president delivers a **State of the Union Address**, which sets forth the programs, policies, and legislation that he or she wants Congress to enact. The president also sends Congress a budget proposal, recommending how the federal government should raise and spend its money.

Representative of the Nation As one of two nationally elected officials in the government, the president represents—in a way that no member of

CONSTITUTIONAL GOVERNMENT *In October 1994 President Bill Clinton visited U.S. troops in Kuwait.* ***What are the president's responsibilities as commander in chief?***

Congress can—*all* of the people. As President Woodrow Wilson wrote, "He [the president] is the representative of no constituency, but of the whole people. When he speaks in his true character, he speaks for no special interest." President Harry Truman stated a similar idea: "The president is the only lobbyist that 150 million Americans have. The other 20 million are able to employ people to represent them . . . but someone has to look out after the interests of the 150 million that are left." (The population of the United States at the time was around 170 million.)

As the nation's main representative, the president is often the focus of political attention. This becomes most apparent during crises. For example, the president often travels to the site of a natural disaster—such as a hurricane in Florida

Comparing Governments

The French Prime Minister

In most countries with a parliamentary system of government, the prime minister—rather than a monarch or a president—is the chief executive. Prime ministers generally are involved in both domestic and foreign policy. The French parliamentary system, however, is organized somewhat differently. In France, the president, who is elected by the people, and the prime minister, who is appointed by the president but is responsible to the Parliament, share executive powers. The president largely manages foreign affairs, while the prime minister takes responsibility for the daily operations of the government.

Another unusual characteristic of the French parliamentary system is that the prime minister is allowed to hold other government positions while helping run the nation. For example, several French politicians in recent years have served as mayor of a city while also serving as prime minister. Many people in France believe that such combinations are a good way to stay in touch with the public while serving as the nation's executive.

CITIZENSHIP *President Bill Clinton awards John H. Johnson, chief executive officer of Johnson Publishing, the Presidential Medal of Freedom.* **What duties must the president assume as the country's chief of state?**

or an earthquake in California—to show national concern. "In times of crisis," one observer has noted, "citizens expect their president to be personally on duty and in charge."

Chief of State As chief of state the president symbolizes the United States and its people. This means that the president represents the nation when meeting with foreign leaders both at home and abroad. In this role, the president engages in **diplomacy**, or the art of conducting negotiations with foreign countries. Such diplomacy builds international ties that further U.S. economic and security interests.

In the role of chief of state, the president also performs many ceremonial duties. These include awarding medals to citizens who have made notable contributions to society, lighting the nation's Christmas tree, and opening the professional baseball season by throwing the first pitch.

WORLD AFFAIRS *President Bill Clinton and First Lady Hillary Rodham Clinton greet Russian president Boris Yeltsin and his wife, Naina Yeltsin, at a White House state dinner in 1994.* **Why is it important for the president to establish friendships with foreign leaders?**

Foreign-Policy Leader Related to the role of chief of state is that of foreign-policy leader. As the head of one of the most powerful countries in the world, the president must give constant attention to the nation's **foreign policy**—its plans for dealing with other countries. The goals of U.S. foreign policy are to promote trade and friendship with other countries while maintaining the security of the United States. (The goals and principles of U.S. foreign policy are more fully explained in Chapter 10.) The president's special role in foreign affairs is suggested in the Constitution by the role as commander in chief and the power to negotiate treaties with foreign nations. Also, the Constitution states that the president must take an oath to "preserve, protect and defend the Constitution of the United States." Congressmembers are not required to take an oath, suggesting that the president has a special responsibility for national security.

Party Leader As the leader of his or her political party, the president makes speeches to help other party members who are running for public office. The president also helps the party raise money for its political campaigns, candidates, and programs.

Qualifications and Terms of Office

You now know the roles that the president must play once in office. What qualifications, though, must a person have to reach the presidency, and what are the terms of office?

Formal Qualifications Article II, Section 1, of the Constitution states that the president must

★ be a native-born U.S. citizen,
★ be at least 35 years of age, and
★ have been a U.S. resident for at least 14 years.

The Constitution contains no other formal qualifications for the presidency.

Presidential Background In addition to fulfilling the above formal qualifications, the people who have become president also have shared similar personal backgrounds. For example, all presidents to date have been white, male Christians. This pattern shows signs of changing, however. In 1984 Geraldine Ferraro was the Democratic nominee for vice president. Also in 1984 and again in 1988, Jesse Jackson, an African American, made a strong bid for the presidency. In fact, recent polls

CONSTITUTIONAL GOVERNMENT *President Franklin D. Roosevelt was the only U.S. president to serve more than two terms in office. Here, an interest group advertises its support of Roosevelt's campaign for his third term.* **Which amendment to the Constitution established a two-term limit for the presidency?**

specified. After serving two terms, George Washington stated that he did not wish to be considered for a third term and stepped down. All presidents afterward followed this two-term tradition until Franklin D. Roosevelt, who was elected to a third term in 1940 and a fourth in 1944.

To keep one person from holding the nation's highest office for such a long time, in 1947 Congress proposed the Twenty-second Amendment, which the states ratified in 1951. This amendment set forth a constitutional two-term limit for the presidency.

Salary and Benefits Currently the president earns $200,000 a year, plus $50,000 for official expenses and additional allowances for travel and entertainment. Congress sets the president's salary. However, to prevent Congress from using the power to influence the president, a change in salary cannot take place until the beginning of the next presidential term.

The presidency carries several benefits in addition to salary. The president and his or her family live in the White House, a stately mansion that features both offices for White House staff and private living quarters for the presidential family. For special meetings and vacations, the president may use Camp David, a mountain retreat in Maryland.

To travel to Camp David and anywhere else in the world, the president has a fleet of cars, helicopters, and airplanes, including the presidential jet, *Air Force One*. One story has it that when President Lyndon B. Johnson began boarding one of two helicopters and an aide informed him that his was the other one, Johnson replied, "They're all mine."

Presidential Succession The Constitution states that if the president dies, resigns, or is removed from office, the vice president becomes president. This constitutional provision has been invoked nine times—eight times when the president died in office and once when he resigned.

What would happen if both the president and the vice president should die or resign? The

suggest that a majority of Americans would vote for a qualified woman, African American, or Jewish American for president.

In addition, most of the nation's 41 presidents have been highly educated. Of the 24 presidents who served during the 1700s and 1800s, when few people went to college, 15 were college graduates. All twentieth-century presidents except for Harry S Truman attended college, and several earned advanced degrees. (President Truman earned a law degree—law schools did not require an undergraduate degree at the time.)

Terms The Constitution sets the president's term of office at four years. Originally, however, the *number* of terms a president could serve was not

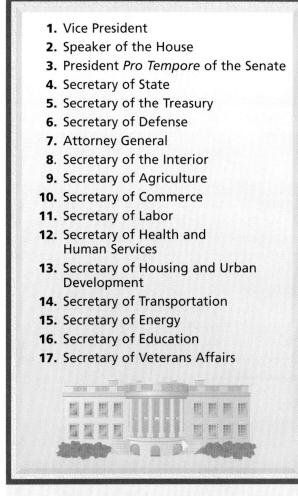

Presidential Succession

1. Vice President
2. Speaker of the House
3. President *Pro Tempore* of the Senate
4. Secretary of State
5. Secretary of the Treasury
6. Secretary of Defense
7. Attorney General
8. Secretary of the Interior
9. Secretary of Agriculture
10. Secretary of Commerce
11. Secretary of Labor
12. Secretary of Health and Human Services
13. Secretary of Housing and Urban Development
14. Secretary of Transportation
15. Secretary of Energy
16. Secretary of Education
17. Secretary of Veterans Affairs

The chart above lists the order of succession for the presidency if the president should die or resign. **Which cabinet member is fourth in line for the presidency?**

Constitution gives Congress the right to decide **presidential succession**, or who should fill the presidency and in what order. According to a law passed by Congress in 1947, presidential succession after the vice president is as follows: Speaker of the House of Representatives, president *pro tempore* of the Senate, and the members of the cabinet—in the order in which their departments were created.

If the president is succeeded by the vice president, who becomes the new vice president? Until 1967 no one did—the office remained empty until the next presidential election. In 1965, however, Congress proposed the Twenty-fifth Amendment, which the states ratified in 1967. The amendment provided for the president to nominate a new vice president.

The new law was tested six years later, when Vice President Spiro Agnew was forced to resign after he pled no contest to income tax evasion. It was later determined that he also had received illegal payoffs from construction company executives while he was governor of Maryland and vice president. President Richard Nixon nominated Gerald Ford to fill the office. When Nixon resigned later that same year as a result of Watergate, Ford became president. Ford nominated Nelson Rockefeller as his vice president, creating a situation in which neither the president nor the vice president was elected by the people. The nominee takes office only if approved by a majority vote of both houses of Congress. The Twenty-fifth Amendment also states that the vice president should serve as acting president if the president is too ill to serve.

SECTION 1 — REVIEW

1. Define the following terms: State of the Union Address, diplomacy, foreign policy, presidential succession.

2. Describe the president's role as representative of the nation. What are the other roles of the president?

3. What formal qualifications must a person fulfill to be president?

4. What are the terms and benefits of the presidency?

5. **Thinking and Writing Critically**
   Examine the chart on this page. Do you agree with the current order of presidential succession? If a president dies or resigns from office, should the vice president assume the presidency, or should a new presidential election be held? Explain your answers.

6. **Applying** POLITICAL FOUNDATIONS
   Conduct an Internet search for the White House's home page. Make a list of the information you find there.

PRESIDENTIAL POWERS

Political Dictionary

executive order
executive privilege
alliance
executive agreement
diplomatic recognition
reprieve
pardon
commutation

Objectives

★ What are the president's executive and foreign-policy powers?

★ What judicial and legislative powers does the president have?

★ How has presidential power grown over the years?

Many people believe that the president has the power to "run" the nation. This impression, however, is not shared by presidents themselves. Contemplating the transition of his successor, Dwight Eisenhower, from the military to the White House, President Truman said, "He'll sit here, and he'll say, 'Do this! Do that!' *And nothing will happen*. Poor Ike—it won't be a bit like the Army." President John F. Kennedy liked to quote William Shakespeare's play *Henry IV*, in which one character boasts, "I can call spirits from the vasty deep," to which another replies, "Why so can I, or so can any man; But will they come when you do call them?"

Presidents may have felt so limited partly because it is Congress that makes the laws. The president's role regarding domestic policy is often merely to try to influence the legislature. As you will learn, however, the president does have decisive and far-reaching foreign-policy powers, and presidential power has grown over the years. In addition, as Chapter 9 explains, the president has the power to influence U.S. economic policy through his or her recommendations regarding the nation's spending plan.

Executive Powers

The president's executive powers are simple and yet far-reaching. They include carrying out laws and appointing officials. Presidents also have claimed an additional power, executive privilege.

Executing Laws Article II, Section 3, of the Constitution states that the president "shall take care that the laws be faithfully executed." This simple phrase gives the president great powers. Because laws passed by Congress are generally quite broad, the president has a great deal of freedom in interpreting how to carry out and enforce them.

One way that the president exercises this power is by issuing **executive orders**—detailed instructions, regulations, and rules that state how to carry out and enforce legislation. Executive orders have the force of law.

Appointing Officials The president's executive powers also include appointing officials. As the

CONSTITUTIONAL GOVERNMENT *Madeleine Albright, the first woman to be appointed secretary of state, was sworn into office on January 24, 1997.* **What constitutional power does Congress have over the president's cabinet appointments?**

Constitution states, the president "shall nominate, and, by and with the advice and consent of the Senate, shall appoint ambassadors, other public ministers, and consuls, judges of the Supreme Court, and all other officers of the United States, whose appointments are not herein otherwise provided for." By appointing people to fill key positions in government, the president can influence the government's priorities and policies.

The president's appointment power is limited to key officials, such as the heads of the major executive departments and agencies and other policy-making officials. Most federal employees are hired under a civil service merit system, which is more fully explained in Chapter 8. Their jobs are out of reach of the president.

The president's appointment power is checked by the Senate, which confirms or rejects appointments of many high-level government officials. The Senate has used its power to refuse presidential appointments only rarely.

Executive Privilege Perhaps the most controversial executive power is the president's occasional refusal to give Congress information that it has requested. Although the term was first used in 1955, presidents since George Washington have based such refusals on the idea of **executive privilege**, or the president's right not to hand over documents or to testify regarding matters that he or she believes are the executive branch's confidential business.

The most dramatic case of executive privilege happened during the Watergate investigation in 1973. When the Senate began investigating the case, President Richard Nixon claimed executive privilege, announcing that none of his aides would be allowed to testify before the Senate Watergate Committee. Afterward, when the Senate learned of the existence of tape recordings of White House meetings, Nixon again claimed executive privilege and refused to hand over the tapes. After a nearly one-year struggle, the Supreme Court ruled that executive privilege did not apply in the case and that Nixon must hand over the tapes.

The debate over executive privilege continues. Some argue that certain matters, such as delicate negotiations with foreign countries, often must be kept secret. Others, however, believe that Congress must have access to all the material it needs to oversee agencies and to write legislation.

From *Herblock Special Report* (W.W. Norton, 1974). Reprinted by permission.

March 27, 1973

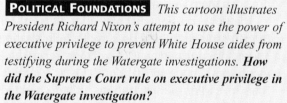

POLITICAL FOUNDATIONS *This cartoon illustrates President Richard Nixon's attempt to use the power of executive privilege to prevent White House aides from testifying during the Watergate investigations.* **How did the Supreme Court rule on executive privilege in the Watergate investigation?**

Diplomatic Powers

Although many officials in the Department of State and other agencies help conduct U.S. foreign policy, the president is the main person responsible for the nation's foreign policy. The president has assumed this leading role partly because of the speed with which foreign-policy decisions must be made, particularly during crises. A large body such as Congress, by requiring debate and majority agreement, would on the other hand move too slowly to handle many foreign-policy situations.

Making Treaties With the advice and consent of the Senate, the president has the power to make treaties, or agreements, between the United States and other countries. Treaties include peace agreements to end wars and trade agreements that set up economic ties and terms of trade. Another kind

Linking

Government and Journalism

The President and the Media

Few photographs exist of President Franklin D. Roosevelt in a wheelchair. Yet the president, who contracted polio when he was 39 years old, relied on a wheelchair to move around. Roosevelt disliked being photographed in his wheelchair, and the press respected his wishes. "There was an unspoken code of honor" among members of the press, writes historian Doris Kearns Goodwin.

At the time, most people did not know that President Roosevelt was in a wheelchair. Why did the press hold to this "unspoken code"? Roosevelt had a good working relationship with the press, in part because he held frequent press conferences. Members of the press respected his wishes, and he provided them with information for their stories.

The news media today play a far different role than they did during the Roosevelt administration. The actions and personal lives of more recent presidents have been much more closely examined than in earlier administrations. What changed? The Watergate break-in, which led to President Richard M. Nixon's resignation, was perhaps the single event that changed the relationship between the media and the president. Investigative journalism, a technique popularized by reporters who exposed the Watergate scandal, often focuses on uncovering negative stories about the lives of high-level officials.

Is this justified? How much does the public have the right to know about the nation's president? These are highly debated questions in today's media-focused world. Television news and newspaper headlines are the public's foremost sources of knowledge about the president. This information helps shape the public's view of the president and opinions on issues. During his administrations, President Bill Clinton has been plagued by stories on Whitewater, Travelgate, and his use of the White House for campaign fundraising. These stories have portrayed the president in less than favorable ways. Some people say

President Ronald Reagan speaks to members of the press on the lawn at the White House.

that the media focus too much attention on the personal lives of presidents when providing this information. Others argue that the job of the media is to act as a watchdog over political leaders.

As the public has gained greater access to information about the activities of the president, the relationship between the president and the media has become less friendly and respectful. Presidents have argued that the media's coverage is too critical, and the media claim that the public has a right to know what the president is doing.

In spite of these criticisms, the president does receive many benefits from media coverage. Increased access to media has allowed recent presidents to influence public support for their policy agendas, for example. In addition, major television coverage of the presidential speeches allows the president to publicly announce his or her legislative agenda for the year. During times of crisis, the president can use the media as a tool to rally the public's support. In essence, the media enable the president to establish a relationship with the public.

What Do You Think?

1. Do you think the public has a right to know information about the president's personal life? Explain your answer.
2. Do you think that the media place too much emphasis on negative stories? Why?

Military Powers

The Constitution states that only Congress can declare war. As commander in chief of the armed forces, however, the president may send U.S. forces anywhere in the world that there is danger to the United States. In this role the president may order troops, warships, and fighter planes to faraway places. The president also makes recommendations to Congress about the military's size and equipment needs. In the 1990s, for example, President Clinton recommended to Congress that the numbers of U.S. soldiers, naval vessels, and long-range bombers be reduced.

WORLD AFFAIRS *President Richard Nixon and Soviet president Leonid Brezhnev signed the SALT treaty in 1972.* **For what reason might a president sign a treaty with another country?**

of treaty forms **alliances**—agreements between two or more countries to help each other for defense, economic, scientific, or other reasons.

Making Executive Agreements Not all issues among countries need be worked out through treaties, however. The president and the leader of a foreign government may arrange a more informal understanding, or **executive agreement**. These agreements cover a variety of areas such as educational and scientific exchange programs, joint economic ventures, and economic assistance. In 1995, for example, through an executive agreement with Mexican president Ernesto Zedillo, President Clinton arranged for a loan of $20 billion to Mexico.

The use of executive agreements has grown in recent years in part because they allow presidents to make foreign policy without going through Congress's slow-moving treaty approval process. Congress needs only to be officially notified of the agreement within 60 days.

Recognizing Countries The president also has the right to establish **diplomatic recognition**, or to determine whether the United States officially recognizes a government as the proper representative of its country's people. To recognize a foreign country means to set up official relations with that nation's government.

Committing Troops Presidents have committed U.S. soldiers to foreign duty for many reasons. In 1992 President George Bush sent U.S. troops to Somalia to help keep the peace and pass out food to starving people. In 1994 President Clinton sent soldiers to Haiti to help restore democracy in that country. These situations involved little in the way of conventional warfare.

War Powers Act Presidents have, however, sent U.S. troops into battle—in Korea, Vietnam, and many smaller conflicts. Though they were not declared wars, these conflicts involved all of the costs of a declared war, including sending soldiers into combat. As a result, Congress has sometimes challenged presidential power to commit U.S. soldiers to battle. Presidents have responded by saying that their authority to do so stems from their constitutional powers as commander in chief.

Congress pressed the issue, however, and in 1973 passed the War Powers Act. This act requires that soldiers sent abroad by the president be brought back within 60 days unless Congress approves the action. This time may be extended to 90 days if needed to ensure the safe removal of U.S. troops. Some critics of the act argue that it gives the president a power not stated in nor intended by the Constitution—the power to conduct undeclared war for 60 to 90 days without congressional approval. Others believe that the act

Careers in Government

The Military

Many young people—men and women alike—find a rewarding career in the military. In 1775, when George Washington took command of the country's first army, soldiers learned to load muskets and fire cannons. In contrast, today's military is one of computer-operated tanks and sophisticated jet fighters. Although combat preparedness is still a major aspect of military training, today's military jobs also include those requiring technical expertise in fields such as communications, electronics, and medicine. The role of the military—to defend the nation—remains unchanged, however.

Military personnel at the Satellite Operation Center near Denver, Colorado, keep an eye on missiles around the world.

The U.S. armed forces is made up of five branches—the Army, Navy, Air Force, Marine Corps, and Coast Guard. Each branch employs personnel in occupations that range from meteorology to equipment maintenance. Military employees are provided with specialized, complex training, and each branch has its own training programs.

An enlistee is trained in one of the more than 2,000 military occupation specialties, which include such jobs as rocket specialist, air traffic controller, emergency medical technician, illustrator, and computer programmer. Enlistees enter the armed forces by enrolling in a branch of the military. Many enlisted men and women enter the military after graduating from high school.

Military officers, however, are usually college educated. Officers in all branches of the military

except the Coast Guard can train in the Reserve Officer Training Corps (ROTC), which is offered at colleges and universities. Graduates completing the four-year ROTC program leave college as officers. Officers in all branches are trained to perform functions such as combat leadership, technical support in electronics and computers, and military intelligence.

Military officers also may train at one of the country's five service academies—the U.S. Military Academy, the U.S. Air Force Academy, the U.S. Naval Academy, the U.S. Coast Guard Academy, and the U.S. Merchant Marine Academy—all of which are now open to women. In addition, Officer Candidate School (OCS) and state-controlled military schools, such as the Citadel and Virginia Military Institute, provide officer training.

---

was necessary, however, to limit the president's powers as commander in chief.

In fact, the act did not end the debate over committing U.S. troops. In 1991 President Bush sent U.S. soldiers to the Persian Gulf to lead a ground and air attack on Iraq, which had invaded its neighbor Kuwait in late 1990. American troops, along with troops from several other countries, defeated Iraq and won back Kuwait's independence. Some people criticized the Persian Gulf operation because it took place without Congress's having issued a declaration of war. Others have pointed out,

however, that Bush did meet with Congress about sending U.S. troops to the area and that Congress issued a statement supporting the operation.

Judicial Powers

As you know, the Constitution gives the president the power to appoint Supreme Court justices with the approval of the Senate. How much influence does this power give presidents over the Court? Conservative presidents do tend to appoint justices with conservative ideals, just as liberal presidents tend to appoint justices with liberal ideals. Once on the Court bench, however, justices often stray from these labels. Several presidents have been dismayed when one of their Court appointees handed down a decision that was the opposite of what they expected it to be. Supreme Court justices, unlike other presidential appointees, cannot be removed from office by the president once they are seated. Thus, the appointment power does not place Supreme Court justices under presidential control.

The president's judicial powers also include the appointment of all other federal judges, and granting reprieves, pardons, and commutations. A **reprieve** postpones the carrying out of a person's sentence. It allows a convicted person to gather more evidence or to appeal for a new trial. Reprieves often are granted in death penalty cases. A **pardon** grants forgiveness to a convicted criminal and frees the person from serving out his or her sentence. A **commutation** lessens the severity of a convicted person's sentence.

Legislative Powers

In addition to the preceding executive powers, the president also holds several legislative powers. He or she can influence congressional action by recommending legislation, vetoing legislation, and lobbying congressional members.

Recommending Legislation According to the Constitution, only members of Congress may actually introduce bills. Congress and the public, however, have come to expect the president to play a key role in setting the legislative agenda. For example, President Woodrow Wilson presented to Congress a legislative reform program that he called the "New Freedom." Among the proposed reforms were the lowering of a high protective tariff and the creation of the Federal Reserve system.

The State of the Union Address has become the president's major opportunity for proposing a

POLITICAL PROCESSES *President George Bush meets with U.S. soldiers in Saudi Arabia during Operation Desert Storm in 1990.* **What restrictions does the War Powers Act place on the president's power to send soldiers abroad?**

legislative program. This speech tends to outline the president's priorities in broad terms. The details of the legislative program usually are contained in the president's annual budget, which proposes how much money government will spend and on what programs. (The president's role in the budget process is more fully explained in Chapter 9.)

Vetoing Legislation The veto power is largely a preventive measure. It does not enable the president to produce legislation, but it can help undo laws with which he or she disagrees. Because vetoes are difficult to override, the president can sometimes use the threat of a veto to pressure Congress into modifying a bill. In addition, as noted in Chapter 6, the line-item veto increases the president's power by allowing him or her to veto certain parts of a spending bill without vetoing the entire measure. As noted in Chapter 6, however, the constitutionality of the line-item veto had yet to be ruled on by the Supreme Court by mid-1997.

Lobbying Presidents lobby members of Congress on behalf of certain bills by making personal telephone calls and by inviting members of Congress to the White House. Presidential lobbying typically takes place just before final floor consideration—

POLITICAL PROCESSES *Speaker of the House Newt Gingrich, President Bill Clinton, and Senator Bob Dole meet at the White House to discuss the problems with the federal budget.* **How does the president work to gain the support of members of Congress for certain programs and policies?**

particularly if the count is so close that a handful of votes could make the difference. Of course, some presidents have used this power more than others. President Lyndon Johnson, for example, called members frequently. In fact, he once called to lobby a senator at 2:30 A.M. Johnson began the conversation by asking how the member was doing. "I was just lying here waiting for you to call me, Mr. President," came the sarcastic reply.

Sometimes a president will offer support or threaten to withhold support for a project that is crucial to a member's district in order to pressure the person into backing a particular bill. More often, however, presidential lobbying involves wooing, not threatening. For example, Donald Regan, a close adviser to President Ronald Reagan, described the president's lobbying efforts by saying that "the President never bullied, never threatened, never cajoled [sweet-talked]. It was always: Let me explain why I'm for this bill, and I hope that we can count on your vote."

Growth of Presidential Power

As noted in Chapter 3, many of the delegates to the Constitutional Convention believed that executive power was necessary for effective government, but they feared creating an executive that was too strong. As a result, they placed several

checks on the president's powers. Nonetheless, the power of the presidency has grown—in large part because of the individuals who have held the office.

Early Presidents President George Washington, determined to establish the new government's role as representative of the American people, set out to make the president a symbol of federal authority. During 1794's Whiskey Rebellion, when a ragtag band of farmers in western Pennsylvania rose up to oppose a federal tax on liquor, Washington himself accompanied more than 12,000 militia partway to the scene of the rebellion. This display of military might was meant to show how much force the president could summon to ensure that people obey federal laws.

BORN TO COMMAND.

OF VETO MEMORY.

HAD I BEEN CONSULTED.

KING ANDREW THE FIRST.

The Granger Collection, New York

CONSTITUTIONAL GOVERNMENT *Some presidents have pushed their power to the limits of what the Constitution allows. In this cartoon, published in 1832, President Andrew Jackson is portrayed as a royal leader with little respect for the Constitution.* **Why is it important that Congress and the Supreme Court check the president's power?**

The third president, Thomas Jefferson, was the model of the president as a strong executive. This was unexpected of a man who had earlier expressed concerns about the power of the office. One way that Jefferson increased presidential power was through foreign affairs. In 1801, for example, he sent U.S. naval ships to the Mediterranean Sea to take action against the Barbary pirates, who were demanding that U.S. commercial vessels pay increasing amounts of money to sail along northern Africa without being attacked. Some regard Jefferson's action as the first example of an undeclared presidential war.

In addition, Jefferson acted beyond the expressed powers of government when he bought the Louisiana Territory from France in 1803. First, the Constitution does not mention any power to purchase foreign lands. Second, Jefferson signed an agreement to buy the territory before he got congressional approval to make the purchase. Jefferson defended his action by arguing that if he had not acted swiftly, France might have retracted its offer to sell the territory.

President Andrew Jackson cast himself as a champion of the common citizen in his campaign against the Bank of the United States. Declaring the bank a symbol of economic privilege, Jackson vetoed congressional legislation intended to renew the bank's charter and made the bank an issue in the presidential election. "Never before," wrote two political analysts, "had a chief executive gone to the people over the heads of their elected legislators." This image of the president as representative of the people has become a defining part of the presidency today.

The Modern Presidency

Modern presidents have used frequent speeches and media attention to try to reach the people. One of the earliest presidents to do so was Theodore Roosevelt. Roosevelt took advantage of these tools, traveling around the country making direct appeals to the public on legislation. The press covered his

POLITICAL PROCESSES *President Theodore Roosevelt frequently made speeches and used the press during his presidency.* **How have the media helped to shape the image of modern presidents?**

speeches, thus further drawing the public's attention to Roosevelt's ideas. Presidents ever since have followed Roosevelt's path.

Woodrow Wilson might be considered the first president to act the way that someone living today expects a president to act. For the most part, Wilson merely extended techniques Roosevelt had used. He lobbied Congress directly, installing a telephone line between the White House and Congress, and held regular press conferences. In addition, as you read earlier, Wilson proposed an entire legislative program to Congress.

President Franklin D. Roosevelt went on to refine the techniques that were used by Theodore Roosevelt and Woodrow Wilson. He took advantage of the technology of radio by broadcasting "fireside chats" to Americans. In addition, Roosevelt proposed the most thorough legislative agenda in U.S. history to try to bring the country out of the Great Depression. One result of Roosevelt's actions was a tremendous increase in public interest in the president and his ideas. This increased public response shows that the president was becoming the focus of attention in the political system.

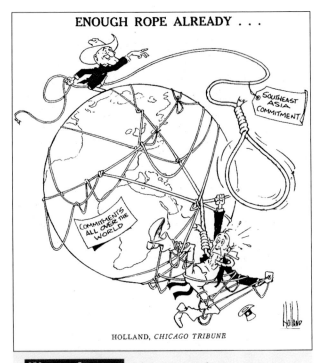

ENOUGH ROPE ALREADY . . .

SOUTHEAST ASIA COMMITMENT

COMMITMENTS ALL OVER THE WORLD

HOLLAND, *CHICAGO TRIBUNE*

WORLD AFFAIRS *The cartoon above comments on President Lyndon B. Johnson's decision to commit U.S. troops abroad.* **What does this cartoon say about the consequences of that decision?**

The Imperial Presidency Many people began to fear that the power of the presidency was expanding dangerously during the presidencies of Lyndon Johnson and Richard Nixon in the 1960s and early 1970s. Both of these presidents, for example, committed thousands of U.S. soldiers in the undeclared war in Vietnam, initially without congressional approval. The use of such seemingly unrestrained power led many people to claim that the office had become "the imperial presidency." (Congress did, however, approve the funds for these troops after they had been sent.)

Concerns over presidential power peaked with the Watergate case, in which President Nixon helped cover up the illegal break-in of Democratic Party headquarters by members of his own re-election committee. Nixon resigned to avoid facing impeachment charges for abusing the powers of the presidency.

The Presidency Today Distrust of the president and of government in general certainly remains higher than before the events of the 1960s and 1970s. This distrust is reflected in an increase in the number of investigations of government actions. Investigations such as the Iran-contra affair, Whitewater, and Travelgate regularly splash across newspaper headlines.

Some people argue that the search for acts of government wrongdoing has become a thin disguise for political witch-hunts, distracting the president and Congress from their duties. Still, such investigations act as a vital check on government power. Despite the many accusations and investigations that have tarnished its image, the presidency remains the focus of the U.S. political system and the most powerful office in the world.

SECTION 2 — REVIEW

1. Define the following terms: executive order, executive privilege, alliance, executive agreement, diplomatic recognition, reprieve, pardon, commutation.

2. What are the president's executive powers? Why is executive privilege such a source of controversy?

3. What diplomatic and military powers does the president hold? Why did Congress pass the War Powers Act?

4. How can the president influence the judiciary? Congress?

5. Describe how Woodrow Wilson helped establish the modern presidency. What changes took place in Franklin D. Roosevelt's presidency?

6. **Thinking and Writing Critically** Do you think the presidency has become too powerful an office? Are there enough checks on presidential power? Explain your answers.

7. **Applying** **CONSTITUTIONAL GOVERNMENT** Why might investigations of White House actions affect people's trust in government? Name some examples of these investigations. Do they affect your opinion of the presidency?

PRESIDENTIAL NOMINATION AND ELECTION

Political Dictionary

nominate
electoral college
elector
caucus
convention
primary election
general election
party platform
plank
popular vote
plurality

Objectives

★ What is the electoral college?
★ How are presidential candidates chosen?
★ How are convention delegates chosen?
★ What is the format for conventions?

Have you made up your mind about running for president? Even if you fulfill the formal qualifications listed in Section 1, you must leap one more hurdle to become an official candidate—securing your party's nomination.

Nominating candidates—proposing people to run for an elective office—is the first step in the process of choosing the president. The Constitution makes no mention of how presidential candidates should be nominated. While the framers did design a system for choosing the nation's president and vice president, they did not anticipate how the U.S. political system would develop.

Electoral College

When first discussing how the president would be selected, the framers found themselves in disagreement. Some believed that the president should be selected by popular vote, while others thought that Congress should choose the president. The system finally agreed upon was the **electoral college**—a special body made up of people selected by each of the states—which votes for the president and vice president. (See the chart below for a description of how the framers intended the electoral college to work.)

In the Constitution, the framers planned for each **elector**—or electoral college member—to cast two ballots. One ballot, or electoral vote, had to be cast for a person who was not a resident of the elector's state. The person who received the majority (more than half) of the votes was president, and the person who received the next-highest number of votes

The Original Plan of the Electoral College

1. Each state has the same number of electors as it has senators and representatives.

2. In their respective states, electors vote for two candidates—one of whom may not be a resident of the electors' home state.

3. A list of these candidates is presented to Congress, and the number of votes for each candidate is counted.

4. The person who wins the majority of electoral votes becomes president.

5. The person having the second-greatest number of electoral votes becomes the vice president.

6. If two candidates tie for first place in the electoral vote, or if no candidate wins a majority of the votes, the president is chosen by the House of Representatives, with each state having one vote.

7. If a tie occurs for second place, the Senate chooses the vice president.

CONSTITUTIONAL GOVERNMENT *The framers' original plan for the electoral college was changed by the Twelfth Amendment.* **What were the flaws of the original plan?**

would be the vice president. Each state had as many electoral votes as it had members of Congress.

The first two elections under the plan worked smoothly—George Washington was unanimously elected twice. As political parties developed during the 1790s, however, the system began to show flaws.

Instead of electors each selecting the person they considered to be best for the job, they began nominating only members of their own political party. The rules governing the electoral college did not account for this change, which led to some difficult situations. During the election of 1796, for example, Thomas Jefferson lost to John Adams by only three electoral votes. He thus became Adams's vice president, despite the fact that they were members of rival parties.

By the election of 1800 the lines between political parties were firmly drawn in the electoral college. Thus, the electors, who were chosen according to their party affiliation, voted exclusively for their own party's candidates in the election.

During the election of 1800, a majority of the electors chosen were members of the Democratic-Republican Party. When they voted, they chose, per electoral college rules, two people—Thomas Jefferson and Aaron Burr. Jefferson was the party's choice for president, and Burr the party's choice for vice president.

Because each elector cast one ballot for Jefferson and one for Burr, however, Burr and Jefferson were tied. Following the Constitution, the election was then thrown to the House of Representatives, which tied 35 times before its members finally chose Jefferson as president and Burr as vice president. To prevent such a situation in the future, Congress passed and the states ratified the Twelfth Amendment in 1803–04. The amendment stated that the president and vice president would be elected with separate ballots. It did not, however, change any other part of the electoral college.

Nomination Procedures

As you have read, the framers did not establish a system for nominating the presidential and vice presidential candidates, only for electing them once nominated. For this reason, the process for nominating candidates has changed a great deal throughout U.S. history.

The Granger Collection, New York

POLITICAL PROCESSES *In 1800 Thomas Jefferson (right) was chosen as president, and Aaron Burr (left) as vice president, after 35 tie votes by the House of Representatives.*
What major change did the Twelfth Amendment make to the original plan?

Early Nominating Procedures During the early 1800s, the parties chose presidential candidates in congressional caucuses. A **caucus** is a meeting of people, such as members of a political party, who gather to make decisions on political courses of action. These meetings, which went on behind closed doors, were criticized by many voters, who believed them to be unrepresentative. For this reason, the states replaced the congressional caucus as a means of nominating presidential candidates by the 1820s. (Caucuses are more fully explained in Chapter 19.)

Conventions The death of the caucus led to the rise of another means of nominating presidential candidates—**conventions**. These party gatherings are held to nominate candidates, determine rules that govern the party, and make decisions about the party's stance on issues of the day. The first one held—a National Republican Convention—nominated John Quincy Adams in 1828. In the election of 1832, all three parties in the running used a national convention to nominate presidential and vice presidential candidates. The procedure is still used today.

Conventions are attended by delegates—people elected or appointed to select a party's candidates. Delegates generally are selected through one of two means—presidential primaries or state caucuses.

Presidential Primaries

As you have read, conventions are now used for nominating presidential candidates. Before the national conventions are held, however, most states hold presidential primary elections to determine who will be the convention delegates. **Primary elections** are elections held before the general election that determine the candidates for each party. After the national conventions, voters actually choose officials in a **general election**.

Presidential primaries generally serve two functions: to select delegates to the convention, as mentioned above, and to show voters' preferences for presidential candidates. In some states the primaries serve only one of these functions; in others they serve both. It is important for candidates to know what kind of primary a state holds, as it may affect how candidates spend their campaign time and resources.

In some states' presidential primaries, party members vote for their choice of presidential candidates only. Delegates to the national convention are awarded to the candidates, based on the results of the primary. This system is called a "binding presidential preference" system. In states with "beauty-contest" primaries, voters choose their favorite candidate, but actual selection of the delegates to represent each candidate takes place independently. In yet other states with "delegate selection" systems, voters choose only the delegates to the convention, without indicating which candidate the delegates will support.

POLITICAL PROCESSES *President Bill Clinton and Vice President Al Gore accepted their bid for a second term in office at the Democratic National Convention in 1996.* **What role do national conventions play in the nominating process?**

Finally, in some states voters express both a preference for presidential candidate and vote for a slate of delegates. These states include New Jersey, Pennsylvania, Vermont, West Virginia, and Illinois.

Some states award delegates to candidates based on the percentage of the votes the candidates receive in the primary. For example, in Kentucky, the top four candidates who have at least 15 percent of the vote are awarded a certain percentage of the delegates.

In just a few states—West Virginia, Illinois, Pennsylvania, and New Jersey—the candidate who receives the greatest percentage of the votes receives all of that state's delegates at the national convention. In these "winner-take-all" states, a candidate can actually win less than half of the votes and still win all of the delegates for that state. For example, if there are three top candidates, and one receives 40 percent of the vote, another 35 percent of the vote, and the third 25 percent of the vote, even though the top candidate won only 40 percent of the vote, he or she still gets all of that state's delegates at the convention.

Caucuses

Some states hold party caucuses instead of or in addition to presidential primaries. (Some states also hold local or state conventions.) Caucuses usually originate at the local level. These meetings are held on the same day at places around the state and are open to any party supporter. Many states, however, have systems that hold additional caucuses at the county, congressional district, and state level before making final decisions on candidates. The caucuses also elect delegates to the national convention.

Turnout in caucuses is lower than in primaries because people often need to stay an entire evening to participate in a caucus meeting but only a few minutes to vote in a primary. State law, not convenience, however, determines whether the parties choose presidential convention delegates by primary or by caucus.

The Nominating Season

The presidential nominating season usually starts with caucuses in early February of each presidential election year and ends with the last primaries in early June. Some states begin their nomination process earlier than others do, and the order is important. The decisions of voters and financial contributors in states with primaries later in the year may be affected by the results of earlier primaries. The front-loading of primaries—the scheduling of primaries early in the year—can therefore have a great effect on the outcome of the election. The momentum gained in winning or making a strong showing in early primaries—even in small states with few electoral votes—can boost a candidate to the front of the pack. Likewise, a poor showing weeds out many candidates early in the game.

Over time, front-loading has become increasingly significant. States such as California, once proud because their June primaries gave the candidates the last chance to face off against one another, began to see their primaries become unimportant because front-loading had already determined a winner. As a result, in 1996 California and several other states moved up their presidential primary dates to March.

POLITICAL PROCESSES *Citizens of Runnells, Iowa, meet at the local fire station to vote in a caucus for the presidential election.* **Why are primaries generally better attended than caucuses?**

Indeed, understanding the importance of early momentum, presidential candidates have been looking for increasingly earlier chances to gain victories. Some people, hoping to shorten presidential nomination contests, have proposed holding a national primary on a single day.

National Conventions

Though the candidates for each party may already be determined after the primaries, it is at the national party conventions where the candidates are officially chosen. Party conventions are gigantic, boisterous events filled with tradition. The only formal business of a convention is nominating presidential and vice presidential candidates and agreeing on the party's views on issues of the day. Conventions, however, also try to unify the party for the coming campaign through informal events and party-oriented rallies. As a result, many conventions take on a carnival-like atmosphere. Delegates and other attendees wear festive, multicolored hats and carry signs; members of the party make rousing speeches; and music and balloons fill the air.

Still, the conventions do have official party business to conduct. The format of the convention includes opening speeches, the adoption of a party platform, floor demonstrations, and a state-by-state roll call for the presidential and vice presidential nominations.

Speeches Conventions at times can seem like one long speech. Influential figures in the party give speeches about the party and about the broad themes that the party supports. The most important speech is that of the keynote speaker, who presents the themes that the party will feature in the forthcoming presidential campaign.

Party Platform The biggest controversy at conventions generally centers around approving the **party platform**, or the party's positions on issues of the day. The platform is made up of several **planks**—each of which represents the party's position on a single issue.

Platforms often lead to bitter disagreement among groups within a party—as the abortion issue has among conservatives and moderates in the Republican Party. Party leaders generally attempt to settle disagreements before the convention, both to keep delegates from bickering on prime-time

POLITICAL PROCESSES *General Colin Powell spoke at the 1996 Republican Convention.* **How do political parties use national conventions to promote party unity?**

television and to keep the party from appearing splintered. Sometimes, however, the conflicts make their way into the convention. Finally, delegates vote on whether to adopt the party platform.

Floor Demonstrations At one time, conventioneers held spontaneous demonstrations on behalf of their candidates. Now, however, these demonstrations are carefully planned, with exuberant music and a display of floating balloons. Party leaders strictly control the length of floor demonstrations to keep them from interfering with other events the party wants to have broadcast on prime-time television.

State-by-State Roll Call Though the balloting for the nomination of presidential and vice presidential candidates could be done much more quickly by computer, the state-by-state roll call of the delegates is one tradition that has lasted. Each state's party leader is called upon one at a time, at which point he or she announces how the state's vote will be distributed.

Some states require that the state's primary winner receive all of the state's delegates. Others allow their delegates to be split among two or more candidates. In any case, a candidate must receive over 50 percent of the convention's votes to become the party's nominee. If no candidate receives this high a percentage on the first ballot, additional ballots are taken until a majority candidate emerges.

CASE STUDY

Conventions: From Proving Ground to Media Event

POLITICAL PROCESSES National conventions were once a place where several of a party's candidates could present themselves and explain their positions before the convention delegates. In fact, for most of the history of conventions, the nomination of the party's presidential candidate was undetermined at the convention's start—except in the case of an incumbent president running for re-election, who was usually renominated. For many years, most delegates were more loyal to local party leaders than to a certain candidate. In an era leaders had little contact with one another before the convention. Thus, it was at the conventions where these leaders would compromise with one another to gain a majority for one candidate.

It often took numerous ballots before a majority of delegates could agree on a candidate. Have you ever heard of Champ Clark? He was the front-runner entering the Democratic convention of 1912. On the forty-sixth ballot, however, he lost to Woodrow Wilson. At the Democratic convention of 1924, it took 103 ballots to nominate John Davis. It generally took the Democrats more ballots than it did Republicans because until 1936 the Democrats required a two-thirds convention majority for nomination.

Since 1952, however, neither party has taken more than one ballot to nominate a candidate. Airplane travel and inexpensive long-distance telephone service have made it easier for local party leaders to discuss the possible nominees before reaching the convention floor. In addition, today the vast majority of delegates are elected in primaries that determine their votes. No longer decision-making bodies, conventions thus have become coronations of the candidate who led in the primaries and caucuses, as well as a launching pad for the general election campaign. They are designed to give favorable media exposure to the candidate and to the party's platform.

POLITICAL PROCESSSES *Delegates count votes for the nomination of Bob Dole and Jack Kemp at the 1996 Republican National Convention in San Diego, California.* **What percentage of votes must a candidate receive to become a party's nominee?**

The Election

Once the candidates are chosen, they campaign for several months until the election, which is held on the first Tuesday after the first Monday in November. This period is filled with speechmaking, personal appearances, and other campaigning by the

Comparing Popular and Electoral Votes

WINNER DID NOT RECEIVE THE MOST POPULAR VOTES

Year	Candidate	Popular Vote	Electoral Vote
1824	* John Quincy Adams	105,321	84
	Andrew Jackson	155,872	99
	Other Candidates	90,869	78
1876	* Rutherford B. Hayes	4,033,950	185
	Samuel Tilden	4,284,757	184
1888	Benjamin Harrison	5,444,337	233
	Grover Cleveland	5,540,050	168

CLOSE POPULAR VOTE

Year	Candidate	Popular Vote	Electoral Vote
1884	Grover Cleveland	4,911,017	219
	James G. Blaine	4,848,334	182
1960	John F. Kennedy	34,227,096	303
	Richard M. Nixon	34,108,546	219
	* Harry F. Byrd		15
1968	Richard M. Nixon	31,785,480	301
	Hubert H. Humphrey	31,275,166	191
	George C. Wallace	9,906,473	46
1976	Jimmy Carter	40,828,929	297
	Gerald R. Ford	39,148,940	240

* 1824—Elected by the House of Representatives because no candidate won a majority

1876—An electoral commission set up to rule on contested election results in three states gave Hayes the presidency.

1960—Received electoral votes but no popular votes

Source: *The World Almanac*

According to the rules of the electoral college, a presidential candidate can win without the most popular votes. The popular vote in several presidential races has been very close. **Does the electoral vote always reflect the popular vote?**

candidates. (The process of political campaigning is more fully explained in Chapter 19.) Finally, on election day, citizens go to the polls to vote for the candidate of their choice—or do they?

Electoral College and the Popular Vote As you have learned, U.S. voters do not cast their votes directly for the president and vice president. Instead, the **popular votes**—votes cast by the general public—are cast for slates of electors who are pledged to the candidates for whom

people wish to vote. Candidates who receive a **plurality**—or most—of the popular votes receive all of that state's electoral votes. For this reason, a close national popular vote may still result in one candidate's winning a large majority of the electoral votes.

Criticisms of the Electoral College In all but three elections, the winner of the national popular vote has been elected president. The fact that the electoral college system allows a candidate

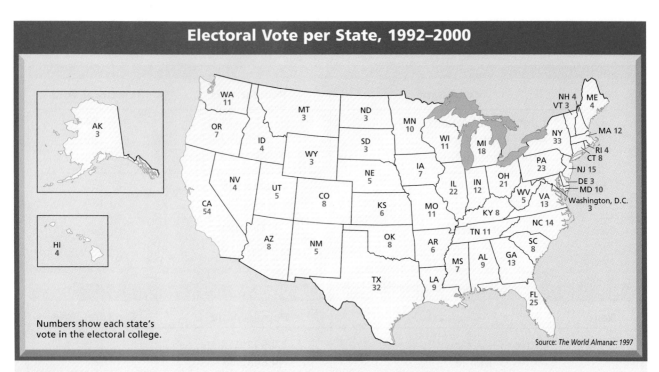

Electoral Vote per State, 1992–2000

Numbers show each state's vote in the electoral college.

Source: *The World Almanac: 1997*

States get the same number of electoral votes as their representation in Congress.
Which state has the greatest number of electoral votes?

who did not receive the most popular votes to win an election, however, has caused many people to criticize the electoral college.

Other criticisms of the college also have arisen. Some people are wary of the fact that the electors are not required to vote for the candidate to whom they are pledged, making it possible for the electoral college to disregard the popular vote (although this happens very rarely). In addition, many people feel that the electoral college system is weak because a strong bid by a third-party or an independent candidate might prevent either major-party candidate from winning a majority. In such a case, the House of Representatives—instead of the people through their electors—would decide the election. Although there have been suggestions for revising or eliminating the electoral college to address the criticisms that have been voiced, elections are still decided by electoral votes.

SECTION 3 — REVIEW

1. Define the following terms: nominate, electoral college, elector, caucus, convention, primary election, general election, party platform, plank, popular vote, plurality.

2. Why was it necessary for the framers to create the electoral college? How did they expect the electoral college to work?

3. How have the nomination procedures for presidential and vice presidential candidates changed over time?

4. How are delegates to national conventions selected?

5. **Thinking and Writing Critically**
Do you think the criticisms of the electoral college are valid? Why or why not?

6. **Applying** CONSTITUTIONAL GOVERNMENT
Imagine that you are one of the framers of the Constitution. How do you think the president and vice president should be selected? Briefly outline your reasoning.

CHAPTER 7 — SUMMARY

SECTION 1 The president plays a number of key roles, including chief executive, commander in chief, agenda setter, representative of the nation, chief of state, foreign-policy leader, and party leader. Some of these roles are outlined in the Constitution. Others have been assumed and expanded over the years by the presidential officeholders.

The formal qualifications for the presidency are few, but the benefits and responsibilities are great. The president serves a four-year term and may serve no more than two terms. The order of presidential succession is set by Congress.

SECTION 2 The president has decisive and far-reaching executive, diplomatic, and military powers, including executing laws, appointing officials, making treaties and executive agreements, recognizing foreign countries, and committing U.S. troops. The president also has key judicial and legislative powers. The latter allow the president to influence congressional legislation. All of these powers have grown greatly—in large part because of the people who have held the presidential office.

SECTION 3 The framers of the Constitution did not set a means for *nominating* presidential candidates, only for *choosing* the president and vice president.

Because the framers did not state *how* candidates would be nominated, nomination procedures have changed. Until the early 1800s the parties used congressional caucuses to nominate candidates for president and vice president. Parties later switched to national conventions to nominate candidates, a process still in use. Conventions are attended by delegates who are chosen by either presidential primary or caucus.

Depending on the state, presidential primaries generally serve two functions: choosing delegates for the conventions and showing voter preference. Some states hold caucuses that perform these functions as well.

In recent campaigns, an increasing number of presidential primaries and caucuses have been scheduled for early in the year, leading to a relatively quick elimination of the weaker candidates. For this reason, the candidates for both major parties generally are known long before the national conventions.

The format of the national conventions includes speeches, the adoption of a party platform, floor demonstrations, and a state roll call of votes for the candidates. The candidate who wins the nomination then campaigns for several months before the general election is held.

The electoral college, not the popular vote, actually chooses the president and vice president. The electoral college has been criticized for three primary reasons: that a candidate can win the election even if he or she does not win the popular vote, that a state's electoral votes do not have to reflect its popular vote, and that a strong bid by a third-party or independent candidate could mean that neither major-party candidate receives the majority of the electoral votes, throwing the election into the House of Representatives. These criticisms, however, have not led to reform of the electoral college system.

Government Notebook

Review what you wrote in your Government Notebook at the beginning of the chapter about the presidents you remember. Now that you have studied this chapter, can you find within your recollections any examples of the president's roles, qualifications, and powers? Record your answer in your Notebook.

CHAPTER 7

REVIEW

REVIEWING CONCEPTS

1. What are the benefits of being president? How long is a presidential term of office?

2. How are presidential and vice presidential candidates nominated?

3. What are the president's five main powers? Give an example of each.

4. Describe the roles of the president. Are any, in your opinion, more important than the others?

5. What qualifications must you have to run for president?

6. What is the electoral college? Why is it sometimes criticized?

THINKING AND WRITING CRITICALLY

1. **CONSTITUTIONAL GOVERNMENT** What amendment made it impossible for a president to serve more than two terms? Should presidents be allowed to serve more than two terms? Explain your answer.

2. **CONSTITUTIONAL GOVERNMENT** The Constitution gives the president the power to appoint government officials, with Senate approval. Do you think that this power gives the president too much influence on the government? Why or why not?

3. **POLITICAL PROCESSES** Why do you think the framers of the Constitution did not establish guidelines for nominating the president? Explain your answer.

4. **PUBLIC GOOD** What system for electing the president would better serve the public good: the electoral college system or a direct popular vote? Why?

CITIZENSHIP IN YOUR COMMUNITY

Each state follows a different schedule and system for selecting delegates to the presidential nominating conventions. Research the nominating system of your state. Create a brochure informing citizens about these procedures. Be sure to include information on how delegates are selected, when the nominating event is usually held, and the rules for placing third-party candidates on the ballot. You may want to include a chart illustrating how your state's system works.

INDIVIDUAL PORTFOLIO PROJECT

Imagine that you are an adviser to the top officials of a country that is planning to hold its first presidential election. The country's leaders want to use the office of the U.S. president as a model for its executive office. You have been asked to brief key government leaders on the role of the president in the U.S. political system. Write a report describing the roles and duties of the president. You may want to include examples of activities associated with each role.

THE INTERNET: LEARNING ONLINE

Conduct an Internet search for information about the president and vice president. For example, try to find the e-mail addresses for both the president and vice president, recent legislation signed by the president, and recent speeches given by the president or vice president.

You might start by using search words such as *president of the United States, U.S. vice president,* and *executive branch.* List the sources of information you find. Create a flyer with instructions on how to find information about the president and vice president on the Internet, making sure to include the Internet sites you visited.

PRACTICING SKILLS: UNDERSTANDING CHARTS AND GRAPHS

Study the line graph below, which illustrates the percentage of female delegates to national conventions between 1944 and 1992. Read the labels on the graph, and answer the questions below.

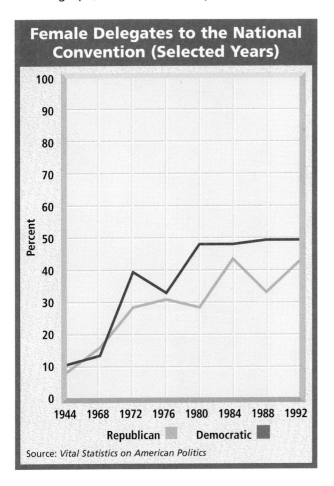

Female Delegates to the National Convention (Selected Years)

Source: *Vital Statistics on American Politics*

1. Which election year shows the greatest decrease in the percentage of female delegates to the Democratic convention?

2. In which two election years were more than 40 percent of the delegates to the Republican convention women?

3. Which party held a national convention with an equal number of male and female delegates? When did this convention take place?

PRESIDENT DWIGHT D. EISENHOWER'S FAREWELL ADDRESS

On January 17, 1961, President Eisenhower gave a Farewell Address in which he described his hopes for the future of the country. Read the following excerpt and answer the questions.

" *Throughout America's adventure in free government, our basic purposes have been to keep the peace, to foster progress in human achievement, and to enhance liberty, dignity, and integrity among people and among nations. . . .*

As we peer into society's future, we—you and I, and our government—must avoid the impulse to live only for today. . . . We cannot mortgage the material assets of our grandchildren without risking the loss also of their political and spiritual heritage. . . .

Down the long lane of the history yet to be written America knows that this world of ours, ever growing smaller, must avoid becoming a community of dreadful fear and hate, and be, instead, a proud confederation of mutual trust and respect. . .

. . . As one who has witnessed the horror and the lingering sadness of war—as one who knows that another war could utterly destroy this civilization which has been so slowly and painfully built over thousands of years—I wish I could say tonight that a lasting peace is in sight.

Happily, I can say that war has been avoided. Steady progress toward our ultimate goal has been made. But, so much remains to be done. As a private citizen, I shall never cease to do what little I can to help the world advance along that road. "

1. According to President Eisenhower, what are the basic purposes of American government?

2. What presidential responsibility did Eisenhower see as increasingly important?

3. What do you think Eisenhower meant when he said that the world is "even growing smaller"?

CHAPTER 8

EXECUTIVE BRANCH AT WORK

Is the orange juice in your refrigerator really orange juice? Thanks to the Food and Drug Administration (FDA), an agency in the executive branch, you can be sure that if a carton says it contains 100 percent orange juice, the product inside is indeed pure orange juice. If the product is less than 100 percent orange juice, the FDA requires that the total percentage of juice in the beverage be declared on the information panel on the container. Such a beverage may be called an orange juice drink, instead of orange juice.

Regulations like this affect almost every part of your daily life—from the food you eat to the clothes you wear to the compact disc player you buy. Among other things, regulations make sure that products are safe for you to use, that you are not discriminated against in the workplace, and that your savings deposits are insured. This chapter looks at how the executive branch is organized to meet these and other goals Congress has set by law.

Government Notebook

Look around your home tonight, and list in your Government Notebook all of the products you think are affected by federal regulations.

EXECUTIVE OFFICE OF THE PRESIDENT AND THE CABINET

Political Dictionary

secretary
attorney general

Objectives

★ How is the Executive Office of the President organized?
★ What is the role of the vice president?
★ How does the cabinet help carry out the work of the executive branch?

To learn how the executive branch carries out its duties, you first need to know how it is organized. Two key parts of the executive branch are the Executive Office of the President and the cabinet.

Executive Office of the President

The Executive Office of the President is made up of several separate organizations, including the White House Office, the National Security Council, the Office of Management and Budget, the Council of Economic Advisers, and the National Economic Council. In addition, the vice president has taken on a key role in helping the Executive Office carry out its work.

White House Office A striking feature of the modern presidency is the growth of the White House Office staff. George Washington's staff consisted only of personal assistants, including nephews, whom he paid out of his own pocket. As one political observer noted of early presidents, they lacked "even so much as a receptionist or a personal guard to control access to [their] person."

As a result, early presidents spent much of their day meeting with visitors who came in off the street—"vendors, wayfarers, curiosity-seekers, and bearers of grievances of every conceivable [imaginable] sort." Not until after the Civil War did Congress appropriate funds for the president to hire White House personal staff and groundskeepers. Until then, he had to pay for them out of his own salary.

Today the White House staff serves as the president's personal staff and close advisers. They are appointed by the president without Senate confirmation. A chief of staff manages all of the White House staff and controls access to the president.

The people under the chief of staff are organized into groups that each handle a separate area, including national security issues, domestic policy, speechwriting, relations with Congress, and dealings with the press and the public. Given the influence of the media today, the White House press office is critical to a president's success. The press secretary, who heads the office and often presents televised briefings to the press, is one of the most visible members of the White House staff.

Speechwriting also is crucial to a president's success, particularly since speeches are a major means by which the president reaches the general public. President Warren Harding hired the first

POLITICAL PROCESSES *The White House chief of staff has many assistants, such as the two shown here, to help manage the White House.* **What are some of the responsibilities of the people who work under the chief of staff?**

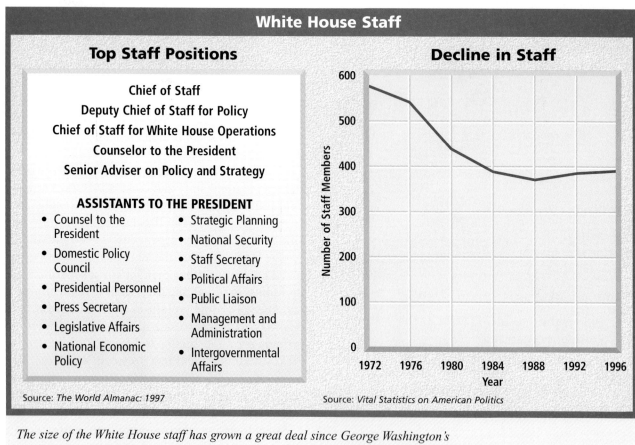

White House Staff

Top Staff Positions

Chief of Staff
Deputy Chief of Staff for Policy
Chief of Staff for White House Operations
Counselor to the President
Senior Adviser on Policy and Strategy

ASSISTANTS TO THE PRESIDENT

- Counsel to the President
- Domestic Policy Council
- Presidential Personnel
- Press Secretary
- Legislative Affairs
- National Economic Policy

- Strategic Planning
- National Security
- Staff Secretary
- Political Affairs
- Public Liaison
- Management and Administration
- Intergovernmental Affairs

Source: *The World Almanac: 1997*

Decline in Staff

Source: *Vital Statistics on American Politics*

The size of the White House staff has grown a great deal since George Washington's administration. The chart on the left shows some of the chief assistants the president relies on for support. The chart on the right shows how White House staff numbers began to decline in the 1970s as presidents' staffing priorities changed. **Which member of the White House staff might handle the president's media relations?**

presidential speechwriter, called a literary clerk, in 1921. Prior to that, presidents generally wrote their own speeches.

Through President Lyndon Johnson's administration, important speeches were usually written by a senior adviser to the president, not by someone with the title "speechwriter." The task of speechwriting has now become a separate and distinct staff function. Speechwriters work on the Inaugural Address, as well as the annual State of the Union message and the greetings that presidents give to people—ranging from returning astronauts to college baseball champions—who are invited to meet the president at the Rose Garden, which is located outside the Oval Office.

An important part of the White House staff's work deals with the complicated day-to-day operation of the presidency. The Scheduling and Advance Office, for example, plans presidential trips. Once a site is selected, this office handles a mountain of details—from the exact timing and

route of the president's motorcade through city streets to the location of television cameras at speaking engagements.

Answering telephones and mail also are major jobs in the White House. Under President Bill Clinton, for example, the White House received some 20,000 letters a week. In 1993 it became possible to send the White House electronic mail. During the first nine months after the system was put in place, the White House received some 125,000 e-mail messages.

National Security Council The National Security Council (NSC) was set up in 1947 to improve coordination among the government departments that deal with national security issues—particularly the Central Intelligence Agency (CIA) and the Departments of State and Defense. At first the NSC was made up of representatives from the various agencies as well as a permanent council staff. In 1949, however, the

Citizenship in Action

President Clinton recognizes the outstanding service of several young people at a White House awards ceremony.

Presidential Recognition

Each year, the president honors teens around the country for their community service and scholastic efforts. For example, in 1994 President Bill Clinton issued Proclamation 6674, making January 16, 1994, "National Good Teen Day," saying that young people "deserve our recognition and appreciation" for their community service. Presidential administrations support the awards programs that have been established to honor the accomplishments of certain teens.

On January 28, 1997, in a ceremony at the U.S. Capitol in Washington, D.C., the President's Environmental Youth Award was presented to the Mighty Duck Savers—a group of eight young women. The group earned the award for its efforts toward making people "aware of the threat humans pose to some animal life."

One of the Duck Savers' main goals was to clean up Culler Lake, an important duck habitat in Frederick, Maryland. In addition to cleaning up the lake, the young women worked to educate people about the dangers of feeding bread to ducks. For more than three years, these young volunteers created T-shirts, stamps, brochures, and signs informing the public that feeding bread to ducks encourages them to eat anything resembling bread, including harmful objects such as white plastic trash. The young women suggested that people feed the ducks cracked corn, a safe alternative to bread. As a result of their efforts, the city put up informational signs and cracked-corn dispensers around the lake.

The annual Presidential Scholars Program recognizes the scholastic talent of young people. In 1996, for example, 2,700 high school seniors from across the nation were selected to be part of the prestigious program. As a part of the selection process, the scholars were asked to submit an essay in which they held a conversation with any person in history. One scholar, 17-year-old Joshua Goodman, wrote an essay in which he held an imaginary debate with John C. Calhoun, vice president of the United States from 1825 to 1832. The debate centered on the issue of states' rights versus those of the federal government.

Goodman advanced to become one of 500 semifinalists before being named a winner by a 32-member, presidentially appointed commission. The Harvard-bound New Yorker was among 141 graduating seniors chosen as Presidential Scholars. A perfect score on his Scholastic Aptitude Test (SAT), in addition to an exceptional essay, helped Joshua win the honor.

Presidential Scholars are invited to Washington, D.C., for a medallion ceremony with the president. Goodman and his fellow winners were also treated to a performance in their honor at the Kennedy Center for the Performing Arts.

What Do You Think?

1. Does presidential recognition of young people's accomplishments promote community involvement? Why or why not?
2. Why is the support of programs that recognize the contributions of outstanding individuals part of the president's role?

WORLD AFFAIRS *In 1997 Vice President Al Gore met with Korean president Kim Young Sam (right front) during a tour of Asia. **Why do you think that vice presidents have become more involved as public spokespersons for the president in recent years?***

Treasury Department, the National Security Council, and the OMB—in advising the president on economic policy.

National Economic Council In January 1993 President Bill Clinton signed an executive order establishing another executive branch advisory body—the National Economic Council—to provide guidance on economic policy. The main goal of the council is to coordinate economic policy in the same way that the National Security Council coordinates advice on U.S. foreign policy. At the top of the council's list of duties is to monitor and advise the president on U.S. trade and industrial technology.

The Vice President The Constitution states that the vice president is to preside over the Senate and to be first in line of succession to the presidency. As head of the Senate, the vice president can vote on legislation only when the senators' votes are tied, which does not happen often.

For many years the vice president's role in government did not amount to much more than the above two functions. The first vice president, John Adams, said of the position:

❝ My country has in its wisdom contrived [invented] for me the most insignificant office that ever the invention of man contrived or his imagination conceived. ❞

Usually asked to perform ceremonial tasks, such as representing the president at the funerals of foreign leaders, past vice presidents were seen rarely and heard even less.

Today, however, presidents often give their vice presidents an active role in and responsibility for a specific policy area. President Clinton, for example, had Vice President Al Gore head an effort to reduce government waste and help agencies run more smoothly. Vice presidents also have become more involved as public spokespersons for the president. Given these developments, the office is often seen as a path to the presidency itself. In fact, many vice presidents later run for president, with 14 out of 45 having received their party's nomination thus far. Some vice presidents,

council was reorganized and placed in the Executive Office of the President. A national security adviser, who is appointed by the president, heads the NSC staff.

With this change, the NSC staff became part of the president's staff, and the national security adviser assumed a prominent role in making national security decisions. For example, when U.S. soldiers were sent in to stop a civil war in 1965 in the Dominican Republic, President Lyndon Johnson sent his national security adviser to hold talks with local political groups. This was the first time a national security adviser traveled to another country to take part in negotiations.

Office of Management and Budget Because executive branch agencies must submit their budget requests to the Office of Management and Budget (OMB), this office is one of the president's key tools for influencing these agencies. For example, OMB could potentially withhold funding for a program that the president considers ineffective. The OMB staff also helps prepare the president's annual budget recommendations to Congress.

Council of Economic Advisers The Council of Economic Advisers was set up in 1946 to give expert economic advice to the president. It is made up of three members and a staff of about 40. The council participates with many other groups—such as the White House staff, the

Executive Branch Organization

PRESIDENT

EXECUTIVE OFFICE OF THE PRESIDENT

- White House Office
- Office of the Vice President
- Office of Management and Budget
- Council of Economic Advisers
- Office of National Drug Control Policy
- Office of the U. S. Trade Representative

- Council on Environmental Quality
- Office of Science and Technology Policy
- Office of Administration
- National Security Council
- Office of Policy Development
- National Economic Council

VICE PRESIDENT

CABINET DEPARTMENTS

Department of Agriculture	Department of the Interior
Department of Commerce	Department of Justice
Department of Defense	Department of Labor
Department of Education	Department of State
Department of Energy	Department of Transportation
Department of Health and Human Services	Department of the Treasury
Department of Housing and Urban Development	Department of Veterans Affairs

Executive offices and cabinet departments were organized to help the president make and enforce policy in all areas of government. **Which executive offices and cabinet departments advise the president on economic policy?**

including Al Gore, have even run for president before becoming vice president.

Role of the First Lady

POLITICAL PROCESSES   The role of the first lady is difficult to define. Some first ladies have taken an active role in the country's policy making. Others have promoted social causes. But each first lady has had to determine for herself how to define her role.

In the 1992 presidential campaign, Hillary Rodham Clinton took an active role in campaigning for her husband's election. During his first year in office, President Clinton gave his wife a key role in domestic policy making, naming her as head of the Task Force on National Health Care Reform, the most influential position ever awarded to a first lady. In this position, she sought to reorganize the nation's health care system.

Hillary Clinton is not the first presidential spouse to take an active role in politics, however. Eleanor Roosevelt paved the way by serving as President Franklin D. Roosevelt's "eyes and ears." Since he was partially paralyzed, President Roosevelt had difficulty traveling and relied on his wife to gather information about the needs of the people. Eleanor Roosevelt traveled the country, investigating the working conditions of Appalachian miners and migrant laborers in California. Her schedule was filled with a daily newspaper column, a weekly radio broadcast, lectures, and other responsibilities. Her activities brought her further into the public eye than any previous first ladies had been.

Many first ladies have used their visibility to advance various social causes. For example, Lady Bird Johnson embraced environmental issues and the beautification of the nation's interstate highways. The National Wildflower Research Center in Austin, Texas, is part of her legacy. Rosalyn Carter crusaded for mental health programs. Nancy Reagan established the Just Say No campaign against drug use, and Barbara Bush promoted national literacy programs.

Some people believe that while working with charities is an acceptable role for the president's spouse, helping to establish national policy is not because the president's spouse has not been approved by the Senate as most high-level policy makers are. "I think the only answer is to be who you are and do what you do," Hillary Clinton said. Whether or not elected officials will act to limit the role in the future remains to be seen. Either way, however, the role will vary, depending on the experience, background, and interests of the person who performs the role.

The Cabinet

In addition to the Executive Office of the President, there are 14 cabinet departments that assist the president in carrying out the work of the executive branch. The heads of cabinet departments are called **secretaries**, the one exception being the **attorney general**, who is the head of the Department of Justice.

Cabinet departments are divided into units that perform the actual work of the government. These units may be called bureaus, administrations, offices, agencies, or services. Examples include the Occupational Safety and Health Administration (OSHA) in the Department of Labor, the Internal Revenue Service (IRS) in the Department of the Treasury, and the Patent and Trademark Office and the Minority Business Development Agency in the Department of Commerce.

Before the tremendous growth of the Executive Office of the President, the cabinet was the president's main advisory body. As the Constitution states, the president might "require the opinion, in writing, of the principal officer in each of the executive departments, upon any subject relating to the duties of their . . . offices." George Washington relied heavily on his cabinet as a body of advisers. He even requested that some of the members of his cabinet—Henry Knox, Alexander Hamilton, and Thomas Jefferson—meet with one another if important matters arose when he was traveling.

More than 200 years later, however, the cabinet's role as an advisory body is much less significant. Cabinet meetings are now infrequent, and those that do occur are mainly ceremonial. Some secretaries, however, are still frequently consulted by the president—in particular, the attorney general and the secretaries of state, defense, and the treasury. The president relies more on these cabinet members' advice because their departments deal with areas of key

Comparing Governments

Census Counting in the United States and Canada

Once every 10 years the U.S. Department of Commerce's Bureau of the Census takes a head count of the U.S. population. The census does much more than just count people, however. It also gathers information about them, including their age, occupation, ethnic origin, and whether they live in a city or rural area. In this way, the census provides an update on the ever-changing face of U.S. society. Perhaps the most important use of census information, however, is to determine the distribution of congressional representation among the states.

Canada also holds a census every 10 years. The first census in what is now Canada was taken in 1666, when Louis XIV ordered a population count of New France. Today, the Canadian census is used to determine boundary readjustments of electoral districts.

Census counting rarely draws much media attention, but in 1996 the Canadian census made world news when it tallied the number of hours that men and women spend on household chores. Initial analysis of the census results revealed that in Canada, women do two thirds of this work.

The new census questions are the result of what some call the "kitchen table revolution," a campaign to recognize the contributions of women in the home. Some consider the 1996 Canadian census to be a first step in gaining benefits such as pensions for women who work at home without pay.

POLITICAL PROCESSES *Here President Clinton meets with members of his cabinet.*
Why does the president rarely meet with all cabinet members at the same time?

national concern, including crime, foreign affairs, the military, and economic concerns.

Why do current presidents rely so little on the cabinet for advice? One reason is that they rely heavily on the advice of members of the White House staff, as you have read. Another is that cabinet meetings are both impractical and time-consuming. If the president needs advice on what position to take in trade negotiations with Japan, for example, he or she might consult with the secretary of commerce individually. However, a meeting including the secretary of veterans affairs and other cabinet members who may have

limited knowledge of the issue at hand would make little sense.

In addition, cabinet departments, like many other organizations, tend to be territorial. To protect their budgets and areas of influence, cabinet secretaries and their staffs may offer advice that is more beneficial to their specific areas of concern than to achieving the president's goals or to serving the public good. For example, officials in the Department of Health and Human Services might recommend improvements in health coverage programs without considering their costs, which is the concern of the Treasury Department and the OMB.

SECTION 1 — REVIEW

1. Define the following terms: secretary, attorney general.

2. Name and describe the six main divisions in the Executive Office of the President. What is the newest group within this office?

3. How has the role of the vice president changed over time?

4. How is the cabinet organized? Why do presidents no longer rely on cabinet meetings for advice?

5. **Thinking and Writing Critically**
   Do you think first spouses should play a role in making policy decisions? If so, should their "appointment" to a policy area be confirmed by the Senate? Explain your answer.

6. **Applying POLITICAL PROCESSES**
   Conduct an Internet search using the name of the U.S. vice president as a search word. What information do you find? In what activities has the vice president recently been involved?

THE FEDERAL BUREAUCRACY

Political Dictionary

bureaucracy
bureaucrat
public comment
independent agency
regulatory commission
government corporation
civil servant
spoils system
merit system

Objectives

★ How do government agencies help carry out the work of the executive branch?

★ Why does Congress set up independent agencies?

★ How are government positions filled?

The many agencies of the executive branch are important to the running of the government. In other words, these agencies perform much of the actual work of government. Most of the federal government consists of the cabinet departments. In addition, there are a number of independent agencies. Together these organizations make up the federal **bureaucracy**—a highly organized system of people and their work. People who work in a bureaucracy are called **bureaucrats**.

Government Agencies' Work

How do government agencies help the executive branch carry out its duties? They do so by advising the president and Congress on policy decisions and by making and carrying out the rules and regulations needed to enforce the law.

Advising Government Officials Most of the government's expert knowledge is found in the executive branch agencies. Why is this so? Many mid- to lower-level employees in these agencies stay in their jobs until they retire. As a result, the agencies have a deep pool of experience and continuity that is needed for studying and managing the huge, complex programs of the federal government. These agencies share their knowledge by generating reports and statistics that the president and Congress need in order to make policy and legislative decisions.

Making Rules The rules made by executive branch agencies have the force of law, though they usually carry only civil, not criminal, penalties for any violations. Over the years, agencies have passed a tremendous number of rules, which appear in the Code of Federal Regulations. As of 1997 this publication ran to more than 204 volumes.

Agencies must follow set procedures for issuing a rule. For example, an agency cannot issue a rule without first giving notice and allowing a period for **public comment**, during which

POLITICAL PROCESSES *Here a member of the Peace Corps, an executive branch agency, talks to children in Ecuador.* **What duties do other executive branch agencies perform?**

interested parties can give their opinions on the proposed rule. After notification, the public has at least 30 days to submit written comments. For key proposals, however, agencies almost always hold public hearings as well, at which experts and other witnesses testify and deliver research reports.

The publication of a final rule must be accompanied by a "statement of reasons" explaining why each provision was adopted, as well as the evidence supporting those decisions. In addition, rules may be challenged in court. By allowing outside forces to examine the rule-making process, government provides a check on agency power.

The process from proposal to completion may take a long time and involve as much as 5,000 pages of recorded notes. Rule-making proceedings usually last a year or more. It is easy to see how citizens who want government to act quickly might become upset at what they see as the grinding—or spinning—of wheels. It is also understandable that the businesses, workers, and consumers whose lives are directly affected by a particular rule insist on its being thoroughly considered.

Implementing Rules Even after laws are passed and rules are written, government agencies still have a great deal of work to do. They must implement, or carry out, the rules they have created. This can be a difficult task. The Social Security Administration must provide checks to more than 43 million people each month. The armed forces must organize a fighting force of thousands of vehicles, weapons, and soldiers. The National Institutes of Health must decide who receives grants for medical research. The Immigration and Naturalization Service must patrol the nation's borders. To accomplish these enormous tasks, agencies employ an army of people.

Independent Agencies

The executive branch agencies outside the cabinet departments are called **independent agencies**. Congress creates these agencies to help the president carry out the work of the executive branch. They are independent in the sense that they are separate from the cabinet departments—often because they perform duties that do not fall under the scope of a cabinet department or because they serve the interest of several departments. Thus,

they function best as separate and independent organizations.

Today there are more than 60 independent agencies. They include the Social Security Administration, which runs the Social Security system; the Equal Employment Opportunity Commission (EEOC), which hears job discrimination claims; the Environmental Protection Agency (EPA), which monitors air, water, and ground pollution; and the National Aeronautics and Space Administration (NASA), which runs the nation's space program. Other examples include the Central Intelligence Agency (CIA) and the Peace Corps.

Regulatory Commissions Some independent agencies have a greater degree of autonomy, or self-rule, than others. The agencies that act with the least direction from the White House are called **regulatory commissions**—independent agencies that have the power to establish and enforce regulations.

Regulatory commissions maintain so much independence because of their leadership. They

POLITICAL PROCESSES *Family members of victims of a plane crash attend a hearing held by the National Transportation Safety Board.* **What are the functions of independent regulatory commissions?**

are usually headed by a set number of commissioners from each party who are appointed by the president for fixed terms and confirmed by the Senate. In fact, many commissioners serve longer than do the presidents who appoint them. Regulatory commissions are more strongly influenced by Congress than the White House but, on the whole, act independently of both.

Why is it particularly important that regulatory commissions be free of political pressure? The commissions monitor and police key areas of national interest. Members of these commissions thus must be free from political pressures so they can make unbiased and well-reasoned decisions.

There are around a dozen regulatory commissions, including the Securities and Exchange Commission (SEC), which regulates the stock market; the Federal Trade Commission (FTC), which oversees business practices; and the National Labor Relations Board (NLRB), which

PUBLIC GOOD *The Food and Drug Administration requires pharmacies to provide customers with prescription-drug information sheets.* **How does this regulation promote the public good?**

puts a stop to unfair labor practices. Other examples include the Nuclear Regulatory Commission (NRC) and the Consumer Product Safety Commission (CPSC).

Government Corporations Some of these independent agencies—called **government corporations**—are run as nonprofit businesses. By far the largest of these corporations is the U.S. Postal Service. Others include the Federal Deposit Insurance Corporation (FDIC), which guarantees people's bank deposits, and the Tennessee Valley Authority (TVA), which provides affordable electricity to many rural areas in the South. Believing that these corporations run more efficiently than most other government agencies, many people argue that new government corporations should be set up to take over agency functions such as the nation's air traffic control system. Government corporations generally are set up when an agency's business is mostly commercial, when an agency generates its own income, and when the agency's work requires more flexibility than government agencies usually have.

Government Employees

The question of how the federal government fills government jobs has long been a source of controversy. Will effective government best be achieved by lifetime employees or by political appointees who share the views of each newly and democratically elected administration? Will a government run by people owing their jobs to the party in power lead to corruption?

These questions have been answered differently at different times. As you will see, government positions today are filled with both politically appointed and nonappointed **civil servants**—people employed by the federal government.

The Spoils System Between 1789 and 1828 the number of federal employees was extremely small. Positions were primarily filled by wealthy citizens who stayed at their jobs despite changes in presidential administrations.

In 1829, however, when Andrew Jackson took office as president, a new system emerged. Jackson passed out a large number of government jobs to his political supporters. He believed that people who held office permanently might

PRINCIPLES OF DEMOCRACY *Many people criticized the way in which federal employees were selected under President Andrew Jackson.* **What was this cartoonist's opinion of the spoils system?**

turn their public offices into private property and become a type of aristocracy. Believing in the abilities of ordinary citizens, Jackson stated that the government jobs were "so plain and simple that men of intelligence may readily qualify themselves for their performance." Jackson decided that the policy of keeping agency officials in their jobs permanently should be replaced by a policy of rotation in office. He believed that democratically elected officials should bring into office with them people who share the ideas for which a majority of the electorate voted.

This policy, of course, benefited Jackson by giving him more power and influence over government policies. As one senator stated it, Jackson's doctrine was like the doctrine of governing the behavior of victorious armies—"to the victor belong the spoils of the enemy." Soon,

Jackson's system came to be known as the **spoils system**.

Pressure for Reform After the Civil War, critics of the spoils system began a movement for reform. They pointed out that the quality of government service dropped as inexperienced and even incompetent people were appointed to jobs just because they had worked for the winning candidate. The spoils system, reformers argued, led to a government driven by personal benefit rather than public spirit. Furthermore, the spoils system symbolized a decline in moral standards and a rise in the worship of money, which they believed had gotten out of hand during the business expansion that took place after the Civil War. Stopping the spoils system was crucial, in their view, to raising the nation's moral well-being.

The reform movement grew during the 1870s, particularly after several corruption cases. One of the most damaging was the discovery of the Whiskey Ring, a group of officials—including President Ulysses S. Grant's personal secretary—who took bribes from distillers wanting to avoid paying an alcohol tax. Even with these cases, however, reform might have failed had it not been for the assassination of President James

PUBLIC GOOD *Federal employees such as air traffic controllers often are required to pass an examination before they are hired for a government job.* **How has the merit system ensured that all applicants for federal jobs have an equal opportunity to be hired?**

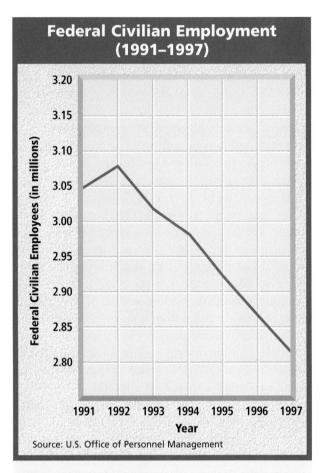

Federal Civilian Employment (1991–1997)

Federal Civilian Employees (in millions)

3.20
3.15
3.10
3.05
3.00
2.95
2.90
2.85
2.80

1991 1992 1993 1994 1995 1996 1997

Year

Source: U.S. Office of Personnel Management

This graph illustrates the changes in federal civilian employment. The number of civilians employed by the federal government has decreased since 1992. **What was one of the reasons for the downsizing of the federal work force in the 1990s?**

Garfield in 1881. He was killed by a man who had tried unsuccessfully for a spoils job in the new administration.

The Pendleton Act The reform movement led to the Pendleton Act of 1883, which gradually replaced the spoils system with a more rational one. Under the **merit system**, federal employees secure jobs through competitive exams and then stay on the job even after new presidents take office.

At first, the Pendleton Act applied the merit system to only about 10 percent of government employees, but it was slowly expanded to cover most of the government workforce. In 1897 President William McKinley strengthened the goals of the Pendleton Act with an order prohibiting the dismissal of employees hired through the merit system, except for good cause. Even so, a larger number of officials continued to be appointed politically in the United States than in most other democracies.

Political Appointees Merit system civil servants make up the bulk of the executive branch agencies' workforce. A small portion—about 3,000—of top agency officials are political appointees. Of these, some 1,100—cabinet secretaries, deputy secretaries, undersecretaries, assistant secretaries, and various agency heads—are appointed by the president. Around 700 must be confirmed by the Senate. The remaining 2,000 are named by the presidential appointees themselves, also without the Senate's approval.

It is no longer true, if it ever was, that most political appointees are unqualified and receive their jobs only as a reward for work in a presidential campaign or because they belong to a powerful interest group. A few political appointees may fit that description, but they are the exception rather than the rule. Political appointees, especially those in top positions, are generally well educated. Many have had prior government experience as well.

Civil Service Today The number of federal employees, has been fairly constant for about 25 years, though efforts at downsizing have steadily decreased this number throughout the 1990s. In addition, given steady population growth, the percentage of federal employees as part of the population as a whole has dropped.

As of 1993 there were 4.4 million federal employees, including political appointees and the military, making the federal government the single largest employer in the country. Many people believe that the majority of these employees work shuffling papers at a desk in Washington, D.C.

Actually, government jobs are as diverse as are the government's tasks. Federal workers include soldiers, police officers, drug agents, accountants, engineers, firefighters, rescue workers, park rangers, biologists, chemists, physicists, and doctors. Also, less than 16 percent of civil servants work in the Washington, D.C., area.

Most cabinet departments and many individual agencies have offices in federal buildings in 10 regional centers that the federal government runs across the United States: in Boston, New York City, Philadelphia, Atlanta, Chicago, Dallas/Fort Worth, Kansas City, Denver, San Francisco, and Seattle. (Some agencies put their regional offices in other cities, however.)

In addition, many government agencies have small local offices. For example, the Social Security Administration has more than 1,300 local offices that receive applications for Social Security cards and benefits, as well as answer questions from citizens. If you live in a city or large town, you might look in your telephone directory (under *U.S. government*) to find out what federal agencies have offices located in your city.

Downsizing of the Federal Government

With rising pressure for smaller, more efficient government, President Clinton announced in 1993 that the federal government would shed 272,900 workers by 1999, the first major downsizing of the federal workforce in decades. In 1994 Congress approved a proposal to offer selected federal employees "buyouts"—cash payments for voluntary retirement—similar to those that many private companies have used to reduce the size of their workforces.

The results of these efforts have been significant. By March 1997 the federal workforce numbered 2,807,077, down from 3,038,041 in January 1993. While most of these were civilian positions in the Department of Defense, the nondefense workforce also was cut significantly. All but one

POLITICAL PROCESSES *The federal government employs people in many different professions. These federal workers are scientists who inspect fruit trees and other crops.* **Do most federal employees work in Washington, D.C.?**

of the executive branch departments saw cuts in their staffs. The Agriculture Department, for example, was cut 15 percent, or by 17,136 workers, and the Department of the Interior also was cut 15 percent, or by 11,522 workers.

SECTION 2 — REVIEW

1. Define the following terms: bureaucracy, bureaucrat, public comment, independent agency, regulatory commission, government corporation, civil servant, spoils system, merit system.

2. Who sets up the independent agencies of the executive branch? What types of activities do these agencies oversee?

3. What are the three main tasks of the government agencies?

4. How has the civil service system changed over time? What government positions are filled by political appointees?

5. **Thinking and Writing Critically**
   How do you think most government positions should be filled—with career civil servants who are required to take a civil service exam and compete for jobs or with political appointees who share the views of the president? Explain your answer.

6. **Applying** POLITICAL PROCESSES
   Conduct an Internet search for some of the agencies mentioned in this section. Are some of these agencies at work in your community? If so, which ones? What kind of work do they perform? What information do they provide on their Internet sites?

THE EXECUTIVE BRANCH AND THE PUBLIC GOOD

Political Dictionary

privatization

Objectives

★ Is the presidency too powerful?
★ What are some common criticisms of government agencies?

Just as Congress has its critics, so does the executive branch. The principal criticisms of the executive branch center around the power of the presidency and the size, complexity, and maze-like procedures of the executive branch agencies.

The Presidency and the Public Good

One of the most powerful offices in the world, the presidency holds a great potential for abuse of power. For many years people have debated whether the president has too much power and what are appropriate ways of maintaining or reducing it.

Growth of Presidential Power Some critics charge that the president today is exactly what the framers wished to avoid—a sort of elected monarch. These people believe that the growth of presidential power has upset the checks and balances set up by the Constitution. Is this the case?

The president holds far-reaching foreign-policy powers, though they can be checked by Congress.

However, Congress has the power to decide domestic matters by passing laws, though the president can affect domestic policy by influencing, and creating public pressure on, Congress.

As noted in Chapters 5 and 6, the locally elected members of Congress provide a special voice for local concerns. The president, as a nationally elected official, balances this viewpoint by representing all of the nation's people. Thus, just as it is vital that Congress represent local concerns, it is crucial that the president have a strong enough voice and powers of office to represent the concerns of the country as a whole. This check and balance promotes the public good.

Reliance on Public Support Another criticism of the presidency is that in trying to act effectively as a representative of the nation, the president must work to gain majority support for policies. As noted in Chapter 7, Andrew Jackson was the first president to appeal directly to the public for support of his policies. Modern presidents have sharpened Jackson's technique by using more sophisticated and influential tools to help them reach the public.

Why do critics believe that such actions might harm the public good? While trying to gain public support, the president can spend a great deal of time on media relations—becoming more concerned with image than with the substance of

POLITICAL PROCESSES *Ronald Reagan, like other modern presidents, carefully prepared for public appearances.* ***How much time do you think presidents should spend on media relations? Why?***

Presidential Aide

Long days and a lot of responsibility—that is how one might describe the job of a presidential aide, whose role is to make the president's job easier. Though each president determines how heavily to rely on aides for assistance, high-level aides, such as the White House chief of staff, usually play a powerful role in assisting the president. The chief of staff often meets with the president several times a day; sets the president's daily schedule; arranges all of the president's trips; screens telephone calls, memos, and letters; and supervises the writing of speeches.

Presidential aides assist the president in almost every area of the job, from formulating policy to dealing with the media. Aides often work an average of 12 hours a day and six or seven days a week. Although presidential aides work difficult hours, they do receive significant benefits. High-ranking aides have a great deal of power and prestige. They also enjoy other fringe benefits, such as large offices, the use of a chauffeur-driven car, and gourmet meals prepared by White House chefs.

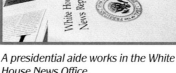

A presidential aide works in the White House News Office.

Only a small percentage of the president's aides hold high-profile positions that bring "celebrity" status. Most of the president's staff work behind the scenes, assisting high-level aides with their responsibilities. Lower-level aides answer phones, write letters, help prepare speeches, research legislation, and answer questions from the media. All presidential aides are appointed by the president and generally are well educated and civic-minded. While some aspire to political careers, others simply enjoy the experience of working for the nation's most important leader.

---

governing. In other words, as a president spends more time trying to present one side of an issue to the public, the facts and the importance of the issue can easily get lost in a battle of images. As Donald Regan's memoir of the Reagan presidency states,

> ❝ Every moment of every public appearance was scheduled, every word was scripted, every place where Reagan was expected to stand was chalked with toe marks. The President was always being prepared for a performance. ❞

The amount of time that a president spends presenting a certain image varies, and determining the degree to which such efforts affect the public good is difficult. No matter what the effect, however, the media will continue to play a large role in presidential politics.

Government Agencies and the Public Good

The executive branch agencies perform much of the day-to-day work of the government. As a result, they also receive the lion's share of criticism. Two major criticisms of these agencies are that they are staffed with nonelected officials and that they are inefficient.

Nonelected Officials Most of the millions of federal employees are civil servants. This means that much of the work of the government is carried out by nonelected officials. As critics point out, this situation contradicts a basic democratic idea: that government rules should be made by representatives of the people. Unless the people elect the rule makers, they cannot make sure that the government's rules promote the public good.

© Tribune Media Services, Inc. All rights reserved. Reprinted with permission.

HERE'S A WHITE HOUSE MEMO ASKING US TO CUT DOWN ON WASTE. MAKE SIX COPIES. FILE ONE AND CROSS-FILE THE OTHERS. SEND COPIES TO OUR STAFF IN TRIPLICATE. ASK THEM TO FILE ONE, CROSS-FILE ONE AND SEND ONE BACK INITIALED. MAKE SIX COPIES OF THE INITIALED MEMO, FILE ONE AND CROSS-FILE THE OTHERS. SEND A LETTER TO THE WHITE HOUSE OUTLINING WHAT ACTION WE'RE TAKING. MAKE SIX COPIES FOR OUR FILES AND SEND IT IN TRIPLICATE TO OUR STAFF. HAVE THEM INITIAL ONE AND FILE THE OTHERS. WHEN THE INITIALED LETTER IS RETURNED MAKE SIX COPIES AND....

FEDERAL PROCUREMENT OFF.

PRINCIPLES OF DEMOCRACY *The cartoon above criticizes the wastefulness and inefficiency of federal agencies.* **According to this cartoonist, what is one of the causes of government inefficiency?**

Many critics of government agencies even believe them to be armies of arrogant bureaucrats who issue endless commands and trample civil liberties without having to answer to the people. Is this an accurate assessment?

In reality, delegating power to nonelected officials in government agencies is a democratic choice made by elected officials. Consider the many people who visit a certain doctor for an illness and instead see a physician's assistant who was hired by the doctor. This assistant is not the person whom the patients have "elected" to see. However, these patients may trust their doctor to hire only competent assistants, just as many voters trust Congress to make sure that the agencies to which it assigns rule-making powers will promote the public good.

One still may ask, however, whether this delegation of power promotes the public good or is simply unavoidable, given the high number of government activities and the time limits on members of Congress. There are in fact positive reasons for giving decision-making powers to agencies. Most elected officials are generalists concerned with a variety of issues. Agency officials, however, often devote their careers to just a few policy issues. Sensibly, these employees are given responsibility for areas in which they are experts.

Keep in mind also that government agencies do not work unchecked. Congress creates, oversees—and can dissolve—agencies. In addition, the Office of Management and Budget (OMB), guided by the elected president, has control over the administration of the agency budgets. These checks ensure that agencies do not run wild in making and implementing rules.

Inefficiency People sometimes criticize government agency officials not for making too many rules, but for accomplishing too little. For example, a hurricane slams into the Atlantic coast, and the Federal Emergency Management Agency (FEMA) does not send relief quickly enough. In this case "the bureaucracy" might be denounced as being wasteful and inefficient.

However, most large organizations, public or private, are in some ways inefficient. Some civil servants are arrogant, some incompetent, and some wasteful. To paint all government officials in this image, however, is inaccurate.

Many government agencies in fact operate effectively. The Environmental Protection Agency (EPA) has secured much cleaner air than the country had just 15 years ago. The Customs Service rapidly processes piles of paperwork on imports. Remember also that government agencies often tackle the hardest problems—if it were easy and

PUBLIC GOOD *The federal government funds programs to clean up pollution in the Florida Everglades.* **Do you think that government has found effective solutions to problems such as air pollution?**

profitable to deal with poverty and crime, the private sector would likely have done so long ago.

Improving Agency Management

While often successful, not all government agencies are managed as well as they could be and therefore do not promote the public good as well as they might. How can agency management be improved? Some people believe that the government should use performance measures, contract out some government functions, and turn others over to private companies.

Performance Measures One suggestion for improving agencies is to increase their accountability for their performance while giving them greater discretion in how best to do their job. In 1993 Congress attempted to implement this solution by passing the Government Performance and Results Act, which required agencies to set strategic goals, measure performance, and report on their progress in meeting those goals.

For many programs, measuring these accomplishments is a simple matter. People who call a Social Security hot line can be surveyed to find out how satisfied they are with the way their questions were answered. The amount of time it takes to process a veteran's benefit application can be measured. These sorts of standards can be used to rate agencies' performance and pinpoint areas needing improvement.

What about cases in which performance measures are more complicated? For example, how should a school's performance be measured? A survey of student satisfaction might show only a dislike for homework. Looking at scores from the Scholastic Aptitude Test (SAT) would show only how well prepared some students were for admission into college. To fully evaluate a school, the Department of Education can develop a bundle of performance measures that take into account student, parent, and teacher satisfaction; SAT scores; graduation rates; and so on. Using performance measures becomes even more complicated when people disagree about what feature of performance is most important—should the government look first at how well a school prepares the brightest students or at whether it minimizes the dropout rate?

Some of the changes that performance measures require can be difficult for government agencies to make, but these changes may present opportunities for the people working in the agencies. Results-oriented performance standards give people clearer goals for which to strive and greater freedom in deciding how to do their jobs.

Contracting Out Many people argue that government agencies are incapable of operating efficiently enough. The solution, they say, is to contract out as many government functions as possible. When government contracts out work, it hires a private company to produce a good or perform a service. For example, a city government might contract out its garbage collection to a private company, Acme Trash. Acme collects the garbage, and the city pays Acme with tax dollars. Thus, although a private company performs the service, the government retains the right to oversee the company's work.

Government in fact already contracts out many responsibilities. Private companies develop weapons systems for the Department of Defense, and the government buys services such as building management and debt collection from private firms. This practice is similar to that of private companies that contract out some functions to other private companies. Many companies, for example, hire advertising agencies to prepare marketing materials, and law firms to provide legal services.

POLITICAL PROCESSES *NASA's Jet Propulsion Laboratory, located near Pasadena, California, is managed by the California Institute of Technology.* **Why do some people think that contracting out government work is a good solution to inefficiency?**

PUBLIC GOOD *In many states, trash collection and recycling services are provided by private companies.* **What government services in your community do you think could be better provided by a private company?**

Contracting out, however, is unlikely to work in all instances. There are several government activities—such as diplomacy and the arrest of criminals—that are undertaken in the name of the people of the United States as a whole and should not be handled by private parties. Do citizens, for example, want the U.S. Embassy in Tokyo staffed by employees of Diplomacy, Inc.? Would these employees represent the U.S. public or their company? In other cases, the performance of a job by U.S. government employees has symbolic value. By hiring its own rangers, the National Park Service shows that the national parks are the property of all U.S. citizens.

In addition, contracting out also presents its own problems. For example, the government has had great difficulties in dealing with defense contractors. On occasion, weapons systems created by these companies have not performed up to expectation. Because so few companies can make submarines and fighter planes, the government often has little leverage over the companies. In turn, as private companies, the defense contractors have conflicting goals—promoting the public good and trying to make as much profit as possible.

Privatization Another possible solution to problems in agency management is **privatization**—the turning of an entire government function over to a private company. In the case of city garbage collection, privatization would mean the government would no longer collect taxes to pay for garbage collection. Instead, Acme Trash would not only collect the garbage but also charge customers directly.

What services might be privatized? Rather than having the Forest Service manage the national forests, the Department of the Interior could sell them to private owners. Rather than having a national space program, space exploration could be left to private companies. In these cases, though, the forests might be cut down for timber, and space exploration might be stopped because of its enormous costs. By removing agencies from their role as overseer, some people argue that privatization takes away a major motivation for the companies to promote the public good.

SECTION 3 — REVIEW

1. Define the following term: privatization.

2. Why do some people say that the presidency is too powerful? What is a possible effect of the president's reliance on public support?

3. Describe the major criticisms of government agency management.

4. What is the difference between contracting out a government service and privatizing it?

5. **Thinking and Writing Critically**
   What kinds of government functions, if any, do you think should be privatized? How would privatizing these functions promote—or threaten—the public good? Explain your answers.

6. **Applying PUBLIC GOOD**
   As you have read, the president relies on public support to strengthen his or her position. Modern technology, such as television and the Internet, enables the president to get political messages out quickly and easily. Consider recent news stories that you have heard or read about the president. In your opinion, how are the stories influenced by the president's efforts to project a certain image?

SECTION 1 The executive branch is organized in two main parts: the Executive Office of the President and the cabinet. The Executive Office is made up of several separate organizations, including the White House Office, the National Security Council, the Office of Management and Budget, the Council of Economic Advisers, and the National Economic Council. The vice president also has taken on a key role in helping the Executive Office carry out its work.

The 14 cabinet departments assist the president in carrying out the work of the executive branch. The heads of cabinet departments are called secretaries, with the exception of the attorney general, who is head of the Department of Justice. Cabinet departments are divided into units—the bureaus, administrations, offices, agencies, and services—that carry out the actual work of the government.

Before the growth of the Executive Office of the President, the cabinet was the president's main advisory body. Today, however, the president relies mainly on some department heads, as well as the Executive Office staff, for advice. Another reason that the president relies so little on the cabinet for advice is that cabinet meetings are impractical and time-consuming. In addition, cabinet departments can be territorial and may tend to try to protect their budgets at the expense of other agencies' projects.

SECTION 2 The cabinet departments combine with the independent agencies of the executive branch to make up the federal bureaucracy. Independent agencies are set up by Congress and include regulatory commissions and government corporations. Government agencies advise the president and Congress on legislation as well as make and implement rules to carry out federal law.

Government agencies are staffed by civil servants. The bulk of them are merit system employees, while about 3,000 top officials are political appointees. Today there are more than 4 million federal government employees, including political appointees and the military.

SECTION 3 There are several criticisms of the executive branch. The first major criticism concerns the power of the presidency. Many people believe that the president is too powerful. Although the president's foreign-policy powers are indeed far-reaching, his or her powers overall are greatly checked by Congress. In addition, a strong president is necessary to check congressional powers.

A second criticism of the executive branch relates to its attempts to represent majority opinion. Many people believe that the president, in trying to gain public support for his or her policies, spends too much time on media relations and his or her image. These people argue that when this occurs, the facts and importance of an issue can get lost in a battle of images.

The executive branch also is criticized for the size, complexity, and procedures of its agencies. However, executive branch agencies are more efficient than people give them credit for being. Government has attempted to improve agency management in several ways, such as by adopting performance measures and contracting out and privatizing some government functions.

Government Notebook

Review what you wrote in your Government Notebook at the beginning of the chapter about the products in your home that are affected by federal regulations. Now that you have studied this chapter, would you revise your list? Research which agency in the executive branch is responsible for regulating each product you have listed. Record your findings in your Notebook.

REVIEW

REVIEWING CONCEPTS

1. How has the role of the vice president changed in recent years?

2. Of what elements does the Executive Office of the President consist?

3. What functions do independent agencies serve? Name three of these agencies.

4. Describe one major criticism of the presidency.

5. What is a civil servant? What is a political appointee?

6. What is the role of the cabinet?

THINKING AND WRITING CRITICALLY

1. **POLITICAL PROCESSES** Do you think the president should rely on the advice of the White House staff rather than executive branch agencies in the policy-making process? Why or why not?

2. **POLITICAL PROCESSES** Do you think the privatization and contracting out of government functions, such as developing weapons systems, is a good solution to inefficiency in the federal government? Explain your answer.

3. **PUBLIC GOOD** Why is it important for regulatory commissions to be free from political pressures? How could political influence over regulatory agencies jeopardize the public good?

CITIZENSHIP IN YOUR COMMUNITY

Many cabinet departments have offices located in cities and towns across the country, giving the public better access to important services. The Department of State, for example, has visa and passport offices located in many major U.S. cities. Check the local telephone directory for the community offices of a cabinet department of your choice. Then research the services provided by these offices. Afterward, use the information you gather to create a brochure informing the public of the community services provided by the cabinet department you selected.

INDIVIDUAL PORTFOLIO PROJECT

With a group, create a handbook on federal regulatory commissions. Your guide should list three or four of the commissions that oversee business and labor issues and briefly describe the functions of each. Be sure to include specific examples of regulations implemented by each commission. Your handbook should be clearly written, well designed, and easy to follow. You might want to use photos to illustrate the different types of goods or services regulated by the commissions.

THE INTERNET: LEARNING ONLINE

Conduct an Internet search to find information about the president's cabinet. Specifically, look for the names and e-mail addresses of the current cabinet members. You might start by using search words such as *executive departments, president's cabinet,* and the name of each executive department. After making a list of the current cabinet members and their e-mail addresses, send an e-mail message to one of the cabinet members, requesting information about the department he or she heads.

PRACTICING SKILLS: CONDUCTING RESEARCH

The table below displays information on volunteer and community service work among young people. Read the labels and study the figures in the table to answer the questions that follow.

	Almost Every Day	At Least Once a Week	Once or Twice a Month	A Few Times a Year	Never
Percentage of High School Seniors Participating in Volunteer or Community Service Work: 1984–1994					
1984	2.6	7.4	14.1	44.9	31.0
1986	1.7	8.4	14.0	44.9	31.0
1988	2.6	6.3	13.4	45.4	32.3
1990	1.8	6.9	13.0	43.3	35.1
1991	2.4	5.9	14.6	44.6	32.4
1992	2.8	7.4	16.5	41.7	31.6
1993	2.7	8.0	15.0	44.0	30.3
1994	3.2	7.6	17.2	44.8	27.2

Source: University of Michigan Institute for Social Research

1. In which year did the highest percentage of high school seniors volunteer almost every day?

2. Between 1990 and 1994, did the amount of volunteer work and participation in community affairs by high school seniors increase or decrease?

3. According to these statistics, in which year did the smallest percentage of high school seniors perform volunteer work?

ANALYZING PRIMARY SOURCES

A PRESS BRIEFING

In 1997 Madeleine Albright became the first female secretary of state. As a member of the president's cabinet, the secretary of state is responsible for advising the president on the country's foreign policy. The following excerpt is from a press briefing at which Albright presented the U.S. Department of State's annual report on human rights. Read the excerpt and answer the questions that follow.

> *I'm pleased today to release officially the State Department's Annual Country Report on Human Rights. These reports reflect the American people's commitment to high standards of respect for human dignity and freedom for all people. . . .*
>
> *When human rights standards are observed, sustainable economic progress is more likely; violent conflicts are easier to prevent; terrorists and criminals find it harder to operate, and societies are more fully able to benefit from the skills and energy of their citizens.*
>
> *In such an environment, Americans are safer, and we are more likely to find good partners with whom to pursue shared economic, diplomatic, and security goals. That is why human rights are and will remain a key element in our foreign policy, both in our bilateral [two-sided] relationships and in our leadership with international organizations. . . .*
>
> *Open economic and political systems contribute to national well-being in a host of ways. Women and men who are free to think for themselves and who have fair access to the levers of economic and political power will be more productive and have a more stabilizing impact than those whose creativity is shut down. . . .*
>
> *We live at a time when democratic principles and respect for human rights have greater reach than at any previous time in history. This is due not simply to what governments have done but to what people around the world have done either within their own countries or through non-governmental organizations to elevate, monitor, and enforce human rights standards.*

1. What is more likely to occur when human-rights standards are observed?

2. How do open economic and political systems contribute to national well-being?

3. Why is it important for the U.S. government to set a standard for human rights?

CHAPTER 9

ECONOMIC POLICY

Imagine that you are preparing to start a T-shirt-manufacturing company and have to find a way to finance it. You know that you can raise money from selling the T-shirts, but how do you go about making them in the first place? You need to buy fabric and equipment to produce the T-shirts and hire people to design and sew them. You also need managers to coordinate these employees.

All of this is just to create the T-shirts. You still have to find a place to keep them, stores to buy them, and a way to transport them to the stores.

As you can see, running an individual company involves hundreds of fundamental decisions. Now imagine the process that the U.S. government must go through to finance its operations. It can raise money through taxes and other means, but that is only part of the process. Lawmakers must then decide how to spend the money in a way that will provide for the public good of the more than 260 million people in the United States. In recent years the federal government has spent as much as $1.5 trillion annually trying to accomplish this task. In this chapter you will learn about how the government raises and spends that money.

Government Notebook

In your Government Notebook, describe what impact you think the government's economic policies have on your daily life.

RAISING REVENUE

Political Dictionary

revenue
tax
exemption
deduction
excise tax
estate tax
gift tax
customs duty
standard of living

Objectives

★ What are the major types of federal taxes?
★ How does the federal government collect taxes?
★ What sources of revenue, other than taxes, does the federal government have?
★ What factors have affected the political debate over tax policy in recent decades?

As you can imagine, the federal government cannot develop and sustain its programs without **revenue**—the income it collects. Today, **taxes**—charges laid on individuals and businesses by a government—are the federal government's primary source of revenue.

Federal Taxes

For fiscal year 1996, federal taxes totaled just over $1.4 trillion. (A fiscal year is a 12-month financial period that might or might not follow the regular calendar year. The federal government's fiscal year begins on October 1 and ends on September 30.) The federal government relies on several types of taxes for revenue. The graph on this page shows the percentage of revenue that each tax generates.

Individual Income Tax The individual income tax makes up the federal government's largest source of revenue. Around 45 percent of all federal revenue currently comes from this tax. The individual income tax is levied on a person's taxable income, including wages or salaries, business profits, tips, interest, and dividends (payments received as a return on an investment). It is a progressive tax, which means that it takes a larger percentage from a high-income person than from a low-income person.

The income tax is not assessed on a person's entire yearly income. Rather, taxable income is the sum of all sources of a person's income minus certain deductions and exemptions. Each taxpayer is allowed a standard **exemption**—an amount of income upon which the government does not levy a tax. Plus, other exemptions exist for each dependent—or additional person reliant on the taxpayer's income—for example, a child.

Deductions are amounts that the government allows taxpayers to subtract from their taxable income. For example, the government allows people who have borrowed money to pay for a home to deduct interest payments on the loan from their taxable income. If a person has an income of

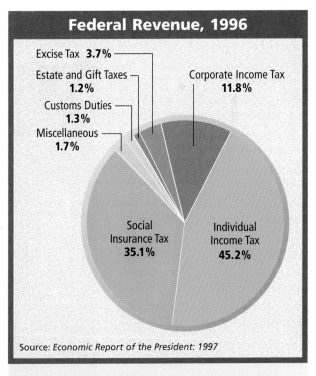

Federal Revenue, 1996

Excise Tax **3.7%**
Estate and Gift Taxes **1.2%**
Customs Duties **1.3%**
Miscellaneous **1.7%**
Corporate Income Tax **11.8%**
Social Insurance Tax **35.1%**
Individual Income Tax **45.2%**

Source: *Economic Report of the President: 1997*

Federal revenue comes from several sources. The social insurance tax and the individual income tax make up more than four fifths of this revenue. **What type of tax makes up the smallest percentage of federal revenue?**

CITIZENSHIP *People who have borrowed money to pay for a home are allowed to deduct interest payments on their loan from their taxable income. **What other types of income tax deductions does the government allow individuals?***

$50,000, interest payments totaling $5,000 would reduce taxable income to $45,000. A person may also deduct certain charitable donations. In addition, certain kinds of income are nontaxable; for instance, interest income that is earned on money that has been borrowed by a state or local government is not taxable.

Most employees pay individual income taxes through a payroll deduction system. Under this system, employers withhold a certain amount of money from an employee's pay and forward it to the Internal Revenue Service (IRS)—the branch of the Treasury Department in charge of tax collection. This "pay-as-you-go" system also applies to people who are self-employed. Self-employed people make quarterly payments to the IRS based on the amount of income they expect to earn over the calendar year. Overpayments are typically refunded in the next calendar year.

Do you recognize the date April 15? This day—Tax Day—inspires dread in many people around the country. On or before April 15, all U.S. residents who earned taxable income in the preceding year must file their tax returns with the IRS. Tax returns list all sources of a person's income, any exemptions and deductions the person can legally claim, and the amount of money that he or she owes to or is owed by the IRS.

Corporate Income Tax A corporation—a form of business organization—also must pay a federal income tax. The corporate income tax is based on a corporation's net income—that is, all income earned above the cost of maintaining the business.

The corporate income tax is the most complicated federal tax because of the numerous deductions that the government allows a corporation to take. Many of these tax breaks are granted to help achieve certain national goals. For example, to promote industrial growth, the government may allow a corporation to deduct the costs of expansion and modernization. In addition, corporations may deduct a certain percentage of their charitable donations.

Corporate income taxes are the federal government's third-largest source of revenue. In 1996, for example, corporate income taxes accounted for 11.8 percent of all federal revenue.

PUBLIC GOOD *Corporations may be allowed to take tax deductions for modernizing their equipment and facilities. **What other types of deductions can corporations take?***

Social Insurance Taxes In addition to the revenue it receives from income taxes, the federal government collects huge sums of money each year to finance two social welfare programs:

★ Old-Age, Survivors, and Disability Insurance (OASDI)—or Social Security—and
★ Medicare, which provides health care to the elderly, regardless of their income level.

These social programs are funded through taxes collected under the Federal Insurance Contributions Act (FICA). FICA taxes are paid by both the employee and the employer. As with individual income taxes, FICA taxes are withheld from workers' pay. The employer matches the amount paid by the employee and sends the full payment to the government. Self-employed people must pay the entire FICA tax themselves, although they can deduct 50 percent of the money paid in FICA taxes from their taxable income.

Excise Taxes The government also receives revenue from **excise taxes**, which are levied on the manufacture, sale, or consumption of certain goods or services. The federal government places excise taxes on such goods and services as tobacco, gasoline, alcohol, and telephone systems. In 1996, excise taxes accounted for around 4 percent of federal revenue.

An excise tax is a regressive tax, for it charges all taxpayers the same rate. Because the excise tax imposes the same tax on everyone purchasing a certain good or service, it takes a larger percentage of a lower income than it does of a higher income.

Estate and Gift Taxes The federal government also generates revenue through estate and gift taxes. An **estate tax** is a tax placed on a deceased person's assets when they are transferred to someone else. Federal estate taxes are levied on all such assets worth more than $600,000 (to be gradually increased to $1.2 million over the next few years). A **gift tax** is a tax placed on the transfer of certain gifts of value to individuals. Gift taxes are paid by anyone giving gifts the total value of which exceeds a certain amount in a given year. Federal estate and gift taxes account for only about 1 percent of total federal revenue.

Customs Duties Also known as tariffs or import duties, **customs duties** are taxes levied by the federal government on goods brought into the United States from abroad. The United States collects these duties not only to raise revenue but also to protect U.S. business, agriculture, and industry from harmful foreign competition.

The Constitution gives Congress the power to levy customs duties. Congress has, in turn, authorized the president to raise or lower these duties by certain percentages, as well as to make agreements with foreign countries to help reduce trade barriers. The president's decisions generally are based on the recommendations of the U.S. International Trade Commission (ITC). If the president does not follow the recommendations of the ITC, Congress can override presidential decisions by a two-thirds vote.

Before the introduction of the federal income tax, customs

CONSTITUTIONAL GOVERNMENT *Consumers must pay an excise tax each time they purchase goods such as gasoline, tobacco, and alcohol.* **What type of a tax is an excise tax?**

POLITICAL FOUNDATIONS *Customs duties are placed on goods brought into the United States from abroad. Congress has the power to levy customs duties.* ***Why does the U.S. government collect customs duties?***

duties were the most important source of revenue for the United States. Today, however, customs duties amount to only about 1.3 percent of federal revenue.

Nontax Revenue

Taxes are not the only source of revenue for the federal government. In fact, in 1996 the net federal receipts—the total amount of money raised by the federal government—included more than $25 billion in nontax revenue.

This money comes from several sources. The main source of nontax revenue is composed of earnings by Federal Reserve banks. (The Federal Reserve system and its role in the U.S. economy are more fully explained in Section 2.) Fees and fines collected by various government agencies also provide revenue for the federal government.

Do you have a passport? Whenever you pay the processing fee for a federal service such as a passport, you are contributing to federal revenue. Other nontax revenue includes fees paid for patents, trademarks, or copyrights; fines imposed by the federal courts; and money earned from the sale or lease of federal lands.

Politics of Making Tax Policy

When lawmakers create tax policy, they must address two questions: How high should taxes be, and what tax advantages should be offered? These questions have been answered in different ways during U.S. history. In tax debates during recent decades, Democrats—motivated in part by the desire to fund government programs to aid less-advantaged citizens—generally have favored higher and more progressive taxes. Many Democrats also have opposed tax advantages for the wealthy. Republicans generally have favored lower taxes.

The most significant feature of the tax debate since the 1970s, however, has been growing public opposition to taxes. By the late 1970s, disillusionment with government led people to question the usefulness of much government spending. Around the same time, supply-side economics was gaining support among Republicans. Supply-side economists argued that taxes should be cut to stimulate economic growth. According to this view, if less income were taxed, people would produce more because they would get to keep more of their earnings.

In 1980 Jack Kemp, then a Republican member of Congress from Buffalo, New York, persuaded presidential candidate Ronald Reagan to adopt the supply-side theory. Reagan made the call for a cut in income taxes one of the major themes of his campaign. Reagan won the election, and—because Democrats were unable to resist the public's tax-cutting zeal—in 1981 he got Congress to accept a 25 percent cut over three years.

The tax cut of 1981 was one of two major changes in tax law during Reagan's presidency. The other change was the Tax Reform Act of 1986. Income tax rates were slashed again and made less progressive. This time, many tax advantages enjoyed by the wealthy also were repealed. One might say the legislation reflected the main ideas of each party—Republican support for low tax rates and Democratic opposition to tax advantages for the wealthy.

In 1990, huge budget shortfalls that had appeared in the late 1980s inspired compromise on a tax increase, which Congress passed and President George Bush signed. In 1993 President Bill Clinton unveiled a plan for taking further action to reduce the budget shortfalls. The

Democrat-dominated Congress responded by passing a sharp increase in the top income tax rate, affecting about 1.2 percent of all taxpayers. After the elections of 1994, however, when Republicans became a majority in Congress, tax cuts were back on the national agenda. As you will learn in Section 4, Congress and the president reached an agreement on modest tax cuts within the framework of a plan to balance the budget by the year 2002.

Tax Policy and the Public Good

Tax policy decisions affect both the U.S. **standard of living**—that is, how well people in general are doing —and the distribution of economic benefits. People disagree about whether or not government should redistribute wealth through taxes. Supporters of redistribution argue that the natural distribution of the income and wealth produced by the U.S. economy is unfair. Unequal opportunities and sometimes sheer luck have too big an impact on economic success, they say. Therefore, the government should equalize wealth through income redistribution.

Opponents of income redistribution make several counterarguments. First, they hold that the

Courtesy of David Horsey, Seattle Post-Intelligencer.

PUBLIC GOOD *Some people believe that government should redistribute wealth through taxes.* **What criticism does this cartoon make of government tax policy?**

uneven distribution of income broadly reflects important differences in people's efforts to earn a living as well as in their contributions to society. They also argue that redistribution schemes hurt economic growth and hence tend to reduce people's overall standard of living. High taxes on wealthy individuals take away some of the personal benefit from their economic endeavors and thus discourage them from making larger contributions to society.

SECTION 1 — REVIEW

1. Define the following terms: revenue, tax, exemption, deduction, excise tax, estate tax, gift tax, customs duty, standard of living.

2. What type of tax generates the most revenue for the U.S. government? What are the other types of taxes?

3. Explain the pay-as-you-go system of tax collection. How do self-employed people pay taxes to the federal government?

4. What are the primary sources of the federal government's nontax revenue?

5. Discuss the issues that have influenced tax policy in recent decades. How have Republicans and Democrats differed in their views?

6. **Thinking and Writing Critically**
   In addition to raising revenue, what purposes might excise, estate, and gift taxes serve?

7. **Applying** CONSTITUTIONAL GOVERNMENT
   The federal government's power to tax is stated in the Constitution. Why might it be necessary to have such powers outlined in the Constitution? Explain your answer.

INFLUENCING THE ECONOMY

Political Dictionary

free enterprise
recession
inflation
fiscal policy
monetary policy
disposable income
Federal Reserve system
reserve requirements
discount rate
open-market operations
bond
Keynesianism
deficit
monetarism

Objectives

★ How is the U.S. economy organized?
★ What are the goals of economic stabilization policy?
★ What tools does the U.S. government use to stabilize the economy?

The ways in which the U.S. government chooses to spend $1.5 trillion a year directly affect the overall national economy. There is more to economic policy, however, than just raising money and spending it on government programs. The government also attempts to stabilize the economy and promote economic growth.

The two main goals in economic stabilization are full employment and low inflation. The government uses two tools to achieve these goals: fiscal policy and monetary policy. It also uses industrial policy to promote growth in the economy. This chapter will explain just what each of these terms means. To understand how government economic policies work, however, you must first understand how the U.S. economy is organized.

Organization of the U.S. Economy

The United States has what is known as a **free-enterprise** economy—one in which business can be conducted freely, with little government intervention. A free-enterprise system is dependent on a market in which goods and services are exchanged freely.

Free-Enterprise System The free-enterprise system of the United States is based on five main rights:

★ to own private property and enter into contracts,
★ to make individual choices,
★ to engage in economic competition,
★ to make decisions based on self-interest, and
★ to participate in the economy with limited government involvement and regulation.

A major benefit of the free-enterprise system is that it produces what consumers want. If consumer demand for blue jeans is higher than that for formal gowns, for instance, more jeans

POLITICAL FOUNDATIONS *In a free-enterprise system, individuals can choose which goods and services they want to buy.* ***Why do some people believe that private ownership and free markets provide the best environment for economic growth?***

will be produced than gowns. In addition, producers who offer lower-quality jeans at the same price as their competitors' higher-quality jeans will likely sell little merchandise or even go out of business. Supporters of free enterprise believe that private ownership and free markets will provide the best environment for economic growth, because businesspeople wanting to make money are driven constantly to look for new things to produce or better ways to produce them.

Government and the Economy Economic policy in the U.S. free-enterprise system often has been a source of political controversy. The basic political disputes involve the extent to which government should intervene in the operation of the free market (such as when consumer demands shift from American-made products to goods made abroad). The free market leaves some people unemployed or with low-paying jobs. Some people believe that government should address this problem by making the distribution of income and wealth more even. Others believe that government should reduce the pain when disruptions occur.

In addition, although the free market usually works well to achieve economic growth, many people think that there are situations in which government intervention can produce stronger economic growth than the free market can when left alone. Similarly, some argue that the government should play a role in stabilizing the economy by taking steps to lessen the cycles of boom and **recession**—economic downturns—that many economists see as characteristic of a free-market system.

Democrats have traditionally favored greater government intervention in the economy. In general, they support greater equality in income and do not believe as strongly that the free market will solve all economic problems. These ideas gain greater electoral support from lower-income voters, who are more likely to suffer from economic disruption or instability. Republicans have been inclined toward minimizing government involvement, a policy often called laissez-faire (French for "let [the people] do [as they will]"). Laissez-faire policy reflects a greater belief in the ability of the market to create high overall standards of living, as well as a worry that government intervention tends to hurt rather than help the economy. Support for laissez-faire policy often comes from higher-income voters, who have more of a cushion against economic disruption or instability.

Stabilization Goals

The terms *economic growth* and *economic stabilization* mean different things to the U.S. economy. Economic growth determines a country's long-term standard of living. It determines whether a country will achieve more wealth or remain poverty-ridden. Economic stability involves changes in unemployment and **inflation**—the general rise in prices that often accompanies economic booms. Economic growth rates determine how high the economic airplane is flying; economic stability determines how bumpy the ride is. It is possible for a growing economy to be unstable. Likewise, it is possible for a poor country to have a low rate of inflation and unemployment.

The government attempts to fulfill two main goals with a stabilization policy. These are full employment and low inflation.

Full Employment Full employment is an obvious goal for government because people need income to survive. During economic downturns, employment levels drop, sometimes dramatically. Loss of a job can cause serious problems even for two-income households, which can have difficulty paying all of their monthly bills—such as payments on a home loan—on a single income. In addition, unemployment hurts the general public because it lowers the total output of the economy.

Low Inflation During economic upswings, harmful, inflationary pressures can develop. Thus, stabilization policy is designed to avoid major growth booms in the economy, as well as recessions.

Inflation creates significant problems, such as hindering economic growth. It pushes up interest rates beyond the level justified by the current rate of inflation, as banks cushion themselves against the risk of even higher inflation in the future when the borrowed money will be paid back. Because higher interest rates mean an increased cost of borrowing money, they discourage investment in new plants and equipment.

Inflation also has significant psychological effects. When prices start going up rapidly, people feel insecure, as if an earthquake were shaking under them. In a famous line many people think was a key element in his landslide victory in the 1980 presidential campaign, Ronald Reagan asked during a televised debate with President Jimmy Carter, "Are you better off today than you were four years ago?" In fact, the numbers showed that many people *were* better off: real per capita spendable income in 1980 was nearly 7.5 percent higher than when Carter took office in 1977, and the unemployment rate was lower. A lot of people *felt* worse, however. The biggest reason was that inflation had been running at a rate of more than 10 percent.

Tools for Economic Stabilization

Government may use both fiscal and monetary policies to deal with unemployment and inflation. **Fiscal policy** is a set of government spending, taxing, and borrowing policies used to achieve desired levels of economic performance. **Monetary policy** is a set of procedures designed to regulate the economy by controlling the amount of money in circulation as well as the level of interest rates.

Fiscal Policy The federal government uses the budget to develop fiscal policy through its taxing and spending plans. By increasing spending or by lowering taxes, the government can increase the overall level of demand for goods and services in the economy, thereby putting more money into a slow-moving economy and stimulating growth. On the other hand, the government may decide to decrease spending if a rapidly growing economy produces inflation.

In addition to adjusting spending, the federal government also uses taxation as a tool for stabilizing the economy. If unemployment is very high, for example, the government may respond by cutting taxes. A tax cut will increase people's **disposable income**—the amount they have to spend after accounting for financial obligations such as taxes—and allows businesses to keep more of their profits. When people have more money, demand for goods and services rises. When businesses have more, they are able to invest money and hire more workers, thus decreasing unemployment.

If inflation is high, however, policy makers may raise taxes. Higher taxes reduce a person's disposable income and a corporation's net profits. This reduces the amount of money people spend and slows business activity, which, in turn, tends to lower prices.

Monetary Policy The second way in which the federal government tries to influence the economy is through its monetary policy. Monetary

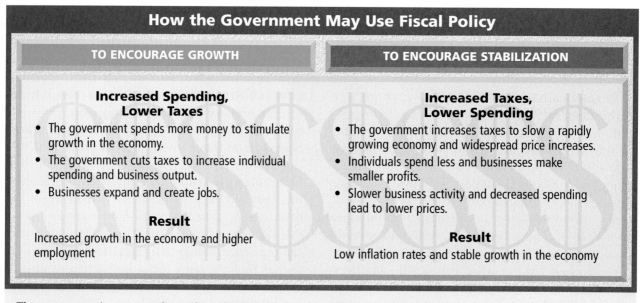

How the Government May Use Fiscal Policy

TO ENCOURAGE GROWTH	TO ENCOURAGE STABILIZATION
Increased Spending, Lower Taxes	**Increased Taxes, Lower Spending**
• The government spends more money to stimulate growth in the economy.	• The government increases taxes to slow a rapidly growing economy and widespread price increases.
• The government cuts taxes to increase individual spending and business output.	• Individuals spend less and businesses make smaller profits.
• Businesses expand and create jobs.	• Slower business activity and decreased spending lead to lower prices.
Result	**Result**
Increased growth in the economy and higher employment	Low inflation rates and stable growth in the economy

The government's taxing and spending plans may be used to achieve different results.
What results may be achieved if the government increases taxes?

Raising the Minimum Wage

Thirteen million Americans work in minimum-wage jobs in the service, retail, and agricultural industries. Many of these people, often trying to support a family as well as themselves, applauded congressional efforts in 1996 to raise the minimum wage.

President Bill Clinton backed the plan. "If we value work, if we value families, we ought to raise the value of the minimum wage. Now is the time to put politics aside . . . and help lift the lives of millions of America's workers." However, 1996 also was an election year, and the proposal to raise the minimum wage became entangled in politics. Politicians, business owners, economists, and the public aired differing views about the government's role in helping workers and the possible economic impact of the legislation.

Many restaurant owners predicted that raising the minimum wage would make earning a profit extremely difficult—"I would probably end up out of business," concluded Nevada pizzeria owner Sandra Murphy. The National Restaurant Association warned that raising the minimum wage would mean that many minimum-wage workers would lose their jobs, because these workers did not produce enough to justify a higher wage. Economists warned that because employers would have to pay more to employees, fewer new jobs would be created.

Some politicians agreed with restaurant owners and strongly opposed the wage hike. Senator Don Nickles, for example, criticized it as the response of a heavy-handed federal government interfering in the free market. Bob Dole, the Republican presidential candidate in 1996, accused the Democrats, most of whom supported the increase, of caving in to pressure from labor unions.

The American Federation of Labor–Congress of Industrial Organizations (AFL–CIO)—the nation's largest labor union—did endorse the wage increase. The union noted that the minimum wage had not increased since 1991. Union leaders argued that minimum-wage workers' pay, when adjusted for inflation, was near a 40-year low. They predicted that raising the minimum wage would ease poverty and help lower taxes by enabling people to rely less on food stamps and other public assistance.

Both sides of the debate used economists' studies to support their position. Supporters of a minimum-wage increase pointed to research showing that the 1990 and 1991 minimum-wage increases caused little if any job loss. Critics of the wage hike, however, emphasized studies that predicted the increase would reduce the number of minimum-wage jobs by 20 percent.

In this war of conflicting numbers, public support proved the most important. Polls showed that 80 percent of Americans favored an increase in the minimum wage. Eventually, Republicans joined with Democrats to pass the measure. In August 1996 President Clinton signed into law a two-step increase in the minimum wage, which brought the minimum wage to $5.15 in September 1997.

Many workers received an increase in their wages after Congress passed a bill to raise the minimum wage.

What Do You Think?

1. Do you think that the 1996 minimum-wage increase promoted the public good? Why or why not?
2. What were the major arguments against the minimum-wage increase?

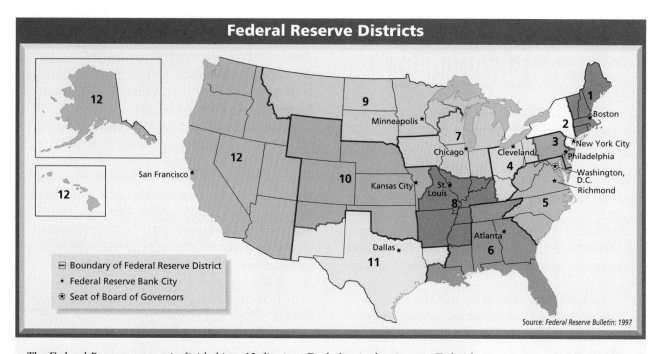

Federal Reserve Districts

Boundary of Federal Reserve District
★ Federal Reserve Bank City
⊛ Seat of Board of Governors

Source: Federal Reserve Bulletin: 1997

The Federal Reserve system is divided into 12 districts. Each district has its own Federal Reserve bank, which is owned by other banks in the district. **In which Federal Reserve district is your state located?**

policy is controlled through the **Federal Reserve system**—or the "Fed"—which is the central banking system of the United States. The Fed, created by the Federal Reserve Act of 1913, is an independent government agency.

The Fed is not a bank like your neighborhood bank. You cannot set up an account there. It gives out no automated teller cards, and it will not lend you money. Rather, the Fed is a "central bank" that controls how much money is in circulation. The Fed is organized unlike any other government agency. It is made up of 12 regional Federal Reserve banks and thousands of privately owned member banks.

The Fed's two main decision-making bodies are the Board of Governors and the Federal Open Market Committee (FOMC). The Board of Governors, located in Washington, D.C., heads the Federal Reserve system. It is made up of seven members who are appointed by the president and confirmed by the Senate for 14-year terms. The chair of the Board of Governors is also appointed by the president. The board supervises the Fed's banking services and issues policies that regulate the U.S. money supply. It also oversees the activities of the district and member banks and approves the appointments of their presidents. The FOMC steers the strategy of the Fed's monetary

policy. The seven members of the Board of Governors and the president of the Federal Reserve Bank of New York are permanent members of the FOMC. The remaining four members are presidents of district Federal Reserve banks who serve one-year terms on a rotating basis.

The Federal Reserve system is divided into 12 geographic districts, each of which houses one Federal Reserve bank. The 12 district banks, which are not operated for profit, perform regulatory functions for banks in their district. After subtracting their operating costs, the district banks send their yearly income to the U.S. Treasury.

Each Federal Reserve bank is owned by other banks in the district, which buy stock in the district bank. These banks are called member banks. There are around 9,700 commercial banks in the United States. Of these, more than 3,700 are members of the Federal Reserve system.

Making Monetary Policy

The Federal Reserve uses three tools to implement monetary policy. These are

★ reserve requirements,
★ the discount rate, and
★ open-market operations.

Reserve Requirements The first tool the Fed uses to implement monetary policy involves rules for banks. These **reserve requirements** determine the minimum amount of money that a bank must keep on hand at all times and thus not lend out to its patrons. By raising reserve requirements, the Fed lowers the amount of money that banks can lend, thereby decreasing the money supply in the economy. A lowering of reserve requirements has the opposite effect.

The Fed rarely changes reserve requirements, for to do so creates uncertainty in the banking system. Changes may also make it more difficult for banks to make long-term loans and investments.

Discount Rate A second tool that the Federal Reserve uses is the **discount rate**—the interest rate that it charges to banks. Remember that the Fed is a banker's bank. If a bank wants to borrow money so that it can, in turn, loan the money to a person or business, it can do so by borrowing from the Fed. The lower the discount rate, the more inclined banks are to borrow from the Fed; the higher the rate, the less inclined they are. Thus, because the overall money supply in the U.S. economy increases when banks lend more money to customers, the Fed can influence the economy by adjusting the discount rate.

The Fed also sets the federal funds rate—the interest rate at which banks can borrow funds from each other. Raising or lowering the federal funds rate can encourage or discourage banks from borrowing from each other. Although it does not affect the money supply directly, raising or lowering the federal funds rate does have an impact on banking and the economy in general.

Open-Market Operations The most common way the Federal Reserve influences the economy is through **open-market operations**—the purchase or sale of bonds in order to finance the operations of government. **Bonds**, or securities, are certificates issued by a government to a lender from whom it has borrowed money. By buying or selling these bonds, the Fed is able to increase or decrease the money supply in the economy.

When the Federal Reserve buys government bonds from private investors, the money supply increases because the Fed pays by adding funds to the general economy. In contrast, when the Fed sells bonds, it tightens the money supply by accepting funds that had been in circulation.

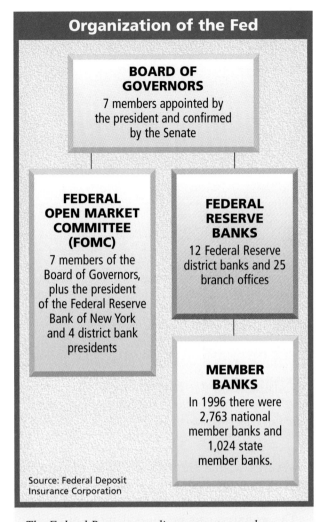

Organization of the Fed

BOARD OF GOVERNORS
7 members appointed by the president and confirmed by the Senate

FEDERAL OPEN MARKET COMMITTEE (FOMC)
7 members of the Board of Governors, plus the president of the Federal Reserve Bank of New York and 4 district bank presidents

FEDERAL RESERVE BANKS
12 Federal Reserve district banks and 25 branch offices

MEMBER BANKS
In 1996 there were 2,763 national member banks and 1,024 state member banks.

Source: Federal Deposit Insurance Corporation

The Federal Reserve supplies money to member banks across the country. Member banks must follow the rules and regulations established by the Fed. **Which branch of the Fed steers overall monetary strategy?**

Monetary Versus Fiscal Policy

Monetary policy can work much faster than fiscal policy. Fiscal policy is tied to annual budgets and involves a lag between when an economic problem occurs and when shifts in fiscal policy are actually felt. A change in monetary policy, on the other hand, works much more quickly, since a change in policy is effective immediately.

Remember that fiscal policy is made entirely by the president and Congress. They decide how much to tax and how much to spend. Monetary policy, however, is controlled by an independent agency that is not elected by the people. For this reason, some people believe that the Fed's role in making economic policy is too great. Others,

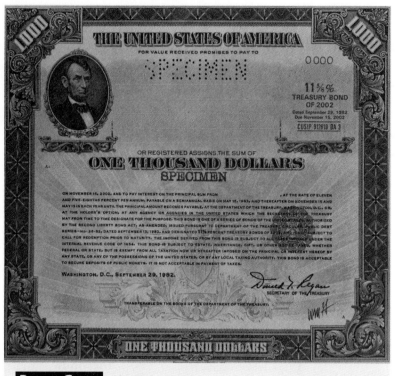

PUBLIC GOOD *The Federal Reserve influences the economy by buying and selling bonds.* **What happens to the money supply when the Fed sells government bonds?**

attention to issues of long-term economic growth.

The economic doctrine supporting active government stabilization is most often called **Keynesianism** (KAYN-zee-uh-ni-zuhm), after John Maynard Keynes. Keynes was a British economist who called for the government to stimulate the economy during the Great Depression of the 1930s. The basic argument that Keynesians make is that active government stabilization policies can counteract instability in the normal operation of a free-market economy. In response to an economic slowdown, Keynesian fiscal policy calls for the government to run a budget **deficit**—or let expenses exceed revenue—and to use its monetary policy to provide low interest rates to stimulate the economy.

The high point for Keynesianism came during the 1960s. In 1963 President John Kennedy proposed a tax cut, hoping that consumers would respond by spending more money and thus stimulating the economy. The proposed tax cut was not to be offset by government spending cuts, however, and would therefore result in a budget deficit. Kennedy hoped that the deficit would eventually disappear as the economy improved.

The tax cut, which was actually passed during President Lyndon Johnson's administration, contributed to increased economic growth and seemed to support Keynesian ideas. Loosening restrictions on spending made it possible to expand spending on public aid while running budget deficits.

During the 1970s Keynesian doctrine became subject to growing intellectual and political challenges. The benefits of the economic boom in the years after the Kennedy-inspired tax cut were increasingly undercut by inflation. Then in 1973 an increase in oil prices after an embargo by oil-producing nations resulted in a mixture of high inflation and lower economic growth. In this climate, Milton Friedman, a University of Chicago professor and leading economic conservative, popularized **monetarism**.

Monetarists argue that a market economy, working properly and left alone, most likely will operate at full employment and low inflation.

however, say that the lack of political pressure ensures that the Fed will do what is best for the economy, not what is best for a political party.

The country can be guided most effectively when fiscal and monetary policy are used together. For example, if inflation is the most important economic problem, monetary and fiscal policies should work together to curb demand and thus reduce prices. The Fed would need to reduce the money supply and the availability of credit, while Congress and the president would need to agree on a fiscal policy that involves decreased federal spending, increased taxes, or both.

Economic Policy and the Public Good

Between the 1930s and the 1960s the most important economic policy debates between Democrats and Republicans involved stabilization policy. Democrats wanted government to play an active role in stabilizing the economy, and Republicans opposed such a role. During the last two decades, stabilization policy debates have become less important as political leaders have turned their

They believe that economic downturns—including the Great Depression—have occurred not because of economic instability, but because mistaken government policies have intervened in the economy's operation and drastically cut the supply of money. Monetarists believe that government's only role in terms of economic stabilization should be to keep the money supply expanding at a steady pace to accommodate economic growth.

Industrial Policy and Economic Growth

Stabilization policy aims to even out the bumps in the economy. By contrast, over the past 15 years there also have been debates about whether government aid (often called industrial policy) can increase overall economic growth.

When the phrase *industrial policy* was introduced in the early 1980s, it frequently referred to attempts to prop up declining industries. Arguments on behalf of aid to such industries involve maintaining the current number of jobs in these inefficient industries rather than improving the overall economy. In recent years, however, the phrase has been used almost exclusively to refer to aiding "industries of the future." These industries—particularly high-tech ones such as computer technology, semiconductors, telecommunications, and biotechnology—hold promise for future economic growth. Supporters suggest that aiding such industries would improve overall economic growth by allowing these new industries to move forward more quickly.

Supporters of industrial policy also have argued that Japan has successfully followed a bold policy to target important industrial sectors, particularly those involving high-tech consumer goods. They also point to various internationally successful sectors of the U.S. economy, such as agriculture, computer technology, biotechnology, and aviation, which have benefited both from significant government research money and from government purchases (particularly for defense). Industrial policy supporters argue that if such industries are not supported by the government, they will lag behind their global competitors in basic scientific research and development, for market forces alone will not support such future-oriented endeavors.

On the other hand, opponents of industrial policy have expressed skepticism about the ability of government to improve on the operation of the free market. They hold that the government cannot do a better job than private investors in picking the economic winners of the future and should thus stay on the sidelines.

The most insistent criticism of industrial policy has to do with the way the U.S. political system works. Even if a good case might be made for industrial policy in theory, opponents argue, pork-barrel politics and interest group influence are likely to result in the wrong industries being chosen for government help.

SECTION 2 — REVIEW

1. Define the following terms: free enterprise, recession, inflation, fiscal policy, monetary policy, disposable income, Federal Reserve system, reserve requirements, discount rate, open-market operations, bond, Keynesianism, deficit, monetarism.

2. Describe the organization of the U.S. economy.

3. What two factors are most important in making economic policy?

4. What is the difference between monetary and fiscal policy?

5. **Thinking and Writing Critically**
Consider the institutions involved in making both fiscal and monetary policy. Why is it important that these two types of policies be used together?

6. **Applying PRINCIPLES OF DEMOCRACY**
Conduct an Internet search on the Federal Reserve system. You may want to consult the chart on page 201 that shows the organization of the Fed to find search words that you might use. Briefly describe the information you find.

THE FEDERAL BUDGET

Political Dictionary

federal budget
Office of Management and Budget
Congressional Budget Office
resolution
reconciliation

Objectives

★ How has the federal budget-making process changed over the years?
★ What role does the president play in planning the budget?
★ Why are attempts at reducing the budget politically controversial?

In 1789 Congress created the Treasury Department as one of the original executive departments. Alexander Hamilton, the first secretary of the treasury, established the role of the federal government in the economy by promoting a form of national economic planning. Hamilton believed that the country required a national spending program based on the priorities and needs of the nation as a whole. The executive branch would submit departmental estimates of funding to Congress, asking for the money needed to carry out the programs. Today, the U.S. national spending program is known as the **federal budget**.

Changes in the Budget Process

Though the idea of preparing a federal spending plan came from Alexander Hamilton, the means by which the budget is prepared has changed dramatically over the past two centuries. In fact, the budgetary process as it now stands is fairly new. Before the early 1900s the United States had no formal system for planning how to spend the revenues that it collected. Each federal department simply

issued requests for funds as the money was needed. By the early 1900s many people in government, including President William Howard Taft, were calling for a more orderly budget process.

Budget and Accounting Act of 1921 A significant step in reforming the national budget process was made in 1921 with the passage of the Budget and Accounting Act. This legislation gave a newly established Bureau of the Budget the power to raise or lower agencies' spending requests before they were sent to Congress.

Office of Management and Budget In 1939 the Bureau of the Budget was moved from the Treasury Department to the Executive Office of the President. This made it easier for the president to influence the budget and thus increased the president's role in making economic policy. The position of director of the **Office of Management and Budget** (OMB)—as the bureau was renamed in 1971—has cabinet-level status.

Congressional Budget and Impoundment Control Act of 1974 The process by which Congress examines the president's budget proposal has changed considerably over the last two decades. For nearly 200 years, there was no process by which Congress could consider the budget as a whole. Congress never voted on overall

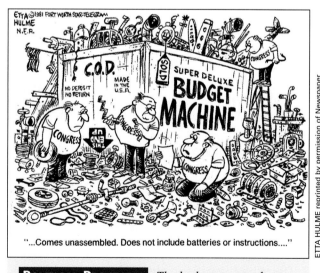

"...Comes unassembled. Does not include batteries or instructions...."

POLITICAL PROCESSES *The budget process has undergone numerous changes over the past 100 years, yet it is still a complex procedure that does not always run smoothly.* **What does this cartoon imply about Congress's ability to prepare the budget?**

ETTA HULME reprinted by permission of Newspaper Enterprise Association, Inc.

PUBLIC GOOD *One of President Bill Clinton's campaign promises was to provide funding to public schools for Internet access. Here, President Clinton and Vice President Al Gore visit a computer facility at a public school.* ***What is the president's role in the preparation of the budget?***

year's budget to determine which areas of government should receive more, or less, funding than last year. That is, if an agency received an appropriation of $1 billion last year and is asking for $1.1 billion this year, examination typically will not center on the $1 billion, but on whether the additional $100 million is justified.

President's Role The budget process begins with the Office of Management and Budget's guidelines about the overall fiscal situation that detail the kinds of programs the president wants to support or reduce. Each agency then uses those guidelines to develop a spending proposal, which is considered by OMB. Two considerations tend to drive OMB's evaluation of a proposal: keeping spending in line and remaining loyal to the president's priorities.

Members of the OMB staff review the agencies' requests and present their overall recommendations to the president. Over the next several months, each federal agency, OMB, and the president review and negotiate a working budget proposal. Upon completion, the budget proposal is submitted to Congress before the established deadline, which is February 1.

Appropriations Process According to the U.S. Constitution, "No money shall be drawn from the Treasury, but in consequence of appropriations made by law." Once the president's proposed budget has been submitted, Congress takes the lead in the budgetary process. It must draft and approve spending and revenue bills for the coming fiscal year. As noted in Chapter 6, spending for a program must first be authorized, and then funds are appropriated for it. Authorizations and appropriations are arrived at after a long process of review, debate, and compromise.

The Budget Committees of both the House and Senate set overall spending targets and revenue goals, based at least partly on the president's proposal. Congress then must pass a resolution setting

spending levels but rather on a series of separate appropriations bills for different agencies over several months. This made it difficult to compare one appropriation with another. In theory, a member could vote in favor of every proposal to spend money and against every proposal to levy taxes.

To amend this situation, Congress passed the Congressional Budget and Impoundment Control Act of 1974, which limited presidential impoundments and set ceilings for the budgets each year. (An impoundment is a refusal by the president to spend funds that Congress has authorized and appropriated.)

The 1974 Budget Act created budget committees in the House and Senate to allow Congress to review the president's budget proposal more systematically. The law also created the **Congressional Budget Office** (CBO) to provide economic data, information, and analysis to both houses of Congress.

Preparing the Budget Today

When preparing a budget, agencies do not begin with a blank slate. Rather, they—and the president and members of Congress—look over the previous

Economist

On a given day, economists at the Congressional Budget Office (CBO) might be called on by Congress to analyze the potential economic impact of a major bill, prepare a report on how the economy will fare in the next five years, and strategize about how to reduce the deficit. At the General Accounting Office (GAO), economists might wade through the budget of a government agency, looking for ways to cut costs.

Aside from colleges and universities, the federal government is the largest employer of economists. State and local governments also employ many economists to work in areas such as welfare and urban economics, monetary and fiscal policy, and industrial organization. Other economists work at universities as teachers and researchers. In addition, economists work for businesses and industries in areas such as finance, marketing, and economic growth and development.

People with skill at crunching numbers may find a position in economics fulfilling. Laura D'Andrea Tyson—an economics professor at the University of California at Berkeley and former chair of the National Economic Council (NEC)—became an economist for several reasons. "I felt (economics) was a wonderful combination of being able to be engaged in public-policy problems and, at the same time, use my analytic skills," she explained.

In 1993 Tyson became the first woman to serve as chair of the Council of Economic Advisers. As chair, she advised the president on tough issues such as the budget deficit and health-care reform. She also testified before Congress on economic

Laura D'Andrea Tyson was the chair of President Clinton's Council of Economic Advisers and, later, of the National Economic Council. She now teaches economics at the University of California at Berkeley.

issues. In 1995 she joined the NEC, taking on the high-pressure job of coordinating the president's overall economic strategy.

Most people who go on to become economists first sharpen their analytic skills by earning a college degree in economics. Many also pursue advanced degrees. Economists in key government posts, such as those Tyson has held, have extensive research and teaching experience as well.

In a time when the federal government is spending billions of dollars a day, the number-crunching skills of government economists are increasingly important in helping create sound public policies. With the government facing such high-stakes issues as eliminating the deficit, reforming welfare, and promoting economic growth, government economists at all levels will continue to be in high demand.

forth these goals. A **resolution** is a formal declaration or statement that does not require the signature of the president and does not have the force of law. In the case of the budget, Congress passes a concurrent resolution—a formal declaration by both houses. This resolution details the complete federal spending and tax plan for the upcoming fiscal year. Congress must complete the concurrent resolution for the next fiscal year by April 15,

although it may later revise the resolution. Congressional review of the budget continues with extensive hearings by the committees and subcommittees that have jurisdiction over the programs or agencies to be funded. Legislators examine agencies' requests and hear testimony from administration officials.

The various congressional committees, overseen by the House and Senate Appropriations

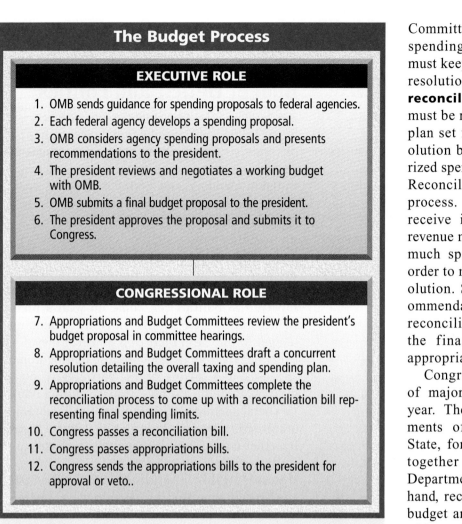

The Budget Process

EXECUTIVE ROLE

1. OMB sends guidance for spending proposals to federal agencies.
2. Each federal agency develops a spending proposal.
3. OMB considers agency spending proposals and presents recommendations to the president.
4. The president reviews and negotiates a working budget with OMB.
5. OMB submits a final budget proposal to the president.
6. The president approves the proposal and submits it to Congress.

CONGRESSIONAL ROLE

7. Appropriations and Budget Committees review the president's budget proposal in committee hearings.
8. Appropriations and Budget Committees draft a concurrent resolution detailing the overall taxing and spending plan.
9. Appropriations and Budget Committees complete the reconciliation process to come up with a reconciliation bill representing final spending limits.
10. Congress passes a reconciliation bill.
11. Congress passes appropriations bills.
12. Congress sends the appropriations bills to the president for approval or veto..

The budget preparation process requires members of the legislative and executive branches to complete several steps. **What is the role of OMB in this process?**

Committees, then prepare detailed spending and tax legislation but must keep within the limits set in the resolution. This process is called **reconciliation**, because the bills must be reconciled not only with the plan set forth in the concurrent resolution but also with already authorized spending for existing programs. Reconciliation thus is a two-step process. First, Budget Committees receive instructions on how much revenue needs to be generated or how much spending needs to be cut in order to meet goals set out in the resolution. Second, the committee recommendations are combined in a reconciliation bill that represents the final spending limits for all appropriations.

Congress passes a limited number of major appropriations bills each year. The funding for the Departments of Commerce, Justice, and State, for example, may be grouped together into one bill. The U.S. Department of Defense, on the other hand, receives a large portion of the budget and therefore has its funding addressed in a separate appropriations bill. After passing both houses, the appropriations bills go to the president for final approval or veto.

SECTION 3 — REVIEW

1. Define the following terms: federal budget, Office of Management and Budget, Congressional Budget Office, resolution, reconciliation.

2. Why was it necessary to revise the federal budget-making process in the early 1900s? What changes have been made to the process?

3. Who is responsible for making the original budget proposal for the federal government? How is that duty executed?

4. What groups are involved in the budget-making process after submission of the original proposal? What influences these groups' decisions in the appropriations process?

5. **Thinking and Writing Critically**
How do the changes in the federal budget-making process reflect the greater complexity of the federal government itself?

6. **Applying** POLITICAL PROCESSES
Conduct an Internet search for the types of appropriations that Congress will pass this year. What types of programs will be funded by each appropriation?

DEFICIT SPENDING AND THE ECONOMY

Political Dictionary

gross domestic product
entitlements
national debt
Gramm-Rudman-Hollings Act

Objectives

★ What factors cause the federal government to operate at a deficit?
★ How does the national debt influence the U.S. economy?
★ In what ways do the national debt and the federal deficit influence each other?

In this chapter, you have learned how the government takes in money and how decisions are made to spend it. What you may also know, however, is that the government at times has spent a lot more money than it raised. This has led to the accumulation of a huge national debt.

Federal Deficit

As you have read, if the government spends more than it takes in, in both tax and nontax revenue, the budget is in deficit. Between 1789 and 1932, two thirds of federal budgets showed a surplus, meaning the government raised more revenue than it spent. Since 1932, however, the budget has shown a surplus only eight times.

As noted in Section 1, at the beginning of Ronald Reagan's first presidential term in 1981, individual income taxes were cut 25 percent. Overall government spending continued to rise, however. As a result, between 1981 and 1982 the deficit increased by about 62 percent. The next year it again grew by around 62 percent. By 1983 the deficit was around 6 percent of the **gross domestic product** (GDP)—the total dollar value,

or price, of all finished goods and services produced within a country during one year.

Budget Deficit and Politics

The budget deficit became a major political issue in the 1990s. Deficit reduction, however, has been difficult for three main reasons: political disagreements over which programs to cut, uncontrollable spending, and a reluctance of the general public to accept either tax increases or major spending cuts in programs.

Political Disagreements Budget cutting involves making tough choices about which programs to cut and by how much. Almost everyone involved in politics can come up with a plan to reduce the deficit significantly by producing a budget in line with their own political views. For example, Democrats may propose cutting defense spending and raising taxes, particularly on the wealthy. Republicans may propose cutting domestic social spending. The problem lies in obtaining a political majority for a plan that fairly distributes the pain of deficit reduction to all groups.

Uncontrollable Spending Much of the budget consists of so-called uncontrollable spending—a term that refers to spending based on the government's prior legal commitments. This type

THE DEFICIT SEEMS TO BE LEVELING OFF.

...AND LOOKS LIKE EVENTUALLY IT WILL START GOING DOWN AGAIN

Toles © 1992 The Buffalo News. Reprinted with the permission of Universal Press Syndicate. All rights reserved.

POLITICAL PROCESSES *Many citizens are concerned about the size of the deficit yet are opposed to spending cuts.* **What point of view is illustrated in this cartoon?**

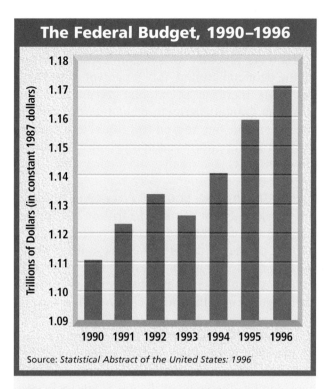

The Federal Budget, 1990–1996

Trillions of Dollars (in constant 1987 dollars)

Year	Value
1990	1.11
1991	1.12
1992	1.13
1993	1.13
1994	1.14
1995	1.16
1996	1.17

Source: *Statistical Abstract of the United States: 1996*

The federal budget increased significantly between 1990 and 1996. Uncontrollable spending makes budget cutbacks difficult. **How much did the budget increase between 1993 and 1996?**

of spending occurs each year without specific appropriation.

Major examples of uncontrollable spending include (1) payments on the national debt; (2) current payments under contracts the government has signed in the past (for example, the government must pay rent on any buildings it leases); and (3) **entitlements**, or benefits that federal law requires be given to all persons who legally qualify for them (for example, benefits from Social Security and Medicare, as noted in Section 1).

In 1995 about 58 percent of the budget consisted of entitlements. The largest entitlements are Social Security (mostly pensions for elderly people), Medicare (health-care benefits for elderly people), and Medicaid (health-care benefits for the poor). Other important entitlement programs are veterans' benefits, crop support payments to farmers, food stamps, civilian and military retirement, unemployment insurance, and government-backed loans for college students.

Many budget debates of recent years have been over entitlement programs, particularly Social Security, Medicare, and Medicaid. Senior citizens have been well organized in opposing entitlement

cutbacks. They argue that such cuts not only would break the government's promise to provide the entitlements but also would hurt the disadvantaged. Supporters of entitlement cutbacks argue that the nation simply can no longer afford to spend as much on Medicare and other programs as it has in the past. Many of the recent deficit reduction proposals have involved lowering entitlement benefit levels (as with college student loans and Medicare) or ending a program's entitlement status entirely (as with welfare).

Reluctant Public People usually oppose higher taxes and are generally unhappy that the government spends such huge amounts of money overall. However, at the same time, widespread

Comparing Governments

Budget Deficits Around the World

At about $107 billion, the 1996 U.S. budget deficit dwarfed the budget shortfalls of many other industrial nations. Yet by another measure the 1996 deficit seems rather small, having made up only 1.4 percent of the nation's gross domestic product (GDP). Even Japan, which in recent history has boasted budget surpluses, racked up a budget deficit in 1995 that was 3.9 percent of its GDP.

In the early 1990s, widening budget deficits in Europe caused so much concern that leaders of the 15 Western European nations agreed to a common economic goal. The 1993 Maastricht Treaty—which aimed to establish a common currency among European Union members—required members to reduce their 1997 budget deficit to no more than 3 percent of their GDP. In 1996, experts predicted that more than half of the European nations would overshoot this deficit mark.

Many nations' deficits have similar causes—higher spending on social programs, growing unemployment, a stubborn economic recession. To address these concerns and to balance their books, governments around the world will have to make difficult choices.

PUBLIC GOOD *Students planning to attend college may apply for government-backed student loans. Student loans are just one form of entitlement program funded by the federal government.* **What is one group that has opposed entitlement cutbacks in recent years?**

public support for costly government programs has been consistent. Part of the reason that politicians have difficulty cutting spending is the public's reluctance to allow favored programs to be scaled back or eliminated.

The National Debt

When the government's expenditures are higher than its revenue, it must borrow money to make up the difference, thus increasing the debt. The **national debt** is the sum of all money the U.S. government owes as a result of borrowing.

The Size of the National Debt The national debt has skyrocketed from about $908 billion in 1980 to $5.18 trillion in 1996. Just how much money is $5.18 trillion? If you wanted to pay off the national debt by paying $1 million a day, it would take you more than 14,000 years—and that does not even include interest payments.

Interest Payments on the Debt If you were to borrow money from the bank, you would have to pay back the amount you borrowed, plus any interest that had accumulated. The federal government also must pay interest on the money it borrows.

About 15 percent of the current federal budget consists of interest payments on the national debt. As recently as 1980, interest payments on the debt constituted only 9 percent of the budget. This increase in interest payments stems from the dramatic growth of budget deficits. In turn, part of the reason for the huge budget deficits is the enormous amount owed in interest each year.

The Debt and the Economy As you can imagine, a national debt of some $5 trillion has serious implications for the U.S. economy. Huge budget deficits can cause foreign investors to lose faith in the U.S. dollar. If foreign investors believe that U.S. deficit spending is out of control, they may exchange their dollars for a currency that appears to be more stable, such as the Japanese yen. This action, in turn, causes the U.S. dollar to lose some of its value in relation to other currencies.

In recent years, because the deficit has shrunk considerably, the value of the dollar has increased. When the government borrows billions of dollars to finance deficit spending, the investment funds that are available for the economy in general decrease substantially. In other words, there is a limited amount of money available to be borrowed. When the government borrows huge amounts of money, the competition for the remaining available funds causes interest rates to rise, which in turn slows down the economy.

Balancing the Budget

The issue of how to address the budget deficit has long been a matter of debate. In 1997, however, the president and Congress agreed on a plan to balance the budget by the year 2002. As the history outlined below shows, such attempts have been made before, and it remains to be seen whether this plan will in fact lead to a balanced budget.

Gramm-Rudman-Hollings Act In response to the huge budget deficits of the 1980s, Congress passed the Balanced Budget and Deficit Reduction Act of 1985, known as the **Gramm-Rudman-Hollings Act** (GRH). The legislation was designed to force Congress and the president to work together to reduce the mounting budget deficits.

The GRH required the president's budget staff and the Congressional Budget Office to produce

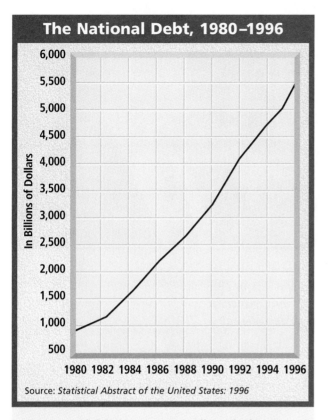

The National Debt, 1980–1996

In Billions of Dollars

Source: *Statistical Abstract of the United States: 1996*

The national debt has grown rapidly in the last several years. **How can a debt of this size affect the economic growth rate?**

a joint report on the budget. This report would include estimates on how much the proposed budget would exceed expected revenue and how much the budget would need to be cut to meet deficit reduction targets. An official in the General Accounting Office (GAO), called the comptroller general, would then be allowed to make budget cuts if the president and Congress could not agree on how to do so. In 1986, however, the U.S. Supreme Court ruled that this method of cutting spending was unconstitutional. In response, Congress amended the procedures and moved the dates for achieving a balanced budget from 1991 to 1993.

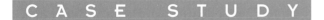

C A S E   S T U D Y

Budget Enforcement Act

POLITICAL PROCESSES By 1990 the Gramm-Rudman-Hollings (GRH) Act had come under attack in the halls of Congress. Critics of the balanced budget law charged that it just was not working,

because budget makers were getting around the law by clever accounting tricks.

Still committed to tackling the deficit, members of Congress worked out new legislation to reform the budget process. President George Bush signed the Budget Enforcement Act (BEA) into law in November 1990.

The BEA changed the budget process in many ways. Instead of focusing on just one year, budget makers are now required to predict what will be included in the budgets of the next five years. The act also established what are known as "pay-as-you-go" (PAYGO) restrictions. PAYGO restrictions require that any increase in spending be paid for by an increase in taxes and that any decrease in taxes be offset by spending cuts. The law set specific limits on spending for defense, social programs, and foreign aid. That way, money saved in one area cannot be spent in another. The BEA also establishes the maximum amount of the deficit for each year.

Despite the strict new spending rules, the deficit soared to record highs in 1991 and 1992. A recession and large increases in social spending not covered by the BEA caused the leap. Though the BEA alone has not eliminated deficits, it has proved to be an important tool in curbing out-of-control spending.

Balanced Budget Amendment Some lawmakers believe that a constitutional amendment requiring a balanced budget is ultimately the only way to solve the deficit problem. In March 1997, however, the Senate rejected a proposed constitutional amendment that would have required the federal government to maintain a balanced budget each year. (The House had previously passed a similar measure.) Many lawmakers, as well as President Clinton, who called the balanced budget amendment "both unnecessary and unwise," were against the amendment. They argued that a balanced budget should come by reaching a mutually agreed upon budget proposal, not by amending the Constitution.

POLITICAL PROCESSES *U.S. Representative John Kasich, chairman of the House Budget Committee, stands near the National Debt Clock, located in front of the Ohio state house. Kasich strongly supported a Balanced Budget Amendment to the Constitution.*
What are some arguments made by critics of the Balanced Budget Amendment?

The 1993 Clinton Plan The budget deficit began a steady decline in 1993. An important step in the turnaround was an economic package proposed during President Clinton's first year in office and adopted over Republican congressional opposition. The plan increased taxes on wealthier Americans and decreased spending on some programs.

In 1996 the budget deficit stood at just 1.4 percent of GDP, the lowest percentage in almost 20 years. Currently, the annual U.S. deficit as a percentage of the GDP is among the lowest of industrialized nations. (See Comparing Governments on page 209.) Low inflation (which reduces interest rates and thus interest payments on the national debt) and strong economic growth (which increases tax revenues) have helped lower the deficit.

Balanced Budget Act of 1997

Lawmakers have continued to work on means to eliminate the deficit entirely. In August 1997, President Clinton signed into law the Balanced Budget Act of 1997. The act was intended to eliminate budget deficits for the first time in 30 years. President Clinton said about the act that it "prepares Americans to enter the next century, stronger than ever. By large, bipartisan majorities in both Houses, we have risen to that challenge."

SECTION 4 — **REVIEW**

1. Define the following terms: gross domestic product, entitlements, national debt, Gramm-Rudman-Hollings Act.

2. What is uncontrollable spending? What other factors cause a budget deficit?

3. Why is the national debt a concern for the United States?

4. How does the accumulation of debt contribute to the deficit?

5. **Thinking and Writing Critically**
In the 1990s the president and Congress faced an ongoing debate over the Balanced Budget Amendment. Why do you think this issue has posed such a problem?

6. **Applying** **PUBLIC GOOD**
Make a list of the most effective methods that you think the federal government could use to reduce the deficit. What might be the arguments against some of these means?

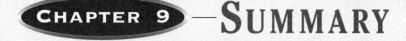

CHAPTER 9 — SUMMARY

SECTION 1 Taxes are the federal government's primary source of revenue. There are several different kinds of taxes—the individual income tax, the corporate income tax, social insurance taxes, excise taxes, estate and gift taxes, and customs duties. The federal government also generates revenue from several nontax sources. These include fees, fines, and earnings of the banks in the Federal Reserve system.

Tax policy is politically controversial. Democrats generally have favored higher and more progressive taxes and have opposed tax advantages for the wealthy, while Republicans generally have favored lower taxes.

SECTION 2 The U.S. economy is a free-enterprise system in which economic policy is controversial. The basic political disputes involve the extent to which government should intervene in the operation of the free market. Democrats generally have favored greater government intervention, while Republicans have been inclined toward minimal government involvement.

The goals of economic stabilization are full employment and low inflation. The tools that the government uses to achieve these goals are fiscal and monetary policy. Fiscal policy is a set of government spending, taxing, and borrowing policies used to achieve desired levels of economic performance. Monetary policy is designed to regulate the economy by controlling the amount of money in circulation. The government also uses industrial policy to promote economic growth. Supporters of economic aid to industries have argued that this aid should be applied to industries of the future because these industries, particularly high-tech ones, hold great economic promise.

SECTION 3 The budget process has changed a great deal during the 1900s. Today, the budget process begins with the Office of Management and Budget's setting guidelines about the overall budget situation. Each agency uses those guidelines to develop a spending proposal. The staff of the OMB reviews the agencies' requests and submits a recommendation to the president. After all changes are made, the president's proposal is submitted to Congress.

Congress then reviews the proposal, and congressional committees work to draft a concurrent resolution based on it. After reconciling all congressional recommendations and changes made to the original proposal, spending limits are set in a reconciliation bill, which both houses of Congress must pass. Congress then passes a limited number of appropriations bills. Afterward, they go to the president for approval or veto.

SECTION 4 In recent decades the federal government has consistently spent more than it takes in, causing the budget to be in deficit. The budget deficit became a major issue in the 1990s. Deficit reduction has been difficult because of political disagreements over which programs to cut, increased uncontrollable spending, and a reluctance of the general public to accept either tax increases or spending cuts.

To support deficit spending, the government must borrow money. This has caused a huge national debt. Politicians recently have focused on how to balance the budget, and a plan for achieving a balanced budget by 2002 was adopted in 1997.

Government Notebook

Review what you wrote in your Government Notebook at the beginning of the chapter. After reading the chapter, do you believe the government is more or less involved in the economy than you originally thought? Record your answer in your Notebook.

CHAPTER 9

REVIEW

REVIEWING CONCEPTS

1. Define tax deductions and give several examples.

2. What are the two primary social welfare programs financed by the federal government?

3. Name and describe the main policies that government uses to stabilize the economy and promote economic growth.

4. What three tools does the Fed have for creating monetary policy? Describe how each is used.

5. How did the Congressional Budget and Impoundment Control Act change the way the president's budget proposal is considered?

6. Define uncontrollable spending and list three examples.

THINKING AND WRITING CRITICALLY

1. **PUBLIC GOOD** Should government redistribute wealth through taxes? Write a paragraph that states and supports your opinion on the issue. Be sure to consider how tax policy decisions affect the standard of living in the United States.

2. **PRINCIPLES OF DEMOCRACY** Why do you think that individual rights are a key element of the free-enterprise system?

3. **POLITICAL PROCESSES** Why is it important for Congress to examine overall spending rather than separate appropriations? How has the creation of the Office of Management and Budget helped increase the president's role in making economic policy?

4. **PUBLIC GOOD** Why do you think the public is reluctant to support cuts in public spending? How does deficit reduction promote the public good?

CITIZENSHIP IN YOUR COMMUNITY

As noted in this chapter, the individual income tax is a major source of federal revenue. The Internal Revenue Service (IRS) provides several aids to citizens filing federal tax returns. For example, the IRS maintains hotlines people can call for answers to their questions about filing taxes. It also has established an Internet site that enables people to file their returns electronically. Create a pamphlet for citizens in your community, providing information on filing federal tax returns. Include information on where they can pick up tax forms and the types of tax preparation assistance available in your community.

INDIVIDUAL PORTFOLIO PROJECT

Imagine that you are a member of the Board of Governors for the Federal Reserve system. The chair of the Board of Governors has asked you to prepare a handbook for foreign governments interested in setting up a national bank system similar to the Fed. In the handbook, describe both how the Fed is organized and the regulations that it places on member banks.

PRACTICING SKILLS: UNDERSTANDING CHARTS AND GRAPHS

The circle graph, or pie chart, on page 191 illustrates the various sources of federal revenue. The graph has seven "slices" that together represent total federal revenue in 1996. Read the labels on the graph, and study the relative size of the slices to answer the questions that follow.

1. What three types of taxes account for the largest portion of total federal revenue?

2. Approximately what fraction of total federal revenue comes from the corporate income tax?

3. What percent of federal revenue comes from estate and gift taxes?

THE INTERNET: LEARNING ONLINE

Conduct an Internet search to learn more about the Balanced Budget Amendment. You might start with search words such as *federal budget, federal spending,* and *Balanced Budget Amendment.* What information is available on Web sites? Are individuals expressing their opinions on the amendment? Is information on both sides of the debate available on the Internet? Write a paragraph describing the information you find.

ANALYZING PRIMARY SOURCES

NOTES ON THE NEW DEAL

The theories of British economist John Maynard Keynes have greatly influenced the economic policies of many countries. In 1934 Keynes visited President Franklin D. Roosevelt. While in the United States, Keynes recorded his thoughts on the New Deal, Roosevelt's plan for helping the United States cope with the effects of the Great Depression. Read this excerpt from Keynes's notes and answer the questions that follow.

❝ *These are a few notes on the New Deal by one who has come here on a brief visit of pure inquisitiveness—made under the limitations of imperfect knowledge, but gaining, perhaps, from the detachment of a bird's-eye view.*

My purpose is to consider the prospects rather than the past. . . . I am in sympathy with most of the social and reforming aims of this legislation; and the principal subject of these notes is the problem of consolidating economic and business recovery. . . .

Obstacles can [not] be overcome in a day or by a stroke of the pen. The notion

that, if the government would retire altogether from the economic field, business, left to itself, would soon work out its own salvation, is, to my mind, foolish; and, even if it were not, it is certain that public opinion would allow no such thing. This does not mean that the administration should not be assiduously [diligently] preparing the way for the return of normal investment enterprise [business]. But this will unavoidably take time. When it comes, it will intensify and maintain a recovery initiated by other means. . . .

I believe that there is much devoted and intelligent work in progress there [in Washington], and that the fittest ideas and the fittest men are tending to survive. In many parts of the world the old order has passed away. But, of all the experiments to evolve a new order, it is the experiment of young America which most attracts my own deepest sympathy. For they are occupied with the task of trying to make the economic order work tolerably well, while preserving freedom of individual initiative and liberty of thought and criticism.

The older generation of living Americans accomplished the great task of solving the technical problem of how to produce economic goods on a scale adequate to human needs. It is the task of the younger generation to bring to actual realization the potential blessings of having solved the technical side of the problem of poverty. The central control which the latter requires involves an essentially changed method and outlook. The minds and energies which have found their fulfillment in the achievements of American business are not likely to be equally well adapted to the further task. That must be, as it should be, the fulfillment of the next generation. ❞

1. What did Keynes believe public opinion would not allow?

2. According to Keynes, why is it hard to make the economic order work tolerably well, while preserving freedom of individual initiative?

3. What task did Keynes say the older generation of living Americans accomplished?

FOREIGN POLICY AND NATIONAL SECURITY

The way the United States interacts with the rest of the world affects more of your daily life than you probably imagine. For example, the odds are very good that you have purchased products that were made in foreign countries. You were able to do so because the U.S. government's foreign-policy decisions help to maintain free and open trade with other nations. Are you hoping to visit a foreign country someday? Once again, your ability to do so hinges upon U.S. foreign policy. The goals and history of U.S. foreign policy, and what it means to you, are the focus of this chapter.

Government Notebook

In your Government Notebook, list as many ways in which countries interact as you can. How do you think the government goes about monitoring this interaction?

GOALS AND PRINCIPLES OF U.S. FOREIGN POLICY

Political Dictionary

national security
trade embargo
isolationist
realism
internationalist
neoisolationist
idealism

Objectives

★ What are the goals of U.S. foreign policy?
★ What principles have historically guided U.S. foreign policy?

The United States currently recognizes and maintains relations with more than 180 countries throughout the world. The government determines its interactions with these nations through its foreign-policy decisions. As noted in Chapter 7, a nation's foreign policy is its plan for shaping economic, diplomatic, military, and political relationships with other countries. Historically, several basic goals and principles have guided U.S. foreign-policy decisions.

Foreign-Policy Goals

As you will learn later in this chapter, the actual policies for maintaining foreign relations have changed dramatically throughout U.S. history. The fundamental goals of U.S. foreign policy, however, have remained somewhat constant. These goals include maintaining national security, supporting democracy, promoting world peace, and providing aid to people in need. In addition, since the mid-1930s establishing free and open trade has become another consistent goal of U.S.

foreign policy, as the United States trades goods and services with many of the world's nations.

Maintaining National Security The most important goal of U.S. foreign policy is to preserve **national security**—that is, to protect the rights, freedoms, and property of the United States and its people. The United States must consider national security foremost when dealing with foreign countries.

Supporting Democracy As you know, since its creation the United States has been a democratic country. A strong belief in democracy often has led the United States to aid other democratic nations as well as those moving toward democracy.

Promoting World Peace U.S. foreign policy also is based on the goal of promoting and maintaining world peace. The more nations are at peace, the less likely the United States will be drawn into an existing conflict. To advance this goal, the United States sometimes becomes actively involved in resolving disputes between other countries.

Providing Aid to People in Need As a world leader, the United States often has assumed the responsibility of providing humanitarian and other relief to foreign countries. This aid might come in the form of money, food, or military assistance.

WORLD AFFAIRS *The United States often becomes involved in promoting peace in troubled areas of the world, such as South Africa. **Why is ensuring that other nations are at peace important to U.S. foreign-policy goals?***

WORLD AFFAIRS *In 1928 U.S. secretary of state Frank Kellogg signed the Kellogg-Briand Pact. All countries entering into this agreement officially renounced war as a foreign-policy tool.* **Why do you think that many countries signed this pact?**

In 1992, for example, the United States sent soldiers to Somalia. Many people in the East African nation were suffering from starvation as a result of famine. Much of the food sent there by international relief organizations was being stolen at the direction of various warlords. U.S. troops were sent to help the food reach famine victims and break the power of the warlords. This type of humanitarian support not only provides aid to people in need but also aims to help maintain social and political stability in foreign countries.

Establishing Free and Open Trade The United States trades goods and services with most of the world. Thus, one of the main concerns of U.S. foreign policy is establishing and maintaining strong global economic ties. The nation's leaders have attempted to do so through free-trade policies—the exchange of goods and services across national borders without restrictions, such as high tariffs.

Free trade's greatest economic benefits include increasing the size of the market to which domestic businesses can sell their goods and giving U.S. consumers a chance to buy goods from around the world. Politically, trade can also be a powerful tool. For example, from 1985 to 1991, the U.S. government used a **trade embargo**—a stoppage of commerce and trade—against South Africa to pressure that nation to end its practice of apartheid, or racially motivated political and economic segregation designed to ensure white minority rule.

Principles of Foreign Policy

The question of which basic principles should guide the formation of U.S. foreign policy has been controversial throughout the nation's history. In making foreign policy, two basic questions must be answered:

★ How active should the United States be in world affairs?
★ What guidelines should be used to evaluate U.S. activities abroad?

These questions have been answered in different ways at various points in U.S. history. In general, the United States has followed four basic approaches to foreign policy: isolationism, realism, neoisolationism, and idealism.

Isolationism The **isolationist** doctrine reflects the view that a nation should tend to its domestic affairs rather than to international affairs. Supporters of isolationism believe that

★ the United States has many domestic problems, and U.S. policy makers should focus on those exclusively;
★ most countries think primarily about their own interests, so the United States should too;
★ being in a militarily defensible location, the United States does not need to become involved in other nations' affairs; and

★ staying out of other countries' affairs will keep the United States out of war.

Isolationism was the main philosophy behind U.S. foreign policy during many periods of U.S. history, particularly during the 1800s and the 20 years between World War I and World War II. Since World War II, isolationism has had very little support among foreign-policy scholars or policy makers in Washington, as it became less practical in the post–World War II world.

Realism Some of the most serious criticisms of isolationism have come from backers of **realism**, probably the most dominant U.S. foreign-policy doctrine since World War II. Realists and isolationists both believe that U.S. foreign policy should be evaluated by how well it promotes U.S. national interests. However, realists strongly disagree that the U.S. national interest is best promoted by isolationism. Instead, they argue for an **internationalist** approach—the taking of an active role in international affairs—to promote U.S. interests. Realists believe that this approach should include military intervention when necessary.

Realists believe that isolationism ignores the reality of world affairs. They say that many countries are dangerous and are ruled by aggressive leaders trying to dominate other countries. In addition, realists say that because no world government exists to resolve international disputes satisfactorily, a nation's only tool for stopping an aggressive country is action—alone or in alliance with like-minded nations.

Thus, realists conclude that by avoiding participation in world affairs, the United States could become a victim of another nation's aggression. They argue that the United States must be strong and prepared for war, thereby achieving peace by scaring off aggressors.

Finally, some realists argue that the United States must

sometimes use force simply to show that it is militarily strong. A refusal to act in a certain situation might cause potential aggressors to believe that the United States is unable to defend itself. At the same time, realists hold that for the most part the United States should not use force unless vital national interests—such as national security or opportunities to trade with other countries—are at stake.

In the view of realists, vital interests matter more than similar belief systems when it comes to choosing alliances with other nations. The United States's primary goal should be to gain allies that are militarily strong and strategically located and that can help in preventing the expansion of hostile countries. According to this view, the United States should not hesitate to ally itself with countries whose values may differ from U.S. values or to oppose countries, if necessary, whose values it shares. For this reason, realism is sometimes called power politics or realpolitik, which means "realist politics."

Neoisolationism People who adhere to the **neoisolationist** doctrine think that the United

WORLD AFFAIRS *Secretary of State Cordell Hull (third from left) led the U.S. delegation to the 1933 Pan American Conference in Uruguay. At the conference, U.S. leaders declared that the United States would not intervene in South American politics.* **Why do some people argue that the United States should stay out of other countries' affairs?**

States should keep its foreign involvement to a minimum, not only for the good of the United States but also because such involvement is likely to be bad for other nations in whose affairs the United States would intervene. The prefix *neo,* or new, serves to distinguish this doctrine from traditional isolationism, which focuses only on the interests of the United States.

In support of their view, neoisolationists cite several U.S.-backed governments in the 1960s and 1970s, saying that they did not have popular support. Even when the motives behind the support were good, neoisolationists argue, it failed to help most people in those countries. Neoisolationists believe that the United States should not interfere in other countries' internal affairs—a principle called noninterference. They argue that even people being kept down by oppressors should be left to attempt to overthrow their rulers without outside help. They warn that the people of a small country may resent a strong foreign government's intervening in their affairs, even if it is acting against the domestic oppressor.

Finally, neoisolationists believe that it is ethically necessary to avoid war. In their view, to engage in involvement in another nation's affairs not only violates the rights of that nation's people but also may lead to war.

Idealism Supporters of the doctrine of **idealism** argue for an internationalist foreign policy, but unlike realists, their internationalist motivations are based on what is good for other countries as well as for the United States. They believe that decision makers should take into account the interests and rights of people both inside and outside the United States. Idealists oppose injustice and tyranny around the world and believe that the U.S. government should support democratic values everywhere. Although to a lesser extent than realism, idealism has heavily influenced U.S. foreign policy. For example, the United States has acted many times to put a stop to violations of human rights, as in Haiti in 1994.

Idealists tend to work for international cooperation as well as for economic and humanitarian assistance to less-fortunate foreign countries. They also support efforts to promote friendship and cooperation across borders, particularly among nations sharing democratic values.

Like neoisolationists, but unlike realists, idealists believe that supporting tyrannical governments is wrong—even when doing so might protect the nation's vital interests. Idealists argue that support for tyrannical governments in a world where many people strongly believe in humanitarian ideals is likely to both make enemies abroad and reduce support for an active foreign policy within the United States.

Finally, idealists believe that U.S. foreign policy should protect American ideals. In particular, the actions of the United States should be associated with defense of human rights.

Some idealists are less inclined to support the use of force than are realists, instead preferring nonmilitary international action, such as economic boycotts or the withholding of economic aid from nations with tyrannical governments. Other idealists support U.S.

PUBLIC GOOD *Protesters march in front of the White House with signs criticizing U.S. government inaction in Bosnia.* **Why do idealists believe that foreign-policy makers should take into account the interests of people both inside and outside of the United States?**

military action in foreign countries, perhaps even more readily than realists, because they are willing to use force to stop injustice and not just to protect vital national interests.

During the 1990s the United States was involved in Somalia, Bosnia, and Haiti. All of these countries were of little military or economic importance to the United States but their people were suffering. Isolationists, neoisolationists, and most realists opposed the U.S. actions there, but idealists supported them.

U.S. Foreign Policy and the Public Good

Although there are plenty of exceptions, Republicans today are generally either realists or isolationists, while Democrats generally are either neoisolationists or idealists. Each of these foreign-policy principles has a limited scope, so the public good is often best promoted by making trade-offs among them. Idealism tends to focus on ethics in U.S. foreign policy, but it could be argued that it would be foolish not to support a strategically located foreign government—even if its values were not the same as Americans' values— if this would stop a worse aggressor from taking

Mike Luckovich *Atlanta Constitution*

WORLD AFFAIRS *The cartoon above portrays the United States and Europe as uninterested bystanders rather than as a bulwark, or strong protection, against the abuse of people's rights in other countries.* **Why do you think U.S. involvement in Bosnia was opposed by isolationists, neoisolationists, and most realists?**

over other nations. Such an argument would, however, violate strict idealist principles.

Similarly, isolationists and neoisolationists stress the cost and horror of war, but many people believe that the United States could pay a heavy price for allowing others to dominate the world. On the other hand, some foreign-policy analysts suggest that force should be used only when it would serve a vital national interest *and* a moral cause.

SECTION 1 — REVIEW

1. Define the following terms: national security, trade embargo, isolationist, realism, internationalist, neoisolationist, idealism.

2. List and explain the primary goals of U.S. foreign policy.

3. Explain the principles that drive foreign policy. Which principle has the greatest influence in the present-day United States?

4. **Thinking and Writing Critically**
   Do you think that it is important for the United States to consider a combination of approaches when making its foreign policy? Why or why not?

5. **Applying** **WORLD AFFAIRS**
   Why do you think people disagree over the principles of foreign policy? Do you think they also disagree over its goals? Explain your answer.

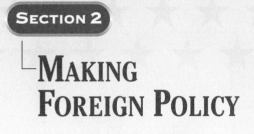

MAKING FOREIGN POLICY

Political Dictionary

presidential doctrine
summit conference
embassy
consulate
ambassador

consul
Foreign Service
passport
visa

Objectives

★ Why does the executive branch have greater influence over foreign policy than does any other branch of government?

★ How does the U.S. Department of State affect foreign policy?

★ How is the U.S. Department of Defense organized?

★ What are the roles of the Central Intelligence Agency and Congress in making foreign policy?

The executive branch generally takes the most influential role in foreign-policy decision making. The main figures within the executive branch that have influential foreign-policy roles are the president, the Departments of State and Defense, and the Central Intelligence Agency. In addition, the National Security Council plays an important role in coordinating activities that involve national security.

Role of the President

The president generally is considered the nation's most influential foreign-policy decision maker. This influence comes from several sources.

Influence Through General Acceptance

Much of the president's control over foreign policy comes from the general acceptance that presidential influence in this area is appropriate. That is, both the people of the United States and the U.S. Congress generally have accepted that the president should assume the leading role in matters of foreign policy. This has happened for various reasons.

As noted in Chapter 7, the primary reason that the people and Congress have allowed the president to assume this authority is that dealing with foreign governments and international crises often requires decisiveness and speed. A president can respond more quickly than can a large body such as Congress.

Even when urgency is not an issue, Congress generally has accepted greater presidential influence over foreign policy. For example, of the five declarations of war in U.S. history, two (War of 1812, Spanish-American War) were initiated by Congress. The others (Mexican War, World War I, World War II) were initially requested by the president. As the country's top nationally elected official, the president is typically regarded as the most appropriate national spokesperson in foreign affairs.

Presidents also have asserted their leadership in foreign policy by issuing foreign-policy statements. These **presidential doctrines** do not pass

WORLD AFFAIRS *President Clinton met with foreign leaders during the 1993 Pacific Rim Summit in Seattle, Washington. **Why has the president assumed the leading role in matters regarding foreign policy?***

through the legislative process and are intended to set the direction of foreign policy. Such doctrines do not have the force of law, so specific steps to carry them out must be taken through legislation or budgetary appropriations. Presidential doctrines do set a strong guideline for future decisions, however. Similarly, presidents may hold **summit conferences**—meetings between the heads of state of two or more nations. The statements made or understandings reached at these meetings do not have the force of law but strongly influence public debate.

Influence As Commander in Chief
As commander in chief, the president can make important foreign-policy decisions. In this capacity, presidents also can undertake military action in times of crisis without seeking congressional approval.

Presidents have used this power not only in ordering short-term military strikes but also in committing military forces to serve in what have been called undeclared wars. Undeclared wars, such as the Korean War and the Vietnam War, are longer military actions that are undertaken without an official congressional declaration of war. In addition, the United States has engaged in more than 100 limited military actions.

Influence Through Executive Agreements
As noted in Chapter 7, presidents also can negotiate executive agreements—formal understandings with foreign governments. These agreements do not require ratification by the Senate. Generally, such agreements have been minor, often involving implementation details on already signed treaties. There have, however, been significant exceptions. Twentieth-Century examples include President Franklin Roosevelt's trading 50 aging destroyers to British prime minister Winston Churchill for 50 air bases in British territory in the Western Hemisphere in 1940, before U.S. entry into World War II. Another example is the General Agreement on Tariffs and Trade (GATT)—trade agreements among most of the world's nations—which began in 1947.

Role of the U.S. Department of State

The U.S. Constitution gives the president the authority, with the advice and consent of the Senate, to make treaties, appoint diplomatic officials, and receive foreign delegates. To help the president execute these duties, Congress established the U.S. Department of State in 1789. The head of the State Department, the secretary of state, is the highest-ranking member of the cabinet and fourth in line for presidential succession.

The mission of the State Department is to promote good relations between the United States and other countries. The State Department generally opposes the use of force to solve serious conflicts, preferring to make every possible effort at diplomacy. The department is responsible for maintaining diplomatic relations with approximately 180 countries throughout the world. Included in its duties are establishing and maintaining **embassies**, or diplomatic centers, and **consulates**, which deal with U.S. commercial interests. The department also issues passports and visas.

Organization and Structure
The State Department is organized into bureaus dealing with U.S. relations with specific regions of the world (Europe and Canada, East Asia and the Pacific, the Middle East and South Asia, Africa, and Latin America) and bureaus dealing with foreign-policy issues including human rights, drug trafficking,

WORLD AFFAIRS *This building of unusual design is the U.S. embassy in Lima, Peru.* **Why does the United States maintain embassies in other countries?**

Foreign-Service Officer

In her long career in the Foreign Service, Ruth Davis—the principal deputy assistant for consular affairs and a former U.S. ambassador to the African nation of Benin—has met with major international figures and seen the world. Not only has she chatted with King Juan Carlos of Spain and dined with opera singer Luciano Pavarotti, she also traveled to Tokyo to help make the final bid for holding the 1996 Olympic Games in Atlanta, Georgia. Foreign-service officers (FSOs) like Davis get an insider's look at other governments and cultures while helping to shape and carry out U.S. foreign policy.

Applicants to the foreign service must pass a series of difficult tests to become officers. The written portion of the foreign-service examination tests the applicant's knowledge of U.S. and world history, government, economics, and English grammar. An all-day oral exam, a thorough background check, and a medical examination also are required.

Though a college education is not mandatory, most FSOs have a bachelor's degree, and more than half have earned advanced degrees. College courses in economics, history, government, geography, literature, business, environmental studies, and foreign languages are recommended for potential officers.

Those accepted into the Foreign Service go through orientation and months of training, including language courses, before their first two- to four-year tour overseas. To advance in the service, officers must work at a consulate or embassy and show fluency in at least one foreign language. Officers later choose to specialize in administrative, consular, economic, or political areas. FSOs usually alternate tours of duty overseas with short-term assignments in Washington, D.C.

Once overseas, the main duties of FSOs include collecting data, writing reports, and meeting with key officials. Embassy staffers develop and maintain close contacts with government officials, educators, the media, and business and community leaders in their host countries. These contacts help the officers collect reliable information and gain cultural insights inaccessible to most other Americans.

Officers in the Foreign Service go through extensive training to gain the skills necessary to be diplomatic representatives of the United States.

international economic and business affairs, and environmental and scientific matters.

Maintaining Embassies and Consulates One main duty of the State Department is to organize and maintain offices abroad. The United States maintains an embassy in about 160 foreign countries. An **ambassador** is the chief diplomatic official at each embassy. He or she acts as a personal representative of the U.S. president. Ambassadors usually are appointed based on their foreign-service records. In many cases, however, they are political appointees, receiving their posts as a reward for supporting the president or a particular political party.

The embassy staffs assist the ambassadors in executing their duties. These duties include keeping the United States informed of events in, and explaining U.S. laws and policies to, the host country, as well as transmitting official communications and negotiating diplomatic agreements between the two countries.

To protect U.S. commercial interests in foreign countries, the United States maintains consulates in many of the world's major commercial centers.

Each consulate is headed by a **consul**, who also is appointed by the president and confirmed by the Senate. Consuls' primary goals are to promote U.S. trade and commerce and assist American citizens with travel-related matters or other problems. They also and issue immigration and tourist visas to travelers to the United States.

The State Department maintains a staff of nearly 25,000 employees. Of those, more than 15,000 work at U.S. embassies and consulates around the world. The men and women of the State Department who serve abroad form what is called the **Foreign Service**.

Issuing Passports and Visas A **passport** is a formal document issued by a government to one of its citizens for travel to other countries. The State Department is responsible for issuing passports to U.S. citizens. No citizen may legally leave the United States—except for trips to Mexico, Canada, and some other nearby nations—without a passport. A passport entitles a person to all of the privileges established by international laws and treaties.

The State Department also issues **visas**—seals that are placed on foreign passports and that entitle their holder to enter the United States. The U.S. government requires that all visitors to the United States obtain a visa. Most countries of Western Europe, however, require only a passport.

Role of the U.S. Department of Defense

The State Department supervises all of the diplomatic activities of the United States. The supervision of U.S. military activities, however, is handled by the Department of Defense.

To maintain the U.S. military, Congress established the War Department as one of the three original executive departments during George Washington's first term as president. In 1797 the Navy Department was established, and national defense functions were divided between the War Department and the Navy Department until the 1940s. The National Security Act amendments of 1949 placed all branches of the armed forces under the authority of one government office, called the U.S. Department of Defense (DOD). The DOD is headed by a secretary of defense, with individual secretaries supervising the Army, Navy, and Air Force.

Organization of the DOD The DOD is a huge establishment with global responsibilities. Its headquarters are in the Pentagon, a massive building that covers around 34 acres outside of Washington, D.C. It employs more than 800,000 civilians and more than 1.4 million members of the armed forces.

The DOD is not only larger than any other department, but it also must follow the strictest

POLITICAL PROCESSES *The Pentagon, one of the world's largest buildings, is located in Arlington, Virginia. It contains the offices of thousands of civilian and military personnel.*
Which cabinet department's headquarters are located in the Pentagon?

guidelines. This is because the framers of the Constitution were well aware of the dangers that could result from a military state. That is, if the military were to take control of the government, the ideals of democracy might be jeopardized. To prevent the nation's military from interfering with free government, the framers determined that the military would be under civilian control.

As you know, the Constitution states that the president is the commander in chief of all U.S. armed forces. The secretary of defense, the deputy secretary, and the secretaries of the three armed services are all civilians, as are most of their staff. Thus, the military is at all times subject to civilian authority.

Joint Chiefs of Staff Although the DOD is headed by civilian leaders, recommendations about military actions come from military advisers. The most influential military advisers in the United States are the members of the Joint Chiefs of Staff. The president, the vice president, and the secretaries of defense and state seek consultation on military matters from this group on a regular basis.

The group includes only five people: the chair, the Army chief of staff, the chief of naval operations, the Air Force chief of staff, and the Marine

Corps commandant, who is present only when Marine Corps matters are at issue. The chair is selected by the president and serves as the nation's top military officer.

Role of the Central Intelligence Agency

Foreign-policy decisions are sometimes made with the aid of information gathered by the Central Intelligence Agency (CIA), which Congress created by the National Security Act of 1947. Congress's goal was to create a single organization responsible for providing the president with foreign intelligence—information about the activities of other governments. Broadly speaking, the CIA, which is an independent government agency within the executive branch, undertakes three kinds of activities: gathering information related to national security, analyzing that information, and briefing the president and the National Security Council (NSC) on its findings. In addition, the CIA sometimes engages in covert, or secret, operations. Covert operations are efforts to promote U.S. foreign-policy goals through sometimes unconventional means, such as by supporting political parties or rebel factions in other countries. Covert actions are controversial and are often supported by realists but opposed by idealists and neoisolationists.

One major task of the CIA is to predict for policy makers how foreign governments will behave and what their defense capabilities are. For example, the CIA might attempt to predict whether Russia's government will remain stable and friendly, or to determine if North Korea has nuclear weapons. To analyze these situations, the CIA uses both open sources (including foreign newspapers and consultations with academic experts) and secret intelligence operations.

National Security Council

As noted in Chapter 8, the National Security Council (NSC) was set up in 1947 to improve coordination among the government departments that deal with national security issues—in particular the CIA and the Departments of State and Defense. A national security adviser, who is appointed by the president, heads the NSC staff, which is part of the Executive Office of the President.

PUBLIC GOOD *The Joint Chiefs of Staff, shown here in 1996, frequently consult with the president and other executive officials on military matters.* **Why is the Department of Defense not headed by a military leader?**

WILSON PULLS LAGGARD CONGRESS INTO PREPAREDNESS
Kirby in the New York *World*, 1916

POLITICAL PROCESSES *In 1917 President Woodrow Wilson asked Congress for a declaration of war against Germany. The cartoon above illustrates the reluctance of Congress to organize for and declare war.* **How has Congress's power to declare war been undercut in the past?**

Role of Congress

As you have read, the executive branch assumes the greatest responsibility for foreign policy. The Constitution, however, grants crucial foreign-policy powers to Congress. These powers include the power to declare war, appropriate money for national defense, and ratify treaties.

Declaring War The U.S. Constitution balances the president's power as commander in chief with Congress's power "to declare war," "to raise and support armies," and "to provide and maintain a navy." However, as noted, the United States has had two major undeclared wars and more than 100 limited military engagements that were not declared by Congress. Thus, Congress's constitutional power to declare war has in many ways been undercut.

Appropriating Money Congress's greatest source of influence in foreign-policy making lies in its constitutional authority to appropriate government funds. Congress has the final authority over the funding of government services—including national defense. Likewise, Congress is responsible for any appropriations related to financial aid to foreign countries.

Ratifying Treaties According to the Constitution, the president must seek the "advice and consent" of the Senate in making treaties with foreign countries. Altough the president often negotiates treaties without the benefit of congressional advice, treaties only become official with Senate approval by at least a two-thirds vote.

Confirming Appointments The final constitutional foreign-policy power granted to Congress involves the confirmation of the president's diplomatic appointments. Article II of the Constitution states that presidential foreign-affairs appointments, such as those for consuls and ambassadors, must be approved by the Senate. This power is another check on the actions of the president.

★ SECTION 2 — REVIEW

1. Define the following terms: presidential doctrine, summit conference, embassy, consulate, ambassador, consul, Foreign Service, passport, visa.

2. What are the sources of the president's influence in the foreign-policy arena?

3. Why did Congress establish the U.S. Department of State? What role does this department play in foreign policy today?

4. Why is the U.S. Department of Defense headed by nonmilitary personnel?

5. **Thinking and Writing Critically** Why is the president—rather than a military officer—the commander in chief?

6. **Applying** **POLITICAL PROCESSES** Conduct an Internet search on the Department of Defense. Outline the information you find.

SECTION 3

HISTORY OF U.S. FOREIGN POLICY

Political Dictionary

Monroe Doctrine
Truman Doctrine
containment
détente
glasnost
perestroika

Objectives

★ What principle shaped leaders' foreign-policy decisions in the early years of the United States?
★ What is containment?
★ What significance did the expansion of communism have on U.S. foreign policy?

As noted in Section 1, U.S. foreign policy historically has been based on four basic approaches—isolationism, realism, neoisolationism, and idealism. How the United States turns these principles into policy, however, has changed dramatically over the past 200 years, as has its role in the world.

Isolationist Policies

During the 1800s the United States was a minor participant in world affairs. Foreign policy during this period was based on neutrality in European wars, a principle that was formally established by President Washington in his Farewell Address in 1796.

In 1823 the **Monroe Doctrine** turned this principle of neutrality into an official foreign-policy agenda. The doctrine also stated, however, that the United States would not tolerate European interference in the Americas:

❝ The American continents, by the free and independent condition which they have assumed and maintain, are henceforth not to be considered as subjects for future colonization by any European powers. . . . We should consider any attempt on their part to extend their system to any portion of this hemisphere as dangerous to our peace and safety. ❞

Rise to World Power

By the late 1800s the United States had become one of the most important industrialized nations in the world. As companies produced increasing numbers of goods, the desire for global markets and international relationships became evident. The United States began pulling away from its isolationist policies and embracing the principles of internationalism. As the rest of the world became more important to the United States, Americans became interested in preserving stability in other nations. This shift to international involvement began with the Spanish-American War, which redefined the United State's role in the world.

POLITICAL FOUNDATIONS *The Spanish-American War, fought in the Philippines and Cuba, marked a turning point in foreign affairs.* **How did the Spanish-American War change U.S. foreign policy?**

Spanish-American War of 1898 Although it lasted a mere four months, the Spanish-American War of 1898 was a turning point in U.S. history. Cubans, discontented with Spanish rule, were in rebellion. Stories of Spain's brutal treatment of Cuban civilians, together with the sinking of the *Maine*—a U.S. ship that had been based in Cuba to protect U.S. interests—led the United States to declare war on Spain in April 1898. U.S. involvement in the war reflected both idealist principles—American sympathy with the struggle for Cuban independence—and realist principles—growing support for U.S. expansion in other areas of the world.

The U.S. victory was decisive, winning independence for Cuba and possession of Guam, Puerto Rico, and the Philippines for the United States. Having gained control of overseas territories, the United States emerged from the war as a world power.

World War I After the Spanish-American War, the United States attempted to return to its isolationist policies in its dealings with Europe. The outbreak of war in Europe in 1914, however, threatened all U.S. foreign-policy goals, particularly that of promoting democracy. President Woodrow Wilson, an idealist, saw the European war as a struggle between the democracy of Britain and the monarchy of Germany. In his words, it was a war to make the world "safe for democracy." He argued that a peace settlement should be followed by the creation of a League of Nations, an international organization dedicated to stopping further aggression. President Wilson hoped that the establishment of the league would make World War I the last of its kind.

Leaders of America's European allies had a different idea. They used victory to claim territory and repayment from the defeated nations, rather than making the world democratic or ending war. The League of Nations was created, but the U.S. Senate rejected U.S. membership in it in an effort to return the country to an isolationist era. The United States then returned to practicing isolationist principles—at least until until December 1941.

World War II Realists and idealists supported U.S. involvement in World War II from the beginning. Germany and Japan were militarily aggressive and posed a possible threat to U.S. security. In addition, both nations had oppressive governments. Some

isolationists, however, remembering the brutality of World War I, denounced U.S. involvement. Attempting to respect these sentiments, President Franklin Roosevelt announced U.S. neutrality at the war's outbreak but in fact supported the Allied cause in many ways.

When Japanese planes attacked the U.S. naval base at Pearl Harbor, in the Hawaiian Islands, on December 7, 1941, President Roosevelt called for a declaration of war on Japan, and Congress issued it. The United States and the other Allies won the war in 1945. The war left Europe in ruins, while no fighting took place on the U.S. mainland, leaving the United States the most powerful nation in the world. This position was enhanced by the development of the atomic bomb by American scientists, giving the nation unmatched military technology.

Cold War

As noted in Section 1, one goal of U.S. foreign policy is to promote democracy. Another goal is national security, which may be jeopardized by powers opposing U.S. interests. At the end of World War II, the Soviet Union threatened the realization of these goals. As a result, U.S.-Soviet relations became so strained that one speechwriter coined the term *Cold War* to describe the hostility between the two nations.

Origins of the Cold War At the end of World War II, the Soviet Union, in part because it feared the emergence of a strong postwar Germany, used its troops to establish control over Eastern Europe and the eastern part of Germany. To consolidate their control, the Soviets set up governments based on communism—a political and economic philosophy that puts government in control over a nation's industries and farms, as well as over most aspects of citizens' lives. (The ideas of communism are more fully explained in Chapter 22.)

In March 1947 President Harry Truman issued a "declaration" of the Cold War. In a speech that set forth what came to be known as the **Truman Doctrine**, Truman announced a basic U.S. foreign-policy strategy that would remain in place for the next 40 years—**containment**. Containment reflected idealist and realist principles and was based on the view that communism threatened democratic values and that Soviet expansion must be stopped.

Major Events of the Cold War

1947	• President Truman issues a declaration known as the Truman Doctrine, establishing containment as the primary goal of U.S. foreign policy.
1949	• The Soviet Union takes complete control of Eastern Europe. • The Soviet Union explodes an atomic bomb. • Chinese Communists led by Mao Zedong win control of China.
1950	• The Korean War begins when North Korea invades South Korea.
1959	• Rebels led by Fidel Castro gain control of Cuba and seek help from the Soviet Union.
1961–73	• U.S. troops fight in the Vietnam War in an effort to support the noncommunist South Vietnamese government.
1962	• The Soviet Union secretly installs nuclear weapons in Cuba.
1972	• Nixon becomes the first U.S. president to visit China. • Nixon and Brezhnev negotiate the first Strategic Arms Limitation Talks (SALT I) agreement.
1987	• Mikhail Gorbachev initiates a series of reforms known as glasnost and perestroika.
1989	• East Germany announces it will dismantle the Berlin Wall.

Many critical events occurred during the period of hostility between the United States and the Soviet Union known as the Cold War. **Why was the United States involved in military conflicts in several foreign countries during the Cold War?**

The primary goal of containment was to keep the Soviet Union from setting up communist governments outside of Eastern Europe. Containment was based on the theory that if Soviet expansion could be stopped, communism might eventually collapse.

By 1949 the Soviet Union had taken complete control of Eastern Europe. Previously, U.S. leaders had taken some comfort in knowing that the United States was the only nation possessing nuclear weapons. This feeling of security was not to last, however. In September, 1949 President Truman announced that the Soviet Union had exploded an atomic bomb. The two most powerful nations in the world had now joined a destructive atomic arms race that would eventually lead to fears of global nuclear war. Preventing such a war became the primary concern of foreign-policy makers.

In addition, the focus of the Cold War had expanded to areas outside of Europe. In 1949, Communists led by Mao Zedong seized control of China. Communist governments in North Korea, Cuba, and Vietnam soon threatened U.S. containment efforts as well.

Korean War After World War II, Korea, a country on a peninsula adjacent to China, had been divided into two parts: a communist north and a noncommunist south. In 1950 North Korea invaded South Korea in an attempt to bring the south under communist rule. In response, troops from the United States and other nations were sent by the United Nations to help defend South Korea. Within a few months these troops had not only repelled the attack but moved into North Korea. Communist China, however, became worried by the approach of U.S. troops near its border and sent its own soldiers. The bloody war continued for three years, with neither side gaining a lasting advantage. On July 27, 1953, an armistice was finally signed; actual peace terms, however, have never been negotiated.

Cuban Missile Crisis The event that came closest to sparking a nuclear confrontation during the Cold War took place in Cuba. By the late 1950s many Cubans resented the United States, which had dominated their island-nation for decades. In 1959 Cuba's pro-American dictator was overthrown by a group of rebels led by Fidel Castro, who appealed to Cubans' widespread anti-Americanism. Opposed by the United States, Castro turned to the Soviet Union for help.

WORLD AFFAIRS *President John F. Kennedy met with Russian leaders in October 1963. At the time of this meeting, the Soviets had already placed nuclear weapons in Cuba.* **What actions did President Kennedy take when he found out about the weapons?**

In 1962 the Soviet Union began secretly installing nuclear weapons in Cuba. When this operation was discovered, President John F. Kennedy announced a naval blockade to stop ships carrying missiles to Cuba. If the Soviet Union were able to install nuclear weapons in Cuba, it could easily threaten the United States with nuclear destruction. For the first time, a direct confrontation occurred between nuclear-armed powers. Six tense days after Kennedy announced the blockade, the Soviets agreed to withdraw the missiles. The incident was known as the Cuban missile crisis.

CASE STUDY

U.S. Foreign Policy Toward Cuba

WORLD AFFAIRS The United States played a dominant role in Cuban affairs until Fidel Castro gained power in 1959. These close ties originated with U.S. support of Cuba during the Spanish-American War of 1898. After the war, U.S. soldiers stayed in Cuba for three years.

The United States continued to be involved in the island's affairs. By the 1950s Americans owned most of Cuba's mines and cattle ranches and controlled

half of its sugar production. The United States bought much of Cuba's sugar, and Cubans purchased American-made manufactured goods. Cuba's thriving gambling casinos and resorts attracted American vacationers.

The 1950s marked a crucial point in U.S.-Cuban relations. Soon after Cuban army leader Fulgencio Batista (fool-hayn-syoh bah-TEE-stah) took control of the government by force in 1952, the United States granted his government formal diplomatic recognition. U.S. business leaders supported the dictator, who prevented a rebellion in March 1952 from disrupting business operations.

Fidel Castro's 1959 revolution led to strained relations between the United States and Cuba. Castro's communist government took over American-owned land and businesses, and the two countries soon broke off diplomatic relations. In 1961 the United States organized a group of Cuban exiles to invade Cuba and remove Castro from office. The invasion, known as the Bay of Pigs, was an embarrassing failure for the United States.

In the decades after the invasion and the missile crisis, the United States continued efforts to weaken Castro's government through an economic blockade. American officials also persuaded other nations to suspend trade with the island. In March 1996, U.S. trade restrictions were strengthened when President Clinton signed into law the Cuban Liberty and Democratic Solidarity Act, known as the Helms-Burton Act; it has not been enforced, however. Despite U.S. opposition, Castro has held power for close to 40 years and poses a continuing challenge to U.S. diplomacy.

Vietnam War The Cold War left many scars on the United States. None, however, are more visible

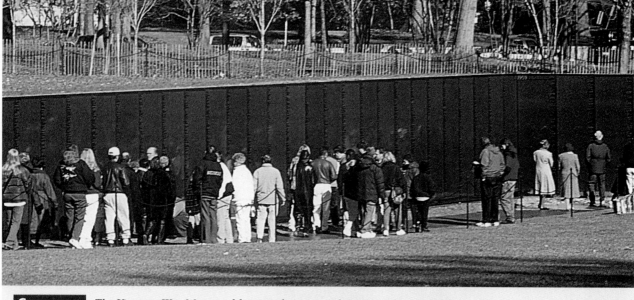

CITIZENSHIP *The Vietnam War Memorial honors the men and women who served in the military during the Vietnam War.* **How did the Vietnam War and the continual fear of communist expansion influence U.S. foreign policy?**

than those left by the Vietnam War. U.S. troops fought in Vietnam from 1961 to 1973—making it the longest war in U.S. history.

In the years that followed World War II, a nationalist movement arose in Vietnam, then a colony of France. The Vietnamese nationalists, made up primarily of communist forces, fought the French and won their independence. In the truce agreement that followed, Vietnam was divided, creating the communist North and the noncommunist South.

In 1959 the Communists helped begin a rebellion in South Vietnam. President Dwight Eisenhower responded by providing military and economic assistance to the anticommunist government. This assistance increased under President John Kennedy's administration. In 1965 President Lyndon Johnson further escalated U.S. involvement in the conflict by committing large numbers of combat troops to support the government of South Vietnam and by ordering the bombing of North Vietnam.

In 1969, in response to mounting public opposition to the conflict, President Richard Nixon began scaling back the number of U.S. troops in Vietnam. Nixon tried to win the war through increased bombing against North Vietnam and by mining and blockading North Vietnamese ports. U.S. troops left Vietnam in 1973, and in 1975 the U.S.-backed South Vietnamese government surrendered. By that time more than 58,000 Americans had been killed or were missing in action, and many who returned home suffered tremendous emotional, physical, and psychological scars from the war.

Détente The horrors of Vietnam and the continual fear of further communist expansion dominated U.S. thinking about foreign policy for more than a decade. President Nixon and his foreign-policy adviser Henry Kissinger took a realist approach. Believing that the war had weakened the United States, Kissinger wanted to decrease tensions with communist nations. The resulting policy was known as **détente**, a French word meaning "relaxation." The policy was targeted at the Soviet Union but applied to China and other communist nations as well.

The key elements of this strategy were the Strategic Arms Limitation Talks (SALT) and Nixon's 1972 visit to China. His visit, the first by a U.S. president, was a dramatic event for two reasons. First, the United States had not established diplomatic relations with China's communist government since it had come to power in 1949. Second, the United States had spent two decades trying to isolate China from the rest of the world. The purpose of his visit, President Nixon said, was "to seek normalization of relations between the two countries."

Later in 1972, Nixon met in Moscow with Soviet premier Leonid Brezhnev. They signed the first SALT agreement. SALT was a treaty in which both sides agreed to limit the production of certain nuclear weapons. Despite the mutual agreements, however, the arms race dragged on and the Soviet Union continued its aggressive policies. Détente was followed by a return to containment and a massive military buildup during the 1980s.

The Collapse of Communism The late 1980s marked perhaps the most dramatic shift in global relations in modern history—the collapse of communism. Events leading up to this collapse began in the Soviet Union when new leaders tried unsuccessfully to modernize their nation's decaying political and economic system through a series of political reforms.

Relations between the United States and the Soviet Union improved dramatically after Mikhail Gorbachev became the general secretary of the Communist Party's Central Committee in 1985 and the Soviet president in 1988. At that time, the Soviet Union had been suffering from economic and political problems for years. Gorbachev, believing that his country needed massive change, initiated a program of reforms in 1987 that expanded freedoms and reformed the political process. These programs called for greater openness (**glasnost**) and economic restructuring (**perestroika**). In 1989 Gorbachev decided not to block anticommunist movements in Eastern Europe. As a result, all the communist governments there collapsed within several months.

Perhaps the period's most dramatic moment occurred on November 9, 1989, when East Germany declared that it would open its border with the West. This action led to the destruction of the most notorious symbol of the split between Eastern and Western Europe—the Berlin Wall. (The wall had been built in 1961 to separate communist East Berlin, the capital of East Germany, from democratic West Berlin, which was technically part of West Germany.) Armed police had patrolled the border between the halves of the city, as well as that between East and West Germany,

WORLD AFFAIRS *President Richard Nixon and China's premier Zhou Enlai review troops of China's Red Army during Nixon's famous trip to China in 1972.* **What message did Nixon hope to send to Chinese leaders by visiting their country?**

for decades. After the dismantling of the wall, the two countries agreed to unify, re-forming the nation of Germany in October 1990.

In response to the dramatic turn of events, a group of Soviet generals and old-line Communists tried to overthrow Gorbachev in August 1991. The revolt collapsed after several days of a pro-Gorbachev strike led by Boris Yeltsin, president of Russia, the largest republic in the Soviet Union. Within months, the Soviet Union had dissolved.

By the 1990s China and Vietnam, while retaining their communist political structure, were adopting market-oriented economic policies, and even Vietnam was seeking friendship with the United States. The only traditional communist countries left in the world were Cuba and North Korea.

SECTION 3 — REVIEW

1. Define the following terms: Monroe Doctrine, Truman Doctrine, containment, détente, glasnost, perestroika.

2. How did the Monroe Doctrine shape foreign policy? When did U.S. foreign-policy makers abandon the principle of isolationism?

3. What was the focus of the Truman Doctrine? How did the principles in the doctrine shape foreign policy for more than 40 years?

4. List the events that led to the end of the Cold War. Why did the Cold War end?

5. **Thinking and Writing Critically** How do you think the development of nuclear weapons changed U.S. foreign policy?

6. **Applying WORLD AFFAIRS** Do you think nations should become involved in other nations' affairs? Under what circumstances might this be necessary? Explain your answer.

FOREIGN AID AND ALLIANCES

Political Dictionary

foreign aid
Marshall Plan
U.S. Agency for International Development
defense alliance
collective security
North Atlantic Treaty Organization
multilateral treaty
bilateral alliance

Objectives

★ How does providing foreign aid to other nations help the United States?
★ What defense alliances does the United States maintain today?
★ How do alliances and foreign-aid programs promote the public good?

The foreign policy of the United States changed dramatically after communism ceased to pose a significant threat to U.S. national security. Promoting foreign-aid programs and maintaining defense alliances, however, remain critical factors in U.S. foreign policy.

Foreign Aid

Every president since World War II has supported **foreign aid**—economic and military assistance to foreign countries. U.S. foreign aid began in the early 1940s with the Lend-Lease program, which supplied money and military supplies to U.S. allies during World War II. Since then, the United States has spent about $500 billion in foreign economic and military aid—an

impressive amount but only a very small portion of total U.S. expenditures over the last 50 years.

Critics of foreign aid, particularly isolationists, argue that U.S. tax dollars should be used exclusively to help people at home. Others add that much foreign aid is wasted on inefficient government projects and often provides money to corrupt rulers, rather than contributing to the development of strong market-based economies.

By contrast, supporters of foreign-aid programs contend that by providing economic assistance to foreign nations, the United States is actually promoting the public good not only of other countries but of the United States as well. This argument is based on the idea that some friendly countries need and deserve our help.

Furthermore, the governments of countries with weak economies might fall to forces hostile to the United States; whereas, if strengthened by foreign aid, such countries can eventually become good markets for U.S. goods. Germany, for example, a former recipient of U.S. foreign aid, has imported more than $20 billion of U.S. goods annually in recent years.

The Marshall Plan The most significant U.S. effort at providing financial assistance to foreign nations occurred through an aid program that was proposed by George Marshall, the secretary

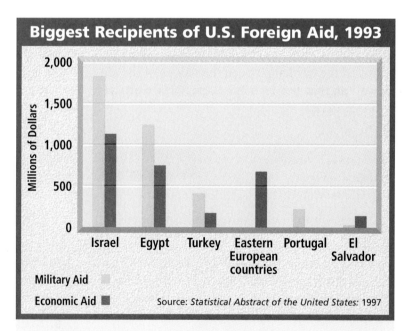

Biggest Recipients of U.S. Foreign Aid, 1993

Military Aid
Economic Aid

Source: *Statistical Abstract of the United States: 1997*

This graph shows how much economic and military aid some countries received from the United States in 1993. **Does the United States give more in military aid or economic aid to these countries?**

WORLD AFFAIRS *Workers in Haiti stack food sent by the United States as humanitarian aid.* **How does USAID help the United States achieve its foreign-policy goals?**

of state under President Harry Truman. The **Marshall Plan** was an economic assistance program that poured around $13 billion into the 16 nations of Western Europe between 1948 and 1952. During this period these nations were suffering because of the financial burdens of World War II. The Marshall Plan restored them to economic health.

USAID Prior to the 1960s, foreign-aid programs were implemented individually. That is, no central institution existed for assessing the need for, and the possible benefits of, providing aid to foreign nations. Since 1961, however, the **U.S. Agency for International Development** (USAID), part of the State Department, has been responsible for implementing most U.S. foreign-aid programs. The agency works to help achieve U.S. foreign-policy goals in five principal areas— promoting economic growth, advancing democracy, delivering humanitarian support to victims of disasters, promoting public health, and protecting the environment.

Alliances and Pacts

In addition to providing aid to foreign countries, the United States pursues its foreign-policy goals by establishing alliances and pacts with foreign nations. **Defense alliances** are agreements in which nations pledge to come to each other's aid in case of attack. A primary goal of these

Ranking the United States in Global Giving

In the early 1960s the United States was spending more than any other industrial nation on aid to developing countries. By 1995, however, the United States had cut these expenditures, falling to fourth place—behind Japan, France, and Germany—in the total amount of money spent on foreign aid. Moreover, the United States ranked last among the leading industrial nations in the amount of foreign aid it gave as a percentage of gross national product (GNP)—the total dollar value of all final goods and services produced during one year by the residents of a nation.

The size of the U.S. economy, however, allows the nation to contribute a much higher *amount* than most countries. Countries with relatively small economies—such as Portugal, Ireland, and New Zealand—cannot possibly contribute as much as the United States, even though they might give a more generous portion of their GNP. In 1994 the United States contributed .15 percent of its GNP to poor countries, compared to the .45 percent average among the rest of the world's 21 high-income countries.

The United States is not the only country to cut its foreign-aid expenditures. Many other industrialized countries, including Japan, Italy, and Germany, have been forced to reduce foreign aid because of severe budget restrictions. As the largest contributors of foreign aid tighten their belts, major recipients feel the loss.

Citizenship in Action

Amnesty International's Power to Liberate

Since 1948 the United Nations Universal Declaration of Human Rights has been the international standard for fair treatment of people. Many countries have incorporated the standards proclaimed in this document into their national laws. Although the declaration has prompted worldwide efforts to protect human rights, some countries continue to abuse these rights.

Amnesty International, an organization established in 1961, works to bring human rights abuses to light. Part of Amnesty International's efforts include massive letter-writing campaigns to pressure governments to end the abuse, torture, and unfair imprisonment of their citizens. In the process, Amnesty International volunteers have discovered that sometimes a simple letter can have the power to liberate.

Amnesty International volunteers in Boston, Massachusetts, decorate T-shirts as part of a project to inform the public of human rights abuses.

Amnesty International has about 200,000 members around the world, including more than 30,000 U.S. high school and college students. These students sponsor lectures, discussions, and even art exhibits to educate fellow students about human rights. In Minneapolis, Minnesota, for example, a group of middle and high school students studied poems, songs, and pictures illustrating the worldwide struggle for human rights. Then they created a large outdoor sculpture of four figures with interlocking arms and covered it with statements appealing for tolerance, respect, peace, and human rights.

College students in the organization have drawn on the many resources on their campuses to promote human rights. At Mary Baldwin College in Virginia, Kate Shunney knew that her fellow students had the energy and abilities to further Amnesty's mission.

During an orientation to educate students about the group's worldwide efforts, Shunney explained the letter-writing campaigns and told the stories of Asian refugees, exiled Soviet political objectors, and Holocaust survivors. Her speech attracted many new members to the local chapter of Amnesty International. In one year, the energetic group sent some 300 letters to political leaders around the globe, helping to free nearly a dozen prisoners.

These simple hand-written letters from students and other Amnesty members of all ages communicate several powerful messages. They not only draw attention to human rights abuses; they also show that people working together can make a difference in the lives of prisoners in seemingly hopeless conditions. The success of the letter campaigns shows that communication and education are a key to protecting human rights around the world.

What Do You Think?

1. Why do you think Amnesty International depends on thousands of volunteers around the world to promote its efforts to free people who are unfairly imprisoned?
2. In what ways are letter-writing campaigns an effective tool in fighting human rights abuses?

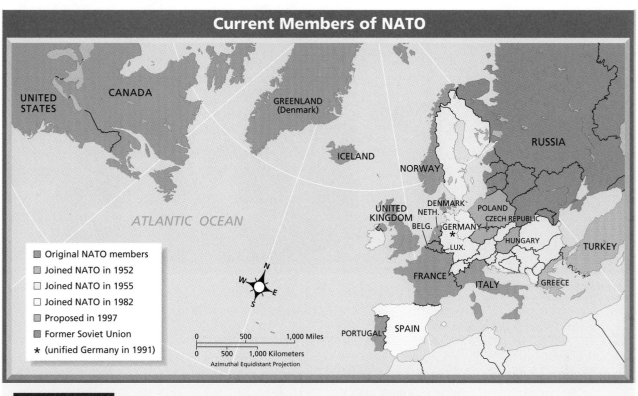

Current Members of NATO

UNITED STATES

CANADA

GREENLAND (Denmark)

ICELAND

NORWAY

RUSSIA

ATLANTIC OCEAN

UNITED KINGDOM

DENMARK
NETH.
BELG.
LUX.
GERMANY
*

POLAND
CZECH REPUBLIC
HUNGARY

TURKEY

FRANCE

ITALY

GREECE

PORTUGAL

SPAIN

■ Original NATO members
□ Joined NATO in 1952
□ Joined NATO in 1955
□ Joined NATO in 1982
■ Proposed in 1997
■ Former Soviet Union
* (unified Germany in 1991)

N W E S

0   500   1,000 Miles
0   500   1,000 Kilometers
Azimuthal Equidistant Projection

WORLD AFFAIRS *NATO was formed in 1949 when several countries signed a treaty to create a unified defense of Western Europe and North America.* **Which three countries joined NATO in 1997?**

alliances is **collective security**, the ensuring of peace through the guarantee of mutual defense. Treaties that the United States and other nations have signed to achieve this goal include the North Atlantic Treaty Organization, the Rio Pact, and the Organization of American States. In addition the United States is a member of the United Nations, a worldwide forum with more than 180 member countries, that was designed to resolve disputes and achieve other important international goals. (The United Nations is more fully explained in Chapter 23.)

North Atlantic Treaty Organization In 1949, four years into the Cold War, the Western nations formed the **North Atlantic Treaty Organization** (NATO). NATO was only the second alliance that the United States had ever joined in peacetime. The goal of NATO was to create a unified defense of the North Atlantic area, composed of Western Europe and North America. All member countries agreed that "an armed attack against one or more of them in Europe or North America shall be considered an attack against them all."

NATO is an example of a **multilateral**

treaty—an agreement signed by several countries. Today NATO includes the original 12 members—the United States, Canada, the United Kingdom, France, Italy, Portugal, the Netherlands, Belgium, Luxembourg, Denmark, Norway, and Iceland—plus Greece and Turkey, which joined in 1952; Spain, which joined in 1982; and Germany, which joined in 1990 (replacing West Germany, which had joined in 1955).

For more than 40 years the focus of this alliance was mutual defense against Soviet aggression. In the post-Cold War era, however, NATO's focus has shifted to expanding cooperation with new partners in Central and Eastern Europe and in the former Soviet Union. In July 1997 three Eastern European countries—Poland, the Czech Republic, and Hungary—were approved for membership in 1999 by the existing members.

Rio Pact The Inter-American Treaty of Reciprocal Assistance of 1947, known as the Rio Pact, is a defense agreement signed by 22 republics in the Americas. The agreement states that "an armed attack by any State shall be considered as an attack against all American States."

WORLD AFFAIRS *Philippine president Elpidio Quirino (left) and U.S. president Harry Truman (right) watch as Secretary of State Dean Acheson signs a mutual defense pact in 1951.* **What is the purpose of bilateral alliances?**

Organization of American States Like the Rio Pact, the Organization of American States (OAS) is a mutual agreement among the republics in the Americas. OAS, however, is concerned with resolving economic—rather than military—disputes. It also is responsible for implementing the Rio Pact's terms for safeguarding the Americas against attack.

Bilateral Treaties of Alliance The United States is an active partner in various **bilateral alliances**—security agreements between two nations. For example, the United States still adheres to the 1951 U.S.-Japan Mutual Security Treaty—which allows it to maintain land, sea, and air forces in Japan, in return for agreeing to protect Japan in a time of crisis. In addition, the bilateral alliance supports the foreign-policy goal of open and free trade. The United States also maintains bilateral treaties with the Philippines, signed in 1951 as well, and South Korea, approved in 1954.

Since the signing of these treaties, the issues that most affect U.S. foreign-policy decisions have changed dramatically, particularly with the end of the Cold War during the late 1980s and 1990s. Even so, these and other treaties remain vital to the realization of U.S. foreign-policy goals.

SECTION 4 — REVIEW

1. Define the following terms: foreign aid, Marshall Plan, U.S. Agency for International Development, defense alliance, collective security, North Atlantic Treaty Organization, multilateral treaty, bilateral alliance.

2. What are the benefits, both foreign and domestic, of providing foreign aid? Are there drawbacks, in your opinion?

3. With what countries does the United States maintain defense alliances?

4. Why does the United States maintain defense alliances during times of peace?

5. **Thinking and Writing Critically**
   Do you agree with the U. S. policy of providing aid to less-developed countries? Explain your answer.

6. **Applying** WORLD AFFAIRS
   Conduct an Internet search for information on USAID. Which countries are the largest recipients of its programs today?

CHAPTER 10 — SUMMARY

SECTION 1 There are several fundamental goals of U.S. foreign policy. These include maintaining national security, supporting democracy, promoting world peace, providing aid to people in need, and establishing free and open trade.

U.S. foreign policy must answer the question of how active the United States should be in world affairs and determine which guidelines should be used to evaluate U.S. activities abroad. These questions have been answered differently at various points in U.S. history. The United States has generally followed one of four basic approaches to foreign policy: isolationism, realism, neoisolationism, or idealism. Republicans generally are either realists or isolationists, and Democrats generally are either neoisolationists or idealists. Each principle has a limited scope, so the public good is often best promoted by making trade-offs among them.

SECTION 2 The executive branch takes a more influential role in making foreign-policy decisions than does Congress. The main figures within the executive branch that have critical foreign-policy roles are the president, the U.S. Departments of State and Defense, and the Central Intelligence Agency. The National Security Council also plays an important role in coordinating foreign policy.

The president is generally the most influential decision maker in U.S. foreign policy. This influence comes from three sources— the American people's and Congress's general acceptance of the president in this role; the presidential role as commander in chief, and executive agreements.

SECTION 3 Early U.S. foreign policy reflected isolationist sentiments. A shift to international involvement began with the Spanish-American War of 1898. The United States won a decisive victory in this war and emerged as a world power.

Afterward, U.S. leaders returned to an isolationist policy until World War I began. After the war, the country again tried to return to an isolationist policy, but the Japanese bombing of Pearl Harbor in 1941 led to U.S. involvement in World War II.

After World War II the communist Soviet Union began expanding its control over Eastern Europe, threatening the U.S. goals of promoting democracy and of maintaining national security. Hostility between the United States and the Soviet Union came to be known as the Cold War.

The United States tried to stop communist expansion worldwide by following a policy of containment. The Korean War, the Cuban missile crisis, and the Vietnam War were results of U.S. attempts to stop communist expansion. Communism collapsed in the late 1980s, however, with the fall of communist governments in a number of Eastern European nations and eventually in the Soviet Union.

SECTION 4 The foreign policy of the United States has changed dramatically since the fall of communism. Promoting foreign-aid programs and maintaining defense alliances remain critical factors in foreign policy. Foreign aid began with the Lend-Lease program and continued with the Marshall Plan. Today, most foreign aid is administered by the U.S. Agency for International Development. The United States also is involved in several defense alliances and pacts, the most significant of which is NATO.

Government Notebook

Review the list that you made in your Government Notebook. After reading the chapter, do you find that there are ways in which countries interact that you did not consider? Record your answer in your Notebook.

CHAPTER 10
REVIEW

REVIEWING CONCEPTS

1. What is a trade embargo? Why is trade a powerful political tool?

2. How has the use of presidential doctrines expanded the president's power in foreign-policy decision making?

3. What foreign-policy goals affect the United States's relationships with other countries?

4. In what way did the United States change its foreign-policy approach after the bombing of Pearl Harbor?

5. How did the Marshall Plan help ease the economic hardships of Western Europe after World War II?

THINKING AND WRITING CRITICALLY

1. **WORLD AFFAIRS** How do you think the horrors of the Vietnam War changed the way the public views the use of force as a tool for resolving international conflict?

2. **CONSTITUTIONAL GOVERNMENT** Considering that the CIA sometimes has used covert operations in the execution of its activities, do you think that there is potential for an abuse of power? Why or why not?

3. **POLITICAL PROCESSES** How have technological advances in communications and transportation helped shape foreign policy over the last 100 years? In what way have these advances changed how the public views the United States's relationships with other countries?

4. **PUBLIC GOOD** How do the U.S. government's efforts to build good relations with other countries promote the public good? Do you think that technology has helped the United States build strong relationships with other countries? Why or why not?

CITIZENSHIP IN YOUR COMMUNITY

With a group, research foreign-aid organizations in the United States. What types of assistance or aid do they provide to other countries? What countries are the biggest recipients of this aid? How many community, state, and national volunteers work for each organization? Do these organizations need more volunteers, supplies, and monetary contributions? How can you and other students become involved in efforts to help people in other nations? You might want to create charts and graphs to present the information you collect to your class.

INDIVIDUAL PORTFOLIO PROJECT

Write a newspaper editorial expressing your views on which principle of foreign policy should most guide U.S. decision makers. Review the basic approaches to foreign policy outlined in Section 1 of this chapter. Then select one approach or a combination of approaches that you support. In your editorial, write a clear argument for why this approach best promotes U.S. national interests. You might want to include specific examples of successful foreign policies using the approach you selected.

PRACTICING SKILLS: LEARNING FROM VISUALS

Editorial cartoons have been used for hundreds of years to influence public opinion about economic, political, and social issues. Two important techniques that cartoonists use to express their message are caricature—the creation of drawings that exaggerate or distort physical features—and symbolism—the use of an image to represent an idea, feeling, or object.

Using the following guidelines, study the editorial cartoon on page 221 to determine its significance and meaning. Then write a brief paragraph explaining your interpretation of the cartoon.

1. Identify the subject by reading the labels and speech balloons.

2. Identify the symbols and caricatures (for example, identify any representative figures characterized in the cartoon).

3. Determine what action is taking place. What is the significance of this action?

4. What overall message is the cartoonist trying to convey?

THE INTERNET: LEARNING ONLINE

Conduct an Internet search to find out more about the president's current foreign-policy goals. See if you can find information on recent summit conferences or official meetings between the president and other world leaders. You might start with search words such as *U.S. foreign policy, summit,* and *trade policy.* Create a fact sheet on one policy goal you research. In addition, list the Web sites you use to gather information about this policy goal.

ANALYZING PRIMARY SOURCES

TRUMAN DOCTRINE

The Truman Doctrine, announced by President Harry Truman in 1947, set forth containment as the basic U.S. foreign-policy strategy. For the next 40 years the United States concentrated on stopping the spread of communism. Read the following excerpt, and answer the accompanying questions.

❝ *One of the primary objectives of the foreign policy of the United States is the creation of conditions in which we and other nations will be able to work out a way of life free from coercion [pressure]. This was a fundamental issue in the war with Germany and Japan. Our victory was won over countries which sought to impose their will, and their way of life, upon other nations. . . .*

The peoples of a number of countries of the world have recently had totalitarian regimes forced upon them against their will. The government of the United States has made frequent protests against coercion and intimidation. . . . I must also state that in a number of other countries there have been similar developments.

At the present moment in world history nearly every nation must choose between alternative ways of life. The choice is too often not a free one.

One way of life is based upon the will of the majority, and is distinguished by free institutions, representative government, free elections, guarantees of individual liberty, freedom of speech and religion, and freedom from political oppression [persecution]. The second way of life is based upon the will of a minority forcibly imposed upon the majority. It relies upon terror and oppression, a controlled press and radio; fixed elections, and the suppression [limiting] of personal freedoms.

I believe that it must be the policy of the United States to support free peoples who are resisting attempted subjugation [conquering] by armed minorities or by outside pressures. . . . I believe that our help should be primarily through economic and financial aid which is essential to economic stability and orderly political processes. ❞

1. Do you think that the "primary objectives of foreign policy of the United States" are the same today as in 1947?

2. Do you think that it is important for the United States to help other countries avoid the second way of life described by President Truman?

3. What types of aid are essential to economic and political stability? Do you agree with President Truman's opinion that the United States should primarily use economic aid to help other countries? Explain your answer.

Writing Presidential Speeches

Imagine that you and your classmates are speechwriters for the president of the United States. The president's chief of staff has asked you to write a speech for a press conference about an upcoming foreign-trade summit with Prime Minister Kaya Nikano of Libertaria. The purpose of the summit is to negotiate an agreement that would reduce trade restrictions and establish a free-trade zone between the two countries. The president wants to use this press conference as a tool to gain public support for the summit and the trade agreement. He has already spent much time discussing the summit goals with his cabinet and other high-level advisers. To help you in writing the speech, the president's chief of staff has sent you a memo outlining the key elements to include and has provided copies of the summit agenda, policy recommendations from presidential advisers, and a letter from Prime Minister Nikano. You will find those documents on the following pages.

After you review the documents, answer the accompanying questions in your Government Notebook. Your group also may want to conduct some outside research to gather additional statistical or historical information on the factors that contribute to successful economic and trade agreements between the United States and other countries. Use this information to make comparisons between past foreign policies and one that could lead to strong trade relations with Libertaria.

After you have finished reviewing the documents, work with other group members to write a speech for the president to give at the press conference. In the speech, be sure to clearly state the purpose of the summit and the president's goals for the treaty negotiation. You may want to include some of the statistics that the president's advisers have provided. Discuss how the summit and impending agreement will improve the economic outlook for the United States by creating strong international trade relations.

Consider having one group member read the speech to the rest of the class as part of a discussion on the president's role in the development of foreign and economic policy.

OFFICE OF THE PRESIDENT OF THE UNITED STATES

STAFF MEMORANDUM

To: Staff Speechwriters
From: Chief of Staff

The president will be attending a press conference on April 15 where he will be speaking to the press and the public about the upcoming free-trade summit with Prime Minister Kaya Nikano in Paris. This press conference is crucial for setting the tone for the summit. The speech must clearly establish the president's goals and agenda for the summit and show how accomplishing them will heighten domestic prosperity.

The broad goals of the Paris Free-Trade Summit are to
• open new markets,
• create a free-trade area, and
• improve the quality of life for the people of both countries.

The president's speech must emphasize that a free-trade treaty will enable the United States to increase its gross domestic product by
• expanding the export of domestic goods and services and
• creating more high-wage jobs.

Please carefully review the policy recommendations of Secretary of Commerce James Lin and U.S. Trade Representative Alice Brooks before preparing this speech. Both recommendations include statistics that clearly show the projected economic growth that would result from a free-trade treaty with Libertaria. Please examine the summit agenda for a more detailed description of the summit goals.

The speech should stress the importance of this treaty in the future growth and development of the U.S. economy. This speech will be an important tool of the president in generating broad public support for the free-trade agreement. Public support for the agreement may be key to gaining congressional approval. I appreciate your assistance and look forward to reading this speech.

Thank you

The President's Paris Free-Trade Summit Agenda

The focus of the Paris Free-Trade Summit agenda is to build on the good political and trade relations that already exist between Libertaria and the United States. We aim to seek a higher level of openness and cooperation and to address current trade restrictions maintained by both countries. We are committed to creating a trade agreement that is mutually supportive. In pursuit of these goals, we will construct a long-term plan for further negotiations and agreements. Priority at this summit will be given to
• promoting high-tech U.S. exports;
• supporting high-growth U.S. export industries, particularly those requiring highly skilled labor;
• eliminating barriers that adversely affect the creation of new jobs and the maintaining of existing—particularly high-wage and high-skill—jobs;
• opening markets for Libertarian exports; and
• creating an agenda for further trade negotiations with Libertaria over the next 10 years.

PUBLIC POLICY LAB

SECRETARY OF COMMERCE
James Lin

The goals of the free-trade summit must reflect the inter-dependence of the U.S. and Libertarian economies in a global market. The long-term economic prosperity of the United States will be significantly affected by the economic development and stability of the countries with whom we establish strong trade relations.

Identifying the major foreign consumers of U.S.-made goods is crucial to U.S. economic policy. The growth of the U.S. economy relies on increased consumption of U.S. exports. Consider the following statistics on Libertarian consumption of U.S.-made goods. For every dollar Libertaria spends on exports, 47 cents goes toward goods made in the United States. Libertaria maintains trade barriers that are approximately two times higher than ours, yet the United States sold almost $100 billion worth of goods in Libertaria last year. If current trends in trade between the United States and Libertaria are maintained, by the year 2008 the United States will sell more to Libertaria than to Europe or Japan.

I strongly recommend that the president concentrate significant efforts on building strong trade relations with the major consumers of U.S.-made goods. This can only be done by negotiating mutually beneficial trade agreements with those countries, one of which is Libertaria. By working to ensure the economic growth and development of our trade partners, we secure our own country's future economic growth.

◀ WHAT DO YOU THINK?

★ What role do exports play in the growth of the U.S. economy?

★ How may a free-trade agreement affect the future consumption of U.S. exports?

★ Why is it particularly important for the health of the U.S. economy that the United States have good relations with Libertaria?

U.S. TRADE REPRESENTATIVE

Alice Brooks

Policy Recommendation

The major goal of the upcoming Paris Free-Trade Summit is economic growth. This goal can be accomplished only through creating economic opportunity, particularly through new jobs. The creation of high-wage, high-quality jobs is essential to improving Americans' standard of living.

Libertaria is a major consumer of U.S.-made computers and electronics. An increased effort to build strong trade relations with foreign consumers of such goods is essential to the growth of U.S. industry. By making the rules fair and breaking down trade barriers, the United States will be able to export more of its goods to this market. By the year 2005, given appropriate diplomatic efforts, U.S. exports could increase 35 percent. By concentrating on opening up the market for high-tech goods, the United States could create 150,000 new jobs in the high-tech industry. High-skill jobs such as these pay about 16 percent more than do other manufacturing jobs in our economy.

Economic stability and growth—not only for the United States but also for our trading partners—depends on the diligent efforts of government leaders to create and move forward with a strategy that is based on creating high-wage, high-skilled jobs through opening markets and reducing barriers. The successful outcome of this summit relies on the ability of the president and Prime Minister Nikano to negotiate an agreement that will stimulate both countries' economies.

WHAT DO YOU THINK? ▶

★ Do you think that the public is concerned about how trade agreements will affect employment in the United States? Explain your answer.

★ Why does Alice Brooks think that opening new markets for high-tech goods is essential to the growth of the U.S. economy?

★ Why might foreign-policy specialists recommend a focus on the creation of more high-skill jobs?

FROM THE DESK OF KAYA NIKANO

Dear Mr. President:

In response to your most recent correspondence, I wish to ensure that you and I have a clear understanding of the central matters concerning trade relations between the United States and Libertaria.

Countries entering into a free-trade agreement must be willing to accept foreign products into their market. If the consumers in Libertaria are going to be able to buy U.S.-made goods, they must be able to generate income by the sale of goods and services in the United States. To increase economic integration and free trade, we must work together with private industries and financial institutions to promote productive investment and trade. We must move toward lifting trade barriers.

Libertaria has made monumental progress in economic development and stability over the last 10 years. The debt burden has been reduced to a manageable level, and we have the fastest-growing economy in the Western Hemisphere. The United States has played a key role in helping Libertaria reach its current level of prosperity through investment and other economic aid. Our aim in the next several years is to open markets for U.S.-made goods and services, as well as establish markets in the United States for our exports.

Creating a mutually beneficial trade environment should be given careful attention, encouragement, and support. I look forward to our meeting as a vital step toward achieving this goal.

Sincerely Yours,

Kaya Nikano

Kaya Nikano

▲ WHAT DO YOU THINK?

★ Why do you think Prime Minister Kaya Nikano believes that removing trade regulations is key to developing better trade relations?

★ How might the United States benefit from establishing strong trade relations with one of the world's fastest-growing economies? What would Libertaria gain from a free-trade agreement with the United States?

THINGS TO DO

1. Discuss group members' notes on the documents presented for review.

2. Create an outline summarizing the main goals for the summit. You may want to start with a list of basic points and statistics.

3. Determine the main theme of the president's speech—for example, opening new markets for

U.S. exports, creating new jobs in the United States through increased trade, or building close trade relations with foreign countries.

4. Prepare a speech to be delivered at the press conference, explaining why the free-trade summit is important to the U.S. economy. Support your argument with statistical information from this assignment.

UNIT

4

PUBLIC POLICY LAB

Do police officers have the right
to search people's homes without a search warrant? Find out by
reading this unit and taking the
Public Policy Lab challenge on
pages 290–93.

THE JUDICIAL BRANCH

THE FEDERAL COURT SYSTEM

In *Federalist Paper* "No. 78," Alexander Hamilton stated that "the judiciary is beyond comparison the weakest of the three departments of power." The legislature controls lawmaking and spending, and the executive "holds the sword of the community." In contrast, courts have "no influence over either the sword or the purse; no direction either of the strength or of the wealth of the society." Courts cannot even enforce their own decisions, but must depend on "the aid of the executive."

Hamilton's opinion might be different were he to see the judiciary at work today. Both the lower federal courts and the Supreme Court have expanded their powers significantly since the 1700s. This increased power has sparked a debate over the judicial branch's role in promoting the public good.

Government Notebook

In your Government Notebook, make a list of the things in your daily life that you think might be affected by Supreme Court decisions.

SECTION 1

THE LOWER COURTS

Political Dictionary

precedent
strict constructionist
loose constructionist
jurisdiction
original jurisdiction
district court
court of appeals
circuit
appellate jurisdiction
brief
senatorial courtesy

Objectives

★ What are the role and the authority of the lower courts?
★ How are the lower courts organized?
★ How are lower-court judges selected?

The federal court system consists of the lower courts and the Supreme Court. The Supreme Court is more fully explained in Section 2. This section discusses the lower courts—their role, authority, organization, and judges.

Role of the Courts

The lower federal courts perform the day-to-day work of the judicial branch. That is, they hear and decide thousands of cases that are brought to the federal court system each year. In performing this duty, the courts resolve disputes, set precedents, and interpret the law.

Resolving Disputes The lower courts hear "cases and controversies," reviewing and resolving specific disputes between specific parties. For example, suppose you apply for a job at Acme, Inc., but are not hired because the company has

an illegal, discriminatory hiring policy. You, as a job applicant of Acme, may contest the company's policy in court. If you had not applied to Acme, however, and only had heard about its policy from a friend, you could not sue Acme merely on general principles as a concerned citizen. Rather, the law allows only people who have suffered a specific injury to bring suit.

Setting Precedents Although the courts rule only on specific cases, their decisions can have much broader and more far-reaching consequences. This is because in addition to announcing their specific decisions, the courts also provide the legal grounds, or reasoning, for these decisions. These grounds serve as **precedents**, or guiding principles, for determining what is legal in situations that involve similar issues. Judges, lawmakers, government officials, companies, and citizens look to these precedents to guide their actions.

Interpreting the Law What philosophy should judges apply when resolving disputes and setting precedents? Some people are **strict constructionists**. They believe that laws and the Constitution should be interpreted strictly according to the words they contain. If any wording is vague, the courts should examine the historical record to determine the authors' intended meaning. These records might include transcriptions of debates over bills and proposed amendments, discussions and debates at the Constitutional

"Maybe I'm in the minority here, but aren't we becoming obsessed with constitutionality?"

CONSTITUTIONAL GOVERNMENT *Some judges believe that the Constitution should be interpreted strictly according to the words it contains. **What tools do the courts use to interpret the meaning of any vague wording in the Constitution?***

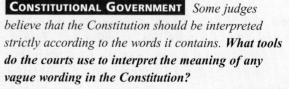

© 1997 Robert Mankoff from The Cartoon Bank. All rights reserved.

Convention, and documents such as the *Federalist Papers*.

For example, Article I of the Constitution gives Congress the power "to regulate commerce . . . among the several states." A review of historical records shows that the framers wanted to prevent states from setting their own rules regarding trade and business with other states. Such practices had damaged the national economy under the Articles of Confederation. Strict constructionists argue that the framers did not mean for Congress to use this power to design other business regulations, such as minimum-wage laws. They instead believe that the proper way to address changing circumstances is not by reinterpreting the Constitution and the laws passed by Congress but by passing constitutional amendments or new laws.

Other people prefer a "living Constitution." These **loose constructionists** believe that the Constitution and other laws must be interpreted in light of current political and social conditions. In other words, judges should consider *current* standards in applying to specific cases the general intentions of the documents' authors.

For example, the Eighth Amendment to the Constitution prohibits "cruel and unusual punishment." A punishment is considered cruel if it inflicts more pain or humiliation than the lawbreaker deserves, given the nature of the crime. When the framers wrote these words, public beatings were in common practice. Examples of what society considers cruel have changed over the years, however, and today most people would consider public beatings to be cruel and unusual. Loose constructionists thus argue that the courts should now interpret the Eighth Amendment to mean that public beatings are unconstitutional.

Authority of the Courts

Article III of the Constitution states that "the judicial power of the United States shall be vested in one supreme Court, and in such inferior courts as the Congress may . . . establish." The First Congress used this constitutional power to set up a system of federal courts under the Judiciary Act of 1789. Congress was given the power to establish the lower federal courts, but the courts receive their **jurisdiction**, or authority to interpret and administer the law, from the Constitution.

Lower federal courts have **original jurisdiction**—the authority to hear a case's

Extent of the Jurisdiction of Lower Courts

The lower courts hear cases in which

- a person is accused of disobeying the U.S. Constitution,
- a person is accused of violating a U.S. treaty,
- a person is accused of breaking federal laws passed by Congress,
- the U.S. government or a U.S. citizen is charged with an offense by a foreign nation,
- a person is accused of committing a crime on a U.S. ship at sea,
- a U.S. ambassador or other foreign-service official is accused of breaking the laws of the country in which he or she is stationed,
- a person is accused of committing a crime on certain types of federal property, and
- a citizen of one state brings a lawsuit against a citizen of another state.

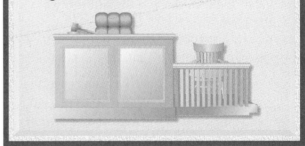

The Constitution outlines the jurisdiction of the nation's courts. Federal courts administer the law for many types of federal crimes. **Why do you think that the federal courts hear cases in which a citizen from one state sues a citizen of another state?**

initial trial—only over cases arising under the Constitution and other federal laws, and over those involving diplomats, treaties, state governments, the U.S. government, and citizens of other countries or of more than one state. (See the chart on this page for the extent of lower courts' jurisdiction.)

In addition, a few special types of disputes, which are discussed in Section 2, fall under the original jurisdiction of the Supreme Court. All other disputes are left to state, county, and municipal courts, which are discussed in Unit 7.

Government and Philosophy

Philosophy and the U.S. Court System

"You and I, my dear friend," wrote Constitutional Convention delegate John Adams to a fellow delegate, "have been sent into life at a time when the greatest lawgivers of antiquity (ancient times) would have wished to live." Few people, he concluded, had the chance to create their own laws. To write these laws and—just as importantly—build the court system to uphold them, the delegates at the Constitutional Convention drew on the writings of political philosophers dating back to the ancient Greeks.

The writings of Aristotle, a Greek who lived from 384 to 322 B.C., provided the basic ideas on the functions and purpose of government. Aristotle argued that the main goal of government should be to promote the public good, a novel idea for his time. He believed that law and justice helped people achieve a good life. "For man, when perfected, is the best of animals," he argued, "but when separated from law and justice, he is the worst of all."

Later philosophers echoed Aristotle's belief in the connection between the law and the public good. In his *Two Treatises of Government* (1690),

English philosopher John Locke agreed that people formed governments to preserve the public good. In exchange for giving up some of their liberties, people accepted their government's "right of making laws . . . and of employing the force of the community in execution of such laws." Courts and laws protected individual rights and property, rather than threatening citizens' liberty.

Baron Charles de Montesquieu, a French philosopher, believed that the main aim of government should be to promote liberty. He argued that government could most effectively achieve this goal by dividing its authority among executive, legislative, and judicial branches.

In *Spirit of the Laws*, published in 1748, Montesquieu called for this bold concept of the separation of powers to defend people's freedom from a too-powerful government. He argued that a combined executive and legislative branch would abuse its power and destroy liberty. He also stated that the judiciary would become too powerful if joined with the legislative branch, which was a common practice at the time.

The writings of Locke and Montesquieu particularly influenced the framers of the Constitution. In the *Federalist Papers*, James Madison praised Montesquieu's separation of powers as an "invaluable precept (precious principle) in the science of politics." Thomas Jefferson, advising a friend who wanted to study law, also "generally recommended" Montesquieu's *Spirit of the Laws* and cited Locke's "little book of Government" as "perfect as far as it goes."

Drawing on these philosophers, the framers of the Constitution created a separate court system that sought to protect liberty as it enforced the Constitution. As a separate body, the judiciary could check the power of the legislative branch, which the framers saw as the greatest threat to liberty. Judges could make sure that legislators did not create new laws that violated the Constitution.

The Granger Collection, New York

In 1748 Baron Charles de Montesquieu published Spirit of the Laws, *in which he argued for the separation of government powers.*

What Do You Think?

1. How did Montesquieu build upon Aristotle's belief that the main goal of government should be to promote the public good?
2. In what ways could a judiciary combined with the legislative branch become too powerful?

Lower Court Organization

The lower courts are divided into district courts and courts of appeals. These two types of courts play different roles in the legal system. The lower court system also includes several specialized courts.

District Courts The trial courts of the federal system are called **district courts**. These courts are assigned to specific geographic areas and have original jurisdiction over federal cases that arise there. The District of Columbia has one district court, and each state has from one to four, generally depending on the size of its population.

District courts engage in the oldest and most fundamental judicial activity—making a decision in a dispute. Any trial decision is based on the *facts* of the case (the specifics of what happened) as well as the *law* (the general, established rules of society). The basic task of district courts is to determine the facts and then reach a verdict by applying the law to them.

Cases are tried before a district court judge and a jury, though the defendant can waive, or give up, the right to a jury. Both sides support their position by providing evidence, some of which may be supplied by witnesses. In criminal cases a U.S. attorney from the Justice Department serves as the prosecutor. In civil cases the opposing parties are represented by their own attorneys. Some district court civil cases are tried before a jury as well as a judge, though the right to a jury is typically waived in such cases.

Courts of Appeals Appeals of cases from the U.S. district courts are heard by the **courts of appeals**. Although about one third of district court decisions are appealed, only around one fifth of them are actually reviewed. The remainder are settled out of court.

There are 13 U.S. courts of appeals, each of which covers a large judicial district called a **circuit**. The 50 states are divided into 11 circuits. There is also a circuit for the District of Columbia and a Federal Circuit, which hears certain kinds of cases involving federal agencies. The Federal Circuit has jurisdiction over all states and territories. Each court of appeals has a total of 6 to 28 judges. There are no juries in a court of appeals, so cases are heard by the judges alone. Usually, only three of a circuit's judges hear any one case, although some important cases may be decided by the entire court.

Appeals courts were established to give individuals who have received an unfavorable decision another chance to be heard. This opportunity is

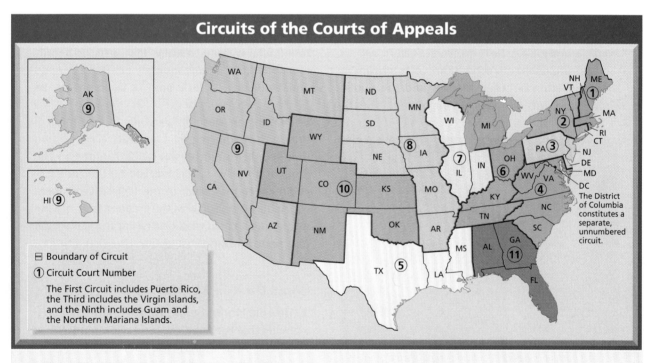

Circuits of the Courts of Appeals

☐ Boundary of Circuit
① Circuit Court Number

The First Circuit includes Puerto Rico, the Third includes the Virgin Islands, and the Ninth includes Guam and the Northern Mariana Islands.

The District of Columbia constitutes a separate, unnumbered circuit.

The U.S. federal court system is divided into 13 circuits, including one for the District of Columbia and a federal circuit. **In which circuit court is your state located?**

Special Courts

- U.S. Court of Claims
- U.S. Court of International Trade
- U.S. Court of Appeals for the Armed Forces
- U.S. Territorial Courts
- U.S. Tax Court
- U.S. Court of Veterans Appeals

These special courts were established by Congress to handle specific types of cases. **What court handles cases in which a veteran of the U.S. armed services brings a lawsuit against the federal government?**

rooted in the U.S. legal and cultural tradition. The appeals courts' **appellate jurisdiction** means they have the power to review cases previously decided by a lower court.

Appeals courts are limited in the scope of their examination. They may not review a trial's determinations of the *facts,* such as whether a defendant robbed a store. Therefore, no new facts are presented to a court of appeals. Rather, courts of appeals may review only issues of *law,* such as whether a defendant's confession to a robbery was legally obtained. They only determine whether the person appealing the case received his or her full rights under the law during the district court trial.

Thus, courts of appeals do not hold another trial of the cases they review. Judges make their decisions based on two types of information: the written record from the district court trial and **briefs**, or written legal arguments, submitted by both sides in the case. Thus, whereas a district court trial is basically an oral proceeding, an appeal is basically a written one, although oral arguments are often allowed.

There are a variety of decisions that the judges may make in an appealed case, including reversing the decision, affirming it, or sending the case back to district court for a retrial if the court finds that an individual's legal rights were not fully protected. If the court of appeals finds that his or her rights were observed and the law was properly applied to the facts, it upholds, or affirms, the district court's decision. If it finds that the law was not properly applied, the court of appeals reverses the lower court's decision.

Other Courts In addition to the district courts and courts of appeals, Congress has set up several special courts to handle specific types of cases. For example, the U.S. Claims Court hears cases involving money claims against the federal government. (See the chart on this page for a list of special courts.)

Federal Judges

Most federal judges, not including those who preside over special courts, serve for life, although Congress can impeach and convict them for serious crimes. The framers established life terms for these judges so that they could remain independent of political pressure.

Delegates at the Constitutional Convention discussed various methods for choosing federal

Comparing Governments

Russian Courts

After 74 years of communist rule, the Soviet Union disbanded in 1991, and Russia, a former Soviet republic, became independent. As part of the restructuring of its government, Russia is struggling to build a democratic court system. Yet many judicial practices from the old system remain. For example, illegal tactics are often used by investigators to gather evidence, which prompts defense attorneys to ask for the dismissal of large portions of the testimony.

In 1993 Russia adopted a new constitution and set out to reform the courts. Under the new constitution, people accused of a crime have the right to a jury trial, the right to a lawyer, and the right to an appeal. The constitution also includes strict new standards for collecting evidence.

However, the courts are still a long way from putting the reforms into effect. Only about 1 trial in 4,000 is a jury trial. Significant opposition to jury trials comes from police officers and prosecutors, who complain that such trials are expensive and bring fewer guilty verdicts.

POLITICAL PROCESSES *Burnita Shelton Matthews was the first woman to be appointed U.S. district court judge. President Harry Truman appointed her to the District of Columbia federal district court in 1949.* **Who handles most of the nominations for district court judges?**

District Court Appointments By far the largest number of judicial appointments are those to the district courts. Because there are so many district court positions, the nominations of district court judges are handled mostly by the Department of Justice and by White House staffers, not by the president.

The traditional principle in making district court nominations has been **senatorial courtesy**. That is, the executive branch allows senators in the president's party to approve or disapprove each potential nominee for a position in a district in their state before the official nominations are made. The other senators then almost always follow the lead of those senators and approve the nominee. In return for this courtesy, the Senate confirms almost all of the president's nominations for the district courts.

Courts of Appeals Appointments Individual senators have less influence over appeals court nominations. Appeals court appointments involve several states, so senatorial courtesy does not play a role.

On the other hand, because of the vital role of courts of appeals in interpreting the law and setting precedents, the Senate examines appeals court nominations far more carefully than those for district courts. Another reason for this closer examination is that appeals court judges are more likely to wind up serving on the Supreme Court. For example, seven of the nine current Supreme Court judges formerly served in the U.S. courts of appeals.

judges. Some favored a system in which the president would have independent appointment powers, while others feared that this would give the president too much power. The resulting compromise established the same system as that used for appointing top officials of the executive branch: nomination by the president and approval or rejection by a simple majority of the Senate. Today this selection process varies somewhat, depending on the position being filled.

SECTION 1 — REVIEW

1. Define the following terms: precedent, strict constructionist, loose constructionist, jurisdiction, original jurisdiction, district court, court of appeals, circuit, appellate jurisdiction, brief, senatorial courtesy.

2. Describe how the lower courts resolve disputes, interpret the law, and set precedents.

3. What are the functions of the district courts and the courts of appeals? List the special federal courts.

4. How does judicial appointment differ for district courts and courts of appeals?

5. **Thinking and Writing Critically**
   Why might some people say that loose constructionist interpretations endanger the integrity of the Constitution?

6. **Applying** **CONSTITUTIONAL GOVERNMENT**
   Conduct an Internet search for information on the appeals process in the federal courts. Briefly describe the information.

SECTION 2

THE SUPREME COURT

Political Dictionary

writ of *certiorari*
docket
amicus curiae brief
majority opinion
concurring opinion
dissenting opinion
stare decisis

Objectives

★ How has the role of the Supreme Court changed over time?
★ How are Supreme Court justices appointed, and what are their terms of office?
★ How does the Supreme Court operate?

As noted in Chapter 5, Pierre-Charles L'Enfant designed the capital of Washington, D.C., in 1791. L'Enfant's original plans for the city did not include a building for the Supreme Court. In a revised plan, though, L'Enfant did include a home for the Court—in marshland about halfway between the Capitol Building and the president's mansion. This building was never constructed, however, because of the high cost of draining the marsh. Such an expense was viewed as unjustified due to the Court's small size and small caseload.

Lacking other quarters, the Supreme Court met in chambers in the Capitol Building. (During one year, while the Capitol was under construction, the Court met in a tavern.) In 1824 a newspaper reporter described the Court's quarters in the Capitol as "not in a style which comports [is consistent] with the dignity" of the Supreme Court, complaining that "the room is on the basement story in an obscure [unnoticeable] part of the north wing. . . . A stranger might traverse [cross] the dark avenues of the Capitol for a week, without finding the remote

corner in which Justice is administered to the American Republic." The Supreme Court did not gain its own building until 1935.

This modest position of the Supreme Court has changed considerably. Today the Court is held in higher esteem, with a far-reaching impact on the public policies that influence people's day-to-day lives. For example, the Supreme Court's decisions affect where you go to school, the conditions where you work, the laws protecting your environment, and where and when you may vote.

Development of the Supreme Court

Initially, the Supreme Court was part of the weakest branch of government. Over time, however, the Supreme Court has become in some respects the most powerful institution in the country.

The Early Years Much of the first session of Congress was taken up with discussion of the organization of the judicial branch. The result was the Judiciary Act of 1789. This law established the three-level structure of the federal courts, which are made up of district courts, courts of appeals, and the Supreme Court.

CONSTITUTIONAL GOVERNMENT *The construction of the Supreme Court building was completed in 1935.* **Where was the Supreme Court housed before its permanent quarters were finished?**

CONSTITUTIONAL GOVERNMENT *John Jay
(1745–1829) was the first chief justice of the Supreme
Court. This portrait of him was begun by artist Gilbert
Stuart and is believed to have been finished by John
Trumbull.* **What is the role of the chief justice?**

President George Washington appointed a number of distinguished people, many of whom had been present at the Constitutional Convention, to serve on the Court. The first chief justice—the justice who presides over the Court—was John Jay, a coauthor of the *Federalist Papers* and a leader in New York's battle over ratification of the Constitution.

During its early years the Supreme Court was considered a fairly insignificant institution. Antifederalist views against the judiciary were still strong, and many people felt that Jay's Court lacked the right to serve as the nation's highest judicial body. During the first decade the Court heard only around 50 cases. Unsurprisingly, given the lack of Court activity, Jay's position was a part-time job. In fact, in 1794 Jay took off to lead a U.S. diplomatic mission to Britain, and he was a candidate for governor of New York while sitting on the bench. After winning that election in 1795, Jay resigned from the Court. Asked to return as chief justice in 1800, Jay declined, stating his belief that the Court could never "obtain the energy, weight, and dignity which were essential to its affording due support for the National Government."

The Marshall Court The modest role of the Court changed abruptly with John Marshall's 1801 appointment as chief justice. The Court handed down several landmark decisions during the time that Marshall served as its chief (1801–35), including *Marbury* v. *Madison,* which established the principle of judicial review. As noted in Chapter 3, judicial review gives the Court the final voice in deciding the constitutionality of government laws and policies.

Through this and other decisions, Marshall made the Supreme Court a significant force in government. These decisions gave the Court the power to influence whether and how Congress and the president may pursue specific public policies.

The Justices

Who are the Supreme Court justices who make these far-reaching decisions? How long do they serve and how are they appointed?

Supreme Court justices do not have to meet any constitutional age or professional requirements, such as having had experience serving as a lawyer or a judge. However, all Supreme Court justices have had legal training, and today most are graduates of top law schools and have previously served as federal judges.

The Constitution does not state the size of the Supreme Court. Rather, the number of justices is set by Congress. The Judiciary Act of 1789 set the number of justices at six. The current number of nine justices was set in 1869. The chief justice, who presides over the group, is the highest judicial officer of the United States.

Like other federal judges, Supreme Court justices serve for life, although they, too, may be impeached by Congress for serious crimes. Typically, justices have chosen to stay on the Court up to an advanced age—often into their seventies and eighties. During the 1800s a majority died in office. More recent justices almost always have retired. The average age of justices retiring from the Court since 1970 is 78.

Several justices have continued serving despite serious illnesses, often because they did not want a president with political views that were different from their own to nominate their successor. For example, Justice Harry Blackmun retired in 1994 at age 85, purposely staying in office long enough to give a president closer to his political ideology—Democrat Bill Clinton, as it turned out—the chance to make an appointment to replace him. Also fearing that he might be replaced by a conservative appointee if he retired, Justice Thurgood Marshall once told his clerks, "If I die, prop me up and keep on voting."

Justices of the Supreme Court

	Year Appointed	President by Whom Appointed
Chief Justice		
William H. Rehnquist	1972*	Nixon
Associate Justices		
John Paul Stevens	1975	Ford
Sandra Day O'Connor	1981	Reagan
Antonin Scalia	1986	Reagan
Anthony M. Kennedy	1988	Reagan
David H. Souter	1990	Bush
Clarence Thomas	1991	Bush
Ruth Bader Ginsburg	1993	Clinton
Stephen G. Breyer	1994	Clinton

*Appointed as chief justice in 1986 by President Reagan

The president has the power to appoint justices to the Supreme Court. **Which of the justices was appointed most recently?**

Terms

The Supreme Court's regular annual term begins on the first Monday in October. Justices hear cases throughout the year until summer recess, usually the last week in June.

Court Appointments

Supreme Court justices, including the chief justice, are appointed by the president with the approval of the Senate. In view of their importance and contrary to the previously mentioned procedure of appointing lower court judges, these nominations have the president's personal attention. Unlike cabinet appointments, though, the opportunity to appoint justices to the Supreme Court is not guaranteed to every president. Such appointments depend on a vacancy occurring in the Court. All but four presidents, however, have had the chance to make at least one appointment. These appointments have become among the most important ones that presidents make. After all, because justices usually serve very long terms, a president's judicial appointments can influence national politics for years after he or she leaves office.

Presidential nominations to the Supreme Court never have been approved automatically by the Senate. In fact, between 1789 and 1996 the Senate refused to confirm or took no action on 28 of 148 Supreme Court nominees. Such negative reactions were more common in the last century than in this one, however. For example, five of the six justices nominated by President John Tyler and three of the four nominated by President Millard Fillmore were either rejected or not acted upon. In contrast, only 7 of the 63 nominations between 1900 and 1996 met this fate.

Although the number of rejections has decreased significantly in this century, the degree of care with which the Senate examines appointments has increased. Since 1939 the Senate Judiciary Committee has subjected nominees to intense background investigations and lengthy public hearings to examine their personal lives and legal views. As a result, several nominations have produced bruising political battles that ended with dramatic final votes broadcast on television. As recently as 1991, for example, hearings for the appointment of Clarence Thomas, who faced charges of sexual harassment by a former co-worker, were broadcast on television for days and received front-page newspaper coverage.

CASE STUDY

Packing the Court

CONSTITUTIONAL GOVERNMENT In 1935 and 1936 the Supreme Court declared unconstitutional about a half dozen pieces of federal legislation regulating business. These laws had been passed under President Franklin D. Roosevelt's New Deal program to fight the Great Depression of the 1930s.

Frustrated by the Court's overthrow of key legislation, President Roosevelt proposed at the beginning of his second term in 1937 to change the Court fundamentally by raising the number of justices up to 15. His proposal would have allowed presidents to nominate an additional justice to the Court each time a justice who had served at least 10 years reached the age of 70. It was no coincidence that between 1933 and 1937 four of the justices—each around 70 years old—had formed a voting block that declared much of President Roosevelt's legislation unconstitutional.

Opponents denounced the idea, saying that it would give the president the power to "pack" the

Court with justices who were friendly to him. The new plan was never tested, however. Within three months of Roosevelt's presenting his proposal, but before it was considered in congressional committees, the Court upheld the constitutionality of two key pieces of Roosevelt's legislation—on labor and the minimum wage. As a result, Roosevelt backed off from pushing for his court-packing plan, which Congress later rejected decisively. The verdicts were the result of one justice—Owen Roberts—shifting his opinion to support Roosevelt's legislation. "A switch in time," as a contemporary saying put it, had "saved nine."

Roosevelt eventually achieved his goal of influencing the Court's composition, however. During the next few years, all of Roosevelt's judicial opponents on the Court either died or resigned. This allowed Roosevelt to appoint a total of nine justices with ideals closer to his own.

CONSTITUTIONAL GOVERNMENT *Here, the U.S. Supreme Court justices assemble for a portrait. Standing (left to right): Ruth Bader Ginsburg, David Souter, Clarence Thomas, and Stephen Breyer. Sitting (left to right): Antonin Scalia, John Paul Stevens, William Rehnquist, Sandra Day O'Connor, and Anthony Kennedy.* **How are Supreme Court justices selected?**

The Supreme Court at Work

How does the Supreme Court decide which cases to hear, and how are cases argued before the Court? Once a case is selected, it goes through five stages: briefs, oral argument, conference, preparation of opinions, and announcement of decisions.

Choosing Cases The Supreme Court serves chiefly as an appeals court, reviewing cases that have been tried and appealed in the lower federal courts, and decisions of the highest state courts that involve alleged violations of the Constitution or other federal laws. Twelve percent of the cases heard by the Supreme Court have come from the state courts. The Supreme Court does, however, have original jurisdiction in cases that involve these listed situations

★ diplomatic representatives of other nations,
★ disputes between two or more states, and
★ disputes between a state and the federal government.

Compared to the president and Congress, the Supreme Court might seem to have little control over what it considers. The president and members of Congress may pursue public policies addressing any number of possible issues—from job growth and civil rights to health-care reform and protection of the environment. In contrast, the Supreme Court may not take such initiative. It may act on only the "cases and controversies" that are appealed to it by others.

The Supreme Court is not merely a cork bobbing in the currents, however. On closer inspection, it has considerable control over which issues it considers. Each year thousands of cases on many public policy issues are appealed to the Court. The Court can choose to hear—or, more often, not to hear—any case from among this vast pool. Thus, the Court has the freedom to set its agenda by addressing cases that involve the public policy issues it believes are most pressing. Similarly, the Court also can shape public policy by refusing to hear a case, thus quietly supporting the lower court's decision.

Who May Appeal Anyone may appeal a high state court or federal appeals case to the Supreme Court if a violation of the U.S. Constitution is

Careers in Government

RESEARCHER CD-ROM

Law Clerk

Like the Supreme Court, the lower federal courts employ law clerks. These lawyers gain an insider's view of judicial decision making as they work with federal judges on important legal issues.

Law clerks in the federal district courts help judges try a wide range of civil and criminal cases, involving everything from civil rights violations to drug smuggling. Law clerks in the appeals courts research cases decided in the district courts. Special federal courts such as the U.S. Tax Court and U.S. Court of Veterans Appeals also employ law clerks who assist judges with cases.

Law clerks spend much of their time in law libraries, researching legal issues.

Before judges make a decision, law clerks put in countless hours summarizing the case or appeal at hand, researching the legal issues involved, and writing down their conclusions. They often prepare the judge's final written draft of the decision, review and proofread the argument, and check the accuracy of the document.

The application process for federal clerkships is extremely competitive. Judges require that clerks have a law degree, and often they must have passed the appropriate state bar exam. In making decisions about whom to hire, judges weigh the applicants' grades, writing ability, work experience, recommendations from professors, and extracurricular activities.

About 12 percent of graduating law students begin their careers as clerks for either federal or state courts. According to Supreme Court clerk Julia Shelton, "Clerkships are a great way to make the transition from law student to lawyer." Clerks get direct experience in the major areas of the law and learn from an experienced judge.

Many lawyers go on to use the experience they gain during their one- or two-year clerkships to further their law careers. Private law firms heavily recruit lawyers who have had experience as federal clerks. Other former clerks go on to distinguished careers in government service or teaching.

charged. Unlike the lower courts of appeals, however, the Supreme Court is not required to hear an appeal.

Most petitioners who appeal to the Supreme Court do so by requesting a **writ of *certiorari*** (suhr-shuh-RAR-ee). In legal terms the Supreme Court "grants *cert*" if it agrees to hear the appeal and "denies *cert*" if it refuses. Four of the nine justices must agree to grant *cert* for an appeal to be heard by the Court. If such an agreement is reached, the case is placed on the Court's **docket**, or schedule. If, however, the Supreme Court denies *cert,* the lower court decision is left standing. The Court does not have to provide a reason for denying *cert.*

Although the number of appeals has grown dramatically over the years, the number of cases the Court has agreed to hear has steadily declined—from an average of around 180 a year between 1981 and 1987 to only 80 in 1996. Even at its highest, however, this number is far below the number of decisions made by Congress, let alone the number made by executive agencies.

Most participants in a case are represented by a lawyer who is a member of the Supreme Court bar. To be admitted into this group, a lawyer must have been a member of a state bar for at least three years and must be known to be of good moral and professional character.

Filing Briefs The lawyer for each party in the case generally files a written brief. When the federal government is a party, its brief is filed by

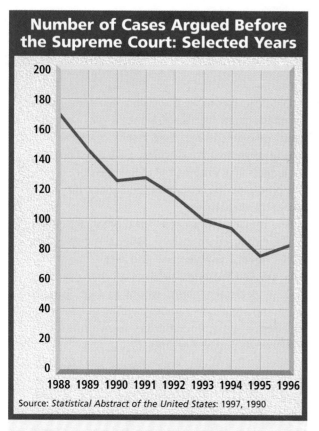

Number of Cases Argued Before the Supreme Court: Selected Years

Source: *Statistical Abstract of the United States: 1997, 1990*

The Supreme Court hears many cases each year. **Why do you think that the number of cases the Court agrees to hear has declined since 1988?**

the solicitor general of the United States, an official of the Department of Justice.

Groups that are greatly affected by a case but are not one of the parties involved may be granted the Court's permission to file **amicus curiae** (uh-MEE-kuhs KYOOR-ee-eye) **briefs**. (*Amicus curiae* means "friend of the court" in Latin.) These briefs state the group's concerns and arguments regarding the case. For example, the federal government may be allowed to file an *amicus curiae* brief in a water rights disagreement between two states, as this issue involves the nation's water supply.

These briefs usually make arguments relating the case to precedents and to provisions in the Constitution, other federal laws, and state laws. Sometimes, however, briefs make an argument about why a certain decision would make good public policy. For example, in *Brown* v. *Board of Education of Topeka,* a brief presented psychological data about the harmful effects of segregation on the social development of African American children. This information formed a

significant part of the Court's reasoning for outlawing segregation in public schools.

Oral Argument The most dramatic stage of a Supreme Court case is the oral argument that lawyers make before the justices. In the early years of the Supreme Court, there were no written briefs, only oral argument. Because no time limits existed on oral arguments, some of them went on for days. In 1848 the Court imposed its first limit on the length of oral argument—eight hours per case. Limits have since been tightened further and now stand at 30 minutes per side, except in rare cases of extreme importance.

The Court uses an official timer to time lawyers' arguments. When a red light goes on, the chief justice notifies the lawyer that his or her time is up. Chief Justice Charles Evans Hughes supposedly stopped lawyers in midword when their time expired. A later chief justice, Warren Burger, referred to this practice by stating that the Court is "more liberal now. We allow a lawyer to finish the sentence . . . provided, of course, the sentence is not too long."

During oral argument, lawyers seldom have the chance to make prepared speeches. Rather, justices often interrupt them to ask questions about the case. The public may witness this process, but because the number of seats in the courtroom is extremely small, only a few people may witness the entire argument, while others are allowed to listen

CONSTITUTIONAL GOVERNMENT *The photo above shows the timer used in the Supreme Court to time lawyers' oral arguments.* **How many minutes does each side have to present its argument?**

for only about three minutes before being ushered out to make way for the next group. People are seated to view Supreme Court proceedings on a "first-come, first-served" basis.

Conference The justices meet in private conference twice a week to review petitions for new cases, debate current cases, and conduct other Court business. The chief justice presides at this conference and is first to speak, offering his or her views. The remaining justices then present their views, in order of seniority on the Court. The atmosphere of the conferences varies from case to case, but discussion of cases is limited to some degree. Some controversial cases may involve greater dialogue among the justices. After the newest member of the Court has spoken, a tally of the votes is generally taken (unless the justices have all made their votes clear during their initial comments). The decision reached during this conference can change, however, as the justices prepare the Court's official opinion, or decision, on the case.

Preparing Opinions When the chief justice votes with the majority of the justices, he or she decides who will draft the Court's opinion. Otherwise, the most senior justice voting with the majority makes the assignment. The assignment of a justice to an opinion can have a decisive effect on the Court's ruling in a case. An opinion that is drafted by a fairly liberal justice will be much different from one drafted by a fairly conservative justice. Thus, the chief justice or senior justice assigning the case must take such considerations into account, particularly if the preliminary vote on a case is close. An opinion written by a moderate justice may have a better chance of keeping—and maybe increasing—majority support for the ruling.

The chosen justice writes a draft opinion and circulates it among the other justices for comment. During this process, justices often discuss the content of the opinion, negotiating about whether the grounds, or reasoning given for the opinion, should be changed.

The eight justices reviewing the draft opinion can endorse—or refuse to endorse—the draft depending on whether certain changes are made in the grounds for the opinion. Through such negotiations, votes on the case's outcome may shift from what they had been in conference, affecting the size of the majority supporting the Court's decision or changing the decision itself.

CONSTITUTIONAL GOVERNMENT *The room shown in the photo above is the Supreme Court justices' conference room. Justices meet here to review petitions for new cases. **What role does seniority play in the Supreme Court justices' procedure for reviewing petitions?***

There are three main kinds of opinions that the Court may issue in a case. Most cases include a **majority opinion** that reflects the views of the majority of the Court—both on the outcome of the case and on the grounds for deciding it. A justice may also issue a **concurring opinion** that agrees with the majority *outcome* but disagrees with all or part of the *grounds* stated in the majority opinion. A concurring opinion instead offers other grounds for the decision. A justice also may issue a **dissenting opinion** that disagrees with the one reached by the majority and explains the grounds for the dissent. In addition, in some cases the Court will issue a plurality decision, in which justices agree on a certain result but disagree on the grounds for the decision. In such instances the Court will issue no majority opinion, only a series of separate opinions in which justices explain the reasons for their votes.

Dissenting opinions often are addressed more to Supreme Courts of the future than to the present court. One study shows that about three fourths of Supreme Court decisions that overrule earlier Court precedents are based on previous cases' dissenting opinions.

The Supreme Court rarely reverses its decisions, however. Most justices place great weight on ***stare decisis*** (STER-ee di-SY-suhs), or upholding precedents set by earlier courts. (*Stare decisis* is a Latin

CONSTITUTIONAL GOVERNMENT *Clerks for the Supreme Court justices often use the reading room in the Court library.* **What are the primary responsibilities of law clerks in the Supreme Court?**

Justice Horace Gray began the practice of hiring law clerks in the Supreme Court in 1882. Each year, he hired at his own expense a new law school graduate to assist him. Gradually, the practice spread. Usually, clerks serve one year, although this has not always been so. A clerk to Justice Pierce Butler served for 16 years in the 1920s and 1930s.

Clerks generally read the cases that are appealed to the Court and make recommendations about which ones the Court should hear. Clerks also help draft the justices' opinions. A clerk's role in this task depends on the justice for whom he or she works. A clerk to Justice Louis Brandeis said of their division of labor, "He wrote the opinion; I wrote the footnotes." Other clerks write almost all of an opinion, with the justices making editorial changes.

term meaning "let the decision stand.") For example, some experts believe that some of the more conservative justices on the current Court disagree with the *Roe* v. *Wade* decision, which supports women's right to an abortion. However, say the experts, these justices have refused to vote to revisit and overturn the decision because their support of *stare decisis* has outweighed their views on the constitutionality of the right to an abortion.

Justices' Staffs Writing and rewriting opinions is a time-consuming, lengthy process. To help in this enormous task, justices employ a personal staff of clerks. Compared to congressional and presidential staffs, each justice's staff is tiny. At its largest, a justice's staff generally consists of four law clerks, two secretaries, and one messenger.

Announcing Decisions Although justices once read lengthy parts of their opinions in public sessions, they no longer do so. Also, before 1965, Court decisions were announced only on Mondays. Today they are announced on other days as well, to allow more media coverage. Decisions also are now announced earlier in the day to make it easier for reporters to meet press deadlines. The Supreme Court does not hold press conferences, however, to explain its rulings or to answer questions about them.

SECTION 2 — REVIEW

1. Define the following terms: writ of *certiorari,* docket, *amicus curiae* brief, majority opinion, concurring opinion, dissenting opinion, *stare decisis.*

2. How did the Marshall Court increase the power of the Supreme Court?

3. What roles do the president and the Senate play in appointing Supreme Court justices?

4. Describe what happens to a case once it is granted *cert* by the Supreme Court. How many cases does the Court hear each year?

5. Thinking and Writing Critically
Do you agree with the current practice of appointing Supreme Court justices to life terms? Is the Court less responsive to the people because its members are not elected? Explain your answers.

6. Applying **CONSTITUTIONAL GOVERNMENT**
Why is it important that presidents are unable to pack the Court? If each president were allowed to add to or change the Court's membership at will, what might happen to its decisions?

THE COURTS AND THE PUBLIC GOOD

Political Dictionary

judicial restraint
judicial activism

Objectives

★ What are the main criticisms of the judiciary?
★ How can the courts' power be checked?

The judiciary, like the other branches of the federal government, has its share of critics. The two main criticisms of the courts are that federal justices are appointed rather than elected and that the courts often overstep their powers. Are these criticisms valid? How is the courts' power checked?

Appointment Versus Election

As you have learned, Supreme Court justices and other federal judges serve for life. Although they may be impeached by Congress for serious crimes, once on the bench they are largely immune from the actions of the president, Congress, and other outside influences. Interest groups do submit briefs in some court cases, but they neither contribute money to judges and justices nor target them in lobbying campaigns as they do in the case of presidential and congressional candidates.

Critics charge that a system in which justices can make unpopular decisions and still keep their positions for life invites the abuse of judicial power. Instead of putting power into the hands of elected officials who must answer to the people, the current system of judicial appointment results in an enormously powerful judiciary that answers to no one.

Are the critics right? Are the courts capable of ignoring many of the outside influences that affect other institutions of U.S. government? In fact, when interest groups have tried to lobby the courts through demonstrations and letter-writing campaigns, the courts have criticized these attempts to influence their decisions and refuse to submit to political pressure. In addition, judges do not participate in party politics. Justice Sandra Day O'Connor, for example, declined an invitation to appear as a guest of honor of the National Federation of Republican Women at that party's 1984 convention.

Few people would agree, however, that this independence of the courts has resulted in the abuse of judicial power. The framers set up a free judiciary in the Constitution so that judges could make decisions based on the public good, including protecting minority rights, rather than simply bowing to the wishes of the majority. Elected justices would undoubtedly fear handing down unpopular decisions that might prevent them from being re-elected. As one observer notes, "Few American politicians would care to run on a platform of desegregation, pornography, abortion, and the 'coddling' of criminals." (In this context "pornography" refers to expansive court decisions regarding free speech, and "coddling of criminals" refers to expansive decisions regarding the constitutional rights of convicted criminals.)

POLITICAL PROCESSES *In 1981 Sandra Day O'Connor, the first female Supreme Court justice, was sworn into office. She is shown here on the day of her swearing-in with President Ronald Reagan and Chief Justice Warren Burger.* **Why are Supreme Court justices appointed rather than elected?**

In addition, although the courts do maintain much independence, they are not wholly unresponsive to the public. Long-term changes in the Supreme Court's opinions generally follow long-term public opinion trends. Many of those changes are determined by new personnel on the Court. That is, as public opinion shifts on issues, voters elect new presidents with contemporary views who in turn appoint justices with similar views. As a result, the Court's opinions also shift, although with a bit of a lag, as justices serve much longer terms than presidents and generally value continuity in the Court's decisions.

The combination of changes in opinion and new justices on the Court therefore is critical to how strictly the court will adhere to precedent. This is why the courts have reversed themselves on some issues, such as segregation. By reflecting the change in public opinion on certain issues, the courts show some responsiveness to the needs and wishes of the majority.

Judicial Restraint Versus Judicial Activism

Another criticism of the courts is that they have overstepped their constitutional powers. It is true that since the 1960s the intervention of the federal courts in the administration of government programs, for example, has grown dramatically. The courts have become involved in the management of state prisons, schools, mental health facilities, and many other institutions. Consider the following examples.

In 1969 a federal judge ruled that an Arkansas prison's officials did not fulfill their constitutional duties to protect inmates. Prisoners had filed numerous petitions, saying that they were housed in overcrowded dormitories, clothing was inadequate, and the food was insufficient. Agreeing with many of their complaints, the federal district court ordered the state to improve conditions.

In school desegregation cases, judges often have issued detailed orders telling school districts how to run their school system. In one 1986 case a judge ordered Kansas City to scrap its existing school system and to spend more than a billion dollars for various school improvements. The city's taxpayers funded the cost of the improvements.

In Alabama in 1971, Judge Frank Johnson ruled that the state's mental health system in effect unconstitutionally denied adequate treatment to patients. In his ruling, Johnson issued orders, developed in cooperation with mental health experts, for specific actions that the state was to undertake. In addition, Johnson ordered that state funds necessary to carry out his court order were to have priority over nonessential state functions in the state's budget and said that he himself would ensure that the funds were provided if the legislature failed to appropriate them.

Not surprisingly, rulings such as these have been controversial, sparking a debate over the judiciary's role. Critics argue that courts should not establish priorities for a state's budget because this is a legislative responsibility and because the courts are inexperienced in the running of government agencies. Critics also fear that such intervention prevents states and communities from pursuing the policies that best meet the specific needs of their citizens. In general, these critics support **judicial restraint**,

POLITICAL PROCESSES *The courts have ruled that school districts must provide bilingual education to students whose first language is not English.* **What are some other examples of federal courts' intervention in the administration of government programs?**

or a limited use of judicial power.

In contrast, those who support judicial intervention, or **judicial activism**, believe that judges should intervene when unacceptable conditions have been ignored or constitutional rights have been violated. Judicial activism can take many forms, however. In the early 1900s, for example, judges taking an activist role struck down legislation designed to protect children from harsh labor conditions. In recent years, conservative justices have held some federal laws unconstitutional for violating the principles of federalism.

As noted in previous chapters, Congress tends to represent the concerns of localities and organized groups, while the president advances the concerns of the nation as a whole. Like Congress, the federal courts sometimes give special weight to intense concerns of a minority of the population. Unlike Congress, however, the courts allow people to have their interests heard even if they are not well funded or well organized like the interest groups that lobby members of Congress. As a result, many people believe that judicial activism is sometimes necessary to ensure that the views and rights of the minority are heard and protected.

CONSTITUTIONAL GOVERNMENT *The Sixteenth Amendment overturned a Supreme Court ruling that declared the federal income tax unconstitutional.* **How can Congress check the Supreme Court's power?**

Checking the Courts' Power

The Constitution provides important checks on the judiciary's power just as it does for the other branches of government. Among the more important of these checks are the president's and Senate's power to appoint and confirm justices. In addition, Congress can check court decisions by amending the Constitution and sometimes by simply passing suitable laws. States and individuals sometimes have even attempted to check the courts' power illegally by refusing to obey judicial decisions.

Passing Amendments If the Supreme Court rules that a certain policy violates the Constitution, Congress could legalize the policy by passing a constitutional amendment. At least 3 of the 27 amendments to the Constitution have been passed in direct response to Supreme Court decisions:

★ the Eleventh Amendment, which deals with lawsuits against a state, overturned one of the Supreme Court's first decisions;
★ the Sixteenth Amendment, which authorizes a federal income tax, overturned a Supreme Court ruling that declared such a tax to be unconstitutional;
★ the Twenty-sixth Amendment, which lowers the voting age to 18 in national elections, overturned a Court decision stating that Congress had no constitutional power to set the voting age.

Refusing to Obey Court Decisions As you recall from the beginning of the chapter, Alexander Hamilton noted in the *Federalist Papers* that the courts have no "sword" with which to enforce their decisions. Rather, they must rely on the executive branch for enforcement.

As a result, court rulings sometimes have been resisted, gotten around, or ignored. President Andrew Jackson, for example, when balking at a Supreme Court decision regarding the applicability of Georgia law over Indian lands, supposedly remarked "[Chief Justice] John Marshall has made his decision; now let him enforce it."

CONSTITUTIONAL GOVERNMENT *U.S. Army troops escort African American students from Central High School in Little Rock, Arkansas, in 1957. In some states, federal troops had to enforce the Supreme Court's decision to integrate public schools.* **Why do you think there have been so few challenges to Supreme Court decisions?**

Recent examples include resistance by some state governments in the 1950s and 1960s to Supreme Court decisions calling for the integration of public schools. In some of these instances, the president was forced to call out federal troops to enforce the Supreme Court's decisions.

What is surprising, however, is not that some court decisions have been resisted but just how few challenges there have been. Even powerful groups and individuals have acknowledged the courts' authority over them. No president, for example, has ever defied a Supreme Court decision regarding him personally. The most dramatic court order to a president was the unanimous 1974 Supreme Court decision ordering President Richard M. Nixon to deliver transcripts of tape recordings of White House conversations about the Watergate cover-up. Nixon accepted the decision and delivered the transcripts, which revealed his part in the cover-up of the Watergate break-in and forced his resignation a few days later.

★ ★ ★ ★ ★ **SECTION 3** — **REVIEW**

1. Define the following terms: judicial restraint, judicial activism.

2. What are the advantages and disadvantages of the appointment system for federal judges?

3. Describe the argument over judicial restraint and judicial activism.

4. What action can possibly check the courts' power? What other checks exist on the judiciary?

5. **Thinking and Writing Critically**
   Do you support judicial restraint or judicial activism? Why?

6. **Applying** **CONSTITUTIONAL GOVERNMENT**
   Refer to President Andrew Jackson's comment regarding the Supreme Court's power to enforce its decision. How is such an attitude dangerous to the power of the Court? What might happen if today's executive branch assumed such an attitude?

CHAPTER 11 — SUMMARY

SECTION 1 The judiciary, which consists of the lower courts and the Supreme Court, has expanded its powers significantly over the nation's history. The lower courts perform the day-to-day work of the judicial branch, hearing and deciding the thousands of cases that are brought before the federal court system each year. In performing this duty, the courts resolve disputes, set precedents, and interpret the law. The courts' jurisdiction, or authority to interpret and administer the law, is established by the Constitution.

The lower courts are divided into district courts and courts of appeals. The district courts are the trial courts of the federal system. The courts of appeals hear appeals of cases from the district courts. In addition, Congress has set up several special courts to handle specific types of cases.

Federal judges serve for life, although Congress can impeach and convict them for serious crimes. Judges are nominated by the president and approved by the Senate. By far the largest number of judicial appointments are those to the district courts. These nominations are handled by the Department of Justice and by White House staffers. The executive branch, however, allows senators in the president's party to approve or disapprove each potential nominee for a position in a district in their state before the official nominations are made. This practice is called senatorial courtesy.

SECTION 2 At its creation, the Supreme Court did not hold the power and influence that it holds today. Although L'Enfant made plans to construct a building in which to house the Court, these quarters were never built, and the Court met in the basement of the Capitol. The Court heard few cases in its early years. This changed after John Marshall became chief justice, however. One of the most critical decisions of this period was *Marbury* v. *Madison*, which established the principle of judicial review.

The Supreme Court is the highest court of appeals in the nation. Anyone may appeal a case to the Supreme Court from a federal appeals court or from a state supreme court if a violation of the U.S. Constitution is charged. The Supreme Court does not have to hear any specific case, however. Any case that the Court agrees to hear undergoes five stages. These stages are briefs, oral argument, conference, preparation of opinions, and announcement of decisions.

As with other federal court judges, Supreme Court justices serve for life. They are appointed by the president and approved by the Senate. Justices employ a personal staff of clerks to help them in their work.

SECTION 3 The judiciary, like the other branches of the federal government, has its share of critics. One criticism of the courts is that judges are appointed rather than elected. This system, however, ensures an independent judiciary whose decisions are not influenced by a desire to be elected. A second criticism is that the courts often overstep their powers. Vital checks are in place, however, to prevent judicial abuse of power.

Government Notebook

Review what you wrote in your Government Notebook at the beginning of this chapter about the areas of your daily life that are affected by Supreme Court decisions. Now that you have studied this chapter, how would you revise your list? Are there any additional areas that you would include? Explain your answer in your Notebook.

REVIEW

REVIEWING CONCEPTS

1. How has the Supreme Court's power changed since the late 1700s?

2. Describe the organization of the lower federal courts.

3. What is the selection process for lower-court judges? Supreme Court justices?

4. How do the executive and legislative branches check the Supreme Court's power?

5. Describe the process a case goes through in the Supreme Court.

6. Name some common criticisms of the judiciary.

THINKING AND WRITING CRITICALLY

1. **POLITICAL PROCESSES** Do you think that the principle of senatorial courtesy is an efficient method for nominating and appointing district court judges? What problems could occur if senatorial courtesy were no longer practiced? Why does the principle of senatorial courtesy not play a role in appeals court nominations?

2. **POLITICAL PROCESSES** What are the arguments for both judicial restraint and judicial activism? If you were a Supreme Court justice, which would you practice, and why?

3. **CONSTITUTIONAL GOVERNMENT** Do you think that the Supreme Court places too much emphasis on *stare decisis*? Explain your answer.

4. **PUBLIC GOOD** The president appoints federal judges and the Senate confirms them. How does this sharing of power promote the public good?

CITIZENSHIP IN YOUR COMMUNITY

Research the U.S. district courts in your state. How many districts does your state have? In which district do you live? Who are the judges in your district? Where in your state are the district courts located? Create a poster containing the information you gather. Be sure to include a list of the judges in your district. You might also want to include photographs of the judges.

COOPERATIVE PORTFOLIO PROJECT

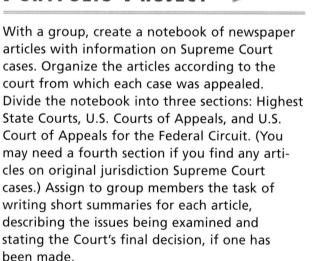

With a group, create a notebook of newspaper articles with information on Supreme Court cases. Organize the articles according to the court from which each case was appealed. Divide the notebook into three sections: Highest State Courts, U.S. Courts of Appeals, and U.S. Court of Appeals for the Federal Circuit. (You may need a fourth section if you find any articles on original jurisdiction Supreme Court cases.) Assign to group members the task of writing short summaries for each article, describing the issues being examined and stating the Court's final decision, if one has been made.

PRACTICING SKILLS: UNDERSTANDING CHARTS AND GRAPHS

An effective way to visualize the structure of the federal court system is to use an organizational chart. Organizational charts have two basic parts: boxes and lines. Study the chart on the following page. The boxes represent certain types of courts and the lines represent the flow

The Federal Court System

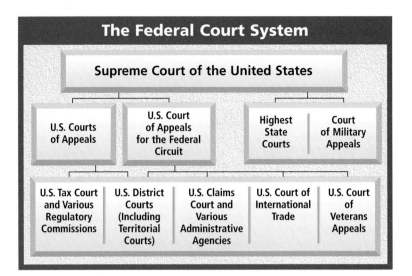

Supreme Court of the United States

| U.S. Courts of Appeals | U.S. Court of Appeals for the Federal Circuit | | Highest State Courts | Court of Military Appeals |

| U.S. Tax Court and Various Regulatory Commissions | U.S. District Courts (Including Territorial Courts) | U.S. Claims Court and Various Administrative Agencies | U.S. Court of International Trade | U.S. Court of Veterans Appeals |

of authority. Examine the chart and answer the following questions.

1. Which court reviews cases appealed from the highest state courts?

2. The U.S. Court of Appeals for the Federal Circuit hears cases from which four different types of courts?

3. Which court reviews cases appealed from the U.S. Tax Court?

THE INTERNET: LEARNING ONLINE

Conduct an Internet search for information on the federal courts. You might start with search words such as *U.S. federal courts, Supreme Court,* and *U.S. judicial system.* Sketch a World Wide Web page titled "Learning About the Federal Courts." On the page, illustrate how citizens could use the Internet to learn about the federal court system. Be sure to include the addresses of the sites you find and brief descriptions of the information available at those sites.

ANALYZING PRIMARY SOURCES

BROWN V. BOARD OF EDUCATION OF TOPEKA

As you have read, the Supreme Court ruled against public school segregation in the 1954 case *Brown v. Board of Education of Topeka,* leading to the integration of U.S. schools. Read the excerpt from the Court's majority opinion, and answer the questions that follow.

"These cases come to us from the States of Kansas, South Carolina, Virginia, and Delaware. They are premised [based] on different facts . . . but a common legal question justifies their consideration together. . . . In each of the cases, minors of the Negro race . . . seek the aid of the courts in obtaining admission to the public schools of their community on a nonsegregated basis. In each instance, they had been denied admission . . . under laws requiring or permitting segregation according to race. This segregation was alleged [claimed] to deprive the plaintiffs of the equal protection of the laws under the Fourteenth Amendment. In each of the cases other than the Delaware case, a . . . federal District Court denied relief to the plaintiffs on the so-called "separate but equal" doctrine. . . .

In approaching this problem, we . . . must consider public education in the light of . . . its present place in American life. . . .

We come then to the question presented: Does segregation of children in public schools . . . , even though the physical facilities and other "tangible" [material] factors may be equal, deprive the children of the minority group of equal educational opportunities? We believe that it does. . . .

To separate them from others . . . solely because of their race generates a feeling of inferiority as to their status in the community that may affect their hearts and minds in a way unlikely ever to be undone."

1. On what basis have the federal district courts denied relief to the plaintiffs?

2. What right is guaranteed under the Fourteenth Amendment?

3. How is the decision in this case an example of judicial activism?

CHAPTER 12

THE U.S. LEGAL SYSTEM

How do you regard the laws that govern your community and nation? Some people may see laws as restricting their freedom. Most believe that laws generally serve positive functions in U.S. society, such as preserving order and protecting property.

For example, laws determine who receives certain benefits and who does not. Laws create government programs—such as highway construction, flood control, and Social Security—and the organizations to administer them. In addition, laws forbid certain behaviors that harm people or their property—for example, murder or burglary. Laws also make it difficult for government officials to make random decisions that may negatively affect people.

✎ Government Notebook

In your Government Notebook, make a list of ways—both positive and negative—that laws affect your everyday life.

SECTION 1

U.S. LAW

Political Dictionary

common law
statutory law
statutory interpretation
constitutional interpretation
administrative law
felony
misdemeanor
plaintiff
defendant

Objectives

★ What is common law, and where did it originate?
★ What is statutory law?
★ Whom does administrative law govern?
★ What is the difference between civil law and criminal law?

As you know, laws govern people's conduct. You may not realize, however, that there are several types of U.S. law, including common, statutory, constitutional, and administrative. Many of these laws can be further classified as criminal or civil laws. Together, these laws help ensure that both governmental actions and standards of social conduct promote the public good.

Common Law

Common law, also called judge-made law, is a body of law based on judicial rulings in earlier cases. The common-law system first developed in England during a period when very few written laws existed. When conflicts arose to which no law applied, judges had to make decisions based on their individual sense of fairness. Judges in other jurisdictions who recognized these rulings as fair then used them in similar cases. As noted in Chapter 11, this acceptance of earlier court decisions is known as *stare decisis*.

The U.S. legal system today incorporates this common-law heritage. For example, common law includes much of the law applied to cases in which one person blames another for injury and sues for damages. To help decide these cases, judges developed the principle that a defendant must generally have acted negligently, or irresponsibly, before he or she could be required to pay damages to an injured party. Thus, someone whose non-negligent actions harmed another person would not have to pay damages.

The term *negligence* has been applied to many different types of cases, and there are different levels of negligence. For example, officers of federally chartered banks have been charged with negligence for approving large loans that were not repaid and caused the banks to fail. Other professionals, such as stockbrokers, can be charged with negligence if their apparent failure to perform according to the standards of their profession causes a harm, such as an investor's losing large amounts of money.

POLITICAL FOUNDATIONS *English judges dressed in their traditional robes and wigs march in a procession. How does the U.S. legal system incorporate the English common-law tradition?*

Both judges and lawyers rely on precedents, or earlier rulings, in their interpretations of the law, thus ensuring stability and predictability in the legal system. Because they have been tested repeatedly in different court cases, rulings based on common-law precedents are given as much respect as rulings based on legislative statutes.

Statutory Law

Statutory law consists of laws (also called statutes) passed by city councils, state legislatures, and Congress—the lawmaking bodies of local, state, and national government. Statutory law serves a variety of purposes. For example, statutes may be passed to create or abolish government programs, increase or decrease the penalty for a crime, or change the salaries of government workers.

In making rulings, courts often must decide the meaning of laws that legislatures have passed, a process referred to as **statutory interpretation**, or statutory construction. Statutes are valid as long as they are not found to be in conflict with the Constitution.

PUBLIC GOOD *Administrative law applies to agencies such as the Occupational Safety and Health Administration (OSHA).* **What other agencies operate under administrative law?**

Constitutional Law

Constitutional law has supreme standing over all other types of law. A court can hold invalid any statutory or common law that contradicts a constitutional provision.

Ruling on the intended meaning of phrases in the Constitution is called **constitutional interpretation**. As noted in Chapter 11, judges often have to interpret the Constitution because its language is broad on many important points. This lack of clarity has allowed the Supreme Court to use its power of judicial review to reach expansive or narrow interpretations of the Constitution each time it hears a case.

Administrative Law

Administrative law includes both the regulations made by executive departments and independent agencies and the laws that govern their actions. Examples of agencies that operate under administrative law include the Federal Trade Commission, the Environmental Protection Agency, and the Food and Drug Administration.

Agencies are part of the executive branch, and they also act as agents of Congress by helping to carry out congressional legislation. Their power is limited in two ways, however. First, the Constitution places the same restrictions on agencies that it places on the president and Congress. Second, Congress determines the structure and powers of all agencies, and the president appoints their top leadership, with the advice and consent of the Senate.

The power that Congress delegates to these agencies comes in three forms. First, Congress authorizes agencies to make rules and regulations that fill in the details of legislation. For example, the Food and Drug Administration (FDA) determines which food additives are safe for human consumption and makes regulations regarding their use. Second, Congress authorizes agencies to enforce the rules they make. For example, the FDA can fine companies that use a food additive it has outlawed. Third, Congress authorizes agencies to attempt to resolve disputes that arise over their enforcement measures. The agencies can also represent the government in court cases that result from those disputes. A food company that believes it has been wrongly fined can demand an agency hearing on the matter. If dissatisfied with this ruling, the company can appeal to a federal court, which hears arguments from both the company and the agency.

Because agency officials are not elected, some people argue, these agencies have too much power, and as a result, they adopt many unfair regulations. Administrative law is intended to ensure that agencies do not abuse their power.

Criminal and Civil Law

Statutory laws can be further classified as either criminal or civil. As noted in Chapter 4, criminal law covers actions that are forbidden by a society's government and punishable by imprisonment, while civil law

POLITICAL PROCESSES *In 1996, after several churches in the South were burned, federal investigators stepped in to determine the cause of the fires. Here, FBI and Bureau of Alcohol, Tobacco, and Firearms agents inspect the site of a church near Turner, Arkansas.* **What other types of crimes might federal agents investigate?**

Comparing ⟶ Governments

The Power of the Courts

By establishing the power of judicial review in *Marbury* v. *Madison*, the Supreme Court created for itself a much more powerful tool than any held by high courts in other democratic nations at the time. Historically, national governments did not grant their highest courts the power to cancel a law made by the national legislature. Britain's High Court of England, for example, to this day has no power to cancel laws made by Parliament.

Since World War II, however, judicial review has been established in the constitutions of several countries other than the United States, such as Germany, Japan, and India. In addition, the French during this period established a Constitutional Council with the right to cancel Parliamentary laws that it found to be in conflict with the national constitution.

covers private disputes, such as ones involving personal injury or the breaking of a contract. People found to be at fault in civil law cases must pay fines or settle the dispute according to the law, but they are not subject to imprisonment.

Criminal Law Criminal law covers two main types of crime—felonies and misdemeanors. **Felonies** are serious crimes, such as murder, rape, or burglary. **Misdemeanors** are less serious crimes, such as resisting arrest.

Most felonies and misdemeanors are covered by state laws and deal with crimes against people and property. Some crimes, however, are covered by federal law. Crimes against the national government—evading income tax, counterfeiting U.S. currency, and threatening the life of the president, for example—are federal crimes. Other federal crimes include illegal actions that take place across state lines and offenses such as kidnapping, drug trafficking, bank fraud, the shooting of migratory birds out of season, drunken driving on government land, illegal possession of a firearm, and carjacking. Denial of a person's civil rights under the Constitution also is a federal crime.

Crimes are more than private disputes; they are considered an offense against society as well as against an individual victim. To find a person

PRINCIPLES OF DEMOCRACY *Civil law cases involve the settlement of disputes between two or more parties. The above cartoon gives a humorous look at how some of these cases might be considered extreme or unnecessary.* **What is the reason for lawsuits regarding contracts?**

another for causing some harm. A party generally files a suit to seek a remedy— money, property, or an action. In civil cases the party bringing the suit is known as the **plaintiff**, while the party against whom the suit is brought is known as the **defendant**. In a civil case a party does not have to prove beyond a reasonable doubt that a wrong was committed. Rather, civil cases are generally decided in favor of the party whose position is supported by most of the evidence that is presented.

Three major categories of civil law involve contracts, torts, and property law. Contracts are legal promises made between two or more parties. When one side breaks a contract, another side may sue, or bring a lawsuit against, the contract breaker. Torts are harms that one party causes another and for which the victim may receive damages. Tort lawsuits often involve accidents, such as car wrecks. Property law involves violations of the rights one has as an owner of land or other personal property.

guilty of a crime, guilt must be established beyond a reasonable doubt. This means that a person cannot be convicted of a crime unless very little doubt exists about his or her guilt.

Civil Law Civil law involves disputes in which one private party brings a lawsuit against

---

SECTION 1 — REVIEW

1. Define the following terms: common law, statutory law, statutory interpretation, constitutional interpretation, administrative law, felony, misdemeanor, plaintiff, defendant.

2. What is the origin of U.S. common law?

3. Who makes statutory laws?

4. To whom do administrative laws apply? What purposes do these laws serve?

5. What is the difference between civil and criminal law? Give two examples of offenses that break each kind of law.

6. **Thinking and Writing Critically**
People can file lawsuits against those who cause them harm. Why is this right necessary to protect people? How might this right be abused?

7. **Applying** **CONSTITUTIONAL GOVERNMENT**
Think about the laws that you follow every day, such as traffic laws or laws that determine how many days schools are in session and when your school day begins and ends. Into which category or categories do these laws fall? List the other types of law that you have not mentioned and give one example of each.

THE CRIMINAL JUSTICE SYSTEM

Political Dictionary

county
bail
bond
indictment
grand jury
information
arraignment
no-contest plea
petit jury
voir dire
peremptory challenge
sequester
subpoena
hung jury
plea bargain

Objectives

★ Who enforces criminal laws?
★ What process does an accused person go through after his or her arrest?
★ What is a plea bargain?

People sometimes violate the law. The job of the criminal justice system is to stop these violations and to punish lawbreakers. The criminal justice system of the United States consists of three parts: police, courts, and corrections. In this section you will learn about the role of the police and the courts in the criminal justice system. The corrections system will be discussed in Section 3.

Police

More than 500,000 police officers enforce the law across the country. They work at the local, state, and national levels, and their jobs involve many responsibilities. Not only do they protect highways and neighborhood streets and maintain peace and order, they also investigate, arrest, and book people accused of crimes.

Organization The police system in the United States is highly decentralized. Though the system exists at the local, state, and federal levels, most law enforcement agencies are located in counties, cities, and towns. (**Counties**—divisions within a state that function as units of government over a particular area—are more fully discussed in Chapter 21.) At the county level, the county police or sheriff's department is the main law enforcement agency. Its duties include preserving order, enforcing court orders, and patrolling areas within the county. Town and city police perform a similar function within town and city limits. At the state level, police patrol state highways and have the responsibility for enforcing some state laws.

The United States, unlike some other countries, does not have a national police force. However, some national agencies, such as the Federal Bureau of Investigation, do help enforce federal laws and aid local authorities in detecting local crimes and catching offenders. Federal offenses in which these agencies would become involved include kidnapping, the attempted assassination

PUBLIC GOOD *Police officers patrol the streets of Austin, Texas, on bicycles.* **How do the duties of police officers employed by a city or county differ from the duties of a state police officer?**

of a president, mail fraud, bank robbery, and the hijacking of an aircraft.

Arresting Suspects After a criminal act has been committed, police officers must make decisions about a number of factors before making an arrest. First, they must investigate the crime and then decide whether there is enough evidence to arrest someone. If they did not witness the crime, they may need to obtain an arrest warrant—or court authorization—before an arrest can be made. Second, they must decide what level of control or force is necessary to make the arrest.

Police officers may use force sometimes, but not more than is necessary to do their job effectively, whether making an arrest, controlling a crowd, or fulfilling any other police function. In general, the use of lethal, or deadly, force is forbidden unless an officer or other person is threatened with serious bodily harm or death. In some states, however, an officer may use lethal force against a suspect who is fleeing after an arrest, even if the arrest was only for a misdemeanor offense.

Because of three significant Supreme Court cases, *Gideon* v. *Wainwright, Miranda* v. *Arizona,* and *Escobedo* v. *Illinois,* the police cannot question people without informing them of their constitutional rights to remain silent and to secure the services of an attorney. (The rights of the accused are more fully explained in Chapter 14.) After an arrest, the accused is "booked" at the police station, where his or her picture and fingerprints are taken. These are then used to check the person's identity and examine criminal records to determine whether he or she has been previously arrested or convicted.

Courts

Once the police arrest and book someone for a crime, he or she then awaits appearance in court. The accused person's first court proceeding after an arrest must be held as soon as possible, unless there is good cause for delay.

Appearance in Court At the initial hearing, a judge determines whether there is sufficient evidence to hold the person and possibly sets **bail**—an amount that the accused must deposit with the court to be released from jail while awaiting trial. The bail money—called a **bond**—is held as security to ensure that the accused will not flee from

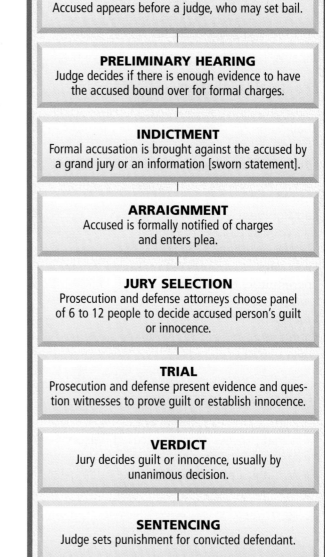

The Legal Process

APPEARANCE IN COURT
Accused appears before a judge, who may set bail.

PRELIMINARY HEARING
Judge decides if there is enough evidence to have the accused bound over for formal charges.

INDICTMENT
Formal accusation is brought against the accused by a grand jury or an information [sworn statement].

ARRAIGNMENT
Accused is formally notified of charges and enters plea.

JURY SELECTION
Prosecution and defense attorneys choose panel of 6 to 12 people to decide accused person's guilt or innocence.

TRIAL
Prosecution and defense present evidence and question witnesses to prove guilt or establish innocence.

VERDICT
Jury decides guilt or innocence, usually by unanimous decision.

SENTENCING
Judge sets punishment for convicted defendant.

Each step in the legal process is necessary to guarantee that the rights of the accused are protected. **How many people are selected to serve on a jury?**

the jurisdiction of the court. It is returned when the accused appears for the trial.

Even though people are presumed innocent until proved guilty and the Eighth Amendment prevents judges from setting "excessive bail," the Supreme Court has ruled that people do not have the *right* to be released on bail. To protect the community from people accused of serious crimes, judges may set high bail or refuse to set bail at all.

Preliminary Hearing Many states give accused people the right to appear at a preliminary hearing, though they may give up that right. At a preliminary hearing the judge will review a copy of the complaint, which is the written statement of the facts of the case. The judge will then determine whether there is reason to believe that an offense was committed and that the defendant is the one who committed it.

The preliminary hearing is largely one-sided, with the prosecutor trying to persuade the judge that there is sufficient reason for the case to go to trial. If the judge determines that there is enough evidence, the accused will then answer formal charges at the next stage of the process.

Indictment The **indictment**, or the formal accusation against the accused, is the next step in the process after the initial appearance in court or the preliminary hearing, depending on the jurisdiction. In the federal courts and in about half of the states, a person is indicted by a grand jury. A **grand jury** is made up of 12 to 23 people who decide if the government has enough evidence to try an accused person on formal charges.

Grand jury meetings are closed to the public, and only the prosecutor is allowed to present evidence. Grand juries almost always accept the prosecutor's recommendation to begin formal criminal proceedings. They can also act as powerful investigative tools because they can call any person to appear as a witness before them and can order any person to produce documents and papers related to the case. (The grand jury system is more fully explained in Chapter 14.)

States that do not use the grand jury system indict by an information. An **information** is an affidavit, or sworn statement, in which the state's prosecuting attorney declares that there is sufficient evidence against the accused to justify trying the case.

Arraignment At **arraignment**, the accused is formally notified of the charges against him or her and is asked to enter a plea of guilty or not guilty. Most states also permit a **no-contest plea**, which comes from the term *nolo contendere,* or "I will not contest it." The major difference between a guilty plea and a no-contest plea is that with a no-contest plea, the accused does not deny committing the offense but does deny that the offense involved any moral wrongdoing.

In some instances a not-guilty plea can later be changed to a guilty plea, and a guilty plea can sometimes be withdrawn. If the accused pleads not guilty, a trial will be scheduled. Sometimes, however, he or she accepts a plea bargain, in which case there will be no trial. (You will learn more about plea bargains later in this section.)

CONSTITUTIONAL GOVERNMENT *The jury (seated, top left) and judge listen to the court proceedings of a trial.* **How is a grand jury different from a petit jury?**

State Trial Judge

Every Friday, California state trial judge Peter Mirich takes a helicopter or ferry from San Pedro, California, to Santa Catalina, an island just off the California coast. There he presides over a small municipal court and hears cases typical of a popular resort town, ranging from falsifying a fishing license to disturbing the peace. In the afternoon the judge may perform wedding ceremonies.

On the mainland, Roosevelt Dorn, also a California state trial judge, looks over the rap sheet—a list of criminal charges—of a 13-year-old who has stolen a car. Judge Dorn sternly lists the probation rules the teenager must follow to stay out of jail. A few cases later, the judge smiles at a young man who has completed his probation and graduated from high school. In this court Judge Dorn's stern attention may make an important difference in a young person's life.

Judge Peter Mirich, flying to Santa Catalina in a private helicopter to preside over the city's municipal court

Judges Mirich and Dorn are just 2 of some 12,000 state, county, and municipal trial court judges in the country. State courts handle around 27 million criminal and civil cases per year in the United States. State court judges weigh the evidence that is presented, apply the appropriate laws, and decide penalties. In jury trials, judges also must instruct the jurors on how to apply the law to the evidence.

At the municipal court level, judges try misdemeanor cases and civil cases involving minor monetary damages. Municipal court judges also hold preliminary hearings to decide if defendants charged with felonies should be tried in a superior court. Superior court judges handle felonies and civil cases with higher monetary damages. They also run juvenile and family courts.

Judges have a college education and a law degree. Many also have years of experience practicing law. Although any type of lawyer may become a judge, district attorneys—also known as prosecuting attorneys—are particularly likely to be selected as judges because of their courtroom experience.

The process of selecting judges varies from state to state. In some they are elected; in others they are appointed by state governors or legislatures. Once selected, judges may serve for fixed terms or until mandatory retirement. In some states, judges may serve many terms, and sometimes they move up from the municipal courts to superior courts. Judges generally enjoy the challenges of applying the law and carrying out justice. California superior court judge Barbara Lane describes her job as stimulating and enjoys it so much that she says, "I should pay to come in here."

Jury Selection In the criminal justice system a defendant has the right to a trial by jury. A trial jury, sometimes called a **petit** (PEHT-ee) **jury**, is a panel of people who live in the community and are chosen to hear a case to determine a person's guilt or innocence. In the federal courts and in all but two states, a trial jury is made up of 12 people. Trial by jury is the defendant's right under the Sixth Amendment to the Constitution. However, the

defendant may choose to give up this right in favor of a "bench" trial—a trial held before a single judge.

If the defendant chooses a jury trial, the lawyers from both sides must agree on the people to serve on the jury, as well as any alternates, from a pool of citizens summoned for jury duty. To guide them in their selections, the lawyers engage in the process called *voir dire* (VWAHR DIR), meaning "to speak the truth," in which they question each potential juror and may ask the judge to dismiss anyone they believe holds a strong opinion about the case. For example, if the defendant is a stockbroker, any potential jurors who appear hostile to stockbrokers may be dismissed.

In addition, the defense lawyer or prosecuting attorney may dismiss a juror without giving a reason by issuing a **peremptory challenge**. Such challenges are used when a potential juror's presence on the jury might harm the defense's or prosecution's chances of winning, but no reason for dismissal would satisfy the judge. Usually each side is limited to about six peremptory challenges.

Once members of the jury are chosen, they are sworn in and the trial begins. In cases that receive a lot of publicity, the jury may be **sequestered**, or kept in isolation, in a hotel during the trial. In an attempt to keep their viewpoints from being influenced by outside information, sequestered jurors are allowed neither to speak about the case with family or friends nor to watch television, read newspapers, or observe other media.

Trial Both sides in a criminal trial have the right to call witnesses to testify about the case. If a witness will not come to the court voluntarily, he or she may receive a **subpoena**—a court order requiring the person's presence.

The lawyers ask their own witnesses questions in a process called direct examination, and they question the other side's witnesses in a process called cross-examination. The judge also may question the witnesses. Witnesses must respond to every question, unless answering the question will reveal their participation in a crime. The right not to answer such questions is protected by the Fifth Amendment. (The Fifth Amendment is more fully explained in Chapter 13.) Similarly, defendants in a criminal case are not required to testify, though they may choose to if they wish.

After the prosecution has presented its case, the defense routinely asks for a dismissal of the charges on the grounds that the evidence is insufficient to prove beyond a reasonable doubt that the defendant is guilty. If the judge sustains the motion, the defendant is acquitted—or freed from the charges. If the judge rejects the motion, the defense can take one of two actions. It can rest its case, hoping that its cross-examination of the prosecuting witnesses raised enough reasonable doubt

CONSTITUTIONAL GOVERNMENT *Former football star O. J. Simpson was tried in both a criminal court case and a civil court case for the deaths of his former wife and her friend.* **Under what circumstances may a person be tried twice for the same charges?**

to result in an acquittal. Or, if the defense feels the need to make a stronger case, it can present its own witnesses. In this case, however, the prosecution may call additional witnesses to rebut—or contradict—the defense's new witnesses.

In the final step of the process, the lawyers make their closing arguments to the jury. The defense also will renew its motion to dismiss the charges, giving the judge a final opportunity to acquit the defendant before the case is submitted to the jury to decide the defendant's fate.

The Verdict The judge tells the jury to decide on a verdict of guilty or not guilty, and in most states the verdict must be reached unanimously. If the defendant is found guilty, he or she will face sentencing. The verdict may be appealed, however, by claiming that errors were made in the trial. If the verdict is overturned on appeal, the defendant may receive a new trial or the prosecution may drop the case.

In states requiring a unanimous verdict, the presence of one or more jurors who vote differently from the majority results in a **hung jury**—a jury that is unable to reach a verdict. In the event of a hung jury, the state may either retry the defendant on the same charge or else on a lesser charge.

This is the only circumstance under which the government can try a defendant twice for the same offense. (Under the Fifth Amendment, it is illegal to retry someone for a crime of which he or she has been acquitted.) A person may, however, be tried on a criminal charge by a state and then be tried for a similar charge in a civil, rather than a criminal, case. As noted in Section 1, criminal laws deal with actions that are forbidden by society, while civil laws deal with disputes between private parties. Thus, a person accused of killing someone, for instance, can be charged in a criminal court for murder and in a civil court for causing pain and suffering to the victim's relatives.

Sentencing In state, local, and federal courts, after a person has been convicted of a crime, he or she receives a sentence. Sentencing statutes vary considerably from state to state. In recent years legislatures and sentencing commissions have moved toward establishing specific sentencing guidelines for each crime, rather than leaving judges to choose a sentence within broad, unspecified guidelines.

After a defendant in a criminal trial is found guilty by a jury or a judge, the prosecuting and defense attorneys suggest a sentence they consider appropriate. The defense lawyer is likely to emphasize the defendant's good record and chance to become a productive member of society, while the prosecution is likely to emphasize injuries to society or to the victim and the victim's family, as well as any prior criminal record the defendant might have. In some jurisdictions the defendant and the victim or family of the victim may have the opportunity to speak as well. Then, also considering information from a probation report, if applicable, the judge makes a sentencing decision.

The judge does not need to explain how he or she decided on the sentence, and the sentence cannot be appealed as long as it falls under proper legal guidelines. Sentences for the same crime can vary greatly because the range of sentencing guidelines is generally very broad, and each judge has great leeway in determining the sentence for a crime.

Plea Bargaining Some defendants avoid going to trial by accepting a **plea bargain**—agreeing to plead guilty to a less serious charge, which generally results in a shorter sentence than he or she would receive if found guilty in a jury trial. In the U.S. criminal justice system today, more than 90 percent of convictions are obtained through a plea bargain. The Supreme Court upholds plea bargains so long as defendants understand the charges, know that they are giving up their rights to a jury trial, and realize that they are acknowledging guilt for a crime.

Those who support the use of plea bargaining argue that trials usually are costly and sometimes lengthy. Also, no matter how strong the case is against the accused, there is always a chance in a jury trial that the defendant may be found not guilty. With a plea bargain, finding the defendant guilty is a certainty. In addition, the courts already have far more cases pending than they can possibly try. Opponents of plea bargaining argue that it allows those who are guilty to avoid adequate punishment. They also criticize plea bargaining on the grounds that it deprives a person of his or her right to a fair trial.

★★★★★★★★★★★★ **SECTION 2** — **REVIEW**

1. Define the following terms: county, bail, bond, indictment, grand jury, information, arraignment, no-contest plea, petit jury, *voir dire*, peremptory challenge, sequester, subpoena, hung jury, plea bargain.

2. What role do police play in the criminal justice system?

3. What happens after a person is arrested and booked?

4. What are plea bargains? Why are some people opposed to them?

5. **Thinking and Writing Critically**
   Why is it important for police to follow certain procedures when they make arrests?

6. **Applying** CONSTITUTIONAL GOVERNMENT
   Why would some people accused of crimes be more inclined to accept a plea bargain than to have a jury trial?

CORRECTIONS

Political Dictionary

probation
parole
capital punishment
juvenile delinquent

Objectives

★ What are the various sentencing options in the criminal justice system?
★ What is parole?
★ Why is capital punishment controversial?
★ What happens to juvenile offenders after their arrest?

O nce a person has been convicted of a crime in the United States, various types of sentences may be imposed. In some instances, people who have not committed a serious crime may be placed on probation. More serious offenders generally are imprisoned. Some of the most serious offenders, however, may receive the death sentence.

Juvenile offenders are treated differently in the criminal justice system than are adults. Although juvenile offenders have some of the same rights and receive some of the same punishments as adults, their correction, or punishment, is often handled in a much different manner.

Probation

Around 60 percent of all persons convicted of crimes in state and federal courts are sentenced to probation. Under a sentence of **probation**, someone found guilty of an offense remains free but under supervision. Supporters of probation argue that it benefits both the defendant and society. The probationer retains his or her freedom, and society does not have to pay the high cost of imprisonment.

When sentencing an offender to probation, a judge hopes that the person will use the freedom

to become more responsible and avoid future crime. The defendant may be on probation for several years and may be required to participate in a drug treatment or other kind of program, maintain employment, or stay in school. The judge determines the length and terms of probation, as well as how closely the offender will be monitored by authorities. If the offender violates certain set conditions, a judge may revoke probation and instead impose a prison or jail sentence.

Imprisonment

More serious or repeat offenders usually are not placed on probation, but are imprisoned. In the mid-1990s approximately 1.3 million people were in U.S. prisons and jails. A prison is a state or federal correctional institution where inmates serve a sentence of a year or more (for felonies). A jail generally is a county or local institution where accused persons await trial, sentencing, or transfer to another correctional institution. A jail may also house convicted persons who are serving sentences of less than one year (for misdemeanors).

The organizations that run prisons at the state and federal levels usually are called departments of correction. These departments decide if offenders

CONSTITUTIONAL GOVERNMENT *Some criminal offenders are required to perform community service as a part of their sentence.* **What are some of the conditions of probation that an offender might be required to follow?**

Largest U.S. Prison Inmate Populations (end of 1995)

Prison System	Number of Inmates
California	135,646
Texas	127,766
Federal	100,250
New York	68,484
Florida	63,879
Ohio	44,677
Michigan	41,112
Illinois	37,658
Georgia	34,266
Pennsylvania	32,410

Source: *World Almanac: 1997*

Prison populations in many states are so large that officials are searching for solutions to the problem of overcrowded prison facilities. **What are some alternatives to imprisonment that may help address the problem of overcrowded prisons?**

should be sent to a maximum-, medium-, or minimum-security prison or jail. They base their decisions on the offenders' age, how dangerous they are, and how likely they are to attempt to escape. In theory, the jail or prison to which a person is sent depends on the crime committed. However, state prisons are so overcrowded today that many state prisoners are now housed in county or city jails.

Although most people agree that lawbreakers should be removed from society for a period of time, they often disagree on the reasoning behind imprisonment. There are usually four major arguments for putting people behind bars—it serves as a form of retribution, as rehabilitation, as a deterrent to other would-be criminals, and as a form of protection for society.

When people say that imprisonment is proper retribution for a crime, they mean that it is a deserved punishment for a crime committed against society. They argue that it would be wrong not to punish people who have significantly harmed others.

Some people believe that imprisonment is a deterrent to future crime. They argue that the threat of a prison term will keep people from committing illegal acts.

The third major argument for imprisonment is that it will rehabilitate a convicted criminal. People who believe that prison is a form of rehabilitation hold that the purpose of imprisonment is to reform criminals and then free them to become law-abiding members of society.

Finally, some people feel safer knowing that a convicted criminal is off the streets. They say that putting a criminal behind bars keeps him or her from committing other crimes, therefore serving to protect members of the community.

Parole

After serving part of their sentence, many prisoners are eligible for **parole**—early release from prison. The amount of time an offender must serve before being eligible for parole varies greatly from state to state. Every state, however, maintains a parole board to determine when and if a prisoner will be released. Each board's members are chosen by the governor of its state. Parole boards typically meet with a prospective parolee at the prison to determine if he or she is eligible for parole. This process also involves examining the prisoner's previous record and the facts of the crime for which he or she was imprisoned. If parole is denied, the prisoner remains in prison, but may be reviewed for parole at a later date set by law.

An inmate who is granted parole must fulfill his or her parole terms until the time remaining on the sentence is served (minus any time subtracted from the sentence for the good behavior of the inmate while in prison). The parole agency may require that the parolee receive counseling, be tested for illegal drug use, attend school, or avoid certain people or places. If the parolee violates the terms of his or her parole, the parole agency will re-evaluate the case to decide whether to cancel parole and send the offender back to prison.

Capital Punishment

The most serious offenders may receive **capital punishment**—the death penalty. Capital punishment is legal in 36 states and is usually reserved only for people convicted of murder.

PUBLIC GOOD *Camp Sandhill, located near Patrick, South Carolina, is a private juvenile correction facility that houses 32 boys.* **How has the treatment of juvenile offenders changed since the 1800s?**

Capital punishment sentences are passed far more frequently than they are carried out. Although only about 30 executions take place each year, almost 3,000 inmates currently sit on death row. The sentence in many death penalty cases is eventually reversed or reduced.

Capital punishment is a highly controversial topic in the United States. Research, however, indicates that a majority of Americans support its use in at least some instances. Reflecting this sentiment, Congress—in the 1994 crime bill—increased the number of offenses subject to the death penalty.

Supporters of capital punishment frequently argue that people who commit the worst crimes deserve to die. They also suggest that would-be killers will be less likely to commit murder if they know that they might face death if caught. Supporters further argue that the death penalty is less expensive than life imprisonment.

Opponents of capital punishment argue that cost savings are offset by the fact that in the United States, offenders on death row spend years appealing their cases. These appeals are very expensive and may in some cases cost more than life imprisonment. Opponents also argue that the

death penalty has not worked in preventing people from committing horrible crimes, and most importantly has sentenced innocent people to death in some instances. But possibly the most controversial charge leveled by opponents is the claim that capital punishment is discriminatory. In support of this claim, they note that African Americans receive the death penalty in a much higher proportion than do whites in cases involving similar circumstances. (Capital punishment is further discussed in Chapter 15.)

Juvenile Crime

Young people are responsible for a large number of the nation's crimes. Each state has special laws that apply to **juvenile delinquents**—or young offenders. The legal definition of a juvenile varies across the country. It can range anywhere from under 16 to under 21 years of age, depending on the state. Separate criminal justice agencies designed to deal with juvenile offenders first emerged in the 1800s. Before that time, juveniles at least 14 years old were fully accountable for their crimes and could be tried in adult courts. They could be sentenced to adult prisons and even

Citizenship in Action

Teen Court

The 17-year-old defendant sat nervously in the witness chair. Facing the judge and jurors, the prosecuting attorney described the crime: vandalism to a vehicle. The jurors listened attentively to the facts and chose the maximum punishment: 25 hours of community service, payment for damage to the car, and four weeks of service as a juror.

Though this sounds like a scene from a regular courtroom, this particular court was different. The attorneys, jurors, and most of the key courtroom personnel were teenagers, just like the defendant. These peer courts, known as teen courts, allow young, first-time offenders and some second-time offenders to be heard by a jury of their peers.

Teen courts provide a legal alternative to the juvenile court system. In most teen courts the defendants—some as young as 7 years old and others as old as 19—have already pleaded guilty to misdemeanor charges in a juvenile court. These juveniles come before a teen court only because the judges who heard their initial trials sent them there.

The crimes with which the juveniles are charged include shoplifting, vandalism, violation of curfew, truancy, and possession of alcohol or drugs. Sentences might include hours of community service or repayment to the victim. Defendants also might be required to attend an alcohol, drug, or violence prevention workshop and to obey a curfew. Defendants may also have to write letters of apology to their victims or sometimes even a research paper. Many teen courts also require service on a teen court jury.

Teen courts often issue harsher sentences to their peers than regular juvenile courts do. For example, a Kentucky teen court sentenced a teenager to 90 hours of community service, four months of jury duty in teen court, and a one-month curfew for carrying a concealed weapon. The teenager appealed the sentence in a standard, juvenile court and received only a $50 fine and two days of service on a teen court jury.

The success of teen courts stems from a number of factors. Teen court defendants must examine their actions and take into account the effect of their actions on others. Teen courts also give teenagers a second chance. Once the defendant completes his or her sentence, the court clears the charge from the defendant's criminal record.

Perhaps the most important factor, however, is positive peer pressure. In teen court, defendants receive punishment from teenagers just like themselves. "The kids who are the prosecuting and defense attorneys and the kids who sit on the jury take it very seriously," says Bill Ferchland, a lawyer who has served as a teen court judge. "And that means that the defendants take it seriously."

Teen courts allow young defendants the opportunity to have their cases heard by a jury of their peers.

What Do You Think?

1. Do you think that teen courts are an effective legal alternative to standard courts?
2. Why do you think many teens volunteer their time as attorneys, jurors, or personnel in teen courts?

to death. During the late 1800s, however, many people believed that the juvenile justice system needed to be reformed and that young people should be given special attention rather than receiving the same punishments as adults. Today's juvenile court is based on the idea that the government must assume the role of parent to juveniles accused of crimes.

Juvenile Court Treatment of juvenile offenders today varies depending on the offense, and some states even try juveniles as adults if they commit serious crimes such as murder. Juveniles who are arrested are taken to a juvenile detention center that is separate from the adult jail. Most states deny bail to juveniles, and judges must decide whether to release a juvenile based on the likelihood that he or she might flee or pose a threat to the community.

Although juveniles have the right to an attorney and are presumed innocent until proved guilty, in the past they have had no right to a trial by jury. In recent years, however, about one quarter of the states have passed legislation allowing trial by jury for many juvenile offenses.

Juvenile Corrections Juveniles who are found guilty beyond a reasonable doubt may be sentenced to probation, to community service, or to pay a fine. (See the Citizenship in Action feature, opposite page.) They also may be required to serve time in a juvenile detention center. The judge decides the length of the sentence, but the juvenile must be released when he or she reaches adulthood. Instead of giving juveniles probation or time in a detention center, some states are experimenting with juvenile "boot camps." These camps are designed like military boot camps and are intended to provide a structured environment where juvenile offenders can learn positive social values.

CASE STUDY

Boot Camps

PUBLIC GOOD The first "boot camps" for criminal offenders were established in 1983 in Georgia as an alternative to jail, prison, or juvenile detention centers. Often modeled after boot camps used to train military recruits, most of these programs have incorporated many typical military features, such as drill instructors, barracks-style housing, and military-style uniforms.

Boot camps vary widely in time spent per day on military drill, discipline, and physical labor. Camps in Pennsylvania require juveniles to spend only 10 percent of their day on these activities, while camps in South Carolina require 80 percent. Other activities that are emphasized include education, counseling, and physical fitness.

In the mid-1990s there were about a dozen juvenile camps in at least 10 states. Most boot camp programs range from 90 to 120 days. One study of such boot camps, including those for adults, found that between 3 and 42 percent of those attending either drop out or fail and that most of those do so in the first weeks of a program. Another study of boot camps discovered

Possible Juvenile Court Penalties

- Warned and dismissed
- Required to attend appropriate counseling or youth assistance programs
- Required to pay for damages
- Placed on monitored probation
- Required to perform community service
- Sent to a youth corrections facility (Sentences range from 30 days to until the offender turns 21 years old.)
- Fined $15 to several hundred dollars plus court costs

Sentences for juvenile offenders vary depending on such factors as the severity of the crime and the offenders' juvenile record. **How does the treatment of juvenile offenders differ from the treatment of adult offenders?**

PUBLIC GOOD *Juvenile offenders sentenced to boot camp are often required to perform military drills such as marching.* **Why are boot camps less expensive than prisons?**

that between 7 and 52 percent of offenders are expelled from boot camps as a part of disciplinary action. The percentage varies so widely because different camps tolerate different levels of misconduct.

Boot camps have proven to be an effective alternative to incarceration in some ways, but not in others. The positive aspects of boot camps include maintaining inmates' physical fitness and improving their education. Also, boot camps spend less money per inmate than do prisons. Unfortunately, boot camps have not reduced the rate of people who revert to criminal behavior upon being released from custody. In addition, boot camps have only proved to be less expensive than prison because they keep offenders for shorter periods of time. In the long run, however, boot camps may be a better option than prisons if they succeed in improving educational performance, physical conditioning, and attitudes of offenders.

Many people believe that the juvenile justice system needs a massive overhaul. Some believe that all juveniles should receive the same rights granted to adults in criminal proceedings, such as the right to trial by jury. Others believe that juvenile justice is far too lenient, given that young males under the age of 21 commit the highest number of offenses.

SECTION 3 — **REVIEW**

1. Define the following terms: probation, parole, capital punishment, juvenile delinquent.

2. What are some of the advantages of probation?

3. What are some of the opposing opinions concerning the death penalty?

4. Are juvenile offenders treated in the same manner as adult offenders? Explain your answer.

5. **Thinking and Writing Critically**
   What do you think about the practice of allowing prisoners to be released on parole? Explain your answer.

6. **Applying** **CONSTITUTIONAL GOVERNMENT**
   What alternatives to imprisonment do you think might be effective in helping to solve prison overcrowding and prevent crime?

CHAPTER 12 — SUMMARY

SECTION 1 There are several types of U.S. law, including common, statutory, constitutional, and administrative. Laws are further classified as criminal or civil.

SECTION 2 The criminal justice system consists of three parts: police, courts, and corrections. There are hundreds of thousands of police across the country, at local, state, and national levels. When a criminal act has been committed, police are responsible for arresting suspects. Police must follow certain procedures when a person is arrested.

After an arrest the suspect is "booked" at the police station and awaits his or her first appearance in court. At the initial hearing a judge may allow a person to post bail. Some states then hold a preliminary hearing.

The next stage is the indictment. Around half of the states have indictment by grand jury. Others have indictment by information. After the indictment is the arraignment, during which the accused is formally notified of the charges and then enters a plea.

A not-guilty plea is followed by a trial, at which the first step is jury selection. Once the jury is selected, the trial begins. Sometimes, juries are sequestered in an attempt to keep their viewpoints from being influenced by outside information.

During the trial, both sides can call witnesses. After the witnesses testify, the lawyers make their closing arguments to the jury, which then determines a verdict. A jury that cannot agree on a verdict is considered hung, and the case can be retried. After a guilty verdict, the judge hands down the sentence.

In some instances, a person may accept a plea bargain instead of going to trial. Some of those who support plea bargaining argue that trials can be lengthy and costly. Those opposed to plea bargaining say that it allows criminals to avoid adequate punishment, while others argue that it deprives a person of his or her right to a fair trial.

SECTION 3 A sentence may take several forms. Some offenders are placed on probation, or allowed to remain in society while being supervised. More serious offenders and repeat offenders may be imprisoned. After serving part of a prison term, a person may be eligible for parole. If a person is denied parole, he or she remains in prison and is reviewed again at set intervals. If granted parole, the person will remain so until the entire sentence is fulfilled. If parole is broken, he or she may be returned to prison.

In some states, people convicted of the most serious crimes may receive a sentence of capital punishment, or the death penalty. Capital punishment is a highly controversial topic in this country.

Many of the nation's crimes are committed by juvenile offenders. Juvenile delinquents are treated differently from adult offenders in most cases. The juvenile court is different from the regular court; most juvenile offenders, for example, do not have the right to trial by jury. The judge sets a juvenile's sentence and determines its length, but when the juvenile reaches adulthood, he or she must be released. In some cases, juveniles receive probation. In others, they are sent to juvenile detention centers. Some states also are experimenting with juvenile "boot camps" to rehabilitate young offenders.

Government Notebook

Review the list in your Government Notebook of positive and negative ways that laws affect your everyday life. In what ways do you think the U.S. legal system works to protect most Americans? In what ways do you think it is effective, and in what areas do you see need for improvement? Explain your answers in your Notebook.

CHAPTER 12
REVIEW

REVIEWING CONCEPTS

1. How are criminal and civil laws different?

2. Name the four main types of law.

3. List the steps that an accused person typically goes through after being booked by the police.

4. What is the difference between a felony and a misdemeanor? Give an example of each.

5. What are the major arguments for and against capital punishment?

6. In what ways are juvenile offenders treated differently than adults?

THINKING AND WRITING CRITICALLY

1. **CONSTITUTIONAL GOVERNMENT** What are some of the reasons that constitutional law takes precedence over other types of law?

2. **PRINCIPLES OF DEMOCRACY** Do you think that all accused people should have the right to stay out of jail until their trial? Why or why not?

3. **POLITICAL PROCESSES** Why do you think that some states require their juries to unanimously agree on a verdict?

4. **PUBLIC GOOD** Do you think that the treatment of juveniles in the U.S. court system promotes the public good? Why do you think juveniles are treated differently from adults? Explain your answer.

CITIZENSHIP IN YOUR COMMUNITY

Look for newspaper, magazine, television, and radio reports of unusual sentences imposed on people convicted of crimes. Keep a log of the reports, and select a case in which you think the sentence is particularly effective or ineffective. Cut out the related articles and take notes about the details of the case. Write a letter to the editor of a local newspaper expressing your opinions about the sentence. Be sure to include arguments that explain why you think the sentence is effective or ineffective.

INDIVIDUAL PORTFOLIO PROJECT

Research the career of a certain state or federal judge. Where did that person attend law school? What jobs did he or she have before becoming a judge? Was he or she appointed or elected to the court? What are some of that judge's important rulings? You might want to begin your research by checking your library's card catalog or conducting an Internet search. After you have completed your research, write a one-page biography on the judge you selected. If possible, include a photograph of the judge with your biography.

PRACTICING SKILLS: CONDUCTING RESEARCH

Create a chart that illustrates the different types of laws that make up the U.S. legal system. Divide the chart into four sections. In a separate section of the chart place a label for each type of law: common, statutory, constitutional, and administrative. Under each section, include information about the origin of the type of law and examples of specific laws. Be sure to include information on how laws may be further classified as either criminal or civil law where appropriate.

THE INTERNET: LEARNING ONLINE

Conduct an Internet search to find statistics on the prison inmate populations for each state. You might start by using the search words *prison inmate populations* and *Department of Justice.* After you find these statistics, draw a map of the United States showing the inmate population for each state. Highlight the states with the highest and lowest inmate populations with a specific color. Include a list of Internet sites you visited to gather the information used in the map.

ANALYZING PRIMARY SOURCES

LEWIS V. UNITED STATES

Sandra Day O'Connor was appointed to the Supreme Court by President Ronald Reagan on September 21, 1981. As the first female Supreme Court justice, her appointment was a significant event for the Court.

The following excerpt from the Court's opinion in *Lewis* v. *United States,* written by Justice O'Connor, clarifies some circumstances under which a person is not guaranteed a jury trial. Read the excerpt and answer the questions that follow.

66 *Petitioner [the person making the appeal to the Supreme Court] was charged with two counts of obstructing the mail. . . . Each count carried a maximum authorized prison sentence of six months. Petitioner requested a jury, but the magistrate judge granted the Government's motion for a bench trial. She explained that because she would not, under any circumstances, sentence petitioner to more than six months' imprisonment, he was not entitled to a jury trial. . . .*

The Sixth Amendment guarantees that [in] all criminal prosecutions, the accused shall enjoy the right to a speedy and public trial, by an impartial [unbiased] jury of the State and district wherein the crime shall have been committed. . . .' It is well established that the Sixth Amendment, like the common law, reserves this jury trial right for prosecutions of serious offenses, and

that 'there is a category of petty crimes or offenses which is not subject to the Sixth Amendment jury trial provision'. . . .

Petitioner argues that, where a defendant is charged with multiple petty offenses in a single prosecution, the Sixth Amendment requires that the aggregate [total] potential penalty be the basis for determining whether a jury trial is required. Although each offense charged here was petty, petitioner faced a potential penalty of more than six months' imprisonment; and, of course, if any offense charged had authorized more than six months' imprisonment, he would have been entitled to a jury trial. The Court must look to the aggregate potential prison term to determine the existence of the jury trial right, petitioner contends, not to the "petty" character of the offenses charged.

We disagree. The Sixth Amendment reserves the jury trial right to defendants accused of serious crimes. . . . We determine whether an offense is serious by looking to the judgment of the legislature, primarily as expressed in the maximum authorized term of imprisonment. Here, by setting the maximum authorized prison term at six months, the legislature categorized the offense of obstructing the mail as petty. The fact that the petitioner was charged with two counts of a petty offense does not revise the legislative judgment as to the gravity [seriousness] of that particular offense, nor does it transform the petty offense into a serious one, to which the jury trial right would apply. We note that there is precedent at common law that a jury trial was not provided to a defendant charged with multiple petty offenses. 99

1. Where is it established that the right to a jury trial is reserved for prosecutions of serious crimes? Why do you think that this right is reserved for cases involving serious crimes?

2. Although he was charged only with petty offenses, why did the petitioner in *Lewis* v. *United States* argue for the right to a jury trial?

3. What was the Supreme Court's ruling in this case? What was its reasoning behind the ruling?

Judging an Appeal

You and the other members of your group are sitting judges on a federal court of appeals. Your panel is hearing an appeal of a case in which the defendant, John Goode, has been convicted in a federal district court of participating in a crime ring. This ring was shown to have transported stolen goods across state lines, a federal offense.

Goode claims that he is innocent, and his attorney, Mary Kelly, has challenged her client's conviction. She is basing her client's appeal largely on rights guaranteed in the Fourth, Fifth, and Eighth Amendments to the U.S. Constitution. To support her client's case, Kelly has submitted the following documents as evidence for your panel to examine: a legal brief stating her arguments in asking the court of appeals to send the case back to federal district court for retrial, copies of the applicable amendments, and a transcript of the arresting officer's testimony in Goode's trial. In addition, the prosecutor in Goode's trial, Will Gordon, also has supplied a legal brief opposing Kelly's motion for a new trial.

You will find these documents on the following pages. After you have finished reviewing the information in each of the documents, answer the accompanying questions in your Government Notebook. When you have reviewed all of the information, compare notes with other judges on your panel and arrive at a decision in favor of or against sending Goode's case back to district court. Your written legal opinion should address the arguments made by Kelly, as well as how they affected your decision.

Fourth Amendment to the U.S. Constitution

The right of the people to be secure in their persons, houses, papers, and effects, against unreasonable searches and seizures, shall not be violated, and no warrants shall issue but upon probable cause, supported by oath or affirmation, and particularly describing the place to be searched, and the persons or things to be seized.

EXHIBIT 2

Fifth Amendment to the U.S. Constitution

No person shall be held to answer for a capital or otherwise infamous crime, unless on a presentment or indictment of a grand jury . . . ; nor shall any person be subject for the same offense to be twice put in jeopardy of life or limb; nor shall be compelled in any criminal case to be a witness against himself, nor be deprived of life, liberty, or property, without due process of law; nor shall private property be taken for public use, without just compensation.

EXHIBIT 3

Eighth Amendment to the U.S. Constitution

Excessive bail shall not be required, nor excessive fines imposed, nor cruel and unusual punishments inflicted.

◄ WHAT DO YOU THINK?

★ Identify five things the Fifth Amendment specifically forbids. Why do you believe the protection against self-incrimination is important?

★ What does the Eighth Amendment guarantee? How has the Supreme Court ruled on the right of accused people to be released on bail? Do you agree with the Supreme Court's position?

FEDERAL DISTRICT COURT
TRANSCRIPT

Case: *The United States v. John Goode*

EXHIBIT 4

Date: May 31, 1998

Transcript:

EXCERPT FROM THE TESTIMONY OF LT. JOEL R. THEODORE, AN OFFICER IN THE CITY POLICE DEPARTMENT, UNDER CROSS-EXAMINATION BY DEFENDANT'S ATTORNEY:

KELLY: Lt. Theodore, why did you go to the home of the defendant, Mr. Goode, on February 2 of this year?

THEODORE: Well, I had been providing security at a Groundhog Day ceremony, and I got to thinking about the crime ring we had busted the year before. During a trial of one of the members of that crime ring last year, Mr. Goode had refused to testify about his connection to the defendant, claiming the Fifth Amendment right not to incriminate oneself. Well, that sounded to me like Mr. Goode was guilty of taking part in the ring's criminal activity and did not want to admit it. Second, one of his neighbors told me at the Groundhog Day ceremony that Mr. Goode had been selling a lot of new televisions from his home in the last two days. I decided that I needed to drive over to Mr. Goode's house and check it out.

KELLY: But you did not get a search warrant to do that, did you?

THEODORE: No, I did not. I thought that if I went to get a search warrant from a judge, Mr. Goode would have time to sell the last of the televisions I suspected had been stolen when he was part of the crime ring the year before. I thought I needed to go over to his house right away.

KELLY: You have testified that Mr. Goode would not let you in the door but that you could see five new televisions in his living room. And then you forced your way into the house without a search warrant. Is that right?

THEODORE: Well, yes. I thought I had reason enough to go in without a search warrant because I saw what I believed was evidence of a crime. After I checked the televisions out, I discovered that serial numbers on them matched those of stolen televisions from the year before. I then arrested Mr. Goode and took him to the police station.

WHAT DO YOU THINK? ▶

★ Do you believe that Lt. Theodore's search violated Goode's rights? Explain your answer.

★ Why did Lt. Theodore go to Goode's house?

PUBLIC POLICY LAB

No. 12-789
In the Federal Court of Appeals

John Goode

v.

United States

BRIEF OF APPELLANT

My client, Mr. John Goode, is appealing in federal district court his conviction of participating in the transportation of stolen goods across state lines. We are appealing Mr. Goode's conviction on the following grounds.

First, the arresting police officer entered the appellant's home, searched the premises, and arrested him without either a search warrant or an arrest warrant. In doing so, the arresting officer violated Mr. Goode's rights as protected under the Fourth Amendment to the U.S. Constitution.

Please see Exhibit 4, which is an excerpt from the district court testimony of Lt. Joel Theodore. We believe that Mr. Theodore did not have sufficient evidence to justify a search warrant in the first place. In addition, if he did have such evidence, we believe he was required by the Constitution to request a search warrant from a judge before entering Mr. Goode's home.

Second, Mr. Goode's refusal to testify in an earlier trial of suspected members of the crime ring in question—a refusal that was based on his Fifth Amendment right not to incriminate himself—was used as evidence against him in his trial. For example, in his testimony, Lt. Theodore mentioned Mr. Goode's refusal to testify, saying that it revealed his guilt in a crime about which he wished to remain silent for fear of incriminating himself. In addition, in his summation the prosecuting attorney at Mr. Goode's trial also told jurors that they could assume Mr. Goode's refusal to testify, either at his trial or at earlier trials, was basically an admission of guilt.

Finally, the presiding federal judge in Mr. Goode's trial ordered bail for the defendant set at $500,000. We believe the bail was excessive and therefore a violation of the Eighth Amendment to the U.S. Constitution. As a result of this excessive bail, Mr. Goode—whose bank accounts contain only about $10,000—was unable to secure his release from jail prior to his conviction.

Based on these arguments, we believe Mr. Goode's case should be sent back to federal district court for retrial. Thank you.

Respectfully submitted,

Mary Kelly

Mary Kelly
Attorney-at-Law

▲ WHAT DO YOU THINK?

★ On what grounds are John Goode and his lawyer appealing his conviction? Do you think Mary Kelly presents convincing arguments for why this case should be sent back for retrial?

★ Do you believe that Goode's use of the Fifth Amendment's protection against self-incrimination was improperly used to convict him of a crime? Why or why not?

★ Why was Goode unable to secure his release from jail? Do you think the bail was excessive or justified?

★ Why does the government believe that searching John Goode's home and arresting him without a search warrant was justified?

★ Do you believe that refusing to testify in your own trial should be taken as an admission of guilt? Why or why not?

★ Why might the judge believe that Goode would flee the country if he were able to post bond? For what other reasons might the judge set a high bail?

No. 12-789
In the Federal Court of Appeals

John Goode

v.

United States

Brief of Appellee

The government believes that Mr. Goode's appeal of his conviction for participating in the transportation of stolen goods across state lines should be rejected by the court of appeals. The arguments presented by Mr. Goode's attorney, on examination, do not justify sending the case back for retrial in federal district court.

Mr. Goode's argument that his rights under the Fourth Amendment were violated when Lt. Theodore searched his home without a search warrant and arrested him without an arrest warrant are weak. Based on information provided by a neighborhood witness and on his own suspicions that Mr. Goode was involved in a crime ring, Lt. Theodore had every reason to believe that Mr. Goode might get rid of important evidence if the search were delayed. By waiting, Lt. Theodore would have allowed Mr. Goode to flee the scene and escape arrest.

Second, Mr. Goode's refusal to explain under oath his connections with the crime ring that was broken last year was a legitimate cause for suspicion that he was guilty of a crime. If Mr. Goode were not involved in a crime, what objection should he have to testifying in court? Our use in court of his refusal to testify in an earlier trial, then, was justified.

Finally, the $500,000 bail set for Mr. Goode prior to his trial was justified. The high bail was based on the judge's concern that Mr. Goode had the resources to leave the country and would try to do so if he were able to post bond.

We believe, then, that Ms. Kelly has failed to justify sending Mr. Goode's case back for retrial in federal district court.

THINGS TO DO

1. Review with other judges in your group the notes you have taken and answers you have given about the information presented in this activity.

2. You might want to conduct some outside research to help you in deciding whether or not to grant John Goode's appeal for a retrial. Search for information about how the Supreme Court has applied the Fourth, Fifth, and Eighth Amendments to similar cases. You might also want to conduct an Internet search.

3. When you have finished your research and have debated the case with other group members, take a vote of the judges to determine your decision. Then work with other judges to prepare a written decision on the matter, explaining your court's decision and addressing the arguments made by the opposing attorneys. Your formal, written decision should be typed or neatly handwritten. Consider presenting the decision to your class.

UNIT
5

PUBLIC POLICY LAB

Do reporters have to follow certain procedures when writing news stories? Find out by reading this unit and taking the Policy Lab Challenge on pages 360–63.

294

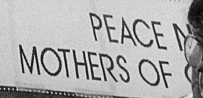

RIGHTS AND RESPONSIBILITIES

The Granger Collection, New York

CHAPTER 13

FUNDAMENTAL FREEDOMS

Do you read a newspaper or a magazine in your free time? Did you watch your favorite television show last night? Do you attend a place of worship? Have you ever written a letter to the editor of the local newspaper or to a government official about an issue?

What do all of these activities have in common? Each involves freedoms that are protected by the First Amendment. These and other protections found in the Bill of Rights guarantee fundamental freedoms to you and other residents of the United States.

Government Notebook

The First Amendment protects the freedoms of religion, speech, the press, assembly, and petition. Are these rights without limit? What restrictions do you think the government may place on these rights? Write your answer in your Government Notebook.

FREEDOM AND THE BILL OF RIGHTS

Political Dictionary

civil liberty
alien

Objectives

★ How does the Constitution protect civil liberties?

★ Whose civil liberties does the First Amendment guarantee?

★ What is the role of laws and the courts in balancing individuals' civil liberties with the interests of the community?

As noted in Chapter 2, several states made strong recommendations that a bill of rights be added to the Constitution upon its ratification. President George Washington also supported adding a bill of rights to the Constitution. James Madison, although he had originally thought a bill of rights unnecessary, took the lead in the first session of the initial Congress in developing the amendments. Twelve amendments were originally proposed for ratification by the states. The two amendments that were never ratified dealt with how members of the House of Representatives would be apportioned among the states and how congressmembers would be compensated for their service.

About 18 months passed before the necessary three quarters of the states agreed to ratify the Bill of Rights. Massachusetts, one of the states that originally had called for a bill of rights as a condition for signing the Constitution, was one of three states that did not ratify the Bill of Rights when it was proposed in Congress. Connecticut ratified it only in 1932, Georgia and Massachusetts in 1939. (Of course, because three quarters of the states had ratified the Bill of Rights, it applied to all states in the Union, even though it had not yet been ratified by all.)

Curiously, the adoption of the Bill of Rights was not seen as an earthshaking event at the time, as is indicated by the text of a letter Thomas Jefferson sent to the states on March 1, 1792, in his official capacity as secretary of state. The letter listed the adoption of the Bill of Rights after a law Congress had passed regulating fishing! Today, however, most people in the United States understand the profound impact the Bill of Rights has had on the rules of the U.S. political system and the content of U.S. public policies.

Civil Liberties

The Bill of Rights is designed to protect people's civil liberties. **Civil liberties** are basic individual rights and freedoms that are protected from government violation. When drawing up the Bill of Rights, members of the initial Congress specifically wanted to guarantee freedom of speech, assembly, and religion in order to protect individual rights and prevent a tyranny of the majority. These freedoms are considered to be among the most fundamental civil liberties. In listing these rights in the First Amendment, the framers conferred upon them a special place in the American consciousness. They believed that respecting these freedoms was among the most important duties of government and society.

POLITICAL FOUNDATIONS *Shown here is President George Washington arriving for his inauguration in 1793. It was during Washington's presidency that the first 10 amendments were added to the Constitution.* ***Which civil liberties did the drafters of the Bill of Rights particularly wish to guarantee?***

Careers in Government

Civil Rights Lawyer

In 1971, civil rights attorneys Morris Dees and Joseph Levin joined civil rights activist Julian Bond to found the Southern Poverty Law Center. The center is a nonprofit organization staffed by lawyers who specialize in providing legal assistance to victims of civil rights violations and racially motivated crimes.

Well-known defenders of the civil rights of poor citizens, the center's lawyers battle to fulfill the promise of the Civil Rights Act of 1964. Their caseload involves everything from challenging segregation in recreational facilities to acquiring better medical care and social services for the poor. In one successful case, civil rights lawyers at the center helped gain financial compensation for a cotton mill worker who had contracted a lung disease as a result of an unsafe job environment. In addition, this case led to the creation of federal laws regulating working conditions in cotton mills.

Civil rights lawyers such as those employed by the Southern Poverty Law Center spend years studying and preparing for a career in law. Lawyers must earn a college degree and graduate from a law school approved by the American Bar Association. In addition, potential lawyers must pass the bar exam of the state in which they plan to practice law. Passing the bar exam generally requires months of preparation. After completing the necessary education and certification, some

Morris Dees, cofounder of the Southern Poverty Law Center, works to provide legal assistance to victims of civil rights violations.

new lawyers work with well-established lawyers and law firms to gain experience.

Many people interested in a career in law turn to the federal government. Its dozens of departments and agencies employ attorneys who work in many fields of law, including civil rights. For example, the Equal Employment Opportunity Commission (EEOC), created by the 1964 Civil Rights Act, hires lawyers to defend people fighting discrimination in the workplace.

To whom do First Amendment freedoms and other constitutional protections belong? In several of its amendments, the Bill of Rights refers to the "right of the people," but nowhere does it define who the people are. In addressing this issue the Supreme Court has ruled that the protections granted by the Constitution are not limited to U.S. citizens. For the most part, these constitutional protections also guarantee the civil liberties of **aliens**, or resident noncitizens. The government may, however, limit some civil liberties of aliens who reside in the United States.

Balancing Rights and Interests to Promote the Public Good

Although the Constitution guarantees civil liberties, it does not guarantee absolute freedom to do as one wishes. The freedom to assemble with others in pursuit of a goal, for example, does not give people the freedom to riot, which would violate other people's right to safety. Recognizing the responsibilities that come with freedom is part of being a good citizen.

How are one person's civil liberties balanced with the rights of others and the interests of the majority? What happens, for example, when a person's religious beliefs necessitate behavior that is illegal? Who decides if the freedom of the press to report on a criminal investigation threatens the accused's right to a fair trial?

The government tries to answer questions such as these by passing laws that balance individual liberties with the rights and interests of society. The Supreme Court then uses its power of judicial review to determine whether government actions and laws violate constitutional protections.

The Supreme Court's approach to cases involving civil liberties has been influenced by two views. One view holds that the liberties protected by the Bill of Rights, particularly those of the First Amendment, are absolute, or without limit. Those who subscribe to this point of view argue that the First Amendment's statement that "Congress shall make no law" restricting free speech means that *all* federal laws that restrict free speech in any way are unconstitutional.

However, the government often passes laws that set boundaries on an individual's rights so others' rights or interests are not threatened. This reflects a second view—that the Supreme Court's role is to decide whether the government has promoted the public good by properly restricting a civil liberty to protect others' rights, or majority interests.

The Supreme Court has often chosen this latter approach. Throughout this and the next two chapters, you will see how the Court and the rest of the federal government have tried to ensure a proper balance of liberties.

LIBERTY'S CROWN

Courtesy of Karl Hubenthal, Los Angeles Herald-Examiner.

CONSTITUTIONAL GOVERNMENT *This political cartoon illustrates the liberties protected by the Bill of Rights. Many of these rights are found in the First Amendment.* **Why do you think that the cartoonist placed these rights on the spikes of the Statue of Liberty's crown?**

★ ★ ★ **SECTION 1** ★ — **REVIEW** ★ ★ ★

1. Define the following terms: civil liberty, alien.

2. What part of the Constitution protects the civil liberties of people in the United States?

3. Does the Constitution guarantee aliens' civil liberties? How has the Supreme Court ruled on government's restricting the civil liberties of aliens?

4. Why is a balance between individual liberties and majority interests that conflict with them important? Who decides whether restrictions on individual liberties promote the public good?

5. **Thinking and Writing Critically**
   What kinds of liberties do your parents or guardians grant you? Do you, for example, have the freedom to borrow the car or to participate in group activities after school? What kinds of responsibilities come with these liberties?

6. **Applying** **CONSTITUTIONAL GOVERNMENT**
   Make a list of the freedoms found in the First Amendment. Why might the framers have determined that these freedoms are among people's most fundamental rights?

FREEDOM OF RELIGION

Political Dictionary
Establishment Clause
Free Exercise Clause

Objectives

★ How has the Supreme Court interpreted the Establishment Clause to define the relationship between religion and public schools?
★ How does the Supreme Court decide if government aid to religious groups is constitutional?
★ Why has the Supreme Court allowed tax exemptions for religious groups?
★ How has the Free Exercise Clause been interpreted?

Religion is a part of many people's lives in the United States. In the early 1990s, for example, surveys showed that nearly 70 percent of people in this country were members of a church, synagogue, temples of various faiths, mosques, and other places of worship. The freedom to choose your religious beliefs, or to hold no religious belief, is a basic civil liberty guaranteed by the First Amendment.

The Establishment Clause

One way the Constitution guarantees freedom of religion is through the First Amendment's **Establishment Clause**. This clause states that "Congress shall make no law respecting an establishment of religion." Under the Establishment Clause the government may not act in ways that establish an official religion, that favor one religion over another, or that favor religion generally.

At the time the Bill of Rights was written, most countries supported one official religion. Even most of the North American colonies had official religions. After U.S. independence, support grew in the states to put an end to official religions. Many U.S. citizens thought that their young country was too diverse to allow religious beliefs to be imposed on people. As a result, religious freedom was included in the First Amendment. Later, Thomas Jefferson wrote in a personal letter that the First Amendment established "a wall of separation between church and State."

Whether the Establishment Clause does indeed build such a wall has been controversial. As cases about this subject have arisen, the Supreme Court has worked to define the line separating government and religion. Many such establishment cases have involved prayer in public schools, government aid for religious organizations, and government tax policies toward religious bodies.

Religion in Public Schools Religion in public schools has been a source of heated debate, and the Supreme Court's rulings have varied according to the case and the time period in which it was heard. Some states, for example, once allowed programs in which students could attend voluntary religion classes during school hours. However, in 1948 in *McCollum* v. *Board of Education,* the Court ruled

CONSTITUTIONAL GOVERNMENT *All citizens of the United States have the freedom to worship as they choose. **Why is the U.S. government prohibited from establishing an official religion?***

that an Illinois religious instruction program unconstitutionally established religion because it received official support. In a later case, the Court ruled in favor of a school that permitted students to leave campus to receive religious instruction outside the school grounds.

Some of the most controversial decisions about the Establishment Clause involve prayer in schools. Officially sponsored prayers once were common in U.S. public schools. In the 1962 case *Engel* v. *Vitale,* however, the Supreme Court ruled that this practice violated the Establishment Clause. The Court said that all officially sponsored prayer in public schools, even when participation was voluntary, represented unconstitutional official support for religion. Other Court decisions since 1962 have kept public schools from sponsoring religious activities, such as Bible readings and moments of silence for meditation or prayer.

The Court has not ruled, however, against students praying on their own in school. In fact, students are free to pray on their own at any time and in any place—in or out of school. Religious works also may be used in public schools as part of literature courses and other nonreligious studies.

Nevertheless, criticism of the Supreme Court's decisions on school prayer has been strong. Critics have argued that prayer and religious study are vital to teaching morals and values. Some have tried to pass constitutional amendments that would allow public schools to set aside time for voluntary prayer. In addition, Congress acted in 1984 to allow student religious groups to meet in public schools. Under the 1984 Equal Access Act, student religious groups have the same right as other student groups to use public school buildings for meetings. The Supreme Court ruled that the Equal Access Act was constitutional as long as the clubs are created and led by students.

Government Aid for Religion The Supreme Court also has heard establishment cases about government aid for religious organizations, such as parochial (puh-ROH-kee-uhl) schools. Parochial schools are elementary and high schools run by churches and other religious groups.

People who believe in giving government aid to parochial schools argue that the families of students in these schools are required to pay taxes to support the public education system and that these taxes should go to the schools that their children attend, parochial or public. By lowering tuition costs, government aid to parochial schools also would make it easier, they argue, for families to exercise their right to choose their children's schools. Currently, government aid does help parochial schools provide some services, such as buses.

Opponents of government aid argue that sending children to parochial schools is a financial burden that families freely choose and should handle on their own. They also argue that government aid would violate the Establishment Clause because it would support religious education.

SHOE

SHOE © Tribune Media Services, Inc. All rights reserved. Reprinted with permission.

POLITICAL PROCESSES *Although the Constitution protects citizens' right to practice their religion by attending parochial school, the government does not provide financial assistance to families who send their children to private schools. Some people have proposed a school voucher program that would provide a certain amount of government assistance to these families.* **Would you support legislation establishing this program?**

Drawing upon principles of past rulings, the Supreme Court in 1971 established in *Lemon* v. *Kurtzman* a three-part test for deciding if a government law aiding a religious body violates the Establishment Clause. Under the *Lemon* test a law must

★ have a secular, or nonreligious, purpose;
★ neither advance nor limit religion; and
★ not result in excessive government involvement with religion.

Instances of government aid that have passed the *Lemon* test include providing special education teachers and transportation to and from school. The Supreme Court has ruled that such aid, although perhaps indirectly supporting religion, promotes important nonreligious goals, including securing the welfare and safety of children.

Taxes and Religion The Establishment Clause has also affected the way tax laws are written. Federal, state, and local governments do not tax property owned by churches and other religious organizations if it is used for religious purposes. Supporters of this policy have argued that taxing churches and other religious properties would in effect allow the government to limit the freedom of religion.

Other people have argued, however, that tax exemptions for religious property violate the Establishment Clause. These people believe that tax exemptions provide official support for religion by giving it a privilege not enjoyed by other organizations. Some people also argue that such tax exemptions unfairly increase property tax rates by placing the entire tax burden on the nonexempt. The Supreme Court consistently has sided with those who support tax exemptions for religious property. In 1970 the Court ruled in *Walz* v. *Tax Commission* that tax exemptions help the government take a neutral approach toward religion, neither supporting it nor restricting it. In other decisions, however, the Court has said that the government may refuse to grant a tax exemption to a religious organization practicing racial discrimination. In such cases the Supreme Court has tried to balance the need to prevent discrimination with the protection of religious freedom.

POLITICAL FOUNDATIONS *Many towns and cities in the United States decorate public buildings with religious and nonreligious displays during holidays.* **What has the Supreme Court said about this practice?**

Custom and Religion In spite of the separation of church and state, many official U.S. symbols and customs involve religion. The money you use, for example, bears the phrase *In God We Trust.* During certain holidays your local government may sponsor a religious display on publicly owned property. How does the Supreme Court apply the Establishment Clause to these situations?

The Supreme Court has ruled that these references to God and to religious beliefs do not support religion as much as they recognize many Americans' deeply held beliefs. The Court has used this reasoning to rule, for example, that chaplains may open sessions of Congress and of state legislatures with a prayer. In addition, holiday displays in which nonreligious figures such as Santa Claus share space with religious symbols like nativity scenes are constitutional. In general, the Court has held that these long-practiced customs do not violate the Establishment Clause.

The Free Exercise Clause

In addition to the Establishment Clause, the First Amendment guarantees freedom of religion through its Free Exercise Clause. The **Free Exercise Clause** states that "Congress shall make no law . . . prohibiting the free exercise" of religion. This clause protects the right of a person to hold any religious beliefs he or she chooses. The right to *believe* as one wishes, however, is not the same as the right to *behave* as one wishes.

The Supreme Court has ruled that religious practices may be restricted if they threaten the health and safety of others or if they violate social standards and constitutional laws. For example, in 1879 the Court ruled in *Reynolds* v. *United States* that Mormons could not engage in bigamy—the act of marrying one person while legally married to another. The Court said that even though bigamy was (at the time) allowed by the Mormon faith, federal law prohibited the practice. The Court also has allowed the government to require vaccinations for children whose parents' religious beliefs forbid such medical practices. In this case, the Court valued protecting citizens' health over preserving the absolute free exercise of religion.

The Court has, however, supported some religious practices that violate the law but do not threaten the public interest. In a 1972 case, Wisconsin officials argued that requiring all children to attend school is a vital public interest. Amish families, who reject many modern practices for religious reasons, argued that schooling after the eighth grade threatens their beliefs. The Court, considering that few Amish children lived in the community, ruled that the state's requirement threatened Amish religious freedom more than an exemption for the Amish threatened the state's interest in educating its citizens.

CASE STUDY

Religion and Saluting the Flag

CONSTITUTIONAL GOVERNMENT Another issue concerning free exercise of religion involved pledging allegiance to the U.S. flag. In 1943 the Supreme Court ruled that people could not be forced to salute the flag if doing so would violate their religious beliefs. In *West Virginia State Board of Education* v. *Barnette*, Jehovah's Witnesses objected to their children's saluting the flag. The Witnesses argued that their religion did not allow them to pay homage to the U.S. flag, which they saw as an object of worship.

The Supreme Court had ruled against the Witnesses in a similar case just three years earlier. In *Minersville School District* v. *Gobitis*, the Court ruled that a community's interest in using the flag to encourage patriotism and national unity was more important than a person's religious beliefs.

In 1943, however, the Supreme Court decided that refusing to salute the flag posed no danger to patriotism and public order. What had changed? In part, the Court was reacting to the persecution of Jehovah's Witness children that had occurred as a result of the *Minersville* decision. In addition, forcing people to believe and act according to government rules had become a sensitive issue. At the time, the United States was at war with countries ruled by totalitarian dictatorships that controlled every aspect of their citizens' lives. The Court did not base its decision against forced saluting on the Free Exercise Clause, however. Rather, it determined that requiring people to say the Pledge of Allegiance violated their First Amendment guarantee of free speech.

SECTION 2 — REVIEW

1. Define the following terms: Establishment Clause, Free Exercise Clause.

2. Under what circumstances does the Supreme Court allow government aid to religious groups?

3. Describe the debate over tax exemptions for religious organizations.

4. Does the Free Exercise Clause allow all religious practices?

5. **Thinking and Writing Critically** How would you describe the "wall of separation between church and state"? How high is it? What is it made of—solid granite or chain links? Explain your answers.

6. **Applying CONSTITUTIONAL GOVERNMENT** Why might changing times influence the Supreme Court's decisions concerning religion in schools?

FREEDOM OF SPEECH AND OF THE PRESS

Political Dictionary

treason
sedition
prior restraint
shield law
libel
slander
obscenity
symbolic speech
draft
hate speech

Objectives

★ What challenges exist in balancing individuals' freedom of speech with the need to protect national security?

★ What boundaries exist on the media's freedom of expression?

★ How does the First Amendment affect symbolic speech and hate speech?

In 1579 John Stubbs published a book in England criticizing a proposed marriage of Queen Elizabeth. Because criticizing the country's leaders was not allowed at the time, the government ordered that Stubbs's right hand be cut off at the wrist so that he could never write again.

Today such a book might be a tame addition to the shelves of your local bookstore. This is because the First Amendment guarantees freedom of speech and freedom of the press in the United States. These freedoms are among the most cherished liberties assured by the Bill of Rights. The freedom to express your opinions, popular or not, in speech or in print, is vital to a democracy.

As with freedom of religion, the Supreme Court has applied the First Amendment guarantees of free speech to government laws and actions. At times the Court has interpreted the First Amendment to strike down *any* laws that limit free expression. At other times the Court has tried to promote the public good by balancing free speech with other liberties. Although finding this balance sometimes means setting boundaries on expression, people in the United States still enjoy great freedom to speak out and express their ideas.

Freedom of Speech and National Security

National security is one area in which the Supreme Court has allowed the government to establish boundaries on free speech. As you know, the Constitution gives the government the authority to protect the nation against foreign powers and domestic threats. It is largely this latter responsibility that has sparked questions about balancing free speech with national security.

Treason and Sedition One form of domestic threat is treason. **Treason** is the act of aiding and comforting an enemy of the United States in a time of war—for example, spying on one's government for a foreign power. Article III, Section 3, of the

CONSTITUTIONAL GOVERNMENT *A group of young people protests the U.S. government's involvement in the Vietnam War.* **In what kinds of cases has the Supreme Court allowed government to limit free speech?**

Constitution gives Congress the authority to punish people found guilty of treason. What about acts committed during peacetime?

The government has answered this question differently over time. For example, Congress has passed laws restricting speech that criticizes government. Many of these laws specifically address **sedition**—the use of language that encourages people to rebel against lawful government. Several people in U.S. history have in fact been accused of endangering the nation's security through seditious language.

Whether a statement is seditious is debatable, of course. Some people might think that a particular criticism of the government encourages others to work against unfair government policies, but others might consider it seditious. In cases of sedition, then, the Supreme Court has had to decide how to balance the security interests of the nation with individuals' right to free speech.

Alien and Sedition Acts The first laws against sedition were passed by Congress in 1798, just seven years after the adoption of the Bill of Rights. Among other things, the Alien and Sedition Acts made it illegal to say anything "false, scandalous [disgraceful] and malicious [spiteful]" against the government or its officials. The acts were aimed at opponents of President John Adams and his Federalist supporters, and in fact, only opponents of the Federalists were ever convicted under the laws. One such opponent, a congressman, was jailed for four months and fined $1,000. Newspaper editors also were jailed or fined for their critical words.

Opposition to the Alien and Sedition Acts was strong from those who believed that the acts violated the First Amendment's freedoms of speech and the press. The Alien and Sedition Acts were never tested in the courts, however, and Congress allowed them to expire in 1801. In that same year President Thomas Jefferson pardoned all those who had been convicted under the acts, and Congress voted to refund the fines that had been paid.

Clear and Present Danger After the assassination of President William McKinley by an anarchist in 1901, public opinion began to favor legislation punishing seditious acts. Then in 1917 and 1918, after the United States had entered World War I, Congress again passed sedition laws forbidding verbal attacks on the government. By the end of World War I, 32 states had laws against

Comparing Governments

Freedom of Speech in Singapore

As you know, the First Amendment of the Constitution guarantees that "Congress shall make no law . . . abridging the freedom of speech, or of the press." Although laws in the United States restrict certain types of speech, people can legally express unfavorable comments about the U.S. government.

Not all nations share this freedom. In Singapore, criticism of the government in the press is forbidden. A federal statute in Singapore protects freedom of speech but restricts people from saying anything that the courts identify as disrespectful of judicial authority, harmful to someone's reputation, or an "incitement to any offense." In 1994, for example, the nation's Supreme Court found the *International Herald Tribune* and its distributors guilty of having criticized three of Singapore's high-ranking government officials in a newspaper article. Although the newspaper published letters of apology for the article, it was fined $678,000 for breaking the law.

sedition-related offenses. More than 1,900 people were prosecuted for such offenses, and more than 100 newspapers and periodicals were censored for publishing items considered seditious. Congress also passed laws against using language that might encourage someone to disobey military orders or to avoid required military service. In 1919 the Supreme Court upheld the conviction of a man who had been prosecuted under these laws. The man had been arrested for handing out documents urging others to avoid required military service. In this case, *Schenck* v. *United States,* the Court established a key rule for drawing the boundaries of constitutional protections for free expression: the clear-and-present-danger test.

Under the Court's clear-and-present-danger test, the First Amendment did not cover expressions that were closely connected to the committing of an illegal action. "The most stringent [strict] protection of free speech," wrote Justice Oliver Wendell Holmes in the Court's majority opinion, "would not protect a man in falsely shouting fire in a theatre and causing a panic." The danger posed in the *Schenck* case was that encouraging men to disobey orders or to refuse military service might harm the nation's ability to defend itself in war.

In the 1969 case *Brandenburg* v. *Ohio* the Supreme Court made the clear-and-present-danger test less restrictive by ruling that simply expressing a belief that the government should be overthrown or that violence might be necessary to achieve certain goals is protected by the First Amendment. To convict a person of sedition, the government must prove that a person's words are meant to encourage *actively* the violent overthrow of the government or are likely to *succeed* in encouraging others to commit violence.

Freedom of Speech and the Media

The government and the courts also have tried to find a balance between the media's freedom of expression and other rights and interests. Media, as you know, include newspapers, magazines, books, television, radio, motion pictures, and computer networks. How has the media's right to freedom of expression been defined?

Prior Restraint With few exceptions, the First Amendment has been interpreted to forbid the government from using **prior restraint**, or stopping someone from expressing an idea or providing information. The case that established this rule against prior restraint involved a Minnesota law designed to keep newspapers from publishing sensational articles about government corruption. In 1931 the Supreme Court ruled in *Near* v. *Minnesota* that the law was a form of censorship. As such, it violated the

Fourteenth Amendment's Due Process Clause, which—according to the Supreme Court—extends the First Amendment's free-press protections to the states.

In other prior-restraint cases the courts have allowed the media to publish material that public officials considered secret. In 1971, for example, the Supreme Court ruled that the government could not prevent the *New York Times* and other newspapers from publishing the Pentagon Papers. These classified, top-secret government documents, secretly copied and given to the newspapers, discussed controversial and previously secret accounts of U.S. involvement in the Vietnam War. The Court did not accept the government's argument that publishing the papers would harm national security. In the Pentagon Papers case the justices did, however, state that the government could use prior restraint when it could give compelling reasons for doing so.

CONSTITUTIONAL GOVERNMENT *In 1971 the Supreme Court upheld the New York Times's right to publish the Pentagon Papers.* **Under what conditions can the government restrict a newspaper's right to publish top-secret documents?**

Trials There are also some boundaries on the rights of the press during court trials. News reporters often have used the First Amendment guarantee of a free press to avoid giving testimony about the identities of their news sources or about information they have discovered in their work. Reporters fear that sources would be less likely to give information if they might be publicly named in court.

Federal courts, however, have refused to accept the argument that the First Amendment protects reporters from naming their sources. In 1972 the Supreme Court ruled in *Branzburg* v. *Hayes* that the First Amendment did not excuse reporters from the responsibilities that all citizens have to testify about information applicable in a court proceeding.

Some states have passed **shield laws** that allow reporters to protect the identity of their sources from state courts. In addition, many reporters who have been summoned to federal courts or to state courts without shield laws have gone to jail rather than reveal information about their sources.

Libel The Supreme Court also has ruled that abusing the freedom of speech to harm the character and reputation of others unjustly is not protected by the First Amendment. **Libel** is a written statement or visual presentation that is defamatory, or unjustly harms another person's character and reputation. **Slander** is verbal defamation.

Libel cases most often involve the news media. The 1964 Supreme Court case *New York Times* v. *Sullivan* established guidelines for determining when a public figure has been libeled. In that case, the *New York Times* and a group of African American clergymen had published a newspaper advertisement that harshly criticized some Alabama state officials' reactions to protests against racial discrimination. Some of the statements in the advertisement were false, and the state officials sued for libel.

The Supreme Court, however, decided that the officials had not been libeled. In a landmark ruling, the Court established a standard for libel involving public officials. The Court ruled that to be libelous, a false statement about a public official must reflect "actual malice" on the part of the author. That is, such a statement cannot be found libelous unless someone proves that it was made "with knowledge that it was false or with reckless disregard of whether it was false or not." The Court later extended this standard to public figures who are not officials—for example, celebrities.

CONSTITUTIONAL GOVERNMENT *Many states have shield laws that allow reporters to protect the anonymity of their sources.* **Do reporters have a responsibility to avoid libel?**

The argument for the *Sullivan* standard stems from the view that free expression in the media helps monitor possible government abuses. Making it easy to sue successfully for libel might make the media more hesitant to publish hardhitting stories involving government officials. Nevertheless, courts have allowed the government to establish some boundaries on free expression through libel laws.

Obscenity The First Amendment does not protect obscenity. In general, an **obscenity** is something sexually indecent and highly offensive. In legal terms, however, defining obscenity is a difficult task for the courts because different people find different things offensive. Nevertheless, in the 1957 case *Roth* v. *United States* the Court ruled that obscenity was something "utterly without redeeming social value." In the 1973 case *Miller* v. *California* the Supreme Court redefined obscenity as material

★ in which the major theme would be judged to appeal to indecent sexual desires by the average person applying "contemporary [current] community standards";
★ that shows in a clearly offensive way sexual behavior not allowed by state laws; and

★ that is "lacking serious literary, artistic, political, or scientific value."

Even with these factors, determining what is obscene is difficult because personal and community standards vary. In another case that same year the Supreme Court ruled that a Georgia community could not use its local standards to ban the motion picture *Carnal Knowledge*— which starred several well-known and respected actors—for obscenity. The ruling seemed to limit the extent to which a local community's standards could differ from what the Court thought of as "national" standards. In doing so, the ruling further complicated the question of whether something is obscene or protected speech.

The Supreme Court has ruled, however, that sexually explicit material involving children is not protected expression regardless of whether it meets the three-part test for obscenity. Congress and the states have passed laws against such material. In 1996 Congress also passed a law restricting obscenity on the Internet, the first such major law affecting communication via computers. Critics went to trial to challenge the law, and the Supreme Court ruled in 1997 that it was unconstitutional.

Licensing Radio and television stations generally have fewer First Amendment protections against government actions than do newspapers, magazines, and other print media. This is true in part because radio and television broadcast over airwaves owned by the public. To operate, radio and television stations must receive a license from the Federal Communications Commission (FCC).

In fact, in 1934 the FCC developed a set of rules that radio and television stations must follow in order to receive an FCC license. Even though the FCC could not censor broadcasters or restrict the First Amendment protections of broadcast news reporters, the FCC could subject the renewal of a station's license to the various rules that it or Congress set. For example, stations had to restrict the broadcast of violent or sexually explicit material during certain times of the day, particularly during "family hour," the first hour of prime-time programming. In addition, broadcasters had to operate under what was known as the equal-time doctrine. This policy required that opposing political candidates be given equal time on a station to state their views.

These restrictions were gradually cut back in the 1970s and 1980s, however, partially in response to the development of cable and satellite broadcasting and greater public access to the media. Interestingly, the courts have ruled that cable television stations have broader First Amendment protections than do other broadcasters. This is because cable programming is not broadcast over public airwaves. Many people, including some members of Congress, have petitioned broadcasters to reinstate family hour programming and to return to the original FCC standards.

False Advertising The courts take a more definite stand on limiting freedom of speech when it relates to commercial advertising. In particular, courts have ruled that the government may

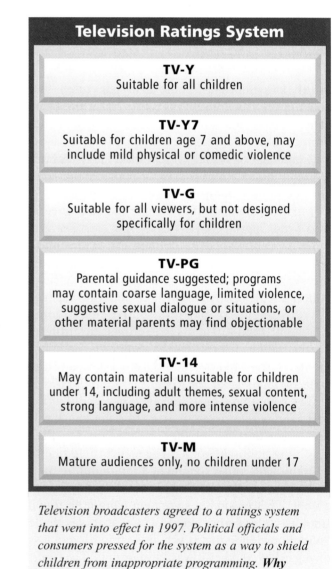

Television Ratings System

TV-Y
Suitable for all children

TV-Y7
Suitable for children age 7 and above, may include mild physical or comedic violence

TV-G
Suitable for all viewers, but not designed specifically for children

TV-PG
Parental guidance suggested; programs may contain coarse language, limited violence, suggestive sexual dialogue or situations, or other material parents may find objectionable

TV-14
May contain material unsuitable for children under 14, including adult themes, sexual content, strong language, and more intense violence

TV-M
Mature audiences only, no children under 17

*Television broadcasters agreed to a ratings system that went into effect in 1997. Political officials and consumers pressed for the system as a way to shield children from inappropriate programming. **Why might some people criticize this rating system?***

Citizenship in ➔ Action

The Tinkers' Silent Protest

In 1965 three students—13-year-old Mary Beth Tinker, 15-year-old John Tinker, and 16-year-old Christopher Eckhardt—made a choice that would bring them to the attention of the Supreme Court. These young people were part of a group that decided to silently protest the U.S. government's involvement in the Vietnam War by wearing black armbands during the holiday season. They took this action to mourn the deaths of soldiers killed in the war.

When Des Moines school district officials learned of the group's plan, they feared that the controversial nature of the protest would cause a disturbance in the schools. The school board adopted a policy banning the wearing of the armbands. Students who arrived at school wearing one of the symbols of protest would be asked to remove it. Any student who refused would be suspended from school until he or she agreed to return to school without the armband.

Mary Beth and John Tinker display the armbands they wore to protest the U.S. government's involvement in the Vietnam War.

In mid-December, Mary Beth, John, and Christopher came to school wearing black armbands. The students were sent home and suspended. They then refused to return to school without the armbands until after New Year's Day, the end of the group's planned period of protest.

Shortly after this incident the students' fathers filed a complaint in district court, asking that the school officials and school board be prohibited from disciplining the students for their actions. The court dismissed the complaint and supported the board's policy on the grounds that it was adopted to prevent disturbances in the classroom. The Tinkers appealed the case, but the court of appeals upheld the district court's ruling.

The Supreme Court agreed the following year to hear the case. In *Tinker v. Des Moines Independent Community School District*, the Court ruled that wearing an armband is symbolic speech and as an expression of opinion is protected by the First Amendment. The Court found no evidence to support the school board's claim that it had acted to prevent disturbance in the schools. The board did not prove that the wearing of the armbands had interfered with school discipline.

Furthermore, the Court ruled that in order for school officials to ban an expression of opinion, they must show evidence that their actions were not based merely on fear of the expression of controversial or unpopular opinions. In the Court's majority opinion, Justice Abe Fortas stated, "Students in school as well as out of school are 'persons' under our Constitution. They are possessed of fundamental rights which the State must respect, just as they themselves must respect their obligations to the State." The Court, however, did not prohibit schools from limiting students' rights to express themselves, but merely required them to provide a constitutionally valid reason for restricting students' speech.

What Do You Think?

1. What limits should be placed on students' rights to express themselves in their schools?
2. Have you ever expressed your opinions in your school? What forms of expression did you use?

pass laws against false advertising. The courts have agreed that false or misleading advertising works against the public interest. For example, the First Amendment does not protect an ad that exaggerates the health benefits of a product or that makes claims about a product that may do nothing beneficial or may actually harm someone.

For many years federal courts ruled that the right to free expression did not apply to business advertising. The Supreme Court ruled in 1942, for example, that business advertising was commercial, as opposed to "pure," speech. As such, it was not protected by the First Amendment. In later years, however, the Court extended some protections to business advertising, such as ads for professional services. The government may still restrict false advertising and advertising that is not in the public interest—for example, cigarette ads on television.

Freedom of Speech and Individual Behavior

Debate over free speech is not limited to national security issues and the media. The Supreme Court also has applied First Amendment protections to cases that involve personal conduct and those that involve speech that expresses hatred.

Personal Conduct Some of the most difficult questions about what forms of expression are protected by the First Amendment involve personal conduct. The Supreme Court has ruled that some conduct is a form of symbolic speech that is protected by the First Amendment. **Symbolic speech** is an action meant to deliver a message.

Deciding which actions are examples of protected symbolic speech, however, has been difficult for the Supreme Court. In fact, the Court has ruled that not all conduct designed to communicate a message is protected by the First Amendment. In the 1968 case *United States* v. *O'Brien*, for example, the Court ruled that burning a draft card was not protected symbolic speech. The **draft** was a policy requiring men to serve in the military. Destroying a draft card was against the law. In the 1960s and early 1970s, a number of men around the country burned their draft cards to protest U.S. involvement in the Vietnam War. In the *O'Brien* decision the Court ruled that it could not accept "the view that an apparently limitless variety of conduct can be labeled 'speech.'"

CONSTITUTIONAL GOVERNMENT *Demonstrators in Baltimore, Maryland, burn draft files in protest of the Vietnam War.* **Why did the Court rule that burning draft cards is not protected by the Constitution?**

One year later, however, the Court ruled that students in an Iowa high school could wear black armbands to protest the Vietnam War. In the 1969 case *Tinker* v. *Des Moines Independent Community School District,* school officials argued that the issue was one of conduct, not the right to free expression. (See Citizenship in Action, page 309.) School officials claimed that the armbands would cause discipline problems. The Supreme Court ruled, however, that wearing the armbands sent a political message and was thus a form of symbolic speech protected by the First Amendment. The Court also determined that no disruption had actually occurred.

In addition to the *Tinker* case, the Supreme Court has also ruled that laws may not restrict other forms of symbolic speech. For example, in 1989 and 1990 the Court ruled that state and federal laws against burning the U.S. flag as a form of protest violated the right to free speech. The Court said that the First Amendment protected freedom of expression even when a vast majority of people disagreed with the particular form of expression—in this instance, flag burning.

Hate Speech In addition to symbolic speech issues, the Supreme Court in recent years has addressed cases involving rules to curb hate speech. Supporters of such rules define **hate speech** as the expression of hatred or bias against a person, based on characteristics such as race, sex, religion, or sexual orientation. During the late 1980s many colleges passed rules that prohibited hate speech.

Various federal courts have ruled that many hate speech rules are unconstitutional because they are so vague that a reasonable person could not know what speech the rules actually limit. Some students and teachers, for example, were reluctant to express their opinions for fear of punishment. The courts also have declared as unconstitutional some hate speech rules that banned certain language, such as racist opinions, simply because it offended some people.

Supporters of hate speech rules point to the 1942 case of *Chaplinsky* v. *New Hampshire,* in which the Supreme Court said that using "insulting or 'fighting' words" that are likely to cause a fight or other physical disturbance are not protected by the First Amendment. Some of these supporters propose that future hate speech rules should be limited to restricting these types of "fighting words." Colleges continue to struggle to uphold the sometimes conflicting values of the First Amendment and respect for the dignity of all groups of people.

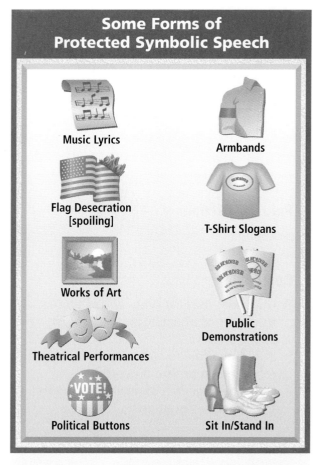

Some Forms of Protected Symbolic Speech

Music Lyrics

Armbands

Flag Desecration [spoiling]

T-Shirt Slogans

Works of Art

Public Demonstrations

Theatrical Performances

Political Buttons

Sit In/Stand In

The forms of symbolic speech illustrated in this chart are protected by law. **Under what conditions might the Supreme Court restrict these forms of symbolic speech?**

SECTION 3 — REVIEW

1. Define the following terms: treason, sedition, prior restraint, shield law, libel, slander, obscenity, symbolic speech, draft, hate speech.

2. What is the clear-and-present-danger test? How does it affect the relationship between free speech and national security?

3. What guidelines did the Supreme Court establish for deciding whether a public figure has been libeled? In what other ways are the media's First Amendment rights limited?

4. What kinds of actions qualify as symbolic speech? Why has the Supreme Court ruled against many hate speech rules?

5. **Thinking and Writing Critically**
   Suppose that a group wants to place a newspaper advertisement that insults various racial groups and calls for policies that discriminate against people in those groups. How would you determine whether or not the First Amendment protects the language used in the ad? If you were the newspaper's editor, would you publish the ad? Why or why not?

6. **Applying** **CONSTITUTIONAL GOVERNMENT**
   Why might a reporter choose jail over revealing a source? How do state shield laws protect journalists' sources? Why do you think that many states do not have shield laws?

FREEDOM OF ASSEMBLY AND PETITION

Political Dictionary

picketing

Objectives

★ How does the First Amendment protect the rights of assembly and petition on public property?

★ How is the freedom to demonstrate restricted on private property?

★ How does freedom of assembly support freedom of association?

Perhaps you have seen people demonstrating in your community for laws to protect the environment or seen them passing out flyers calling for lower taxes. Or maybe you have seen news reports of people addressing a meeting of your local government about traffic laws or zoning issues. You might know someone who has joined with others to march in front of a business to demand higher wages or better working conditions.

What gave these people the right to demonstrate and to address government officials about their concerns? The people in each of these examples exercised their rights of assembly and petition. Along with freedoms of religion and speech, the rights of assembly and petition are protected by the First Amendment. As with other First Amendment liberties, however, the government may act to promote the public good by balancing these freedoms with conflicting considerations.

Demonstrations and Protests

Demonstrations and protests are among the most common examples of the rights of assembly and petition. Such gatherings include abortion protests, marches in support of equal rights, and parades honoring certain groups or causes. The purpose of many of these demonstrations is to persuade government officials and others to pursue certain goals.

As with other civil liberties guaranteed by the Bill of Rights, the freedom to demonstrate peacefully is protected from the actions of the federal government, as well as from state and local governments. In some cases, however, the courts have allowed governments to set boundaries on the freedom to assemble, in order to protect the rights of others.

Assembly and Public Property It has long been recognized that the freedom to demonstrate on public property may be regulated in the interest of keeping order and shielding people from loud noise, blocked streets, and other intrusions. Such restrictions are called time, place, and manner

POLITICAL PROCESSES *Picketing on public property such as a public sidewalk in front of a business is permitted.* ***Do businesses have the right to prohibit picketing on their private property?***

regulations. The courts have said that these rules must be applied fairly and that they may not be used as a means to restrict a specific group's freedom to demonstrate.

One example of a time, place, and manner regulation is a parade permit that local governments may require people to obtain before holding demonstrations on public streets. Such a permit identifies the location and route of the parade or demonstration, as well as the time it will occur. The permit process allows local authorities to develop procedures for managing traffic flow and to prepare for problems that might occur during the demonstration.

In some cases the courts also have allowed governments to regulate demonstrations for reasons of public safety. Police may halt demonstrations that turn violent, for example, and arrest those responsible for the violence. In doing so, the police are protecting the safety of others.

The Supreme Court also has allowed laws prohibiting demonstrations in jails and restricting demonstrations that would disrupt school activities. These laws are allowed because such demonstrations would interfere with critical activities, such as maintaining control of jails and educating children.

The courts have ruled against other restrictions on public assembly, however, even ones that attempted to prevent highly unpopular activities in a community. In 1978, for example, the Illinois Supreme Court ruled that officials in Skokie, Illinois—a largely Jewish suburb of Chicago—could not stop members of a neo-Nazi party—a U.S. version of the Nazi Party—from parading through the city. In the 1930s and 1940s the Nazi government in Germany was responsible for the murder of millions of Jews as well as others. Among Skokie's residents were Jews who had survived Nazi persecution, as well as relatives of the Nazis' victims. Before the ruling, local officials had attempted to stop the neo-Nazi parade for fear that it might lead to violence and to enforce several Skokie ordinances imposing criminal penalties on certain kinds of speech and assembly. The U.S. Supreme Court refused to review the state court's ruling, however, which had stated that the First Amendment protected the neo-Nazis' right to assemble. Therefore, the neo-Nazis were allowed to march.

Assembly and Private Property Among the strongest boundaries on freedom of assembly are those involving demonstrations on private property. The First Amendment right of assembly does not give people the right to use others' private property, such as a business or residence. In 1972, for example, the Supreme Court ruled in *Lloyd Corporation* v. *Tanner* that a shopping mall could prevent people who were on its private property from passing out literature opposing U.S. involvement in the Vietnam War. Such activities, however, could take place on the public sidewalks and streets outside the mall.

In some circumstances, private businesses also may prevent picketing on their property. **Picketing**

PRINCIPLES OF DEMOCRACY *Any group of individuals that wants to demonstrate on public property must first obtain a permit. Government officials have occasionally attempted to prevent controversial groups from demonstrating, as was the case in Skokie, Illinois, during the 1970s.* **What are the restrictions that regulate public demonstrations called?**

is walking or standing in front of a place of business or other property, often holding signs urging others not to buy the company's products or asking others not to cross the picket line to work for the company. Although picketing may be prohibited on the company's property, it is allowed on the surrounding public property.

Peaceful Association

The First Amendment's guarantee of free assembly has been used for more than protecting the right to demonstrate. The courts also have interpreted the freedom of assembly to mean that people have a right to associate with various groups without interference from the government.

A key Supreme Court ruling involving the right of free association was the 1958 decision in *National Association for the Advancement of Colored People (NAACP)* v. *Alabama*. The NAACP is an organization that was founded in 1909 to work for equal rights for African Americans. The 1958 case reached the Supreme Court after the state of Alabama fined the

PRINCIPLES OF DEMOCRACY *The First Amendment's guarantee of free assembly has also been interpreted to mean that people have the right to associate with various groups without government interference. The above photograph shows a meeting of the NAACP.* **What did the Supreme Court rule in the NAACP v. Alabama case?**

NAACP for not providing government officials a list of its state members. The Court ruled that Alabama officials could not force the NAACP to provide the names of its members. Such a rule, the Court said, violated the right of people to associate and organize in pursuit of a lawful goal without interference from the government.

SECTION 4 — REVIEW

1. Define the following term: picketing.

2. What are time, place, and manner regulations? What is the purpose of such restrictions on the right to demonstrate on public property?

3. What role did the 1972 Supreme Court case of *Lloyd Corporation* v. *Tanner* play in applying the First Amendment's guarantee of freedom of assembly to demonstrations on people's private property?

4. How is freedom of association protected by the First Amendment?

5. **Thinking and Writing Critically** How do officials at your school regulate student assemblies? In what ways are the regulations similar to time, place, and manner regulations that government officials set for public demonstrations?

6. **Applying** **CONSTITUTIONAL GOVERNMENT** Why do courts uphold the right to stage a public demonstration or to march even for groups whose views might be offensive to others in the community? Do you agree or disagree with their decisions?

SECTION 1 The Bill of Rights guarantees civil liberties for residents of the United States. Civil liberties are basic individual rights and freedoms that are protected from government violation.

Among these liberties are the First Amendment freedoms of religion, speech, the press, assembly, and petition. The government and the courts balance these individual liberties with conflicting rights, and with the interests of the community. In finding this balance, the government promotes the public good.

SECTION 2 Freedom of religion is guaranteed by two clauses of the First Amendment. The Establishment Clause prohibits government from acting in ways that establish an official religion, that favor one religion over another, or that favor all religions. The Establishment Clause affects such issues as religion in public schools, government aid for religion, and tax laws regarding religious property. It does not, however, prevent some customs in the United States that reflect religious beliefs.

The Free Exercise Clause prohibits the government from passing laws that restrict people's right to choose their own religious beliefs. In establishment cases the courts have helped define the relationship between government and religion. In free exercise cases, the courts have restricted the government's ability to force people to obey laws that conflict with their religious beliefs. The courts have, however, upheld such laws when public health concerns are involved.

SECTION 3 The First Amendment also guarantees free speech. The Supreme Court, however, has ruled that not all forms of expression are protected by the First Amendment. For example, the government has established boundaries on freedom of speech when it comes to national security. The Court has restricted free expression that represents a "clear and present danger" to national security or to the safety of individuals. The courts have ruled that some forms of symbolic speech are protected by the First Amendment. In recent years, the courts also have addressed cases involving rules to curb hate speech—the expression of hatred or bias against a person, based on characteristics such as race, religion, gender, and sexual orientation.

The First Amendment does not protect libel, slander, obscenity, or false advertising. Furthermore, the government may regulate radio and television broadcasting.

SECTION 4 Individuals' freedom of assembly and freedom of petition are protected under the First Amendment. Demonstrations and protests are among the most common examples of the rights of assembly and petition. In general, these rights allow people to demonstrate peaceably on public property. Property owners may prohibit demonstrations on their private property, however.

The courts also have interpreted the freedom of assembly to protect the freedom of association. By extension, therefore, people have the right to associate with various groups without government interference.

Government Notebook

Review what you wrote in your Government Notebook at the beginning of this chapter about the ways that government may restrict First Amendment rights. Now that you have studied this chapter, how would you revise your answer? Why is it important that these rights are not without limit? Record your answers in your Notebook.

REVIEW

REVIEWING CONCEPTS

1. How does the Supreme Court apply the clear-and-present-danger test to free-expression cases? In what ways may government set boundaries on free speech in the media?

2. How are civil liberties guaranteed in the U.S. Bill of Rights? Do aliens have the same rights as citizens in the United States?

3. How is the freedom of assembly applied on public property and on private property? How does the freedom of assembly protect the right of association?

4. How is symbolic speech protected by the First Amendment? What is the difference between the free expression that is restricted by many hate speech rules and that which the courts have called fighting words?

5. What is the importance of the Establishment and Free Exercise Clauses of the First Amendment? Under what conditions do the courts allow the government to aid religious organizations?

6. What is the role of the courts in finding a proper balance between individuals' civil liberties and some wider public interest? Why is this balance difficult to achieve?

THINKING AND WRITING CRITICALLY

1. **CONSTITUTIONAL GOVERNMENT** Imagine that you are visiting a country where freedom of religion is not a right. The country does protect a free press, however, and a newspaper has asked you to write an editorial favoring religious freedom. Write a short editorial explaining why religious freedom is valued in the United States.

2. **CONSTITUTIONAL GOVERNMENT** Although some states have shield laws that allow reporters to protect their sources, many state courts and all federal courts do not excuse reporters from the responsibility of testifying about information important in a court proceeding. Do you think that news reporters should always be required to testify in criminal cases about the identities of their news sources? Explain your answer.

3. **PRINCIPLES OF DEMOCRACY** Why are freedom of speech and freedom of the press important in a democracy? Do you think that the government places too many limits on these freedoms? Why or why not?

4. **PUBLIC GOOD** Recall what you learned about the debate between people who believe First Amendment rights are absolute and people who believe those rights should be balanced with other considerations. What do you think? Should First Amendment rights ever be restricted? In what kinds of situations should this occur? Explain your answer.

CITIZENSHIP IN YOUR COMMUNITY

Working with others in your group, create a Media Guide that lists and describes the various kinds of media that exist in your community. Include addresses and other identifying information for television and radio stations, newspapers, and magazines. In addition, list the addresses of any libraries that offer their patrons access to the Internet. You might want to include information on classes that teach patrons how to use the Internet. Illustrate the guide with various images and other art, and consider giving it to a visitor's center to distribute to tourists and to new residents.

INDIVIDUAL PORTFOLIO PROJECT

Create a Free Press Handbook that student reporters might use as part of their training to become broadcast or print journalists. The handbook should describe how the First Amendment affects various parts of the media, including information about the kinds of restrictions that the courts allow to be placed on free expression.

PRACTICING SKILLS: CONDUCTING RESEARCH

To understand the importance of federal laws and Supreme Court decisions you must be able to identify cause-and-effect relationships. To identify cause and effect, look at why an event took place and what happened as a result of the event. Often more than one cause can trigger an effect, and one cause can result in multiple effects.

Create a chart showing the cause-and-effect relationship among the Supreme Court cases listed below. If there are multiple causes or effects, list them all in the chart. The chart should be clear and easy to follow.

1. *Engel v. Vitale*
2. *West Virginia State Board of Education v. Barnette*
3. *Schenck v. United States*

THE INTERNET: LEARNING ONLINE

In 1997 the Supreme Court ruled as unconstitutional the Communications Decency Act, a law restricting obscene material on the Internet. Conduct an Internet search for information about this ruling. You might start with search words such as Reno *v. American Civil Liberties Union, Supreme Court and Communications Decency Act,* and *obscenity law.* Then design your own Web site entitled The Internet and the Law. Write a short editorial for your Web site explaining whether you agree with the Court's opinion that the law unjustly limits free expression. Include links to applicable Web sites about law that you found in your search.

ANALYZING PRIMARY SOURCES

LETTER TO THE DANBURY BAPTISTS

Thomas Jefferson believed that the First Amendment created a wall separating church and state. In a letter written to the Committee of the Danbury Baptist Association in Connecticut on January 1, 1802, Jefferson offers his opinion on the necessity of a law that specifically forbids government from favoring one religion over another. Read the excerpt from the letter and answer the questions that follow.

" *Believing with you that religion is a matter which lies solely between man and his God, that he owes account to none other for his faith or his worship, that the legislative powers of government reach actions only, and not opinions, I contemplate [think] with sovereign [greatest] reverence that act of the whole American people which declared that their legislature should 'make no law respecting an establishment of religion, or prohibiting the free exercise thereof,' thus building a wall of separation between church and State. Adhering to [obeying] this expression of the supreme will of the nation on behalf of the rights of conscience, I shall see with sincere satisfaction the progress of those sentiments [beliefs] which tend to restore to man all his natural rights, convinced he has no natural right in opposition to his social duties.* "

1. How do government powers reach religious actions, but not religious opinions? Why do you think that it is important for people to be allowed to form religious opinions without government intervention?

2. To which "act" is Jefferson referring when he states that "that act of the whole American people which declared that their legislature should "'make no law respecting an establishment of religion . . .'"?

3. How does a law that prevents government from establishing a religion and guarantees all people freedom of religion protect people's rights?

CHAPTER 14

ASSURING INDIVIDUAL RIGHTS

If you like to watch police shows on television, you probably know what it means when one officer says to another, "Read them their rights." At that point, the officer explains to the criminal suspects a list of constitutional rights that protect people accused of crimes. These include, for example, the right to remain silent and the right to be represented by a lawyer.

The Constitution requires government to follow certain procedures—such as reading rights to a suspect—and to pass fair laws in order to assure the protection of many civil liberties. These liberties include freedom from unreasonable police action, the right to privacy, and fair treatment when accused of crimes.

Government Notebook

When do you think police may search people, their cars, or their homes? When may school officials search students or their lockers? Write your answers in your Government Notebook.

PROTECTING INDIVIDUAL LIBERTIES

Political Dictionary

due process
procedural due process
substantive due process
police power
search warrant
probable cause
exclusionary rule

Objectives

★ What does the term *due process* mean?
★ How is procedural due process different from substantive due process?
★ How do the Fourth Amendment and due process protect people's security against unreasonable state action?
★ How does the Bill of Rights protect people's privacy?

As noted in Chapter 13, the First Amendment secures many of the fundamental freedoms that people living in the United States enjoy. Additional individual liberties are protected by other constitutional amendments. The Fifth Amendment, for example, is vital to securing citizens' basic liberties. It states that the federal government may not take away anyone's "life, liberty, or property, without due process of law." **Due process** refers to government's duty to follow fair procedures set by law when carrying out government functions.

Due Process of Law

How do the courts decide whether the government has acted with due process? The courts have recognized that the concept of due process can be broken down into two parts: procedural due process and substantive due process. The courts use both of these aspects of due process to determine whether government uses its police power reasonably.

Procedural Due Process According to the concept of **procedural due process**, government must apply a law fairly and act according to procedures and rules set by that law. As noted in Chapter 13, time, place, and manner regulations guide the holding of parades. These rules help government protect public safety and manage the use of public streets. A government that does not carry out these rules fairly and according to law has not acted with due process.

For example, suppose a group named Save Our City asks for a permit to hold a demonstration. The group wants to protest the city's lax pollution control laws. City officials, however, refuse to give the group a permit unless it agrees to hold its demonstration at 6:00 A.M. outside of the city limits—ensuring that few people will see the group's efforts. Save Our City responds by taking the city to court. The group argues that city

POLITICAL PROCESSES *Part of the responsibility of government is to carry out rules fairly and to keep the peace. Government must, however, practice procedural due process in performing these roles.* **How may government officials use their power to restrict people's freedom of speech and assembly?**

officials have unfairly and unreasonably used their authority to restrict the group members' freedom of speech and assembly.

In this case, the court must determine whether or not city officials have unfairly used the law's procedures, perhaps to keep critics of the city's pollution laws from being heard. If the city officials have unfairly administered the law, then they have not acted with procedural due process.

Substantive Due Process The court also may consider whether the city's time, place, and manner regulations are fair and reasonable in the first place. In doing so, the court is applying a second aspect of due process, referred to as **substantive due process**. Applying substantive due process involves considering whether or not a law is fair and reasonable and whether or not it unjustly restricts constitutional freedoms.

Applying substantive due process to the Save Our City case means asking whether government should be involved at all in deciding how groups conduct demonstrations. As noted in Chapter 5, government does have good reasons for establishing time, place, and manner regulations—for example, the management of traffic flow and the protection of public safety. Therefore, the court would likely rule that the law on giving out parade permits has met the standard of substantive due process. Nevertheless, city officials still must observe procedural due process by applying the law fairly and reasonably.

Due Process and the States

Originally, the Fifth Amendment's Due Process Clause and the rest of the Bill of Rights protected people from federal government actions only. The framers assumed that bills of rights in state constitutions would ensure that state governments did not violate people's rights.

Just after the Civil War, however, the Fifth Amendment's protections were extended to state actions by the Fourteenth Amendment. This amendment sought to ensure the rights of freed slaves by granting

them—as well as everyone else born or naturalized in the United States—U.S. citizenship and hence the right of due process. Anticipating that the southern states might refuse to recognize that African Americans had the right to due process, Congress added a provision declaring the states may not "deprive any person of life, liberty, or property, without due process of law."

In the 1925 case of *Gitlow* v. *New York,* the Supreme Court issued the first in a series of rulings clearly stating that the freedoms in the Bill of Rights are protected from the actions of both the federal *and* state governments. The Court used as its justification the Due Process Clause of the Fourteenth Amendment.

Gitlow involved a man who had called for overthrowing the government. The Supreme Court upheld New York State's right to punish the man for breaking a law forbidding people from plotting such action. For the first time, however, the Court also ruled that, in general, the First Amendment does protect a person's right to free speech from being violated by the states. Following *Gitlow,* other Supreme Court rulings firmly established that the states must respect the fundamental freedoms guaranteed by the Bill of Rights.

PUBLIC GOOD *Bailiffs of a superior court in Massachusetts escort a prisoner into a courtroom for his trial.* **How may the exercise of police power restrict some individual liberties?**

American Legal Traditions

You probably recall reading about certain court rulings in which judges helped justify their decisions by citing previous rulings. As noted in Chapter 12, judges often use this body of rulings to make decisions on situations for which no written laws exist. This so-called common law constitutes an important part of the legal systems not only in Great Britain but also in many of its former colonies, including Canada, Australia, and New Zealand. Common law also plays a significant role throughout all of the United States except Louisiana.

Because its early settlers were French, Louisiana's legal system developed from French civil law. The French civil law system, known as the Code Napoleon, developed during the early 1800s. At that time, French emperor Napoleon Bonaparte combined France's civil laws into one code that joined the traditional law of northern France, the Roman-influenced law of southern France, and newer ideas that had emerged during the French Revolution. By replacing France's regional statutes, the Code Napoleon became that country's first national body of law.

In England, common law evolved over centuries, beginning in the 1100s with the monarch's royal courts. Judges and lawyers recorded the cases at first in annual reports and later in ongoing records. New court decisions were then bound by those made previously. The decisions that were cited in new cases soon became known as common, because of their widespread impact. Thus, the English courts are called common-law courts.

Common-law courts were not the only source of justice available to citizens. English citizens also were able to petition the monarch for justice. If citizens felt that they would not receive a fair decision in a common-law court, for example, they might ask the monarch to intervene. He or she often assigned the job of hearing petitions to the lord chancellor, England's highest legal

The use of common law to determine rulings on cases for which no written law exists was adopted by many of Great Britain's former colonies, including the United States.

authority. Eventually, courts of equity were established in the 1300s to hear cases not addressed by common law. These courts, which chancellors administered, added flexibility to the common-law system.

Sometimes the two systems came into conflict, as when a chancellor declared a common-law ruling unfair or inappropriate and refused to enforce it. In an attempt to solve the problem, King James I declared that equity rule was superior to common law. However, equity and common law eventually merged in 1873 to form one legal system.

The system of common law was transported to the English colonies in America by the colonists and later spread to the individual states. Each state (except Louisiana) developed its own version of common law to deal with its own cases. Over time, however, much of what was once common law has been made into statutory law. Common law and equity law, which also came to America with the colonists, began to merge in most legal systems throughout the United States in 1848.

What Do You Think?

1. Imagine that you are a lawyer preparing a court case. Why is knowledge of common law important to your preparation?
2. Should judges always consider previous rulings in deciding a court case? Why or why not?

In short, the due process clause limits the government's **police power**—or its authority to promote and to protect the health, safety, and welfare of the people. This power is exercised primarily by state and local governments.

Exercising police power, such as fighting crime, often restricts some individual liberties. To fight crime, police may, for example—if following proper procedures—enter homes or limit people's freedom by jailing them. To prevent abuse of police power, the Constitution requires government to act within the framework of the Bill of Rights.

Protecting People from Government Intrusion

The Constitution further protects individual liberties by protecting people from government intrusion. The Fourth Amendment guarantees "the right of people to be secure in their persons, houses, papers, and effects, against unreasonable searches and seizures." In other words, government cannot use its police power in ways that unjustly subject citizens to government interference.

PUBLIC GOOD *Police officers may search people's personal possessions, including their vehicles, if they have probable cause to do so.* **Why are police not required to obtain a warrant to search a car?**

Security at Home The Fourth Amendment requires authorities to respect the security of private homes. This means, for example, that police must follow set rules in entering and searching homes and in seizing any contents for use as evidence in a criminal trial. One of these rules states that, except under certain circumstances, police cannot search a home without first obtaining a written order from a judge. This **search warrant** allows police to enter a home or other private property to search for specific items.

Before a judge will issue a search warrant, police must show that they have reasonable grounds, or **probable cause**, for requesting one. If, for example, a police officer sees someone deal drugs and then enter a certain home, or has information from a reliable source that the home contains illegal drugs, that officer has probable cause to request a warrant to search for illegal drugs.

Authorities do sometimes enter a private home without a warrant and seize items as evidence for a criminal case. In such instances, however, judges typically rule that the evidence is tainted, or illegally obtained. Under what is referred to as the **exclusionary rule**, tainted evidence—no matter how strong—is barred from use in court. In the 1961 case *Mapp v. Ohio,* the Supreme Court extended the exclusionary rule to state trials.

Since the early 1970s, however, the Supreme Court has identified some exceptions to the exclusionary rule. Tainted evidence may be used in a trial if, for example, a police officer, acting in "good faith," obtained a search warrant that turns out to be invalid. The Court also has ruled that tainted evidence that could have been legally obtained anyway can be used in court.

In addition, the Court has ruled that police do not need to obtain search warrants in certain cases. For example, police do not need a warrant to search through garbage that people have placed outside their home for trash collection. Police also may seize evidence that is "in plain view" even if it is not listed in the search warrant used to enter the home.

CASE STUDY

Gun Control

CONSTITUTIONAL GOVERNMENT One of the most debated issues of constitutional interpretation involves the Second Amendment, which states that "a well-regulated militia, being necessary to the security of a free state, the right of the people to keep and bear arms, shall not be infringed." Some people believe that the amendment supports Americans' right to own a gun or other firearm to protect themselves and their homes.

Others argue that firearms are dangerous and need to be restricted. About 38,000 Americans are killed by firearms each year, some 1,400 of them accidentally. The solution, many people believe, lies in gun control, or regulations on the ownership of firearms. Gun control supporters believe the Second Amendment's purpose is to allow citizens to bear arms only as part of a "well-regulated militia." The debate over gun control remains heated.

In 1939 the Supreme Court ruled in *United States* v. *Miller* that the federal government could restrict the transportation of certain kinds of firearms, such as sawed-off shotguns and machine guns. In addition, the Court has allowed states to pass some gun control measures.

Several recent federal and state gun control measures have restricted the sale and ownership of firearms. In 1994 the federal government banned the sale of certain kinds of assault weapons. In 1993 Congress passed the fiercely debated Brady gun control law, which requires a five-day waiting period for buying handguns, and gives local authorities time to determine if a buyer has committed a felony and is thus prohibited from owning a firearm. Congress anticipated replacing the waiting period in five years with a computerized database that would allow authorities to check almost instantly if potential gun buyers have criminal records. In June 1997 the Supreme Court struck down the part of the Brady law that required local law enforcement officials to perform these checks, saying that Congress could not force the states to assist with the administration of federal programs.

CONSTITUTIONAL GOVERNMENT *State and federal laws regulate the sale and ownership of firearms.* **How do some people use the Second Amendment to argue that government should not restrict citizens' right to own firearms?**

Personal Security The Fourth Amendment prevents police from conducting unreasonable searches of people and their possessions. The Supreme Court has ruled, for example, that police cannot stop people in public and search them unless the officers involved have reason to think that the suspects are armed or dangerous. On the other hand, the Court has allowed employers to require workers to submit to drug testing, considering it a reasonable way to protect public health and safety.

© 1997 Arnie Levin from The Cartoon Bank. All rights reserved.

"There are indications that little Tommy is being naughty. But not enough for me to authorize a wiretap."

PRINCIPLES OF DEMOCRACY *Protections outlined by the Fourth Amendment limit the way in which government can intrude on individual liberties.* ***What must police do in order to tap a telephone?***

the use of electronic devices known as wiretaps. Are there circumstances under which the use of these devices violates Fourth Amendment rights?

In 1928 the Supreme Court ruled that law enforcement authorities could use wiretaps to listen to private telephone conversations without search warrants. In that case, *Olmstead* v. *United States,* the Court stated that wiretapping was not a form of illegal search and seizure because it did not involve breaking into a private home.

Later, the increased number and sophistication of such devices led the Supreme Court to change direction on this issue. In 1967 the Court ruled that authorities cannot listen to private telephone conversations without first obtaining a warrant. In addition, Congress has passed laws against using electronic devices to listen to private conversations without a warrant.

The Supreme Court has allowed police greater leeway in conducting searches of people's personal possessions—including cars, boats, and other vehicles—than in searching homes. A police officer may, for example, search a car without a warrant if he or she has probable cause to believe it contains illegal drugs or weapons. The Court recognizes that because a car can be driven away, delaying a search until a warrant is obtained might give a suspect the opportunity to destroy or get rid of evidence.

Police also may stop drivers at random to check whether they are intoxicated. The Supreme Court has allowed such checkpoints because it considers their use a reasonable way to protect public safety from the dangers posed by drunk drivers.

Security and Private Communication Fourth Amendment protections have been extended to private communications between people. Listening to private conversations is considered a form of search and seizure. One way that police may "seize" private telephone conversations is through

Student Rights Fewer restrictions apply to authorities searching students or their possessions. In 1985, for example, the Supreme Court ruled that school officials did not need a warrant to search students' possessions. The case of *New Jersey* v. *T.L.O.* involved a 14-year-old New Jersey student who school officials believed had broken school rules on smoking. An official searched the student's purse and found marijuana, along with evidence indicating that she had smoked and sold some of it.

The Supreme Court ruled that school officials had acted properly to guard students' health and safety and to keep order. To conduct searches of students or their possessions the Court said, school officials need only "reasonable" grounds to suspect a student has broken the law or school rules.

Protecting the Right to Privacy

The Constitution does not specifically address the issue of privacy. The courts, however, have determined that the Bill of Rights provides a right of privacy against the government's police power. In

CONSTITUTIONAL GOVERNMENT *Supreme Court justice Louis Brandeis argued that the Court should not allow the government to wiretap people's telephones without a warrant. **What is the current Court ruling on this issue?***

1928 Supreme Court justice Louis Brandeis, writing for the minority, argued that the Court was wrong to allow government to wiretap telephones without a warrant. The framers, Brandeis wrote, "sought to protect Americans in their beliefs, their thoughts, their emotions and their sensations." In doing so, he said, the framers recognized the people's "right to be let alone—the most comprehensive of rights and the right most valued by civilized men."

Some 37 years later, in the *Griswold* v. *Connecticut* case, the Supreme Court agreed with Brandeis's view by ruling that the Constitution does guarantee a right of privacy. The 1965 case involved a state law that prohibited the use and promotion of birth control devices. The Court said that such laws violated a married couple's "zone of privacy created by several fundamental constitutional guarantees."

Some judges and constitutional scholars argue that the right to privacy does not exist because it is not specifically mentioned in the Constitution. These opposing views about the right to privacy have played a leading role in the bitter controversy over abortion. In 1973 the Supreme Court ruled in *Roe* v. *Wade* that laws restricting a woman's freedom to have an abortion in the first three months of pregnancy violate her right to privacy. Many people strongly oppose the Court's ruling in *Roe* and argue that government should ban abortion.

Over time the Court has revisited the abortion issue, and since 1989 has allowed state governments to place certain restrictions on the right to have an abortion. One such restriction prevents unmarried females under the age of 18 from having an abortion without the approval of their parents or a judge.

SECTION 1 — REVIEW

1. Define the following terms: due process, procedural due process, substantive due process, police power, search warrant, probable cause, exclusionary rule.

2. How do procedural and substantive due process affect government in establishing time, place, and manner regulations?

3. How does the Fourth Amendment protect "the right of the people to be secure in their persons, houses, papers, and effects"?

4. How did the 1965 case of *Griswold* v. *Connecticut* affect the right to privacy?

5. **Thinking and Writing Critically**
   Government uses its police power to promote and to protect the health, safety, and welfare of the public. How do schools use rules to achieve these same goals for students? Be sure to include examples of such rules.

6. **Applying** CONSTITUTIONAL GOVERNMENT
   As you have read, the right to privacy is not specifically guaranteed in the Constitution. Do you think that it should be? Can officials search lockers at any time in your school? What sorts of rights to privacy should students have, if any? Explain your answers.

RIGHTS OF THE ACCUSED

Political Dictionary

presentment
Miranda Rule

Objectives

★ How does the Constitution protect the right of *habeas corpus* and protect against bills of attainder and *ex post facto* laws?

★ How do requirements for bringing charges before grand juries protect the rights of people accused of crimes?

★ How does the Fifth Amendment protect against self-incrimination?

As you have learned, the government uses its police power to prevent crime and to arrest people who break the law. Even though these actions are needed to protect the public, the use of police power must not violate the constitutional rights of people who are accused of crimes. Upholding accused people's rights may make it harder at times for government to bring about justice. These rights, however, reflect the framers' desire to protect innocent people from being wrongly convicted of crimes.

Writ of *Habeas Corpus*

The Constitution states that authorities cannot hold a person in jail without showing good reasons for doing so. Specifically, accused people have a right to a writ of *habeas corpus*. As noted in Chapter 5, this writ is a court order that requires police to bring a person accused of a crime to court and to show good reasons for keeping him or her in jail. (*Habeas corpus* is a Latin term meaning "you have the body.") The right to a writ of *habeas corpus* is guaranteed by Article I, Section 9, of the Constitution.

The Constitution allows the federal government to suspend the right to *habeas corpus* only "when in cases of rebellion or invasion the public safety may require it." President Abraham Lincoln believed such a case existed when he suspended the right during the Civil War. Lincoln took it upon himself to suspend *habeas corpus,* even though the Constitution lists that power in Article I, which deals with the powers of Congress. Despite some opposition to Lincoln's action, Congress approved it in an 1863 law. In 1866, however, the Supreme Court ruled in *Ex parte Milligan* that Lincoln and Congress had acted improperly and that neither had the power to suspend *habeas corpus* in areas that were not

Constitutional Protections for Those Accused of Crimes

1. **Writ of *habeas corpus*** Police must appear in court with the accused and show good reason to keep him or her in jail.

2. **Bill of attainder** The government may not pass laws directed at specific individuals.

3. ***Ex post facto* laws** The government may not pass laws that punish people for actions that were legal when they took place.

4. **Grand jury** A person accused of a federal crime must be brought before a panel of citizens who decide if the government has enough evidence to try him or her on formal charges.

5. **Self-incrimination** An accused person cannot be forced to provide evidence to support a criminal charge against himself or herself.

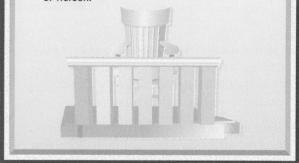

*The Constitution outlines specific protections for people accused of crimes. These protections make it more difficult for the government to wrongly convict innocent people. **Why is it important that accused people be protected against self-incrimination?***

in open rebellion and in which civilian courts still functioned.

Bills of Attainder

As noted in Chapter 5, the Constitution also states in Article I, Sections 9 and 10, that neither Congress nor a state government can pass bills of attainder, or laws that are directed against a specific person. The Supreme Court has ruled that a law can be considered a bill of attainder even if it prescribes a form of punishment other than imprisonment. In the 1946 case *United States* v. *Lovett,* the Court overturned a congressional act that prohibited three specified federal government employees from collecting a salary. The men had been suspected of having political beliefs that many people considered harmful to the United States. The Court ruled that the law punished the men by withholding their salaries even though they had not been found guilty of a crime. The law was thus found to be an unconstitutional bill of attainder.

Ex Post Facto Laws

The Constitution also prohibits authorities from punishing people for actions that were legal at the time they took place. As noted in Chapter 5, the Constitution states in Article I, Sections 9 and 10, that the federal and state governments cannot pass *ex post facto* laws, or laws that apply to actions that took place before those laws were passed. For example, government may not pass a law today that outlaws buying foreign automobiles and then punish people who bought a foreign car yesterday. The prohibition against *ex post facto* laws applies only to laws that may impose punishment or other penalties.

Grand Juries

The Fifth Amendment protects the rights of all people accused of federal crimes by requiring that their case be brought before a grand jury. As noted in Chapter 12, a grand jury is a panel of citizens who decide if the government has enough evidence to try an accused person.

In a grand jury proceeding the attorney for the government presents its case against the accused. If the grand jury agrees that the government has enough evidence to support its case, it may return a "true bill of indictment" that calls for a trial. If the government's evidence does not satisfy the grand jury, the accused person is not sent to trial and can no longer be kept in police custody.

Less often, a grand jury will decide to conduct its own investigation rather than accept evidence from a government attorney. If the grand jury believes its own investigation has found sufficient information to send an accused person to trial, it may issue a **presentment**, or formal report authorizing a trial.

The Fifth Amendment's requirement for a grand jury applies only in federal cases, although some states do have their own grand juries to consider cases against people accused of state crimes. In other state cases, however, no grand jury is convened. Lawyers for the state simply bring formal charges in what is called an information. As noted in Chapter 12, an information is an affidavit, or sworn statement, in which the state's lawyer declares that there is sufficient evidence against the accused to justify trying the case.

Self-Incrimination

The Fifth Amendment also protects against self-incrimination, stating that people accused of crimes cannot be forced to provide evidence against themselves. Thus, accused people may legally refuse to testify at their own trials if such testimony might incriminate them. They also cannot be forced to incriminate themselves when being questioned by law enforcement officials. The 1936 case *Brown* v. *Mississippi,* for example, involved an incident in which police had tortured a suspect to force a confession. The Supreme Court ruling in the case stated that police may not physically force a criminal suspect to confess to a crime. Other cases have established that police may not threaten people or use other methods to force them to incriminate themselves.

The Supreme Court also has ruled that police must inform criminal suspects of their right to refuse to answer questions. This requirement—known as the **Miranda Rule**—stems from the 1966 case *Miranda* v. *Arizona.* The case involved Ernesto Miranda, who, after two hours of police questioning, confessed to kidnapping and raping a woman. The Court ruled that his confession could not be used in a trial because the police had not effectively advised him of his rights to remain silent and to consult with a lawyer. The Court also determined

Miranda Rights

Before asking you any questions, it is my duty to advise you of your rights:

1. You have the right to remain silent.

2. If you choose to speak, anything you say may be used against you in a court of law or other proceeding.

3. You have the right to speak with an attorney before answering any questions, and you may have an attorney present with you during questioning.

4. If you cannot afford an attorney and you want one, an attorney will be provided for you free of charge.

5. Do you understand what I have told you?

6. You may also waive the right to counsel and your right to remain silent, and you may answer any question or make any statement you wish. If you decide to answer questions, you may stop at any time to consult with an attorney.

PUBLIC GOOD *Criminal suspects who are arrested must be informed of their Miranda rights before police may question them.* **Why do you think the Supreme Court believed that suspects should be informed of their right to an attorney?**

that police should have informed Miranda that a lawyer would be provided for him if he could not afford one and that anything he said could be used against him in court.

Today police across the country inform criminal suspects of their "Miranda rights" before questioning them. Suspects, however, may decide to give up these rights and answer police questions. The statements that criminal suspects then freely make, even confessions, may be used against them in court.

Critics of the Miranda Rule have argued that the requirement ties the hands of police officers by making it harder for them to carry out their duties. These critics also argue that some people who are guilty of crimes are released from jail simply because a police officer did not properly inform the accused person of his or her rights to silence and to a lawyer.

Supporters of the Miranda Rule, however, say that it protects innocent people from being tricked or brutally forced into confessing to crimes they did not commit. Although over time the Supreme Court has allowed some exceptions to the Miranda Rule, the Court has generally supported the principle that accused people cannot be guaranteed their rights without being informed of them by police.

Note that protections against self-incrimination do not allow criminal suspects to refuse to be fingerprinted and photographed, to participate in a police lineup, or to submit to blood and other tests commonly used in an investigation. These are all considered proper parts of the evidence-gathering process.

SECTION 2 — REVIEW

1. Define the following terms: presentment, Miranda Rule.

2. What does the right of *habeas corpus* protect? How do prohibitions against bills of attainder and *ex post facto* laws help ensure that government passes fair laws?

3. What must the government prove when taking a case before a grand jury?

4. What are the Miranda rights of people accused of crimes in the United States? What methods of gathering evidence do not violate the constitutional protection against self-incrimination?

5. Thinking and Writing Critically
You may have heard of accused people who "plead the Fifth." This phrase indicates that they are using their Fifth Amendment right to refuse to respond to questions whose answers might incriminate them. Why should people not assume that pleading the Fifth is an admission of guilt?

6. Applying **CONSTITUTIONAL GOVERNMENT**
Examine the chart above that lists the Miranda rights of the accused. Why is it important that certain rights be extended to people accused of crimes?

ENSURING FAIR TRIALS AND PUNISHMENTS

Political Dictionary

change of venue
bench trial
double jeopardy

Objectives

★ Which amendments of the Bill of Rights help guarantee the right to a fair trial?

★ In what ways does the Bill of Rights protect convicted criminals from excessive punishments?

As noted in Section 2, the Constitution requires government to respect the rights of the accused during investigations. Similarly, government must respect a person's right to a fair trial and must act fairly when punishing people convicted of crimes.

The Right to a Fair Trial

What provisions of the Constitution regarding a fair trial must the government respect? The Fifth, Sixth, Seventh, and Eighth Amendments together establish the following: the right to a speedy and public trial, the right to trial by jury, the right to an adequate defense, and restrictions on trying a person twice for the same crime.

Speedy Trial The Sixth Amendment guarantees the right to a speedy trial. This means that the period of time between the filing of formal charges and the start of a trial must be reasonable. Starting a trial as soon as possible keeps an accused person who cannot or will not post bail from being held in jail for an unnecessarily long period of time. Speedy trials also reduce the

chance that evidence may be lost and that witnesses may forget what they saw or heard.

Sometimes long delays are unavoidable, however. In some cases the accused person's attorney may ask for a delay to prepare a more thorough defense. Sometimes a court already has a full docket, or schedule, which delays starting a trial.

As noted in Chapter 12, judges may allow an accused person to be released on bail while awaiting trial, and the Eighth Amendment keeps judges from setting excessive bails. Defining *excessive* is difficult. In general, the courts have said that an excessive bail is one greater than is necessary to assure the appearance of the accused person in court. After the trial begins, the bail money is returned.

Public Trial The Sixth Amendment also guarantees the right to a public trial. Public trials help prevent abuses of the law by allowing the public to witness, or check on, the proceedings. Even though judges may keep some people out of the courtroom to maintain order and to ensure that witnesses and the jury are not influenced unfairly, they may not keep members of the general public from attending the trial.

CONSTITUTIONAL GOVERNMENT *In accordance with the protections specified in the Sixth Amendment, members of the general public are allowed to attend trials.* **How do public trials help prevent abuses of the law?**

Public trials also function as a kind of laboratory for citizens to see how the justice system works. Indeed, much of the media use this argument to justify their presence in the courtroom.

A current debate involving the media centers on whether or not the courts should allow trials to be televised. Federal court proceedings are not televised, but television cameras are allowed in courtrooms in 47 states. One of the most famous televised trials took place in 1995, when a California jury found former football star O. J. Simpson not guilty of murder charges. Millions of people watched the trial on cable and broadcast television.

The extensive and sensational media coverage of the Simpson trial spurred the debate over television cameras in the courtroom. Journalists argued that the public had a right to view the court proceedings. Opponents argued that allowing the media into the courtroom enabled reporters to sensationalize the case and influenced the conduct of the trial. To prevent the trial's massive media coverage from influencing members of the jury, the judge ordered that jury members be sequestered in a hotel when they were not in the courtroom. For these reasons, many people argued that television cameras should be kept out of courtrooms in the future.

PUBLIC GOOD *News media outside the Los Angeles courthouse await the reading of the verdict at the O. J. Simpson trial.* **How did the media coverage of the Simpson trial change the way that many people feel about having television cameras in a courtroom?**

Comparing ····▶ Governments

The Right to a Speedy Trial

Imagine spending eight long months in prison while waiting to stand trial for a crime you did not commit. Fortunately, the U.S. Constitution is designed to protect people from such an ordeal. In France, however, where the right to a speedy trial is not constitutionally guaranteed, prisoners endure an average of nearly eight months behind bars while awaiting trial.

For serious crimes, officials can hold a suspect for an unlimited period if he or she is considered a flight risk or a threat of some kind. With 40 percent of its 55,000 prisoners currently awaiting trial, France has one of the highest rates of pretrial imprisonment in Europe.

Trial by Jury As you have learned, the Constitution prevents the government from finding someone guilty of a crime without due process of law. One element of due process is the right to a trial by an impartial jury. The Sixth Amendment and Seventh Amendment—as well as Article III, Section 2, of the Constitution—all guarantee the right to a trial by jury.

As noted in Chapter 12, a trial jury, or petit jury, usually is made up of 12 people. The trial must be held in the district in which the crime was committed, and the panel of jurors must represent a fair cross-section of the community. To make sure that juries are representative, jurors are chosen at random from lists of registered voters or other such official lists. The Supreme Court has ruled that people cannot be kept off a jury based on their race, sex, economic status, national origin, or religion.

Accused people who believe that they cannot receive a fair trial in the community where the crime took place may ask for a **change of venue**, or that their trial be moved to another location. For example, a trial might be moved if media coverage of the crime has biased potential local jurors against the defendant. Such an instance occurred with the trial of Timothy McVeigh, who was accused of bombing a government building in

Oklahoma City. McVeigh's trial was moved to Denver, Colorado.

Federal cases must be decided by unanimous verdicts. A few states, however, allow most criminal cases to be decided by less than a unanimous vote of jurors. In cases involving disputes over civil laws, many states allow jurors to reach a verdict with a less-than-unanimous vote, usually two thirds or three fourths.

An accused person may give up the right to a trial by jury in favor of a **bench trial**, in which a judge decides the case. Judges, however, may refuse to grant requests for a bench trial.

CONSTITUTIONAL GOVERNMENT *People accused of a crime have the right to be represented by a lawyer.* **What did the Supreme Court say in** Gideon v. Wainwright *about this right?*

Adequate Defense The Sixth Amendment guarantees defendants the right to an adequate defense. This means that people accused of crimes have the right to

★ be informed of the charges against them,
★ question witnesses against them in court,
★ present their own witnesses in court, and
★ be represented by counsel—a lawyer.

In 1932 the Supreme Court ruled that the last right listed—the right to counsel—was so critical that in cases involving capital offenses, or crimes punishable by death, the government must appoint lawyers for people who cannot afford them. The Court said that without a lawyer, even an innocent person "faces the danger of conviction because he does not know how to establish his innocence." In 1938 the Supreme Court ruled that in all federal cases, the government must provide a lawyer for people who cannot afford to hire one.

Then, in the 1963 case *Gideon* v. *Wainwright,* the Supreme Court issued a landmark ruling regarding the right to counsel in state courts. The case involved a man named Clarence Gideon, who had been convicted in a Florida court of breaking into a pool hall with the intent to commit a misdemeanor. At his trial, Gideon claimed that he was too poor to afford an attorney and requested that one be provided. The judge refused, and Gideon was convicted.

While serving a five-year sentence in a Florida state prison, Gideon mailed a petition about his case, written on borrowed paper, to the Supreme Court. The Supreme Court agreed to hear his case, and there Gideon argued that the state of Florida had violated his Sixth Amendment right to counsel by not providing him with a lawyer.

The Supreme Court agreed. Speaking for the Court, Justice Hugo Black wrote that "any person [hauled] into court, who is too poor to hire a lawyer, cannot be assured a fair trial unless counsel is provided for him. This seems to us to be an obvious truth." The Court ruled that in federal and state criminal cases involving serious crimes, the court must appoint a lawyer to represent an accused person who cannot afford one. Gideon later was found not guilty in a new trial in which he was represented by a state-appointed lawyer.

In 1972 the Supreme Court extended the right to counsel even further. It ruled that an accused person cannot be sent to jail for any offense unless he or she has either been represented by counsel or voluntarily given up that right. This ruling covers all cases that could involve imprisonment, no matter how minor the crime.

Double Jeopardy The Fifth Amendment provides protection against **double jeopardy**, or

Court Reporter

No television courtroom drama would be complete without the prominently placed court reporter, whose fast-paced typing provides a constant accompaniment to the court proceedings. In real life as well, the court reporter—like the judge and jury—is a standard fixture in the U.S. courtroom. The job of the court reporter, or court stenographer, is to record the court's proceedings word for word, usually using abbreviations and other shorthand techniques. As the court reporter types, the steno machine—which allows words to be typed with only one stroke rather than several—spits out a steady stream of symbol-covered paper that resembles cash register tape.

By the end of the much-publicized O. J. Simpson trial, two court reporters—now almost celebrities as well—typed an estimated 3 million words, or 30,000 pages, of court transcripts. Today's court reporters take advantage of the latest technology. Keyboards are often linked to a computer system that gives judges and lawyers an immediate transcript of the proceedings, and allows the court reporter to communicate with them without interrupting the trial.

Court reporters use abbreviations and other shorthand techniques to record court proceedings.

Simpson-trial court reporter Christine Olson became interested in court reporting as a high school senior. "I could type 100 words a minute on a manual typewriter," she says with pride. According to Olson, studying piano as a child helped give her the dexterity needed to become a master of the keyboard.

Those interested in a court-reporting career should investigate degree programs offered at business colleges or community colleges. While an interest in law might make the job more appealing, manual dexterity and knowing how to type are essential.

---

being tried more than once for the same crime. If a person is found not guilty of a crime in a state court, for example, the state cannot put him or her on trial again for the same crime. Similarly, if the person is found guilty, the state may not put him or her on trial again in order to win a harsher punishment.

Double jeopardy does not include, however, situations in which a person breaks both a state and a federal law with the same act. This might happen, for example, in cases involving federal and state laws made to control the possession and use of illegal drugs. In addition, if a person breaks several state or several federal laws when committing a crime, he or she may be tried separately on each charge. For example, a person who breaks

into a home to steal a computer and then sets fire to the house may be tried separately for illegally entering the home, for stealing the computer, and for setting fire to the house.

Protections against double jeopardy also do not apply to cases in which a jury fails to deliver a verdict in the first trial. A person may be tried again in a second trial that is considered a continuation of the first trial.

Providing for Fair Punishment

What happens to people who have been found guilty of crimes in fair trials? What protections does the Bill of Rights provide for convicted people? The Eighth Amendment protects people convicted of crimes from "cruel and unusual punishment." Defining what is cruel and unusual, however, is difficult. The debate over the death penalty, for instance, has been particularly fierce.

Cruel and Unusual Punishment Deciding which punishments are cruel and unusual is difficult for many reasons. Different people have varying opinions about what is cruel. Also, societal standards change over time. For example, do you think that whipping a convicted criminal is cruel? The Massachusetts officials who put such punishments into law during the 1700s certainly believed at the time that they were appropriate. Proposing such punishments today, however, likely would prompt an outcry, for most present-day Americans would consider them unusually harsh.

Just as the Supreme Court has established guidelines for dealing with other civil liberties issues, it has also set guidelines for applying the Eighth Amendment's prohibition against cruel and unusual punishment. In the 1910 case *Weems* v. *United States,* for example, the Court ruled that a Coast Guard officer had been punished too harshly for stealing money. Using an old law, a lower court had sentenced the officer to 15 years of hard labor in chains and fined him nearly seven times the amount of money he had stolen.

In overturning the sailor's punishment, the Supreme Court argued that societal standards are critical in deciding what is cruel and unusual. The Eighth Amendment, the Court said, "is not fastened to the absolute but may acquire meaning as public opinion becomes enlightened by humane justice."

Federal courts also have applied the Eighth Amendment in cases involving living conditions and overcrowding in prisons. In 1969, for example, a federal court found that parts of the Arkansas prison system violated the Eighth Amendment because of poor living conditions, including inadequate clothing and food for prisoners. In addition, during the early 1990s the federal courts oversaw more than 80 percent of federal prisons, in order to ensure that prisons met adequate standards for cell space, food, and clothing.

Capital Punishment As noted in Chapter 12, one of the most controversial issues involving the Eighth Amendment is capital punishment, or the

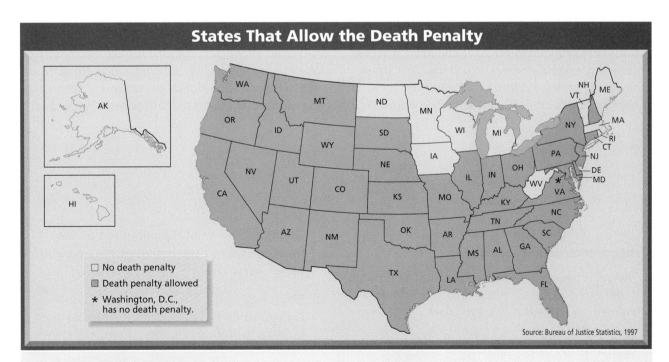

States That Allow the Death Penalty

☐ No death penalty
■ Death penalty allowed
★ Washington, D.C., has no death penalty.

Source: Bureau of Justice Statistics, 1997

*Since 1976 the Supreme Court has approved several laws that allow capital punishment. **What 1972 Supreme Court case ruled that capital punishment laws across the country violated the Eighth Amendment?***

death penalty. The Supreme Court has considered cases involving the death penalty since the 1800s. In the 1890 case *In re Kemmler,* for example, the Court ruled that the death penalty was not cruel and unusual punishment.

In general, until the early 1970s the Supreme Court refused to find any law unconstitutional that allowed government to hand out death sentences to people convicted of serious crimes. In the 1972 case *Furman* v. *Georgia,* however, a sharply divided Court ruled that the capital punishment laws enforced by states across the country violated the Eighth Amendment. In that case, several justices said that many death penalty decisions were influenced by racism and other factors that made such punishments inconsistent—and thus unfair—in their application.

Over the next few years, states changed their capital punishment laws to address the Supreme Court's concerns. In 1976 in *Gregg* v. *Georgia,* the Supreme Court ruled in favor of a new Georgia law allowing the death penalty. The law called for a two-step process in cases involving capital punishment. First, a jury decides whether the accused person is guilty or innocent. If the jury finds the

PRINCIPLES OF DEMOCRACY *Florida attorney general Robert Shevin argued in* Profitt v. Florida *that the death penalty may prevent some criminal behavior.* **What 1890s Supreme Court decision ruled that some forms of the death penalty were not cruel and unusual punishment?**

accused person guilty, it then decides whether the death penalty should be imposed. The jury—or in a bench trial, the judge—also must consider whether any other circumstances involved in the case make the death penalty an inappropriate punishment. In addition, the state's highest court automatically reviews each death penalty case.

Since 1976 the Supreme Court has approved other laws allowing capital punishment. In addition, new state and federal laws passed in 1994 increased the number of crimes that are punishable by death.

SECTION 3 — **REVIEW**

1. Define the following terms: change of venue, bench trial, double jeopardy.

2. Why is a speedy and public trial vital to protecting the rights of accused people? What are other characteristics of a fair trial?

3. Why is defining "cruel and unusual punishment" difficult? How has the Supreme Court suggested that cruel and unusual be defined?

4. Why did the Supreme Court rule against the death penalty in 1972? How did the state of

Georgia's new capital punishment process meet the Court's requirements for a constitutional law allowing the death penalty?

5. **Thinking and Writing Critically** Do you think the death penalty is cruel and unusual punishment? Why or why not?

6. **Applying** **CONSTITUTIONAL GOVERNMENT** Conduct an Internet search for information on the legal process of a country of your choice. Briefly outline the information.

 **CHAPTER 14** — # SUMMARY

SECTION 1 The First Amendment secures many fundamental freedoms, although additional individual liberties are protected by other constitutional amendments as well. For example, the Fifth Amendment protects people's right to due process of law. Courts have broken due process into two parts—procedural and substantive due process—to use in ensuring that government laws are fair and reasonable and that they are applied according to set procedures and as the Constitution prescribes.

Originally, the Fifth Amendment's Due Process Clause and the rest of the Bill of Rights protected the people from federal government actions only. However, the Fourteenth Amendment to the Constitution extended most Bill of Rights protections to state actions.

The Fourth Amendment requires authorities to protect individuals against governmental intrusion. The Bill of Rights also has been interpreted to protect people's right to privacy, although this interpretation has been controversial.

SECTION 2 People accused of crimes also have rights that are protected by the Constitution. Accused people have the right to a writ of *habeas corpus,* a court order that requires police to bring a person accused of a crime to court and to show good reasons to keep him or her in jail. People also are protected from bills of attainder, laws that punish people without a trial, and *ex post facto* laws, which punish people for actions that were legal at the time they were committed.

In addition, the Constitution requires that all people accused of federal crimes be brought before a grand jury. A grand jury protects the rights of accused people by forcing government to show that it has enough evidence to support its case against them.

The Constitution also protects people from self-incrimination and from unfair questioning by police. The Miranda Rule states that the police cannot question suspects without first informing them of their rights to remain silent and to consult with a lawyer.

SECTION 3 Government must also respect people's right to both a fair and public trial by jury and an adequate defense. The right to a fair trial is established in the Fifth, Sixth, Seventh, and Eighth Amendments, which together establish the right to a speedy and public trial, the right to trial by jury, the right to an adequate defense, and restrictions on trying a person twice for the same crime.

The Constitution also provides certain protections for people who have been found guilty of crimes in fair trials. The Eighth Amendment protects people convicted of crimes from "cruel and unusual punishment." Defining cruel and unusual is difficult, however.

The issue of the death penalty has been controversial for many years. The Supreme Court has considered cases involving the death penalty since the 1800s. In general, until the 1970s the Supreme Court refused to rule that laws allowing government to put people to death were unconstitutional. However, in 1972 a sharply divided Court ruled against the death penalty as it was then being instituted in the states. In 1976, however, the Court upheld a new Georgia death penalty law. Since that year, the Supreme Court has approved other laws that allow capital punishment.

Government Notebook

Review what you wrote in your Government Notebook at the beginning of the chapter about searches by police and school officials. Now that you have studied this chapter, how would you revise your answers? Record your answer in your Notebook.

REVIEWING CONCEPTS

1. How does the writ of *habeas corpus* protect the rights of the accused? Why does the Constitution prohibit bills of attainder and *ex post facto* laws?

2. What is capital punishment? How has the Supreme Court applied the Eighth Amendment to cases involving capital punishment?

3. What is the Miranda Rule? In what way does this rule protect people's right not to incriminate themselves?

4. What is the difference between procedural due process and substantive due process? What role does due process play in protecting the security and privacy of the people?

5. What elements of a fair trial are protected by the Bill of Rights?

6. What role does a grand jury play in protecting the rights of the accused?

THINKING AND WRITING CRITICALLY

1. **CONSTITUTIONAL GOVERNMENT** Imagine that you have been asked to speak to high school students in a country whose government does not respect the rights to privacy and security. Write a short speech explaining the benefits of protecting these rights.

2. **CONSTITUTIONAL GOVERNMENT** One of the ways government uses its police power is by setting a minimum legal age for consuming alcoholic beverages. How do such minimum-age laws protect the health, safety, morals, and welfare of children and young adults? What other laws does government use to protect children and young adults?

3. **PRINCIPLES OF DEMOCRACY** What do you think would happen if the government were allowed to pass *ex post facto* laws? How might such power allow government to punish people unfairly?

4. **PUBLIC GOOD** Create a chart with two columns. In one column, list the rights of an accused person. In the other column, explain what might happen if each right listed in the first column were ignored in a particular trial. Then write a short paragraph explaining why respecting these rights promotes the public good.

CITIZENSHIP IN YOUR COMMUNITY

Working with a partner, research and write a newspaper article on the process in your community that a person accused of a crime undergoes. Talk with a police officer, lawyer, or judge about what happens when a person is arrested and charged with stealing a car or destroying public property, for example. Your article should explain where a suspect is taken after arrest, where he or she is held in jail, where and when a grand jury meets to consider an indictment, where and how soon after indictment a trial takes place, and other information important to the case.

INDIVIDUAL PORTFOLIO PROJECT

Create a pamphlet about due process that private clubs might use in developing rules for their members. The pamphlet should include explanations of procedural and substantive due process as well as suggest policies that clubs might use to ensure that their official actions follow due process. One policy, for example, might forbid a club from holding secret trials of members accused of breaking a rule.

PRACTICING SKILLS: DISTINGUISHING FACT FROM OPINION

One key to evaluating what you see and hear is the ability to distinguish between fact and opinion. A fact is something that can be proved true, and an opinion is a personal belief about what is true. Read the statement below and answer the questions that follow.

> *The Fourteenth Amendment was designed to keep state governments from limiting the rights of former slaves after the Civil War. It is my belief that the Supreme Court has used the Due Process Clause and the Equal Protection Clause to rule improperly on laws made by state and federal governments.*

1. Is the second sentence a statement of fact or opinion?
2. What descriptive words in the passage signal that the writer is expressing a fact or an opinion?
3. If you knew nothing about the Supreme Court, how might this description influence your opinion of it?

THE INTERNET: LEARNING ONLINE

Conduct an Internet search for information about Supreme Court cases involving due process and the rights of the accused. You might use search words such as *Gideon* v. *Wainwright*, *Miranda* v. *Arizona*, and *Brown* v. *Mississippi.* Then create an Internet Docket Sheet that lists these cases, summarizes their significance, and provides Internet locations for finding information about them.

ANALYZING PRIMARY SOURCES

"EQUALITY IN AMERICA"

In 1792 Joel Barlow, a scholar of European political theory, wrote an essay on his views of government responsibility. In his essay he discusses the principles of equality and justice upon which the U.S. government was built. The following excerpt from his essay describes government's responsibility regarding laws. Read the excerpt and answer the questions that follow.

> *A method of communicating instruction to every member of society is not difficult to discover, and would not be expensive in practice. The government generally establishes ministers of justice in every part of the dominion [country]. The first object of these ministers ought to be to see that every person is well instructed in his duties and in his rights; that he is rendered [made] perfectly acquainted with every law, . . . in case he should deem [consider] it unjust; that he is taught to feel the cares and interests of an active citizen, to consider himself as a real member of the state, know that the government is his own, that the society is his friend, and that the officers of the state are the servants of the people. A person possessing these ideas will never violate the law, unless it be from necessity; and such necessity is to be prevented by means which are equally obvious. . . .*
>
> *It is not enough that the laws be rendered familiar to the people; but the tribunals [courts of justice] ought to be near at hand, easy of access, and equally open to the poor as to the rich. The means of coming at justice should be cheap, expeditious [quick and efficient], and certain; the mode of process should be simple and perfectly intelligible to the meanest [lowest] capacity, unclouded with mysteries and unperplexed [not confused] with forms. In short, justice should familiarize itself as the well-known friend of every man; and the consequence seems natural, that every man would be a friend to justice.*

1. What is the first task of a minister of justice? What obstacles might the government face in trying to accomplish this objective?

2. Do you agree that a "person possessing these ideas will never violate the law, unless it be from necessity"? Explain your answer.

3. What does Barlow say should be part of the country's "means of coming at justice"?

CHAPTER 15

PROTECTING CIVIL RIGHTS

Most Americans or their ancestors came to this country from other lands. Many came in search of freedom and opportunity. Others, for whom freedom and opportunity remained distant dreams, were enslaved and then brought to these shores by force. No matter how they or their ancestors came, all have made invaluable contributions to U.S. society. The result is a country with a rich diversity of cultures and talents.

Unfortunately, however, not all Americans have enjoyed equal opportunity or experienced equal justice. In fact, many of the diverse groups of people in the United States have experienced significant challenges. For many, the struggle to win equality is highlighted by the civil rights movement of the 1950s and 1960s. Efforts continue today to fulfill the promise of equal opportunity for everyone in the United States. These efforts are necessary because securing the rights and freedoms guaranteed to everyone by the Constitution is vital to promoting the public good.

Government Notebook

How should government work to prevent discrimination in the United States? Record your answer in your Government Notebook.

SECTION 1

CITIZENSHIP AND IMMIGRATION

Political Dictionary

jus sanguinis
jus soli
naturalization
denaturalization
expatriation

Objectives

★ In what two ways may a person become a U.S. citizen by birth?
★ How does an immigrant become a U.S. citizen?
★ How can a person lose U.S. citizenship?

As noted in Chapter 13, the Constitution guarantees certain fundamental freedoms to all people in this country. Becoming a full participant in the U.S. democratic system, however, requires citizenship. Only citizens, for example, may vote, hold elected office, and serve on juries. The Constitution and Congress have established the ways people may become U.S. citizens and the ways their citizenship may be lost.

Becoming a U.S. Citizen

The framers did not define citizenship in the Constitution. Rather, they assumed that each state would establish rules for becoming state citizens and that those people would be considered U.S. citizens.

Today, however, a person can become a U.S. citizen in only three ways. In two of these, citizenship is determined by birth. The third involves a legal process that is overseen by the U.S. Department of Justice.

By Birth Most Americans become citizens by birth. People can become citizens by birth in two

ways: by being born to U.S. citizens or by being born in the United States or in a U.S. territory.

Congress has long allowed a person born in a foreign country to become a U.S. citizen if at least one of his or her parents is a U.S. citizen. This principle of citizenship by parentage is known as ***jus sanguinis*** (YOOS SAHNG-gwuh-nuhs), a Latin phrase meaning "law of the blood."

A child born in a foreign country whose parents are both U.S. citizens gains citizenship only if one of the parents has resided at some point in the United States or in a U.S. territory. A child who has one parent who is a U.S. citizen and one who is a citizen of another country becomes a citizen only if the parent who is a U.S. citizen has lived in the United States or in a U.S. territory for at least five years. Two of the five must have been after the parent was 14 years old. In addition, the child can only maintain citizenship by living in the United States for two continuous years sometime between his or her fourteenth and twenty-eighth birthdays.

A second way a person can become a citizen is by being born in the United States or in a U.S. territory. This principle of citizenship by birthplace is called ***jus soli*** (YOOS soh-LEE), a Latin phrase meaning "law of the soil." The principle was set into law by the Fourteenth Amendment, which was ratified in 1868 and made freed slaves U.S. citizens. The Fourteenth Amendment states that "all persons born . . . in the United States . . . are citizens of the United States and of the State wherein they reside."

What about children born in this country whose parents are citizens of a foreign country? Are they

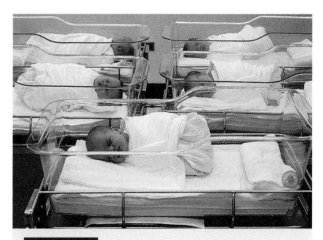

CITIZENSHIP *People can become citizens by being born in the United States or in a U.S. territory.* ***In what other way may people become citizens by birth?***

U.S. citizens? In most cases they are, but only if their parents were under the authority of the United States at the time the children were born. A child born in the United States to parents officially representing a foreign country, for example, is not given citizenship.

Through Naturalization The third way to gain citizenship is through **naturalization**, a legal process by which immigrants become citizens. The naturalization method of becoming a citizen is authorized by the Fourteenth Amendment. Congress, however, passes the laws that outline the naturalization process.

The first part of the naturalization process usually involves entering the United States legally. To do so, foreigners must prove that they can support themselves financially and that they can read and write. They also must prove they do not have certain diseases, mental illnesses, a drug addiction, or a criminal past. Several other restrictions also bar people from entering the United States. One, for example, bars the entry of anarchists, or people who favor the violent overthrow of the government.

Generally, only aliens admitted as permanent residents may become U.S. citizens. Thus foreign visitors, people studying here from abroad, and others who do not plan to live out their lives in the United States do not receive citizenship. Although they are not required to do so, aliens may file a citizenship application and a "declaration of intention." A declaration of intention states that the applicant is over 18 years of age, is planning to give up citizenship in another country, and plans to become a U.S. citizen. Children under 16 automatically become citizens when both of their parents' naturalization has been officially completed. When only one parent has been naturalized, a petition may be filed for citizenship of the child as long as he or she is under 18 and lives with the naturalized parent.

After entering the country legally, an alien can complete the naturalization process only if he or she

★ has been a lawful resident of this country continuously for at least five years (three years if married to a U.S. citizen) and has been physically present in the country for at least half of this period;
★ is at least 18 years old;
★ completes a citizenship application;
★ is able to speak, read, and write English;

★ demonstrates good moral character, belief in the principles of the Constitution, and knowledge of U.S. history and government;
★ supports the order and happiness of the United States; and
★ takes an oath of allegiance to the United States at a swearing-in ceremony.

The U.S. government has occasionally given citizenship to a group of people all at once in a process called collective naturalization. The

How an Alien Becomes a Citizen

PETITION FOR NATURALIZATION

After an alien has lived in the United States at least five years (or three years if married to a U.S. citizen), he or she files an application called a petition for naturalization.

EXAMINATION

A naturalization examiner conducts an examination in which the applicant must show that he or she is a person of good moral character who believes in the principles of the Constitution and supports the order and happiness of the United States. The applicant also must prove that he or she can read, write, and speak English and is knowledgeable about the history and government of the United States. Examinations may be given at a private, designated testing center or at the interview by the immigration examiner.

FINAL HEARING

If the applicant meets all of the qualifications, he or she is granted citizenship at a final hearing. There, the alien swears an oath of allegiance and is given a certificate of naturalization.

*Someone who plans to become a U.S. citizen must go through a lengthy naturalization process. **How many years must someone reside in the United States before he or she can petition for naturalization?***

Constitution's Fourteenth Amendment, for example, collectively naturalized freed slaves and other African Americans. The most common reason for collective naturalization, however, is the acquisition of new territory. When Texas joined the nation in 1845, for example, Congress declared Texas residents naturalized U.S. citizens.

Losing Citizenship

The involuntary loss of U.S. citizenship has occurred only rarely. States may not take away someone's citizenship, though they may restrict some of the rights of a person convicted of a serious crime, usually a felony. A state may, for example, take away a felon's right to vote.

The Supreme Court has ruled that in most cases, the federal government also may not take away someone's citizenship. One Court decision, for example, declared that the federal government may not take away the citizenship of someone who deserts from the military in wartime. The removal of someone's citizenship for desertion, stated the Court, breaks the Constitution's prohibition against cruel and unusual punishment.

The Supreme Court also has limited the federal government's ability to take away citizenship in other situations. Citizens cannot lose their citizenship just by illegally avoiding military service during wartime, nor can naturalized citizens do so simply by returning to their original countries for a few years. Even voting in foreign elections does not automatically cause a loss of citizenship.

PRINCIPLES OF DEMOCRACY *U.S. citizens may vote in elections in a foreign country, such as Nigeria, without endangering their U.S. citizenship.* **What is it called when an individual voluntarily gives up his or her citizenship?**

A court may, however, take away the citizenship of a naturalized citizen who can be shown to have become a U.S. citizen by fraud. A person who lies, for example, about his or her background or provides other false information during the naturalization process may undergo **denaturalization**, or loss of citizenship.

Every citizen has the right to renounce, or give up voluntarily, his or her citizenship, an act known as **expatriation**. A person may give up his or her citizenship in several ways, such as by being naturalized as a citizen of or by pledging allegiance to another country.

SECTION 1 — **REVIEW**

1. Define the following terms: *jus sanguinis, jus soli,* naturalization, denaturalization, expatriation.

2. Are children born to foreign officials in the United States automatically U.S. citizens? How may people become citizens by birth?

3. Why does the Supreme Court severely limit the federal government's ability to take away a person's citizenship?

4. What are some of the ways a person may give up citizenship voluntarily? When may the courts take away the citizenship of a naturalized citizen?

5. **Thinking and Writing Critically**
   What are the requirements for naturalization? Why do you think the U.S. government has such requirements?

6. **Applying** CITIZENSHIP
   Conduct an Internet search for information on the Immigration and Naturalization Service. Make a list of the information you find.

SECTION 2

DIVERSITY AND EQUAL PROTECTION

Political Dictionary

illegal alien
deportation
amnesty
ethnic group
prejudice
discrimination

Objectives

★ How has U.S. immigration policy changed over time?

★ In what ways is the United States an ethnically diverse nation?

★ What are the benefits and challenges of diversity in the United States?

At various times, concern over the number of newcomers arriving in this country has led to efforts to restrict immigration. The diversity brought by immigration has benefited U.S. society in numerous ways. On the other hand, diversity has presented significant challenges, including prejudice and discrimination.

Immigration Policies

You or your ancestors probably immigrated to this country under certain rules. These rules have changed greatly over time, however, with varying limits on the number of foreigners who may come to the United States to live.

Unrestricted Immigration For much of colonial and early U.S. history, there were few immigration rules. Indeed, before the late 1800s anyone who wanted to come to the United States could do so with few or no restrictions.

Why did people come? Throughout the 1800s many came for the land available in the country's vast interior and for jobs in rapidly growing U.S. industries. In fact, so many immigrants arrived during this period that by 1890 they made up nearly 15 percent of the U.S. population.

Over time, tensions developed between immigrants and people already living in the United States. These tensions were caused partly by competition for jobs between immigrant and native-born workers. Differences in cultural traditions, beliefs, and ways of life often caused conflict as well.

Irish immigrants, for example, faced hostility from native-born citizens as well as from other immigrants. The majority of Irish immigrants were Roman Catholics, while most other people in the United States were Protestants. In addition, Irish communities often kept themselves apart by operating their own hospitals, orphanages, and schools. As a result, some native-born citizens feared that Irish immigrants would not become part of U.S. society. Others feared that immigrants might lack respect for the rule of law and threaten the U.S. political system.

Immigration Restrictions Hostility toward immigrants led Congress over time to restrict

CITIZENSHIP *During the 1800s, people from around the world could come to the United States with few immigration restrictions.* **When did the government first start placing restrictions on immigration from certain countries?**

Immigration Officer

It is estimated that around 5 million foreign citizens currently live in the United States illegally. In addition, hundreds of thousands of other immigrants legally enter the country each year. One government agency—the Immigration and Naturalization Service (INS)—is responsible for sorting out these groups, enforcing immigration laws, and naturalizing new citizens. The INS, part of the U.S. Department of Justice, employs more than 20,000 people in about 40 field offices in the United States and abroad.

To meet the many demands facing the agency, INS immigration officers work in a wide variety of fields. Some of the agency's many job titles include border patrol agent, investigations agent, immigration inspector, deportation officer, and computer specialist.

Tasks for each of these jobs may vary a great deal. Border patrol agents, for example, guard about 8,000 miles of international borders to prevent foreigners from entering the country illegally. Plainclothes special agents track down illegal immigrants involved in criminal activity in the United States. Other INS tasks involve serving the many legal immigrants who enter the United States each year. Immigration officers review citizenship applications, administer citizenship tests, process residency applications, and conduct naturalization interviews. In 1995 alone the United States admitted more than 700,000

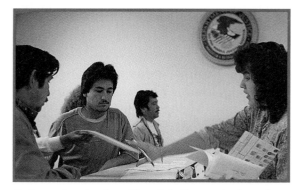

Each year, immigration officers help thousands of people file applications for citizenship. The INS is also responsible for enforcing immigration laws.

immigrants and naturalized 500,000 others as new citizens.

One difficulty with handling so many requests is that the system often gets backed up, causing applicants to feel lost or ignored. In response to paperwork problems, INS directors, such as Detroit District director Carol Jenifer, have worked to speed up the naturalization process and improve communication with immigrant organizations.

Along with communication skills, technical training is very helpful for immigration officers. The INS employs college graduates with a wide variety of degrees, but computer science and criminal justice majors are particularly valued. Fluency in Spanish is also useful. INS commissioner Doris Meissner notes that the INS is "working smarter and applying technology" to help meet the challenges of the future.

immigration. In 1882 Congress passed an act that imposed a tax on those who entered the country and denied entry for convicted criminals, paupers, and people with mental illnesses. Some 20 years later, Congress also banned anarchists from entering the United States.

Also in 1882, Congress for the first time banned all immigration from a particular country—in this case, China. Congress was moved to action partly by native-born workers in California who claimed that the low wages paid to Chinese workers lowered wages for everyone else. For similar

reasons, Japan, because of pressure from the U.S. government, agreed to restrict emigration to the United States beginning in 1900.

Continuing pressures to restrict immigration led Congress to pass laws in 1921 and 1924 setting specific ceilings on the number of immigrants allowed from each European country. The ceilings were based on the national origins of the U.S. population as established in censuses from 1890 and 1910. The largest group of U.S. citizens at that time—around 47 percent—had western and northern European ancestors. Correspondingly,

Congress allowed more immigration from northern and western Europe than from eastern and southern Europe. In addition, the new laws effectively banned immigration from Asia and Africa. Latin Americans were allowed to immigrate to the United States, but they faced strict requirements for coming into the country.

Immigration Policy Today Following World War II, immigration restrictions generally were eased. In the 1950s small numbers of Asians—around 100 per country annually—were allowed to immigrate to the United States. Then in 1965 Congress passed the Immigration and Nationality Act. The new law allowed 290,000 immigrants annually, with 120,000 from the Western Hemisphere and 170,000 from the Eastern Hemisphere. The law was partly designed to reunite U.S. citizens and legal residents with their relatives in foreign countries.

The eased restrictions contributed to dramatic increases in immigration from Asia during the 1970s and 1980s. For example, Asian countries accounted for around 38 percent of all legal immigration to the United States in the 1980s. Many of these immigrants were Filipino. Others were Vietnamese, who began coming to the United States in large numbers during and after the Vietnam War in the 1970s.

Immigration from Latin America also has soared since 1965. By the 1970s more than 40 percent of the legal immigrants to the United States were coming from Latin America. Cuban immigration was highest during the 1960s and 1970s. Today, immigration from Latin America remains at around 50 percent of the total.

The level of legal immigration today is determined by the Immigration Act of 1990, which increased the legal immigration limit to 675,000 a year, not counting refugees. Adjusting this legal limit remains a subject of debate in Congress.

Illegal Immigration One of the most difficult immigration problems in recent years has involved keeping people from entering the United States illegally. In the mid-1990s, for example, about 4 million illegal immigrants were estimated to be living in the United States. Counts of the illegal immigrant population are unreliable, however, because these people must avoid being discovered if they are to remain in the country. These **illegal aliens** came to the United States without legal

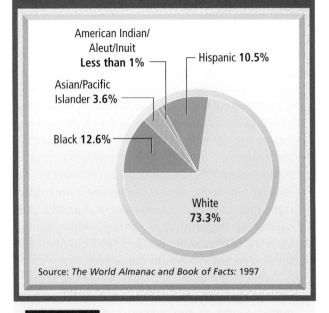

Racial/Ethnic Population of the United States in 1996

American Indian/ Aleut/Inuit **Less than 1%**

Asian/Pacific Islander **3.6%**

Black **12.6%**

Hispanic **10.5%**

White **73.3%**

Source: *The World Almanac and Book of Facts: 1997*

CITIZENSHIP *The United States contains a rich diversity of peoples and cultures. **What are the largest and second-largest nonwhite ethnic groups in the United States?***

immigration papers and by law may not remain here. Any who are caught may be **deported**, or forcibly returned to their countries of origin.

In an attempt to control illegal immigration, Congress passed the Immigration Reform and Control Act of 1986. The law gave illegal aliens a one-time **amnesty**, or general pardon that government gives to people who have broken a law. The 1986 act allowed illegal aliens who could prove they had lived continuously in the United States since before 1982 to apply to stay in the United States as legal residents. The act also outlawed the practice of hiring illegal aliens, a step designed to decrease the flow of illegal aliens by reducing job opportunities for them. In 1994, California voters approved a law that denied state benefits, including public education and medical benefits, to illegal aliens and their children. The measure, however, has been challenged in court.

In 1996 Congress passed additional measures designed to further restrict illegal immigration. This Illegal Immigration Reform and Immigrant Responsibility Act of 1996 increased border controls and provided stronger penalties for creating and using false identification papers. The act also placed additional restrictions on the use of public benefits by aliens, as well as stricter penalties for those who employ illegal aliens.

A Nation of Diversity

Immigration has led to a diverse U.S. population. People and cultures from around the world can be found in many places in the United States, particularly in large urban areas such as Los Angeles and New York City. This great diversity has brought many benefits, as well as some difficult challenges.

Benefits of Diversity The United States contains a rich mixture of peoples, cultures, and traditions from around the world. This diversity provides several advantages. First, the diversity of cultures makes many people's lives richer. Such diversity gives us the chance to enjoy the foods, music, literature, and celebrations of other cultures. Second, the mixture of different ideas and values in a diverse society encourages creativity in many areas, from literature and the arts to business.

The blending of these many cultures and traditions has resulted in a unique U.S. culture. Within this tapestry, however, many distinct cultural traditions survive and flourish. Neighborhoods such as Chinatown in San Francisco, Polish Hamtramck near Detroit, and Little Italy in New York City are examples of the rich diversity that exists in much of the United States.

Each of these neighborhoods is populated largely by one **ethnic group**—a group of people within a nation who share common characteristics such as race, nationality, religion, language, or cultural heritage. U.S. ethnic groups include American Indians, Irish Americans, Italian Americans, Korean Americans, and Jewish Americans. The largest nonwhite ethnic group in the United States is made up of African Americans. More than 33 million African Americans lived in the United States in 1996. More than 27 million Hispanics lived in the United States in the same year. (See the chart on the opposite page.)

Challenges of Diversity Such significant diversity of peoples and cultures has presented challenges as well as benefits. Among these challenges are prejudice and discrimination. **Prejudice** is an opinion formed without careful and reasonable investigation of the facts. Suppose, for example, that a white business owner refuses to hire African Americans because he or she dislikes them. The owner's hiring decisions are not based on a reasonable judgment of each job candidate's skills. Instead, the owner partly bases the decisions on his or her personal prejudice against African Americans. Acts of prejudice like this are called **discrimination**.

Unfortunately, some people do harbor prejudices against people who are different from them, and discrimination too often is the result. In the past, government sometimes was used by powerful majorities to discriminate against people in the minority. Over time, however, various groups have struggled to overcome this discrimination. Particularly in this century, as you will see, much progress has been made in ending discrimination.

SECTION 2 — REVIEW

1. Define the following terms: illegal alien, deportation, amnesty, ethnic group, prejudice, discrimination.

2. What were some of the reasons for the rise in immigration in the 1800s? Why did the federal government restrict immigration during the 1800s?

3. Identify the benefits of diversity in the United States.

4. What are some of the challenges posed by diversity?

5. **Thinking and Writing Critically**
   What are the national origins of some of your ancestors? What are some contributions immigrants from those places of origin have made to the United States? Do you carry on any of the traditions your ancestors brought to the United States?

6. **Applying** CITIZENSHIP
   Conduct an Internet search for the population of your state. In addition, record any information you can find about the ethnic makeup of your state.

STRUGGLE FOR CIVIL RIGHTS

Political Dictionary

civil rights
suspect classification
civil rights movement
segregation
Jim Crow law
de jure segregation
separate-but-equal doctrine
de facto segregation

Objectives

★ What two tests do federal courts use to determine whether laws respect the Equal Protection Clause?

★ How did the Equal Protection Clause help the civil rights movement fight government discrimination?

Much of the progress against discrimination has been made in the courts. Judges have used the Fourteenth Amendment's Equal Protection Clause to prevent discrimination by federal and state governments. This clause has been key in securing all citizens' civil rights, particularly those of African Americans. **Civil rights** are those powers or privileges that governments grant to individuals to guarantee their equal treatment under the law.

Equal Protection of the Law

As you have learned, the Equal Protection Clause is part of the Fourteenth Amendment, which was added to the Constitution after the Civil War to protect the rights of the newly freed slaves. The amendment says that a state government may not "deny to any person within its jurisdiction the equal protection of the laws." In short, the Equal Protection Clause keeps state governments from classifying people *unfairly* and from making

unreasonable distinctions between groups of people. Such classifications imply that government considers it acceptable to treat some people differently from others.

Reasonable Distinction Making sure that people are guaranteed equal protection under the law does not prohibit government from making some distinctions between classes of people. For example, many state governments charge state park visitor fees to pay for the maintenance of the parks. People who do not visit parks do not pay the fees. Thus, in this situation the government has reasonably discriminated, or distinguished, between two groups of people—park visitors and nonpark visitors.

When is discrimination considered reasonable? Today, federal courts generally use two guidelines to decide if government has made fair distinctions between classes of people in specific circumstances. These guidelines are the rational basis test and the strict scrutiny test.

Rational Basis Test The courts recognize that government sometimes has good reasons, or a rational basis, for treating some classes of people differently from others. Differences in treatment are considered valid under the rational basis test

PRINCIPLES OF DEMOCRACY *When the legal drinking age was set at 21, the rational basis test was used to determine that in this case discrimination was reasonable.* **What other guideline is used in determining if discrimination is reasonable?**

CONSTITUTIONAL GOVERNMENT *Some southern schools, such as the Moton School in Virginia, remained legally segregated into the mid-1950s despite the addition of the Thirteenth, Fourteenth, and Fifteenth Amendments.* **What term means segregation by law?**

if they are part of a law that establishes reasonable methods of accomplishing a legitimate goal of government.

The rational basis test can be used to judge many current laws with which you might be familiar. Think about the minimum legal age for drinking alcoholic beverages, for example. This law treats people under 21 differently by prohibiting them from drinking alcohol. Is this discrimination reasonable? Legislators believe that people under 21 have not gained enough life experience to make wise decisions about drinking alcohol. The courts have agreed, stating that these laws pursue a legitimate goal of discouraging irresponsible consumption of alcohol.

Strict Scrutiny Test In cases where government makes distinctions between people based on race or national origin, federal courts have adopted a much stricter standard than that used in the rational basis test. Because such distinctions often reflect prejudice, federal courts automatically presume that they are of suspect, or doubtful, legality. Called **suspect classifications**, these distinctions are immediately considered by the courts to be possible violations of the Equal Protection Clause. In such cases, the courts scrutinize the law strictly.

When courts apply the strict scrutiny test, government must show that a classification is more than just a reasonable method of achieving a legitimate goal. Instead, government must show

that there are compelling reasons that make such a law important to the public interest. The higher standard applied by the strict scrutiny test is much harder for government to meet than the standard under the rational basis test.

To understand the strict scrutiny test, suppose that a city government passed a law requiring a local high school to set up one cafeteria for white students and one for African American students. City officials might argue that such a law was a reasonable effort to minimize disagreements among students of different races. Under the strict scrutiny test, however, the government would have to show that keeping students separated by race served some compelling public interest. The courts in fact have ruled that no compelling reason exists in such a case and have struck down similar laws.

Civil Rights and Equal Protection

The Equal Protection Clause has played a key role in the **civil rights movement**—the struggle by minorities and women to gain in practice the rights guaranteed to all citizens by the Constitution. The movement has a long history and an enduring legacy.

***De Jure* Segregation** Among the most visible examples of government discrimination against

CONSTITUTIONAL GOVERNMENT *During the late 1800s many southern states enacted laws that segregated numerous public places. **Which amendments passed after the Civil War freed slaves and gave constitutional liberties to African Americans?***

decades afterward. This doctrine held that segregation laws did not violate the Equal Protection Clause so long as the facilities reserved for each race were equal to those for the other.

In reality, however, separate facilities often were anything but equal. African American students frequently had access only to older, broken-down schools that were far inferior to those reserved for whites. Efforts to show that the separate-but-equal doctrine was not, in fact, permitted by the Equal Protection Clause became the main goal in the struggle to secure African Americans' civil rights.

African Americans was **segregation**, or mandatory separation of the races. Southern states began enacting segregation policies under the so-called **Jim Crow laws** of the late 1800s.

Jim Crow laws covered nearly all areas of life, particularly in the South. The laws required, for example, separate schools for white students and African American students. Public transportation, public rest rooms, hotels, restaurants, places of entertainment, and other public places also were segregated by law. Even public drinking fountains carried signs reserving some of them for "Whites Only" and others for "Colored," or African Americans.

De jure (DEE joohr-ee) **segregation**, or segregation by law, became policy in the South despite the existence of the Thirteenth, Fourteenth, and Fifteenth Amendments to the Constitution. These three amendments had been passed after the Civil War to free the slaves and to give constitutional liberties to African Americans. For many decades, however, federal courts refused to rule that segregation policies violated constitutional civil rights protections.

One landmark segregation case was *Plessy* v. *Ferguson* in 1896. In that case the Supreme Court upheld a Louisiana law requiring separate railway coaches for white and African American passengers. The *Plessy* decision enshrined the **separate-but-equal doctrine** in U.S. law for

Rolling Back Segregation The fight against the separate-but-equal doctrine continued for many years. Eventually, the Supreme Court turned against Jim Crow laws. In *Sweatt* v. *Painter* in 1948, for example, the Court ruled that a segregated law school for African American students at the University of Texas could not provide students with equal educational opportunities and therefore violated the Equal Protection Clause.

In 1954, civil rights supporters won a major victory. That year, the Supreme Court ruled in *Brown* v. *Board of Education of Topeka* that the segregation of public schools necessarily made for unequal education. A racially segregated school, the Court said, "generates a feeling of inferiority" among African American students "that may affect their hearts and minds in a way unlikely ever to be undone." Therefore, the Court said, "separate educational facilities are inherently [by their very nature] unequal."

In 1955 the Supreme Court ordered states to act "with all deliberate speed" to integrate, or desegregate, their schools. The resistance of prosegregation whites, mostly in southern states, slowed the pace of integration, however. Federal law enforcement officials and federal troops occasionally were used to protect African American students enrolling in formerly all-white schools. Finally, in the 1971 case *Swann* v. *Charlotte-Mecklenburg* the Supreme Court upheld a lower federal court's power to impose busing plans and set racial admission levels to speed desegregation.

Over time the Supreme Court also ruled against legally segregated public transportation, prisons, and other facilities. In fact, it extended its rulings to overturn every state law segregating a public place. In addition, in 1967 the Court ruled in *Loving* v. *Virginia* that state laws banning interracial marriages violated the Equal Protection Clause.

***De Facto* Segregation** Even though *de jure* segregation ended by the early 1970s, the separation of the races has continued. Even today **de facto segregation** (literally "segregation in fact") exists in school systems around the country. In neighborhoods with mainly African American populations, for example, enrollment in local schools often is largely black. Similarly, communities with largely white populations often have local schools in which enrollment is mainly white.

Efforts to eliminate *de facto* segregation often have been bitterly opposed. In the 1970s, for

CONSTITUTIONAL GOVERNMENT *To help eliminate* de facto *segregation the government used busing programs in the nation's schools.* **How did people react to many of these efforts?**

example, many whites reacted with hostility when courts ordered white students bused into black neighborhoods to integrate public schools. African Americans also were bused to schools in white neighborhoods. Some of the strongest reactions occurred in northern cities such as Boston, where violence broke out between black and white high school students. Busing and other means to eliminate *de facto* segregation remain controversial.

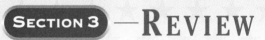

SECTION 3 — REVIEW

1. Define the following terms: civil rights, suspect classification, civil rights movement, segregation, Jim Crow law, *de jure* segregation, separate-but-equal doctrine, *de facto* segregation.

2. How do the rational basis and strict scrutiny tests affect cases involving the Equal Protection Clause?

3. How does legal segregation violate the Equal Protection Clause? In what way did the Supreme Court interpret the Equal Protection Clause differently in *Plessy* v. *Ferguson* and *Brown* v. *Board of Education of Topeka*?

4. **Thinking and Writing Critically**
Think about the places you go for fun outside of home and school—movie theaters, public parks, shopping malls, etc. How would you feel if government laws suddenly barred anyone from your high school from entering these places? How could you use the Constitution to support overturning these laws? Give historical examples to support your case.

5. **Applying CONSTITUTIONAL GOVERNMENT**
Would a law that forbids only blue-eyed people from purchasing goods in a local supermarket or shopping mall be reasonable? Why or why not?

CIVIL RIGHTS LAWS

Political Dictionary

affirmative action
quota

Objectives

★ How have civil rights laws protected the rights of African Americans?

★ How have civil rights protections been extended to other minority groups?

The struggle for civil rights did not end with court victories against segregation. Through marches, protests, and close work with lawmakers, civil rights supporters have gained the passage of key legislation protecting the civil rights of African Americans and other minority groups.

Civil Rights Laws

The first civil rights laws, which were passed in the late 1800s, were not strictly enforced by the courts and did little to protect against discrimination. The growing strength of the civil rights movement in the 1950s and 1960s, however, produced several effective civil rights laws.

Early Laws The first civil rights laws were passed in the 10 years following the Civil War. The Civil Rights Act of 1866 sought to protect African Americans' constitutional rights, such as the right to vote. In addition, an 1875 act outlawed racial discrimination in public places, such as theaters and hotels.

In general, however, these early civil rights laws made little progress in preventing racial discrimination. This failing resulted in large part from court rulings that not only weakened the effects of such laws but also declared many of their provisions unconstitutional.

Failure of Early Laws The federal and state governments' failure to protect African Americans' civil rights was clear by the late 1800s. African Americans accused of crimes, for example, often did not receive fair trials. In addition, many African Americans were lynched, or murdered by mobs acting outside the law. Such lynchings often went unpunished.

The severe discrimination experienced by African Americans gradually persuaded many people that the federal government needed to take a stronger role in protecting individual rights. In response, Congress passed civil rights laws in 1957 and 1960. However, these laws were of limited scope. The failure to pass strong civil rights laws led civil rights supporters to intensify their efforts. Through marches, demonstrations, and boycotts, civil rights supporters pressed Congress for stronger legislation.

Nonviolent Protests One of the earliest boycotts began in December 1955 when Rosa Parks—an African American seamstress in Montgomery, Alabama—was arrested for refusing to give up her seat to a white person on a public bus—as required by city segregation laws. Alabama civil rights leaders responded to the arrest by asking African

PRINCIPLES OF DEMOCRACY *"Sit-ins" such as the one pictured here were used as a nonviolent method of protesting segregation.* ***What were some other forms of nonviolent civil rights protest?***

PRINCIPLES OF DEMOCRACY *Martin Luther King, Jr., waves to a crowd of some 250,000 Americans who had gathered in Washington, D.C., to express their support for the civil rights movement.* **In what year did the March on Washington occur?**

American citizens to boycott the city buses until the city changed the laws. The bus company lost 65 percent of its normal income as a result. The boycott did not end until almost a year later, when the Supreme Court ruled that the segregation of buses was unconstitutional.

Most civil rights supporters conveyed their message through nonviolent protest. In February 1960 in Greensboro, North Carolina, for example, four African American college students staged a "sit-in" at a Woolworth store's lunch counter, which refused to serve black customers. The students entered the store, sat down at the lunch counter, and were refused service. They stayed for a few hours and then left. The next day, they returned to the store and sat for a few more hours. By the fourth day, some whites began participating. During the first six months of the protest, police arrested more than 1,600 participants. The sit-ins, which were almost always led by high school or college students, spread to other southern cities.

Despite their use of nonviolent methods, the protesters often were the victims of violence from others. During 1961, for example, members of the Congress of Racial Equality organized the Freedom Rides—bus trips that both black and white civil rights supporters took to various southern cities to challenge the segregation practices in bus terminals. The Freedom Riders rode throughout the South, intentionally ignoring the segregation signs

in terminals along the way. In Alabama, when buses and their riders were attacked by angry mobs, the local authorities offered little or no protection. In Mississippi, riders were arrested and jailed. In spite of these incidents, the Freedom Riders continued their efforts.

In August 1963 around 250,000 Americans gathered in Washington, D.C., to express their support for the civil rights movement. This March on Washington was led in part by Martin Luther King, Jr.—a dynamic civil rights activist, Baptist minister, and president of the Southern Christian Leadership Conference—who was one of the guiding forces behind the principle of nonviolent protest. It was at this event that King made his famous "I Have a Dream" speech, in which he declared, "I have a dream that my four little children will one day live in a nation where they will not be judged by the color of their skin, but by the content of their character."

Change Takes Hold Such pressures finally led to the passage of the most important civil rights laws in a century. The 1964 Civil Rights Act forbade segregation of public places, such as restaurants, lunch counters, movie theaters, and hotels. The act also extended civil rights protections to minority groups other than just African Americans. It prohibited employers and administrators of any program receiving federal funding from discriminating based on race, national origin, religion, or sex.

In contrast to court decisions on civil rights laws in the 1800s, the Supreme Court ruled that the 1964 Civil Rights Act was constitutional. The Court decided that congressional authority to prevent discrimination in public places came from its constitutional power to regulate commerce among the states. Motels, for example, are considered part of interstate commerce partly because they receive many out-of-state customers. Similarly, restaurants serving out-of-state food are said to be involved in interstate commerce as well.

As a result of the 1964 law, facilities that had once been closed to African Americans opened their doors. Many public schools that had been slow to integrate were pushed into action, fearing that their state's attorney general would file lawsuits against them otherwise. Similarly, agencies that received federal grants for local projects, such as youth programs and public facilities, also were affected by the new law.

Another key civil rights law, the Voting Rights Act of 1965, helped African Americans secure equal opportunity at the ballot box. Among other things, the law prohibited the use of literacy and other tests to decide if a person could vote. These tests had been used to prevent many African Americans in the South from voting. The law also allowed federal agents to help African Americans register to vote in states where they faced discrimination. As a result, between 1964 and 1968 the percentage of registered African American voters in several states rose significantly—from 7 to 59 percent in Mississippi, for example. (Voting is more fully explained in Chapter 19.)

Congress has since passed other civil rights laws as well, including the Civil Rights Acts of 1968 and 1991. The 1968 act prohibited discrimination based on race, national origin, and religion in the advertising, financing, sale, and rental of housing. The 1991 law strengthened protections against discrimination in the workplace.

Extending Civil Rights

The progress made by African Americans has encouraged other groups that are working to end discrimination. These groups include Hispanic Americans, American Indians, Asian Americans, people with disabilities, and women.

Hispanic Americans Hispanic Americans compose a rapidly growing ethnic group in

Comparing Governments

Nonviolent Protests in Burma

As in the United States, nonviolent protest has been used by people around the world who demand fair treatment and civil rights. In 1988, for example, prodemocracy supporters in Burma (now called Myanmar) participated in nonviolent demonstrations against General Ne Win, who had ruled the South Asian country for more than 25 years. The military reacted by crushing the demonstrations and killing thousands of people, while military leaders took over the government.

In response, protester Daw Aung San Suu Kyi (daw awng suhn soo chee) cofounded a prodemocracy opposition party, the National League for Democracy. Suu Kyi bravely spoke out against the military government. As a result of her actions, she was placed under house arrest for six years, and the army arrested hundreds of her supporters. Suu Kyi's efforts drew world attention, however, and she received the Nobel Peace Prize in 1991 in recognition of her nonviolent campaign. Political pressure eventually forced the military government to release her. "We must have the courage to face the bully's challenge," Suu Kyi said, as she vowed to continue her party's nonviolent struggle for democracy. The Burmese military, however, continues to exercise significant political and economic power.

the United States. Hispanic Americans are U.S. citizens or residents who are of Latin American or Spanish descent.

Hispanic Americans have faced discrimination in several areas, such as employment and housing. Progress has been made, however, in extending civil rights to Hispanic Americans. By 1994, Hispanics held nearly 5,500 public offices in the United States, and 17 Hispanic Americans were congresspersons in 1995.

American Indians American Indians today make up around 1 percent of the U.S. population.

For most of U.S. history, the federal government considered American Indians to be conquered peoples with their own separate governments. As a result, they were long denied many civil rights. For example, some American Indians could not vote until 1924, when they were granted U.S. citizenship.

Since the 1960s American Indians have used protests, court cases, and lobbying efforts to secure their civil rights. In 1975, for example, Congress expanded protections of the Voting Rights Act to require that ballots be printed in American Indian languages in communities with large American Indian populations. (The same law required that ballots be printed in Spanish and other languages of large non-English-speaking minority populations where appropriate.)

Asian Americans Like Hispanic Americans, Asian Americans are a rapidly growing ethnic group in the United States. Increasing immigration from Asia, particularly since the 1970s, has fueled this growth.

At different points in U.S. history, racial prejudice has been a source of discrimination against Asian Americans. For example, Japanese Americans on the West Coast, many of them U.S. citizens, were held in detention centers while the United States and Japan were at war with each other during World War II. Like other ethnic minorities, however, Asian Americans today are protected by the civil rights acts of the 1950s and 1960s.

People with Disabilities Civil rights protections were extended again in 1990 with the passage of the Americans with Disabilities Act (ADA). The ADA forbids employers and the owners of public accommodations to discriminate against people with disabilities.

You can see the effects of the ADA in many places. Businesses have installed ramps, widened doors, and made other changes to provide access to people with disabilities. The ADA also mandated establishment of the Telecommunications Relay Service (TRS), which enables people with hearing and speech impairments to communicate by telephone with anyone in the nation.

Women From early in the nation's history, women did not have the same rights as men. Except for the Nineteenth Amendment, which

CONSTITUTIONAL GOVERNMENT *The Americans with Disabilities Act prohibits discrimination against people with disabilities.* **What effects of the ADA can you see in your school?**

gave women the right to vote in 1920, the Constitution contains no references to people's sex. Because of this lack of clearly stated constitutional protections, courts once regularly ruled against claims of sex discrimination in employment and other areas. Courts also refused to rule against the practice of excluding women from juries. In a 1961 case, for example, the Supreme Court ruled that such exclusions were proper in light of the place of women at "the center of home and family life."

Efforts to win equal rights for women have made significant progress, however. The civil rights acts of the 1960s, for example, included protections against sex discrimination. In addition, in the 1971 case *Reed* v. *Reed* the Supreme Court for the first time ruled against a law that discriminated against women. The case involved an Idaho law that gave fathers preference over mothers in deciding who should administer the estates of children who had died. In later cases the Court ruled that government must have strong reasons for making legal distinctions between men and women.

Progress toward equal rights for women has brought many changes to U.S. society. Since 1979,

Citizenship in Action

Many students from the University of California at Los Angeles protested the end of affirmative action in the state university system.

Speaking Out on Affirmative Action

Affirmative action programs at businesses and universities seek to provide special consideration for minority applicants during the making of hiring, admissions, or scholarship decisions. Supporters of affirmative action argue that these programs create a more diverse environment at school or in the workplace and help to compensate for social inequalities that have hindered minorities. Opponents, however, believe that such programs have served their purpose and are no longer necessary. As a result, many of these programs have recently been challenged as unfair or unconstitutional.

College students across the country have joined this heated debate. The 1995 decision by the University of California board of regents to end affirmative action in the state university system created an uproar. Thousands of students from the Los Angeles campus (UCLA) protested, demanding that the decision be repealed. Other students, such as African Student Union member Shauna Robinson, organized a public forum designed to educate students about the need for affirmative action.

Protests then spread to other California college campuses, where student organizations worked to influence opinion on affirmative action. Despite these efforts, the ban on affirmative action remains in effect.

California students also formed groups supporting the regents' decision. One such group was Students Against Affirmative Action and for Equality, which argued that admissions criteria involving race were unnecessary. This group suggested that alternative criteria such as financial hardship would be more impartial and would still help many minority students.

The controversy in California spurred many groups around the country to action. After attending a protest by UCLA students, civil rights leader Jesse Jackson urged young African Americans throughout the country to defend affirmative action policies. He accused young people of having become "much too comfortable" and called on them to protect hard-won civil rights.

High school students around the nation also joined the debate. *United Youth of Boston,* an independent high school student newspaper, published articles discussing affirmative action. Inspired by the reports, students at Boston's Madison Park High School organized forums on racism, poverty, and education.

The status of affirmative action is still uncertain. A 1997 poll taken by the Joint Center for Political and Economic Studies suggested that African Americans age 18 to 25 were more likely to support affirmative action than older African Americans or whites. More than 80 percent of the whites polled and about half of the African Americans and Hispanics were against preferential treatment for minorities. No matter what decisions local, state, and federal government make on affirmative action, the debate over the subject has encouraged many students to explore and discuss their rights and responsibilities as U.S. citizens.

What Do You Think?

1. What is your opinion of affirmative action programs at universities?
2. What were some of the ways in which college students worked to educate the public about affirmative action?

PRINCIPLES OF DEMOCRACY *Protesters march by the New York Public Library during a parade for women's suffrage in the early 1900s.* **In what year were women guaranteed the right to vote?**

for example, women have outnumbered men on college campuses. In addition, women now work in occupations that once were closed to them, including medicine, law, and engineering.

CASE STUDY

Affirmative Action

CONSTITUTIONAL GOVERNMENT Some people have argued that discrimination cannot be ended unless government and private industry adopt affirmative action programs. **Affirmative action** refers to policies that are used to help end the effects of both historical and continuing discrimination, particularly in jobs and education. A business, for example, may take affirmative action by making special efforts to hire and to promote ethnic minorities and women to help make up for their having been denied equal employment opportunities in the past.

Supporters argue that such measures are one of the best ways to ensure that minorities and women have the same opportunities that others have. Without such efforts, they argue, minorities

and women would continue to earn less money, as well as hold fewer high-level jobs in top companies and fewer positions in certain fields. For example, although women have made great strides in recent years, they hold only 10 percent of the positions on the directing boards—the highest decision-making bodies—of the 500 top-performing companies in the United States.

Affirmative action policies sometimes include numerical goals and timetables for hiring women and minorities and for granting them admission to colleges and universities. Opponents argue that establishing numerical goals—or **quotas**—based on race or sex is unfair. They state that reserving a share of jobs or places in universities based on overall representation in the population contradicts the principle that choices for such positions should be based on merit.

As a result, the setting of quotas has been particularly controversial. Opponents point out that a white male who is the most qualified person for a particular job might not be hired if the employer must fill the slot with someone of a different ethnic background or sex. Some people believe that in

CONSTITUTIONAL GOVERNMENT *People disagree about affirmative action policies.* **What issue has been particularly controversial in policies surrounding affirmative action?**

doing so, the employer discriminates against white males and thus engages in reverse discrimination.

The Supreme Court has agreed with some of these arguments. In 1978 the Court ruled in *Regents of the University of California* v. *Bakke* that

a California medical school could not reserve for minority applicants a certain number of seats in an entering class. Such a quota, the Court said, violated the Equal Protection Clause and the 1964 Civil Rights Act because it treated people differently based on their race. The Court did rule, however, that race could be one of the factors schools can use in admitting students.

Supporters and opponents of affirmative action continue to argue over how much consideration race and sex should be given in making employment and admissions decisions. The Supreme Court has added to the confusion at times by allowing quotas in some cases but not in others.

Affirmative action supporters have recently seen setbacks in the courts and in the political arena. In 1996 the Supreme Court refused to overturn a ruling by a lower federal court that backed away from the *Bakke* standard by ruling in *Hopwood* v. *University of Texas* that a law school could not use race as a factor in deciding which students to admit. Later that year, California voters approved a constitutional amendment that forbids race and sex preferences in all public agencies, including universities. (See Citizenship in Action, page 354.) As a result of these and other events, the future of affirmative action is unclear.

SECTION 4 — **REVIEW**

1. Define the following terms: affirmative action, quota.

2. Identify the key civil rights laws of the 1960s. How does each one help protect the civil rights of African Americans?

3. What groups other than African Americans have faced discrimination in the United States? In what ways have people in these groups won civil rights protections?

4. **Thinking and Writing Critically**
   Do you think affirmative action is an appropriate tool for overcoming the effects of past discrimination? Why or why not?

5. **Applying** **CONSTITUTIONAL GOVERNMENT**
   Conduct an Internet search using the search words *affirmative action*. Note any Supreme Court cases involving affirmative action that you find mentioned in your search.

SECTION 1 Becoming a full participant in the U.S. democratic system requires citizenship. The Constitution and Congress have established the ways people may become U.S. citizens—by birth or through naturalization.

A court may take away the citizenship of anyone who can be shown to have become a U.S. citizen by fraud. In addition, a citizen may renounce his or her citizenship.

SECTION 2 Immigration has benefited U.S. society in numerous ways. The resulting diversity, however, also has presented significant challenges, including prejudice and discrimination.

During much of colonial and early U.S. history, immigration to America was unrestricted. Over time, tensions developed between immigrants and people already living in the United States. Hostility toward immigrants eventually led Congress to pass various acts restricting immigration. Following World War II, however, some restrictions were eased. Today, immigration is determined by the Immigration Act of 1990.

One of the most difficult immigration problems in recent years has involved keeping people from entering the United States illegally. In an attempt to control illegal immigration, Congress passed the Immigration Reform and Control Act of 1986. It passed additional measures in 1996.

The diversity that arises from immigration brings many benefits to the United States. It makes people's lives richer and encourages creativity in many areas by stimulating a mixture of ideas and values.

SECTION 3 The Fourteenth Amendment's Equal Protection Clause keeps state governments from unfairly classifying people and from making unreasonable distinctions between groups of people. Today, federal courts generally use two guidelines to decide if government has made fair distinctions between classes of people—the rational basis test and the strict scrutiny test.

The Equal Protection Clause has played a key role in the civil rights movement. Among the most visible examples of government discrimination against African Americans was segregation. The fight against segregation lasted for many years. Even though *de jure* segregation ended in the 1970s, *de facto* segregation still exists in many places around the country. Busing and other efforts to desegregate schools remain controversial today.

SECTION 4 Through marches, protests, and close work with lawmakers, civil rights supporters have gained the passage of key legislation protecting civil rights. Although civil rights laws were initially passed in the late 1800s, they were not strictly enforced. Stronger civil rights laws in the 1950s and 1960s, however, have protected civil rights more effectively. In recent years the progress made by African Americans has encouraged other groups working to end discrimination. These groups include Hispanic Americans, American Indians, Asian Americans, people with disabilities, and women.

> ✎ **Government Notebook**
>
> Review what you wrote in your Government Notebook at the beginning of the chapter about the ways government should work to prevent unfair discrimination. Now that you have studied this chapter, would you revise your answer? Do actual government methods match those that you listed? Does government do more or less than you believe it should? Record your answers in your Notebook.

REVIEW

REVIEWING CONCEPTS

1. What guidelines do courts use to determine whether government laws violate the Equal Protection Clause? What role does the Equal Protection Clause play in protecting the civil rights of African Americans?

2. In what three ways may a person become a U.S. citizen? How can a person lose U.S. citizenship?

3. Describe U.S. immigration policy during the United States's first 100 years as a nation. How has immigration policy changed since then?

4. What benefits and challenges does diversity present the United States?

5. Why were civil rights laws of the 1950s and 1960s more successful than earlier civil rights laws? What groups besides African Americans do civil rights laws protect from discrimination?

THINKING AND WRITING CRITICALLY

1. **CONSTITUTIONAL GOVERNMENT** Why must the government show compelling reasons for passing a law that has suspect classifications? Why do you think the courts created the strict scrutiny test?

2. **CITIZENSHIP** How diverse is the community in which you live? In what ways has your state or community been shaped by various cultures?

3. **CONSTITUTIONAL GOVERNMENT** Why do you think that *de facto* segregation is difficult to combat? What efforts has the government made to eliminate this type of segregation? Have these efforts been effective?

4. **PUBLIC GOOD** Imagine that you were a participant in the civil rights movement of the 1950s and 1960s. Write a short newspaper editorial explaining why a law should be passed to forbid segregation in public places.

THE INTERNET: LEARNING ONLINE

Conduct an Internet search for information about civil rights issues today. You might start with search words such as *civil rights, Civil Rights Act,* and *affirmative action.* Create a list of the sites that contain information about civil rights. Afterward, include your list in a short library brochure entitled "Civil Rights: An Internet Guide." Your brochure also should include other information, such as names of online news groups and online chat groups that would be helpful to people who want to learn more about civil rights issues today.

CITIZENSHIP IN YOUR COMMUNITY

Working with a group, choose an event of the civil rights movement of the 1950s and 1960s, such as the 1963 March on Washington. Then write a script for a documentary commemorating that event. Be sure to include important details about the event, such as when and where it took place, who the key participants were, and its impact on the civil rights movement. You may want to include photos of the event to illustrate your script.

INDIVIDUAL PORTFOLIO PROJECT

Use the library and other resources to identify important individuals in the struggle for civil rights—for example, Martin Luther King, Jr. Create a biographical sketch of one of these people, including his or her background, accomplishments, and role in the civil rights movement. In addition, include illustrations and a list of resources readers can use to learn more about the person.

PRACTICING SKILLS: CONDUCTING RESEARCH

Statistics, such as those regarding a country's population, often are presented in tables or charts. By reading across the rows and down the columns, you can quickly glean information about the topic at hand.

Statistical tables enable people to analyze numerical data easily, see relationships, and make comparisons. Study the table below and then answer the questions that follow.

Foreign-Born Population in the United States

Country of Origin	Estimated Population	Percentage of U.S. Foreign-Born Population
Mexico	6.7 million	29.1%
The Philippines	1.2 million	5.2%
China/Taiwan/Hong Kong	816,000	3.5%
Cuba	797,000	3.5%
Canada	695,000	3.0%
El Salvador	650,000	2.8%
Great Britain	617,000	2.7%
Germany	598,000	2.6%
Poland	538,000	2.3%
Jamaica	513,000	2.3%
Dominican Republic	509,000	2.2%

Source: *The World Almanac: 1997*

1. What is the subject of the data in the table?

2. What specific information does the table contain about the foreign-born population of the United States?

3. From which country does the largest percentage of the foreign-born population come?

ANALYZING PRIMARY SOURCES

LETTER FROM BIRMINGHAM JAIL

Martin Luther King, Jr., led the civil rights movement of the 1950s and 1960s. In 1963 King was jailed because he refused to obey a court order to put an end to civil rights demonstrations in Birmingham, Alabama. While in jail, he wrote this letter to several clergy explaining why he could not agree to end the demonstrations. Read the excerpt from the letter and answer the questions that follow.

❝ *We know through painful experience that freedom is never voluntarily given by the oppressor [persecutor]; it must be demanded by the oppressed [people who are persecuted]. Frankly I have never yet engaged in a direct action movement that was 'well timed,' according to the timetable of those who have not suffered unduly [excessively] from the disease of segregation. For years now I have heard the word 'Wait!' It rings in the ear of every Negro with a piercing familiarity. This 'wait' has almost always meant 'never.' It has been a tranquilizing Thalidomide [sedating drug], relieving the emotional stress for a moment, only to give birth to an ill-formed infant of frustration. We must come to see with the distinguished jurist of yesterday that 'justice too long delayed is justice denied.' We have waited for more than 340 years for our constitutional and God-given rights. The nations of Asia and Africa are moving with jet-like speed toward the goal of political independence, and we still creep at horse and buggy pace toward the gaining of a cup of coffee at a lunch counter.* ❞

1. Why did King believe that waiting for the right time to protest segregation was not the wisest choice?

2. What is the meaning of the statement "justice too long delayed is justice denied"? Do you agree with this statement? Why or why not?

3. How does King believe waiting for freedom has affected African Americans?

Reporting the News

Imagine that you are part of a team of newspaper reporters that has been assigned by your editor to investigate a major story. Together you have uncovered important evidence concerning an upcoming trial that your newspaper will be covering. The story involves charges that a local representative to your state's legislature has broken state law by using campaign funds for personal purposes. In fact, investigators charge that during a recent election the representative diverted more than $300,000 in campaign funds to his personal bank account.

On the following pages you will find various documents and notes that your team has gathered to help you in deciding how to write the story. One of those documents is a newswriting guide that points out the important elements of a news story. A sample newspaper article has been included along with this guide as an example of how to write a news story.

Other information includes a list of facts put together from each reporter's research. In addition, you will find notes that two reporters have taken during interviews with sources. Finally, you will find a letter from the state attorney general, who has concerns about the newspaper's coverage of the case.

After your group has reviewed the information on the following pages, answer the accompanying questions in your Government Notebook. When you have finished, use your answers and the information presented here to write the story. In doing so, your team must decide what information to use and then prepare a memo to the editor explaining why you have chosen to use some pieces of information but not others.

The Daily Post

ELEMENTS OF A NEWS STORY

A news story is a factual explanation of details surrounding a noteworthy event. Unlike an editorial, a news story does not include the opinion of the reporter. In fact, the reporter must strive to write a balanced story that takes no position on the facts of the case.

A news story contains the following elements:

Headline

Every reporter writing for *The Daily Post* should suggest a headline for his or her story. Headlines are short titles that summarize the story's subject. Headlines should not be complete sentences.

Byline

The byline is the name of the reporter or reporters who have written the story.

Dateline

The dateline is the location of the news story: NEW YORK, ALBUQUERQUE, or our hometown, CHARLESTOWN.

Lead

The lead is the first sentence of a news article. In general, the lead tells the reader not only who did what and where, but also when and how it was done.

Body

The rest of the article, called the body, tells the reader the "why" behind the story. The body is made up of paragraphs and includes quotations from sources and applicable details about the story's subject. Paragraphs should be short—no more than two or three sentences.

SAMPLE

Large Company to Hire More Workers

By Ruby Chang

CHARLESTOWN—The president of the largest employer in the Charlestown area announced Tuesday that the company will be adding more than 500 jobs over the next year.

Compurama will hire more workers because sales of the company's computers are increasing rapidly, said Juan Vasquez, the company's president. Compurama currently employs 2,000 people.

"It looks like our efforts to improve the design of our products are really paying off," Vasquez said.

The company began to improve its product line last year. Sales of the company's newest product, the CyberRama computer, have increased 50 percent over the last year, Vasquez said.

"Customers really seem to like the faster speed and extra features we have put into the CyberRama computer," Vasquez said.

One source, who asked not to be identified, said that Vasquez still is interested in selling Compurama even though its sales have increased. Vasquez denies that he wants to sell the company.

Facts of the campaign story:

- Darryl Stevens is serving his second term in the state House of Representatives.

- Stevens raised $500,000 for his last campaign. He is accused of using $300,000 of that money to purchase a new lakefront home.

- Stevens's trial is set to start on June 20, which is next week.

- Recent interviews with an anonymous source (code-named "Deep Pockets") and a former police officer (Sherry Tate) indicate that Stevens might be guilty but that police may have acted improperly in the investigation.

- Tate was dismissed from the force for conduct improper for a police officer.

- This state does not have a shield law.

◀ WHAT DO YOU THINK?

★ What new information have you collected from interviews that might interest readers? Why would such information make a good lead for your story?

★ The trial is set to start next week. How do you think publicity from your news story might affect potential jurors?

★ What is a shield law? Why is it important to know that your state has no such law?

June 3 interview w/ "Deep Pockets" (staff member in Stevens's office; can't use name; fears losing job; Stevens won't comment)

Q: Is there evidence that Stevens used campaign money for personal use?

A: Just before last November's election, I saw a check for $300,000 that was made out to Representative Stevens personally. The check was drawn on his campaign's account.

Q: Do you know what the money was used for?

A: I remember that Stevens had earlier told various staff members that he needed a lot of money to buy a new house at the lake. Shortly after the election, he told the whole staff that he had purchased a lake house and would be moving in after Christmas.

Q: But do you know for sure that the $300,000 check from his campaign was used to buy the new house?

A: Well, no, I don't. But how else would he be able to come up with $300,000 so fast? And it's very suspicious that he got the check just a few weeks before buying the house.

June 4 interview with Sherry Tate, former Charlestown police officer (can't confirm this information with other sources; police chief says Tate is wrong)

Q: How did Charlestown police find out that Representative Stevens might have broken the law?

A: The police chief suspected that Stevens might use campaign money for personal purposes. Another police officer told me that the chief ordered him to tap Stevens's phones. In phone conversations with a friend, Stevens mentioned that he had gotten $300,000 from his campaign to buy a house at the lake.

Q: Did the police get a search warrant to tap Stevens's phones?

A: The officer told me that no search warrant was issued.

Q: The police chief says that he did not order Stevens's phones to be wiretapped.

A: Then the chief is a liar.

Q: Will the recorded telephone conversation be used in court?

A: I doubt it. The recorded conversations helped the police discover other evidence indicating that Stevens had broken the law.

▲ WHAT DO YOU THINK?

★ How believable is the anonymous staff member from Stevens's office? Did he or she personally see a check to Stevens from the campaign's account?

★ Do you think the staff member's suspicions about how the money was used is newsworthy? Why or why not?

★ What has the Supreme Court said about wiretapping telephones? Should the police chief have obtained a search warrant if he wanted to tap Stevens's phones?

★ How believable is Sherry Tate? Did she personally witness the police chief order Stevens's phones to be tapped?

★ Do you think that printing Tate's charge that the chief is a liar might be libelous? Why or why not?

STATE OFFICE OF THE ATTORNEY GENERAL

Editor
The Daily Post
2254 State Street
Charlestown, Rhode Island 02813

Dear Editor:

It has come to my attention that reporters from your newspaper are preparing to write a story on the upcoming trial of Representative Darryl Stevens. I have a number of concerns about this possible story.

First, there is the possibility that further publicity in your area on this topic will make it difficult for Representative Stevens to get a fair trial. If potential jurors read the story in your newspaper, they might form their own conclusions before the trial even begins. I insist that you withhold the publication of any other stories about the case until after the trial.

Second, I have learned that one source for the upcoming story has requested that he or she not be named. If the anonymous source has applicable information about the case, he or she should testify about it in open court rather than anonymously in your newspaper. Therefore, your reporter must supply the source's name and address to the proper authorities. I remind you that this state currently has no shield law.

Finally, information your reporter has gathered indicating that the police chief acted improperly in any way cannot be confirmed by us or other sources. If that information is used in the story, you probably can expect that the police chief will sue you for libel.

Sincerely,

Dwonna Jones

Dwonna Jones
State Attorney General

◄ WHAT DO YOU THINK?

★ What is prior restraint, and what has the Supreme Court ruled on it? Does the attorney general have the right to demand that the newspaper not publish the story?

★ Should you reveal the name of "Deep Pockets" so that he or she can be called to testify in court? What has the Supreme Court said about such cases? Would you be willing to go to jail for refusing to identify an anonymous source?

★ What has the Supreme Court said about libel? Is the police chief a public official? Do you think that publishing the improper wiretapping charge and the charge that he is a liar would show reckless disregard for the truth? Why or why not?

THINGS TO DO

1. Review the information from this activity and the answers that you have written in your Government Notebook. Research the Supreme Court's rulings on freedom of the press.

2. Decide what information should be used in the story you will write about the Stevens case. Consider whether you should tell your readers that you have or have not been able to confirm the information given by your sources.

3. Consider what information you should include in the story's lead. Then plan how to use other information and quotations for the body of your story.

4. Write your story about the Stevens case. Make sure to provide a balanced story that does not include your opinion.

5. If you use information from the anonymous source or from the former police officer in your story, explain why such information was necessary. If you include information about the improper wiretapping charge, explain why you believe your story does not libel the police chief.

UNIT
6

PUBLIC POLICY LAB

How do presidential candidates prepare for televised debates? Find out by taking the Public Policy Lab challenge on pages 454–57.

The U.S. Political System

PUBLIC OPINION

How many times have you been asked the question "What do you think?" Consider all the times a teacher has called on you in class. Think about the hours you spend with your friends and family trying to decide what to do or what to wear. In each of these instances, your teachers, friends, and family asked you for your opinion about something—a novel, a problem, a shirt, a movie. They asked because your opinion matters to them.

Your opinions—and those of other citizens—also matter to government officials. People in office and those running for office are keenly interested in finding out what the constituents in their district think. By making your opinions heard, you can influence not only government but also laws that affect you.

✎ Government Notebook

In your Government Notebook, list all the times in one day that you express your opinion. What forms does your opinion take? Think not only about what you say and write but also about the choices you make in clothes, classes, and activities.

WHAT IS PUBLIC OPINION?

Political Dictionary

public opinion
ideology
political socialization

Objectives

★ What is public opinion, and how does it shape political events?
★ What factors influence public opinion?
★ What is the media's role in influencing public opinion?

Consider the following scenario. Your friend comes to you during the day at school and tells you that he likes a certain girl and wants to ask her out on a date. He wants to know what you think he should do. You tell your friend that in your opinion the best idea is to walk up to her and casually ask her to go to a movie with him. Your friend takes your advice. He asks her out, she accepts, and they make plans. Because he valued your opinion, your friend took your advice. In other words, your opinion influenced your friend's actions.

Just as your friends, family, and teachers want to know your opinion about certain things, public officials want to know what you and the rest of the public think about important local and national issues. The collective opinion of large numbers of people is called **public opinion**.

Role of Public Opinion

In a democracy, government officials respect public opinion as the voice of the majority of the people. Thus, by making their opinions heard on specific issues, people can influence the government policies that affect them.

Consider the antiapartheid movement in South Africa. For many years, black South Africans were suppressed by apartheid, a government system of racial segregation that restricted where they could live and work and that denied them the right to vote. After years of often violent demonstrations against the government and strong actions by other nations, the leaders of South Africa began to allow multiracial elections in 1994. Nelson Mandela, black nationalist leader of the African National Congress Party, was elected president. The pressure of international public opinion had helped to force an end to apartheid.

As a citizen in your own community, you might agree or disagree with certain laws. Have officials in your community ever passed laws about which you had strong feelings? If so, did you express your opinion? In some communities, teens have expressed their opinions about laws by speaking before or writing letters to their city councils. If public opinion about an issue is strong enough, it may cause the law to be changed.

Forms of Public Opinion

How can government officials, researchers, and others concerned with public opinion tell what people's views are? One way is by examining people's

WORLD AFFAIRS *Nelson Mandela, South Africa's president, led the antiapartheid movement in that country.* **How can people living in democratic countries influence government policies?**

Citizens Registered and Voting in Federal Elections, 1964–1996

Year	Voting Age Population	Registered	Voted	Percent of Voting Age Population Who Voted
1964	114,090,000	73,715,818	70,644,592	61.92%
1968	120,328,186	81,658,180	73,211,875	60.84%
1972	140,776,000	97,328,541	77,718,554	55.21%
1976	152,309,190	105,037,986	81,555,789	53.55%
1980	164,597,000	113,043,734	86,515,221	52.56%
1984	174,466,000	124,150,614	92,652,680	53.11%
1988	182,778,000	126,379,628	91,594,693	50.11%
1992	189,529,000	133,821,178	104,405,155	55.09%
1996	196,511,000	146,211,960	96,456,345	49.08%

Source: Federal Election Commission

In federal elections only around half of the eligible voters exercise their right to vote.
In what year did the percent of eligible voters who voted in federal elections drop below 50 percent?

participation, in the political process. One obvious way people participate in politics is by voting. Citizens who are 18 or over, have not been convicted of a felony, and have taken the time to register are eligible to vote. Unfortunately, only around half of the eligible voters take the time to vote in presidential elections. In other elections, turnout is even lower.

People participate in the political process in ways other than voting, however. No matter what your age and even if you are not a citizen, you can speak out or write about political issues, demonstrate, sign a petition, write a letter to a public official, or join an interest group that has specific political goals. Some people donate money or time to political candidates and interest groups. Through all these forms of political participation, people make their views known.

Influences on Public Opinion

You now know how people express their political opinions, but what helps form those opinions in the first place? Ideology, family, school, and the media all influence how people form their opinions.

Ideology One factor affecting people's viewpoints on certain issues is their **ideology**—or basic set of political beliefs. By conducting interviews, political scientists have discovered that

many people do maintain a set of basic beliefs about freedom, opportunity, and equality, and that this ideology influences their political ideas about both issues and candidates.

You have probably heard relatives or friends speak of themselves as liberal, conservative, or moderate. These are different types of ideology. In general, a person with a conservative ideology believes that in order to promote the public good, government should be less involved in people's lives, while someone with a liberal ideology believes that government should actively protect and advance the general welfare of citizens. A moderate usually holds some liberal and some conservative beliefs.

Political Socialization Some of people's earliest influences, such as family and school, affect how they form their opinions. In fact, family beliefs, ideas learned in school, job experiences, and influences from income, education, age, gender, race, and geographic region all combine to produce a person's **political socialization**. This process helps determine how someone's political opinions will develop over his or her lifetime.

The political socialization process starts very early. Research by political scientists has shown that people develop some basic political preferences as children. Many children can name some countries they like and do not like by the age of six. Studies

Government and Psychology

Politics and the Mind

Why would anyone want to know your emotions on election day? When considering how to vote, you base your decisions partly on personal factors, such as feelings, personality traits, and values. Political psychologists study these factors to help them determine how people make political decisions.

By scientifically studying the public's thoughts and behavior, political psychologists analyze how people form political beliefs and make decisions about political issues. One of the earliest political psychologists was Harold Laswell. In 1930 Laswell published a study arguing that people act according to personal motives when making political decisions. In particular, Laswell thought that many people who had feelings of inferiority sought political power to prove their own worth.

In 1960, Angus Campbell's book *The American Voter* presented the results of surveys in which voters were asked questions about their ability to influence politics. This study showed that people who felt they could bring about political changes were more likely to vote than those who did not feel that their efforts could result in change. This theory was supported by a 1963 study listing a number of other psychological factors that also encouraged voting. These factors included a strong sense of identification with a political party, interest in specific issues or candidates, and concern about the results of an election.

Political ideology has also been a focus of political psychology. During the 1940s a group of researchers studied the psychological influences on fascism and anti-Semitism. The study found that people who joined the Nazi Party had harsh, impulsive personalities, favored strict punishment. and tended to blame others—in that case, Jews—for their problems. Supporting these findings, a study in the United States during the 1960s showed that people who felt powerless, isolated, and dissatisfied were more likely to hold extreme views.

Political psychologists also study psychological socialization, or how people's emotions, opinions, and behavior make them part of a larger society. In 1971 psychologist Joseph Adelson studied the development of political thought in adolescents, based on a theory developed by psychologist Jean Piaget. Adelson noted that different stages in children's mental development coincided with changes in political attitudes. The most dramatic changes appeared in children between the ages of 12 and 16, with older adolescents better able to think abstractly about politics.

The political development that teens undergo often reflects their upbringing. Psychologist Judith Gallatin's 1980 study showed, for example, that parents play an important role in the formation of their children's political views. This role is more pronounced when both parents hold similar political beliefs and when political discussion is encouraged in the home. Gallatin's study also showed that teenagers raised in unusually strict or lenient families are less likely to be aware of political issues and tend not to be involved in politics.

Political psychologists analyze why some people participate more actively in the political process than others.

What Do You Think?

1. Why might voting be more common among people who believe that their actions can lead to political change?
2. What factors other than parental interest might influence a teen's political beliefs? Explain your answer.

CITIZENSHIP *Most U.S. citizens learn to say the Pledge of Allegiance in school at a young age. As adults many citizens continue to promise loyalty to their country by reciting the pledge.* **In what other ways does political socialization occur?**

Media Another major factor influencing public opinion is the media. Consider your daily activities. Do you spend time watching television or listening to the radio? If so, you may find that the media—magazines, newspapers, television, radio, and books—influence your opinions. The media provide people with much of the knowledge they use to form their opinions.

The media's influence on public opinion has grown over the years with the development of radio and television. Before television became popular, researchers in the 1930s and 1940s studied politicians ability to affect people's opinions through radio speeches. Radio was used often by the great political speakers of the age, such as President Franklin Roosevelt and British prime minister Winston Churchill. Adolf Hitler, dictator of Germany from 1933 to 1945, also used radio to rally support for his policies. Through radio, politicians had found a way to influence the way these people thought about the issues.

With the rise of television, media's ability to affect public opinion became even greater. One way television affects public opinion is by giving priority to certain issues. "The media do not affect *what* people think," it has been said, "but rather what they think *about*." In fact, some studies have shown that people tend to rank an issue as more important if it has received a high degree of evening news coverage.

In one study conducted in New Haven, Connecticut, for example, researchers had different groups of people watch television news broadcasts for a week. The broadcasts were the same as the actual national news shown each night, but with a few changes. One group of viewers saw a large number of stories on problems with U.S. defense capabilities, and a second saw a large number of stories about defense, inflation, and pollution. A third saw many stories about arms control, civil rights, and unemployment, and a fourth about unemployment only. (The stories, which were taken from earlier newscasts, were inserted into the newscasts without the viewers' knowledge.)

The researchers found that viewers who saw more stories on the targeted problems were more likely than the other groups to rate these problems as major national issues. As you can see from this study, the media play a considerable role in influencing people's opinions. You will learn more about the media, as well as how they affect the public good, in Section 3.

have shown that children as young as fourth grade frequently have political party preferences. In many cases these choices reflect the political beliefs of the children's parents or guardians.

School is also a significant part of the socialization process. In school you learn about your government, how it was founded, and why it is a good system. You also learn to say the Pledge of Allegiance, in which you promise loyalty to your country.

Other influences, such as those arising from regional background and income, also affect how people form their opinions. For example, people with low incomes are often more likely than those with high incomes to back government programs that provide health care, stimulate job growth, or redistribute income. Though regional opinion differences have lessened over the years, southerners do tend to be more conservative on moral and social issues than people in other regions of the country.

Recent research suggests that the key period in forming political beliefs is during the late teens or early twenties. At this time, people have new experiences, meet new people, and live more independently of their parents. People are open to new influences during that period, and therefore are more likely to be affected by major political events (such as wars or economic crises) and by popular ideas of the day.

The Nature of Public Opinion

There are two key features that influence the nature of public opinion. These are how strongly people feel about an issue and with which side of the issue people identify.

Strength of Opinion How strongly people feel about an issue is one factor that may determine the nature of public opinion. When answering a question such as "Are you for or against the death penalty?" people generally would say either, "I support it" or "I oppose it." The answer to such a question, however, would not reveal the *strength* of the opinion held. Because some issues matter a great deal more to some people than to others, determining the strength of people's opinions is important to understanding the nature of public opinion—strength of opinion can influence someone's vote, as well as how politically active the person will be regarding an issue.

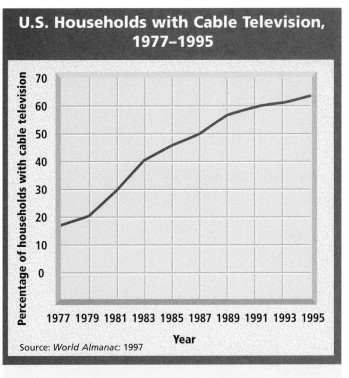

U.S. Households with Cable Television, 1977–1995

Source: *World Almanac: 1997*

With the rise of television's popularity, the media's influence has increased. **How do media affect people's opinions?**

Face of the Issue Which side of the issue a person identifies with is also an important factor when measuring public opinion. Just about every public policy the government might adopt has attractive and unattractive qualities. Environmental policies can preserve nature, for example, but by forcing factories to spend money on pollution control devices they can also make products more expensive. Not surprisingly, most people want both a clean environment and less expensive products. Nonetheless, people often take a stand on a particular side of an issue. Someone who hears about an environmental policy during a broadcast on air pollution would be more likely to support the legislation than someone who hears about it in connection with rising prices for consumer goods. Politicians, interest groups, and political parties frequently try to encourage people to see the "face" of the issue most favorable to their cause.

SECTION 1 — REVIEW

1. Define the following terms: public opinion, ideology, political socialization.

2. How can public opinion affect politics?

3. How do school, family, and ideology relate to public opinion?

4. How do media affect public opinion?

5. What two factors determine the nature of public opinion?

6. **Thinking and Writing Critically**
   Would the United States still be a representative democracy if policy makers ignored public opinion? Explain.

7. **Applying** PUBLIC GOOD
   Name some important issues that you have seen or heard covered in the media recently. How much does the media affect your opinion about these issues? Do you think that the media has accurately reportd information on the issues?

MEASURING PUBLIC OPINION

Political Dictionary

polling
exit poll
sampling
sampling error

Objectives

★ What is polling, and how is it used to determine public opinion?
★ What types of polls exist?
★ What are some of the main concerns in conducting a poll?

Have you ever filled out a questionnaire on the food service in the school's cafeteria or on a theme for a school dance? If so, you were responding to a poll. **Polling**—surveying a population on an issue—is the most reliable way of determining what the public thinks. In this case the pollsters at your school hoped to find out what you and other students thought about the cafeteria food or the dance. In a similar way, pollsters around the country survey people about their opinions on such things as presidential candidates and government policies.

Polling

The history of polling stretches back to the last century, but modern polling started in the 1930s and is now a regular feature of political life in the United States. Pollsters have asked Americans questions about almost everything—not only about politics but also about whether they snore or believe in the predictions of fortune-tellers.

There are several kinds of polls in use today, and they have varying levels of reliability. The most reliable polling methods were pioneered in the 1930s by George Gallup.

Origins of Polling George Gallup is the founder of modern political polling. While working on his doctoral degree, Gallup became convinced that the survey method that newspapers and other organizations were using was inaccurate. Many of the polling questions being asked were open-ended, failing to probe residents for specific, detailed answers. For example, one poll might ask respondents which sections of the newspaper they read. Some people, embarrassed to admit that they read only the comics and not the editorial page, would answer falsely.

Gallup developed a polling method that involved, in this instance, going through each section of the newspaper to determine which sections interested the respondent. In this way the respondent could express interest in each section separately. (In response to an early Gallup poll revealing that not only children but also adults read the comics, the *Des Moines Register and Tribune* decided not to cut back, but to expand its comic section.)

Gallup gained fame in 1936 by attacking the presidential poll that a weekly magazine called the *Literary Digest* had conducted since 1916. The magazine polled voters by mailing out millions of ballots to people whose names had been gathered from lists of automobile and telephone owners. In 1936 the *Digest* predicted that Republican Alfred

POLITICAL PROCESSES *Pollsters often ask citizens about their political opinions.* **How can open-ended polling questions lead to inaccurate survey results?**

PUBLIC GOOD *Telephone interviews are a quick and inexpensive method for conducting polling surveys.* **What are other common types of polls?**

M. Landon would win over Democrat Franklin D. Roosevelt.

Gallup claimed that the methods used in the *Digest* poll were flawed and that the poll was unrepresentative of all voters. He made this determination because the lists on which the poll was based did not include low-income voters, who at that time were less likely to have cars or telephones. Gallup then declared that his own poll would produce more-accurate results. He backed his claim by declaring that if he were proved wrong, he would refund the money that newspapers had paid for the columns he had written. Gallup predicted that Roosevelt would win the election with 54 percent of the vote.

The *Literary Digest* poll was in fact flawed, and for just the reason that Gallup had mentioned. The *Digest*'s faulty prediction became perhaps the most famous polling blooper ever, for Roosevelt won the greatest landslide victory in U.S. history up to that point. (Actually, even Gallup's poll was off, underestimating Roosevelt's victory by 7 percent.)

With the success of his 1936 presidential poll, Gallup launched a career as the pioneer of modern polling. Gallup had better results than other pollsters because he used a more scientific method of polling. That is, he polled a group of people who better represented the U.S. population as a whole. Gallup's success firmly established

statistical sampling methods in opinion polling. This kind of scientific polling has become increasingly complex and more accurate as pollsters have developed better techniques.

Types of Polls The most common types of polls are in-person interviews, telephone interviews, and mail questionnaires. In-person interviews were common in the early days of polling and are still used by a few polling organizations, such as the one founded by Gallup. Most polling organizations, however, have abandoned in-person interviews for telephone interviews, which are quicker and less expensive.

Mail questionnaires have also been popular for many years. Some early mail questionnaires used "straw ballots," which people could clip out of a newspaper, fill out, and drop in the mail. Mail polls are inexpensive and allow more questions, but generally fewer people respond to them. In some cases, however, researchers who have carefully selected the population they will be polling have used them with much success.

In 1967 the Columbia Broadcasting System (CBS) pioneered another technique—the exit poll. An **exit poll** surveys a fraction of voters in randomly selected voting precincts after they have cast their ballots. This allows pollsters to discover how people actually voted without waiting for the official votes to be counted.

The use of exit polls has been criticized in recent elections. In 1980, for example, a television network using exit poll results declared Ronald Reagan the winner of the presidential election while people on the West Coast were still voting. (Because of the time zone difference, polls on the East Coast had already closed.) This early announcement, it was argued, discouraged people from voting, thereby possibly influencing the outcome of other West Coast races, such as those for congressional seats. Today, television networks generally do not broadcast a state's exit poll results while people in that state are still voting.

Conducting Polls

If pollsters are to gain reliable results from a poll, they must follow certain guidelines. Getting accurate results depends on how people are chosen to participate in the poll, the type of poll that is used, proper question wording and order, and how familiar the public is with the issue.

Pollster

Pollsters conduct surveys on public opinion for many kinds of clients, ranging from political groups to media organizations to business interests. The information they collect can help shape public policy, change corporate plans, and inform the public on important issues. They may conduct polls over the phone, through the mail, on the Internet, or in person.

Some pollsters work as independent consultants. For example, Frank Luntz is an independent pollster whose firm assists Republican candidates for public office. Luntz earned undergraduate and graduate degrees in political science before starting his own business in 1991. In 1994 he guided the polling work that helped Republicans prepare their Contract with America. He then became one of House Speaker Newt Gingrich's advisers on public opinion.

Luntz's job requires him to travel extensively and work long hours. He meets regularly with clients to plan polling strategies and discuss poll results, and he watches television shows and listens to popular music to keep in touch with public attitudes.

Other independent pollsters help businesses test public opinion before marketing new products. Some help local organizations and charities determine the best ways to conduct fund-raising drives or serve the needs of the community. In this way, unpopular initiatives might be avoided or modified before the public votes on them.

Many pollsters work for companies that supply

Pollsters need to know how to listen and communicate well in order to gather accurate information.

news media with polling information. Often these companies work according to tight deadlines, creating poll questions on current news events and conducting polls to characterize public opinion as it changes in response to events.

Some pollsters work for nonpartisan organizations. These pollsters provide information on public views to politicians, journalists, scholars, and public interest organizations. Their goal is to educate the public and help civic leaders create better public policies.

Pollsters must have strong writing and analytical skills to create unambiguous questionnaires and to interpret the results accurately. In addition, pollsters need a clear knowledge of current events so that they can ask questions on important subjects at the appropriate times. They also need to be good communicators and listeners to determine what their clients need to know.

Sampling Modern public opinion polls depend heavily on accurate **sampling**—or the choosing of a group of people to participate in a poll. To get a poll result that accurately reflects the total population's opinion, participants must be chosen at random.

Good polling relies on the randomness of the sample much more than its size. The 1936 *Literary Digest* poll, for example, had a sample of more than 2 million, but came up with inaccurate results because the sample was not random. Many national polls try to determine the opinions of almost 200 million potential voters by questioning only 1,500 respondents. Some people doubt the validity of such polls. Indeed, when Americans once were polled about whether national polls with 1,500 respondents could be accurate, only 28 percent thought they could be, while 56 percent said they could not.

Hundreds of election polls have proved, however, that such a sample size can indeed give accurate results. As one political scientist points out, cooks test soups by sampling only one spoonful from a large pot, and doctors test blood by drawing a single drop from a whole body. Mathematical proofs have demonstrated that a small random sample can accurately represent the opinions of hundreds of millions of people.

A sample cannot, however, reveal with certainty what the *exact* distribution of opinion in response to a question would have been if everyone in the population had been surveyed, instead of just a sample. The uncertainty that sampling introduces is called **sampling error**. The likely size of the possible error, which can be determined through statistics, is expressed as a percent above and below a poll's result. For example, a poll might find that candidate A leads candidate B by 55 percent of the vote to 45 percent. If the sampling error were 5 points, however, candidate A might get between 50 to 60 percent of the vote while candidate B might get 40 to 50 percent.

Question Wording The wording of a poll's questions can lead to inaccurate results. Questions that make a one-sided statement and ask poll respondents to agree or disagree with it tend to get biased results.

For example, suppose someone in your school conducts a poll worded in this way: "All students should be allowed to go off campus for lunch. Do you agree or disagree?" Because of how the statement is phrased, most students being polled would probably agree. Now consider this wording: "Some students believe that the school day should start 30 minutes earlier so that there would be extra time to leave campus for lunch. Other students believe that the school should keep the shorter day and continue to hold lunch in the cafeteria. Which belief comes closer to your opinion?" Even though both questions are asking about the same situation, your answer to the second one might be different because it presents more information.

Certain words also can affect results. For example, in a poll about how to cut government

"OUR LATEST POLL SHOWS THAT 68% OF THE VOTERS THINK THAT 91% OF THE POLLS ARE INACCURATE 71% OF THE TIME -- PLUS OR MINUS THREE PERCENTAGE POINTS."

RICHMOND TIMES-DISPATCH · 9/18 · ©1988 · BROOKINS

Gary Brookins, 1988, *Richmond Times-Dispatch*. Reprinted by permission.

PUBLIC GOOD *Television networks often broadcast the results of exit polls and public opinion polls.* **Why is randomness more important than sampling size in getting accurate polling results?**

budgets, only 8 percent of the respondents identified "aid to the needy" as an area for cuts. When the poll referred to this budget area as "public welfare programs," however, 39 percent supported cuts. Why the change? The two terms bring up very different images in respondents' minds. "Aid to the needy" calls up a picture of human suffering. In contrast, "public welfare" has become negatively associated with people who take advantage of government welfare programs.

Keep wording's effect on responses in mind when analyzing poll results. Those who wish to use poll results to advance a particular viewpoint can manipulate question wording to create inaccurate results.

Question Order Just as different ways of wording a question can affect a poll's response, so can the order in which questions are asked—even if the wording is unchanged. The earlier questions in a poll may lead people to see an issue in a certain way, thus possibly affecting how they answer later questions.

Think about the following situation. A pollster is conducting a poll during a presidential election year. The economy is in a slump. The order of the pollster's questions is as follows: 1) How well do you think the country is doing these days? 2) What do you think of President Pat Hartley's economic policies? 3) Are you going to vote for President Hartley in the election? The pollster's questions

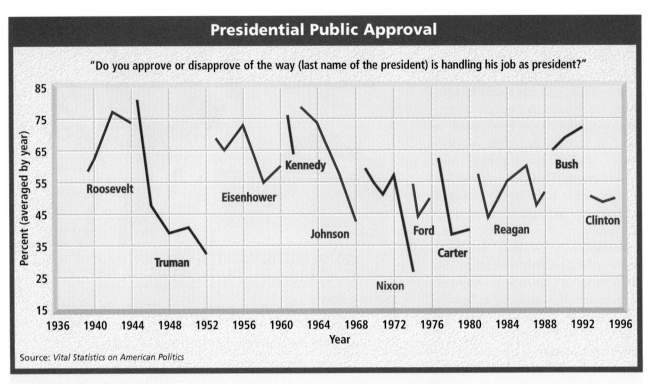

Presidential Public Approval

"Do you approve or disapprove of the way (last name of the president) is handling his job as president?"

Source: Vital Statistics on American Politics

For more than 50 years citizens have been polled about how well they feel the president is handling his job. **Which president experienced the most dramatic drop in his approval rating during his time in office?**

remind the respondent that the country is in an economic slump and suggest that President Hartley might be somehow responsible. The respondent thus is more likely to have a negative response to the question about voting for President Hartley.

Timing When a poll is held also can affect its results. Public opinion often can change dramatically, particularly on new issues. Early polls on such issues often are poor predictors because people have not yet developed strong opinions.

For example, polls sometimes are conducted very early during a presidential race. These polls may give a misleading impression of how people will actually vote. After all, as the events unfold and people find out more information, their opinions about candidates often change. As a result, you should be cautious about results of early polls.

SECTION 2 — REVIEW

1. Define the following terms: polling, exit poll, sampling, sampling error.

2. How is polling significant in determining public opinion?

3. Describe the four main types of modern polls.

4. How can a poll's sampling affect its results?

5. **Thinking and Writing Critically**
Your school newspaper has just printed the results of a poll about upcoming student elections. To determine the poll's accuracy, what questions should you ask about how the poll was conducted? Explain your answer.

6. **Applying POLITICAL PROCESSES**
Think of an issue about which you would be interested in knowing your fellow students' opinions. Write two different questions regarding the issue that you believe will get two different responses. How do you change wording to get two different answers?

THE MEDIA AND THE PUBLIC GOOD

Political Dictionary

censorship
bias
objectivity

Objectives

★ What is the role of the media?
★ What are some criticisms of the media?
★ What are the checks on media influence?

O n what do you rely to gain information about what is going on in the world around you? If you want information about your school, you might read your student newspaper. If you are looking for news about the music world, you might read *Spin* magazine or watch MTV.

As you can see from these examples, one role of the media is to provide information. By fulfilling this and other roles, the media help promote the public good. The media are not, however, without their critics and limitations.

Role of the Media

As noted in Chapter 13, the First Amendment guarantees freedom of the press. The news media have constitutional protection from government **censorship**—the control of information or speech. This protection of the press, the framers believed, promotes the public good by allowing the media to provide information and to serve as a watchdog over government officials and policies. These are the most important roles of the media, whose freedom enables them to determine how much coverage to give to each story.

Informing the Public The media's role as a source of information is significant because they provide facts that people in a democracy need to

make wise decisions about their government. "Were it left to me to decide whether we should have a government without newspapers, or newspapers without a government," wrote Thomas Jefferson in 1787, "I should not hesitate a moment to prefer the latter." By providing information to citizens, the media play a key role in promoting the public good.

C A S E   S T U D Y

"Rock the Vote" and "Choose or Lose"

POLITICAL PROCESSES One way that the media can promote the public good is by encouraging citizen participation in elections. In 1990, for example, MTV began airing public service announcements urging viewers to register to vote and to head to the polls. Spots featured pop singer and actress Madonna, rapper Ice-T, and the members of the band R.E.M.

The ads were part of the music industry's Rock the Vote campaign. "The idea is to raise the political consciousness (awareness) of kids and to make voting hip," explained Jody Uttal, cofounder of the campaign. Part of Rock the Vote involved organizing record stores to pass out voter registration materials. Campaign workers also registered thousands of voters at college campuses and at Lollapalooza, a multiperformer concert tour.

CONSTITUTIONAL GOVERNMENT *The Constitution guarantees freedom of press. This freedom allows the media to provide information free from government control.* **Why is the media's role important in a democracy?**

In 1992 MTV also began a political awareness campaign called Choose or Lose. Journalist Tabitha Soren hosted forums with Democratic candidate Bill Clinton and Republican president George Bush. The forums covered issues of concern to young people, including education, the economy, crime, race relations, and AIDS. For the 1996 presidential elections, MTV outfitted a bus for a cross-country voter registration drive. Sporting a Choose or Lose banner that featured quotes from celebrities, the bus stopped at college campuses and rock concerts to register voters. After registering, potential voters signed a pledge promising to "rock the system by exercising my right to vote."

These media campaigns targeted at young people have had mixed results. In 1992 about 42 percent of eligible voters between the ages of 18 and 24 turned out at the polls—a significant increase from the 33.2 percent of 1988. Four years later in 1996, however, the number of young voters had dropped to about 30 percent.

Serving As a Watchdog In its watchdog role the media check the power of government and other institutions, such as business and sports. They do so by investigating and exposing abuses of power by people who are harming the public good to benefit themselves.

Defending the public against "special interests" is a critical part of this role. For example, suppose that the media run a story about how a company is trying to get the government's permission to build a pollution-generating factory near a community's water supply. Without the media's coverage of this story, the public might have been totally unaware of the company's efforts. By informing the public, the media help serve as a balance, allowing the voice of the majority to be heard.

Acting As a Gatekeeper Keep in mind that the media—as information providers—also act as a gatekeeper. Because too much happens in the world for every topic to be covered completely the media must select which stories to report and how much importance to assign to them. For example, should an account of a hurricane in the Caribbean

Comparing
Governments

The Cuban Press

Authoritarian governments around the world generally silence any criticism from the press. In Cuba, for example, all newspapers as well as radio and television stations are owned by the government. Journalists who criticize the policies of the nation's communist leaders are fired from their jobs. Many are arrested and imprisoned.

In October 1995, for example, Cuban police arrested journalist Olance Nogueras Roce for writing a story on safety problems at a nuclear plant. He was charged with "publishing false information contrary to international peace." Many other Cuban journalists also have been threatened and had their equipment and files seized.

Despite such harassment and the threat of arrest, some Cuban journalists have founded the Independent Press Bureau of Cuba to market stories outside the country. Independent journalist Yndamiro Restano hopes to establish a free press in Cuba. "It is the only way we can help change our system from an authoritarian government to a democratic one, without violence," he says.

be a newspaper's lead story instead of a report on newly released national economic statistics? How much broadcast airtime or front-page coverage should the passing of the federal budget receive in comparison to a plane crash in a foreign country? By making these decisions, the media direct the public's attention to areas they consider important. In the process, the media serve to promote the public good by enabling people to avoid sifting through mountains of detail just to find out what the big news stories are.

Criticisms of the Media

For the media to promote the public good, they must be fair in providing information and different viewpoints to the public. Many people question whether the media succeed in their roles as gatekeeper and watchdog. Some critics accuse members of the media of letting bias—personal judgment or prejudice—interfere with their role of informing the public. These critics believe that members of the media too often represent their own personal opinions. Actually, the way events are selected and covered, and with what kind of emphasis, does depend in large part on the judgment of the people who gather the news and decide which stories to publish or broadcast. In addition, some critics believe that by presenting too many negative stories, relying on visual imagery, and focusing on nonsubstantive issues, the media fail to promote the public good as well as they should.

Objectivity

The ability to report both sides of an issue without bias is called **objectivity**. Being objective is essential if the media is to provide information fairly and accurately.

Some people question whether objectivity in the media is even possible. They point out that there are many facts connected with any story. At a presidential press conference, for instance, the facts include not only what the president says but also how he or she says it and what he or she avoids saying. In determining which parts of the conference to report, and what (if any) comments to make about them, the reporter has to decide what is important. This decision opens the door for bias to affect how a story is covered or even if it is covered at all.

Are the critics right? Are the media biased? Just as some members of the general population act on their biases, some members of the media allow their personal opinions to affect their reporting. Many other members of the media, however, do strive to report only what they believe to be newsworthy, based on general standards rather than personal bias, or what they believe their readers and viewers would want to know. In the end, citizens as well as the media are responsible for judging information. You, as a consumer of news, must be alert to the possible bias of a journalist, broadcaster, or other media figure, and keep it in mind when evaluating reported information.

Negative Focus

Many critics also charge that the media focus on negative or sensational stories just to draw audience attention. A larger television audience or newspaper circulation usually means higher advertising revenues. Some people

"REMEMBER — THIS CHANNEL IS ALWAYS PLEASED TO GIVE AIR TIME TO A BROAD SPECTRUM OF EDITORIAL RESPONSES WHICH AGREE WITH US."

© 1999 by Sidney Harris.

PUBLIC GOOD *Although many members of the news media strive for objectivity in their reporting, critics argue that unbiased reporting may not be possible.* **Why might it be difficult for members of the media to be completely objective in their reporting?**

believe that to gain such revenue, the media concentrate too heavily on reporting bad news and problems and on exposing the flaws of politicians and officials.

For example, a study of election coverage of the 1992 presidential campaign concluded that all three candidates received more negative than positive coverage. In fact, according to one analysis, coverage of presidential candidates has become much more negative over the last 30 years. By making policies and institutions seem to work more poorly than they actually do, a negative focus can cause citizens to lose faith in government's ability to handle public problems.

Probably the major reason for the negative tone in journalism concerns newsworthiness—that is, whether or not an event makes a good story. The *unusual* is what is considered news. When social institutions are working as they should, they make no news. In most cases, they make news only when something goes wrong. Thus, the saying "No news is good news" is true: good news tends not to be news!

Though many people dislike this negative focus, others argue that it is necessary for keeping citizens informed about the problems surrounding public officials and institutions. These people believe that the media's importance as a watchdog outweighs any effects of a negative focus in the media.

Visual Imagery Another criticism of television is that to gain reader or viewer interest, it relies too much on pictures instead of the ideas behind an issue. Because stories often seem more powerful when accompanied by strong imagery, some critics fear that important stories without good pictures might be ignored by television.

For example, the crisis in the savings and loan industry in the 1980s was not a very "visual" story. It could show no storm-ravaged coasts, no blazing fires, no dying victims. Thus, though the crisis ended up costing taxpayers almost $150 billion, it received little television news coverage. Some critics say that it might have received more attention if the story had been a visual one.

"Horse-Race Coverage" Other critics believe that reporters tend to focus on "horse-race coverage" of politics. By this they mean, for example, that a president's likely success in *passing* an energy policy proposal through Congress often receives more attention than what the policy actually *involves*. Coverage therefore focuses on which side is "winning"—the president or Congress. This, critics argue, draws attention from the ideas behind an issue and indicates media's failure to do their job.

Checks on the Media

Despite the above criticisms, the media do promote the public good in an important way. They provide information and, through the watchdog role, preserve a balance among government officials, institutions, and the public. At the same time, media's powerful influence on public opinion does have some natural limitations.

One limitation is that the media tend to reinforce the beliefs that people already hold rather than create new ones. For example, some researchers have found that people tend to expose themselves just to those media that support their opinions. Think again about where you find information about the subjects in which you are interested. *You* choose what magazines to read, what stations to listen to, and what shows to watch. In each of these cases you probably choose magazines, stations, and shows that reflect the tastes and opinions that you already hold.

Another limitation on any undue power of the media is that people do not always pay attention to what is on television or in the newspapers. One study found that as much as 40 percent of the time that a person's television set is on, he or she is doing other things. Many people talk with one another, read, or play games, while television merely serves as background noise. Regarding newspapers, most people pay close attention only to the stories that truly interest them.

If citizens are to take advantage of the media's role in promoting the public good, they must recognize the criticisms while working to remain informed. Taking the shortcomings of the media into account, you as a media consumer must analyze the information you receive and use it to make educated decisions about officials, policies, and institutions that affect your everyday life.

★★★★★ **SECTION 3** — **REVIEW** ★★★★★

1. Define the following terms: censorship, bias, objectivity.

2. What roles do the media play in influencing public opinion?

3. What factors can prevent the media from performing their roles effectively?

4. What are the natural limitations on the media's influence?

5. **Thinking and Writing Critically**
   Think about your school newspaper. What role does it perform? Does a school newspaper have certain limitations that other papers do not? Explain your answer.

6. **Applying** PUBLIC GOOD
   What role does the media play for you and other people in your age group? Is this a positive or negative role?

SECTION 1 Public opinion is the collective opinion of large numbers of people. It represents the voice of the majority of the people in the country. Because public officials in a democracy must be concerned with what the majority of the population thinks, public opinion is an important factor in forming government policies.

Government officials, researchers, and others concerned with public opinion can tell what people's opinions are by examining their political participation. The ways in which people participate in the political process include voting, speaking or writing about political issues, demonstrating, and joining interest groups.

People form their opinions based on various factors. Their ideology—or basic political beliefs—greatly influences their opinions. Other factors—such as family and school, job, income, education, age, gender, race, and geographic region—combine in a process called political socialization to affect a person's opinions on issues. In addition, the media—magazines, newspapers, television, radio, and books—provide people with much of the knowledge they use to form their opinions.

SECTION 2 Researchers measure public opinion through polling. Polls gained greater reliability with the scientific methods developed by George Gallup in the 1930s. Gallup determined that the survey methods used by newspapers and other organizations at that time produced inaccurate results. Gallup used a more scientific polling method, and his success firmly established statistical sampling as a foundation of modern opinion polling.

The various types of polls, all with varying levels of reliability, include in-person interviews, telephone interviews, and mail questionnaires. In addition, the so-called exit poll surveys a fraction of voters in randomly selected voting precincts after they have voted.

Sampling, question wording and order, and timing affect a poll's accuracy. If sampling is not done at random, the poll will not be accurate. Likewise, if the wording of a question or the order of the questions is misleading, the poll will be inaccurate. Finally, timing can play a big role in a poll's results.

SECTION 3 The media's great influence on public opinion often inspires questions about their role and whether or not they promote the public good. The media serve three main functions—informing the public, acting as a gatekeeper, and serving as a watchdog. In performing these roles, however, the media have been subjected to many criticisms. They are sometimes criticized for their negative focus, a lack of objectivity, and too heavy a reliance on visual imagery and "horse-race coverage" to make an interesting story.

The media's influence does have some limitations. People tend to seek only those sources of information that reflect their own viewpoints. Another limitation is that many people do not always pay attention to what is on television or in the newspapers. An active and informed citizen must be aware of the criticisms of the media while relying on the news to stay knowledgeable about the issues affecting his or her community.

Government Notebook

Review what you wrote in your Government Notebook at the beginning of the chapter about your opinions. How do your opinions on such things as clothes or classes affect the people around you? What caused you to form your opinions on these issues, and where do you get your information? Record your answer in your Notebook.

REVIEW

REVIEWING CONCEPTS

1. Define public opinion, and explain how it relates to the political process.

2. How is public opinion measured?

3. What are some of the factors that influence public opinion?

4. What is the media's role in politics, and does it benefit the public good? Explain your answer.

5. What issues must one consider when conducting a poll or examining its results?

6. Why do some people feel that the media fail to fulfill their role?

THINKING AND WRITING CRITICALLY

1. **CITIZENSHIP** What factors have influenced your political beliefs the most? Do you think that one factor has influenced your political opinions more than others? Explain your answers.

2. **POLITICAL PROCESSES** Do you think that television networks should be allowed to broadcast exit poll results while people are still voting? Why or why not?

3. **PUBLIC GOOD** Do you think that people should be skeptical of "straw poll" results? Give an example of a poll with probable sampling error whose results you have seen or heard. What polling method was used?

4. **PUBLIC GOOD** What kinds of stories most commonly make headlines? Do you think that giving the most prominent coverage to such stories promotes the public good? Explain your answers.

CITIZENSHIP IN YOUR COMMUNITY

With a group, create a questionnaire on an issue that is important to young people—for example, television rating systems or funding for higher education. Before beginning, you might find it useful to examine the common polling pitfalls discussed in Section 2. Have the members of your group poll their family or friends to find out how they feel about the issue you selected. Compare the results of all group members and combine them into one report.

INDIVIDUAL PORTFOLIO PROJECT

Interview one classmate, one family member, and one adult friend or teacher about their political beliefs, or ideology. Ask questions that focus on the government's role in U.S. society and the international community, as well as on freedom, opportunity, justice, and equality. Be sure to ask each person the same questions in the same order. After you have conducted the interviews, write a paper comparing the ideologies of each person. Answer the following questions in the paper:

★ What were the major differences in ideologies?
★ What were the similarities?
★ Were there values shared by all three people?

THE INTERNET: LEARNING ONLINE

Conduct an Internet search for the results of a political public opinion poll. You might start with search words such as *public opinion, political polls,* and *surveys.* Create a chart outlining the results of the poll. Also, write down both the list of questions asked in the poll and the address of the Web site where you found the information.

PRACTICING SKILLS: UNDERSTANDING MEASUREMENT CONCEPTS AND METHODS

Study the chart below, which shows the results of a 1994 survey of high school seniors concerning their life goals. Then answer the questions that follow.

Goals Rated by Seniors as Extremely Important

PERSONAL GOALS	
Having a Good Marriage and Family Life	76%
Being Successful in My Line of Work	63%
Having Lots of Money	26%

SOCIAL GOALS	
Making a Contribution to Society	24%
Working to Correct Social and Economic Inequalities	14%
Being a Leader in My Community	14%

Source: Bachman, J. G.; Johnston, L. D.; and O'Malley, P. M. "Monitoring the Future: Questionnaire Responses from the Nations' High School Seniors," 1994

1. What additional information do you need to determine the accuracy of this poll?

2. Which personal goal did the smallest percentage of students rate as extremely important?

3. Which social goal did the highest percentage of students rate as extremely important?

4. Which personal and social goals would you rate as extremely important?

ANALYZING PRIMARY SOURCES

SPEECH ON NATIONAL SERVICE

As you have read, George Gallup developed public opinion polling methods that achieve more accurate results than earlier methods. Although Gallup died in 1984, the Gallup Organization, Inc., continues to conduct public opinion polls across the United States and in other countries. Gallup's son, George Gallup, Jr., is now co-chairman of the organization. In the following speech, he discusses public opinion on national service. Read the excerpt and answer the questions that follow.

❝ As far as the American people are concerned, national service on a broad scale is an idea whose time is long overdue. In fact, if a national referendum were held today on whether young men should be required to give a year of service to the nation—in either military or non-military work—the proposal would likely win heavy support. Even greater enthusiasm is found for voluntary programs. In fact, a Gallup Poll found more than eight in ten Americans (83 percent) in favor of setting up a voluntary national program that would permit young people of both sexes to enroll in the military forces or in non-military service projects.

All age groups show high levels of support for giving young people a choice of offering a year of their time following high school or college. In fact, the 18-to-24-year-old age group favors the idea even slightly more (87 percent) than the general public.

Gallup surveys reveal the types of projects the public thinks could be undertaken with a program of national service, including:

- *literacy training for children*
- *conservation, public works, and anti-pollution programs*
- *working with law enforcement agencies in their efforts to rehabilitate youthful offenders*
- *disaster-relief*
- *working with senior citizens in joint volunteer programs. ❞*

1. What percentage of Americans are in favor of a voluntary national service program?

2. Which projects does the public think should be the focus of a national service program?

3. Are you in favor of setting up a national service program? Why or why not?

INTEREST GROUPS

What do members of the American Frozen Food Institute and the National Hot Rod Association have in common? Probably very little as far as their groups' interests are concerned. They do, however, have at least one common trait—they are both members of interest groups.

Like a team or club, interest groups are made up of members who have common goals and—often—intense concerns. Unlike teams or clubs, however, interest groups' goals often are far-reaching and political. In this chapter you will learn about the different types of interest groups, as well as the ways in which they promote their goals.

Government Notebook

In your Government Notebook, write a list of the kinds of groups you think qualify as interest groups. What do these groups have in common? Write your answer in your Notebook.

ROLE OF INTEREST GROUPS

Political Dictionary

agribusiness
trade association
labor union
public interest group

Objectives

★ What is an interest group?
★ What are the functions of interest groups?
★ What are the types of interest groups?

Throughout history, people have organized groups to promote their views on issues that concern them. As noted in Chapter 15, some such groups were made up of African Americans who came together to fight for their civil rights.

Such organized groups, or interest groups, give people a way to work together toward their common goals. As noted in Chapter 5, an interest group is a collection of people acting together to advance a shared concern in the political process. Interest groups serve several key functions in the United States and take several forms.

Functions of Interest Groups

As noted in Chapter 8, public opinion represents the voice of the majority in the political process. Interest groups, however, provide a means by which one segment of the population—typically a minority—can have its intensely held concerns represented in political decision making. They do so in three main ways—by

★ organizing people who share a concern,
★ providing a means of political participation, and
★ supplying information to the public and to policy makers.

Organizing People Interest groups provide a means of organization for people who share strong opinions about an issue. The issue might be one that affects members of the group personally or one that group members believe needs to be addressed to promote the public good. People with strong opinions typically join an interest group in the hope that working with others who have shared concerns will strengthen their cause.

Groups that have banded together to promote their common concerns include farmers, businesspeople, workers, environmentalists, feminists, civil rights activists, and students. People in the fishing industry who disagree with environmentalists over how much commercial fishing should take place may participate in interest groups to make their views heard. Likewise, joining an environmentalist group gives another sector of the population—in this case, citizens concerned about commercial fishing—political strength that they may not have as individuals.

Providing for Political Participation Often when citizens feel strongly about political issues, they want to do more than merely vote for candidates who will represent their concerns. Joining an interest group gives these citizens another way

POLITICAL PROCESSES *Members of the United Farm Workers of America gather at a convention in Fresno, California, to discuss issues concerning their group.* **What are some of the other types of groups whose members have banded together to promote their common cause?**

to take part in the political process—particularly if they are part of a minority viewpoint that is not represented through majority-dominated elections. By working with like-minded people to make their views known to the public and to policy makers, interest group members can affect government actions. As you will learn in Section 2, interest groups have several ways of influencing the political process.

Supplying Information A third function of interest groups is to inform the public about their concerns. For example, if you are curious about a certain industry's effect on air quality, you can contact an environmental interest group. If you want to know what goods and services that industry provides, you can contact a business interest group that represents it. In both cases the interest groups are happy to provide information about their concerns. By doing so, groups that represent the concerns of a minority of the population can draw the attention of the majority to their viewpoints.

Interest groups supply information not only to the public but also to policy makers. In this way, interest groups hope to influence legislation that affects their areas of concern.

Types of Interest Groups

Thousands of interest groups operate in the United States. They range from small local groups to large national organizations, and they represent many concerns. Some seek to inform the public about the needs and concerns of museums, and some organize to support animal rights. These groups may have many members or only a few.

Many interest groups—such as agricultural groups, business groups, labor unions, and professional groups—are formed to address economic concerns. Others are based on social, cultural, or related causes.

Agricultural Groups Because government policies greatly affect agriculture, several interest groups have formed to represent the nation's farmers and agribusinesses. **Agribusinesses** are large companies that run farms, make and distribute farm equipment and supplies, and process, store, and distribute farm crops. Some agricultural interest groups, such as the American Farm Bureau Federation, represent farmers as a whole. Others, like the National Cotton Council of America, represent a particular section of the agricultural industry.

Business Groups Another element of society that operates under heavy government regulation is business. For this reason, businesses—like farmers and agribusinesses—have formed interest groups to advance their own concerns. For example, the Chamber of Commerce of the U.S.A. and the Business Roundtable are nationwide organizations that represent general business interests.

In addition, many businesses maintain specialized interest groups to represent their specific concerns. These interest groups, called **trade associations**, are organizations of business firms within an industry. For example, the snack food and trucking industries both have trade associations that represent their concerns. Though trade

PUBLIC GOOD *Members of the Columbia, Missouri, Chamber of Commerce tour the construction site of a stadium being built on the University of Missouri campus.* **Why have businesses formed interest groups such as the Chamber of Commerce to advance their own concerns?**

associations participate in non-political activities, such as developing product standards, their major function is to represent the political concerns of their industries.

Labor Unions Workers also have formed interest groups to represent them. These **labor unions** are organizations of workers acting together to gain better wages and working conditions. Labor organizations include those for educators and for office workers.

Major union activities involve representing member interests at the workplace, but most unions also are involved in politics. The American Federation of Labor–Congress of Industrial Organizations (AFL–CIO) is a huge collection of many unions that was established in 1955 and currently has more than 13 million members. The AFL–CIO works on a national level to raise the minimum wage, for example, and to secure greater health and other benefits for workers.

Professional Groups Some professions, such as law and medicine, also maintain interest groups to represent their concerns. Among the well-known professional organizations are the American Bar Association (ABA), which works to protect the interests of those in the legal profession, and the American Medical Association (AMA), a group representing those who practice medicine.

Professional groups perform several key functions. In addition to creating standards for the profession, holding meetings, and publishing journals and reports, these groups represent their members' concerns in the political system.

Societal Groups Another type of interest group represents societal groups, such as various ethnic groups, women, and veterans. Societal interest groups include the National Association for the Advancement of Colored People (NAACP), the Mexican-American Legal Defense Fund (MALDEF), the National Organization for Women (NOW), and the American Legion.

TOLES © 1990 The Buffalo News. Reprinted with the permission of Universal Press Syndicate. All rights reserved.

POLITICAL PROCESSES *The goals of interest groups, such as cause-based environmental groups, sometimes conflict with the goals of other groups. The cartoon above provides a humorous look at environmental groups' efforts.* **What tools do cause-based groups use to promote their views?**

These groups are often powerful. The American Association of Retired Persons (AARP), which represents older Americans, has 32 million members. It is the largest organization in the United States after the Roman Catholic Church.

Cause-Based Groups Some groups promote a broad cause, rather than the interest of a certain group of people or businesses. Such causes may include education, a particular field of research, and cultural goals. The National Association for the Advancement of Science promotes scientific research and funding for scientific endeavors. Like professional interest groups, such organizations often hold meetings and publish journals about their topics of concern. These organizations' political goals involve gaining funding for a project and influencing government regulation of the field in which they are interested.

C A S E   S T U D Y

Students Against Drunk Driving

One growing cause-based interest group is Students Against Drunk Driving (SADD). This group works to prevent teenage drinking and driving by raising public awareness and by persuading teens to pledge not to drive under the influence of alcohol.

The organization was founded in 1982 by a high school coach and administrator in Wayland, Massachusetts, after two of his hockey players died in separate accidents. By the mid-1990s SADD had around 4 million members and 20,000 chapters in schools across the country.

Traffic accidents are the leading cause of death for 16- to 20-year-olds. In 1994 almost half of the automobile accidents that took the lives of people in this age group involved alcohol. According to the National Highway Traffic Safety Administration (NHTSA) statistics for 1995, an average of one alcohol-related traffic fatality occurs every 30 minutes. The NHTSA also estimates that about two in every five Americans will be involved in an alcohol-related crash at some point in their lives.

SADD chapters use a variety of strategies to prevent teen drinking and driving. Some chapters have staged public events such as mock crashes, with local police and emergency medical teams helping to simulate the aftermath of a car accident for a student audience. Many chapters sponsor alcohol-free events on prom or graduation night. One of the most important SADD strategies, however, is the Contract for Life. Under the rules of the contract, teens promise to call their parents for a ride home if they or other drivers have been drinking. Parents agree to provide a ride home with no questions or punishment until the following day.

SADD also works with other organizations, such as Mothers Against Drunk Driving (MADD), to influence public policy regarding teen drinking and driving. Members of MADD's Youth in Action program, a group within the organization for people under 21, work with adults to change laws, strengthen enforcement, and publicize efforts to stop teen drinking and driving.

These groups' efforts, combined with the establishment of a nationwide minimum drinking age of 21, appear to have helped save lives. In 1985 about 2,200 drivers age 16 to 20 were involved in fatal alcohol-related accidents. In 1995 that number had dropped to less than 1,000. The decrease in such fatalities was greater for 16- to 20-year-olds than for any other age group.

Other groups promoting particular broad causes include religious groups, environmental groups, gun control groups, anti–gun control groups, and antiabortion and abortion rights groups. The Christian Coalition, the National Rifle Association (NRA), Planned Parenthood, and the National Catholic Welfare Council are all groups that promote causes.

Some cause-based groups refer to themselves as **public interest groups**, or citizens' groups, believing that the policies they pursue would benefit the general public rather than a narrow minority. Public interest groups thus represent people with strong beliefs about what would promote the public good.

The Sierra Club, one of the nation's oldest public interest groups, was founded in 1892 by environmentalist John Muir to work for the preservation of wilderness lands. Today the Sierra Club lobbies for environmentalist causes across the nation.

PUBLIC GOOD *Yosemite National Park, one of the country's oldest national parks, was established as federally protected land in 1890, due in large part to the efforts of Sierra Club-founder John Muir.* ***Why might environmental interest groups also refer to themselves as public interest groups?***

Linking

Government and Sociology

The Influence of Groups on Society

Do you closely follow the news about politics or other public issues? Have you ever passed out flyers or pamphlets to support a particular cause? Have you participated in a debate or discussion on an important political issue? Do you believe that once people reach the age of 18 they should register to vote and cast their ballot on election day? Your answers to these questions provide some insight into how you feel about political participation and how strong your opinions are on various issues that interest you. Why do you feel as you do? What factors are important in helping shape your political beliefs and behavior?

Sociologists believe that the groups we belong to have a strong influence on our attitudes and decisions. Sociologists define a group as two or more people who interact with each other, share expectations, and possess a degree of common identity. Sociologist Emil Durkheim believed that a group could be held together by one of two kinds of forces. The first type of group is held together by similarities, such as belonging to the same family. The second type of group is held together by complementary differences—for example, co-workers who each perform distinct tasks to achieve a shared goal.

Shared interests and desires also form the foundation for interest groups. Students, for example, might join together to support public policies that make it easier for them to afford a college education or to pursue certain degrees. They might try to persuade lawmakers to hold down tuition costs at public universities. They also might pressure Congress to provide more federal aid for those who want to attend college. One group of students at the University of Minnesota at Minneapolis—St. Paul formed Students Against Fee Excess. This organization works to influence school and public policy on

The League of Women Voters is a group of people who share the common goal of promoting political participation through voting.

student fees and tuition. It also educates students on fiscal responsibility in universities.

Groups influence the values, attitudes, and behavior of their members in a wide variety of ways. For example, parents who believe that voting is a civic duty often pass this belief on to their children. Friends planning to attend college may help one another with information about application deadlines or scholarships. The members of a soccer team might rally around a teammate to improve his or her performance.

People frequently do not share all the beliefs of their fellow group members. In addition, as people grow older and have more experiences, they may leave some groups and join others. Despite frequent changes in affiliation and disagreements among fellow members, groups do play an important role in shaping how people think and act.

What Do You Think?

1. Identify some groups to which you belong. How have members of these groups influenced your interests and attitudes?
1. How have your parents and other family members helped to shape your attitudes about government and political participation?

Some Environmental Public Interest Groups

Group	Year Founded	Membership In 1996	Purpose
American Rivers	1973	18,000	To preserve and protect America's river systems
American Wildlands	1977	2,800	To conserve the nation's wildland resources
Climate Institutes	1986	1,500	To act as an international link between the scientific community and policy makers
Coast Alliance	1979	N/A	To increase public awareness of coastal ecology and the value of coastal resources
Ducks Unlimited, Inc.	1937	515,000	To conserve critical wetlands habitat in North America used by waterfowl and a wide variety of other wildlife
Friends of the Earth	1969	35,000	To protect the earth from environmental disaster
National Audubon Society	1905	600,000	To conserve and restore natural ecosystems with a focus on birds and other wildlife
Nature Conservancy	1951	800,000	To preserve biological diversity
Outdoors Unlimited	1965	4,000	To promote multiple-use resource management
Sierra Club	1892	550,000	To promote natural resource protection and conservation of wild areas
Trout Unlimited	1959	85,000	To conserve, protect, and restore trout (and other fish) by influencing the activities of governmental agencies

Source: *Encyclopedia of Associations*

Public interest groups, such as the environmental organizations listed in the chart above, work to promote interests that they believe benefit the majority. **What are some of the interests promoted by the groups listed in this chart?**

Several citizens' groups have been formed by Ralph Nader, a consumer rights supporter. Nader became nationally known in the 1960s for writing *Unsafe at Any Speed*, a book that documents unsafe features of American automobiles. Later, he pioneered the consumer protection organization by forming groups such as the Center for Auto Safety and Public Citizen.

SECTION 1 — REVIEW

1. Define the following terms: agribusiness, trade association, labor union, public interest group.

2. What are interest groups, and what role do they play in the political process?

3. In what way does joining an interest group enable people to participate more fully in the political process?

4. What are the differences between the major types of interest groups? Identify one interest group for each of the major types.

5. **Thinking and Writing Critically**
Consider a school group whose concerns could be addressed by forming an interest group. How might an interest group be better able to achieve results than the school group alone?

6. **Applying POLITICAL PROCESSES**
Conduct an Internet search for information about an issue that concerns you. Are there interest groups on the Internet that address this issue? Write a brief paragraph describing the information you find.

SECTION 2

HOW INTEREST GROUPS WORK

Political Dictionary

endorsement
single-issue voting
lobbying
grassroots lobbying
class-action suit

Objectives

★ In what ways are interest groups involved in the electoral process?
★ What is lobbying?
★ How do interest groups attempt to influence the political process through the legal system?
★ How do interest groups try to shape public opinion?

How might you try to change a school policy that you have concerns about, such as one that keeps students from leaving campus during lunchtime? You might join with a group of students and approach the principal, other school administrators, or the student council.

Interest groups work in a similar way to make their political concerns known. Unlike other political players—such as members of Congress, the president, heads of government agencies, and judges—interest groups do not have the authority to make government decisions themselves. Instead, they seek to *influence* decisions others make. They do this by

★ participating in the electoral process,
★ lobbying members of Congress and government agencies,
★ addressing their concerns through the legal system, and
★ trying to influence public opinion by using the media, demonstrating, and protesting.

Participating in the Electoral Process

One way that interest groups seek to influence the political system is by participating in the electoral process. Their political efforts include endorsing candidates with shared ideas and giving money to campaigns through political action committees.

Endorsing Candidates Interest groups' traditional method of influencing the political process has been through the **endorsement** of—or public declaration of support for—a certain candidate. An interest group will often make these endorsements with the expectation of gaining some influence over the decisions of legislators it helps elect. Interest groups also may withhold their support from and even work to defeat a candidate. This tactic was pioneered as early as 1917 by women's suffrage organizations that targeted a number of senators who were against giving the vote to women.

An interest group commonly keeps track of which elected officials vote for or against legislation that affects its concerns. Then, during elections, the group may tell its members which candidates to vote for—that is, which ones the interest group endorses. One study found that 44 percent of interest groups make congressional voting records known to the members.

How successful are interest group endorsements? Many interest group members do indeed vote for or against a candidate solely because of his or her view on an issue of great concern to the group. This practice is called **single-issue voting**. For example, members of the National Right-to-Life Committee oppose candidates who do not support a ban or limits on abortion, regardless of the candidates' positions on other issues. Members of the National Abortion Rights Action League also practice single-issue voting, opposing candidates solely because they support banning or limiting abortion.

Political Action Committees Interest groups also support political candidates by giving money to their campaigns. With the exception of labor unions, however, interest groups cannot use their own funds, such as members' dues, for campaign contributions. Instead, they contribute through political action committees (PACs).

Top 10 PAC Contributors to Federal Candidates in 1995–1996

1. Democratic Republican Independent Voter Education Committee	$2,611,140
2. American Federation of State, County and Municipal Employees (AFSCME)—PEOPLE	$2,505,021
3. United Auto Workers Voluntary Community Action Program	$2,467,319
4. Association of Trial Lawyers of America PAC	$2,362,938
5. Dealers Election Action Committee of the National Automobile Dealers Association (NADA)	$2,351,925
6. National Education Association PAC	$2,326,830
7. American Medical Association PAC	$2,319,197
8. Realtors PAC	$2,099,683
9. International Brotherhood of Electrical Workers Committee on Political Education	$2,080,587
10. Active Ballot Club, a department of United Food and Commercial Workers International Union	$2,030,795

Source: Federal Elections Commission

POLITICAL PROCESSES *PACs donate money to the campaigns of candidates who share their views.* **What is the maximum amount that a PAC may contribute to a candidate's campaign?**

As noted in Chapter 5, a political action committee is a separate political branch of an interest group that is set up to participate in politics and give money to candidates. Many interest groups now have PACs. By giving money to candidates through a PAC, interest groups hope to elect more officials who share their views. Again, this money is donated in the hope that the legislators an interest group helps elect will attempt to pass legislation favorable to its views.

Though PACs existed as early as the mid-1940s, they grew in number in the 1970s after a change in campaign finance laws. The new legislation limited individual campaign contributions to candidates in an attempt to prevent one person from having too much political influence. At the same time, however, the legislation authorized corporations and interest groups to set up PACs that could give more than individuals could. PACs thus became an attractive source of campaign funding for candidates.

As a result, interest groups' importance in campaign fund-raising increased dramatically. Whereas PACs had contributed about 25 percent of the funds received in 1976 by winners of House races, the figure had increased to about 41 percent by 1988. This number has slowly begun to fall, however. In

1996, PACs contributed around 31 percent of the funds received by the winners of House races.

Individual PACs do not lavish vast sums of money upon single candidates. In fact, even though the maximum PAC donation is set at $5,000, the average donation by PACs in the 1992 congressional election was $1,600. In addition, given huge television fees and other campaign costs, even $5,000 is not a large amount of money. If many companies in the same industry each contribute $5,000 through several PACs, however, the total donations from that industry could be significant.

PACs tend to donate more money to incumbents because they have a greater chance of winning. In some elections, PACs have even paid off campaign debts of candidates who oppose their views, hoping to win these people's support.

Lobbying

A second way that interest groups participate in the political system is by trying to persuade government policy makers to make particular decisions regarding legislation. This **lobbying** is typically carried out by individual lobbyists who represent an interest group's concerns. Lobbyists' actions are protected by the First Amendment to the Constitution,

Careers in Government

Interest Group Director

Many interest groups rely on volunteers or part-time employees to do much of their work. To organize and direct the personnel and resources of an interest group, however, often requires full-time professional managers. Such individuals must be knowledgeable about current politics, skilled at coordinating group efforts, and committed to the causes of the interest groups that employ them. Many start their careers by working for political organizations as interns and participating actively in local political events.

Kirk Clay works for People for the American Way (PFAW), a liberal interest group based in Washington, D.C. There, he helps to advance civil rights issues and other causes. As a regional field coordinator in 1997, the 25-year-old graduate of the University of Cincinnati monitored issues important to PFAW and organized activists in a dozen states. He prepared for his job in part by working as a college intern in the White House. He also worked for the Democratic National Committee, where he helped teach would-be activists how to run political campaigns.

People for the American Way is only one of many organized interest groups whose work is done by paid staff and thousands of volunteers. Many such groups are based in the nation's capital. The executives of these organizations look for job candidates

Kirk Clay, organizer for People for the American Way, gained experience for the job by working for other political organizations.

who are dedicated to the principles of the organization and have the education and training necessary to carry out its work. For example, when the Christian Coalition—a conservative interest group that promotes public policies that support families and traditional values—needed a new executive director in 1997, it hired 31-year-old Randy Tate.

Tate earned a bachelor's degree in economics and political science from Western Washington University. At 22, he was elected to Washington State's House of Representatives, where he served for six years. He then served one full term in the U.S. House from 1995 to 1996 as a Republican in the 104th Congress. Tate sees his job at the Christian Coalition as an opportunity to pursue causes in which he deeply believes.

which gives people the right to request that the government address their complaints.

History of Lobbying
Lobby became a political term in the United States around 1830. It originated to describe the behavior of people who waited in the lobbies of government buildings to talk with legislators. Historically, lobbying has been a negative term, referring to secret meetings in which interest groups try to unfairly influence legislative decisions. Early political cartoons portrayed lobbyists as sinister people who held legislatures in their control. In the 1800s and early 1900s several states enacted strict regulations on lobbying.

Lobbying Today
Today the interaction that lobbyists have with congressmembers and their staff takes place both in private and during public meetings, or hearings. In both settings, lobbyists provide information about the legislation in which they are interested. Hearings often are critical for lawmakers to obtain detailed information previously unknown to them. Most lobbyists are experts on their subjects of concern and have large staffs to perform their research.

In addition to meeting with lawmakers, interest groups also lobby government agencies. After all, laws give only general guidance, leaving the agencies to hammer out the specifics. An

RESEARCHER CD-ROM

POLITICAL PROCESSES *Lobbyists often wait in the halls of capital buildings for an opportunity to speak with certain legislators about policies concerning their group.* **What are some of the tools that lobbyists use to influence public opinion?**

environmental law passed by Congress, for instance, sets general targets for clean air standards. Congress directs the Environmental Protection Agency (EPA) in the executive branch, however, to determine how much nitrogen dioxide may be given off by coal-fired power plants or how much benzene may be given off by automobiles. Lobbyists thus talk not only to members of Congress about the legislation but also to officials at the EPA about its implementation.

Grassroots Lobbying In addition to providing information, many interest groups organize supporters to help further their cause. Much of this support is gathered through **grassroots lobbying**, an organized effort to urge local citizens to try to influence the decisions of Washington policy makers, particularly congressmembers. Because a district's residents choose whether or not to re-elect someone, congressmembers tend to listen to them.

Over the past 20 years, interest groups have become increasingly sophisticated at orchestrating grassroots efforts. This has resulted largely from technological advances. National organizations frequently use computers to forward information to citizens, urging them to contact their representatives about key issues. Lobbyists may even provide targeted "form letters," which computer users can print, sign, and send to their representatives with little effort. Form letters, however, are not considered as effective as other techniques.

Employing the Legal System

A third way interest groups try to influence public policy is through the legal system. In many instances, they file lawsuits regarding their issues of concern. Beginning in the mid-1930s, for example, civil rights interest groups tried to help bring an end to states' racist Jim Crow laws, such as those segregating schools, by filing lawsuits in state courts. (Jim Crow laws are more fully explained in Chapter 15.)

These efforts culminated in the early 1950s, when the National Association for the Advancement of Colored People (NAACP) and its legal arm, the Legal Defense and Education Fund, helped bring suit to integrate a racially segregated school district. The case, *Brown* v. *Board of Education of Topeka,* involved an African American student who was prevented from attending an all-white school. In its 1954 ruling the Supreme Court declared racial segregation of schools to be illegal.

Some legislation passed since the late 1960s, such as the Clean Air and the Clean Water Acts, has contained provisions allowing interest groups to sue government agencies. Typically, suits can be brought when an agency fails to perform some action the law requires it to perform. In a case regarding the habitat of the endangered spotted owl, an interest group called the Oregon Natural Resources Council sued the U.S. Forest Service for supposedly violating the Clean Water Act and other laws.

Interest groups also may initiate class-action suits. **Class-action suits** are brought by one or more plaintiffs on behalf of themselves and all others affected similarly by a particular wrong. Class-action suits allow individuals—each of whose suffering from an injury might be too small to go to court over—to band together to seek compensation. In a famous case in the 1980s, Vietnam War veterans claiming they were harmed by herbicides used by the U.S. Army won a class-action suit against the government and several chemical companies. In the mid-1990s cases were filed against tobacco companies on behalf of people with diseases thought to be linked to cigarette smoking.

Influencing Public Opinion

Another way in which interest groups work to achieve their goals is by influencing public

POLITICAL PROCESSES *The 1994 television ad featuring Harry and Louise tried to persuade viewers that President Clinton's proposed health-care plan was flawed.* **What other means do interest groups use to influence public opinion?**

Today, television is the primary means of advertising. In 1994 an interest group representing health insurance companies used television advertising to combat President Bill Clinton's plan for rebuilding the nation's health-care system. One ad featured a couple named Harry and Louise. In the ad, Harry and Louise expressed concern that the Clinton plan might create several new levels of government. The ad helped defeat national health-care insurance.

Interest groups also encourage favorable stories about their issues of concern. This is called using "free media" (news stories) as opposed to the "paid media" (advertising).

Demonstrations and Protests Television airtime is expensive, so only around one third of all interest groups buy time on television as a means of reaching the public. Other groups stage demonstrations and protests in hopes that the media will cover their actions and bring their cause to the attention of the public.

For example, antiabortion activists have demonstrated in front of clinics that perform abortions. Likewise, environmentalists have made headline news by chaining themselves to trees to block logging trucks. Farmers gained significant media attention by parading down a major avenue in Washington, D.C., on their tractors. Such efforts are commonly rewarded with television news coverage, thus enabling interest groups to share their concerns with millions of viewers.

opinion. Legislators frequently respond favorably to goals that have the support of the majority of the general public. The two main ways in which interest groups try to influence the public are by sending out information through the media and by conducting demonstrations and protests.

Using the Media Interest groups commonly try to influence public opinion through the media, often through advertising. Business interest groups use newspaper and radio advertisements, mailings, and even inserts into monthly electric utility bills.

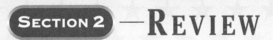

SECTION 2 — REVIEW

1. Define the following terms: endorsement, single-issue voting, lobbying, grassroots lobbying, class-action suit.

2. How do interest groups try to promote their concerns through the electoral process?

3. Why is lobbying an important tool for interest groups?

4. How does the use of lawsuits help further interest groups' concerns?

5. What means do interest groups use to try to influence public opinion? Have you noticed anything in the media, such as television commercials, that might be linked to an interest group?

6. **Thinking and Writing Critically**
If you were to try to change a school policy, which one would it be? In what ways would you try to make your views known?

7. **Applying** **POLITICAL FOUNDATIONS**
Conduct an Internet search for interest groups' home pages. For instance, you might check listings for U.S. dairy farmers or the U.S. steel industry. What do these groups include in their home pages? Why do they want to publicize this information?

INTEREST GROUPS AND THE PUBLIC GOOD

Objectives

★ What are the benefits of interest groups?

★ Why are interest groups criticized?

★ How is interest groups' influence on the political system limited?

As noted in Chapter 16, public opinion is the collective opinion of the majority of the population. You may think that in a democracy, majority opinion should always win out over minority views. What if the *majority* view, however, does not represent what is best for the public good, which covers everyone?

Fearing unfair rule by the majority, the framers of the Constitution set up a framework preventing minority rights from being violated. A key to this framework is the establishment of specific protections for all people—for example, laws guaranteeing property rights and providing for religious freedom. In addition, the framers designed institutions to make it difficult for any group, even a majority, to establish unfair control over government. To accomplish this goal, the framers created a system that would be open to input from many sources. Thus, even interest groups that represent only a small minority have the opportunity to exert a significant influence on government actions. This gives interest groups the opportunity to promote the public good by pushing government to address minority concerns.

As you will see, however, interest groups do not always promote the public good. They sometimes attempt to advance the narrow interests of just a few at the expense of the general population. For this and other reasons, many citizens are critical of interest groups' role in the U.S. political system.

Benefits of Interest Groups

Interest group participation brings two main benefits to the U.S. political system. The first, as stated above, is that interest groups provide a voice for minority concerns in the political system. The second is that they supply information that lawmakers and the general public can use to make informed decisions about policies.

Representing Minority Concerns The major argument on behalf of interest groups is that majority views should not be the only factor that shapes public policy. Why might it be important that minority views be heard in the political system?

Suppose that a city is planning to build a highway. Much of the Oak Heights neighborhood would have to be destroyed to make room for the highway. Though the highway would make life more convenient for many commuters, it also would

PUBLIC GOOD *People representing minority interests can express their views in public meetings such as government hearings.* **What is one major argument on behalf of interest groups?**

significantly disrupt the lives of the people living in Oak Heights. The number of commuters (the majority) is much greater than the number of neighborhood residents (the minority).

Even so, most citizens would probably say that the Oak Heights residents should have their views on the building of the highway considered. Forming an interest group, such as Save Oak Heights, allows the residents to try to convince policy makers and the majority of the public of the importance of protecting their homes.

In such a case, interest groups can perform a key role in promoting the public good, just as they have done throughout U.S. history. Civil rights leaders during the 1950s and 1960s, for example, created groups to bring the injustices of discrimination to the attention of the majority. During the years when it was dominated by Martin Luther King, Jr.'s leadership, the basic strategy of the civil rights movement was to use demonstrations in the South to focus the attention of the country on the injustices of segregation. By giving minority concerns a voice in the political process through lobbying, filing lawsuits, and protesting, interest groups can temper majority rule with appropriate attention to minority concerns.

Providing Information As you learned in Section 1, a key interest group function is to provide information. In this way an interest group may promote the public good by increasing the awareness of officials and the public about its issues of concern. Without such a voice, these issues might not be heard, and the majority might not have the opportunity to lend support to a just minority cause.

As you also learned, members of interest groups often are experts on their subjects of concern and are able to provide detailed information that policy makers and the general public may not otherwise obtain. By providing information, interest groups enable policy makers and the general public to make more informed decisions about public policies.

Criticisms of Interest Groups

Perhaps you have heard someone in your family, your community, or the media say that a certain politician is overly influenced by "special interests." What that person means is that the politician gives interest groups too much control over

Comparing
⤳ Governments

Restricting Interest Groups

In the United States, interest groups have relatively few government-ordered restrictions. In contrast, authoritarian governments often place tight restrictions on interest groups. Such restraints are usually an attempt to limit opposition to the government. Consider, for example, the experiences of interest groups under the communist governments of Poland and China.

Before the fall of communism in Eastern Europe in 1989, Polish workers could not legally join unions that were not sponsored by the government. In the 1980s, however, millions of workers defied this law and joined the independent Solidarity union. Union members demanded freedom of political and religious expression and the right to form free and independent unions. When Poland's first free elections in decades were finally held in 1989, Solidarity candidates received enough votes to take control of the government.

The recent efforts of prodemocracy interest groups in the People's Republic of China were less successful. In 1989 China's communist government ordered the military to put down massive student demonstrations calling for democracy and other reforms. In 1997 China also limited the influence of interest groups in the former British colony of Hong Kong, which had been turned over to Chinese control that year. The Chinese government-appointed Hong Kong legislature approved a law disbanding Hong Kong interest groups that receive political funds from overseas.

his or her policy decisions. Indeed, interest groups often are criticized for having too much sway over the political system. Critics believe that some of these groups gain this control through financial influence.

Financial Influence Interest groups have long been accused of attempting to improperly influence

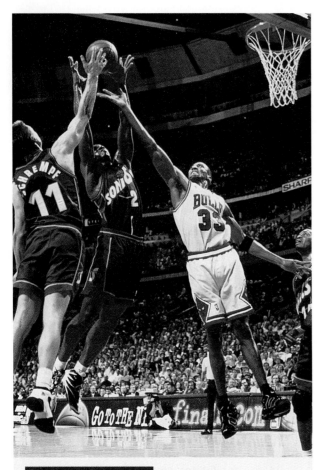

POLITICAL PROCESSES *Some critics accuse interest groups of trying to influence government officials by providing them with entertainment such as tickets to sporting events.* **Why does entertaining no longer play a central role in lobbying?**

officials through favors, entertainment, and financial support. Many people believe that lobbyists actually get their way by buying congressmembers out-of-town trips, tickets to sporting events, and expensive meals. (During the 1800s a lobbyist supposedly remarked that "the way to a man's 'Aye' [vote of support] is through his stomach.") Along with these benefits supposedly come threats of retribution at the next election if members do not give in to the lobbyist's demands. Entertaining, however, played a more central role in earlier lobbying than it does today.

Interest groups' activities today more often come in the form of campaign contributions. Many people see this type of influence as more subtle and dangerous than entertainment. Specifically, many people resent what they see as businesses' and other wealthy groups' practice of providing financial support to elected officials in exchange for political influence. Wealthy and well-educated people can more easily form interest groups than can the disadvantaged, who may feel strongly about an issue but lack the resources to organize.

For example, even with the large increase in interest groups over the last three decades, no powerful interest groups exist exclusively for poor people. For this reason, critics charge that the disadvantaged do not receive the proper voice in the political process.

Excessive Power Many critics also believe that interest groups' financial and ideological influence gives them too much control over government. They believe that the balance between minority and majority views gets lost in U.S. politics. A small interest group that is wealthy, well organized, and vocal about its intense concerns might gain more political power than the majority. Part of the reason for this is that the majority often does not speak out as loudly as a focused minority. On many issues, critics argue, the voice of the majority hardly is heard at all, leaving *only* interest groups to exert influence. What would be a valid input if it were one voice among many, sometimes becomes the *only* voice.

According to some critics, the public policy-making system in the United States enables organized groups to gain excessive influence. For every major policy issue there is a congressional committee legislating on the subject, a government agency implementing the legislation, and one or more interest groups representing people and businesses with an intense concern in the subject. The congressmembers involved joined the committee because the issue at hand is important to them and their constituents. The government agency is staffed largely by people whose life's work centers on the subject. Of course, the interest group also is very concerned with the issue. With these three groups working together to create most public policy, the majority's viewpoint sometimes goes unheard.

An example is the price-support system for farm products such as corn, sugar, and peanuts. The agricultural committees in Congress are dominated by members from rural districts who want to help farmers. The mission of the Department of Agriculture is also to help farmers. Each price support program is backed by an organized farm interest group. These three groups work together to make agricultural policies, while consumers who may want lower food prices (the majority) have trouble being heard.

In such situations government officials certainly hear from several interest groups, but are unlikely to hear from many ordinary citizens. As a result, critics claim, the intense concerns represented by the interest groups gain more weight than the majority concerns represented by public opinion and elections.

This problem, however, usually develops only in fields of public policy that provide large benefits to a small group while the majority loses only a little. For example, tax dollars fund property development subsidies that provide significant new business for the real estate and construction industries in central cities, but cost each taxpayer only a few dollars a year. In such situations, government officials will most likely hear from an interest group in favor of such subsidies but are less likely to hear from many ordinary citizens. With a highly publicized issue that the public cares deeply about, elected officials are more likely to bow to the majority.

Campaign Finance Reform In recent years these criticisms of interest groups' influence over politics have led to demands for campaign finance reform. Congress has been working on campaign finance reform for years, but as of mid-1997 the House and the Senate still had not agreed on a substantive bill.

Some proposals limit the amount of money candidates can spend in campaigns. One problem here is that challengers cannot mount an effective campaign against a current officeholder without spending a great deal of money. Spending limits thus favor officeholders by making it more difficult for challengers to win. Many people believe that officeholders already enjoy many advantages in re-elections and that such legislation would unfairly strengthen their position.

Other proposals support financing elections with public funds, raised through the income tax on U.S. citizens. Public financing, however, has been criticized in light of government's already tight budgets.

Limitations on Interest Groups

Even though few campaign finance reform laws have been passed, there are limitations to interest

groups' influence. First, though interest groups may donate money to a politician's campaign, elected officials often worry that support for "special interest" policies will hurt them with voters. For example, a politician who receives money from the tobacco industry but whose home state is passing significant antismoking legislation will likely be less concerned about tobacco interests than those of his or her state's registered voters.

Overall, evidence suggests that the influence of campaign contributions is less on issues of major significance. Campaign contributions certainly do not dominate congressional votes to the exclusion of other influences.

A second limitation on interest groups' influence is visibility. The increasing aggressiveness of media reporters over the past few decades has made it harder for policy issues to go unnoticed. Interest groups often can only dominate decisions on highly visible issues by gaining majority sympathy for their cause. As long as policy

© 1980 by Herblock in the *Washington Post.*

POLITICAL PROCESSES *Congress has been working for years to pass a campaign finance reform bill that would limit interest groups' ability to influence policy by contributing large amounts of money to politicians' election campaigns.* **What is one of the criticisms of public financing of election campaigns?**

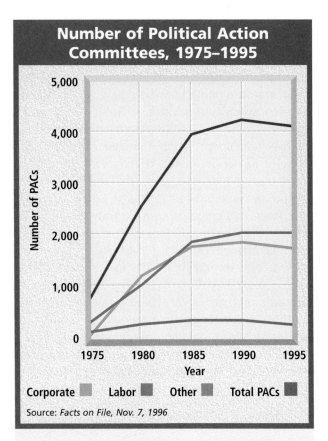

Number of Political Action Committees, 1975–1995

Number of PACs

5,000

4,000

3,000

2,000

1,000

0

1975   1980   1985   1990   1995
Year

Corporate   Labor   Other   Total PACs

Source: *Facts on File, Nov. 7, 1996*

The number of PACs has increased dramatically over the last 20 years. **What has happened to the total number of PACs since 1990?**

concerns. When issues are visible, the ability of interest groups to control legislative decisions depends greatly on their ability to arouse public sympathy for a just cause. When a group is able to make a case for its position, the public will be much more likely to listen to the debate and go on to support that group's position.

Third, interest groups' influence is limited by the competition among them. The dramatic growth in the number and variety of interest groups over the past 30 years has meant that congressional committees and government agencies now hear from many more interest groups in more policy areas.

For example, if the U.S. government decides to set a tariff on imported luxury automobiles, many interest groups will become involved in the debate over the issue. Not only domestic car makers but also businesses who import and sell foreign cars will get involved on different sides of the issue. Even the foreign country where the automobiles are made may become involved in the debate.

Because of this kind of competition, some people believe that the enormous growth in interest groups has actually *decreased* individual groups' influence over U.S. politics. When fewer groups operated, they had more influence because they had less competition for policy makers' attention. As the number of groups competing in a policy area has increased, the ability of any one group to have significant influence over the system has declined.

arguments must be justified in terms of the public good and the debate proceeds completely in the open, interest groups will have trouble dominating the political system with purely selfish

SECTION 3 — REVIEW

1. In what way do interest groups promote the public good?

2. Explain why some people believe that interest groups are a negative influence on the political system.

3. What serves to limit interest groups' influence?

4. **Thinking and Writing Critically**
   Suppose an interest group in your state wants to change the school week from Monday through Friday to Monday through Saturday. Its lobbyists are trying to influence state

lawmakers by taking them to expensive dinners to talk about the issue. What do you think about this situation? Why might some people think that lobbyists' attempts to influence policy makers are unfair?

5. **Applying** POLITICAL PROCESSES
   Conduct an Internet search for listings of public interest groups. Do these groups have a bulletin board where you can leave comments? Do they list an address to which you can send your comments? Prepare a report of your findings.

SECTION 1 An interest group is a collection of people who have banded together to advance a shared political concern. Interest groups perform three main functions in the political process. They organize people who share strong opinions about an issue, they provide an outlet for political participation, and they supply information to the public and to policy makers.

There are several kinds of interest groups. Those that represent economic concerns include agricultural groups, business groups, labor unions, and professional groups. Interest groups that are not based on economic concerns often represent a certain societal group or promote certain causes. One type of cause-based interest group is a public interest group, which claims to represent the interests of society as a whole rather than those of a small group of people.

SECTION 2 Interest groups seek to influence decisions about public policy. One way they try to do this is by participating in the electoral process—by endorsing candidates and contributing money through political action committees.

They also try to gain support for their policy agendas through lobbying—trying to persuade government policy makers to make particular decisions regarding legislation. Today much of the interaction that lobbyists have with congressmembers and their staffs takes place during public meetings and hearings. At that time, lobbyists provide detailed information about the legislation in which they are interested.

Interest groups also use the courts to try to achieve their political goals. To advance or protect their issues of concern, they often file lawsuits, some of which may be filed against the government. The latter are typically brought when an agency fails to perform some action the law requires it to perform. Interest groups may also file class-action suits, which are brought by one or more plaintiffs on behalf of themselves and others affected similarly by a particular wrong.

The fourth way in which interest groups try to influence policy is through public opinion. Legislators frequently respond favorably to goals that are backed by the majority of the general public. Two main ways in which interest groups try to influence the public are by sending out information through the media, often through advertising, and by conducting demonstrations and protests.

SECTION 3 The framers of the Constitution hoped to protect minorities from unfair rule by the majority. For this reason, the Constitution's framework enables interest groups to influence government actions. One benefit of interest groups, therefore, is that they represent minority concerns within the political system. The other benefit is that they provide information to government officials and the public.

Interest groups pose potential problems as well as provide benefits. Many people feel that the groups' financial resources allow them too much control over government policy making. There are limitations to their influence, however. Members of Congress often are more concerned about representing their constituents than about promoting interest groups' issues. In addition, interest groups' competition with one another and their visibility through the media serve to limit their influence.

> ✎ **Government Notebook**
>
> **Review the list of interest groups that you wrote in your Government Notebook at the beginning of the chapter. Now that you have studied the chapter, would you revise your list? Why or why not?**

CHAPTER 17

REVIEW

REVIEWING CONCEPTS

1. What are interest groups? Why do people form them?

2. How do interest groups attempt to influence the political system?

3. What are the different types of interest groups?

4. What functions do interest groups fulfill in the political system?

5. How might interest groups be beneficial to the political system? How might they be harmful?

6. What are the limitations on interest groups' influence?

THINKING AND WRITING CRITICALLY

1. **POLITICAL PROCESSES** Have you ever lobbied for something you wanted? Give an example of a time when you explained your point of view to a parent, teacher, or friend to try to change his or her decision about something. What was the outcome?

2. **PRINCIPLES OF DEMOCRACY** How can interest groups help their members become informed voters? Why do many interest groups spend their time and money educating citizens on legislative issues and candidates?

3. **POLITICAL PROCESSES** Recall the lobbying techniques discussed in Section 2. Which one of these techniques do you think is the most powerful tool for influencing policy makers' decisions? Explain your answer.

4. **PUBLIC GOOD** Do you think that financial resources play too large a role in politics? What limitations have been placed on interest groups' influence? Do you think that these limitations promote the public good? Explain your answers.

CITIZENSHIP IN YOUR COMMUNITY

Working with a group, research the labor unions in your state. What are some of the major industries in your state? Do workers in these industries belong to labor unions? Are there regional offices for these unions in your state? What are some of the major issues that concern members of these unions? You might want to begin your research by checking local telephone directories and by reading your local newspaper. After you have completed your research, write an editorial on how you think labor unions serve the people in your community.

COOPERATIVE PORTFOLIO PROJECT

With a group, make a poster illustrating examples of various types of interest groups. You should include an example of each of the following groups: labor unions, business groups, agricultural groups, professional groups, societal groups, and cause-based groups. You will need to provide membership statistics and a statement of purpose for each group you select. You may want to contact each group to request photos or other visual information such as brochures or pamphlets to attach to your poster.

THE INTERNET: LEARNING ONLINE

Conduct an Internet search for an interest group you might wish to join. You might start by using search words such as *interest groups* and the issue or type of group. When you find the home page of a group you wish to know more about, note the address where you can request information about the group. Is there a postal address or an e-mail address for the group's main office? Using e-mail—or regular mail if no e-mail address is available—write a letter requesting information about the group and how to join.

PRACTICING SKILLS: LEARNING FROM VISUALS

Examine the photograph below, which shows an interest group rallying in front of the Capitol. Then answer the questions that follow.

1. What type of interest group is rallying in this photograph?

2. What details in the photograph give you some clues about the issues in which these people are interested?

3. Why do you think that a member of the media took this photo? What are some techniques used by this interest group to get media coverage of its rally?

ANALYZING PRIMARY SOURCES

CITIZEN HEARING ON CAMPAIGN FINANCE REFORM

The League of Women Voters of the United States, founded in 1920, is dedicated to educating voters and encouraging public participation in government. Today this organization has more than 100,000 members. In June 1997 several of the organization's leaders testified at a congressional hearing on reforming the ways in which political campaigns are financed. Read the following excerpt from the testimony given by the league's president, Becky Cain, and answer the questions that follow.

❝ *Do people discuss the independent expenditure loophole [law allowing interest groups to spend money in support of an election campaign without actually contributing money to a particular candidate] over coffee in the morning? No, probably not. But does this mean they don't care about campaign finance reform? The ballooning activity occurring on this issue at the grassroots level disproves the notion that people don't care.*

They're joining coalitions [organizations], they're volunteering for initiative [proposed legislation] campaigns, they're voting for reform measures in large majorities: in short, citizens are engaging in the process of reforming how we finance campaigns. They care.

Indeed, as one reporter I know put it: voters are desperate for reform.

How is it then that campaign finance reform has stalled at the federal level while it's succeeding at the state level? Why should citizens expect less from the federal government than from state governments?

The answer is, they shouldn't. That's why we need campaign finance reform. . .

The message is that we, citizens, want reform. We deserve reform. We won't expect any less from Congress. ❞

1. Do you think that campaign finance reform is a major issue of concern to voters? Why or why not?

2. What are some citizens doing to work for campaign finance reform? Do you think that these are effective methods for influencing policy?

3. Why do you think that reform might be easier to achieve at a state level than at a federal level?

CHAPTER 18

POLITICAL PARTIES

I f you have ever been a member of a team or club, you know that certain common goals and interests hold a group together. Members of a team share the desire to win a game. Members of a club experience the social bond that comes from interacting with people who share the same interest.

As noted in Chapter 17, interest groups are similar to organized teams and clubs. The reason that people in interest groups join together, however, is to take action on a specific political or social concern. One special kind of interest group is a political party. By belonging to a political party, people can influence elections and the running of government. In fact, political parties are a key way in which citizens participate in the U.S. political system.

Government Notebook

Think about a team or club to which you have belonged. What held the members of that group together? Was there a common set of rules? Were there standards for who could belong? Write a list of these factors in your Government Notebook.

ROLE OF POLITICAL PARTIES

Political Dictionary

electorate
one-party system
two-party system
multiparty system

Objectives

★ What are political parties?
★ What functions do political parties serve?
★ What are the different kinds of party systems?

Imagine this scene. Crowds are roaring. Bands are playing. Banners are waving in the air. Is this the Super Bowl? It could easily be. Or, it might be an election-night bash held by a political party to celebrate its winning candidate. For supporters of a political party, as for fans of a football team, winning is a thrill.

As noted in Chapter 3, political parties are organized groups that seek influence over government power. These parties serve many functions. The way in which they fulfill those functions, however, depends in large part on the kind of party system their country has.

Functions of Political Parties

When the framers were drawing up the Constitution, they did not include information about the functions of political parties. In fact, some parts of the Constitution even suggest that the framers did not intend for this country to have political parties. Many of the framers, including George Washington, feared that political parties might divide the nation by pursuing selfish interests.

Political parties began to form, however, during Washington's administration. In his Farewell Address, he warned the nation against the "baneful [harmful] effects of the spirit of party." He said that the spirit that motivates the formation of political parties creates in the community

❝ jealousies and false alarms, kindles the animosity [hatred] of one part against another, foments [causes] occasionally riot and insurrection [revolt against government]. ❞

Despite Washington's warning, the United States developed what is today one of the oldest systems of popularly based, organized political parties in the world. Why did political parties develop in this country? What role do they play in the U.S. political system? Political parties serve three main functions:

★ assisting the electoral process,
★ organizing the day-to-day running of government, and
★ nominating candidates.

Assisting the Electoral Process As the nation's **electorate**—the body of people entitled to vote—grew, the country needed a system of organization to assist with the electoral process.

The Granger Collection, New York

POLITICAL FOUNDATIONS *George Washington feared that political parties would divide the nation by pursuing selfish interests.* **What is the body of people who are entitled to vote called?**

How do political parties help provide the electorate with this organization?

First, political parties help citizens with the technical aspects of voting. Party workers encourage people to register to vote and to go to the polls on election day. They also raise money for political campaigns and go door to door distributing literature about their party's candidates.

Second, political parties provide a broad stance on major issues. Thus, when a candidate identifies him- or herself as a member of a particular party, voters immediately know much about his or her general political philosophy. For example, some people say that voting for a member of the Democratic Party is shorthand for "I want a government that takes a more active role in society." Voting Republican sends the message that you want government to be less involved in people's lives.

In this way, political parties act as a sort of team leader for voters. Think about how one person often guides a sports team's efforts. If every player on a team made his or her own plans and did not listen to the team captain, it would be difficult for the team to develop a winning strategy. In the same way, political parties provide a basic direction for voters. In doing so, parties gather together individuals with many different concerns by appealing to their broad common goals. This in turn helps the electoral process by making sure that the country is not splintered into so many competing groups that governing becomes impossible.

Third, political parties assist with the electoral process by closely examining the policies pursued by elected officials. In other words, the party out of power watches for any missteps by the party in power and offers alternative policies to voters. By doing so, the party out of power hopes to swing votes to its side during the next election.

Organizing the Government Another function of political parties is to help in the daily operation of the government. How do they do this? Political parties determine leadership in several areas of government. For example, as noted in Chapter 6, congressional leaders and committee members are chosen based on their party affiliation. The membership of committees is based on the number of seats each party holds in the House or the Senate. Therefore, if the Republicans hold more seats in the Senate, they receive more seats on each senatorial committee.

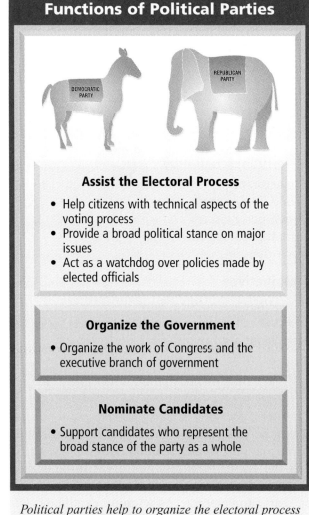

Functions of Political Parties

Assist the Electoral Process

- Help citizens with technical aspects of the voting process
- Provide a broad political stance on major issues
- Act as a watchdog over policies made by elected officials

Organize the Government

- Organize the work of Congress and the executive branch of government

Nominate Candidates

- Support candidates who represent the broad stance of the party as a whole

Political parties help to organize the electoral process by bringing together people who have common political interests. **What are the three main functions of political parties?**

Party membership also is important when it comes to filling positions in the executive branch. A president generally appoints people whose political viewpoints reflect his or her own and those of their political party.

Because their members actually participate in the running of government, political parties take responsibility for government decision making. In this way, the parties are distinct from other interest groups, which pressure the political process only from the outside. These other interest groups simply support a single group of concerns without taking the concerns of others into consideration. Political parties are different. Some of the process of weighing conflicting interests and listening to different ideas occurs within the parties themselves.

POLITICAL PROCESSES *The government of China is controlled by one party—* the Communists. ***Why are some countries dominated by only one party even though other parties are free to participate in elections?***

Nominating Candidates The third major function of political parties is to nominate candidates. When a political party nominates a candidate, it offers him or her its support. Although candidates have their own views about particular issues, they also represent both their party and its broad views, or ideology. The nomination process also reduces the number of candidates to a manageable size.

Types of Party Systems

The way in which a country's political parties fulfill these functions depends to a large degree on the type of party system the country has. There are three major types of party systems: one party, two party, and multiparty.

One-Party Systems A **one-party system** is one in which a single political party controls the government and clearly dominates political activity. In many cases, countries that have a one-party system are dictatorships. For example, the former Soviet Union had a one-party system. The Communist Party alone was allowed to participate in the government. Currently, China has a one-party system—the Communist Party is the only party permitted to take part in the government.

Some countries, such as Indonesia, have one-party systems not because other parties are banned, but because no major opposition has arisen successfully during elections. Opposition does exist in these countries, but the party in power makes it difficult—through rules, and sometimes force—for the opposition to gain power. The party in power in these countries may continue to control the government for many years at a time.

Two-Party Systems Two major parties dominate the government in a **two-party system**. The United States, as you know, has a system dominated by two major parties—the Democrats and the Republicans. Other parties can exist, but two dominate the system.

In a two-party system each major party represents many diverse interests and opinions. Though a party's supporters may vary in their beliefs, they stand behind the overall party message. Voters in two-party systems tend to elect candidates with moderate political views.

As noted in Chapter 7, the United States has a plurality system, meaning that whoever receives the most votes in an election wins. A plurality electoral system generally promotes political moderation, for a party must appeal to a broad range of views to gain a plurality of the vote. To hold power in this system, a party must expand its base beyond the relatively small number of people who have very intense concerns about specific issues and move to satisfy the many people in the middle.

Multiparty Systems A third type of system is the **multiparty system**, in which several parties

Comparing
Governments

Italy's Multiparty System

A strong two-party system has dominated U.S. politics since the early 1800s. Other democratic countries, however, have strong multiparty systems. Before and during World War II, Italy was dominated by dictator Benito Mussolini's Fascist Party. By the war's end, the Fascists had been thrown out. To prevent a return to totalitarianism, Italy adopted a multiparty system. Parties won seats in Parliament based on the percentage of votes they received in elections.

This electoral system encouraged the development of a number of smaller parties, making it difficult for stable coalitions, or combinations of parties, to control a majority of votes in Parliament. As a result, Italy has had more than 50 governments since World War II, even though most of those governments were dominated by the largest party, the Christian Democrats. In contrast, during the same time period the United States has had only 10 presidents, with majority control of the Senate having shifted only five times and majority control in the House only three times.

In 1993 three fourths of Italian voting districts adopted a new system for electing members of Parliament. Even so, Italy still has more than 20 political parties.

try to gain control of the government. In multiparty systems each party's representation in the legislature usually depends on the number of votes the party receives in an election. For example, a party that wins 15 percent of the vote receives roughly 15 percent of the seats in the legislature.

In a multiparty system each party tends to represent a specific region, concern, voter group, or ideology. A country's political landscape might include a Green Party, a Labor Party, or a Peasant Party, for example. By concentrating on a particular issue important to a portion of the population, these parties try to secure at least some representation in the legislature. For this reason, multiparty systems make it possible for a person to join and support a party that reflects his or her *specific* views. In fact, voters in multiparty systems often favor candidates with narrow views.

However, because so many parties share legislative power, multiparty systems sometimes cause government instability. The many parties form governing coalitions that can dissolve or change quickly because their interests are so varied. Think about the saying "Too many cooks spoil the broth." It implies that when too many people are involved in a task, such as making soup, competing visions may clash, resulting in a failed project. Similarly, the existence of many competing parties can make governing virtually impossible.

To reduce the number of parties in their legislatures, many countries with multiparty systems have passed laws requiring that a party receive a minimum percentage of votes before gaining representation. In Germany and some other countries, this minimum is set at 5 percent.

SECTION 1 — REVIEW

1. Define the following terms: electorate, one-party system, two-party system, multiparty system.

2. What makes a political party different from other interest groups?

3. What role do political parties play in the United States?

4. Describe the three main types of party systems.

5. **Thinking and Writing Critically**
   How might an election year in the United States be different if the country had a one-party system? a multiparty system? Explain your answer.

6. **Applying POLITICAL FOUNDATIONS**
   Which type of party system has the most advantages for a democracy? Explain your answer.

SECTION 2

THE U.S. TWO-PARTY SYSTEM

Political Dictionary

realignment
independent
third party
splinter party
ideological party

Objectives

★ Why did political parties develop in the United States?

★ How do the main political parties in the United States today differ from each other?

★ What role do third parties play in the U.S. two-party system?

Have you ever heard of the Natural Law Party of the United States or the U.S. Taxpayers Party? Probably not. Although these parties' presidential candidates received more than 100,000 popular votes in 1996, they are insignificant players in the U.S. political system.

You, like most citizens, are probably more familiar with the Republicans and the Democrats, the two parties that dominate the U.S. political system today. These two parties are the heirs of a long-standing two-party system in this country. These parties do not date back to the country's origins, however.

The U.S. party system has had five distinct periods, with each being characterized by a struggle between two parties. The first three periods involved the Federalists and Democratic-Republicans, the Democrats and Whigs, and the Republicans and Democrats. The two latest periods have been times when support has shifted decisively between Republicans and Democrats. Such periods of **realignment**—the

shifting of the parties' base of support among the electorate—generally are sparked by the development of issues of great public concern.

Early Political Parties

As noted in Section 1, the framers were concerned about the effect of self-interested groups on government. Despite such fears, however, political parties started to form not long after the new government began.

Unlike Congress, the presidency, and the Supreme Court, which were created by the Constitution, parties arose from the actual practice of political life. As the nation's first officials began to run the country and put the Constitution into effect, they differed about which policies the government should follow. The leaders of two major viewpoints organized their supporters into groups (political parties) to better pursue their goals. These groups soon became known as the Federalist and Democratic-Republican Parties.

Federalists and Democratic-Republicans

As noted in Chapter 2, the Federalists and Antifederalists were some of the first interest groups in the United States. Whereas the Federalists favored ratification of the Constitution, the Antifederalists opposed it. The Federalists

POLITICAL FOUNDATIONS *Conflict between Hamilton and Jefferson, both members of Washington's cabinet, led to the formation of the nation's first political parties. **What were the names of these parties?***

The Granger Collection, New York

succeeded in the struggle and in 1789 received many of the positions in the new government under President George Washington.

Soon, however, disagreements arose among the nation's leaders, particularly between Alexander Hamilton, the secretary of the treasury, and Thomas Jefferson, the secretary of state. Jefferson even resigned from Washington's cabinet in 1793 as the tensions mounted.

After his resignation, Jefferson eventually joined with James Madison (a former Federalist) and some of the original Antifederalists in opposition to the policies of Alexander Hamilton and the emerging Federalist Party. Jefferson and his followers included the Antifederalists, who were called Republicans or Democratic-Republicans.

The Federalists and the Democratic-Republicans disagreed about a number of issues. Generally, Hamilton's Federalist Party represented manufacturing and trade interests. Hamilton hoped to use the national government to aid the growth of industry by placing a tariff on foreign manufactured products. He also wished to provide government support for road and canal construction to lower transportation costs for manufactured goods.

In contrast, Madison, Jefferson, and the other Democratic-Republicans regarded farming, not manufacturing, as the backbone of the new nation. They disliked the industrialization and urbanization of the country. Thus, they also opposed government funding for policies and projects that furthered these developments.

Early on in the policy debate Hamilton began to organize congressional support for his programs. His activities were remarkably similar to those of political leaders today. Hamilton and his assistants helped allied congressmembers make their case in debates by providing them with arguments and statistics. He met in private with members, and quietly arranged informal conferences in which his followers could come together. Hamilton also tried to inform and organize nongovernment supporters of his programs.

Congressional opponents, led by Jefferson and Madison, quickly began similar efforts.

U.S. Political Parties

1787	Constitutional Convention takes place; Federalists back Constitution's ratification.
1800	Thomas Jefferson, a Democratic-Republican, defeats John Adams, the last Federalist president.
1828	Andrew Jackson becomes the first Democrat to win presidential election; Jackson's opponents become known as Whigs.
1850	Millard Fillmore succeeds the late Zachary Taylor, becoming the last Whig president.
1854	Republican Party formed as Whigs lose support.
1860	Abraham Lincoln becomes the first Republican to be elected president.
1884	Grover Cleveland becomes the first Democratic president to be elected since the Civil War.
1896	Republican William McKinley defeats Democrat William Jennings Bryan.
1932	Democrat Franklin D. Roosevelt wins the first of four presidential elections; Democrats begin a long domination of Congress.
1952	Dwight Eisenhower becomes the first Republican to be elected president since Herbert Hoover in 1928.
1968	Republican Richard Nixon wins presidency; until the 1992 election, Republicans control White House for all but four years.
1992	Democrat Bill Clinton elected president.
1994	Republicans become the majority party in both the House and Senate for first time since the 1954 elections.
1996	President Clinton is re-elected.

The United States has a two-party political system, although the two parties in power have changed over time. ***In what year did Grover Cleveland become the first Democratic president to be elected since the Civil War?***

Disagreements between the two young parties became so strong that by 1797 Jefferson wrote that "men who have been intimate [close friends] all their lives cross the street to avoid meeting, and turn their heads another way."

Jefferson and Madison continued to build their party and to fight the Federalist policies. In 1796 Jefferson ran for president against Federalist John Adams and was barely defeated. In 1800 he ran again and this time defeated Adams. With that defeat, the Democratic-Republicans established political domination that would last until 1829.

The Democratic-Republicans' control of the White House struck a tremendous blow to the Federalist Party. It suffered a gradual decline, with its original leaders dying and its policies representing an increasingly smaller portion of the population. By 1824 the Federalist Party had basically ceased to exist.

Democrats and Whigs

By the 1824 election the Democratic-Republicans faced some of their own problems. The party had split into factions—those who supported candidate Andrew Jackson and those who supported candidates Henry Clay, John Quincy Adams, or William H. Crawford. Although Jackson won the most popular votes, Adams was chosen by the House of Representatives as president. A lack of popular support, however, plagued Adams's administration, and Jackson remained popular. Four years later, Jackson, leader of the newly named Democratic Party, won a stunning landslide victory in the election of 1828.

Jackson's win led to a new era of competing-party politics. Born in a remote area on the border of North Carolina and South Carolina, Jackson supported the interests of small-business owners, farmers, pioneers, and slaveholders. Opposition to Jackson's policies took form in a new party—the Whigs. The Whigs desired an active role for government, and they supported policies such as protective tariffs and federal improvement programs.

The Democratic Party at that time thought "the government is best that governs least." Party members believed that an active government would create inequality by taking actions that favored some people over others. For example, the Democrats attacked what they considered "special privileges" granted by government to some business interests at the expense of the population as a whole.

The Granger Collection, New York

POLITICAL PROCESSES *The 1858 debate between Democrat Stephen Douglas and Republican Abraham Lincoln helped Lincoln win the presidential election.* **What factors helped the Democrats hold power until the Civil War?**

Government aid to build canals and roads, they argued, came out of tax money paid by all, yet supported projects benefiting only business and industry. The Democrats also opposed tariffs, believing them discriminatory.

This Democratic philosophy appealed to immigrants and the many people developing the rapidly growing young nation's frontier. As a result, Democrats dominated the government most of the time until the Civil War.

During the 1840s and 1850s, however, political unrest began to rise. Democrats and Whigs continued to disagree over tariffs. They also disagreed over slavery, particularly about whether it was to be allowed in the country's newly settled areas. Slavery was in fact the main factor that led to the end of this period of competing-party politics. With southern and northern members present in both parties, tensions made it impossible for the old party system to continue.

After 1852 the Whig party collapsed, and a new party opposed to slavery—the Republicans—arose in 1854. Many northern Whigs, as well as antislavery Democrats, joined the new Republican Party. Though the Democrats won the election of 1856, tensions over slavery, as well as divisions within the party itself, brought an end to Democratic control in 1860 and signaled the rise of the Republicans as the dominant power.

Republicans and Democrats

The Republican Party elected its first president, Abraham Lincoln, in 1860. During Lincoln's term the brewing tensions between the North and South over slavery and other issues erupted into the Civil War in 1861. The changes brought by the election of 1860 signaled another realignment and began a long period of Republican domination that lasted until 1932. Only two Democrats were elected president during that period—Grover Cleveland in 1884 and 1892 and Woodrow Wilson in 1912 and 1916.

Party Support After the Civil War For many years after the war, support for the Republicans and Democrats remained divided according to region and racial and financial concerns. Much of the Republican Party's support stemmed from its stance on slavery during the war. In general, former Whigs, newly freed African Americans, and antislavery Democrats supported the Republicans. The party also embraced the concerns of businesspeople, who wanted government aid for roads and canals, and from pioneers, who hoped for cheap government land.

The Democrats' support, on the other hand, rested with workers in the growing U.S. cities, including the many new immigrants. The party also received support from southerners who, still recovering from the war, resented the Republican stronghold in the North.

During this period, people identified strongly with their party of choice and remained fiercely loyal to it. Indeed, few citizens switched parties, and elections were extremely close. The parties created enough loyalty to produce higher voting turnouts among eligible voters than in any other period of U.S. history.

Election of 1896 The period after the Civil War was one of rapid economic growth and change, with large corporations appearing for the first time. Many farmers, meanwhile, faced difficult economic times.

Although the Democrats lost the election of 1896 and Republican domination continued, the election was a turning point because it brought this new period's economic issues to the forefront. It generally pitted farmers and small-business owners against big business and industry. In doing so, the election served to define the future roles of the Republican and Democratic Parties.

William Jennings Bryan, a congressmember from Nebraska, was nominated as the Democratic

POLITICAL PROCESSES *William Jennings Bryan was the Democratic nominee for the 1896 and 1900 presidential elections. Bryan's candidacy marked a turning point in Democratic Party policy.* ***In what way was this period a political turning point?***

candidate for president after he dazzled his party's convention with an emotional endorsement of rural life. In his speech Bryan declared:

“ Burn down your cities and leave our farms, and your cities will spring up again as if by magic. But destroy our farms and the grass will grow in the streets of every city in this country. . . . You shall not press down upon the brow of labor this crown of thorns. You shall not crucify mankind upon a cross of gold. ”

The Democrats had long been a voice for the poor but had rarely endorsed government action on their behalf. This tradition began to change, however, as the party moved away from its "government is best that governs least" stance.

Republicans were changing as well, adopting policies intended to pave the way for economic prosperity. High tariffs to protect U.S. industry, Republicans argued, would give workers "a full dinner pail."

Representing business and industry interests, Republican William McKinley won a big victory in 1896. Part of the reason for this, however, was a reaction against the economic depression of 1893, which had occurred during President Cleveland's Democratic administration.

The Great Depression With the exception of Democratic president Wilson's two terms, the Republican Party continued its domination of the presidency until the 1930s. The Great Depression, however, brought about another party realignment, which resulted in more than 30 years of Democratic presidents, with the exception of World War II hero General Dwight Eisenhower's presidency.

As the country sank further into the depression, the Democrats rose to power in an effort to help people deal with its painful effects. Franklin Roosevelt and other Democrats fostered their success by building up an electoral base of labor groups, southerners, farmers, and city political organizations.

In a series of bold moves, President Roosevelt sought a cure for the depression in increased governmental activism through a series of programs collectively called the New Deal. The government put millions of unemployed people to work building roads, bridges, and post offices. Roosevelt also sponsored legislation setting up Social Security (an old-age and disability pension system) as well as

legislation making it easier for workers to organize in labor unions. The New Deal programs inspired the new coalition of voters backing Roosevelt to give him even greater support. Republicans opposed Roosevelt's actions and accused him of overstepping the government's powers.

With the New Deal, the reversal of the two parties' traditional roles was complete. Whereas the Republicans (and the earlier Federalists and Whigs) had traditionally stood for big government and increased government expenditures, the Democrats (and the Democratic-Republicans) had always promoted minimal government. Democrats since Roosevelt have been supporters of an active government, and Republicans have favored smaller government.

Political Parties Today The Democrats, with the exception of President Eisenhower's two terms, controlled the presidency until 1968, when Republican Richard Nixon was elected. Though Democrats dominated the Congress until 1994, party control of the presidency has shifted a great deal since 1968. Republicans have won the White House in three out of the first six presidential elections since Nixon left office.

Since the 1960s many political scientists have been predicting a new period of party politics. Evidence up to now, however, does not reveal a major realignment. The major distinction between the parties—with the Democrats supporting "more government" on behalf of disadvantaged groups and the Republicans supporting "less government"—has remained largely unchanged since the New Deal.

Third Parties and Independents

Despite the Republicans' and Democrats' control over the political system since the 1850s, voters in some elections have opted to give significant backing to independent and third-party candidates. An **independent** candidate is not associated with any party. In a two-party system a **third party** is any political party, besides the two dominant ones, seeking to directly participate in government.

Although independent and third-party candidates have enjoyed little success in U.S. political history, there have been times when they have had

Significant Third-Party Presidential Candidates Since the Civil War

Party	Candidate	Year	Issues
Greenback	Peter Cooper	1876	currency reform, labor rights
Greenback	James B. Weaver	1880	currency reforms, labor rights
Prohibition	John P. St. John	1884	antiliquor
Populist	James B. Weaver	1892	currency reform, farm interests
Socialist	Eugene V. Debs	1900–12; 1920	public ownership of property
Progressive (Bull Moose)	Theodore Roosevelt	1912	political and business reform
Progressive	Robert M. La Follette	1924	farm interests, labor interests
Socialist	Norman Thomas	1928–48	public ownership of property
Union	William Lemke	1936	opposition to the New Deal
States' Rights (Dixiecrats)	Strom Thurmond	1948	segregation, states' rights
Progressive	Henry A. Wallace	1948	social reform, opposition to Cold War
American Independent	George Wallace	1968	states' rights
American	John Schmitz	1972	states' rights, crime
Libertarian	Various	1972–96	limited government
Reform	Ross Perot	1996	political and budget reform

Sources: *1997 World Almanac and Book of Facts; Dynamics of the Party System,* James L. Sundquist, copyright 1983, The Brookings Institution

Third-party candidates have run in presidential elections since 1872 but have never won an election. **In what year did Theodore Roosevelt run as the Progressive Party presidential candidate?**

a decisive influence on the outcome of elections. In 1912, when Theodore Roosevelt failed to gain the Republican Party's presidential nomination, he formed a third party called the Progressives to back his bid for the presidency. He did not win the election, but he took so many votes away from Republican candidate William Taft that Democrat Woodrow Wilson won.

In 1992 independent candidate Ross Perot rallied disenchanted voters and campaigned against Republican George Bush and Democrat Bill Clinton. Perot won 19 percent of the vote, more than any independent or third-party candidate had won since Roosevelt's bid for the presidency in 1912. Many people said that Perot's success contributed to Bush's loss in the election, as many Republicans voted for Perot. Perot ran again in 1996 as the Reform Party's candidate, but that time received only 8 percent of the vote. Of the third parties appearing during periods of realignment, the only one ever to replace one of the existing parties was the Republican Party, which replaced the Whigs before the Civil War.

The Reform Party

POLITICAL PROCESSES Ross Perot's independent campaign for president in 1992 and the organization he created to aid his bid were the motivations behind the founding of the Reform Party prior to the 1996 election. Although the party did not nominate candidates for congressional seats, it succeeded in getting its nominee for president—Perot—added to ballots across the country, a difficult task for any third party.

Among other things, the Reform Party called for balancing the federal budget, reforming the way political campaigns are funded, and establishing term limits for members of Congress. The party also pressed for a new tax system and restrictions on lobbying government officials. In his 1992 campaign, Perot had run on the same issues.

Because Perot won 19 percent of the vote in 1992 and was the 1996 nominee of a national party, the Federal Election Commission declared his 1996 campaign eligible to receive federal election funds. As a result, Perot's campaign received $29 million in federal money. The campaigns for Democrat Bill Clinton and Republican nominee Bob Dole each received about $62 million from the federal election fund.

In his first bid for the presidency, Perot spent more than $60 million of his own money. Much of that money went to pay for so-called campaign infomercials. During those half-hour television programs, Perot used charts and other props to explain his concerns about federal spending and the need for various reforms.

Although his 1996 presidential campaign spent less money, Perot continued to use television infomercials. In the end, however, his percentage of the vote fell from its 1992 level. Nevertheless, because he won more than 5 percent of the vote, the Reform Party will be eligible to receive federal presidential election funds for the next campaign in 2000.

Third parties arise because of support for political stances that differ from those held by either major party. People have even formed parties over a single issue. For example, the Prohibition Party formed in 1869 and has nominated a presidential candidate in every election since then. Third parties usually form as a splinter party or as an ideological party.

Splinter Parties People who feel that their party has failed to address their concerns sometimes break off to form a **splinter party**. Examples include not only Roosevelt's Progressive Party but also the American Independent Party, founded by former Democrat George Wallace. Each man ran for president under the banner of his new party.

Ideological Parties The other type of third party is an **ideological party**—a group whose basic political views differ from those of the majority of the population. The Socialists became the only ideological party to gain more than 5 percent of the vote in a presidential election in 1912. The Socialists, who favor government takeover of industry, have run candidates in most presidential elections since then. The ideological Libertarian Party has fielded presidential candidates since 1972. The party promotes individual rights and less government interference in private lives and opposes taxes and U.S. involvement abroad.

SECTION 2 — REVIEW

1. Define the following terms: realignment, independent, third party, splinter party, ideological party.

2. What were the first political parties in the U.S. two-party system? Why did they form?

3. In what ways do the two major U.S. political parties today—the Republicans and the Democrats—differ from each other?

4. What are third parties, and why do people join them?

5. **Thinking and Writing Critically**
What issues are of concern to you in your life? Considering what you have learned about the Republicans and the Democrats, do you believe that either of these parties addresses your concerns? If not, would you join a third party to represent your interests? What kind of a third party would it be?

6. **Applying POLITICAL FOUNDATIONS**
Make a list of the events or changes in ideas that caused periods of political party realignment. In your opinion, are there any current issues that might have long-term effects on support for U.S. political parties? What kind of success might future third parties, such as the Reform Party, have in the U.S. political system? Explain your answers.

PARTY ORGANIZATION

Political Dictionary

party machine
patronage
straight ticket
split ticket
primary election
general election
precinct
ward

Objectives

★ How were early political parties structured, and how did this structure change in the late 1800s?

★ How did state parties change after the decline of local parties?

★ How did national party organization change in the 1900s?

Political parties are set up in tiers—national, state, and local organizations exist for each party. National and state party organizations are strongest today, while local parties are the weakest. This has not always been true, however. In earlier days of party politics, local parties were much stronger than those at the national or state level.

Local Parties

During the mid- to late 1800s, political parties were highly organized at the local level. In large cities, particularly in the North and Midwest, strong local political structures developed as immigration increased and municipal populations grew. By the end of the 1800s, however, many local party structures began to weaken.

Party Machines Local governments during the mid- and late 1800s were dominated by political structures called party machines. A **party machine** is an organized group of individuals who dominate a political party within a geographic area, usually a big city. These people typically use the party's resources to further their own power and control over the political system. Local party headquarters, such as the Democratic Party's Tammany Hall in New York City, have been located in municipal centers of power.

To gain support, party machines assigned small armies of workers to become familiar with residents of a neighborhood well in advance of an election. On election day these workers would urge supporters to go to the polls. Party machines recruited their workers by promising them government jobs as a reward if the party won the election. This system of awarding political favors in exchange for political support is called **patronage**, also referred to as the spoils system.

Big-city party machines also made a point of recruiting newly arrived immigrants. The machines hoped to gain these people's loyalty by helping them deal with unfamiliar bureaucracies and look for work and housing in their new city. The local parties also sought to stoke the pride of these new Americans by giving them leadership positions in the party or in the city.

The Granger Collection, New York

PRINCIPLES OF DEMOCRACY *The caption to this 1871 cartoon criticizing local party machines reads, "As long as I count the votes what are you going to do?"* **During what period were local governments dominated by party machines?**

Local Party Corruption Part of the reason that the party machines were able to maintain their mastery over the political system was through their control of the electoral process. For example, before 1888 the government did not provide a ballot with the names of all parties and candidates. Instead, a local party would print ballots with a list of only its own candidates. A person voted by placing one of these party-produced ballots in a voting box. Because the ballots listed only one party's candidates, the voter was forced to cast a **straight ticket**, or to vote only for candidates from a single party.

Party machines also engaged in illegal voting practices to maintain control over the system. For example, because there was no system of voter registration, party machines could pay supporters to vote several times. A common expression of the time was "Vote early and vote often." Such crooked practices almost guaranteed that a party's candidates would win office.

Elected officials' support and loyalty also helped strengthen early local political parties. In addition, local party organizations were in charge of nominating candidates and of providing the campaign workers to help candidates become elected. Indeed, during the 1800s many people thought it improper for candidates to campaign for themselves, so they relied on local parties to do so on their behalf. If the party machine helped a candidate become elected, he or she would more than likely support the party machine's members.

Party machines frequently financed their operations through crooked deals. In return for offering certain businesses government contracts, the machines would receive financial payments, often called kickbacks. For example, a city government might offer a contract for garbage removal to one business over another. The selected company would receive all of the city's garbage removal business in exchange for money given to the machine or its leaders.

Local Party Reform At the end of the 1800s, an attack on party machines weakened local parties for good. From about 1900 to 1920, a period known as the Progressive Era, reformers led an attack on powerful, self-interested organizations. Many saw big-city party machines as examples of such monster organizations. The reform spirit led to state legislation that severely cut back the power of local party organizations.

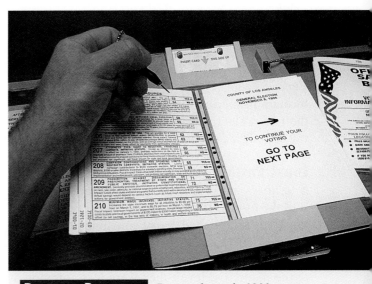

POLITICAL PROCESSES *During the early 1900s, state government officials replaced party-printed ballots with a government-printed ballot.* **What other reforms occurred during the Progressive Era?**

First, state laws introduced a new ballot system. Party-printed ballots were replaced with a government-printed ballot that listed all the parties and candidates. This made it possible for citizens to vote a **split ticket**, or to vote for candidates of different parties for different offices. By reducing the ability of local parties to support individual candidates, split-ticket voting helped to lessen the candidates' loyalty to the local party.

Second, voter registration was introduced. By requiring voters to register, election officials could exercise greater control over who voted—and how many times. This system was designed to make it difficult for party machines to engage in fraudulent election practices.

Third, reforms lowered the number of patronage jobs controlled by mayors and other local officials. This helped ensure that party machines could no longer gather support by securing jobs for their workers.

Last, states passed laws determining how a party could select its candidates. Previously, local party leaders had nominated party candidates for office. The new laws, however, required that party candidates be chosen in primary elections. **Primary elections**, often called primaries, are elections for nominating a party's candidate for office. The primary is held before the **general election**, in which voters actually choose their elected officials. (Types of elections are more fully explained in Chapter 19.)

A party organization whose leadership could choose its candidates had a major tool for assuring candidate loyalty to the machine. Primaries eventually opened up the nominating process. Because the voters now nominated candidates through primaries, candidates were able to create their own election organizations, instead of relying strictly on the local party organization.

Local Parties Today In spite of their limited role, many party machines continued to operate into the 1900s. By midcentury, however, most of the long-established party machines, including New York's Tammany Hall, had ceased to exist.

Although party machines frequently operated at the municipal level, they were less common at the state level and rarely operated at the national level. Today, for the most part, local party organizations have been replaced by strong state and national party organizations and by candidates' personal election organizations.

Where they do survive, local party structures usually are broken up into precinct, ward, city, and county levels. **Precincts** are voting districts into which cities, towns, and counties are divided. In many cities, several precincts may make up a **ward**, a territorial division of city government. These divisions are helpful in organizing the administration of local services, which also may serve as legislative districts for city government elections. Each precinct, ward, city, or county has a distinct party organization or committee. These local political party divisions or committees are subject to the rules and regulations of the state party that oversees them.

State Parties

During the time when local party organization was strongest, national and state party organizations were weak. State parties, however, began to grow in power during the 1900s as the power of local party organizations slowly lost force.

Early State Parties Early state parties were weak and not as well organized as local parties. Instead of having a permanent building as a center of authority, as local parties often had, a state party's headquarters often were located in the home or office of its chief officer. The state party did not receive much funding or support because most citizens participated in politics at the local level. As a result, state parties had little authority compared to local parties.

State Parties Today The growth of state parties during the 1900s coincided with, and in large part was created by, growth at the national party level. Stronger national parties have been able to provide funds and other support to state parties to help finance their operations.

For example, starting in the 1988 presidential campaign, national parties began channeling millions of dollars to state parties without violating any federal campaign finance laws limiting the amount a party could spend on an individual candidate's campaign. The laws allow state party organizations to spend unlimited amounts on "party-building activities." These activities include running voter registration drives, encouraging citizens to vote, and renting or buying facilities for party operations. Campaign finance laws allowed national parties to spend additional money for a presidential campaign by sending money raised at the national level to state party organizations for

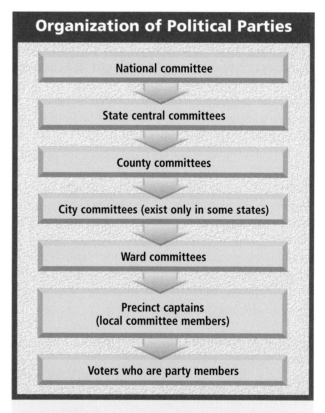

Organization of Political Parties

National committee

↓

State central committees

↓

County committees

↓

City committees (exist only in some states)

↓

Ward committees

↓

Precinct captains
(local committee members)

↓

Voters who are party members

State parties have recently progressed from weak, unorganized groups to powerful, well-funded political weapons. **Why have state parties received more funding from national parties since 1988?**

Party Activist

Working in politics does not always mean running for public office. For Tammy Miller and others who find politics fun and interesting, working for a political party is an attractive alternative.

In 1997 twenty-one-year-old Miller worked as a regional field coordinator for the Republican National Committee (RNC) in Washington, D.C. She served as the national party's contact person for voters, party candidates, and elected officials in her region, the northeastern United States.

Miller answered voter questions about the party and its position on various issues. She also helped Republican candidates and elected officials by researching and providing information about such things as key issues and available campaign resources. "I'm responsible for all the Republican elected officials in my region," Miller says.

Many staff members at the RNC and its counterpart, the Democratic National Commitee, prepared for their jobs with internships at local, state, or national government levels. Miller, for example, worked as an intern for the Nevada County government in California. Working as a budget analyst, she studied such things as how to make government more efficient and how state and federal requirements affect local government.

A few months after joining the RNC as an intern, Miller was hired as a regular staff member during the

Twenty-one year old Tammy Miller works in Washington, D.C., as a party activist for the Republican National Committee.

1996 election campaign. She says that preparing for her job meant "just jumping in and absorbing everything around me and being open-minded and ready to learn."

Some political party activists have earned college and postgraduate degrees in political science, public policy, and other applicable fields. In 1997, while working for the Republican Party, Miller pursued a bachelor's degree through night classes at the University of Maryland.

Miller hopes one day to work as a campaign manager helping talented and intelligent people run for office and pursue worthwhile policies. "I like the idea of organizing and helping people who are qualified get into office," Miller says.

---

such activities. Like national parties, however, state parties could not spend unlimited amounts on the campaign of any specific candidate.

As state parties grew, they began to raise funds through other means as well. Today, state-level political action committees (PACs) provide much of the money that state parties spend on their operations and on candidates. As noted in Chapter 17, a PAC is an organized group that gives funds to parties and candidates who support its interests.

As a result of greater financial strength, state party organization is much more powerful than it once was. Almost every state party has a permanent headquarters and a full-time chairperson, who is

chosen by a central committee of representatives from each county in the state.

Despite increased power, state party organizations have grown more dependent on national party committiees. Because they receive funds from national parties, state parties are subject to national parties' rules and requests. Also, national party leaders sometimes try to persuade state parties to help fund important campaigns in other states.

National Parties

Like state parties, national parties lacked strong organization during the 1800s and early 1900s.

However, during the mid- to late 1900s they transformed into the powerful organizations they are today.

Early National Parties Early national parties did little more than their basic duties—negotiating with the competing party over controversial issues and nominating presidential candidates. Until the early 1960s the Democrats and Republicans had no buildings to serve as permanent national headquarters. Instead, each party rented temporary office space in a building in Washington, D.C. In addition, national parties maintained much smaller staffs than they do today.

National Parties Today The Democratic and Republican Parties today have not only their own headquarters buildings but also television studios in which to record campaign commercials for party candidates and schools in which to teach candidates how to run for office. Each party is run by a national committee with a chairperson and a large staff.

Each party also has two congressional campaign committees, one for the House and one for the Senate, to channel funds to its congressional candidates. These committees are led by members of Congress, rather than by the party's national chair. The congressional committees have great freedom in deciding which candidates to support and how much money to give them. This makes the committees a possible source of party influence within Congress.

Larger national parties with bigger staffs have been able to raise millions of dollars for their

POLITICAL PROCESSES *Both the Republican and Democratic Parties own television studios in which they record campaign commercials.* **Until when, approximately, did both parties lack permanent headquarters buildings?**

candidates. In 1979–80 the national, state, and local Republican Party committees raised about $170 million for the party's candidates, beginning an era in which national political parties began raising a large portion of candidates' campaign funds. For the 1996 election, Democratic Party committees raised $221.6 million, while the Republican Party committees raised $416.5 million.

More money also has meant that national political party organizations have expanded the services they provide. National parties are able to provide candidates with assistance in polling and advertising, for instance. Through polling, parties can find out what voters think about the issues. Through media advertising, parties can make contact with and influence voters on candidates' behalf.

SECTION 3 — REVIEW

1. Define the following terms: party machine, patronage, straight ticket, split ticket, primary election, general election, precinct, ward.

2. Which level of party organization was strongest during the 1800s? What caused this to change?

3. Why did state parties grow stronger in the 1900s?

4. In what ways has the national party organization changed in recent decades?

5. **Thinking and Writing Critically**
   How might advances in technology and communication, such as television and the Internet, help national party organizations become stronger?

6. **Applying** **POLITICAL PROCESSES**
   Conduct an Internet search for information on the political party of your choice. Record the kind of information you find. Do Internet sites provide information about candidates?

POLITICAL PARTIES AND THE PUBLIC GOOD

Objectives

★ What are the common criticisms of the U.S. two-party system?

★ What are the benefits of the U.S. two-party system?

Imagine that you are a registered voter in an election year but are undecided about how to cast your ballot. You have seen several commercials for the candidates on television, but the commercials are brief and do not provide enough information. To whom do you turn?

One place to start is by examining which party each candidate represents. By researching the programs a party supports and its politicians' voting records, you can determine much about the basic political beliefs of its candidates. Although the parties are much criticized, they do help promote the public good in several ways, such as by making it easier to figure out how to cast your ballot.

Criticisms of Political Parties

As noted in Chapter 17, several concerns exist about the effect of interest groups on the public good. Because of their visibility and size, political parties come under even closer scrutiny. The most common criticisms of political parties are that they too often represent special interests, that they are filled with selfish office seekers, and that they are too concerned with "politicking." On the other hand, some political scientists argue that U.S. political parties are too weak.

Special Interests Many people think that parties are influenced too much by special-interest groups. They believe that because these groups

provide money for political campaigns and other party activities, politicians and their parties will make decisions that benefit only the groups rather than promote the public good.

Self-Serving Office Seekers Critics of party politics also have charged that political parties are full of self-serving office seekers, or people interested in personal gain rather than sincerely working on issues. Many have said that politicians and their parties support certain policies only because doing so helps them get elected.

Politicking Many people feel that the frequent bickering between the two major parties is just "politics as usual." Some critics charge that congressional politicking—the posturing between the parties—is often less concerned with real issues and more about which party is winning the public relations race.

Weakness of U.S. Political Parties Finally, some political scientists criticize U.S. political

PUBLIC GOOD *Political parties are criticized for being strongly influenced by special interests rather than working to promote the public good.* **Why are political parties more closely scrutinized today than in years past?**

parties for being what they perceive as too weak. Although the United States has the oldest political parties in the world, it also has about the weakest of any democratic country. Parties in the United States lack strength in several important ways. The two major parties have weak organizations and low voter allegiance, and their elected officials often do not stick together on issues, giving voters the impression that the party lacks unity.

American political parties generally have few organized activities, and the activities they do offer involve a relatively small proportion of the population. By contrast, to join most interest groups, people must fill in application forms, pay dues, and receive a membership card. Only members of the organization may participate in the organization's governance. Even interest groups whose members do not help govern and who do not fill out membership applications or cards usually solicit members by mail.

Similarly, political parties such as the Liberal Democratic Party of Japan and the Christian Democratic Party of Germany have card-carrying, dues-paying members as well as ordinary voters who support the party at the polls. Members provide a core of party workers and loyal supporters who take the party's message to their neighbors or fellow workers. The two major U.S. parties, however, lack such a membership structure.

Furthermore, U.S. legislators of the same party stick together less often than those in most other countries. In many countries there is party discipline in the legislature, with all of a party's representatives voting together on important issues. This does not typically occur in the United States.

Why do political scientists think stronger political parties are important? One answer is voter turnout. A lower percentage of people vote in the United States than in countries with stronger political parties. The reason for this difference, theorize some political scientists, is that citizens with relatively low interest in politics are more apt to vote if exposed to strong parties. Strong parties thus promote high voter participation, whereas weak political parties do not.

PUBLIC GOOD   *Youth organizations, such as the College Republicans, provide political information to young people.* **How can knowing the broad philosophy of a political party be helpful to voters?**

Benefits of the U.S. Two-Party System

Political parties do help promote the public good in four ways. They provide ready information about politics, help to balance the political system by taking into account varied opinions, discourage sudden shifts in political trends, and encourage political participation.

Providing Information Political parties help bring order to the political world. They present political information in a convenient form so that voters do not need to start over every time they encounter a political leader or a political proposal.

Parties provide a political "brand name," in much the same way a soft drink company does for its products. Knowing the broad political philosophy of a party helps you understand where it will stand on certain issues. One reason you may vote for a candidate is that, overall, you support his or her party's views.

Accommodating Varied Opinions Parties help the political system do a better job of allowing for the expression of a wide range of opinions and interests, which is necessary if political decisions are to promote the public good. Each party is made up of both individual voters and organized groups. Therefore, each party must try to consider

Citizenship in ⟶ Action

David Wade, former president of the College Democrats of America, worked to help inform college students about political issues and candidates.

Young Politicians

"The most important thing we could do is to make people care," says David Wade, who as a 21-year-old Brown University student served in 1997 as national president of the College Democrats of America. As a leader in this organization, Wade worked to further the Democratic Party's goals and elect its nominees to political office.

Other such organizations also focus on youth involvement in politics. Teen Republicans and Teen Democrats, for example, organize the efforts of teens who identify themselves as supporters of either the Republican or Democratic Party. The most well-known youth organizations, however, are the College Republicans National Committee, Young Republicans, Young Democrats of America, and College Democrats of America.

Although the College Republicans and the College Democrats limit membership to university students in the United States, the Young Democrats and Young Republicans include any partisans under the age of 35 (for the Democrats) and between the ages of 18 and 40 (for the Republicans). Each of the four organizations boasts tens of thousands of members who are working in thousands of chapters across the country.

The work of these youth organizations focuses on getting young people involved in the democratic process. Doing so helps address some people's concern that young people today care little about politics and the important issues of their time. For example, College Democrats and other youth-oriented political groups keep tabs on issues important to students, such as government policies on college financial aid, tuition rates, and access to education. Members then communicate that information—and the applicable positions of their parties—to other young people. At the same time, they encourage young voters to express their opinions and lobby government officials to support particular policies. "What we've found is that young people really respond to each other," Wade says.

The work of these youth organizations includes more than just keeping young people informed on important issues of the day, however. The organizations also work to register voters, get young people out to the polls on election day, raise money for party efforts, recruit volunteers for party work and campaigns, and provide a variety of community services.

In addition to their work in individual chapters around the country, members of some of these youth organizations also meet in national conventions. These gatherings give members the opportunity to debate issues, propose policies, and share ideas and experiences.

All of these efforts, Wade says, help educate students "so that they can cast a vote on election day or make a call to their congressperson that's reasoned, enlightened, and intelligent." In doing that, these young party members are setting a standard that all voters should follow.

What Do You Think?

1. How can Republican and Democratic youth organizations work together to promote participation in politics?
2. In what other ways can political parties reach out to young citizens and help them take part in the democratic process?

all of its supporters' interests if it is going to continue to receive their support. Including as many interests as possible is important because it means that more citizens are involved in the political system.

Discouraging Sudden Shifts Another benefit of political parties is that they serve as an anchor, making sudden political shifts in response to short-term trends more difficult. Think back to what you learned about multiparty systems in Section 1. By allowing many political parties, multiparty systems enable short-term trends to threaten government stability.

In the United States the two major political parties represent many issues, thus discouraging voters from giving up support for the party and elected officials just because of current trends on *one* political issue. Voters know that even if they disagree with a certain candidate on one issue, he or she represents the broader issues of his or her party. The resulting stability gives elected officials and parties more room to focus on the big picture. This is vital for wise public policies that take a long time to show they are working.

Encouraging Political Participation Many people think of competing political parties as a key part of democracy. In the nondemocratic Soviet Union, for example, only Communist Party members could participate in government. Indeed, the United States would cease to be a democracy if national leaders prevented people with opinions

John Jonik © 1997 from The Cartoon Bank. All rights reserved.

PUBLIC GOOD *Although the two major U.S. parties each have a strong base of support, they are often criticized for holding similar views to each other on many issues.* **How do parties provide political stability in a two-party system?**

different from their own from organizing groups to try to affect government actions.

Participation in political parties is one way for U.S. citizens to take part in the political system—and in their own governing. The United States is a diverse country and political parties provide a way for this diversity to be expressed in the political system.

SECTION 4 — REVIEW

1. What are some of the criticisms of political parties in the United States?

2. Why do some political scientists think that political parties are too weak?

3. How does the U.S. two-party system promote the public good?

4. **Thinking and Writing Critically**
   Why does politicking cause some people to be skeptical about political parties? List at least one important present-day issue that has

caused great disagreement between the Democrats and Republicans.

5. **Applying** **PUBLIC GOOD**
   Imagine that you live in a country with a multiparty system that has seen government control change hands many times in the past 10 years. You have been asked for your opinion on how the political system should change. Would you recommend a system like the U.S. two-party system, or would you keep the multiparty system? Why?

CHAPTER 18 — SUMMARY

SECTION 1 Political parties are organized groups that seek to gain power in the political system. They can serve several functions, including assisting the electoral process, organizing the day-to-day running of the government, and nominating candidates.

These functions vary with the type of party system a country has. There are three major types of party systems: one party, two party, and multiparty. In a one-party system, one political party controls the government and clearly dominates political activity. Many countries with one-party systems are dictatorships. In a two-party system, two major parties dominate the government. The Democrats and Republicans dominate the two-party system in the United States. In a multiparty system, several parties compete for control of the government. Each party's representation in the legislature usually depends on the number of votes the party receives in an election.

SECTION 2 Although the Constitution does not mention political parties, they formed in the United States out of the actual practice of political life. The U.S. two-party system has had five distinct periods, each of which can be characterized according to the parties that were competing for power at the time. These periods involved the Federalists and Democratic-Republicans, the Democrats and Whigs, the Republicans and Democrats, and two major realignments of power between Democrats and Republicans.

Since the 1960s many political scientists have been predicting a new period of party politics. Evidence up to now, however, does not reveal a major realignment. The major distinctions between the parties have remained largely unchanged since the New Deal.

Despite control over the political system by Republicans and Democrats since the 1850s, voters have opted occasionally to give backing to independent and third-party candidates. In a two-party system a third party is any political party, besides the two dominant ones, seeking to directly participate in the government. An independent candidate is not associated with any party.

SECTION 3 There are three levels of party organization in the United States: national, state, and local. Local party organization was originally strongest. Local governments during the mid- to late 1800s were dominated by political structures called party machines, which were often corrupt. Changes in the electoral process, including a new ballot system, voter registration, and the elimination of a large number of patronage jobs, helped end local party domination. State and national party organization grew stronger during the 1900s. Both state and national party organizations today have large staffs and are able to provide more money and better services to candidates.

SECTION 4 U.S. political parties are sometimes criticized for representing special interests, for being filled with self-serving office seekers, and for politicking. Political parties, however, do promote the public good in four ways: by providing readily understandable information, weighing varied interests and opinions to provide a stable balance, making shifts in political trends more difficult, and encouraging political participation.

Government Notebook

Review the list of factors that you wrote in your Government Notebook at the beginning of the chapter. Now that you have studied the chapter, consider which factors on your list might apply to political parties. Explain the reason for your choices in your Notebook.

REVIEW

REVIEWING CONCEPTS

1. What are political parties, and why are they important to political systems?

2. List and briefly explain the historical periods of the U.S. party system.

3. What are the functions of political parties in the United States?

4. How do political parties promote the public good?

5. What are some criticisms of political parties?

6. Was the sphere of party influence strongest during the 1800s at the national, state, or local level? How did this change?

THINKING AND WRITING CRITICALLY

1. **POLITICAL PROCESSES** Do you think that the United States should continue as a two-party system or that it would benefit from switching to a multiparty system? Explain your answer.

2. **PRINCIPLES OF DEMOCRACY** Many people believe that the party system encourages political participation. Do you agree with this opinion? Why or why not?

3. **POLITICAL PROCESSES** One function of political parties is to nominate presidential candidates. George Washington, however, was nominated before political parties developed. How do you think a presidential candidate might be nominated if political parties did not exist? Write a paragraph explaining your theory.

4. **PUBLIC GOOD** What reforms were made in the 1800s to stop corruption in local party machines? How have these reforms improved the voting process and helped voters today?

CITIZENSHIP IN YOUR COMMUNITY

Locate information about the mayor of your city. Is he or she a Democrat or a Republican? What issues were important and what viewpoint did he or she support when campaigning for office? Did he or she make any campaign promises? If so, have they been kept? The Internet often is a good source for finding information about local government, including how to contact your mayor's office. With the information you find, create a poster and display it in your classroom.

COOPERATIVE PORTFOLIO PROJECT

Organize students into two groups to research the Republican and Democratic Parties. Develop brochures that explain the two parties' general views and stances on important issues. Make enough copies to hand out to the 18-year-old students in your school to encourage them to register to vote and to help them become informed voters.

PRACTICING SKILLS: READING MAPS

The map on the next page identifies political party control of state legislatures. Study the map and answer the questions that follow.

1. What percentage of the states have split control of their legislatures?

2. Do Democrats or Republicans control a larger portion of state legislatures?

3. Identify a part of the country in which one party controls several of the state legislatures.

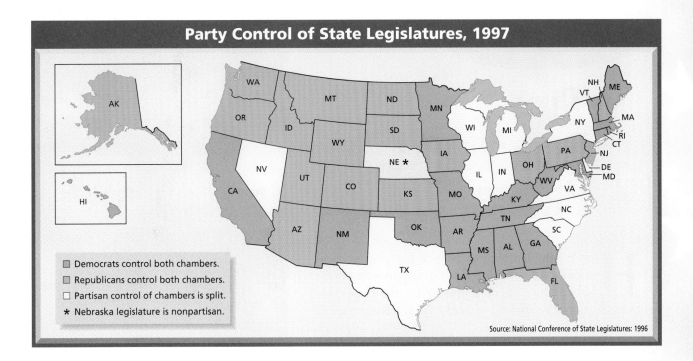

Party Control of State Legislatures, 1997

- ☐ Democrats control both chambers.
- ☐ Republicans control both chambers.
- ☐ Partisan control of chambers is split.
- ✳ Nebraska legislature is nonpartisan.

Source: National Conference of State Legislatures: 1996

THE INTERNET: LEARNING ONLINE

Conduct an Internet search for information about the Reform Party. You might start with search words such as *Reform Party, third party, Ross Perot,* and *Pat Choate.* Make a chart comparing the principles of the Reform Party with the basic beliefs and views of the Democratic Party and the Republican Party. Be sure to include a list of the Web sites you use to gather the information.

ANALYZING PRIMARY SOURCES

THE BUSH-FERRARO DEBATE

In 1984 Geraldine Ferraro became the first female to be nominated for vice president by a major political party. A Democrat, she ran alongside presidential candidate Walter Mondale. At one point during the campaign, Ferraro debated then vice president George Bush. Below is an excerpt from that debate, in which Ferraro identifies some of the major issues of the Democratic campaign. Read the excerpt and answer the questions that follow.

❝ *Being the candidate for vice-president of my party is the greatest honor I have ever had. . . . I wouldn't be standing here if Fritz [Walter] Mondale didn't have the courage and my party didn't stand for the values that it does, the values of fairness and equal opportunity. . . . Do you know when we find jobs for the eight and a half million people who are unemployed in this country and that will be a patriotic act. We'll make our economy stronger. . . . When we reduce the deficits and we cut interest rates, . . . we cut those interest rates [so] young people can buy houses, that's pro-family and that will be a patriotic act. When we educate our children . . . they're going to be able to compete in a world economy and that makes us stronger and that's a patriotic act. When we stop the arms race, we make this a safer, saner world. . . . Those are the keys to the future.* ❞

1. What key issues does Ferraro address?

2. What do you think Ferraro wants to show voters that the Democratic Party values?

3. Are today's candidates and political parties discussing the same issues that Ferraro mentions in this excerpt from her speech? What are some of the major issues discussed by politicians today?

CHAPTER 19

THE ELECTORAL PROCESS

How are the candidates chosen for your school's student council elections? How do you choose from among the candidates? Do the candidates campaign for the student offices? What determines the winners of the elections?

More than likely, your class leaders are chosen in much the same way that U.S. political leaders are chosen by American citizens—through an established electoral process. In this chapter you will learn about the three steps in that process: nomination, campaigning, and election.

Government Notebook

In your Government Notebook, make a list of some of the times this school year that you and your friends or classmates have held a vote to decide a certain issue. On what kinds of things do you generally hold a vote? Explain why voting is an important part of making a decision about an issue.

NOMINATING CANDIDATES

Political Dictionary

direct primary
closed primary
open primary
runoff primary
nonpartisan primary

Objectives

★ What is the first step in the electoral process?
★ In what ways may candidates be chosen for an election?
★ What types of primary elections are held in the states?

W hen casting your vote during an election, you most likely choose from among the candidates listed. But how are the official candidates for an election selected?

As noted in Chapter 7, nominating candidates is the first step in the electoral process. Nomination procedures vary according to local, state, and national election rules. Candidates are nominated in five ways:

★ self-announcement,
★ caucus,
★ convention,
★ petition, and
★ primary election.

Self-Announcement

To nominate by self-announcement, a person simply declares publicly that he or she is running for office. Commonly practiced in the American colonies, this procedure is the oldest means of nomination in the United States.

Today, self-announcement is used most often at the local level. By announcing his or her candidacy,

a person enters the race for office, though there is usually some kind of officially required registration procedure as well.

In some cases a candidate at the national or state level might use self-announcement if he or she is unlikely to secure the nomination of either of the major parties or does not agree with the policies they support. For example, during the 1992 election Ross Perot declared himself an independent candidate for the presidency.

Most ballots are printed with a space for write-in candidates. A write-in candidate is a person who declares that he or she will run for office and then asks people to write his or her name on the ballot when they vote. In states whose official ballots do not provide such a space, voters can request a special ballot to vote for a write-in candidate. Write-in candidates usually fail to achieve a broad base of support and thus rarely, if ever, win.

Caucus

As noted in Chapter 7, the caucus is another long-time means of nominating candidates in America. The earliest caucuses in what is now the United

POLITICAL PROCESSES *Most states stopped using caucuses as a means of nominating state and U.S. legislators by the mid-1800s. Texas, however, still uses this method.* **When were the first caucuses held in the United States?**

States date from around 1725. Community leaders would gather in a home or an official town building to endorse candidates for local offices. Such groups were called caucus clubs. In his diary John Adams described an early caucus:

> " This day learned that the Caucus Club meets, at certain times, in the garret [top-floor room] of Tom Dawes. . . . He has a large house . . . and the whole club meets in one room. . . . There they choose a moderator, who puts questions to the vote regularly; and selectmen [council members], assessors, collectors, wardens, fire-wards, and representatives are regularly chosen before they are chosen in the town. "

Caucuses were held at the state and national levels as early as the 1790s. State legislative caucuses chose candidates for state and local office, while national congressional caucuses chose presidential and vice presidential candidates.

Eventually, as political parties developed, caucuses became functions of the parties and were run by party officials. The meetings, which were not open to the public, were dominated by party leaders. Abuses of the system were frequent, as party leaders used caucuses to further their own goals. Gradually, many voters began to criticize the closed-door caucus meetings.

Because of a rise in voter dissatisfaction, party leaders in most states stopped using the caucus for nominating candidates to the U.S. Congress by the 1820s and for nominating candidates to state office by the 1840s. Today the caucus is still used at the local level in a few states. Some states, including Iowa, still hold caucuses at the national level as well. These caucuses, however, are open to all members of a party—not just to party leaders and influential members of the community.

Convention

As noted in Chapter 7, a convention is a political party gathering held to nominate candidates, set party rules, and create a party platform. By the mid- to late 1800s, party conventions were common at the local, state, and national levels. The delegations were made up of people representing their town, city, county, or state.

Delegates to local conventions chose local candidates as well as delegates to the state convention. In turn, the state convention delegates would choose candidates for state offices and delegates to the national convention. Delegates from each of the states then assembled at the national convention to choose the presidential and vice presidential candidates.

As with the caucuses, conventions eventually were subject to political corruption and control by party bosses, who tried to seat delegates favorable to their views. For this reason many states eventually gave up the convention system for nominating candidates. Today only a few states hold state and local nominating conventions, and these are heavily regulated to prevent abuses. Other states hold conventions only to nominate delegates to the national conventions. The presidential and vice presidential candidates also are still officially chosen by a national convention.

Petition

Another way that candidates are nominated is by petition. Supporters of someone seeking elected office but lacking the endorsement of a major

WRIGHT © Tribune Media Services, Inc. All rights reserved. Reprinted with permission.

POLITICAL PROCESSES *Some critics think that the electoral process has become too complicated and time-consuming for candidates.* **Why did many states stop using the convention system for nominating candidates?**

Campaign Worker

Running election campaigns is a highly professional endeavor. Whether seeking the presidency or a seat on the city council, a candidate turns to professional consultants—expert advice givers—for help in running the campaign. In fact, running campaigns and consulting for them have become steady sources of employment for many people. Consider, for example, Paul Begala, a political strategist with the presidential campaign of Bill Clinton in 1992.

Prior to working on Bill Clinton's 1992 presidential campaign, Paul Begala worked on the campaigns of people running for the Senate and for governor.

Begala entered politics while a student at the University of Texas at Austin, serving as president of the university's students' association in 1982–83. After graduating, Begala went to work for politicians—first as an aide to U.S. Representative Dick Gephardt of Missouri and, in 1983–84, as a U.S. senatorial campaigner during a race in Texas. Begala later worked on campaigns for Senate seats and governorships in Pennsylvania, Georgia, and New Jersey before joining the Clinton campaign.

The work performed by Begala and other campaign workers varies. A typical day may include recruiting volunteers to call potential voters and to walk neighborhoods promoting a candidate. It also may include setting up fund-raising events, preparing speeches, coordinating direct-mail efforts, and helping develop policies and campaign strategies.

Workers may range from students to recent college graduates to seasoned veterans from the campaign trail. Candidates often look for people who have experience, education, or training in politics that might be useful to the campaign. Whatever their backgrounds, however, campaign staff members share a common passion for politics and the candidates and ideals for which they work.

political party can circulate a petition requesting that the person's name be placed on the official ballot. A nominating petition is only valid if it has been signed by a certain number of people registered to vote in the election district in question.

Nomination by petition is most common in local elections. It also is widely used by independent and third-party state and national candidates who have some support from eligible voters.

Primary Election

Today the primary election is the most common way for candidates to gain a nomination for political office. As noted in Chapter 7, primary elections are held before the general election in order to determine the candidates for each party. The primaries give voters, instead of party leaders, the chance to do the nominating.

Nominations for the House and Senate and for state and local office occur through direct primaries. A **direct primary** is one in which the winner is named the party's nominee for the general election. Presidential primaries are not direct—they are followed by a national convention at which delegates elected in the primaries choose a candidate based on the results of the primaries.

The parties do not determine the rules for primary elections. The states do, just as they regulate other features of party organization. The states not only decide who may vote but they also regulate what party organizations may or may not do in primary campaigns. Each state also determines what kind of primary it will hold.

How much influence parties have on the outcome of primaries is also regulated by the states. In about one third of the states, party conventions are allowed to endorse primary candidates. In some states, only candidates running for a state office who receive a certain minimum percentage of the vote at a state party convention may appear on the primary ballot. In others, candidates endorsed by state party conventions appear first on the ballot or with asterisks next to their names. California and Florida go to the opposite extreme, prohibiting party conventions from backing primary candidates.

Closed Primary Fewer than 20 states have closed primaries. A **closed primary** is one in which only the members of a political party are permitted to vote in selecting the party's candidates. Under this system, separate but simultaneous primaries are held for both the Republican and Democratic parties. Democrats wishing to vote Republican and Republicans wishing to vote Democrat must wait for a general election.

Many states with closed primaries, however, have more relaxed rules regarding party affiliation. On the day of the primary, citizens can register for the party in whose nomination process they most want to participate.

Open Primary Most states have what are called open primaries. An **open primary** allows a registered voter to participate in either the Republican or Democratic nomination process just by choosing a party once he or she is in the voting booth. This means that a registered Republican, for example, may vote in a Democratic primary without giving up his or her Republican registration status. In some open primaries, voters may choose candidates from either party for each office open for election.

Runoff Primary Several states have a follow-up primary election if no candidate receives a majority of the votes. In these **runoff primaries**, voters choose between the top vote recipients from the first election. The winner of the runoff primary is then named the party's candidate for the general election.

Nonpartisan Primary A **nonpartisan primary** is one in which all candidates appear on the same ballot. In most cases these candidates are running for city- and county-level offices. For example,

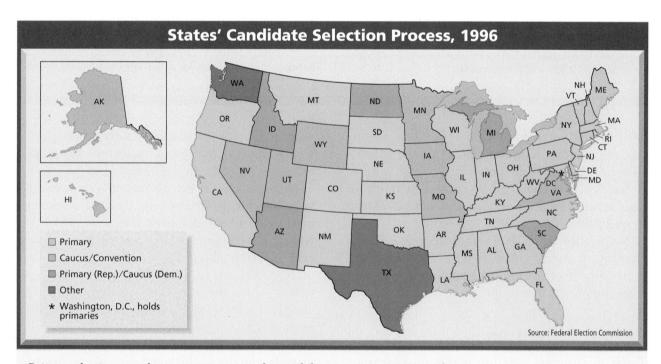

States' Candidate Selection Process, 1996

□ Primary
□ Caucus/Convention
□ Primary (Rep.)/Caucus (Dem.)
■ Other
★ Washington, D.C., holds primaries

Source: Federal Election Commission

Primary elections are the most common way for candidates to gain nomination for political office. Several states, however, use other methods. ***How many states use the caucus/convention system to nominate candidates?***

Citizenship in ⟶ Action

Taking Part in Democracy

In a democracy such as the United States, citizens have many opportunities to get involved in the electoral process. In addition to debating issues, learning about candidates, and voting, they may choose to volunteer for campaign work. In fact, most successful campaigns might have failed were it not for the dedicated work of volunteers who kept the office operating smoothly, worked with voters, and provided other support for candidates and paid staff.

Some people choose to become directly involved in the electoral process by serving as delegates to party conventions. In some states, for example, citizens attend precinct conventions to debate issues and support particular candidates. Citizens also work to become convention delegates at county, district, state, and national levels.

Jo Ann Strickler, for example, ran her own campaign to become a delegate to the 1992 Republican National Convention in Houston. Strickler, then a 22-year-old senior at Virginia Polytechnic Institute and State University, spoke at local county meetings, handed out buttons and signs, shook a lot of hands at the district convention, and organized a network of volunteers to help in her campaign. In the end, her work paid off and she became one of her state's national convention delegates.

In 1992 Marc Glenn, then an 18-year-old high school graduate from Atlanta, also worked hard to become a delegate to the Democratic National Convention in New York City. "The most interesting thing that I learned was that once I decided to get involved, it was relatively easy to become an active part of the American political system," Glenn says.

Strickler and Glenn joined thousands of other delegates at the national conventions. Tens of thousands of others took part in the electoral process by attending conventions at lower levels.

Not all people who are interested in politics become so deeply involved, of course. Some people decide instead to volunteer for a candidate. Others attend debates or campaign rallies. Still others volunteer to work as clerks at polling places, to take people to the polls, or to plan small gatherings in their homes, where candidates can explain their positions on important issues.

Strickler and Glenn say that taking part means more than simply criticizing particular politicians and policies. "It is much easier to criticize from the outside than to wake up at the crack of dawn to hand out campaign literature at the polls or to follow what's going on at Capitol Hill and call your senator and congressperson to let them know how you feel about a certain issue," Strickler says.

Glenn agrees. He asserts that "if a person is bold enough to actively criticize government, then that person is not only *able* enough to take an active role in running it—they are almost *obligated* to become involved in some way."

Mark Glenn was 18 years old when he was selected as a delegate to the 1992 Democratic National Convention in New York City.

What Do You Think?

1. Do you think it is important for citizens to get involved in the electoral process? Explain your answer.
2. In what ways could you and your classmates become involved in the electoral process?

Calvin and Hobbes

by Bill Watterson

CALVIN & HOBBES copyright 1992 Watterson. Reprinted with permission of Universal Press Syndicate. All rights reserved.

PUBLIC GOOD *Around half of the voting-age population does not vote in general elections.*
In general, is voter turnout greater for primary elections or general elections?

candidates for a local judgeship in some states must first receive a nomination in a nonpartisan primary before being placed on a general election ballot.

In some states a candidate who receives the majority of the votes cast in a nonpartisan primary is automatically elected and does not have to run in the general election. If no one wins a majority in the primary, however, its two top vote recipients appear on the general election ballot.

Voter Turnout in Primaries

Turnout in primary elections is generally around one third to one half of that in the general election. Typically, a greater percentage of well-educated, upper-income voters participate in primaries. Some people argue that primary voters also are ideologically more committed than voters in general elections—that Democratic primary voters are more liberal than Democratic voters in general, Republican primary voters more conservative than Republican voters in general. However, evidence gathered by political scientists does not consistently support this proposition. Sometimes primary voters are more extreme, other times not. Factors such as the country's economic situation might be more likely to inspire someone to vote in a primary than would his or her political ideology.

SECTION 1 — REVIEW

1. Define the following terms: direct primary, closed primary, open primary, runoff primary, nonpartisan primary.

2. In what ways have candidates been chosen to run in elections?

3. What are some of the regulations states place on primary elections?

4. Describe the different kinds of primary elections.

5. **Thinking and Writing Critically**
   How do primaries give voters more of a voice in the electoral process than did earlier means of nominating candidates? Why do you think it is important for citizens to have a greater number of opportunities to participate in the political process?

6. **Applying** POLITICAL PROCESSES
   By what means are students in your school nominated for student offices and other positions?

SECTION 2

CAMPAIGNS AND CAMPAIGN FINANCING

Objectives

★ How was early political campaigning different from political campaigning today?
★ What is the role of the media in today's political campaigns?
★ How are campaigns financed?
★ How is campaign financing regulated?

Once candidates have been nominated, the second step in the electoral process—campaigning—begins. The fanfare surrounding political campaigns has been around for almost as long as the country itself. For example, during the 1800s supporters of both the Republicans and Democrats campaigned around the clock to promote their candidates. By day they marched with banners bearing candidates' slogans. At night they often held torchlight parades.

Why do people engage in such extravagant displays? Holding elected office is a high honor in the United States. Candidates must mount elaborate campaigns to convince the electorate that they are right for the job.

Though the reason for campaigning has not changed, the way campaigns are conducted has changed greatly since the 1700s and 1800s. During the 1900s, campaigns changed in three major ways:

★ candidates became more visible,
★ the role of the media became more pronounced, and
★ polling became a key tool.

In addition, campaign spending has skyrocketed to cover increasingly extensive campaigning.

Candidate Visibility

During the 1700s and early to mid-1800s, candidates, particularly those running for president,

were expected to maintain proper form during their campaigns. The political journal *The Nation* described what was generally considered appropriate behavior for a candidate:

66 Etiquette requires that the candidate shall rigidly abstain [keep] from any open efforts to promote his own election, and, indeed, from all discoverable complicity [participation] in such efforts on the part of others. Rigid propriety [properness] . . . seems even to require that he shall preserve complete silence during the [campaign] on all topics of the day, and the summit of dignity and decorum [good form] is only reached by a display of apparent ignorance that any [campaign] is going on, or if going on that he has any particular connection with it. 99

Gradually, as the nation grew, this attitude began to change. In 1896 Democratic presidential

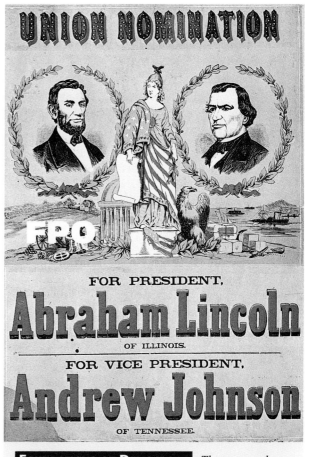

FOUNDATIONS OF DEMOCRACY *The poster above is from Lincoln's 1864 presidential campaign.* **Why do candidates engage in elaborate campaigns during an election year?**

candidate William Jennings Bryan undertook an unprecedented nationwide tour, giving rousing speeches along the way. A new trend in campaigning had begun.

Campaign Appearances

By the first part of the 1900s, presidential candidates were engaging in stunts unheard of only a few years earlier. Woodrow Wilson, for example, got public attention by attending the yearly baby parade in Asbury Park, New Jersey. In 1924 Democratic presidential candidate John W. Davis tried to make points with voters by throwing a pitch to his vice presidential running mate at a baseball game.

Candidates toured large sections of the country by train in what became known as whistle-stop campaigning. While stopping along the way in small towns, candidates would address voters from the rear platform of a train. ("Whistle-stop" was a nickname that railroad workers gave to a town so small that the train stopped there only long enough for the whistle to blow.) According to some observers at the time, Harry Truman won the presidency in 1948 partly because of a vigorous whistle-stop campaign.

Campaigning in Person Today

Campaigning today is a grueling activity that calls for constant travel, speaking, and handshaking. Candidates, particularly those running for president, often spend weeks away from home, traveling from city to city. It can be exhausting—most candidates catch very little sleep, especially during the intense campaigning right before an election. In the final week of the 1996 presidential campaign, for example, Bob Dole stayed up for 96 hours straight to speak at as many campaign rallies as possible before the election. Bill Clinton traveled the country by plane, train, and bus in the 1992 and 1996 campaigns, greeting supporters along the way.

Media Involvement

The early 1900s also brought a greater use of the media in promoting candidates. Presidential campaign organizations began pouring major resources into what were called literary bureaus, working units that generated literature and speeches, explored important issues, and maintained press relations.

With the introduction of new technology, campaigns could rely on not only print but also radio,

PUBLIC GOOD *During his 1952 presidential campaign, Dwight Eisenhower traveled to Mount Holyoke College to meet with students.* **Which presidential candidate of the late 1800s helped to change people's attitudes about campaigns?**

film, and television. When Woodrow Wilson ran for president in 1912, for example, his campaign team produced movies and recordings about him. Radio and television have become a very popular means of advertising in political campaigns.

Early Campaign Advertising Presidential candidates first used television advertising during the 1952 campaign. Dwight D. Eisenhower ran 30- and 60-second political ads, hoping that they would capture viewers' interest much like commercials for household goods, cars, and other products did. In contrast, Adlai Stevenson—Eisenhower's opponent—took a more traditional approach: he simply used television to air half-hour speeches. Unlike Eisenhower's shorter spots, these speeches failed to take advantage of a key feature of television—its ability to quickly and dramatically convey simple ideas and a sense of personality.

Media Campaigning Today Today presidential and senatorial campaigns are conducted largely through the media. The reason is simple: it is far easier to reach millions of voters through media messages than in person. A candidate for national or statewide office can never hope to meet or speak before more than a tiny fraction of a large state's voters, even during an extensive campaign. As political consultant Frank Luntz noted in 1988, "If the two Senate candidates in Florida . . . made ten speeches a day to audiences of 100 persons, it would take eight years to reach every voter."

Because the use of the media increases a candidate's reach, it has become a central campaign strategy. Political media consultants carefully tailor radio and television ads for targeted audiences and plan events whose primary purpose is to gain the candidate coverage on the evening news. In fact, candidates spend an increasing amount of time appearing at events that are staged solely for coverage by the media.

Polling

Polling also became a popular tool of political campaigns during the 1900s. As noted in Chapter 16, polling involves surveying a population on an issue. A major goal of campaign polling is to gain insight into voters' attitudes about a candidate's campaign and views.

For example, suppose that a campaign worker asks voters who oppose Senator Chen a series of questions, such as "Would learning that Senator Chen supports cuts in Social Security benefits lead you to vote for him?" By finding out which of his or her views generate the most voter support, a candidate can create a more effective campaign.

Campaign Financing

Today's extensive campaigns have become very expensive. Bumper stickers, campaign appearances, yard signs, direct mail, buttons, flyers, and above all, television advertising are just some of the campaign tools on which candidates spend money. During the 1996 presidential race the campaigns for Bob Dole and Bill Clinton spent $113 million on advertising in just 13 months.

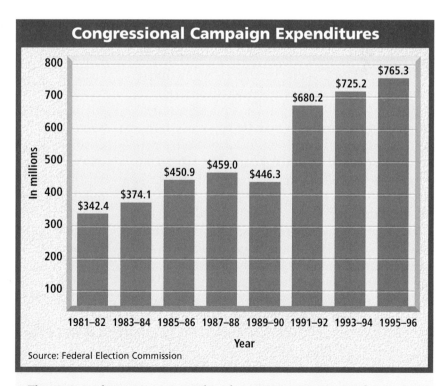

Congressional Campaign Expenditures

Source: Federal Election Commission

The amount of money spent on political campaigns increases each year to keep up with the rising costs of financing a campaign. **How much money was spent on political campaigns in 1991–92?**

As you can see, campaigning today requires huge sums of money. This is particularly true for a candidate challenging an incumbent—a person who already holds the elective office. How can a candidate raise this money? Political parties, political action committees, private donors, and the government supply most of the needed campaign funds. In addition, some candidates spend their own money on their campaigns.

Party Assistance As noted in Chapter 18, one duty of political parties is to raise funds for candidates and their campaigns. Parties do not give equally to all candidates. Rather, they concentrate most of their funds on helping those in the closest races. National party organizations, for example, generally give the most to strong challengers facing incumbent members of Congress or to candidates running for open seats, where the incumbent is not running for re-election.

Political Action Committees Also as noted in Chapter 18, political action committees (PACs) give funds to political parties and their candidates. A PAC contributes money to campaigns in hopes that a candidate who takes office will support the PAC's agenda.

Private Donors Private donors to campaigns vary greatly in their resources and their goals. Some give $5 to a single candidate, while others give thousands of dollars to several candidates. In some cases, wealthy people who give a great deal of money to a campaign may be hoping to influence the candidate's decisions if he or she is elected. In most cases, however, people are just trying to support a candidate who represents their views.

Public Funding Government in some instances provides public money for campaigns, though in limited amounts. Public funding occurs at both the state and the national level. Only presidential and vice presidential candidates receive public funds at the national level, however, and they must follow established fund-raising guidelines.

Personal Financing Some candidates, particularly those running for state and local office, use money out of their own pockets to finance their campaigns. In 1992 Texas billionaire Ross Perot spent about $59 million of his own money on his independent presidential campaign.

Regulation of Campaign Financing

With such large amounts of money changing hands during political campaigns, regulations are needed to make sure that funds are handled properly. These regulations were laid down in the Federal Election Campaign Act of 1972, which has since been amended several times. This act is enforced by the Federal Election Commission (FEC). Regulations that campaigns must follow include financial disclosure, contribution and spending limits, and donor restrictions.

Financial Disclosure Campaign committees are required by law to submit extensive financial reports explaining how much money they have raised and how it was spent. In federal elections these reports are submitted to Congress and the FEC. In state and local elections they are sent to the appropriate state officials. These reports enable officials to make sure that the money is being spent only for legitimate campaign reasons and that candidates do not receive any improper contributions.

Contribution Limits Contributions to a federal candidate's campaign, whether for a primary or general election, are limited to $1,000 for an individual and $1,000 or $5,000 for an organization such as a PAC. Organizations able to contribute as much as $5,000 must have more than 50 contributors, have been registered with the FEC for at least six months, and contribute to five or more candidates in the election at hand. In addition, an individual can give no more than $5,000 a year to a PAC and no more than $20,000 a year to a political party. Individuals can contribute no more than $25,000 overall in a given year, though PACs have no such limit. An important loophole in these restrictions is the ability to donate unlimited amounts of "soft money"— money that is given in support of a party that may not be used for candidates.

Contribution limits are established to prevent any one person or organization from gaining too much influence over candidates, and therefore over government. A person or an organization able to contribute vast amounts to a candidate or party might be able to influence government to promote the interests of a few at the expense of the public good.

PUBLIC GOOD *Ross Perot spent millions of dollars of his own money on his 1992 presidential campaign.* **In the 1996 presidential primary, what was the spending limit for candidates who received matching funds?**

Spending Limits Presidential candidates can receive federal funds if they meet certain requirements, including staying within set spending limits. In a presidential primary campaign, candidates may receive federal funds if they raise $5,000 or more in each of at least 20 states. The federal government matches funds for the first $250 of each contribution received. For example, if a candidate receives two contributions, one for $100 and one for $1,000, he or she would get $350 in matching funds. The federal government does not match PAC or political party donations. The spending limit for candidates receiving matching funds in the 1996 primary campaign was $30.9 million.

A candidate who wins a party's nomination is eligible for public funds for the general election campaign as well. Major-party candidates may not accept private contributions, however, if they receive public funding. A spending limit also applies to the general election campaign—for the 1996 election the limit was set at $61.8 million. The limits are adjusted for inflation. If a presidential candidate does not accept public funds, he or she is not bound by campaign spending restrictions.

Public funding is financed exclusively by a voluntary "check-off" on individual income tax returns, where taxpayers may indicate that $3 of their taxes be set aside for this purpose. (This donation does not increase someone's total tax bill.)

Unlike presidential campaigns, no spending limits have been set for congressional races. Congressional candidates, however, do not receive any public funding.

Donor Restrictions Several restrictions exist on the source of donations to an election campaign. Corporations are forbidden to give money directly, as are labor unions and government contractors. Corporations and other organizations, however, have been able to sidestep this restriction. They donate money to the PACs representing their industries, and the PACs are allowed to spend money on campaigns.

Finally, no campaign may accept donations from a foreign source. During the 1996 presidential election, the Democratic Party came under fire for accepting money from foreign sources. The questionable donations were returned, but led Congress to undertake a broad investigation of political fund-raising practices.

SECTION 2 — REVIEW

1. How were political campaigns that were held in the 1700s and 1800s different from campaigns in the 1900s?

2. How has the media changed the way campaigns are run?

3. How do candidates pay for campaigns?

4. What might happen if campaign financing went unregulated?

5. **Thinking and Writing Critically**
   In your opinion, do laws requiring campaign committees to submit financial reports promote the public good? Explain your answer.

6. **Applying** POLITICAL PROCESSES
   If you were running for office and could spend $60 million on your campaign, what percentage would you spend on advertising? on appearances? Explain your reasoning.

ELECTIONS AND VOTING

Political Dictionary

single-member district
secret ballot
absentee ballot
suffrage

Objectives

★ What are the different types of elections?
★ What determines where, how, and when people vote?
★ What factors determine if a person may vote?
★ What influences the way in which people vote?

Campaigns run right into the final step of the electoral process—the election itself. Even on the day of the election, candidates and their workers continue to hand out flyers, call voters, make appearances, and run advertisements. State laws, however, regulate campaigning on election day as well as throughout the election. Laws made by the states and the federal government also determine the types of elections that may be held, how elections are administered, and who can vote.

Types of Elections

Besides primary elections, in which citizens nominate candidates, there are two main types of elections. These are the general election and the special election.

General Elections As you have learned, U.S. citizens elect their local, state, and national leaders in general elections. The majority of these elections take place in **single-member districts**—electoral districts in which only one candidate can win election to a particular office. For example, in a city, several people from a particular ward or precinct might run for a place on the city council. Only one of the candidates, however, may be elected to the position.

In almost all single-member district elections, the candidate who receives a plurality of the votes is the winner. As noted in Chapter 7, a plurality is the largest number of votes received by a candidate in an election. Whereas races with only two major candidates are decided by a majority, races that typically have more than two candidates are decided by a plurality.

General elections are held on specific days determined by state or federal law. The winner of a general election takes office when the current officeholder's term expires.

Special Elections In addition to general elections, special elections are sometimes called at the state or local level to make a decision by popular vote. Such decisions include whether to institute a tax increase and whom to put into office to replace an official who has died or resigned before the end of his or her term. In some cases, special elections are called to give voters the opportunity to remove an elected official from office. (This process is more fully explained in Chapter 20.)

POLITICAL PROCESSES *Bill Clinton and Al Gore celebrate their 1996 victory with their families at the state house in Little Rock, Arkansas.* **When does the winner of the general election take office?**

Administration of Elections

What determines the types of elections that will be held? Local, state, and federal laws decide not only the types of elections but also when and how they are conducted.

When Elections Are Held

Congressional elections take place every even-numbered year. Congress determined that congressional and presidential elections will both be held on the first Tuesday following the first Monday in November. Presidential elections are held every four years.

The states set the dates for state and local elections. All states but Louisiana hold their statewide elections on the same date as that for federal elections. Several states, however, hold their elections on the first Tuesday after the first Monday in November in *odd*-numbered years. More than half of the states hold elections at the local level on the same date as that for federal elections. A few states hold these elections in other months.

How Elections Are Conducted

On election day, citizens go to their precinct's polling place—or voting site—to vote. Generally, two election judges, or inspectors, and several clerks oversee the election. These officials verify that each voter's name appears on the list of officially registered voters and then either distribute blank ballots or show voters to a voting machine.

Origins of the Ballot System

The United States has not always had the kind of ballot system it has today. Citizens indicated their votes verbally at a public meeting, and their selections were recorded. Later, officials set rules dictating that ballots be printed for elections. However, each political party printed its own ballots. Because these ballots typically differed in size and shape according to party, anyone could tell at a glance for which party's candidates a citizen was voting. This system led to corrupt voting practices, as each political party could pressure voters into choosing its candidates.

Secret Ballot

The ballot system changed in 1888 with the introduction of the secret ballot. Also called the Australian ballot because it originated in Australia, the **secret ballot** allows voters to choose candidates in private. After stepping into a private voting booth, voters can record their votes on a paper ballot or by means of a voting machine.

Absentee Ballot

A person who is seriously ill or unable to go to the polls for some reason can vote by absentee ballot. An **absentee ballot** is a ballot requested by a voter prior to election day. The voter fills out this ballot and mails it in by a certain date. The main use of absentee balloting is by people in the military who are not living in their home district.

PRINCIPLES OF DEMOCRACY *In 1996 Bob Dornan and Loretta Sanchez ran against each other for the congressional seat in California's 46th district.* **How often do congressional elections take place?**

Voting by Mail In a few states, such as Oregon, certain types of elections are conducted through the mail. Citizens receive their ballots in the mail, fill them out, and then mail them back to election officials.

Voting by mail has both pros and cons. On the up side, more people tend to vote in an election if they do not have to go to a polling place. Voting by mail might also reduce costs and streamline the voting process. This method does, however, raise the possibility that someone might tamper with the ballots. People might also mistake the ballots for junk mail and throw them away without realizing what they are. In addition, because some voters do not maintain permanent mailing addresses, not all ballots will reach their desired destinations.

Contested Elections Sometimes, once the ballots have been counted and the results are announced, someone challenges, or contests, the results of the election. For example, a candidate might contest an election if he or she suspects that the votes were miscounted or that the election was conducted improperly. A dispute over an election may be settled in court or by a legislature. In some cases the votes may be recounted.

Voting Requirements

Today, laws regarding who can vote are based on factors such as age, citizenship, residence, and registration status. This has not always been the case, however. At different times in U.S. history, people's **suffrage**, or right to vote, was restricted according to their ownership of property and their ability to pay a poll tax, as well as their race and sex.

Property and Tax Requirements When the Constitution was adopted, all 13 states had laws declaring that in order to vote, a person must own property. Political leaders thought that people had to have a stake in society, or concern for their property, to make wise choices about how the country should be governed. In addition, most states required that eligible citizens pay a poll tax—money paid to cast a ballot—before they could vote. Thus, voting in the late 1700s was restricted to fewer than one fourth of all adult white males.

During a period of political reform in the early 1800s, many states dropped their property requirements. In fact, by 1843, all states had removed all property requirements for voting, allowing almost all of the adult white male population to vote.

African Americans' Right to Vote Laws limiting suffrage to adult white males lasted until several years after the Civil War. Then, in 1870, the Fifteenth Amendment was passed, guaranteeing African American males the right to vote. However, white-run state governments, mostly in the South, made it increasingly difficult for blacks to participate in politics.

Southern leaders typically located polling places far away from where African Americans lived, drew election districts that prevented black majorities, created literacy tests that many blacks could not pass, and in many instances required voters to pay poll taxes. Legal loopholes allowed most adult white males to vote without passing such tests or paying poll taxes. Blacks who opposed the unfair restrictions placed on them were subject to harassment or worse by

CONSTITUTIONAL GOVERNMENT *African American males were guaranteed the vote with the passage of the Fifteenth Amendment.* ***In what ways did some states make it difficult for blacks to vote after this amendment was passed?***

CONSTITUTIONAL GOVERNMENT *Women parade through New York City in 1917 carrying a sign quoting President Woodrow Wilson's support of the suffrage movement.*
Which constitutional amendment guaranteed women the right to vote?

white supremacist groups such as the Ku Klux Klan. As noted in Chapter 15, barriers to black voting were not overcome until the civil rights movement of the 1950s and 1960s.

Women's Suffrage Women also were denied the right to vote for much of U.S. history. The movement for women's voting rights gained force after the Civil War. Supporters of women's suffrage, including Susan B. Anthony and Elizabeth Cady Stanton, organized parades, demonstrations, and protests to bring attention to the issue. These supporters often were criticized, arrested, and even imprisoned for their actions. Their opponents believed that women had no business being involved in politics and that they were not educated enough to vote.

During the late 1800s the Idaho and Colorado state constitutions were amended to give women the vote. By that time, Wyoming and Utah had already written women's suffrage into their territorial constitutions. These victories had little effect on the status of women's voting rights in the rest of the country, however. In 1911 an intense campaign for women's suffrage in California narrowly resulted in an amendment to

that state's constitution. Many people, however, continued to push for an amendment to the U.S. Constitution.

In 1918 President Woodrow Wilson announced his support of the proposed Nineteenth Amendment to guarantee women's suffrage. A year later Congress passed the amendment. It was ratified by the required number of states in 1920.

Voting Requirements Today

Today voting requirements are based on four factors. These are

★ age,
★ citizenship,
★ residence, and
★ registration status.

Age Until 1971 all but four states (Alaska, Georgia, Hawaii, and Kentucky) set the minimum voting age at 21. During the 1960s, many people had argued to change the voting age. They said that if 18-year-olds could legally marry, as well as be drafted to serve in the armed forces, they should be allowed to vote as well.

In 1970 Congress passed a bill lowering the voting age to 18, but the Supreme Court ruled that the law was constitutional only for federal elections. Congress then proposed a constitutional amendment—the Twenty-sixth Amendment—establishing the voting age at 18. The amendment was quickly ratified and applies to *all* elections. In addition, some states allow 17-year-olds to register and vote in primary elections if they will turn 18 before the general election.

Citizenship All states have laws keeping noncitizens from taking part in elections. No voting laws, however, distinguish between native-born and naturalized citizens. On the other hand, many states do bar citizens convicted of serious crimes and those with serious mental illnesses from voting.

Residence Residency requirements for voting vary from state to state, but all states have them. The most common of these requirements says that a person must have been a legal resident in a state for at least 30 days to vote in its elections. Congress also determined in the Voting Rights Act of 1970 that 30-day's residence in a state was sufficient to allow people to vote in a presidential election.

Registration States do not allow any citizen to vote in elections unless he or she has registered. This requirement keeps citizens from voting twice. As voters come to cast their ballots, election workers officially record their names.

PUBLIC GOOD *The Motor Voter Law was passed to allow eligible voters to update their voter registration information in more convenient locations, such as at public assistance agencies.* **How might this law encourage greater voter participation?**

To register, citizens fill out a form that provides information about themselves, such as their age and where they live. After the state checks to see that all voter eligibility requirements have been met, the person is registered.

Some states require that citizens reregister every few years. In most states a voter's registration remains valid unless he or she moves, dies, or does not vote in several consecutive elections.

CASE STUDY

Motor Voter Law

POLITICAL PROCESSES Many people have long argued that simplifying the voter registration process would encourage more citizens to go to the polls. In 1993 those supporters helped persuade Congress to pass and President Clinton to sign the National Voter Registration Act, which made it easier for people to register to vote.

The law, sometimes referred to as the Motor Voter Law, requires states to allow citizens to register to vote, or to update their registration information, when they apply for or renew their driver's licenses. In addition, the law requires that citizens be allowed to register at designated government agencies. These include public assistance agencies and agencies that provide services to people with disabilities. The law also states that citizens must be allowed to register by mail.

Supporters of the bill pointed to the potential benefit of boosting voter turnout. Opponents, on the other hand, argued that looser procedures for registering would make voter fraud easier. Officials in some states also objected to the law in part because Congress did not provide the funding to make the required changes in the registration process.

Nevertheless, supporters have hailed the Motor Voter Law as a success. A total of about 15 million people either registered to vote or updated their registration information in the first 18 months after the law went into effect in January 1995.

Party Identification of U.S. Voters

Year	Democrat	Republican	Independent	Apolitical
1952	57%	34%	6%	3%
1960	52%	36%	10%	2%
1962	54%	35%	8%	4%
1970	54%	32%	13%	1%
1972	52%	34%	13%	1%
1980	52%	33%	13%	2%
1984	48%	39%	11%	2%
1988	47%	41%	11%	2%
1990	52%	36%	10%	2%
1992	50%	38%	12%	1%
1994	47%	42%	10%	1%

Source: National Election Studies, University of Michigan

The chart above shows party identification of U.S. voters during different periods. At what point between 1952 and 1994 did the largest percentage of voters identify themselves as Democrats?

Nearly half, or 8.8 million, of the registration or updating transactions took place in locations where people apply for or renew driver's licenses. Supporters estimated that 15 million new voters would be added to the rolls within two years after the law went into effect.

What effect has the Motor Voter Law had in increasing voter turnout? It is still too early to tell, but turnout during the 1996 general election was not encouraging. Fewer than half of all eligible voters went to the polls that year, down from just over 55 percent in the 1992 presidential election. Still, supporters of the Motor Voter Law say that turnout should increase as more people register.

Voting Behavior

Now that you know how elections are conducted, you may be wondering why people vote the way they do. There are four main factors that influence the way people vote: party identification, personal opinions about the issues, a candidate's record and image, and the voters' personal background.

Party Identification Political party identification is one factor that influences how people vote. Some people absorb their family's political opinions and preferences as children. The party loyalties that are developed early in life may never change.

For others, however, party identification may change as they evaluate the performance of officeholders, or as they respond to certain events. Research now suggests that even voters who have supported one party for a long time may change their party loyalty if they are dissatisfied with their party's performance.

Yet other people choose not to back a particular political party. These people are called independents. (Independent voters are similar to independent candidates in an election. An independent candidate is one who does not represent a political party.) Research shows that the number of people who identify themselves as independents has risen significantly since the 1940s. According to statistics gathered by a series of National Election studies, in 1994 around 35 percent of those polled identified themselves as independents.

Issues People's opinions on certain issues are another factor in how they vote. The issues that are "hot topics" change from decade to decade. Important issues of the 1990s, for example, include abortion rights and taxes. As you probably know, many citizens feel strongly about these two issues and their views about them can affect their party identification and choice of candidates.

Candidate's Record and Image A third factor influencing how people vote is a candidate's record and image. His or her past performance is particularly important. For example, in a presidential election, if people feel the country is headed on the right track, they are more likely to have a positive opinion of the incumbent candidate. If the economy is in a slump or unemployment has risen, however, voters are more likely to have a negative opinion of the incumbent.

candidates according to a perception of their effectiveness, integrity, and leadership ability. In many cases a voter's feeling about the candidate's age and "style" also can affect his or her vote. A younger candidate might receive a greater number of votes from younger voters, for example.

Voters' Background

Studies of voting behavior show that a person's background is another important factor in how he or she votes. As noted in Chapter 16, people develop political opinions over the course of their lifetimes in a process called political socialization. People's individual backgrounds—their age, income, sex, race, education, and

PUBLIC GOOD *Typically, voters evaluate a candidate according to his or her personality and character.* **Why might a candidate believe that meeting with voters in person would help present a positive image?**

Voters in this situation are making their choices based on an overall evaluation of the state of the country rather than just focusing on the incumbent's opinions on certain issues.

Research shows that voters' evaluations of a candidate's personality and character also are critical to voting decisions. Voters typically evaluate

family beliefs—affect how they choose candidates. For example, people who have higher incomes may vote against a candidate who supports higher taxes for the middle to upper classes. Or, as noted above, younger voters might not support an older candidate if they feel he or she cannot relate to their concerns.

 — REVIEW

1. Define the following terms: single-member district, secret ballot, absentee ballot, suffrage.

2. What are the two types of elections besides primary elections?

3. Imagine that it is election day. List the steps you would have to take to vote for the candidates of your choice.

4. How was suffrage limited in early U.S. history? What voting requirements exist today?

5. Name the factors that influence the way you might vote.

6. **Thinking and Writing Critically**
   In your opinion, is a candidate's image an important consideration in an election? How much would issues such as age affect your vote? Why?

7. **Applying** **POLITICAL FOUNDATIONS**
   Conduct an Internet search for information on voting, ballots, elections, and voter registration. Write a paragraph describing the information you find. Be sure to include a list of Internet sites you visit in your search.

CAMPAIGNS AND THE PUBLIC GOOD

Objectives

★ Why do some people criticize the media's role in campaigns?

★ What are the possible effects of negative campaigning?

★ What are some of the benefits of political campaigns?

As you have seen, elections serve an important role in U.S. government. By voting, citizens in effect give their opinions on how the country should be run and who should run it. Many critics, however, question the means by which candidates try to influence voters' opinions to win elections.

A campaign is meant not only to influence voters and get them more interested in an election but also to inform them about the candidate so that they can make educated choices. Critics believe, however, that campaigns' single-minded goal—to win—has led them to misinform more often than inform. In addition, many believe that this drive to win, along with registration requirements and the weakness of political parties, may reduce the level of voter turnout.

It can be argued, however, that campaigns bring issues to the attention of voters in a way that no other political events do. By presenting information about political issues in a format that will attract wide interest, campaigns promote the public good.

Criticisms of Election Campaigns

Campaigns are criticized chiefly for two reasons. First, many people believe that advertising in the media plays too strong a role in campaigns. Second, critics believe that there is too much negative campaigning in today's elections.

Role of Advertising in the Media Much of the criticism of the media's role in campaigns focuses on campaign advertising. In today's world of expensive airtime, campaigns choose to advertise most often in 30-second television and radio spots. How much substance, critics argue, can be communicated in a 30-second spot? A half-minute ad does not really argue a position; it only presents it. Furthermore, a commercial rarely gives a balanced account of what is involved in an issue.

Longer speeches allow for more substance, but they may lose some of the audience. A short spot, on the other hand, can make a point quickly without giving the viewer as much time to tune out. Many viewers, however, tuned in to watch a number of 30-minute infomercials, complete with charts and graphs that candidate Ross Perot ran to present his ideas in the 1992 presidential campaign. These segments differed a great deal from the typical spot format, and yet they received ratings that were competitive with regular network programs.

Negative Campaigning Negative campaigning is nothing new. Even during the country's early years, campaigns printed flyers and banners displaying the claimed faults of the opposing candidates. For example, during the election of 1796, Republicans in Pennsylvania supported

'...Political campaigns have become so simplistic and superficial... In the 20 seconds we have left, could you explain why?..'

Courtesy of Clay Bennett, North America Syndicate.

PUBLIC GOOD *Some critics think that 30-second campaign ads do not contain much substance to help voters make an informed choice about a candidate.* ***Why are long speeches not included in campaign advertisements?***

Comparing Governments

Media and Elections

Some people believe that the broadcast media, particularly television networks, should provide free airtime to political candidates. They think that this would make U.S. election campaigns more fair and more informative for voters.

Such is the case in Russia, where in the early 1990s the government passed a law requiring state-owned television and radio stations to provide one hour of free time each workday to political candidates. Government-subsidized mass media and mass media funded by public institutions must provide equal opportunities for candidates running for office in Russia's State Duma, or lower legislative branch. Political groups have the right to one appearance on state television and one on the state radio. These appearances are scheduled during the three weeks just before election day.

Although political groups each receive the same amount of free airtime, candidates and groups may purchase more. The fees for purchased time are regulated by the government to prevent bias. Even so, Russian political candidates continue to face the problem of unequal media coverage that occurs in U.S. political campaigns.

Thomas Jefferson by passing out a leaflet that read:

❝THOMAS JEFFERSON is a Firm REPUBLICAN, JOHN ADAMS is an avowed [a self-declared] MONARCHIST. . . . Thomas Jefferson first drew the declaration of American independence;—he first framed the sacred political sentence that all men are born equal. John Adams says this is all a farce [an empty display] and a falsehood; that some men should be born Kings, and some should be born nobles. . . . Adams has sons who might aim to succeed their father; Jefferson, like Washington, has no son. ❞

Negative campaigning has become more prominent in recent decades. Although most voters tell pollsters that they oppose negative campaigning, it seems to work. Candidates subjected to it find themselves on the defensive, having to take time and effort away from presenting their own campaign themes in order to fend off attack.

Because of the success of negative campaigning, in many instances campaign workers search for embarrassing quotations, unethical behavior, or contradictory votes that could be used against opponents. By taking particular statements or votes out of context, this practice draws attention away from the opponent's record as a whole.

In many instances campaigns use this information to create negative ads (sometimes called attack ads) to run on television and radio. Some of these ads refer to a candidate's "flip-flops," pointing out how he or she has changed positions on an issue. "Not-on-the-job" ads point out missed legislative votes, while "negative-on-positive" ads dispute something positive an opponent has said about him- or herself, such as a claim about opposing special-interest groups. In recent years, candidates have even run negative ads attacking an opponent for negative campaigning.

Nonvoting

What effect do advertising and negative campaigning have on voters? Many critics feel that today's campaign techniques, along with registration procedures and the weakened condition of the political parties, have caused a decrease in voter turnout. In the 1992 presidential election, for example, only 55 percent of the voting-age population voted. By 1996 this number had shrunk to below 50 percent. This percentage has been decreasing steadily over the past few decades. Turnout is even lower for congressional elections that do not coincide with presidential elections (about 39 percent in 1994).

Voter Alienation Many nonvoters say that they feel alienated by the political system in this country. They feel powerless to change the system and think that their vote does not make a difference in the political process. In addition, some say that the strength of interest groups and contributions of the wealthy play too big a role in the political system.

Furthermore, although negative campaigning is intended to sway voters' opinions, one study reports that some people become less likely to vote after hearing and seeing negative ads. This result might occur because negative campaigning makes them distrust politicians and politics in general, not just the candidates being attacked. By causing fewer people to vote, negative ads detract from the contribution to the public good that campaigns otherwise make.

Registration Requirements

Some people believe that registration requirements discourage some citizens from voting. Before registration procedures were set up, some state governments maintained lists of eligible voters, but others allowed voters to just show up on election day and ask to vote. Registration makes the voting process more difficult because a person must take the time to register beforehand. Up to 30 percent of the voting-age population fails to register by election day.

In 1993, however, Congress passed and President Bill Clinton signed into law the Motor Voter Law, which requires states to make registering to vote easier (see the case study on page 444). To meet the law's mandates, a state must permit citizens to register by mail or when applying for a driver's license or federal or state benefits.

Weakened Political Parties

Another reason for low voter participation is the apparently weakened state of the major political parties. During the late 1800s, when political parties were strong, voter participation was high in campaigns and elections. As political parties grew weaker, however, citizens became less involved in the electoral process. Statistics show that high levels of positive competition between the political parties increase voter turnout for the election in question. Increased competition sparks voters' interest.

VOTER REGISTRATION CARD
(Please type or print)

Date . . . .

1. Name . . . .
                Last   First   Middle Initial

2. Address . . . .
                Street   (Ward No.)

. . . .
          Town/City   Zip Code

3. Mailing Address if different than in 2. . . . .
                            Street

. . . .
        Town/City   (Ward No.)   Zip Code

4. Place and Date of Birth . . . .
                Town/City/State   Date

5. If a naturalized citizen, give name of court where and date when naturalized:

. . . .

6. Place last registered to vote . . . .
                     Street/Town/State   (Ward No.)

. . . .

7. Name under which previously registered, if different from above:

. . . .

8. Party Affiliation (if any) . . . .

I hereby swear, under penalty of perjury, that my permanent established domicile is at the above address, that I am a United States citizen, and that I am 18 years of age or older, and that the information above is true and correct to the best of my knowledge and belief.

E-80552   . . . .
                                                 Signature of Applicant

PUBLIC GOOD *Voter registration helps the government keep the electoral process fair, but it also makes the voting process more difficult.* ***Approximately what portion of the voting-age population is not registered?***

PUBLIC GOOD *John F. Kennedy and Richard Nixon participated in a televised debate during the 1960 presidential campaign.* **How does political debate help voters make more informed decisions?**

Benefits of Campaigns

In spite of the criticisms of campaigns, they do provide services that are necessary to the political process. Among these benefits are the encouragement of political debate and the information they provide to the electorate. Debate and readily available information promote the public good.

Encouraging Debate For voters to make decisions about political issues and candidates, they must be able to weigh conflicting points of view. Political campaigns expose people to opposing viewpoints, thus prompting them to debate the issues. Some campaigns include public debates between the candidates, further fueling discussion among the citizenry.

Providing Information Political campaigns also provide information about candidates and their backgrounds. Some political ads even expose information about an opposing candidate that he or she might not wish to have revealed. Though some of this injurious information may not relate to the issues, in many cases, campaigns do provide facts that voters need in order to be well informed.

Political campaigns provide information to voters in a variety of ways. Many candidates campaign in person—knocking on doors to speak with voters, distributing brochures, and speaking to small groups in homes or clubs. Candidates also send out hundreds of letters directly to voters. These letters usually contain information about a candidate's experience in government office and his or her position on key issues. They may also point out the differences between a candidate's views about the issues and the views of his or her opponents.

Finally, campaign ads provide voters with a significant amount of information in a short period of time. Advertisements often focus on how a candidate's views differ from those of the opposition. By using a variety of campaign tools, a candidate can inform a wide cross section of voters on key campaign issues.

★ ★ ★ ★ ★ **SECTION 4** — **REVIEW**

1. Why is the role of the media in campaigns sometimes criticized?

2. What is negative campaigning, and why do campaigns use it?

3. What are some of the reasons that people might not vote? Why is nonvoting a problem in a democracy?

4. Why are campaigns important to the political process?

5. Thinking and Writing Critically Imagine that you are running for office. Write a 30-second advertising spot describing your beliefs about key issues of the day. Do you feel that 30 seconds is enough time to convey the main points about your views? Explain your answer.

6. Applying **PUBLIC GOOD** Have you ever witnessed negative campaigning during an election year? How does it affect your opinion of the political process?

SECTION 1 The first step in the U.S. electoral process is nomination. There are five ways a candidate can be nominated—by self-announcement, caucus, convention, petition, and primary election. There are different types of primaries: direct, closed, open, runoff, and nonpartisan.

SECTION 2 The second step in the electoral process is the campaign. Since the early years of the United States, supporters of political candidates have conducted elaborate campaigns during election years to try to sway citizens' votes. Though the goal of campaigning has remained the same, its methods have changed a great deal. During the 1900s, candidates became more visible, media involvement became more pronounced, and polling became a key tool. With these new developments came an increase in campaign spending.

Today, campaigns receive funds from several sources: political parties, political action committees (PACs), the government, private donors, and candidates' personal finances. As spending increased, regulation was needed to ensure the proper handling of funds. Thus, campaigns are now required to submit financial reports. Limits have been placed on both how much money individuals and groups can contribute to campaigns and on who can contribute.

SECTION 3 Local, state, and federal laws determine the types of elections that are held, how elections are administered, and who can vote. Besides primary elections, there are two main types of elections: general and special.

Congress determines when congressional and presidential elections are held. The states determine when state and local elections are held. To vote, a citizen goes to a polling place and casts a ballot. In the United States the secret-ballot system protects voters from outside pressures when voting. Citizens who are unable to go to the polls may use an absentee ballot.

Today voting requirements are based on citizenship, age, residence, and registration status. At other times in U.S. history, suffrage has been determined by property ownership and ability to pay a poll tax, as well as by race and sex. African Americans received the vote with the Fifteenth Amendment; women received it with the Nineteenth Amendment.

Voters must be 18 years of age as well as U.S. citizens. Many states also maintain residency requirements that a citizen must meet before voting. States also require that citizens register before participating in an election.

The way people vote is affected by several factors. These include party identification, opinions on issues, the candidate's record and image, and voters' personal backgrounds.

SECTION 4 Election campaigns are criticized for two main reasons: for the role that advertising in the media plays in them and for the negative campaigning that takes place during them. Some critics believe that, in addition to difficult registration procedures and the weakened condition of the political parties, today's campaigning techniques have caused a decline in voter turnout.

Campaigns provide two major benefits, however. They encourage debate within the political system, and they provide information to the electorate. Although some of this information may be part of a negative campaign, in many cases, campaigns do provide facts that voters need in order to be informed.

Government Notebook

Review the list you made in your Government Notebook at the beginning of the chapter. Why is it important that you have a voice in the decisions that you and your friends or classmates make? Write your answer in your Notebook.

REVIEWING CONCEPTS

1. Name the three steps in the electoral process.

2. What is the most common means of nominating candidates today? What are the other means of nominating candidates?

3. How are campaigns financed?

4. How did campaigns change during the 1900s?

5. Why does government regulate campaigns? What rules must they follow?

6. Describe the different types of elections.

7. What are the requirements for voting in the United States today?

8. What limitations existed on voting in the past?

9. Why are campaigns sometimes criticized?

10. What factors might influence a person's vote?

THINKING AND WRITING CRITICALLY

1. **PRINCIPLES OF DEMOCRACY** How were local concerns represented in the national conventions in the 1800s and early 1900s? Do you think local and state conventions should still exist? Explain your answers.

2. **POLITICAL PROCESSES** In campaigning for office, candidates of the past were much less visible than candidates today. How important is it for a candidate to campaign in person? If you were running for office, would you go on a campaign tour? Why or why not? Would you be more or less likely to vote for a candidate you have seen in person? Explain your answers.

3. **PUBLIC GOOD** Describe some of the discriminatory voting regulations in U.S. history. Do you think age requirements are discriminatory? How is the public good promoted by the elimination of discrimination in voter registration? Explain your answers.

4. **PUBLIC GOOD** Imagine that you are running for political office. Is your goal to win at any cost or to inform the public about your platform? Do you think these two goals could go hand in hand? Explain your answers.

CITIZENSHIP IN YOUR COMMUNITY

Imagine that you are the campaign manager for someone in your school who is running for class president or student council representative. Write short speeches or advertisements to read aloud over the public address system, draw posters to display in the school, and create campaign buttons and ribbons to pass out to students. What tactics do you think will be most effective? Why?

INDIVIDUAL PORTFOLIO PROJECT

Two factors that influence the way people vote are party identification and their opinions on the issues. Make a list of some important issues in the 1990s, such as education, taxes, and a balanced budget. Then write your answers to the following questions: What do you think about each issue? Are the current laws concerning each issue effective? (You may need to conduct some outside research about these issues to find out what current laws specify.) What laws do you think should be in place concerning each issue? Based on your answers to these questions, determine whether your answers are more in line with Democratic, Republican, or independent views.

PRACTICING SKILLS: CITIZENSHIP

To register to vote, a person must contact the state or local election office to request a registration form. Most registration forms require basic information such as name, age, residence, and citizenship, as well as a signature to affirm that the information given on the form is correct. Study the voter registration card on page 449, and answer the questions below.

1. What do you think is the main purpose of the Place of Birth section?

2. Why must naturalized citizens provide information about their naturalization?

3. Why might election officials need to know party affiliation?

4. Why is it necessary to know the name under which a citizen was previously registered?

THE INTERNET: LEARNING ONLINE

Conduct an Internet search for information about the Women's Rights Convention held in Seneca Falls, New York, on July 19 and 20, 1848. Who organized the convention? How was it publicized? Who attended? What was accomplished at the convention? Begin by typing in search words such as *Seneca Falls, Women's Rights Convention,* and *Elizabeth Cady Stanton.* With others in your class, re-enact the convention by using the information you gather. Be sure to record the addresses of the Web sites you find.

ANALYZING PRIMARY SOURCES

EIGHTY YEARS AND MORE

Elizabeth Cady Stanton is a well-known women's rights advocate of the 1800s. She helped organize a women's rights movement. Read the excerpt below, from her book *Eighty Years and More,* which describes a time when Stanton attempted to cast her vote before the passage of the Nineteenth Amendment, which gave women the right to vote. Answer the questions that follow.

❝November 2 being election day, the Republican carriage, decorated with flags and evergreens, came to the door for voters. As I owned the house and paid the taxes, and as none of the white males was home, I suggested that I might go down and do the voting. . . . Accompanied by my faithful friend, Miss [Susan B.] Anthony, we stepped into the carriage and went to the poll. . . . When we entered the room it was crowded with men. . . .

The inspectors [men] were thunderstruck. I think they were afraid that I was about to capture the ballot box. One placed his arms round it, with one hand close over the aperture [slot] where the ballots were slipped in, and said, with mingled surprise and pity, 'Oh, no, madam! Men only are allowed to vote.' I then explained to him that, in accordance with the Constitution of New Jersey, women had voted in New Jersey down to 1801, when they were forbidden the further exercise of the right by an arbitrary act of the legislature, and, by a recent amendment to the national Constitution, Congress had declared that 'all persons born or naturalized in the United States, and subject to the jurisdiction thereof, are citizens of the United States and of the State wherein they reside' and are entitled to vote. I told them that I wished to cast my vote, as a citizen of the United States, for the candidates for United States offices. Two of the inspectors sat down and pulled their hats over their eyes, whether from shame or ignorance I do not know. The other held on to the box, and said 'I know nothing about the Constitutions, State or national. I never read either; but I do know that in New Jersey, women have not voted in my day, and I cannot accept your ballot.'❞

1. On what grounds did Stanton base her right to vote?

2. Why were the men so surprised that a woman would attempt to cast a vote in an election?

3. What forbade women to vote in New Jersey after 1801?

Campaign Consultant for a Day

You and other members of your group are campaign consultants, or expert advise givers, who hire out your services to candidates for national office. It is 2000 and presidential candidates, the Democratic nominee and the Republican nominee, are campaigning tirelessly around the country. In addition, they have agreed to a nationally televised debate next month, two weeks before the general election. To help them prepare for their debate, the two candidates are searching for consultants such as yourselves.

On the following pages is information you have gathered on the campaign. This information should guide you in assessing the campaign's important issues. It also should provide some insight into the candidates' positions on those issues. Answer the questions that accompany the information in your Government Notebook.

After you have finished reviewing the information, divide your group into two camps: consultants who will join the Democratic nominee's campaign and those who will join the Republican nominee's campaign. Students on each side must then put together a debate preparation paper for their candidate.

The paper should address three areas: likely debate questions and issues, your opponent's position on those issues, and suggestions for how your candidate can answer the possible questions and persuade the debate audience that his or her positions on the issues are superior. For example, your candidate might emphasize how his or her background would be helpful in tackling tough issues. In addition, you might encourage your candidate to explain to the debate audience how his or her overall philosophical beliefs are revealed by positions taken on specific issues.

When you have finished, share and discuss your debate preparation paper with members of the opposing nominee's campaign.

Each year, PollStats, a national polling firm, conducts 1,500 telephone interviews, asking respondents to identify the country's most important issue. Each annual poll has a sampling error of plus or minus 5 points. The most recent poll was conducted last month in anticipation of the upcoming general election.

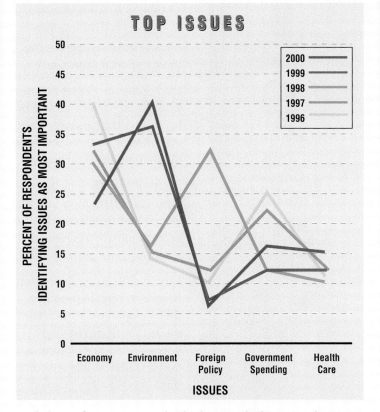

TOP ISSUES

"Of these five issues, which do you believe is the most important facing the United States this year?"

▲ WHAT DO YOU THINK?

★ Using the polling data as a guide, how have U.S. citizens' attitudes changed over the last four years regarding which issues they believe are most important?

★ Why is the *Daily Post* editorial writer concerned about government spending?

★ Using the polling data and the editorial as guides, on what issues do you think the presidential nominees are most likely to be questioned in their upcoming debate? What might some of the questions be?

Candidates Should Focus on Spending

As the general election approaches, we hope the Democratic and Republican nominees for president will focus their campaigns on issues that U.S. voters find important today. In addition, however, the nominees should focus on some issues that likely will become more important over the next four years.

A recent PollStats survey indicates that roughly 40 percent of potential voters believe that the environment is the most important issue facing the United States this year. Support for environmentalism began rising significantly last year, reflecting growing concern over air and water pollution. Congress has since been debating stricter regulations designed to lessen pollution.

At the same time, concern over foreign affairs is low, as it has been since U.S. intervention in the Ziberian civil war ended two years ago. Even the economy is of relatively low concern to respondents, although nearly a quarter of them still identify it as the nation's top issue. As the economy continues to recover from the recession that preceded the Ziberian intervention, U.S. citizens should continue to feel better about their financial situation.

Unfortunately, Democratic presidential nominee George Jenkins and Republican nominee Jeanne Stern have all but ignored another issue we believe will be a bigger concern over the next four years: government spending. After important progress was made toward a balanced budget in the late 1990s, leaders in both parties moved on to other issues. That was a mistake.

With many people in the baby boom generation soon reaching retirement age, government spending—particularly on programs for the elderly—is likely to rise rapidly. In their debate next month we hope the two major party nominees will tell the voters how they plan to address this difficult problem in the coming years.

PUBLIC POLICY LAB

Democratic Presidential Nominee GEORGE JENKINS: Keeping America Working!

Find out more about the Democratic Party and how GEORGE JENKINS WILL KEEP AMERICA WORKING!

About the Democratic Party

Join the Democratic Party

Vice Presidential Nominee Olympia Martinez

Bills Sponsored by George Jenkins

Democratic Youth Organizations

Congressional Elections

State Elections

MEET U.S. SENATOR GEORGE JENKINS, the Democratic nominee for president of the United States. Here is a little background information on the senator who will keep America working!

★ Born: July 4, 1951
★ U.S. Senator, 1991–Present
★ Senate committees: Environment, Public Works, and Budget
★ Author of best-selling book: *The Environment: Making It Work for All of Us*

DEMOCRATIC PARTY PLATFORM

Delegates to the Democratic National Convention this summer adopted a party platform that serves the interests of all Americans. The platform calls for important measures designed to keep our environment clean and to keep workers on the job. These measures include:

★ stronger regulations designed to prevent air and water pollution;
★ a tax cut for the middle class;
★ more federal funding to improve roads, bridges, and railroads that need repair after years of neglect;
★ increased financial aid for students seeking college degrees to help them compete in the economy of tomorrow; and
★ laws that will make it easier for people to purchase health insurance.

WHAT DO YOU THINK?

★ Judging from their backgrounds, on what issues does each candidate appear to have the most experience? Judging from their experience, which candidate might find it easier to address issues that poll respondents believe are the most important this year?

★ During the upcoming debate, what could each candidate do to counter the experience and advantages that the other candidate has in certain areas?

★ Judging from their backgrounds and their parties' platforms, how would you describe each candidate's general philosophy toward government?

★ Other political candidates have used Web sites to promote their campaigns. In fact, the Internet is an increasingly important source of information on politics. Why do you think this is so?

Republicans for JEANNE STERN: Standing Up for AMERICA!

JEANNE STERN

✔ Former U.S. SECRETARY OF STATE
✔ Former U.S. TRADE REPRESENTATIVE
✔ Former U.S. congresswoman and chair of the House Foreign Affairs Committee
✔ Author of *Free Trade and Foreign Policy* and *Business and Environment: Finding Solutions Together*

JEANNE STERN AND THE REPUBLICAN PARTY ON THE ISSUES:

✔ Increase funding for a strong national defense.
✔ Empower the United States to act in its own interests internationally, without interference from foreign governments.
✔ Pass a balanced budget and keep a tight hold on overall government spending.
✔ Cut taxes for the middle class.
✔ Pass fewer regulations that tie the hands of business and hurt the economy.
✔ Encourage business and government to cooperate in finding solutions to pollution problems.

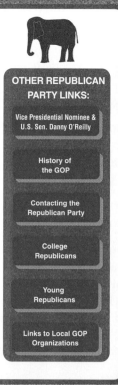

OTHER REPUBLICAN PARTY LINKS:

Vice Presidential Nominee & U.S. Sen. Danny O'Reilly

History of the GOP

Contacting the Republican Party

College Republicans

Young Republicans

Links to Local GOP Organizations

COALITION FOR A CLEAN ENVIRONMENT

The Coalition for a Clean Environment (CCE) works to promote policies that prevent air and water pollution and the wasting of our natural resources. To help inform U.S. voters about the major presidential nominees, we asked the candidates their positions on various environmental issues. Their responses are included in the following voter's guide.

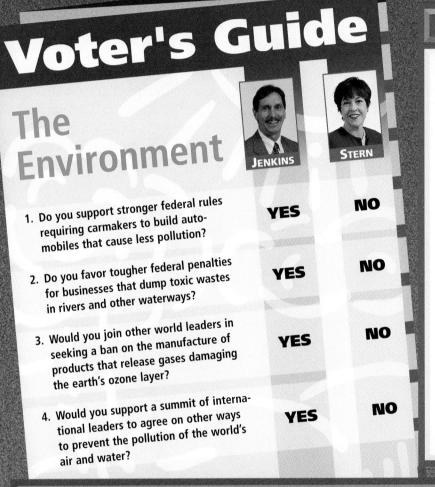

Voter's Guide

The Environment

	JENKINS	STERN
1. Do you support stronger federal rules requiring carmakers to build automobiles that cause less pollution?	YES	NO
2. Do you favor tougher federal penalties for businesses that dump toxic wastes in rivers and other waterways?	YES	NO
3. Would you join other world leaders in seeking a ban on the manufacture of products that release gases damaging the earth's ozone layer?	YES	NO
4. Would you support a summit of international leaders to agree on other ways to prevent the pollution of the world's air and water?	YES	NO

◄ WHAT DO YOU THINK?

★ Review the answers attributed to the candidates in this voter's guide. Which candidate would you expect the Coalition for a Clean Environment to support?

★ The Coalition for a Clean Environment is sending this voter's guide to members across the country. Why do you suppose the organization decided to send out this information?

★ What does this voter's guide really tell you about the candidates' positions? For example, does it tell voters what specific laws and actions Stern opposes and why? What might be some of Stern's reasons for opposing some of the proposals presented here? Does such opposition imply that Stern opposes a clean environment?

THINGS TO DO

1. Divide your group into consultants who support Jenkins and consultants who support Stern.

2. With other consultants for your candidate, discuss the information you have reviewed in this activity.

3. Work with your other consultants to write a debate preparation paper for your candidate. The paper should include a list of questions and issues your candidate can expect during the debate, the opponent's position on those issues, and suggestions for how your candidate can answer those questions and persuade the debate audience that his or her positions on the issues are superior.

4. Finally, share your debate preparation paper with the other consultants. Then consider the following questions. What were the most reliable sources of information about candidates' positions on issues? What other sources of information about the candidates might be available? What are the strengths and weaknesses of each side's debate preparation suggestions? How do you believe your candidate would fare in a debate against his or her opponent?

UNIT
7

PUBLIC POLICY LAB

How can students help fund construction of a new high school? Find out by reading this unit and taking the Public Policy challenge on pages 500–503.

458

STATE AND LOCAL GOVERNMENT

STATE GOVERNMENT

In what state did you take your driving test? If you had sought your license in another state, you might have faced a different test and received a different score. You also might have been able to get your learner's permit at a younger age. If you lived in Virginia, you would have needed to show that you were currently enrolled in school to get a learner's permit.

Why is the driving test not the same across the country? States have the power to set their own rules for obtaining a driver's license as well as for many other actions, such as registering a car, running a public school, paying state college tuition, marrying, and more recently, setting welfare policy. In other words, when you cross state lines, you cross into another government's jurisdiction. So pay attention—the speed limit and many other rules can suddenly change. To heighten your awareness of these changes, think of this chapter as a guidebook to navigating state government.

✎ Government Notebook

What state laws affect you? Think about activities that require licenses, such as driving and fishing, or those that concern people's well-being and safety, such as attending school and wearing seat belts. In your Government Notebook, write a list of state laws that could affect you personally.

THE STATES

Political Dictionary

initiative
referendum
recall

Objectives

★ What is the basis of state governments' authority?

★ In what ways do state governments answer to the people?

★ How do state governments promote the public good?

The 50 states are as diverse as any 50 people you might randomly pick from a crowd on the street. Alaska is 546 times as large in land area as Rhode Island. California has a population of 31.6 million, compared to Wyoming's population of around 480,000. The average annual precipitation in Las Vegas, Nevada, is 4 inches, compared to 67 inches in Mobile, Alabama.

In some ways, however, the states are quite similar. Like the federal government, they all receive their authority to govern from a constitution. In addition, the 50 state governments are all able to answer to the people more directly than can the federal government. The close relationship that a state government is thus able to maintain with the citizens is vital in its helping promote the public good.

State Constitutions

Each state has its own constitution. The state constitutions, however, cannot conflict with the U.S. Constitution, which is the supreme law of the land.

Types of Constitutions Just as the U.S. Constitution reflects the concerns and events of the Revolutionary War period, state constitutions reflect the places and times in which they were written. In other words, both regional and historical traditions may affect a state's constitution. For example, Section XIII of Oklahoma's constitution requires the state legislature to "provide for the teaching of the elements of agriculture, horticulture, stock feeding, and domestic science" in public schools. Oklahoma's framers felt this provision was important, given the high number of people in the state who worked in agriculture when the constitution was drafted.

Each of the original colonies adopted its constitution before or shortly after U.S. independence. Like the U.S. Constitution, these constitutions strive to outline a social contract in the tradition of the political philosopher John Locke. That is, they list the state's responsibilities to the people and vice versa. They are mostly brief and have been revised less frequently than most state constitutions.

In contrast, many other states have constitutions that are quite long and have been revised frequently. In southern states such as Alabama and South Carolina, for example, government officials were forced in the aftermath of the Civil War to rewrite the existing constitutions.

POLITICAL FOUNDATIONS *Oklahoma's constitution requires the legislature to provide for teaching stock feeding in public schools.* **What might affect the contents of a state constitution?**

The constitutions of most western states include provisions enabling the public to keep a relatively high degree of control over the government. For example, the western states established traditions allowing citizens to vote on some laws directly and to remove government officials from their positions before the end of their term. These processes—known as initiative, referendum, and recall—are explained more fully later in this section.

Constitutional Provisions Most state constitutions have been rewritten at least once and some, several times. In fact, since 1775 the 50 states have adopted more than 140 constitutions. Louisiana has had 11 since becoming a state, and Georgia has had 10. In the 1960s and 1970s, ten states adopted new constitutions, which are shorter and more focused than the documents they replaced. In 1982 Georgia became the most recent state to adopt a new constitution.

In addition, the current state constitutions have been amended more than 5,900 times, more than one amendment a year for each state. If the U.S. Constitution had been amended that often, it would have more than 250 amendments instead of just 27.

As a result of these amendments, many state constitutions are quite long—on average, 28,600 words. (The U.S. Constitution has only 7,800 words.) Alabama's constitution, the longest, has 174,000 words—the equivalent of a 687-page final exam essay!

Why are state constitutions so lengthy? Many are packed with details that seem inappropriate to such fundamental documents. One article of the Maryland constitution, for example, establishes conditions for off-street parking in the city of Baltimore. South Dakota's constitution authorizes the state legislature to assess hail insurance on agricultural land, and Minnesota's allows people to sell produce grown in their gardens without a license. The reason for including these detailed elements is often found in history. For instance, short-term events or conditions sometimes inspire provisions that later seem out of date.

C A S E   S T U D Y

The Texas Constitution

CONSTITUTIONAL PRINCIPLES Texas' basic law is among the most amended and longest of the state constitutions. Between its adoption in 1876 and the beginning of 1997, the Texas Constitution was amended 364 times. In addition, state voters rejected 168 other proposed constitutional amendments.

As with other lengthy state constitutions, the Texas Constitution is overloaded with details and specific measures. It is not uncommon, for example, for Texas voters to be asked to approve an amendment affecting the local government of only one or a few specific counties.

Why is the Texas Constitution so unmanageable? In part it reflects the suspicion with which many Texans have long regarded government. This suspicion was particularly strong when the current constitution was adopted in 1876—shortly after the end of Reconstruction and the withdrawal of federal troops that had helped keep a highly unpopular governor in office. As a result, Texas voters must approve constitutional amendments addressing a variety of specific issues, such as interest rates on state bonds, that might better be addressed by elected officials.

There have been a number of unsuccessful attempts to draft a more efficient state constitution. In 1974, state legislators meeting as delegates failed by just three votes to agree on a new constitution. After seven months of work and a dramatic vote that continued up until the final minute of the convention, they were unable to send it to the voters for their approval.

State Government and the People

You now know that each state's government, like the federal government, receives its governing authority from a constitution. Also like the federal government, a state's continued authority to rule rests firmly with the people. Many state governments, however, must answer to their citizens in ways that the federal government need not. In fact, citizens can become more directly involved in state legislative actions than in federal ones. In many states, citizens

Librarian

For anyone doing research, a librarian can be an important source of information. Librarians train extensively to learn how to become guardians of information.

Consider, for example, Kevin Starr, who in 1997 was the state librarian of California. As head of the California State Library, the state librarian provides reference and information services that state officials need to draft legislation and do other important work. The state library also stores historical documents, books, and other materials, and provides other services for use by the general public, government officials, and other libraries.

Starr's education and training prepared him well for his job as California's state librarian. He earned a bachelor's degree from the University of San Francisco, master's and doctoral degrees in American literature from Harvard University, and a master's degree in library science from the University of California, Berkeley.

Not all of this country's approximately 150,000 librarians need such extensive education. Most libraries require librarians to have a master's degree in library science. The degree often is earned through a one- or two-year program. This education helps prepare a librarian for a variety of tasks in public, school, and special libraries such as the California State Library and the Library of Congress. These tasks include selecting, ordering, storing, and properly classifying the books, documents, software, and other materials and equipment that best meet the needs of a library's patrons.

Librarians also help patrons in their research through reference services and by guiding them to appropriate library resources. Increasingly these library resources include access to computers, the Internet, and other electronic information. As a result, librarians are constantly working to further educate themselves so that they can provide the proper assistance needed in the information age.

Librarians must be able to select, store, and properly classify books, documents, software, and other library material and equipment.

can accomplish this by offering an initiative, holding a referendum, and recalling elected officials.

Initiatives Initiatives and referenda are both ways of adopting—or repealing—laws through a direct vote of citizens rather than by the vote of a legislature. (As noted in Chapter 1, such citizen actions are a form of direct democracy.) An **initiative** is a procedure for proposing and enacting state or local laws. If a certain minimum number of registered voters signs a petition backing the bill proposed by an initiative, the bill is placed on a ballot or sent to the state legislature. If voters or legislators approve the initiative, it becomes law. Around half of the states allow initiatives.

There are two kinds of initiatives: direct and indirect. A bill that is proposed by direct initiative is placed directly on a regular or special election ballot to be voted on by the people. A bill proposed by an indirect initiative, on the other hand, goes first to the legislature. If it passes the legislature, it becomes law. If it does not, the voters decide the matter. Only a few states use the indirect initiative.

Over the years almost every imaginable political issue has been the subject of an initiative. In 1918 Montana approved an initiative allowing chiropractors to practice within its borders. In 1972 Colorado passed an initiative to keep state funds from being spent on hosting the 1976 Winter

Olympics. (As a result, those Olympics were not held in Colorado, but in Innsbruck, Austria.) More recent initiatives have addressed issues such as lowering property taxes, denying government benefits to illegal immigrants, and repealing affirmative action programs.

Referenda A **referendum** is a popular vote on a proposal that has already been considered by the legislature. Referenda are submitted to the voters for several reasons. The constitutions of all states but Alabama require lawmakers to submit any constitutional amendments to the voters.

Sometimes a legislature chooses to submit a controversial proposed law to popular vote rather than deciding the matter itself. In addition, citizens may petition for a referendum to overturn a law the legislature has adopted. Forty-nine states allow some form of referendum.

Recalls Like initiatives and referenda, recalls allow citizens in some states to take direct governmental action. A **recall** is a special election to remove an elected official from office before the end of his or her term. Before a recall can be held, however, a certain number of registered

STATES ALLOWING INITIATIVES, REFERENDA, AND RECALLS

STATE	INITIATIVE	REFERENDA	RECALL	STATE	INITIATIVE	REFERENDA	RECALL
Alabama				Montana	x	x	x
Alaska	x	x	x	Nebraska	x	x	
Arizona	x	x	x	Nevada	x	x	x
Arkansas	x	x		New Hampshire		x	
California	x	x	x	New Jersey		x	
Colorado	x	x	x	New Mexico		x	
Connecticut		x		New York		x	
Delaware		x		North Carolina		x	
Florida	x	x		North Dakota	x	x	x
Georgia		x	x	Ohio	x	x	
Hawaii		x		Oklahoma	x	x	
Idaho	x	x	x	Oregon	x	x	x
Illinois	x	x		Pennsylvania		x	
Indiana		x		Rhode Island		x	x
Iowa		x		South Carolina		x	
Kansas		x		South Dakota	x	x	x
Kentucky		x		Tennessee		x	
Louisiana		x	x	Texas		x	
Maine	x	x		Utah	x	x	
Maryland		x		Vermont		x	
Massachusetts	x	x		Virginia		x	
Michigan	x	x	x	Washington	x	x	x
Minnesota		x		West Virginia		x	
Mississippi	x	x		Wisconsin		x	
Missouri	x	x		Wyoming	x	x	

Source: *The Book of States*: 1994

Initiatives, referenda, and recalls are all ways in which citizens, rather than legislatures, can adopt or repeal laws. **What are the two types of initiatives?**

voters must sign a petition requesting such an election.

Recall elections are rare, and the actual recall of an official is even more rare. Why? Elected officials who commit unethical acts are likely to resign or to be censured by their colleagues before a recall can take place. Besides, those who act in highly unpopular ways can be voted out of office in the next regular election, so citizens rarely feel compelled enough to organize a statewide petition drive.

State Government and the Public Good

Some critics of state governments charge that they are large, unresponsive bureaucracies that do not adequately address citizens' needs and concerns. Many people would argue, however, that these criticisms are unfounded. State governments have increased the quality and lowered the cost of some public services. For example, some states have opened offices in shopping malls to allow people to renew their car registration more easily.

Education is another area in which states have tried particularly hard to improve and expand services and opportunities. As a result, all 50 states have seen a dramatic expansion of their state college system. In fact, the research from one study suggests that by the year 2006 college enrollment in the United States will rise to 16.4 million, a 14 percent increase over 1996 college enrollment.

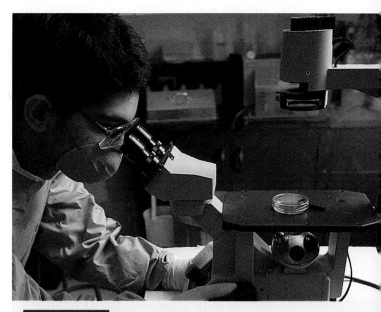

PUBLIC GOOD *Here a researcher at a state university examines a virus through a microscope. State governments have been working hard to improve educational research facilities at public schools.* **How do states determine how well public schools are educating their students?**

To improve their performance, many states also have developed tracking systems that assess how well their governments are fulfilling their responsibilities to citizens. Most states, for example, now use standardized tests to track how well public schools are educating their students. Through these and other inventive methods, states are striving to promote the public good.

SECTION 1 — REVIEW

1. Define the following terms: initiative, referendum, recall.

2. How are the U.S. Constitution and the constitutions of the states similar? How are they different?

3. In what three ways can citizens of a state take direct action to influence the legislative process?

4. What are some of the criticisms of state governments? How have states tried to improve the ways in which they deliver public services?

5. **Thinking and Writing Critically**
   Are any rules in your school subject to a student referendum? Can students propose initiatives? Imagine that you were able to propose initiatives. What rule would you want your school to adopt?

6. **Applying** **PRINCIPLES OF DEMOCRACY**
   Why is it important that states have the power to establish laws for such things as driver's licenses? What problems might occur if the federal government rather than states established such laws?

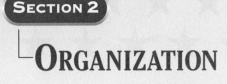

ORGANIZATION

Political Dictionary

governor
jury pool

Objectives

★ How are state legislatures structured?
★ What are the responsibilities of a state's executive branch?
★ How are state courts organized?

Both federal and state governments divide power among legislative, executive, and judicial branches. The organization of the states' branches in many ways mirrors that of the federal government.

State Legislative Branches

Today's state legislatures are different from those of several decades ago. Since then, the powers and makeup of the legislatures have changed, sometimes dramatically.

Terms In most states, senators serve four-year terms, while members of the lower house serve two-year terms. These terms vary from state to state, however, with some senators serving just two years and some lower-house members serving as many as four.

Sessions About 30 years ago, only 20 state legislatures met every year. The other 30 met every two years, often for only three months. Making state law was a part-time job that legislators could perform while running a business, practicing law, or tending a ranch. Perhaps because of the part-time nature of the job, membership turnover was high—generally between 35 and 40 percent in each election.

Today the number of legislatures that meet annually has increased from 20 to 43. Being a legislator, however, still is a full-time job in only nine states (California, Illinois, Massachusetts, Michigan, New Jersey, New York, Ohio, Pennsylvania, and Wisconsin). Turnover among members has declined somewhat, although it is still much higher than the rate for Congress.

Qualifications Like members of Congress, state legislators must be U.S. citizens. They generally also must live in the district they represent. As with terms and sessions, however, age requirements for serving as a state legislator vary across the states. Many states require senators to be at least 25 years of age and lower-house members to be at least 21. In several states, however, the age requirement is only 18 for both houses.

Most state legislators are younger than the average member of Congress. Many politicians start their political careers in state legislatures, later becoming members of Congress, governors, or judges. Indeed, unlike in Congress, where it is not unusual for members to serve 20 years or more, few people choose to make a career out of serving in a state legislature.

How accurately do state legislatures reflect the population as a whole? As of 1996, 21 percent of

POLITICAL PROCESSES *State legislators need to devote a lot of time to their political positions in order to keep up with today's complex system of government.* ***In how many states is being a legislator considered a full time job?***

State Legislatures

STATE	NUMBER OF MEMBERS		SESSIONS	MINIMUM AGE	STATE	NUMBER OF MEMBERS		SESSIONS	MINIMUM AGE
Alabama	Senate	35	Annual	25	Montana	Senate	50	Biennial—odd years	18
	House	105		21		House	100		18
Alaska	Senate	20	Annual	25	Nebraska	Senate	49	Annual	21
	Assembly	40		21					
Arizona	Senate	30	Annual	25	Nevada	Senate	21	Biennial—odd years	21
	House	60		25		House	42		21
Arkansas	Senate	35	Biennial—odd years	25	New Hampshire	Senate	24	Annual	30
	House	100		21		House	400		18
California	Senate	40	Annual, full time	18	New Jersey	Senate	40	Annual	30
	Assembly	80		18		House	80		21
Colorado	Senate	35	Annual	25	New Mexico	Senate	42	Annual	25
	House	65		25		House	70		21
Connecticut	Senate	36	Annual	18	New York	Senate	61	Annual, full time	18
	House	151		18		House	150		18
Delaware	Senate	21	Annual	27	North Carolina	Senate	50	Annual—legal provisions for odd years only	21
	House	41		24		House	120		25
Florida	Senate	40	Annual	21	North Dakota	Senate	49	Biennial—odd years	25
	House	120		21		House	98		25
Georgia	Senate	56	Annual	25	Ohio	Senate	33	Annual, full time	18
	House	180		21		House	99		18
Hawaii	Senate	25	Annual	18	Oklahoma	Senate	48	Annual	25
	House	51		18		House	101		21
Idaho	Senate	35	Annual	18	Oregon	Senate	30	Biennial—odd years	21
	House	70		18		House	60		21
Illinois	Senate	59	Annual, full time	21	Pennsylvania	Senate	50	Annual, full time	25
	House	118		21		House	100		21
Indiana	Senate	50	Annual	25	Rhode Island	Senate	50	Annual	18
	House	100		21		House	100		18
Iowa	Senate	50	Annual	25	South Carolina	Senate	46	Annual	25
	House	100		21		House	124		21
Kansas	Senate	40	Annual	18	South Dakota	Senate	35	Annual	25
	House	125		18		House	70		25
Kentucky	Senate	38	Biennial—even years	30	Tennessee	Senate	33	Annual—legal provisions for odd years only	30
	House	100		24		House	99		21
Louisiana	Senate	39	Annual	18	Texas	Senate	31	Biennial—odd years	26
	House	105		18		House	150		21
Maine	Senate	35	Annual	25	Utah	Senate	29	Annual	25
	House	151		21		House	75		25
Maryland	Senate	47	Annual	25	Vermont	Senate	30	Annual—legal provisions for odd years only	18
	House	141		21		House	150		18
Massachusetts	Senate	40	Annual, full time	18	Virginia	Senate	40	Annual	21
	House	160		18		House	100		21
Michigan	Senate	38	Annual, full time	21	Washington	Senate	49	Annual	18
	House	110		21		House	98		18
Minnesota	Senate	67	Annual—legal provisions for odd years only	21	West Virginia	Senate	34	Annual	25
	House	134		21		House	100		18
Mississippi	Senate	52	Annual	25	Wisconsin	Senate	33	Annual, full time	18
	House	122		21		House	99		18
Missouri	Senate	34	Annual	30	Wyoming	Senate	30	Annual	25
	House	163		24		House	60		21

Source: *The World Almanac:* 1997; *The Book of States:* 1994

their members were women—a far higher percentage than in Congress (11 percent). About 7 percent of state legislators were African American. This figure does not differ much from the percentage in Congress in 1997 (7 percent) but is lower than the percentage of African Americans in the entire U.S. population (about 12 percent). About 2 percent of state legislators were Hispanic, compared with about 3 percent of Congress in 1997 and 11 percent in the U.S. population as a whole. The percentages of Asian Americans and American Indians serving as state legislators are also lower than their percentages in the population.

Salaries For many decades, state legislative salaries were low. As the job became more influential and time-consuming, however, legislators' salaries generally increased. New York offers the highest salary at $57,500 a year, while New Hampshire legislators earn only $200 a year, and Alabama legislators earn $10 a day.

Leadership Except for Nebraska, which has a nonpartisan, one-house legislature, all state legislatures are bicameral, or have two houses. In each house, there is a presiding officer with substantial leadership powers. As in Congress, these leaders assign bills to committees, make committee assignments, and control floor debates.

Committees Committees perform the main legislative work of the states, just as they do for the nation. That is, state legislative committees consider and report on proposed bills.

Bills undergo a legislative committee process similar to that in Congress. First, a member of the state legislature introduces a bill. It is then assigned to and considered in committee. If the bill is approved there, the full state senate and lower house debate it and vote on it.

If different versions of the bill are passed in the two houses, a joint committee will draft a compromise version. The compromise bill is then voted on in both houses and, if passed, sent to the executive branch, where it may be signed into law or vetoed.

Until fairly recently, state legislature committees had little power and no support staff, although today they have a great deal of power. Keep in mind, however, that the power of committees varies from state to state. In some states the legislative committees resemble congressional committees in their scope of influence. In other states, committees are not nearly as strong as in Congress, making it relatively easy to get a bill considered on the floor without committee approval.

As their power has increased, the state legislative committees' staff also has increased. By around 1990 the 50 state legislatures employed more than 33,000 staff members. In most states, committee staff is not divided along party lines, as it is in Congress. Instead, the entire staff serves the committee as a whole, regardless of the members' party affiliations. Gradually, however, partisan staffing is spreading to more states.

State Executive Branches

Every state has a **governor**, or elected chief executive. The qualifications for holding the governorship, as well as the position's terms, salaries, roles, and powers, vary from state to state.

Governors' Qualifications and Terms Each state's constitution lists the requirements for becoming governor. Most states require that the governor be a U.S. citizen. He or she also must have resided in the state in question for a certain length of time. Age requirements vary from state to state, but typically a governor must be at least 30 years of age.

Governors in most states serve four-year terms. In New Hampshire and Vermont, however, they serve only two years. A number of states limit governors to serving two terms. Virginia is more extreme, allowing its governor to serve only one term.

Governors' Salaries As with state legislators, the salaries of governors vary widely. The governor of New York, for example, receives $130,000 a year. In contrast, the governor of Montana earns $59,310. Most states also provide their chief executive and his or her family with a governor's mansion or other official residence in the state capital. In addition, due to the nature and requirements of their job, governors often receive an allowance for travel and related expenses.

Governors' Roles Governors, like presidents, generally take an active role in initiating legislation, preparing budgets, and setting an agenda for the state. In recent years, for example, governors

Constitutional Change over Time

The constitutions of the United States and of each individual state have changed as a result of key events in history. Change in the U.S. Constitution is reflected in its 27 amendments, such as those ending slavery, extending the right to vote, and banning poll taxes. At the state level, change has been reflected in amendments and in complete revisions of some states' constitutions. In fact, some states have been governed by nearly a dozen different constitutions over the years.

What brought about some of these changes? How have historical events affected constitutional government in the states over time? Constitutional measures in the states often have reflected general attitudes and beliefs at the time in which they were adopted. Consider, for example, state constitutions that were adopted before 1820. Remembering more domineering governors that had been imposed on the colonies by the British crown before 1776, state leaders developed constitutions that put strong limits on executive

power. Over time, however, amendments in various states brought a more even balance in power between the two branches of government.

Constitutional change in the decades after the Civil War also reflected the times and historical events, especially in the southern states of the former Confederacy. For example, after the war southern states, under federal occupation, adopted new constitutions that secured legal rights for former slaves. Under those constitutions, African Americans won elections to government offices across the South. For example, between 1869 and 1901 twenty African Americans represented Southern districts in the U.S. House. Mississippi sent two African Americans to the Senate during this period.

Following Reconstruction and the removal of federal troops, however, white southerners who opposed political rights for African Americans returned to power. This brought about another wave of constitutional change across the South. Revised constitutions allowed states to pass laws imposing a form of second-class citizenship on African Americans. These laws included measures for racial segregation and voting restrictions.

For example, Louisiana and six other southern states adopted measures that waived literacy and other eligibility requirements for people eligible to vote before Jan. 1, 1867. Those measures effectively barred most African Americans from voting. How? None had been eligible to vote before 1867, and few had ever received any formal education or could meet other requirements.

State constitutions today still reflect many attitudes that evolved in past eras. Primary and referendum elections, for example, gained popularity during the Progressive era of the early 1900s. Both measures reflected the desire of many people at the time to expand democracy by allowing voters to bypass legislatures to enact popular laws.

The Granger Collection, New York

Pictured here is Hiram R. Revels, who in 1870 became the first African American elected to the U.S. Senate.

What Do You Think?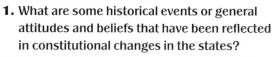

1. What are some historical events or general attitudes and beliefs that have been reflected in constitutional changes in the states?
2. Do you think that the changes made in state constitutions as a result of a key event in history have promoted the public good? Explain.

Terms of Office and Salaries of State Governors

STATE	LENGTH OF TERM (in years)	SALARY	STATE	LENGTH OF TERM (in years)	SALARY	STATE	LENGTH OF TERM (in years)	SALARY
Alabama	4	$87,643	Louisiana	4	$95,000	Ohio	4	$115,762
Alaska	4	$81,648	Maine	4	$69,992	Oklahoma	4	$70,000
Arizona	4	$75,000	Maryland	4	$120,000	Oregon	4	$80,000
Arkansas	4	$60,000	Massachusetts	4	$90,000	Pennsylvania	4	$105,000
California	4	$120,000	Michigan	4	$121,166	Rhode Island	4	$69,900
Colorado	4	$70,000	Minnesota	4	$114,506	South Carolina	4	$106,078
Connecticut	4	$78,000	Mississippi	4	$83,160	South Dakota	4	$79,875
Delaware	4	$95,000	Missouri	4	$94,563	Tennessee	4	$85,000
Florida	4	$104,817	Montana	4	$59,310	Texas	4	$99,122
Georgia	4	$103,074	Nebraska	4	$65,000	Utah	4	$77,250
Hawaii	4	$94,780	Nevada	4	$90,000	Vermont	2	$80,730
Idaho	4	$85,000	New Hampshire	2	$86,235	Virginia	4	$110,000
Illinois	4	$123,022	New Jersey	4	$85,000	Washington	4	$121,000
Indiana	4	$77,200	New Mexico	4	$90,000	West Virginia	4	$90,000
Iowa	4	$98,200	New York	4	$130,000	Wisconsin	4	$101,861
Kansas	4	$80,340	North Carolina	4	$103,012	Wyoming	4	$95,000
Kentucky	4	$86,352	North Dakota	4	$71,042			

Source: *World Almanac: 1997; The Book of States: 1994*

State constitutions outline many aspects of the office of governor such as the yearly salary and the number of terms an individual may hold the office. **What is the salary for the governor of Colorado?**

in several states have taken the lead on issues such as education and welfare reform. Their actions at the state level often have propelled them into leadership roles on these issues at the national level.

In addition, governors today often act as their states' chief ambassadors, working to attract business investment and to encourage the purchase of state exports. Governors frequently become personally involved in negotiations with large companies that are considering locating their offices and factories in the state. Governors even travel to other countries to promote their state to foreign investors and to find markets abroad for its products and businesses.

Governors' Powers As governors' roles have expanded, their powers have increased as well. As noted in Chapter 2, the constitutions of the newly independent American states created weak governorships. Remembering how strong colonial governors had abused their power, citizens of the young country worked to ensure that state

governors would not do the same. This legacy of limiting governors' powers continued well into this century.

For example, most governors' appointment powers are restricted. Unlike presidents, governors seldom may appoint all the agency heads in the executive branch. In almost all states, for example, the attorney general is elected separately from the governor. In addition, voters in many states also elect a lieutenant governor, secretary of state, treasurer, and state auditor or comptroller—whose job is to ensure that no public funds are paid out of the state treasury unless authorized by law.

Most governors do possess one power that traditionally has been withheld from the president— the line-item veto. As noted in Chapter 6, a line-item veto can be used to void specific parts of legislation or budget appropriations while signing the rest of the bill into law. By 1994, governors in 41 states held this power. In 1995 Congress also gave line-item veto power to the president, but a federal judge ruled the legislation unconstitutional. The case was appealed to the Supreme Court. In 1997 the Court ruled that the law's constitutionality could not be decided at that point because the president had not yet exercised the power. With the first exercise of this power by President Clinton in the fall of 1997, the case was sent back to the Supreme Court for review.

State Judicial Branches

As noted in Chapter 11, cases that involve federal laws or the federal government must go through the federal courts. However, most legal rules that affect people's everyday lives are passed not by the federal government but by the states. Therefore, most court cases take place in state courts. In addition, local courts also are established by states to handle matters of state law. During the mid-1990s state and local courts dealt with 99.7 percent of all cases filed in the United States.

Like the federal judiciary, the states maintain two basic types of courts: trial and appeals. The states have also established a number of special courts.

Trial Courts Most states' trial courts, though a part of state government, are organized at the county level. The office of the district attorney or the public prosecutor is in charge of investigating and prosecuting state criminal cases. In many states, criminal cases cannot be brought by the district attorney's office without a grand jury's approval. As noted in Chapter 12, a grand jury is a panel of citizens who determine if the government has enough evidence to put a person on trial.

As noted in Chapter 12, after a grand jury hands down an indictment, a trial—or petit (PEH-tee)—jury hears the case. In almost every state, juries in criminal cases consist of 12 jurors and in most states there can be no conviction in a criminal trial without a unanimous verdict.

As noted in Chapter 12, the jury selection process begins when potential jurors are chosen to come to court. Traditionally, potential jurors were selected using lists that included only one group of people, such as licensed drivers, car owners, or registered voters. This method, however, does a poor job of ensuring representative juries. For example, because poor people and young people are less likely to register to vote than others, they will have a relatively low chance of being called

for jury duty in states that choose potential jurors from lists of registered voters only. As a result, 25 states have begun using multiple sources to compile their jury lists.

In many courts potential jurors sit around the courthouse for a long period of time as part of a **jury pool**, a group of people who might be chosen to serve in a trial. This waiting burdens people because they cannot work or attend classes while part of a jury pool. As a result, many people called as potential jurors ask to be excused from jury duty.

In recent years many state courts have introduced a system called one day, one trial. People selected under this system must appear as a potential juror for only one day. If not chosen as a juror on that day, he or she need not return. If chosen, the person need sit in only the trial for which he or she was selected. The one-day, one-trial system was first used in Houston in 1972. As of the

Comparing
Governments

The Federal Republic of Nigeria

Federal governments in other countries have many similarities to the U.S. government. Sometimes, however, those similarities appear only on the surface and do not truly reflect political reality in a country. This is the case with the Federal Republic of Nigeria, which is located on the southern coast of western Africa.

A former British colony, Nigeria—which has more than 250 ethnic groups—gained its independence in 1960. The country's constitution divides responsibilities among the federal government and 30 state governments and their local councils. State governments, for example, are responsible for medical and health services.

Despite the similarity to the federal system in the United States, however, Nigeria is not a democracy. A series of military governments has run the country—except for a brief period in 1993—since the early 1980s. In 1995, however, the government pledged to turn power over to democratically elected officials within three years.

POLITICAL PROCESSES *West Virginia Supreme Court judges look over the backlog of cases that have flooded their court.* **What courts handle the estates of deceased people?**

* family courts, which handle divorces and child custody and support;
* probate courts, which handle the estates of deceased people;
* juvenile courts, which handle offenses committed by people legally too young to appear in adult criminal courts; and
* traffic courts, which handle cases involving traffic violations.

The Judges Unlike the judges of the federal courts, who are appointed, county trial court judges are usually elected. Even state supreme court judges are elected in almost half of the states. In other states the governor appoints the judges, and in a few, the legislature selects them.

Twenty-seven states have adopted some form of the Missouri Plan for choosing state court judges. Introduced in Missouri in 1940, this plan empowers a nonpartisan commission led by the state bar association to develop a list of candidates qualified to serve as judges. The governor then selects judges from among those candidates, and voters decide at a regularly scheduled election, usually a year later, whether to retain the judges in office.

Most state judges serve limited terms—most often 6 to 10 years. Judges in only one state—Rhode Island—serve for life, as U.S. Supreme Court justices do. In two states—Massachusetts and New Hampshire—judges may serve until age 70, when they must retire. Seated judges in the other states, however, are often re-elected at the end of their terms, enabling many of them to retain their positions for life.

early 1990s, courts serving about 30 states were using this system.

Appeals Courts Cases under state law generally may be appealed only within the state court system. The highest court of appeals in a state is generally called the state supreme court. A state case can be appealed to the federal courts only if it involves a possible violation of the U.S. Constitution or other federal law.

Special Courts In 44 states there are also several special courts with limited jurisdiction, or that handle only specific types of cases. As with most state courts, these special courts usually are organized at the county level and sometimes at the city level. The most common special courts are

---

SECTION 2 — REVIEW

1. Define the following terms: governor, jury pool.

2. How do most state legislatures operate?

3. How have governors' roles and powers changed over time?

4. Describe state trial, appeals, and special courts.

5. **Thinking and Writing Critically**
   What are the advantages and disadvantages of the Missouri Plan for selecting state supreme court judges? Do you think that the advantages of this system outweigh the disadvantages? Explain your answer.

6. **Applying** PRINCIPLES OF DEMOCRACY
   Conduct an Internet search for information on your state's court system. You might start with search words such as *state court system* and your state's name. Outline the information you find.

SECTION 3

STATE BUDGETS AND REVENUES

Political Dictionary

sales tax
sin tax
bond rating

Objectives

★ How are state budgets created?
★ What are the main sources of state revenue?

As the trend toward less federal involvement in state affairs grows, state governments are taking on new responsibilities. Indeed, state governments are currently on the front lines of some of the nation's most difficult challenges, such as making policies dealing with education, drugs, welfare, and crime. As states formulate programs in these areas, they also must find ways to pay for them.

State Budgets

State legislatures generally play a role in the state budget process similar to that played by Congress in the federal budget process. The governor usually presents a budget to the legislature. The members of the legislature then debate the proposed budget and draft their own version, consulting with the executive branch in the process. The legislature draws up a final budget, votes on it, and sends it to the governor for his or her signature.

One key difference between the state and federal budget processes is that most states require by law that the budget be balanced. That is, state spending cannot exceed state revenues. Long before people began clamoring for a balanced-budget amendment to the U.S. Constitution, states had this requirement in place.

Achieving a balanced budget can be challenging during economic downswings, however. Therefore, some states, when revenues are up, hold money in "rainy day" funds set aside for tough economic times. The only exception to the balanced-budget requirement involves long-term bonds used to pay for expensive projects, such as the building of roads, bridges, schools, hospitals, and prisons. As noted in Chapter 9, a bond is a certificate issued by an institution (a government or corporation) in exchange for money borrowed from an investor.

Another difference between the federal and state budgets is the source of government revenue. Unlike the federal government, which depends on the income tax for the largest part of its revenue, states receive money from many sources, including various taxes, fees, federal grants, loans, and lotteries.

State Taxes

Most state governments have sales and income taxes. Some also have severance taxes. States try to keep their tax burdens down because a high tax rate often discourages businesses from locating their operations there.

Sales Taxes A **sales tax** is a tax placed on the sale of a good or service and is charged as a percentage of the sales price. Mississippi adopted the first sales tax in the United States in 1932. Today all but five states—Alaska, Delaware, Montana, New Hampshire, and Oregon—have a sales tax. Rates are generally the same for all goods and range from 3 percent in Colorado and Wyoming to 7 percent in Mississippi and Rhode Island.

Many states exclude some basic items from the sales tax. Half exclude food, and all but six exclude prescription drugs. Other states do not charge a sales tax on items such as clothing, and some do not tax the sale of college textbooks.

Special Sales Taxes Some states have additional sales taxes on certain categories of goods and services. For example, most states have special hotel sales taxes, which are often passed because they are paid largely by visitors from other states. Thus, a state can raise these tax rates without angering state residents. State officials must keep in mind, however, that if such taxes rise too high, businesses may decide to hold their conferences and other travel-related functions in

State Sales and Individual Income Taxes

- ☐ Sales tax only
- ■ Income tax only
- ☐ Sales and income taxes
- ■ No sales or income taxes
- ＊ Income tax on interest and dividends only

Source: *Statistical Abstract of the United States: 1996*

Most states raise revenues by using a combination of sales and income taxes, but some states use either sales taxes or income taxes to raise revenue. **What is the only state to have no sales or income taxes?**

states with lower taxes. Vacationers also might choose a less expensive destination.

Another kind of special sales tax are sin taxes. **Sin taxes** are meant to discourage the purchase of some types of goods, such as liquor and cigarettes. Some states charge as much as 81.5 cents in tax on a pack of cigarettes and $6.50 on a gallon of hard liquor. In 1991, for example, California introduced a type of sin tax on snack foods, such as candy. Although the state does not tax food, the passage of this law removed the sales tax exemption from snack foods. Other items such as alcoholic beverages also lost their exempt status with the passage of the bill.

Income Taxes Wisconsin passed the first state income tax in 1911. Today 43 states have an individual income tax, although 2 of these only tax income from interest and dividends. All states but three—Nevada, Washington, and Wyoming—also have some form of tax on business income. In some states the income tax has a flat rate. That is, all people, regardless of how much money they earn, pay the same percentage of their income in taxes. In other states the rate is progressive, as with the federal income tax. This means that a person's income tax rate rises as his or her income rises.

The highest state income tax is in North Dakota, where people who earn more than $50,000 a year must turn over 12 percent of their incomes.

Severance Taxes Severance taxes are those placed on the extraction of nonrenewable resources, such as oil, coal, and natural gas. This type of tax is paid by a business when it removes such resources from the ground.

Most states raise less than 10 percent of their total tax revenue through severance taxes. States with large reserves of oil and minerals—such as Alaska, Louisiana, Montana, New Mexico, Wyoming, and North Dakota—earn a higher percentage of revenue than other states from severance taxes. In 1996 Alaska took in the highest percentage from this source—63 percent of its total tax revenue.

State Fees

States also charge fees directly to the people who use a particular state service. These types of user fees include highway tolls, auto registration and driver's license fees, fishing and hunting license fees, and state park fees. One of the largest user fees in most states is tuition at state colleges. Some people support this method of financing a government service because user fees remove some of the monetary burden from the general tax payers and place it on those who actually use the service.

Federal Grants

A large revenue source for state governments is federal grants. As noted in Chapter 4, the federal government gives categorical and block grants to the states for many types of projects, such as building schools, roads, and bridges. In 1996 the federal government gave $227 billion in grants to state and local governments. About 40 percent of this money was spent on health services provided by states.

Rapid expansion of federal grants between 1960 and 1980 allowed state and local governments to increase their activities without significantly raising taxes. Many grant programs were set up during President Lyndon Johnson's administration. These grants differed from their predecessors in that they were intended to aid poor people rather than fund public works projects. Some grant programs established during the Johnson administration have been used to fund public education programs for poor students, provide health insurance for those in poverty, and aid in the construction of mass transit systems in cities. A number of the new programs, such as grants to public schools and to local police departments, involved policy areas traditionally reserved to state and local government.

During the early 1980s, however, cutbacks in federal grants created a funding crisis that sent state and local governments scrambling to develop new sources of revenue. Some states, often at the initiative of their governors, have raised taxes in recent years.

Borrowing

Having a mandate to create balanced budgets, most state governments cannot borrow money to fund a budget deficit, as the federal government does. They may, however, borrow in the short term to keep the government running until the budget's predicted tax revenue is collected.

States also may borrow money for longer periods of time to fund lengthy construction projects, such as roads, prisons, college dormitories, and hospitals. Because such construction projects have a long life, lawmakers typically spread their

PRINCIPLES OF DEMOCRACY *Toll roads, such as the one pictured here, charge user fees directly to those who actually use the service.* **What are some other state services that charge a user fee?**

cost out over several years instead of funding them through a single year's budget.

How do states borrow money? They do so by issuing bonds. A state bond indicates that the state is in debt to the bondholder for the amount listed on the certificate. In exchange for loaning money to the state, the bondholder receives interest on the bond. When the bond matures—typically after a number of years—the state returns the amount borrowed to the investor plus interest.

The interest rates a state offers on its bonds vary according to the state's bond rating. A **bond rating**—determined by independent, private organizations—is a measure of how much faith the financial community has in the issuer's (the state's) financial stability. Bond ratings vary from A3 to Aaa (the highest rating issued by Moody's Investors Service). In 1997, for example, Maryland, Missouri, South Carolina, Utah, and Virginia all received Moody's highest rating. States with high bond ratings pay less money in interest because the bondholder is taking on less risk.

Lotteries and Gambling Revenues

In search of ways to raise funds "painlessly," without raising taxes, many states have turned to lotteries and other gambling revenues. In 1964 New

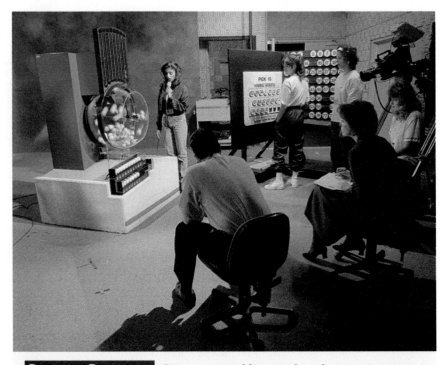

POLITICAL PROCESSES *State-sponsored lotteries have become a source for additional income. State lotteries usually provide 2 to 3 percent of these states' revenues.* **What percent of Nevada's revenue is received from taxes on gambling?**

money in the hope of striking it rich. Early lottery advertising reflected this worry by trying to downplay that the lottery is a form of gambling. Instead, states stressed the worthy causes to which lottery revenues were being applied.

As state budgets grew tighter and tighter, however, and as the popularity of gambling increased, more states adopted lotteries. To maintain interest in the lotteries and to keep sales high, states turned from emphasizing the support of education to enticing buyers with the possibility of huge wealth. As a result, the size of the jackpots started rising astronomically. As of 1994 the largest prize awarded to a single ticket holder in a drawing was $110 million. States also began offering many additional games, particularly "instant winner" lotteries.

Hampshire became the first state in the 1900s to establish a lottery. Today state-run lotteries exist in 38 states, providing about 2 to 3 percent of their total revenue.

At first, state lotteries spread slowly. Many critics objected to them on moral grounds, saying that the government should not encourage gambling among citizens. These critics charged that the lottery was not at all painless, that it encouraged citizens, particularly poor ones, to spend their

To reach more people, the states began selling lottery tickets in additional places, including, in some cases, checkout lines at supermarkets.

Casino gambling is a revenue source in several states, including Nevada and New Jersey. Taxes on gambling in Nevada provide the state with 40 percent of its revenue. In addition, six states have authorized riverboat gambling in dockside casinos. Some states also collect revenue from the horse- and dog-racing industries.

SECTION 3 — REVIEW

1. Define the following terms: sales tax, sin tax, bond rating.

2. How is the state budget process similar to the federal budget process? How is it different?

3. What kinds of taxes do states impose? What are the advantages and disadvantages of each type?

4. Why do states borrow money? How do state government bonds work?

5. **Thinking and Writing Critically**
What advantages do you think sin taxes provide? Name some disadvantages.

6. **Applying** PUBLIC GOOD
Should states raise revenues through lotteries and other forms of gambling? Do you think lotteries are truly a "painless" way to raise money for state programs? Explain your answer.

SECTION 1 The 50 states are similar in many ways. Like the federal government, they receive their authority to govern from constitutions that reflect the places and times in which they were written. State constitutions cannot conflict with the U.S. Constitution.

Furthermore, like the federal government, the states' continued authority to rule rests firmly with the people. Citizens in many states may become directly involved in checking the legislative power of their state government by offering an initiative, holding a referendum, and recalling an elected official. An initiative is a nonlegislative procedure for proposing or repealing a law. A referendum is a popular vote on a proposal that has already been considered by the legislature. A recall is an election to remove an elected official from office.

Some critics charge that state governments are not as responsive to the people as they should be. Most people agree, however, that they are striving to deliver high-quality, cost-effective public services.

SECTION 2 State governments divide their power among legislative, executive, and judicial branches. The powers and makeup of state legislatures have changed in recent decades. In most states the legislatures have gone from meeting every two years to meeting annually.

To serve in a state's lawmaking body, state legislators, like their counterparts in Congress, must meet certain requirements. The main work of the legislative branch is performed by committees that consider and report on proposed bills. State bills undergo a process similar to that of federal legislation in Congress.

The executive branch is headed by the governor, who takes an active role in initiating legislation, preparing budgets, and setting an agenda for the state. Governors' powers were once strictly limited but have increased as states have taken on responsibilities once performed by the federal government.

A state's judicial branch, like the federal court system, has two basic types of courts: trial and appeals. There are also a number of special courts with limited jurisdiction in such areas as child custody, estates, and juvenile or traffic offenses. Most state judges are elected, not appointed.

SECTION 3 State governments are on the front lines of some of the nation's most difficult challenges, such as education, drugs, welfare, and crime. As states formulate policies and programs in these areas, they also must find ways to pay for them. State legislatures generally play a role in the budget process similar to that played by Congress in the federal budget process. A key difference between state and federal budgets, however, is that most states require their budgets to be balanced. For this reason, many states maintain "rainy day" funds.

States receive money from many sources, including sales taxes, income taxes, severance taxes, fees, federal grants, loans, and lotteries and other forms of gambling. Lotteries and gambling have been controversial sources of revenue, as many people feel that the government should not encourage gambling. Lotteries exist in more than half of the states and bring in revenue for services such as education.

Government Notebook

Review the list you wrote in your Government Notebook at the beginning of the chapter about state laws that affect you personally. Now that you have studied this chapter, list as many as you can. Record them in your Notebook.

REVIEW

REVIEWING CONCEPTS

1. What is the difference between an initiative and a referendum?

2. Describe three ways in which state governments promote the public good.

3. Why is the average age of state legislators younger than that of members of Congress? Do you think the age of 18 is an appropriate age requirement to be a state legislator? Explain your answer.

4. How is a bill introduced and passed by a state legislature? What part do committees of the legislature play in this process?

5. States raise revenues by imposing various taxes. Describe some other ways states raise revenues.

THINKING AND WRITING CRITICALLY

1. **PRINCIPLES OF DEMOCRACY** Should states charge a flat income tax or a progressive income tax, like the federal government? Should students with part-time jobs pay the same percentage of their income in taxes as other working citizens? Explain your answers.

2. **POLITICAL PROCESSES** Imagine that an elected official in your state has committed an unethical act. As a registered voter, would you wait for the next election in hopes that the official would not be re-elected, or would you initiate a recall? How would you initiate a recall if you felt it necessary to do so?

3. **POLITICAL PROCESSES** The pay for state legislators varies widely from state to state. How do you account for the huge difference in salaries for legislators in New York and in New Hampshire? What do you think is a fair salary for a part-time legislator? for a full-time legislator? Explain your answers.

4. **PUBLIC GOOD** In addition to trial and appeals courts, the majority of states have a number of special courts. Do you think these family, probate, juvenile, and traffic courts help the judicial system run more smoothly or just make it more complicated? How might these special courts promote the public good? Explain your answers.

CITIZENSHIP IN YOUR COMMUNITY

Research the jury selection process for jury trials in your community. Although procedures for selecting a jury are basically the same across the United States, the process does vary slightly from place to place. Consider the following questions as you conduct your research. How are potential jurors' names selected? How does the court determine a juror's qualifications? How are prospective jurors notified of their jury assignment? Use the information you gather to create a flowchart showing the steps in the jury selection process. Include one or two sentences of explanation for each step.

INDIVIDUAL PORTFOLIO PROJECT

Usually there is no shortage of people who want to run for office in state government. Imagine, however, that not enough candidates have declared their intention to run in your state's next election. To solve the problem, lawmakers have asked you—a clerk in the state government—to place help-wanted advertisements in the state's major newspapers. Write three want-ads describing the jobs of state legislator, governor, and state supreme court justice. Be sure to list the qualifications, terms, and duties of the office in each advertisement.

PRACTICING SKILLS: CITIZENSHIP

Write a letter to one of your state's senators or representatives in order to find out more about the job of being a legislator. You might want to start by looking in your local telephone directory to find out how to contact your state legislators. In your letter, ask for information about the committees on which the congressperson serves and the bills he or she has introduced.

THE INTERNET: LEARNING ONLINE

Conduct an Internet search to locate your state's constitution. You might begin by using search words such as *constitution, state constitution,* and [your state's name] *Constitution.* Browse the document, looking for information about your state's legislative, executive, and judicial branches. How often does your state's legislature meet? How long is each session? What are the requirements for holding the office of governor? Make a poster outlining the information you find. Be sure to include the Web site addresses you find most useful.

ANALYZING PRIMARY SOURCES

GOVERNOR JEANNE SHAHEEN'S INAUGURAL ADDRESS

On January 9, 1997, Jeanne Shaheen was inaugurated as the first female governor of New Hampshire. Read the following excerpt from Governor Shaheen's inaugural address and answer the questions that follow.

❝ *To all of you in this chamber and to every citizen of our great state I pledge my full devotion to the solemn oath I have just taken. . . .*

And so today I invite every New Hampshire citizen to become a part of our history and a part of our future. If you have an idea about how to improve the quality of life in our state, I want to hear it. . . .

I'm going to listen. I'm going to learn. And with your help, we will take action to meet the challenges we face: improving our schools, lowering electric rates, protecting health care, creating jobs, and building our economy. . . .

For too long, we have been paying the highest electric rates in the nation. They constitute [make up] a hidden tax, taking money away from families already struggling to make ends meet. . . .

We have already taken the first steps toward introducing competition into the electric industry. . . . But our task is clear: high electric rates are a threat to our economic future, and they must come down.

We must make sure quality health care is affordable and accessible to all our families. . . . And as our population ages, we must develop alternatives to costly nursing home care, alternatives that allow our senior citizens to remain at home and in their communities. . . .

I will make education a priority—in my budget, in my appointments, and in the full weight and visibility granted by this office. . . .

For now, join me in celebrating this moment. And tomorrow let us begin the quiet, steady work of the people. Let us do it without acrimony [sharpness] or bitterness. Let us do it without petty partisanship [party loyalty]. And let us do it together. Then, we will truly make history. ❞

1. Governor Shaheen addresses New Hampshire's problems with high electric rates, health care, and education. How does she propose beginning to solve these problems?

2. Shaheen urges her peers to work for the people "without petty partisanship." What does she mean by this?

3. Shaheen made history by becoming New Hampshire's first female governor. How does she plan to make history in her work as governor?

LOCAL GOVERNMENT

Local governments play an important role in providing essential services to the public. Take a look around your community—you may not even realize all of the services your local government provides. It may offer fire and police protection, public transit, airports and seaports, and public health services and hospitals.

Tens of thousands of local governmental units operate in the United States today. They vary a great deal in structure—so much so that some people have referred to the organization of local government in the United States as a "crazy quilt pattern" rather than a system. However, within most states, local governmental units share important similarities.

Government Notebook

In your Government Notebook, write a list of services that local government provides to your community.

U.S. COMMUNITIES

Political Dictionary

rural area
urban area
suburb
metropolitan area
megalopolis

Objectives

★ What is a rural area?
★ What historical factors led to the growth of cities?
★ Why did suburbs develop?
★ What is a metropolitan area?

The size and makeup of a community largely determine its government. A city of 1 million residents would of course require many more services and a much larger government than would a town of 650. Governmental diversity is also widespread on the local level because the United States is home to many types of communities. Despite their many unique features, these communities all fit into one or more of the following categories—rural, urban, suburban, and metropolitan.

Rural Areas

Before 1920 a majority of Americans lived in rural areas. A **rural area** is an area with low population density where people live on farms, on ranches, or in small towns. Rural areas usually are dominated by agricultural production, mining, forestry, or ranching. Semirural areas—which make up a related subcategory—usually include a few more towns, sometimes of greater size, than rural areas.

Urban Areas

Today most people in the United States live in **urban areas**, or cities and their surroundings. The first U.S. census, taken in 1790, revealed that only 1 out of every 20 Americans lived in an urban area. By 1920, however, more than 50 percent of Americans were living in urban areas. What sparked such a change?

In the late 1800s and early 1900s immigrants flocked to U.S. cities in search of jobs, which had been brought on by industrial development. Improvements in transportation and communications systems had also spurred the growth of cities, as had the advancement of technology in public works engineering, thus improving urban water supplies and electric utilities, as well as sewers, streets, and bridges. Meanwhile, advances in agricultural technology lessened the need for labor in rural areas, forcing many farmworkers to the cities in search of work. Today around 80 percent of all Americans live in urban areas.

Suburbs

An urban area generally includes **suburbs**—residential areas surrounding a city. While enabling urban areas to support an increasing population, new technology in transportation and communications allowed some people to move from the crowded central cities to the outskirts.

CITIZENSHIP *Today about 80 percent of all Americans live in urban areas such as Denver, pictured here.* **By the 1920s, what portion of the U.S. population lived in cities?**

PUBLIC GOOD *New advances in communications and transportation technology made it more convenient for some people to move from the crowded central cities to suburbs that offered more space.* **What transportation developments helped to speed up suburbanization?**

The earliest commuter suburb, located just outside New York City, was Brooklyn Heights, which developed between 1815 and 1835. The largest U.S. cities, including Philadelphia and Boston, suburbanized rapidly during this period because of the Transportation Revolution, which ushered in widespread use of commuter trains.

With the development of automobiles, suburbanization occurred even more dramatically. Once they were able to afford cars, many people moved to the suburbs and drove to their jobs in the cities. The first large suburbs that catered to automobile commuters appeared around Los Angeles during the 1920s, after city residents voted to borrow money to build an extensive road system.

During the 1960s the nation's suburban population began to exceed that of the central cities. By 1980 about 45 percent of the U.S. population lived in suburbs, while only 30 percent lived in central cities.

Suburban growth has been particularly pronounced in the states of the South and Southwest, known as the Sun Belt. Much of this growth has been caused by the arrival of vast numbers of people from the Northeast and Midwest. They hope to benefit from the Sun Belt states' mild climate, lower energy costs, lower taxes, and job opportunities created by newly developed industries and technologies.

Today Houston is one of the largest Sun Belt boomtowns. From 1945 to 1980, its population rose from 385,000 to nearly 1.6 million. This tremendous growth was partly stimulated by the moving of a large number of oil and energy companies to Houston during the energy crisis of the mid-1970s. Abundant job opportunities drew thousands of new residents each month. In the late 1980s, however, oil prices dropped, triggering a decline in the growth of the city's economy. The economic downturn slowed the population growth rate in Houston and other Texas oil towns.

In contrast to the Sun Belt, during the mid- to late 1970s and early 1980s, cities in the northeastern and midwestern regions of the country experienced a decline in population growth. This area, sometimes called the Rust Belt because of its heavy concentration of steel and automobile

Citizenship in Action

Preserving Part of History

A core responsibility of local governments—rural and urban alike—involves the operation and funding of school systems. Many public school students in turn help promote the public good in their local communities by working to preserve important parts of history.

Students in Calallen Independent School District in Corpus Christi, Texas, for example, have been working for more than 15 years to restore both a one-room schoolhouse built in the late 1800s and a farmhouse built in 1910. Sally Robeau, who teaches Texas history in Calallen Independent School District, sponsors the Junior Historians club and has helped its members recondition the two structures.

Work on restoring the schoolhouse, which had been constructed in Nuecestown—a ghost town near Corpus Christi—began in 1982. The building had been converted decades earlier into a residence. To return the building to its original state, students raised money, helped remove pink stucco that had at some point been applied to the wooden exterior walls, replaced rotted boards, and painted the walls red. Students worked similarly hard to restore the old farmhouse, located in Calallen, installing insulation, building a back porch, wallpapering the interior, and replacing broken and rotted boards.

The students then raised thousands of dollars to move both structures to a common location in Corpus Christi. Some of the money raised for moving and restoring the buildings came from making and selling arts and crafts similar to those used in the late 1800s and early 1900s. The club also has received small grants for its preservation work, but students have raised most of the at least $75,000 spent on the buildings so far, Robeau says. "Every one of the students seems to have a soft spot for the buildings," she says. "They have a sense of ownership."

The students display the buildings during Pioneer Days, an annual two-day event organized by the Junior Historians. At that time, visitors can tour the buildings and view student-made clay pots and other artifacts that are similar to those made a century ago. The schoolhouse also is used for field trips. Robeau says the students will soon have the farmhouse ready for use as a center for researching local history. The house will serve as a museum as well as contain historical files and other information that can be used in research.

Robeau's Junior Historians club is associated with an educational project sponsored by the Texas State Historical Association. The project encourages students to adopt an old building, research its history, restore it, and then apply to have it designated as an official historic site.

Students in one East Texas town adopted their own high school, which features the mission-style architecture that was popular in the 1930s, when it was built. More than 100 other Junior Historians clubs are working to preserve historic sites throughout Texas. Indiana and about six other states have similar programs.

Members of the Junior Historians club of Corpus Christi, Texas, work to restore a schoolhouse that was built in the late 1800s.

What Do You Think?

1. What values do you think students learn when working to preserve historic sites?
2. What historic sites in your community might be candidates for preservation?

CITIZENSHIP *This aerial photograph shows Washington, D.C., which is part of a large megalopolis that stretches north 500 miles to Boston.* **How are megalopolises formed?**

metropolitan statistical areas (MSAs), frequently referred to as metropolitan areas. **Metropolitan areas**—most of which have no single, overall unit of government—are urban areas made up of a central city of 50,000 or more people, its suburbs, and the surrounding counties that depend on it socially and economically. About one third of the metropolitan population of the United States lives in the nation's 12 largest metropolitan areas. These areas include Los Angeles–Long Beach; New York; Chicago; Philadelphia; Washington, D.C.; Detroit; Houston; Atlanta; Boston; Riverside–San Bernardino, California; Dallas; and Minneapolis–St. Paul.

Fueled by high suburban growth, some metropolitan areas have spread far enough to border one another. Together, a group of bordering metropolitan areas constitute a **megalopolis**. Several megalopolises are already well developed in the United States, including one that stretches for 500 miles from Boston to the southernmost suburbs of Washington, D.C. Developing megalopolises include one running from Milwaukee to Pittsburgh and another from Santa Barbara, California, to San Diego and across the border to the southern areas of Tijuana, Mexico.

industries, experienced the effects of high unemployment rates caused by the collapse of the steel industry and a declining demand for American-made automobiles. Many people from this region moved to the South and West in search of jobs.

Metropolitan Areas

By 1970 nearly two thirds of Americans lived in what the U.S. government categorizes as

SECTION 1 — REVIEW

1. Define the following terms: rural area, urban area, suburb, metropolitan area, megalopolis.

2. Why did urban areas grow in size during the late 1800s and early 1900s?

3. What developments spurred the growth of suburbs?

4. What is a metropolitan area?

5. **Thinking and Writing Critically**
   What might be the advantages and disadvantages of living in a city? in a rural area? In what ways might daily life be different for young people living in each of these areas?

6. **Applying** PUBLIC GOOD
   Why might some people rather live in a suburb than in a city? What might be the drawbacks?

LOCAL GOVERNMENT ORGANIZATION

Political Dictionary

township
municipality
mayor-council system
council-manager system
city manager
commission
special district

Objectives

★ What are the four main types of local government?
★ What are the different types of municipal government?
★ What are the functions of a county government?
★ What do special districts provide?

Imagine that you are trying to cross the street near your house, but the street is so busy that you have to wait several minutes to cross. Whom would you contact about constructing a traffic light there? The answer most likely is your local government. As noted in Section 1, local governments provide a range of services—anything from installing signal lights to testing water quality. In these ways, local governments promote the public good by making people's lives easier and safer.

The first thing likely to strike someone studying local governments is just how numerous they are—some 85,000 at last count! Local governments provide several things to the citizens they serve, including a governing body, a legal system, and certain public services. In addition, they usually have the power to collect revenue to finance their operations. Local governments generally are classified according to the type of area they administer—counties, towns or townships, municipalities, and special districts. These governments differ widely in their structure and authority.

Authority of Local Government

In the American system of government, the balance between state and federal authority is a delicate one. The framers of the Constitution took great care to ensure that the states would retain the power to make their own laws.

The Constitution does not, however, address the relationship between state and local governments. Town, city, and county governments are created by the state in which they are located, and their powers are defined by state law.

Local governments generally are established by state charters—documents enacted by a state legislature to create a unit of local government. Localities may exercise only those powers expressly granted to them by the state. Local charters often are very long, because they must detail every local government power.

PUBLIC GOOD *One way in which local governments promote the public good is by establishing local law enforcement agencies to protect public safety.* **What defines the powers of town, city, and county governments?**

States often keep local governments on a short leash. Every state restricts in some way the ability of local governments to tax, frequently by specifying what kinds of taxes they may adopt. Some states even regulate the administration of local governments' finances. Around half of the states, however, grant local governments the power of home rule, which allows them to pass a wide range of legislation without state legislative approval. Home rule is now more common because city government has become much more complicated in today's world, and state legislators are unable to handle individual cities' complexities with the same expertise as local administrators.

County Government

All of the states are divided into counties. In every state but two, counties generally function as units of government over a particular area. In Rhode Island and Connecticut they serve only as judicial or electoral districts. (In Louisiana, counties are called parishes; in Alaska, they are called boroughs.) Counties play a strong role in the local governments of the South and West, which are more rural and less densely populated than some other regions. County government began in the largely agricultural southern colonies, where people often lived far away from one another, with few cities and few city governments.

In 1995 there were 3,097 counties in the United States (including parishes and boroughs). In New England, counties serve mostly as judicial districts, with the towns performing the legislative and executive duties that counties perform in other states. In the Middle Atlantic and midwestern states, counties and townships share the functions of local government. In rural and semirural areas, particularly in the South and West, the county may be the main body of local government.

Cities and towns are bound by state and county laws. Most cities—such as Minneapolis, in Hennepin County; Houston, in Harris County; and Los Angeles, in Los Angeles County—are located in a single county. Other large cities straddle several county boundaries. New York City, for example, sprawls across five counties.

In the states where counties play the strongest role, they generally hold mostly legislative and administrative powers. A county's legislative powers may include regulating the use of county property, establishing requirements for business licenses, and levying taxes. Administrative powers include operating welfare programs, hospitals, schools, and jails; keeping records of deeds, marriage licenses, and other legal documents; and supervising elections. Most county governments also maintain public roads, highways, and recreational facilities, as well as prosecute people accused of committing crimes anywhere within the county's borders, including in its cities.

Towns and Townships

In some parts of the country, particularly the Middle Atlantic and midwestern states, units of government called towns and townships provide services in areas outside major cities. In the United States the town form of government began during the colonial days in New England. Often, these small communities created a central government that combined the authority of the church with the lawmaking power of the community. The town included not only the community buildings but also the farms that the inhabitants established on the outskirts.

Early New England townspeople governed their communities through town meetings. A town's inhabitants would meet in a central

PUBLIC GOOD *Maintaining and repairing roads are primary responsibilities of county governments in many western states.* **In what region of the United States were the first counties established?**

PRINCIPLES OF DEMOCRACY *Town meetings attended by all of the town's inhabitants, such as the one pictured here, have typically been replaced by representative town meetings.* **In what regions of the United States are township governments primarily found?**

location to discuss issues and problems and to vote on how they should be handled. Some small New England towns still operate in this manner. Because of population growth and poor attendance, however, many small towns have abolished the town meeting form of government. Others have moved to a representative town meeting, in which citizens elect representatives to attend the meetings and make decisions.

The town still serves as the major decision-making body in local government in New England. It provides many of the same services that are the responsibility of cities and counties in other parts of the country.

Outside of New England, in states such as New Jersey, New York, and Pennsylvania, communities called **townships** were established. Townships in these states were responsible for some of the same functions as towns in New England—providing roads, schools, and means for assisting the poor, for example. As settlers moved to the West, they established similar townships there to perform the services of local government.

Today, however, township government has generally decreased, as municipal and county governments have taken over many of their functions. Township governments are currently found in only 20 states, primarily in the Northeast and Midwest. They are usually governed by a town meeting and elected officers, or they may have a representative town meeting, as in some New England towns.

Municipalities

Most Americans make their homes in **municipalities**—cities, towns, and villages—with a state charter outlining their powers and responsibilities. Some of the nation's 19,000 incorporated municipalities are large, such as Houston or Chicago, while others are tiny, with nearly 90 percent having populations under 10,000. The smallest municipality is thought to be Valley Park, Oklahoma, which in 1994 had only one inhabitant. Another municipality, Hove Mobile Park, North Dakota, has only two residents.

Municipal governments generally provide services beyond those that county or township governments can provide. They are responsible for basic public services, such operating police and fire departments, initiating garbage collection, and constructing and maintaining sewer systems, streets, parks, and public buildings. Municipalities also adopt zoning laws, which restrict land use by area—so

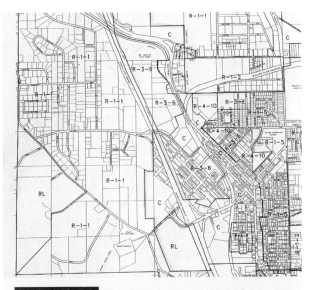

PUBLIC GOOD *This photo shows a typical city zoning map. Municipalities adopt zoning laws that restrict land use by area.* **What services do municipal governments generally provide?**

Basic Forms of Municipal Government

MAYOR-COUNCIL	COUNCIL-MANAGER	COMMISSION
Elected mayor serves as chief executive while separately elected city council serves as legislative body.	Elected city council and often a mayor appoint a professional city manager as chief executive.	Elected commissioners set overall policy while each commissioner heads a city administrative department.

Different forms of municipal government place power into different officials' hands. **In what form of municipal government is the chief executive appointed by an elected city council and often a mayor?**

that fish-processing plants are not located in residential neighborhoods, for example.

There are three basic forms of municipal government in the United States: mayor-council, council-manager, and commission. Although the overall structure of these systems is similar across the country, city governments do vary because each city's charter is designed to meet the specific needs of its various communities.

Mayor-Council Government The **mayor-council system** of city government consists of a separately elected legislature (city council) and chief executive (mayor). Mayors generally serve two- or four-year terms.

In some mayor-council systems the mayor does not play a substantial role. Mayors may lack such powers as veto and appointment, and may also lack the power to create budgets. Called the weak-mayor plan, this form of municipal government became common in the late 1800s and early 1900s, when people feared to give too much power to a single executive and wished to copy the executive branch structure set forth in the U.S. Constitution.

Other cities have what is called the strong-mayor plan, which developed in the late 1800s. This plan is structurally the same as the weak-mayor plan, but gives the mayor more authority. In the strong-mayor plan the mayor holds administrative responsibility and shares policy-making decisions with the council.

In a strong-mayor city the mayor may independently appoint and dismiss department heads without council approval. The mayor also is responsible for carrying out established policies, coordinating the efforts of various departments, preparing the annual budget, and administering it once it is adopted by the council.

City council members typically serve four-year terms and are elected in at-large elections—ones in which the entire city votes for all members. Some cities, however, hold ward elections, in which each ward's residents vote separately for their own council member. Most city councils meet part-time and require their members to attend only one meeting a week. Few councils outside of larger cities maintain any staff.

Council-Manager Government About one third of U.S. city governments operate under the **council-manager system**, in which the public does not elect an independent executive. Instead, the legislature (city council) appoints the chief of the executive branch. The council-manager system is most common in cities with populations between 25,000 and 500,000. Around half of the cities with populations between 250,000 and 500,000 have an appointed executive. Many council-manager cities also have an elected mayor as well, but his or her role is generally limited to the heading of the city council.

The council-manager system executives—called **city managers**—are professionals trained to

City Manager

Experience and training in running the daily affairs of government are not formal job requirements for elected city officials. After all, elected city officials in many communities set general policies but turn over the daily work of municipal government to trained administrators called city managers. In cities that have a council-manager government, the city council appoints the city manager.

One of the most important jobs of a city manager is preparing a municipal budget for the mayor and city council to consider. A city manager's supervision extends to city departments that collect taxes and fees, purchase and maintain equipment, and perform other important duties. With help from the city staff, a city manager also plans for municipal growth by recommending zoning laws and expanding public facilities.

In smaller cities, city managers often must tackle these and other tasks on their own. With a limited number of municipal employees, a small city may rely on its manager to help with such tasks as processing vehicle registration forms, fish and game permits, and other state documents. City managers also must research and write ordinances, respond to citizens' complaints and requests, and prepare reports of city operations.

Applicants for the job of city manager must have a college education and usually a graduate degree in public or business administration. Some positions require city government internships. City managers often start their careers as assistant managers or administrative assistants. City managers generally also need a knowledge of management techniques, experience with computers and various software programs that are used in urban planning and other work, and at least five years of experience working in the field.

One of the jobs of a city manager is to prepare municipal budgets for the mayor and city council to consider.

manage city services in an expert, nonpartisan manner. Typically they have studied public administration in college or graduate school and have risen up the ranks of the city management profession.

City managers are wholly responsible to the council, which can dismiss them at any time. As an appointed official, the city manager is not a political leader, in that he or she does not participate in campaigns or party politics. The city manager does, however, play a role in policy making, which generally involves politics.

Though their roles vary, city managers usually possess the powers of a strong mayor for supervising and directing city government departments. Theoretically, a city manager's primary role is to administer the policies made by the city council. In practice, however, a city manager may become the most influential official in the city, depending on the limits placed on him or her by the city charter.

City managers usually have the right to appoint or remove the heads of various city departments without obtaining the council's approval. They may also act as chief ambassadors and handlers of emergencies (or share these roles with mayors), and prepare and submit executive budgets to city councils. Because city managers are not directly accountable to the voters, some people question whether their power in running city government is too great.

Commission Government A third type of municipal government is the **commission**, which is an elected body that holds both legislative and executive powers. City agencies are managed directly by the commission, which is usually made up of three to nine members. Each commissioner serves individually as the head of a city administrative department, while the commission as a whole makes city policy. Relatively few cities, many of them in Texas and most of them small, have this form of government. The only city with a population over 450,000 that currently has a commission form of government is Portland, Oregon.

Special Districts

About 45,000 local governments are **special districts**—units of government that perform a single service and are generally independent of other units of local government. The boundaries of some special districts coincide with those of a large city, with some special district boundaries extending into a city's suburbs or even into other states. Special districts include seaport facilities, such as the Port of Seattle District, or those in charge of transportation and other important aspects of an urban environment, such the Port Authority of New York and New Jersey.

The most familiar special districts are school districts, which run public schools. Other special districts provide services such as transportation, sewage disposal, and a water supply. These services often are not supplied by a central city because its outlying areas rely on them as well. In addition, special districts sometimes are formed to construct and manage low-rent housing and to undertake other types of urban renewal projects.

Special districts usually are run by commissioners. These public servants are either elected or are appointed by elected officials in city, county, or other local governments.

Metropolitan Government

For years some people have argued that metropolitan areas should have single units of government uniting cities and their suburbs. Supporters of this metropolitan organization argue that metropolitan governments are more cost-effective, can better handle shared problems, and can tax people living in the suburbs who enjoy city services without having to pay for them.

Supporters of metropolitan government have argued that some public services can be produced more efficiently on a large scale than on a small scale. Large sewage disposal plants, for example, can process each pound of sewage for less money than can small plants. Because a metropolitan government can combine operations, it can provide services at a lower cost. Some people also argue that water and air pollution do not respect local boundaries and therefore should be regulated by metropolitan authorities. They also suggest that since transportation systems need to cover an entire metropolitan area, they should be organized under a single government.

Those who support the concept of metropolitan government also point out that it would increase the

Comparing

► Governments

Local Governments in Australia

Australia's local governments, like those in the United States, are often run by local councillors. About 8,300 council members serve in the country's more than 900 local governments. The governments of Australia's six states pass laws establishing and setting the responsibilities for these local councils. Most council seats are elected posts, though a state's governor can, if necessary, dismiss a council and appoint a local administrator.

Responsibilities for local councils are similar to those for local governments in the United States. For example, Australian councils are responsible for keeping track of such local services as road construction and garbage collection. To fund services, local councils levy property taxes. Since the early 1970s they also have received some funding from national and state governments.

Although local councils have some power to set rules for land use and urban planning, state governments generally establish uniform laws that guide the actions of local officials in such matters.

In addition, Australian state governments perform many functions normally handled by local governments in the United States. These functions include maintaining police forces, health services, educational facilities, and public transit systems.

number of people whose taxes go to pay for city expenses. Many suburban residents, particularly those who work in the city, use a variety of city services, such as streets and police protection. A metropolitan government, some people say, would require suburbanites to pay their fair share.

Opponents of metropolitan government disagree. Studies generally do not support the argument that consolidating services makes them cheaper. Opponents also argue that local areas should be allowed to retain their diverse character and not be required to provide the same level of services as other, nearby areas. When local jurisdictions differ in the services they provide and the taxes they impose, people in an area can "shop around" for a community whose services best suit them. In addition, competition for residents encourages local governments to be more responsive.

Only a small number of metropolitan governments have been established in the twentieth century. More frequently, metropolitan areas have established joint councils to discuss and act on common problems. Some proposals for forming metropolitan governments have been voted down by suburban residents who fear that they would be required to pay city taxes and that it would be harder to maintain a high level of public services in their own communities.

POLITICAL FOUNDATIONS *Special districts are formed to provide a single service to the community in which they are located. School districts are the most common type of special district.* **What are some other services that special districts provide?**

CASE STUDY

Consolidating Governments

POLITICAL PROCESSES The growth of suburbs and other communities surrounding large cities often complicates urban planning. As suburbs increase in size, central cities have less room to expand to accommodate their growing populations. In addition, a lack of coordination between governments of central cities and those of surrounding areas creates problems in planning roads, sewage facilities, and other services used by all metropolitan residents.

To ease such problems, some cities and counties have begun to share responsibilities. Several have even consolidated their governments into one metropolitan authority that serves all area residents. Some Consolidated governments include Davidson County–Nashville, Tennessee;

Richmond County–Augusta, Georgia; and Duval County–Jacksonville, Florida. The city of Indianapolis, Indiana, and surrounding Marion County also have a unified government, but few services actually are consolidated.

Portland, Oregon, is another city that has consolidated some of the services in its metropolitan area to better serve residents. In 1977 the Oregon legislature created the Metropolitan Service District (MSD), which includes the city of Portland, 24 neighboring towns and cities, and three surrounding counties. In the mid-1990s the MSD had a population of more than 1.2 million.

Portland and surrounding communities each have their own governments, which provide police and fire protection, community development, and other services. An executive officer and a seven-member council—elected in district elections—set district policy and provide areawide services.

With a budget of $206 million in 1995, the MSD provided land use planning, solid waste management, and water and transportation services. In addition, it operates its own park system, the Metro Washington Park Zoo, the Oregon Convention Center, the Civic Stadium, and the Portland Center

PUBLIC GOOD *Many citizens feel that local governments, although they attempt to provide for the public good, only make people's lives more difficult.* **What is the biggest public service problem that local governments face?**

for the Performing Arts. The state legislature also provided more than $135 million for parkland.

Local Government and the Public Good

Like state governments, most local governments have developed tracking systems to determine how well they are fulfilling their responsibilities to citizens. Some cities, for example, track how quickly potholes are repaired.

The biggest problem that local governments face in delivering services is in adequately meeting the needs of their many communities. Serving urban areas can be particularly difficult, because many solutions to urban problems require increased spending, and people often resist paying higher taxes.

However, some people hold that a more active and informed citizenry will produce local government leaders and alternative solutions that can help improve services without a dramatic increase in spending. The people who live in each local area or community depend on local government to serve them in a variety of ways but may take for granted many of the services local government provides. Though it might be possible for individuals in a community to hire someone to take away the trash, or to protect their neighborhoods from fire and crime, life would be much more difficult if they had to achieve these things alone. People generally find that by working together they receive better and more efficient services.

SECTION 2 — REVIEW

1. Define the following terms: township, municipality, mayor-council system, council-manager system, city manager, commission, special district.

2. What are the differences between the mayor-council form of government and the council-manager form? What is a commission government?

3. What types of services do county governments provide?

4. Why do some people believe that metropolitan areas should be administered by one central government?

5. **Thinking and Writing Critically**
   Why were county governments initially popular in the South?

6. **Applying** **POLITICAL PROCESSES**
   Conduct an Internet search for information on the local governmental organization of a community of your choice. Record the information in a chart.

SECTION 3

REVENUE AND LOCAL SERVICES

Political Dictionary
property tax

Objectives

★ What are the sources of revenue for local governments?

★ What different types of taxes may local governments levy?

★ How do federal and state grants help provide local governments with needed revenue?

★ In what ways do local governments promote the public good?

Unlike the federal government, which depends on federal income taxes for the bulk of its revenue, state and local governments receive most of their money from other sources. Two major sources of revenue are taxes and fees, but local governments also receive extensive state and federal grants. In many cases, local governments also may borrow money to fund major expenditures.

Taxes

The primary method that most local governments use to fund their operations is taxation. A local government's power to tax, however, is limited by the constitution of its state. While local governments' taxation power varies from state to state, citizens generally pay three types of local taxes: property taxes, sales taxes, and income taxes.

Property Taxes The most important source of local government tax revenue is the **property tax**, which is levied on the value of certain kinds of property. About half of property tax revenue goes to pay for schools. The bulk of this revenue is raised by taxes levied on land and buildings, especially

homes, rather than on property such as clothes, furniture, cars, stocks, bonds, or jewelry.

There are two noteworthy features of property taxes. First, property taxes are levied on commercial as well as residential property, but usually not on property belonging to nonprofit or charitable organizations. Thus, a community's ease in raising revenue through the property tax depends on two factors: the value of the houses in the community (which is mostly a function of the community's wealth) and whether the community has a large shopping mall, a factory, or other business with substantial valuable real estate. A small town dominated by a university or other tax-exempt organization will have trouble raising tax revenues because there is not much taxable property. On the other hand, a community that attracts a major shopping mall or a new industry may have an easier time financing its government and meeting the needs of its citizens.

The second noteworthy feature of property taxes is that they generally are based on current property values. This can produce problems

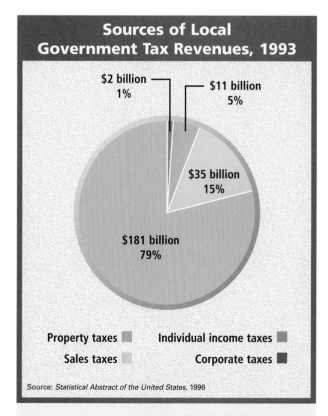

Sources of Local Government Tax Revenues, 1993

$2 billion 1%

$11 billion 5%

$35 billion 15%

$181 billion 79%

Property taxes ■   Individual income taxes ■
Sales taxes ■   Corporate taxes ■

Source: *Statistical Abstract of the United States, 1996*

State and local governments, while they depend heavily on property taxes, receive revenue from a variety of sources. **What source contributes the least to local government revenue?**

when housing values rise. A family of modest means that bought a house 30 years ago may be hurt if soaring property values produce dramatically higher property tax bills.

A problem of property taxes in general lies in the fact that some citizens may own very little taxable property but have large incomes, while others may have low incomes but own a great deal of property. Many people argue that property taxes are regressive and therefore unfair—requiring lower-income people to hand over a larger percentage of their income in taxes than higher-income people are required to pay.

Sales Taxes As noted in Chapter 20, a sales tax is a tax charged as a percentage of the cost of

PRINCIPLES OF DEMOCRACY *To raise revenue, many state and local governments charge sales taxes on a variety of goods and services.* **What items are sometimes exempt from sales taxes?**

services and retail goods. Many items are subject to the sales tax. The local sales tax is relatively new; New York City adopted its first local sales tax only in 1934. Today at least 29 states have authorized their county governments to impose a general sales tax. Some people oppose this tax for the same reason that people oppose the property tax—because it is regressive. Governments sometimes try to ease the effects of the sales tax by exempting essential items such as food, medicine, and clothing.

Income Taxes As noted in Chapter 9, an income tax is a tax levied on an individual's income, including wages or salaries, tips, interest, dividends, and money earned from property. Local governments rely less on personal income taxes than they do on other types of taxes, with only 11 states allowing income taxes at the local level in 1997.

Local governments choose to levy an income tax because it provides much-needed revenue, it is relatively easy and economical to administer, and it is considered by many people to be more equitable than the property or sales tax. In addition, income taxes are collected in the community where the income is earned rather than where the earner resides. This helps local governments—particularly in urban areas where many wage earners work but do not live—because they can collect taxes from both residents and nonresidents of the local community. A local government might, however, drive workers and, potentially, employers out of the city by imposing an income tax.

Fees

In recent years some local governments have come to rely increasingly on user fees, which are typically charged to citizens for the use of parks, recreation centers, other public facilities, parking spaces, mass transit, and utilities. While fees add to local government budgets, they may make services less available to citizens who cannot afford to pay.

On the other hand, some people argue that fees motivate communities to make more economical use of services, thus increasing efficiency and reducing waste. Such motivation does work particularly well for services such as water, which is used extravagantly if no fee or a flat fee—a fee that does not vary according to the level of use—is charged. However, when citizens are charged

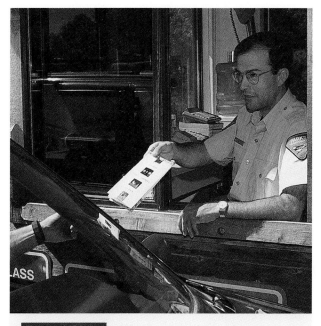

PUBLIC GOOD *Many local governments raise revenue through user fees. Such fees may be charged for admission to county parks.* **For what other services may local governments charge user fees?**

individually for the amount of water they use, they are more likely to conserve.

Grants

As noted in Chapter 4, local governments—like state governments—receive extensive federal grants, called grants-in-aid. During the 1960s the Kennedy and Johnson administrations began increasing the number of grants directly available to local governments. Formerly, the federal government had allocated much more money to state governments to distribute among cities and counties for programs they chose to fund. This change in the administration of federal funding for local governments came partly as a response to lobbying efforts by both the United States Conference of Mayors and the National League of Cities.

Local governments do receive significant revenues through grants from state governments as well. About half of school district funding comes from state grants. Grants help pay for other services as well, including public welfare programs, highway construction and maintenance, and general government support.

As noted in Chapter 4, two types of grants are available to local governments: categorical and block. On a local level, categorical grants might be used for specific purposes, such as vocational education, while block grants would cover public education in general.

Categorical grants can be further classified as project grants, formula grants, or open-ended reimbursements. The process by which the federal government distributes money varies according to the type of grant. To receive a project grant, a local government must submit an application to a federal agency, which can approve or deny the request. In contrast, the federal government distributes formula grants to local governments according to factors established in congressional legislation or administrative regulations. Open-ended reimbursements are federal payments to local and state governments for the expenses arising from the implementation of federal mandates. The federal government typically pays only a portion of the expenses incurred by the mandate; the remaining funds must be provided by the state or local government.

Borrowing

During the 1800s, local governments often managed their finances poorly. For this reason, many state constitutions heavily restrict local governments'

PUBLIC GOOD *Local governments borrow money to finance large projects, such as the Denver International Airport, which is shown under construction in this photograph.* **For what kinds of projects do local governments usually receive grants?**

PUBLIC GOOD *Citizens often have the opportunity to vote in bond elections.* **What are the two types of bonds issued by local governments?**

projects such as the building of schools. Popular referenda are usually required to authorize the use of general-obligation bonds. (As noted in Chapter 20, a referendum is a popular vote on a proposal.) Revenue bonds are usually used to pay for convention centers, city-owned stadiums, utilities, toll roads, and toll bridges and are paid off from the revenue collected through user charges and tolls.

Bonds have been generally considered safe investments since the Great Depression, but they do carry a small element of risk. In late 1994, for example, Orange County, California, was suffering from financial troubles stemming from risky investments by Orange County officials. For some 18 months municipal bondholders were not sure that the county would be able to pay off its debts. In June 1996, however, their worries were over when the county got its finances in order.

In recent years some sellers of local bonds—including Orange County after its financial crisis—have offered insurance to bondholders. The interest rate for insured bonds generally is slightly lower than that for uninsured bonds, but bondholders receive a guarantee that they will be repaid.

ability to borrow money. Although local governments are supposed to maintain a balanced budget, they *can* borrow in anticipation of the revenue they will take in through taxes. They borrow this money through loans from a bank or they issue short-term tax anticipation notes.

Local governments usually issue bonds (which are defined and discussed in Chapter 20) to raise money for large expenditures. Local governments use two types of bonds: general-obligation bonds and revenue bonds. General-obligation bonds rely on the local government's taxing authority for repayment and are usually used to fund long-term

SECTION 3 — REVIEW

1. Define the following term: property tax.

2. Why do some people argue against the use of property taxes?

3. Which type of tax seems fairest: property tax, sales tax, or income tax? Why?

4. For what reason do local governments need to tax citizens?

5. What are some advantages and disadvantages of charging fees for the use of public facilities?

6. **Thinking and Writing Critically**
   Do you think that local government should issue bonds or find other ways to fund necessary services and projects? Explain your answer.

7. **Applying** **POLITICAL FOUNDATIONS**
   Why might some people argue that suburban residents should be required to share in the costs of running the central city on which they depend? Do you think that suburban residents should be forced to share these costs? Why?

CHAPTER 21 — **SUMMARY**

SECTION 1 The size and makeup of a community largely determine its government. Although each is unique, most U.S. communities fit into one or more of the following categories—rural, urban, suburban, or metropolitan.

Today most people live in urban areas, or cities. An urban area usually includes suburbs—residential areas surrounding a city. Suburbs first developed during the mid-1800s.

By 1970 nearly two thirds of Americans lived in what the U.S. government categorizes as metropolitan statistical areas (MSAs), commonly known as metropolitan areas. Metropolitan areas are urban areas made up of a central city of 50,000 people or more, its suburbs, and the surrounding counties that are socially and economically dependent on it.

SECTION 2 Local governments are generally classified according to the type of area they administer—counties, towns or townships, municipalities, or special districts. The authority of local government is determined by the state in which it is located, and its powers are defined by state law.

All of the states are divided into counties. In every state but Rhode Island and Connecticut, where counties serve only as judicial or electoral districts, counties function as units of government over a particular area. Counties play a much stronger role in government in the South and Midwest than they do in the Northeast.

In some parts of the country, particularly in the Middle Atlantic and midwestern states, counties are divided into townships or towns. The town form of government began in the colonial days in New England. The township began in states outside of New England, such as New Jersey, New York, and Pennsylvania, and then spread to the Midwest.

Municipal governments are the most visible local governmental unit. There are three basic forms of municipal government in the United States: mayor-council, council-manager, and commission.

A special district, another type of local governmental unit, addresses a specific need and is generally independent of other units of local government. The most familiar special districts are school districts, which run public schools.

Many people argue that metropolitan areas should have their own units of government. There are several arguments both for and against establishing such a government. Only a small number of such consolidated governments have been established.

SECTION 3 Local governments receive revenue from diverse sources, including taxes, user fees, and state and federal grants. They also borrow funds to provide money for their long-term projects.

The main method most local governments use to fund their operations is taxes. In general, there are three types of taxes—property taxes, sales taxes, and income taxes.

Government fees generally are collected for access to parks, recreation centers, and other public facilities as well as for the use of parking spaces, mass transit, and public utilities. Local governments receive grants from both the state and federal governments.

Most borrowing by local governments is in the form of bonds, which come in two forms—general-obligation bonds and revenue bonds. Other forms of borrowing include short-term bank loans or tax anticipation notes.

> **Government Notebook**
>
> **Review the list that you made in your Government Notebook at the beginning of the chapter. What other services does your local government provide to your community? Add to the list of services in your Notebook.**

REVIEW

REVIEWING CONCEPTS

1. What makes up a metropolitan area?

2. Why has population growth been particularly high in the Sun Belt?

3. How are local governments established? How can state governments restrict the power of local governments?

4. Who runs special districts? What types of services do special districts provide?

5. How are local governments funded?

6. The bulk of property tax revenue comes from taxes on what kind of property?

7. Which sources of revenue do local governments rely on most to fund their schools?

THINKING AND WRITING CRITICALLY

1. **CITIZENSHIP** What form of local government does your community have? Do you think that this form of government adequately serves the needs of the community? Does this form of government encourage citizens to participate in local government? Explain your answers.

2. **PUBLIC GOOD** Many cities have suburbs that depend on city industries for jobs, yet most of these metropolitan areas do not have a *single* unit of government. Imagine that you live in a large city and are a strong supporter of metropolitan government. Write a short speech that you would give at a city council meeting to try to persuade other residents as well as policy makers to adopt your position.

3. **POLITICAL PROCESSES** Local governments assess fees to raise money in order to help fund their operations. What types of fees do you have to pay?

4. **PUBLIC GOOD** Local government provides many necessary services, but some people criticize it for failing to meet the community's needs. In what ways do you think that local government succeeds in promoting the public good? In what ways do you think it fails?

CITIZENSHIP IN YOUR COMMUNITY

Special districts are independent units of local government. They usually provide a specific service or perform a special function. Gather information about the special districts that serve your community or another city in your state. Select one of them to research. What services or functions does it perform? How are officials of the special district selected? How do they determine whether they are meeting the needs of the community? You might want to begin your research by reading articles about the special district in local newspapers or magazines, requesting brochures or other information from the district, and conducting interviews with district officials. Write a two-to-three-page paper and present your findings to your class.

COOPERATIVE PORTFOLIO PROJECT

Colonial New Englanders held town meetings in which they discussed and voted on issues and problems that affected them. Form three groups to research how early New Englanders ran these meetings and what types of issues they addressed. Use the information you find to re-create a town meeting in your classroom. Costumes and props can make the re-enactment more believable. If possible, videotape the performance so you can watch it as a class.

THE INTERNET: LEARNING ONLINE

Conduct an Internet search to learn about the transportation and communications developments that influenced the growth of suburbs in the 1800s and early 1900s. You might want to begin by using search words such as *Henry Ford* and *Model T, James Watt* and *steam engine*, and *Samuel Morse* and *Morse code*. Make a poster with a drawing of the invention you choose to research. Include information about the invention and the inventor, and explain how the invention may have contributed to the growth of suburbs. Remember to list the Web sites that were useful to you in your research.

PRACTICING SKILLS: CONDUCTING RESEARCH

Arrange an interview with the mayor of your city, the city manager, or a city council member to find out more about his or her job, including the necessary qualifications and the everyday duties involved. Prepare for the interview by making a list of questions to ask. Be sure to make eye contact when you ask the questions, and take notes so that you can refer to the answers afterward. If possible, tape-record or videotape the interview to present to the class.

ANALYZING PRIMARY SOURCES

"REINVIGORATING DEMOCRATIC VALUES"

Henry Cisneros, the first Hispanic mayor of a major U.S. city (San Antonio), was appointed secretary of housing and urban development in 1993. In 1990 Cisneros and John Parr, a past president of the National Civic League, cowrote an article addressing the problem of a lack of public participation in government. Read the following excerpt and answer the questions that follow.

❝ *Apart from personal behaviors, current patterns of civic involvement also are shaped by features of our democratic system, such as voter registration and campaign regulation practices—or the availability of the initiative, referendum, and recall—affecting perceptions [awareness] of citizen access to the governance [governing] process. Beyond shortcomings of the campaign process and election practices, the changing nature of our communities, in terms of demographics [population statistics] and economics, also affects citizens' perceptions of both their relationships with their neighbors and the impact they can have on public decision making.*

In alarming numbers, citizens are becoming increasingly disengaged from public affairs, uninterested in the political process and public institutions, and skeptical that government has the talent, resources, and moral courage to solve problems. . . .

Compounding this withdrawal from involvement is that the current practice of democracy also has deteriorated. Evidence of this decline includes political campaigns that focus on personalities rather than public problems . . . and a trivialization of public discourse, characterized by discussion of issues favoring the 'sound bite' over the debate. Popular attention is diverted from serious problems of broad impact . . . to emotionally charged issues appealing to narrow, vocal interests. . . .

The problems confronting us as a nation and as communities require immediate attention. The solutions will not come from government alone. The society we want and can have will be achieved only through the combined effort of involved and concerned citizens and the public, private and voluntary sectors. . . . We must translate our passive anxiety into positive action for constructive change. . . . We must pledge our future to a prescription for strong citizen democracy of responsibility, understanding, consensus [general agreement], and cooperation. ❞

1. According to the authors, what factors help shape public participation in "governance"?

2. Do you think that public participation on a local level can help solve problems facing the country? Explain your answer.

YOUR ASSIGNMENT

Council Member for a Day

Imagine that you and other members of your group serve on a town council in a rural area of your state. Your town has a mayor-council form of government. The mayor and council members are concerned about the lack of space in the town hall to accommodate the current staff and the new town employees whom the council expects to hire next year. In anticipation, the town council has decided to expand the town hall. Now you and other council members are searching for ways to pay for the construction.

The town council must draft legislation that spells out a plan to raise money for the town hall's expansion. If voter approval is necessary for any part of the funding plan, you should include a schedule for bond or other elections.

To help you in drafting the legislation, you and other council members must review important information regarding the town's taxing authority as well as funding options for the construction. That information, which can be found on the following pages, includes these documents: a newspaper clipping about local taxes, a letter about the funding from the mayor to a local newspaper, a state law governing the taxing power of local governments, a rough town budget report, and public opinion polls. When you finish reviewing the information, answer the accompanying questions in your Government Notebook.

You should also consider some other information about your town. First, your town's government already levies local property taxes. Second, because your town is small and located in a rural area, its economy relies largely on agriculture. In fact, your town contains no large businesses, industries, or retail centers. Most town residents have been reluctant in the past to support property tax increases. In addition, small-business owners worry that levying a local sales tax would hurt business. There is also little support for levying an income tax.

After you have reviewed the information in this activity, meet with other council members to debate a course of action. Then prepare legislation that can win a majority of the votes on your council.

ANOTHER TAX INCREASE?

Last spring, for the third time in as many years, our property taxes went up. The increase was only slight, and Forest Park citizens bore it gladly for the sake of the new elementary school. However, with growing talk about a possible sales tax increase or a new local income tax to pay for construction to expand the town hall, people are beginning to grumble.

"We just had a tax increase! I for one am not ready to hand over more of my hard-earned money for some politician's pet project. They should cut some of their current spending to pay for their expansion if they really need it," commented Ronald Walker, a local businessman.

Melanie Hopkins, a cashier at the grocery store, said, "I sure don't want to pay any more taxes. It seems like I hardly have any money left for my family as it is. But my aunt works for the town, and she says that the situation at the town hall is terrible. She has to share an office with three other people, and they can barely walk around all the filing cabinets and office equipment. I'm sure it's a fire hazard, among other things."

Fire Chief Tony Nguyen confirmed Hopkins's suspicion. "It's a fire hazard all right. By state law, I should shut down the town hall. But then who would be running things around here? We need the expansion, but I don't know how we're going to pay for it."

Citizens are largely resistant to a new tax, but according to town officials, the situation at the town hall is urgent. For more information on this issue, see Mayor Mason's letter to the editor on page 3B.

▼ WHAT DO YOU THINK?

★ What reason does the mayor give for overcrowding in the town hall?

★ What options does Mayor Mason offer readers for funding the town hall expansion?

★ Which options do you think would be best for town officials to pursue?

Letters to the Editor

Mayor Urges Support of Town Hall Expansion

I am writing this letter to urge the citizens of Forest Park to support the town hall expansion effort. I hope you will take a few minutes to read my letter, because our community needs to understand the urgent need for more space in town hall.

The main reason the council has decided to expand the town hall is that the building is severely overcrowded. Built 80 years ago, it is designed to accommodate only about 20 employees. Currently, 45 employees are crowded into the building's offices. The town council expects to hire several new employees over the next year.

Why is the number of town employees increasing so quickly? More and more people move to Forest Park each month. Some do so because they like the peaceful lifestyle and beautiful countryside. Others choose Forest Park because it is within easy driving distance of their jobs in nearby cities.

Of course, most people already agree that we need to expand town hall. What is not clear is whether there is enough support to pay for the expansion. It will be expensive. Town officials estimate that it will cost about $300,000 a year to pay off general-obligation bonds for construction.

Forest Park residents will have to pay most of the cost. The choice, of course, is between raising taxes or cutting the budget. If we cut the budget, we must either lay off town employees or decrease the services that the town provides. The only other option is to put the expansion of the town hall on hold.

I believe we must be prepared to pay for construction through higher taxes. Higher taxes will be difficult for many people. Nevertheless, our community needs to have the facilities to continue to provide the services this town needs. Let's all pitch in and help make it happen. I encourage each of you to attend the upcoming town council meetings to let us know what you think about the issue.

Sheila Mason
Mayor

PUBLIC POLICY LAB

Local Government: State Book of Laws

Taxing Authority for Local Governments

A. Municipal Improvements

1. Cities and towns throughout the state have the authority to levy the following taxes to pay for town improvements:
   a. property taxes,
   b. sales taxes, and
   c. income taxes.

2. City and town governments may set tax rates for funding municipal services and maintenance under the following conditions:
   a. revenue from tax rate increases in any one year may not exceed 5 percent of the city or town's current total budget without voter approval;
   b. general elections to decide a tax increase must be held between 30 and 90 days of the local government's approving it; and
   c. revenue from tax rate increases in any one year may not exceed 15 percent of the city or town's current budget with or without voter approval.

▲ WHAT DO YOU THINK?

★ What kinds of taxes may town governments levy to pay for town services or improvements?

★ By how much may city governments raise tax rates annually before they must seek approval from local voters?

★ What is the upper limit of a tax rate increase, even with voter approval?

★ Why do you think state law requires voter approval for tax rate increases of more than 5 percent of the current budget and forbids them above a set limit?

★ You can see in the budget report that the estimated annual cost of paying off general-obligation bonds to expand the town hall is $300,000. Would those annual payments exceed 5 percent of the town's current budget?

 FROM THE OFFICE OF THE TOWN BUDGET DEPARTMENT

TO: Town Council Members
FROM: Jacqueline Soliz, Town Budget Department
RE: Budget Requirements for Town Growth

Per your request during the last council meeting, the Town Budget Department is preparing a report providing rough budget figures regarding current spending and the cost of the proposed expansion of the town hall. The following items are a summary of the main points included in the report:

a. Current annual town budget: $115.5 million
b. Estimated annual cost of proposed town hall expansion: $300,000
c. Possible sources of local revenue:
   • general-obligation bonds, to be paid off by new local sales or income taxes
   • property tax increase of 3 percent
   • decreased spending on an existing program [see below]

Currently, the budget is used to pay for public safety, town administrative services, public health, public recreation and culture, public works, social services, development, and municipal courts.

The full report will be available by the end of the week.

STATE UNIVERSITY
DEPARTMENT OF PUBLIC AFFAIRS

Dear Mayor Mason:

Thank you for asking me to poll residents in your area about expanding the town hall. I hope this information will help you in coming to a decision about how to pay for the construction.

To help me conduct the poll, I contacted graduate students in the Department of Public Affairs and the Department of Economics here at State University. With their help, I conducted two telephone polls in your community last month. The first poll question asked respondents whether they believed an expansion of the town hall was needed. The second question asked respondents their opinions about how the construction costs of the town hall expansion should be funded.

The poll results are shown in the attached two pie charts. If I can be of further assistance, please let me know.

Sincerely,

Peter Simek

Professor Peter Simek
Department of Public Affairs
State University

▼ WHAT DO YOU THINK?

★ What percentage of poll respondents believes that town hall expansion is needed?

★ Review the results of both polls. How likely do you think voters are to approve the use of general-obligation bonds to fund the expansion of city hall?

"Town officials say that the Forest Park town hall does not have adequate space for the current town employees, and the town council expects to hire several new employees this year. To resolve this problem, the council is proposing to expand the town hall. In your opinion, is this expansion necessary?"

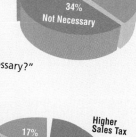

Don't Know 8%
Necessary 58%
34% Not Necessary

"In your opinion, how should the town pay for the expansion of the town hall?"

Higher Property Tax
Don't Know 10%
17%
Higher Sales Tax
26%
2% New Income Tax
45% Budget Cuts

THINGS TO DO

1. Review with the other council members in your group the information and questions in this activity.

2. Work with other council members to decide on a course of action regarding expansion of the town hall. You do not need to provide specific numbers if you decide to increase taxes or levy new ones. For example, you might simply agree to raise property taxes by the amount necessary to cover the construction costs or you may decide to make budget cuts for the necessary amount. You must, however, be prepared to explain the reasoning behind the choices you make.

3. The action you choose must be capable of winning a majority vote of the council. Draft legislation calling for the measures agreed upon by the council. In the legislation, you may write that specific tax rates will be set after a study by the Town Budget Department. Then take a formal and recorded vote of council members. Because it is a formal document, your final legislation should be typed or neatly handwritten and should be accompanied by the mayor's signature and the town's official seal.

4. Present and explain the reasoning behind your legislation to the rest of the class.

UNIT
8

PUBLIC POLICY LAB

How do United Nations ambassadors help solve conflicts among countries? Find out by reading this unit and taking the Public Policy Lab challenge on pages 552–55.

THE UNITED STATES AND THE WORLD

COMPARING POLITICAL AND ECONOMIC SYSTEMS

Do you remember when the Soviet Union dissolved or when the Berlin Wall was torn down? For many people around the world, these events showed the failures and successes of several major political and economic systems.

Varying political and economic systems have long been a feature of human societies. During the 1900s, democracy has flourished in some nations, while authoritarian governments have emerged in others. In some parts of the world, communist revolutionaries attempted to establish a social order without economic classes. In yet others, leaders have worked to establish socialism. As the twentieth century comes to a close, capitalism appears to be either firmly in place or on the rise everywhere. By studying the world's various political and economic systems, one can gain insight into these styles of governing and the cultures that have developed them.

Government Notebook

In your opinion, why might different societies and their leaders form different kinds of political and economic systems? What problems or difficulties might inspire the development of new systems? Write your answers in your Government Notebook.

CAPITALISM

Political Dictionary

entrepreneur
capitalist
factor of production
consumer
competition
supply and demand
profit
self-interest
mixed economy

Objectives

★ What are the four factors of production?
★ In what way is a free-market economy an essential aspect of capitalism?
★ How do supply and demand, competition, and the profit motive affect capitalist economies?
★ How does the U.S. economy differ from Adam Smith's capitalist ideas?

Have you ever thought about starting your own company? If you bought a piece of land, built your own business there, and hired employees to work in the business, you would be an entrepreneur and a capitalist. An **entrepreneur** is a person who takes on the risk of starting, organizing, and operating a business, while a **capitalist** is a person who invests his or her money, land, or machinery in a business. Entrepreneurs and capitalists form the basis of the capitalist system, establishing and maintaining the businesses and industries that drive a free-enterprise economy.

Today the United States, Japan, Mexico, and Taiwan, for example, have some form of capitalist economy. To be classified as capitalist, a country must have an economy geared around some combination of the following principles—private ownership, a market economy, competition, and profit.

Private Ownership Central to the capitalist system is private, or nongovernmental, control over the factors of production. The **factors of production** are the basic resources needed for a country's economy. They include natural resources, human resources, capital resources—such as money and machinery that are needed to produce goods—and entrepreneurship. The factors of production for a shoe factory, for example, would include the land the factory occupies, the factory itself, the machines and materials required to make the shoes, the employees, and the person or people who started and run the business.

Private ownership means that individuals and corporations—rather than the government—own or control the factors of production. In many capitalist societies, governments own some natural resources, such as land, as well as basic public services, such as the postal system and public utilities. However, businesses in the United States and other capitalist nations are owned by individuals and corporations.

The Four Factors of Production

Natural Resources **Human Resources**

Capital Resources **Entrepreneurship**

GRAND OPENING

*The basic resources needed for a country's economy are known as the factors of production. **What are some types of capital resources?***

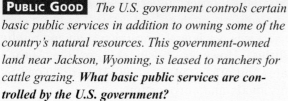

PUBLIC GOOD *The U.S. government controls certain basic public services in addition to owning some of the country's natural resources. This government-owned land near Jackson, Wyoming, is leased to ranchers for cattle grazing.* **What basic public services are controlled by the U.S. government?**

Market Economy A second principle of capitalism is the market economy. In precapitalist economies each family generally produced almost everything it needed, trading with others for items the family could not make itself. In this type of economy, individuals had to perform several jobs in order to make the things they needed. In a free-market economy, however, the products from an individual's labor are not for his or her use alone, but are offered for sale in the market. For example, if you were to pick strawberries as an agricultural worker, you would not take them home for your own use. You would pick the strawberries for your employer, who would pay you for your labor. As noted in Chapter 9, goods and services are exchanged freely in a free-market economy, and the government has little say in what, how, and for whom they are produced.

Critical to free-market economies is the ability of **consumers**, or buyers of products, to choose freely from among goods offered for sale. Consumers therefore actively influence what and how much will be produced, through the pressures their buying decisions put on the market.

Competition and Profit Another essential element of capitalism is **competition**—the effort that sellers of similar products exert in obtaining the

business of consumers. When individuals and corporations must compete in the market economy, they are pressured to produce improved products in order to attract buyers. In a competitive market the prices of goods are determined by two primary factors—supply and demand. Under the laws of **supply and demand**, goods that are in great supply and for which there is little demand tend to have low prices. Conversely, goods that are in low supply and for which there is high demand have high prices.

Another cornerstone of capitalist economies is **profit**—the difference between the revenue received from the sale of a good or service and the costs of providing it. A capitalist system works because the opportunity to earn profits lures people to invest their capital. Industries that generate particularly high profits encourage higher levels of investment. According to the laws of supply and demand, however, an increase in the supply of an industry's products forces down their prices and eventually decreases profits.

Roots of Capitalism

From around the 800s to the late 1300s, economic and social systems in Europe were dominated by feudal monarchies. Feudalism was based on the rule of an aristocratic class of titled landowners—such as barons, dukes, earls, and counts—who answered to a royal family headed by a monarch. As noted in Chapter 1, many people at that time believed that God chose royal families and their heirs to rule over kingdoms and nations. In feudal societies, people's fates depended on the class into which they were born. Moving into a higher class was almost impossible. People who were born peasants almost always lived their entire lives as peasants, working the land for the benefit of the landowners and royal families.

Eventually the feudal order was challenged by a middle class of entrepreneurs that first arose in cities. New theories of government and economics emerged as this rising business class gained influence. Writers and theorists such as Scottish economist Adam Smith, who wrote *An Inquiry into the Nature and Causes of the Wealth of Nations* in the 1700s, popularized ideas about how a free market could regulate economic activity.

Smith stated that everyone in a capitalist economy competes with everyone else to seek the greatest possible advantage from each market transaction. Thus the primary motivation for

The Granger Collection, New York

WORLD AFFAIRS *Scottish economist Adam Smith popularized ideas about how a free market regulates economic activity.* **In what century did Smith publish his major writings?**

it has developed what can be called a **mixed economy**, one in which private enterprise and government action both play a role. The government of a capitalist nation may enact some regulations, but its role in the economy is limited.

As noted in Chapter 9, the government in a capitalist society such as the United States can encourage economic growth by means of fiscal policy—for example, by altering the federal budget or by increasing or decreasing taxes. Conversely, to regulate the nation's economy, the Federal Reserve may use monetary policy, raising or lowering interest

economic behavior is **self-interest**—the impulse that encourages people to fulfill their needs and wants. Self-interest helps the economy grow as businesses compete with each other to provide goods and services to meet consumers' needs and wants. This competition brings about great efficiency because resources are used only to produce the goods and services for which people are most willing to pay. People's pursuit of their own self-interest thus serves as an "invisible hand," guiding the market to promote the public good.

Smith argued that government efforts to regulate prices or restrict free trade interferes with the invisible hand's ability to satisfy consumer wants. He said that the laws of supply and demand would assure that enough goods would be produced to meet the needs of the population. In addition, competition among entrepreneurs would both control profit levels, and also encourage both new and more efficient production methods.

Capitalism in the United States and in Welfare States

The United States does not practice the pure market principles that Smith envisioned. Instead,

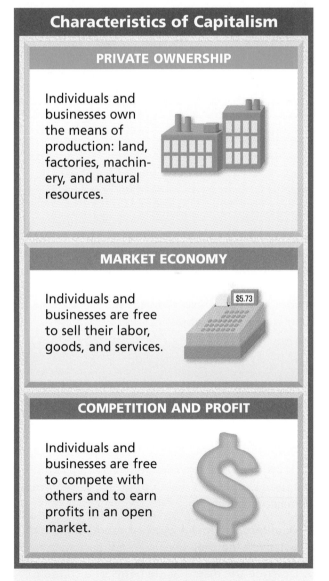

Characteristics of Capitalism

PRIVATE OWNERSHIP

Individuals and businesses own the means of production: land, factories, machinery, and natural resources.

MARKET ECONOMY

Individuals and businesses are free to sell their labor, goods, and services.

$5.73

COMPETITION AND PROFIT

Individuals and businesses are free to compete with others and to earn profits in an open market.

Capitalistic economies are characterized by private ownership, free markets, competition, and profit. **In a capitalist economy, what assures that enough goods will be produced to meet the needs of the population?**

PUBLIC GOOD *In the United States's capitalist economy, the government regulates industry, taxes citizens, and provides social services.* **In what other ways is the government involved in the economy?**

rates to discourage or encourage the borrowing of money. Taxing and spending policies enable the government to provide social services such as education, as well as provide for national defense. The government also may regulate health and safety standards in the workplace.

Otherwise, governments of countries with market economies pass few regulations on the operation of supply and demand. In a capitalist economy such as that of the United States, the government acts as a kind of referee. Although it helps regulate interactions among businesses, it generally does not interrupt the operations of capitalists, business owners, or the market economy. In the United States, private industries have great leeway in decision making, but the U.S. government influences the economy by regulating business practices, taxing citizens, and providing social services. The government also influences the economy in much the same way as a large business does through its purchases of goods and services from the private sector and as an employer of a significant portion of the population.

Many mixed economies today operate under what is called welfare state capitalism—government provides widespread social services financed by taxes. Examples of countries with welfare state capitalist economies include Brazil, Canada, Germany, Mexico, and the United Kingdom.

Welfare state capitalist governments differ from one another primarily in the extent to which they regulate industry, the rate at which they tax businesses and individuals, and the types of social services they provide. In mixed economies, taxes usually fund basic public services, social services such as monetary assistance to the poor, and health care, education, and public housing. Some mixed economies, particularly those in Europe, provide many additional services as well.

SECTION 1 — REVIEW

1. Define the following terms: entrepreneur, capitalist, factor of production, consumer, competition, supply and demand, profit, self-interest, mixed economy.

2. What are the four factors of production, and what role do they play in a capitalist system?

3. Describe the essential elements of a capitalist economy.

4. What are the differences between Adam Smith's capitalist ideas and the way in which the U.S. economy is structured?

5. **Thinking and Writing Critically**
   In what ways do you think capitalism offers people more political and economic freedom? In what ways might it limit those freedoms for some people?

6. **Applying** **POLITICAL FOUNDATIONS**
   Conduct an Internet search to find information on Adam Smith. Use that information to write a short profile of him. Be sure to include details about his life and work, such as the place and dates of his birth and death and the titles of his significant writings.

SOCIALISM

Political Dictionary

socialism
democratic socialism
proletariat
bourgeoisie
communism
nationalization
command economy

Objectives

★ What are some of the basic principles of socialism?

★ What are some nations that have strong socialist traditions?

★ What is a welfare state?

As you have read, capitalism focuses on private ownership, profit, competition, and the operation of the free market. In such a system, people attain different levels of wealth and success, which produces inequality in their standard of living. Some people are quite wealthy, while others are poor. Another economic system attempts to reduce these inequalities of wealth by redistributing money throughout society. Under this system, **socialism**, the government or the people as a whole own, or at least control, the factors of production and manage the distribution of goods. Various types of socialism have been developed to fit different countries' unique cultural, social, economic, and political needs.

History of Socialism

Socialism as an organized political movement began in western Europe in the late 1700s and early 1800s after the Industrial Revolution—when Western countries moved from agricultural to industrial economies. Factories subjected laborers to harsh working conditions and worsened the unequal distribution of wealth. Some political thinkers, including Robert Owen and Charles Fourier, responded by calling for reform to address these economic and social inequalities.

Early socialists sought to expand civil liberties and to secure greater economic equality. They concentrated on expanding voting rights and on establishing the ability of trade unions to bargain collectively with the management of corporations and other businesses. Following the ideas of **democratic socialism**, people sought to use these and other peaceful methods to eliminate capitalism. Industrial factory workers and intellectuals who favored reform worked together in this movement's early political parties. Other political theorists, however, had more revolutionary ideas about political and social reform.

Karl Marx The founder of modern socialist thought is German political and economic theorist Karl Marx, who along with German social scientist Friedrich Engels wrote important works on socialism during the 1800s. These texts criticized capitalism, saying that free markets would enable the wealthy to take advantage of the workers.

Marx urged the **proletariat**—the workers—to violently overthrow the **bourgeoisie**—the people

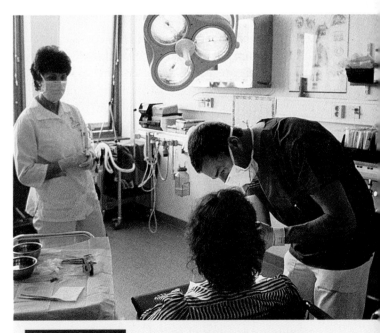

WORLD AFFAIRS *In Sweden, a democratic socialist country, the government provides citizens with health care.* **How did democratic socialists hope to eliminate capitalism?**

WORLD AFFAIRS *Karl Marx (pictured here) and Friedrich Engels wrote the* Communist Manifesto, *which urges workers to overthrow capitalist governments.* **Of what economic and political system do Marx and Engels's theories form the foundation?**

who own the means of production in a capitalist nation. Over time, his ideas formed the foundation of authoritarian socialism, or **communism**, which is based on government ownership or control of nearly all of the factors of production. (Communist doctrine is more fully explained in Section 3.)

Characteristics of Democratic Socialism

Democratic socialism has varied a great deal from nation to nation. In general, however, socialist economies all involve widespread social services and at least some **nationalization**, in which the government takes over industries. In most democratic socialist countries, government ownership is limited to industries of key national concern, such as electric utilities and transportation systems. Individuals are able to influence economic planning through the election of government officials. High taxes are

generally a feature of socialist economies as well. One characteristic that is shared by both socialist and communist countries is that they all operate under command economies, though the organization of this system varies widely among these countries.

Many European nations, including Denmark, Austria, and Sweden, practice democratic socialism. In addition, economies of some less-developed countries, such as India, were traditionally based on democratic socialism. In recent years, many of these economies have moved closer to capitalism.

Social Services and the Welfare State Most socialists believe that government should assure the equal distribution of certain basic social services. For this reason, nations with strong democratic socialist traditions—such as Israel, Sweden, and Australia—have enacted comprehensive social service programs, including old-age pensions, income supplements, health care, child care, unemployment compensation, and supplemental payments to people with children. Socialists also have attempted to expand educational opportunities for all people, eliminate discrimination, replan the layout of towns and cities, tear down slums and build new houses, and rebuild societies by cooperation instead of through competition and profit. As noted in Section 1, a government that provides widespread social services funded by taxes is a welfare state.

WORLD AFFAIRS *This textile-manufacturing plant belongs to the Egyptian government, which owns many of Egypt's major industries.* **Why do socialist countries nationalize industries?**

RESEARCHER CD-ROM

Careers in Government

International Broadcasting Bureau

In 1994 the U.S. International Broadcasting Bureau was established to coordinate all U.S. government international broadcast services. These services include U.S. and international news and programming for listeners around the world.

The most familiar of these broadcast services is Voice of America (VOA). VOA radio began airing on February 24, 1942, to provide news information to listeners in Germany and Nazi-occupied Europe during World War II. VOA remained on air after the war and today broadcasts in 52 languages to about 86 million listeners each week. Since October 1996 VOA also has broadcast television programs. All VOA programming is produced in Washington, D.C.

Every VOA broadcaster must be a fluent speaker of his or her target audience's language. Broadcasters also must possess a wide range of journalistic skills, such as interviewing, writing, and reporting for radio. Many VOA broadcasters pick up their skills while earning a college or graduate degree in print or broadcast journalism.

Most VOA broadcasting job applicants have experience reporting or editing for a news publication, a broadcaster, or a wire service, such as the Associated Press. In addition, applicants must pass an examination that tests their skills and experience, and foreign-language abilities.

A 24-hour hotline provides information about job openings throughout the federal government. Anyone interested in jobs with an International Broadcasting Bureau agency or with any other federal agency should submit a resumé or an official job application to the office in question.

Every Voice of America broadcaster must have a wide variety of journalistic skills and be fluent in the language of his or her target audience.

Nationalization Although democratic socialists do not insist that government control of the means of production is always necessary, some socialist governments try to halt the concentration of wealth through the nationalization of basic industries and services such as banking, transportation, electric power, and mining. Because government operates those businesses, all citizens own them and collectively benefit from any of their profits.

Taxation Although all governments tax their citizens to help pay for government services and programs, under socialism, taxes are extremely high. For example, from the 1920s until 1991, Sweden was solidly socialist, and its taxes were

among the highest in Europe. The Swedish government used the tax revenues to finance comprehensive health insurance, unemployment insurance, retirement benefits, public and college education, public housing, and child care. Although the Swedish standard of living was extremely high, taxes were a source of great controversy. High taxes forced workers to demand higher wages. To cover the cost of these wage hikes, companies increased the prices of their goods. Moreover, tax revenues lagged behind the rising costs of social programs. As a result, the government ran deficits, borrowing heavily to meet its economic and social goals.

In the 1991 election, the Social Democrats lost

Command Economies

Both socialist and communist countries operate, wholly or in part, under what is called a command economy, or planned economy. In a **command economy**, government authorities control some or all of the major economic processes. Prices, for example, are determined by government regulations rather than by the interaction of supply and demand in the marketplace. Decisions about what, when, and by whom goods and services will be produced are made by government officials, often called central planners.

Although both democratic socialist countries and communist countries operate to at least some extent under command economies, the extent to which the government controls the economic activity varies significantly. In a democratic socialist economy, the government controls only a portion of the economy. For example, the government might own and operate telephone networks, public transportation, and postal and shipping services, and heavily regulate only a few industries. As you will learn in Section 3, in a communist country the government owns or controls all areas of the economy.

POLITICAL PROCESSES *The Eastern European nation of Romania operated under a communist command economy before its communist government fell in the early 1990s. Today many of the country's formerly government-owned enterprises have come under private control.* **How much of the economy does the government control in a democratic socialist country?**

control of the government, and a nonsocialist government was formed under the leadership of the Moderate Party. In 1994, however, the Social Democrats once again gained control of the government after winning the election. The government is now working to ease some of the country's economic problems by restructuring government finances. It has launched a government program to limit welfare benefits and turn over the operation of some government services to private firms.

SECTION 2 — **REVIEW**

1. Define the following terms: socialism, democratic socialism, proletariat, bourgeoisie, communism, nationalization, command economy.

2. How do Karl Marx's ideas differ from those of democratic socialism?

3. What are the two main principles of socialism, and why are they important?

4. What are four characteristics of democratic socialism?

5. **Thinking and Writing Critically**
   What features of socialism strike you as being most attractive, and which as least attractive?

6. **Applying** **POLITICAL PROCESSES** Although the United States is a capitalist society, some U. S. government policies have reflected socialist principles. Give some examples of policies that you think reflect socialist principles. Do you think these policies have helped or hurt people in the United States? Explain your answer.

COMMUNISM

Political Dictionary

class struggle
Communist Manifesto
forces of production
relations of production
vanguard
Bolsheviks
Communist Party

Objectives

★ What are some of the basic principles of communism as described by Karl Marx?
★ How did Vladimir Lenin's concept of communism differ from that of Marx?
★ What changes occurred in the Soviet Union under Joseph Stalin?
★ Why did the Soviet Union eventually dissolve?

Since 1917, communist revolutions promising sweeping political, economic, and social change have taken place in countries around the globe. Although most of the resulting communist governments no longer exist, communism has powerfully shaped history and the way people look at power and politics around the world. Nations that have experienced communist rule include Bulgaria, Cuba, China, Hungary, North Korea, Poland, Romania, the Soviet Union, and Vietnam. In the late 1980s most of these countries abandoned communism. Others, such as China, have been slowly changing their economic and political systems to reflect some democratic socialist and capitalist principles. Only Cuba and North Korea remain truly communist.

Communist Thought

As noted in Section 2, Karl Marx is considered the founder of modern socialist ideology; however, his more revolutionary views became the founding principles of an authoritarian style of social-

ism, or communism. Revolutionary leaders from around the world have based their policies and goals on Marxist thought.

Marx's View of History One of Marx's most important contributions to economic thought lies in his interpretation of past events. Marx stated that throughout history all societies have been characterized by **class struggle**—the ongoing competition between economic groups for resources and power. The class struggle in Europe between the 800s and the late 1300s took place between the feudal lords and their subjects. In the capitalist societies that followed feudalism, this struggle has taken place between the bourgeoisie and the proletariat.

In his **Communist Manifesto,** which he cowrote with Friedrich Engels, Marx argued that economic factors have played the dominant role in shaping history. In an agricultural society, land is the basic means of production and those who own it acquire prominence and make up the ruling class. According to Marx, these landowners

WORLD AFFAIRS *Karl Marx argued that class struggle influenced the histories of all societies, as illustrated in this fifteenth-century painting showing property owners vowing service and allegiance to their feudal lord.* **According to Marx, what factors play the dominant role in shaping history?**

had more influence than any governments and other formal organizations in shaping policy, social standards, and values.

Marx believed that because capitalists own the means of production in modern, industrial society, they hold the power. Capitalists not only rule society economically, they also determine its political destiny. In addition, they dominate the law, education, the press, and artistic and literary expression in order to maintain their property ownership.

Concepts of Production
Two other concepts are central to Marx's idea of social change. First, Marx described what he referred to as **forces of production**, the various elements that fuel an economy. The greatest forces of production today are probably technological and scientific knowledge. Marx also discussed the **relations of production**, economic relationships that are affected by social institutions—for example, relations between buyers and sellers.

Marx argued that in a free-market economy the growth of technology and the other forces of production are hampered by capitalism's flawed relations of production. Workers do not get paid enough, and they therefore cannot buy products the economy is able to produce. Economic crisis is the result.

POLITICAL PROCESSES *This Russian propaganda poster depicts the class struggle. The banner on the left reads, "Long live workers' and peasants' Soviet power!" The caption below it reads, "Death to capitalism." The banner on the right reads, "All power to capitalists and death to workers and peasants!" The caption below it reads, "Death under the heel of capitalism."* **What were Marx's primary objections to capitalism?**

Revolution
Marx's primary objections to capitalism were to what he saw as its inefficiencies and injustices. To overcome these problems, Marx argued, workers must stage a violent revolution. Unlike democratic socialists, who believe in peaceful change through elections and participatory democracy, Marxists spoke of a war between the classes. Workers would have to rise up and seize the means of production from the capitalist class. Marx assumed that, over time, people of the working class would develop a consciousness, or awareness, that the capitalists were taking advantage of them. Working-class leaders would then come forth to head revolutionary movements. Marx believed that these working-class movements would develop around the world to defeat capitalism.

Marx assumed that a global communist society would emerge after the revolution. There would be no social or economic classes and no private property, and workers would own the means of production, including transportation, railways, and factories. In addition, the government would no longer serve as an agent of class rule. In a classless society, government would eventually wither away.

Marx's insights into the importance of material conditions and economic systems have helped modern scholars understand social forces much more thoroughly. However, Marx's economic interpretations have proved too general and too simplistic. Even though economic factors are critical to people's interactions with one another, they are not the key factors in all situations. Factors such as ideology, religious beliefs, and nationalism have often played more important roles in social and international conflicts. In addition, Marx's economic predictions about the increasing misery of the working class and the inability of capitalism to accommodate technological progress have proved wildly inaccurate. Furthermore, the governments of the Marxist states that have been established did not wither away, but rather turned totalitarian.

Proletarian Dictatorship
Once a revolution took place, Marx believed that a "dictatorship of the proletariat" would be necessary to make the transition from capitalism to communism. During this transition, Marx thought that the proletariat would need to use force, even terror, to succeed in their communist revolution and abolish both the

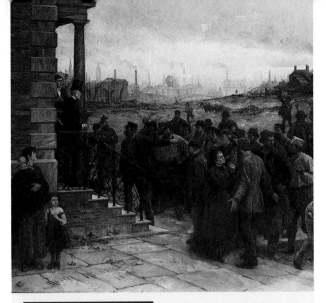

POLITICAL PROCESSES *This 1886 painting by Robert Koehler titled* The Strike *shows workers protesting harsh working conditions.* **How did Marx believe that communism would be established?**

ruling classes and private ownership. Even though Marx hoped for a society in which no class ruled over another, he supported the working class's use of violence against the ruling class to achieve this goal.

For Marx, who argued that this situation could only exist in a communist society where capitalist rulers could not dominate workers, economic equality would be achieved by the elimination of class privileges. Marx further believed that in the highest stage of communism all people would reach a state of full equality.

The World's First Communist Nation

Despite Marx's focus on overthrowing modern capitalism, the first communist nation was not to be a highly developed, industrial society. Instead, the first successful communist uprising occurred in Russia, an economically underdeveloped nation.

Vladimir Lenin Vladimir Lenin, a Russian intellectual and revolutionary, was the most influential communist leader of the early 1900s. Although Lenin considered himself a faithful follower of Marx, he emphasized politics over economics. As a result, he stressed that a **vanguard**—the people he hoped would lead a communist revolution in his country—should form a professionally organized political party. In working toward this aim, Lenin spent 17 years abroad leading and helping develop the **Bolsheviks**, a communist party organization in Russia.

Unlike Marx, Lenin did not believe that a nation had to become a fully industrial society before a revolution could occur. He thought it would be smarter to smash capitalism where it was politically and organizationally weakest—for example, in economically underdeveloped Russia, Asia, and Africa. Also, while Marx believed in a temporary dictatorship of the proletariat, Lenin and the Bolsheviks established a dictatorship *over* the proletariat.

Russian Revolution Led by Lenin, the Bolsheviks successfully overthrew the Russian government in a bloodless revolution in November 1917. The Bolsheviks—who became known as the Russian **Communist Party**—gained support in the early 1900s through their rigorous opposition both to Russia's harsh monarchical government and to the country's bloody involvement in World War I. Opposition to the revolution led to civil war, which lasted until 1920, when the Communists defeated their opponents.

The Communists imposed policies throughout Russia that radically transformed political, economic, and social life. They nationalized banks and businesses and confiscated land, distributing it to peasants in the countryside.

WORLD AFFAIRS *In the early 1900s the Bolsheviks gained the support of Russian citizens by actively spreading propaganda.* **What organization did Lenin and the Bolsheviks form?**

By 1921, however, Lenin recognized that the communist society he had aspired to had not been created—poverty was rampant, and peasant revolts threatened the stability of the nation. Lenin then established what he called the New Economic Policy. This policy was designed to revive the nation's economy by promoting agriculture and industry, and by allowing some private ownership of land and limited free trade.

Spreading Communism Lenin had a more aggressive plan for the spread of communism than Marx had envisioned. Marx believed that economic crises in individual countries would inspire independent communist revolutions that would defeat capitalism. Lenin, however, believed that Russia should be used as a base for supporting communist revolutions in other countries. After seizing power in Russia, Lenin began to organize centers of communist activity throughout the world.

Lenin's ideas about freedom followed from Marx's ideas, but he set them aside in part when he came to power. Lenin believed that the proletariat should have political freedom to organize revolutionary parties before the fall of capitalism. Once the Communist Party took power during the revolution, however, it would have to govern the state ruthlessly and with iron discipline. After the Russian Revolution was complete, Lenin in fact maintained the dictatorship of the Communist Party while concentrating on building a communist nation. Only when the development of communism was complete, declared Lenin, would everyone gain genuine political freedom from the limitations imposed by poverty and inequality. Lenin emphasized that collective freedom, not individual freedom, was his highest priority.

Joseph Stalin Vladimir Lenin died in 1924, two years after Russia had joined with other territories to form a new communist nation—the Soviet Union. The Communist Party established itself as the Soviet Union's only political organization and did not tolerate opposition. Lenin's successor, Joseph Stalin, took the country's dictatorial government to a new extreme. He ruled the Soviet Union with an iron fist for almost 30 years.

Disliking Lenin's move toward free enterprise, Stalin instituted his own economic strategies, the Five-Year Plans. Stalin also focused on developing heavy industry, the military, science, and technology in order to demonstrate to other nations the Soviets' superiority in these areas. He also hoped that these actions would establish the Communists as a stable and accepted force.

Part of Stalin's new policy involved the forced collectivization of agriculture—the combining of small farms into large, government-owned agricultural enterprises. This system was imposed despite widespread peasant opposition. More than 5 million peasant households were eliminated, their property was taken, and millions of peasants were starved to death, killed, or were sent to forced-labor camps. Around 7 million people died from 1929 to 1933 as a result of collectivization and brutality in the labor camps.

WORLD AFFAIRS *The historical photo above shows a Soviet farm where peasants have gathered to hear a speaker talk about the advantages of collective farming.* **Why did Stalin institute his own economic plans?**

Results of the Five-Year Plans Because the Soviet Union had vast natural resources, the Five-Year Plans succeeded in transforming the nation into a world leader in the production of steel, iron, coal, and oil. However, the quality of life for the Soviet people was dismal. The development of agriculture and of consumer goods industries under communist rule was weak. The Soviet Union also had difficulty providing adequate government-owned housing for many of its citizens. In the later years of the Soviet Union, health care also declined. For example, the infant mortality rate increased in the 1970s and 1980s.

In the area of education, however, the Soviet leadership effectively transformed an ill-educated nation into one with almost 100 percent literacy. At first, only 4 years of education were guaranteed for children in rural areas, but eventually, most areas provided 10 years. Adult education programs were common, and by the late 1970s, more than 5 million Soviet citizens attended institutions of higher education each year.

WORLD AFFAIRS *The Soviet Union created a highly effective system of education.* **What effect did the Soviet education system have on the country's literacy rate?**

The Failure of Communist States

Despite its initial promises for improvement, Communist Party rule in the Soviet Union and in Eastern Europe disintegrated in the late 1980s. Not only had the Communist Party failed to achieve its theoretical goal of abolishing economic and social classes, but at least three new classes had risen after the Russian Revolution. In the Soviet Union, the dominant class, made up of only a few hundred thousand families, included government officials, party leaders, military officers, industrial executives, scientists, artists, and writers. The second class, which was made up of

Comparing Governments

Fascism

In contrast to democracy, the central principle of fascism is government's absolute dominance of society. Fascism gained support in the 1920s and 1930s, a period that had been thrown into chaos partly by the great economic and social costs of World War I and by a worldwide economic depression. Many people believed that an extremely powerful government was needed to solve the vast economic and political problems of the day.

In this atmosphere, three fascist leaders emerged in Europe: Benito Mussolini in Italy in 1922, Adolf Hitler in Germany in 1933, and Francisco Franco in Spain in 1939. All three dictators came to power by using some degree of violence.

Once in power, Mussolini, Hitler, and Franco banned all political parties but their own and suspended basic rights and freedoms. In short, the three ruled as absolute dictators, demanding unquestioned obedience from the people, the press, and religious, civic, and social organizations. Today, with fascism a thing of the past, the citizens of these countries enjoy freedom. Germany and Italy are democratic republics and Spain is a constitutional monarchy.

Linking Government and Journalism

The Foreign-Policy Debate

National leaders consider information and opinion from a variety of sources when deciding U.S. policy toward foreign countries. Among the official sources are military leaders, information-gathering organizations such as the Central Intelligence Agency, and elected federal officials. An important but unofficial source of policy influence is the media.

Professional and scholarly journals are particularly influential. Political scientists and other observers analyze foreign-policy issues and suggest courses of action in journals such as *Foreign Affairs* and *Foreign Policy*. These and other, similar journals are highly regarded by many policy makers. Many of the authors of journal articles have had substantial experience in developing foreign policy. Others have an established record of study in the field.

Perhaps the most famous journal article to influence foreign policy was a July 1947 piece in *Foreign Affairs*. The anonymous author, who signed the article "X," was George F. Kennan. Kennan had been a U.S. diplomat and a U.S. State Department adviser on the Soviet Union. His diplomatic experience—particularly in the Soviet Union—made Kennan a respected authority on the issue of U.S.-Soviet foreign policy.

At the end of World War II, U.S. officials debated how the United States and its allies should deal with the Soviet Union. Soviet leaders were expanding their influence and control throughout Eastern Europe and in other regions. In his *Foreign Affairs* article, Kennan argued that, the Soviet Union would eventually collapse under the weight of its unworkable system of communism and cooperate with the United States.

In the meantime, Kennan said, the U.S. government should work—patiently but firmly and over the long term—to contain, or block, the expansion of Soviet control and influence. This policy, which was known as containment, dominated official U.S. foreign policy for more than four decades.

Like Kennan, other former government officials

In 1947 George F. Kennan wrote an article in which he argued that the Soviet Union would collapse and eventually cooperate with the United States.

often publish articles and appear on television and radio news programs to contribute to foreign-policy debates after leaving office. For example, James A. Baker III, U.S. secretary of state under President George Bush, wrote an article for the *New York Times* that stressed the importance of strong U.S. ties with the former Soviet republic of Georgia. Some well-known and widely read columnists and commentators, such as William Safire—a former speechwriter for President Richard Nixon—Anthony Lewis, and George Will, regularly write on policy issues.

The media, then, provides an important national forum for debate on policy issues. In some instances, as with Kennan's 1947 article, journalism proves that the power of the pen can be quite persuasive.

What Do You Think?

1. In what ways does journalism contribute to the making of foreign policy? Why are journals such as *Foreign Affairs* highly regarded by policy makers?

2. Many observers debate public policy and social issues in newspapers and on television. What do you think makes a commentator persuasive?

around 4 to 5 million families, included the intermediary ranks of civilian and military officials, collective farm managers, and some of the better-paid skilled workers and technicians in industry. The third class included the bulk of the population—the common workers and the peasants—who made up more than 50 million families.

The Communist Party ruled everyday life in an authoritarian manner, controlling the military, police, mass media, and government enterprises. People who disagreed with the Communist Party's policies were incarcerated and sometimes tortured. The party's economic decisions had crippled the economy, while the standard of living for most Soviet people increased more slowly than in major free-market nations. By the end of the 1980s, some leaders and disillusioned citizens in both the Soviet Union and Eastern European nations were openly challenging the failing communist system.

WORLD AFFAIRS *Lech Walesa, leader of the Polish Solidarity movement in the 1980s, led his country's fight for government reform.* **In what other former Communist nations did citizens organize movements to demand political reform?**

Eastern Europe The authoritarian governments that the Soviet Union had set up in Eastern Europe after World War II fell apart during this time. As anticommunist resistance in these nations grew, the governments allowed some political reforms. However, these reforms did not stop the demands for change. Movements such as those led by the Solidarity union in Poland demanded multiparty elections and hastened the disintegration of the Communist Party first in Poland, and then in Hungary, the German Democratic Republic (East Germany), Czechoslovakia, Bulgaria, and Romania.

Mikhail Gorbachev As noted in Chapter 10, in 1987 the Soviet government under Mikhail Gorbachev tried to ease some of the unrest in the Soviet Union by implementing perestroika, or "restructuring," and glasnost, or "openness." Gorbachev's policies included greater civil liberties, access to information, and legal restraints on government power. Some economic changes were made to allow greater influence of global capitalist markets. However, these changes only gave the Soviet people a clearer view of what life might be like if communism were completely abandoned.

Gorbachev, believing that his country needed massive change, decided in 1989 not to block the political movements occurring in Eastern Europe. As a result, all of the communist governments there collapsed within several months. In 1991, after months of unrest and an attempted overthrow of Gorbachev's government, the Soviet Union dissolved.

Former Communist Nations Today The transition from communism to democratic, capitalist societies in Eastern Europe and the former states of the Soviet Union has been filled with many difficulties. Political parties have been fragmented and unstable, and ethnic-religious strife in nations such as the former Yugoslavia has been a recurring problem. In some areas, political disorder and crime have grown particularly severe. Many of the existing industries in these countries had been inefficient by world standards and therefore collapsed when forced to compete with business in capitalist nations. The nations of the former Soviet Union and Eastern Europe continue to struggle in their efforts to rebuild their societies. A new, competitive economy seems to be taking root in some places. Nevertheless, the futures of these nations remain uncertain.

China: A Country with Two Economic Systems

WORLD AFFAIRS Like some nations in Eastern Europe and the former Soviet Union, China has experienced significant changes in its economic system in recent years. The handing over of capitalist Hong Kong to communist China in 1997 marked the joining of two different economic systems. Some people believe that this transfer marked the most dramatic chapter in China's decades-long shift away from a communist economy.

For nearly 100 years, Hong Kong had been a British territory and had operated under a free-market system that enabled it to become an economic powerhouse. Before Great Britain gave up control of the colony, China agreed to let this system remain in place.

China itself had already begun moving away from a communist command economy. China's leaders in 1978 introduced reforms that allowed private investment and trade. As a result, China's economy grew rapidly in the 1980s and 1990s.

This rapid economic growth created problems, however. For example, urban crowding increased as people moved from poor rural areas to search for better-paying jobs in the cities. The benefits of economic growth were unevenly distributed, and inflation rates skyrocketed.

China's leaders argued that a strong communist government was needed to keep the country stable during this period of change. Chinese citizens, on the other hand, have increasingly called for political reforms such as democratization and an end to corruption. The government refused these requests. In 1989 government leaders ordered soldiers to forcibly remove prodemocracy demonstrators from Tiananmen Square in China's capital city, Beijing. Thousands were killed, and hundreds more were arrested in the following weeks.

Some people now fear that the Chinese government will treat Hong Kong with similar harshness. Observers, however, believe that Hong Kong's history of political freedom and its powerful economy may speed China's transformation from a communist country to a free, democratic, and capitalist one.

SECTION 3 — REVIEW

1. Define the following terms: class struggle, *Communist Manifesto,* forces of production, relations of production, vanguard, Bolsheviks, Communist Party.

2. In what ways did Marx think that communism would offer greater freedom and equality than did capitalism?

3. How did Vladimir Lenin go about putting communism into practice in Russia?

4. What changes did Joseph Stalin bring to the Soviet Union after Lenin's death?

5. What problems led to the demise of the Soviet Union?

6. **Thinking and Writing Critically**
   Many people now say that the downfall of the Soviet Union proves that communism is a system that can never work in the real world. What factors do you think contributed to the Soviet Union's collapse? In what ways was Marx's theory of communism different from the communism that was applied in the Soviet Union?

7. **Applying** **POLITICAL FOUNDATIONS**
   Conduct an Internet search for nations that have communist governments today. Make a small chart comparing economic and political information.

CHAPTER 22 — SUMMARY

SECTION 1 The United States, Japan, Mexico, and Taiwan have some form of capitalist economy. To be classified as capitalist, a nation's economy must be geared around some combination of the following principles—private ownership, a market economy, competition, and profit.

The roots of capitalism can be found in the works of writers and theorists such as Adam Smith, who believed that self-interest was the primary motivation for economic behavior. Smith argued that government involvement in the economy limits the ability of the market to function in ways that are best for society.

The United States does not have a pure market economy. Instead, it has a mixed economy.

SECTION 2 Another economic system—socialism—tries to eliminate inequality by redistributing wealth. In a socialist system the government or the people as a whole own or control the factors of production and manage the distribution of goods.

Early socialists hoped to change the harsh working conditions and economic inequality resulting from the Industrial Revolution. Socialism eventually divided into two movements—democratic socialism and communism. Democratic socialists believed that capitalism should be eliminated through peaceful methods. Communists believed in a revolution of the proletariat.

The four main characteristics of democratic socialism are public services, nationalization, high taxes, and a command economy. In a socialist state, social services are provided by the government. In addition, some basic industries and services are often nationalized, and taxes are high to help government pay for the services.

SECTION 3 Karl Marx developed modern socialist principles. His more revolutionary views, however, became the founding principles of communism. Marx believed that the capitalist system, in which the capitalists control the factors of production, is unjust. He also thought that workers must stage a violent revolution to eliminate the capitalist system.

The world's first communist state was not a highly developed, industrial society. Instead, an economically underdeveloped nation—Russia—was the first to institute communist principles. Vladimir Lenin was Russia's first communist leader. Unlike Marx, who believed in a dictatorship of the proletariat, Lenin thought that a dictatorship *over* the proletariat was needed to establish a communist system. Thus, under Lenin's direction the Communist Party established itself as the only political organization and did not tolerate opposition.

Joseph Stalin, Lenin's successor, took the country's dictatorial government to a new extreme. Stalin developed a series of Five-Year Plans—forcing the collectivization of agriculture and focusing on the development of heavy industry. By the 1970s and 1980s people in both the Soviet Union and Eastern Europe began to demand change. In spite of changes made by the Soviet government under Mikhail Gorbachev in 1987, communist governments in Eastern Europe collapsed, and the Soviet Union itself dissolved in 1991.

Government Notebook

Review what you wrote in your Government Notebook at the beginning of the chapter about why different kinds of political and economic systems might form. Now that you have finished studying this chapter, do you feel that any of the reasons you listed help explain the establishment of socialist or communist states? Record your answers in your Notebook.

CHAPTER 22

REVIEW

REVIEWING CONCEPTS

1. What are the four principles around which capitalist economies are based?

2. What is government's role in a capitalist economy?

3. Name the three characteristics of a socialist economy.

4. What two concepts are central to Marx's theory of social change?

5. Why did Lenin establish a communist dictatorship after the Russian Revolution?

THINKING AND WRITING CRITICALLY

1. **POLITICAL PROCESSES** How do the basic principles of socialism and capitalism differ? What are some of the benefits and disadvantages of each system?

2. **POLITICAL PROCESSES** How does the operation of a command economy in a democratic socialist country differ from that of a communist country?

3. **POLITICAL FOUNDATIONS** According to Karl Marx, how would a revolution pave the way for a country to make the transition from a capitalist system to a communist system? Why do you think some people would argue that Lenin failed to create a communist society after the revolution?

4. **PUBLIC GOOD** How do the laws of supply and demand determine the price of goods for sale in a competitive market? How is competition beneficial to the development of market economies? Do you think that freedom of choice is important to a capitalist economy? Why or why not?

CITIZENSHIP IN YOUR COMMUNITY

With a group, interview an owner of a small business in your community to find out about setting up a private business. What role do competition and supply and demand play in the operation of the business? What are some of the government regulations that affect the operation of the business? Does the local or state government offer any assistance to people setting up their own business? When you have completed the interview, prepare a presentation for your class. Be sure to include visual images such as charts, graphs, and photographs.

INDIVIDUAL PORTFOLIO PROJECT

Conduct research on a country that operates under a democratic socialist system. What services does the government provide to all citizens? How are these services funded? What are some of the country's largest labor unions? What is the government's role in the operation of the country's major industries? After completing your research, create a poster depicting the economic system of the country you select and write a short article describing its features. Include photos or drawings to illustrate the article.

PRACTICING SKILLS: UNDERSTANDING MEASUREMENT CONCEPTS AND METHODS

The chart on the next page contains the consumer price index (CPI), or cost-of-living index, for a 10-year period. The CPI measures the average change in prices over time. The index is based on the prices of specific goods and services that a typical family purchases on a day-to-day basis. These goods and services include food, shelter, clothing, transportation, and medical services. The figures below were computed by comparing prices for the year indicated with prices from 1982–84. Study the chart and answer the questions that follow.

Consumer Price Indexes, 1986–1996

Percent of Change / Year

Source: Bureau of Labor Statistics, U.S. Department of Labor

1. Which years had the highest and lowest rates of increase?

2. When has the rate of increase ever stayed the same for more than one consecutive year?

3. From 1991 to 1996, what happened to the average change in prices?

THE INTERNET: LEARNING ONLINE

Conduct an Internet search to learn more about Karl Marx. You might start with search words such as *socialist theory, Karl Marx,* and *Communist Manifesto.* Write a one-page biographical sketch of Marx. Be sure to include important details about his life and work, such as the place and dates of his birth and death and the titles of his most important writings. Write down a list of the Web sites you visit.

ANALYZING PRIMARY SOURCES

THE *COMMUNIST MANIFESTO*

Karl Marx and Friedrich Engels wrote the *Communist Manifesto* in 1848 as a call for revolution. Their work has been important to the study of how economic forces impact history. The following excerpt discusses the aims of the Communist Party. Read the excerpt and answer the questions that follow.

It is high time that Communists should openly, in the face of the whole world, publish their views, their aims, their tendencies, and meet this nursery tale of the specter of communism with a manifesto [statement of principles] of the Party itself. . . .

The immediate aim of the Communists is the same as that of all other proletarian parties: formation of the proletariat into a class, overthrow of bourgeois supremacy, conquest of political power by the proletariat. . . .

The distinguishing feature of Communism is not the abolition of property generally, but the abolition of bourgeois property. Modern bourgeois private property is the final and most complete expression of the system of producing and appropriating products that is based on class antagonisms, on the exploitation [unfair use] of the many by the few.

In this sense, the theory of the Communists may be summed up in the single phrase: abolition of private property. . . .

Communists disdain [refuse] to conceal their views and aims. They openly declare that their ends can be attained only by the forcible overthrow of all existing social conditions.

1. What do Marx and Engels say is the immediate aim of the Communist Party?

2. According to Marx and Engels, of what is modern bourgeois private property an expression?

3. What single phrase does the excerpt say sums up the theory of communism?

CHAPTER 23

INTERNATIONAL RELATIONS

Why do you suppose that U.S. government leaders care what happens in other countries? After all, a nation such as North Korea is thousands of miles across the Pacific Ocean from the mainland United States. Similarly, why do efforts to develop forests in South America draw international concern? The answer lies in the recognition that no country is truly isolated from events outside its borders. This interconnectedness can be seen in issues concerning collective security, economics, and the environment.

Government Notebook

In your Government Notebook, write a short paragraph about the importance of understanding how events elsewhere in the world affect the United States.

COLLECTIVE SECURITY

Political Dictionary

interdependence
refugee
nuclear proliferation
international law

Objectives

★ Why is international collective security important?
★ What causes conflicts that challenge collective security?
★ How does growth in the production and ownership of weapons challenge collective security?
★ In what ways does the United Nations help achieve collective security?

Perhaps the most obvious example of the **interdependence**, or mutual reliance, of the world's countries is the struggle for collective security. As noted in Chapter 10, collective security involves ensuring peace by linking nations through mutual defense agreements. Because conflict and the spread of weapons of war are a global threat, many countries are constantly working together to maintain peace.

Working for Security

Why is security so important? Security is vital to a government's ability to perform its functions and promote the public good. A nation unable to secure its borders and protect its citizens may not be able to collect taxes effectively, provide services, protect communities from crime, or maintain a safe and clean environment. In today's interdependent world, security is a collective concern because conflicts often affect regions and countries that are not directly involved in them. Sometimes vast

numbers of people cross international borders to flee war zones, and fighting spreads to regions outside the original area of conflict.

Refugees Conflicts often produce **refugees**—people who flee their community or country to escape war or for economic or political reasons. For example, in 1994 civil war erupted between ethnic groups in Rwanda in east central Africa. Fearing for their lives, hundreds of thousands of refugees fled to neighboring countries such as Zaire (now the Democratic Republic of Congo).

Host countries usually have to help pay for the care of refugees, providing their food, shelter, and protection. Moreover, unsanitary conditions in crowded camps often raise fears about the spread of disease. Because of these burdens, host countries have an interest in helping to end the fighting so that refugees can return home. The U.S. Committee for Refugees estimated that despite all the efforts to restore peace and stability to war-torn regions, at the end of 1995 there were more than 15 million refugees in the world.

Spread of Conflict If fighting spreads within a nation or beyond national borders, it not only may create refugees but also threaten collective security. For example, in the early 1990s fighting broke out among various ethnic and religious

WORLD AFFAIRS *As refugees fled from Rwanda to neighboring Zaire (now the Democratic Republic of Congo) they sought shelter in camps such as the one pictured above.* **What problems did these refugee camps face?**

groups in the former Yugoslav republics, particularly in Bosnia and Herzegovina. European leaders feared that the fighting might spread to neighboring countries. In addition, many of the world's leaders were concerned about "ethnic cleansing"—attempts by the region's Serb population to eliminate local Muslims.

The mounting bloodshed and huge numbers of refugees led European countries and the United States to act. In 1992 troops under the jurisdiction of the United Nations (which you will learn about later in this section) were sent to maintain peace. Their efforts were unsuccessful, and fighting continued. In 1995, however, a peace agreement was signed in Dayton, Ohio. A UN-authorized peacekeeping force made up of members of the North Atlantic Treaty Organization (NATO) was sent in to help keep the peace and enforce a cease-fire.

In 1996 the NATO force was replaced by a UN stabilization force, which was still in place in late 1997. NATO, as noted in Chapter 10, is an alliance of nations originally formed to provide a unified defense of the North Atlantic area—Western Europe and North America. Today, NATO's focus is expanding to include political and military cooperation with new partners in Central and Eastern Europe.

Causes of Conflict

Today, world peace is still threatened by conflicts based on ethnic and religious intolerance, ideological rivalries, and other factors such as competing economic interests. Nations around the world are constantly challenged to contain and stop these conflicts.

Ethnic and Religious Intolerance Many fierce and bloody conflicts around the world have stemmed from ethnic or religious intolerance. Ethnic and racial differences have sometimes sparked violence in the United States. Considering that it has one of the world's most diverse populations, however, the United States has been relatively free of violence based on ethnicity or religion in recent history. Several other countries—particularly in southeastern Europe and in parts of Africa and Asia—have seen many more ethnic and religious clashes.

Persecution, typically fueled by prejudice and hatred, is a primary cause of such conflict. The

WORLD AFFAIRS *Soldiers patrol the border separating North and South Korea.* **How did China assist North Korea during the Korean War?**

Bosnian and Rwandan civil wars are just two recent examples of conflicts stemming from ethnic and religious differences.

Ideological Rivalries Differences in people's ideologies—basic belief systems—have inspired fierce rivalries. Such rivalries have been at the core of many conflicts around the world. In the mid- to late twentieth century, for example, the rivalry between the supporters of communism and those of capitalism and democracy led to a number of civil and regional wars.

Civil and regional conflicts based on ideological differences have at times drawn in countries from other parts of the world. During the 1950–53 Korean War, U.S. and allied troops aided South Korea, which had been invaded by communist North Korea. Communist China supported North Korea with hundreds of thousands of soldiers. Even today, despite the fall of communism elsewhere in the world, U.S. troops remain stationed on the Korean Peninsula, helping to maintain the tense peace on the border between North and South Korea.

Other Causes A violent change in the government of a nation—much like intolerance and ideological rivalry—may also threaten regional security. In 1997, for example, rebels overthrew President Mobutu Sese Seko (moh-BOO-too SAY-say SAY-koh)—the longtime dictator of the African country of Zaire—and created the Democratic Republic of Congo. Supported by aid from neighboring countries, the rebels swept through much of Zaire, storming towns and crushing resistance by the state military. Such conflicts occur when people turn to violence to achieve political and economic aims. Similarly, government corruption and social unrest have often led to violence, as in several Central American nations during the 1970s and 1980s. Violent changes in government and other forms of civil unrest often have important international implications, forcing changes in countries' relationships.

Civil unrest in one country has at times led to international intervention. In 1994, for example, U.S. troops entered the Caribbean country of Haiti to reinstall a democratically elected president who had been overthrown by the military. The intervention came after thousands of Haitian refugees had fled to the United States to escape instability and violence in their country.

The 1990–91 Persian Gulf War is another instance of political and economic interests inspiring outside forces to intervene in a regional conflict. When Iraq invaded Kuwait—a small oil-producing country in the Middle East—the United States and other faraway nations quickly stepped in to defend it. Kuwait's strategic value as an important oil producer and a desire to punish Iraqi dictator Saddam Hussein for his launching of the invasion inspired their actions.

Weapons Proliferation

Another serious threat to international collective security is the increase in the production and ownership of weapons of mass destruction. These include nuclear weapons, chemical and biological weapons, and conventional arms.

Nuclear Proliferation A critical challenge to collective security is **nuclear proliferation**—the spread in the ownership of nuclear weapons. Currently, only the United States, Russia, Great Britain, France, and China acknowledge that they possess nuclear weapons. These nations are known as the nuclear powers. India, Israel, and Pakistan are strongly suspected either of having the capability to produce nuclear weapons or of currently possessing them. Some other countries, including Iran, Iraq, and North Korea, have been suspected of seeking to acquire such weapons.

To assure that nuclear weapons will never again be used in a war, many nations—including the

existing nuclear powers—have worked to stop their proliferation. In the 1968 Nuclear Nonproliferation Treaty, nuclear powers agreed not to transfer nuclear weapons to nonnuclear countries. In turn, nonnuclear signatories to the treaty have pledged not to try to produce or obtain such weapons. Nuclear powers also have worked to prevent nuclear-weapons material from being smuggled out of Russia and other former Soviet republics. World leaders fear that nonnuclear countries or even terrorist groups might purchase such material and attempt to produce nuclear weapons.

In addition, nuclear powers, most importantly the United States and Russia, have agreed to several treaties limiting the production and possession of nuclear weapons. World leaders also have signed treaties banning nuclear-weapons testing in hopes of eliminating potential environmental damage and the further development of such weapons.

Chemical and Biological Weapons Many countries also have worked to limit the production and possession of chemical and biological weapons. These weapons of mass destruction are much easier and more inexpensive to produce than nuclear weapons but are also capable of killing masses of people.

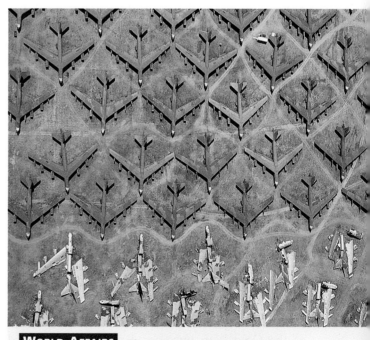

WORLD AFFAIRS *These American aircraft were destroyed in accordance with the U.S.-Soviet Strategic Arms Reduction Treaty.* ***In what year did the nuclear powers agree to the Nuclear Nonproliferation Treaty?***

Countries first used chemical weapons on a large scale during World War I. In that war, mustard gas, which blisters the skin and lungs and causes blindness, killed and horribly wounded many soldiers. More recently, Iraq used chemical weapons in the 1980s in its war against Iran. Several countries also have produced biological weapons, which spread microbes that cause deadly diseases.

Over the years, the horror of chemical and biological weapons inspired a number of agreements to halt their production and use. Many nations agreed to the 1925 Geneva Protocol on Gas Warfare, which outlawed the use of chemical weapons in war. The 1972 Biological Weapons Convention, an agreement signed by some 140 nations, outlaws the development, production, and stockpiling of biological weapons.

The Chemical Weapons Convention, a similar agreement that went into effect in 1997, bans the production and stockpiling of chemical weapons. Although more than 160 countries signed the treaty, the United States was hesitant to join them. Some Americans believed that, as with other arms control agreements, ensuring other nations' compliance would be difficult. Nations that refused to sign were not limited by the ban. Signers would thus be at a disadvantage, because the nonsigners would be the only ones able to possess chemical weapons. Supporters of the treaty argued that ratifying it was necessary to maintaining U.S. prestige around the world and to preventing nations from producing and using such weapons. The U.S. Senate finally ratified the treaty in April 1997.

Conventional Arms Nations have long struggled to restrict the production and possession of conventional arms, such as tanks, artillery, warplanes, and naval ships. In the early 1920s, at the Limitation of Armaments Conference, for example, many of the world's most powerful countries agreed to limit the size of their naval forces. These and other early efforts, however, did not stop the peacetime stockpiling of weapons. During the Cold War, such stockpiling escalated. In 1987 alone, world military spending exceeded $1.3 trillion.

Military spending has declined since the end of the Cold War, however. By 1994 total world military expenditures had dropped to $840 billion, around $280 billion of which was spent by the United States. The decline occurred because of various military reduction agreements, such as the

Top 10 Countries in Military Spending

Country	Billions of U.S. Dollars
1. United States (1995)	$270.6
2. Russia	$98.0
3. Japan	$41.7
4. France	$35.9
5. United Kingdom	$34.9
6. Germany	$29.1
7. China	$28.5
8. Italy (1993)	$20.6
9. Saudi Arabia	$20.5
10. South Korea	$13.5

(Figures are for 1994 except where otherwise indicated.)

Source: *World Almanac: 1997; Statistical Abstract:1996*

Although many countries have signed treaties to limit certain types of weapons, some countries still spend billions of dollars a year on their military. **How much did the United Kingdom spend on its military in 1994?**

1990 Treaty on Conventional Armed Forces in Europe. In spite of such treaties, the increasing level of military spending in some parts of the world, such as the Middle East and South Asia, continues to concern world leaders.

United Nations

As you have seen, the international community has worked in numerous ways to promote collective security. Another important key to collective security has been the work of the United Nations, a worldwide organization of countries that is based in New York City. The United States and 49 other countries founded the United Nations in 1945 after World War II. By the mid-1990s, UN membership had grown to 185 countries.

It is important to remember that the United Nations is not intended to be a world government. Rather, it serves as a forum for settling disputes and accomplishing other important goals, such as protecting human rights, and promoting respect for international law. To organize its efforts to fulfill these goals, the UN Charter established six principal divisions:

- ★ the General Assembly,
- ★ the Security Council,
- ★ the Secretariat,
- ★ the International Court of Justice,
- ★ the Economic and Social Council, and
- ★ the Trusteeship Council.

The General Assembly is made up of all UN member nations. Each member has one vote in the assembly, which decides the UN's budget, member dues, and general policy issues. The assembly also plays a major role in choosing who will sit on various UN councils, including the Security Council.

The UN Security Council investigates international disputes and decides what actions to take to maintain peace or stop aggression. Actions could include the breaking off of diplomatic relations by UN members, the implementing of a trade embargo, or even the use of armed force. The Security Council is made up of 15 members. Five countries—the United States, Russia, China, Great Britain, and France—are permanent members, and each has the power to veto any council decision. The General Assembly elects 10 additional members for two-year terms.

The Secretariat, which is headed by the secretary-general, manages the day-to-day operations of the United Nations. The General Assembly elects the secretary-general for a five-year, renewable term. A nominee cannot assume the office of secretary-general without Security Council approval.

The International Court of Justice, or the World Court, hears legal disputes between countries and gives advisory opinions on international legal questions. The court is composed of 15 judges, each of whom is elected to a nine-year term by the General Assembly and approved by the Security Council.

The Economic and Social Council meets once a year to work on ways to improve people's lives. The council's work includes supervising and coordinating UN social, economic, cultural, health, and educational efforts.

The Trusteeship Council administers any trust territories under UN supervision. The council was formed to help run former colonies that had gained their freedom during World War II but had not yet set up independent governments. Currently, there are no trust territories under UN supervision.

In addition to these divisions, some specialized agencies work with the United Nations to provide its members with medical, agricultural, financial, humanitarian, and technical assistance. For example, the International Bank for Reconstruction and Development, or the World Bank, loans money to countries in need and gives them technical and economic advice to help improve their economies. Another agency, the World Health Organization (WHO), helps governments fight disease. The work of the WHO was instrumental in helping wipe out smallpox—one of the world's most feared and deadly diseases. Today the WHO is a leader in worldwide efforts against AIDS.

Maintain World Peace The primary mission of the United Nations is to maintain world peace by helping to build friendly relationships between countries. The United Nations provides a forum for countries to settle disputes peacefully. In addition, it has worked to keep the peace in a number of tense situations, though not always successfully. UN peacekeeping forces, for example, have intervened between the military forces of Israel and some of its Arab neighbors, with which it has

Judges of the International Court of Justice

Judges	Country
Mohammed Bedjaoui	Algeria
Carl-August Fleischhauer	Germany
Gilbert Guillaume	France
Géza Herczegh	Hungary
Rosalyn Higgins	United Kingdom
Pieter H. Kooijmans	Netherlands
Abdul G. Koroma	Sierra Leone
Gonzalo Parra-Aranguren	Venezuela
Raymond Ranjeva	Madagascar
José Francisco Rezek	Brazil
Stephen M. Schwebel	United States
Shi Jiuyong	China
Shigeru Oda	Japan
Christopher G. Weeramantry	Sri Lanka
Vladen S. Vereshchetin	Russian Federation

Source: International Court of Justice

The International Court of Justice, or the World Court, helps settle legal disputes between countries. **How long is the term of an elected World Court judge?**

WORLD AFFAIRS *The World Health Organization (WHO), a United Nations agency, helps governments combat diseases.* **What other types of assistance does the UN provide its members?**

Korea in 1950 and to drive Iraqi troops out of Kuwait in 1990–91.

Protect Human Rights The United Nations also works to protect human rights. In the Universal Declaration of Human Rights, the United Nations states that respect for human rights and human dignity "is the foundation of freedom, justice, and peace in the world." To that end, the United Nations helps forge international agreements on such things as the prevention of discrimination and promotion of human rights.

The United Nations also provides humanitarian assistance to victims of natural and human-caused disasters. Between 1992 and 1995 the United Nations raised more than $7 billion for disaster-relief programs that helped tens of millions of people worldwide.

Promote International Law In addition, the United Nations promotes respect for **international law**—the rules that govern the relationships among independent countries. International law is established through treaties and other agreements among nations and businesses. The UN's World Court provides a forum for resolving disputes over international law. Furthermore, the United Nations may enforce these rules. For example, it can call on members to limit trade with violators of international agreements.

fought several wars since 1948. The United Nations also authorized a peacekeeping force in Bosnia. In 1997 there were 16 such UN peacekeeping missions around the world.

The United Nations has even authorized the use of force to stop aggression. The organization authorized member countries to defend South

---

SECTION 1 — REVIEW

1. Define the following terms: interdependence, refugee, nuclear proliferation, international law.

2. What are two ways in which conflict can negatively affect countries not directly involved in fighting?

3. How do ethnic and religious rivalries contribute to conflict? What are other causes of conflict?

4. Why are many countries concerned about nuclear proliferation? What other weapons have world leaders sought to limit?

5. What are the goals of the United Nations?

6. **Thinking and Writing Critically** Do you believe the United Nations has an important role to play in promoting world peace? Why or why not?

7. **Applying** WORLD AFFAIRS The United States has been involved in many important peacekeeping missions around the world. Conduct some library research to make a list of UN peacekeeping missions over the past five years. You might find the *Readers' Guide to Periodical Literature* or other periodical indexes helpful in your research. Then write a short paragraph explaining whether or not you believe the missions in question were important to promoting collective security.

SECTION 2

ECONOMIC INTERDEPENDENCE

Political Dictionary

developed nation
developing nation
comparative advantage
trading bloc
trade deficit

Objectives

★ What is the difference between developing nations and developed nations?
★ In what ways have nations worked to promote international trade?
★ Why are U.S. trade deficits a problem?

Interdependence among nations is evident not only in collective security but also in the world economy, where nations often cooperate to create healthy economic relationships. These relationships are strongly influenced by the economic development of the nations involved and the international trade in which they engage.

Economic Development

Nations are at different levels of economic development. The more developed a country is, the greater its influence is likely to be in the interdependent global economy.

Developed Nations Wealthy countries, commonly referred to as **developed nations**, share many characteristics. Among these are high levels of personal income, relatively low unemployment, and healthy manufacturing and industrial sectors. The wealthiest developed countries include the United States, Japan, Germany, France, and the United Kingdom, all of which have gross domestic products (GDPs) of more than a trillion dollars a year.

Developed nations' wealth enables them to strongly influence the economies of other countries around the world. For example, developed nations are the largest consumers of goods and services, making their markets important to producers elsewhere. They also largely determine international economic policies. Through organizations such as the World Bank, developed nations work to create policies and aid packages to improve the economies of poorer countries.

Developing Nations By the late 1990s about four fifths of the world's nearly 6 billion people were living in poorer countries, which are known as **developing nations**. In these countries most people spend much of their working lives just raising enough food to survive. Many of the world's poorest countries are in Africa, Asia, the Caribbean, and Central and South America.

The economic progress of developing and underdeveloped nations is often hindered by factors such as limited health services, poor and crowded schools, high rates of illiteracy, and poor productivity. These problems are often compounded by high rates of population growth. For example, the Democratic Republic of Congo (formerly Zaire), which had a per capita GDP of about $400 in 1996, is home to some 46 million people. This population is expected to double by 2020.

WORLD AFFAIRS *These ships in a port near Mount Fuji carry Japanese imports and exports.*
How does a developed nation's wealth enable it to influence the economies of other countries?

WORLD AFFAIRS *Many problems found in Kinshasa, the capital of the Democratic Republic of Congo, are compounded by its rapidly growing population.* **What do experts predict the population of the Democratic Republic of Congo will be in the year 2020?**

Making Progress Some developing nations have begun to close the economic gap that separates them from developed nations. Although some experienced a severe economic downturn in late 1997, the economies of the Asian countries of China, South Korea, Indonesia, Malaysia, Singapore, Thailand, and Taiwan have grown rapidly since the 1970s. In expanding their production and consumption, these countries have become increasingly important in the global economy. China's more than 1 billion people, for example, provide a huge market for businesses around the world. Chinese exports also have increased dramatically.

This economic expansion was largely brought about by reforms that freed markets and supported private industry. International aid also has helped some countries expand their economies. The World Bank, for example, has loaned billions of dollars for the development of industry.

One of the world's great economic success stories has been Japan. From 1953 to 1966 the country borrowed $857 million from the World Bank. Afterward, the Japanese economy grew rapidly, and by 1970 Japan had begun loaning money to the World Bank to finance development in other countries. However, economic stagnation has overtaken Japan over the last few years.

International Trade

International trade fuels the economic interdependence among nations. It is a major factor in the production and consumption of goods and services in developed and developing nations alike.

The United States strongly supports free trade. As noted in Chapter 10, free trade is the exchange of goods and services across national borders without restrictions, such as high tariffs. Free trade opens foreign markets to domestic businesses and gives consumers access to foreign-made goods.

By rewarding countries for specializing in what they do best, free trade tends to bring about lower-priced and higher-quality goods and services. For example, Kuwait has one of the world's largest reserves of oil. In fact, the Kuwaiti government—which controls most of the country's oil industry—generates much of its income from oil sales to other countries, such as the United States. This income has been used to pay for health care, education, defense, and other services, as well as for improvements necessary for further economic development.

Because Kuwait has no water resources and no land fit for agricultural use, however, it must depend almost wholly on food imports from foreign sources. One of Kuwait's largest food suppliers is the United States, which is the world's leading exporter of agricultural products. Kuwait's experience is an example of the economic principle of **comparative advantage** at work. This principle states that countries should primarily produce goods they can generate at a relatively low cost and purchase goods they cannot.

A great deal of international trade is conducted in regional **trading blocs**—groups of countries that ease trade among their members by setting various rules, such as the reduction of tariffs.

Europe One of the most successful trading blocs is the European Union (EU), which in 1997 had 15 members, including France, Germany, the United Kingdom, and other, mostly Western European countries. The EU grew out of the European Economic Community (EEC), which was established in 1957. Its goal was to create a common market in which goods, services, people, and capital could move freely, regardless of national borders. Member nations hoped that forming economic and political ties would prevent future conflict.

The EU has its own governmental institutions, including the European Parliament, which acts as

WORLD AFFAIRS *Trucks loaded with goods line up to cross the border of Mexico and the United States. In 1992, North American leaders established the NAFTA trading bloc.* **What three countries make up NAFTA?**

a public forum for debate and consideration of issues important to members. With the fall of communism in Eastern Europe, the EU also has strengthened economic relationships with countries there. In 1993 member countries approved the Maastricht Treaty, which committed the EU to creating a common currency by 1999.

North America The United States and two of its most important trading partners, Canada and Mexico, have formed a major trading bloc. In 1992, these countries' leaders signed the North American Free Trade Agreement (NAFTA). NAFTA removed tariffs and other barriers to the creation of a free market among the three countries.

The U.S. Senate ratified the agreement in 1993, but not without overcoming strong opposition. NAFTA opponents argued that tariffs, which raise prices on foreign goods sold in the United States, protect U.S. jobs by encouraging consumers to buy domestic products. In addition, they feared that eliminating tariffs would spur U.S. companies to move their facilities—and thus many jobs—to Mexico, where wages are lower. NAFTA supporters, on the other hand, argued that removing tariffs and allowing free trade would open markets for the sale of U.S. goods, thereby creating more jobs for U.S. workers.

Canadian, Mexican, and U.S. leaders signed NAFTA because they believed free trade would strengthen their countries' economies. Despite an economic crisis in Mexico shortly after NAFTA went into effect, that nation's economy has improved in recent years. NAFTA supporters are now considering expanding the agreement to include other countries in the Americas.

Asia Another important trading bloc is emerging among Asian countries that once were among the world's poorest. As you read earlier, although some experienced a downturn in 1997, the economies of Singapore, South Korea, Taiwan, Thailand, Malaysia, and Indonesia have grown rapidly in recent years. China too has experienced great economic growth since its communist government instituted free-market reforms.

To further encourage trade and economic development in the region, in 1989 many Southeast Asian countries joined with Japan, the United States, and other Pacific Rim countries—nations bordering the Pacific Ocean—to found the Asia-Pacific Economic Cooperation (APEC) group. Although it began as an informal group, APEC has become an important tool in promoting free trade and economic cooperation in Asia.

Asian countries have made other efforts to promote free trade. For example, in 1967 Thailand, Indonesia, Malaysia, the Philippines, and Singapore formed the Association of Southeast Asian Nations (ASEAN) to improve economic and

Careers in Government

U.S. Trade Office Staff

The Office of the U.S. Trade Representative develops international trade and investment policy for the U.S. government. Congress created the office in 1962 and made it a cabinet-level agency in 1974. The head of the office, the U.S. trade representative, is the nation's chief trade negotiator.

Trade office staff members have considerable experience in trade and business. For example, consider the background of Phyllis Shearer Jones, who was appointed as the assistant U.S. trade representative for intergovernmental affairs and public liaison (intermediary) in 1995. In that post, Jones works with businesses and state and local government officials to explain and get suggestions for U.S. trade policies.

Before she joined the staff at the trade office, Jones worked for IBM for almost 19 years. Her most recent post at IBM was as program director of public affairs, trade, and investment in Washington, D.C. In that job, Jones helped formulate IBM's position on several international trade issues, including GATT and NAFTA.

Here, the U.S. trade representative speaks with foreign diplomats. Trade office staff members must have considerable trade and business experience.

Education also played a key role in preparing Jones for her post with the U.S. trade office. She received a bachelor of science degree in economics and a bachelor of arts degree in mathematics from the University of Pennsylvania in 1976. Jones also earned a master's degree in business administration from Harvard Business School in 1980.

---

political cooperation among the nations of the region. Since the group's formation, Brunei and Vietnam have joined, and by 1997 Cambodia, Laos, and Burma (Myanmar) had been identified as possible new members. The ASEAN nations have committed themselves to reducing tariffs and promoting free trade within their region.

Other Trading Blocs Central and South American and African countries also have made efforts to formalize trading relationships. In 1996 the South American countries of Argentina, Brazil, Paraguay, and Uruguay formed a free-trade association known by its Spanish acronym MERCOSUR. Chile and Bolivia have since joined the association. MERCOSUR's members hope to bring in other South American countries and eventually link up with NAFTA.

World Trade Organization Much trade takes place outside geographic trading blocs. The creation of the World Trade Organization (WTO) was an important effort to ease trade restrictions among all countries. Established in 1995, it replaced the General Agreement on Tariffs and Trade (GATT), which had pursued similar goals since 1947. More than 130 countries initially joined. To ensure that overall trade practices benefit all countries, the WTO requires governments to, among other things, lower tariffs and adopt fair trade practices with all other WTO members.

Trade and the United States

Historically, foreign trade played a relatively modest role in the U.S. economy. As a large, geographically diverse nation, the United States could meet most of its needs inside its borders. In the twentieth century, however, foreign trade has become increasingly important.

U.S. exports have grown by leaps and bounds, but since the mid-1970s they have consistently failed to keep pace with imports. This imbalance has created a **trade deficit**, meaning the total value of imports into the United States is higher than the total value of U.S. exports to other countries. Many Americans worry that the large trade deficit is a sign of the country's declining economic status in the world.

The trade deficit is caused by several factors, one of the most important of which involves federal budget deficits. Having run up large budget deficits over the last three decades, the U.S. government has had to borrow increasing amounts of money. Higher interest rates resulting from increased borrowing attracted increased foreign demand for American bonds. As a result of the increased demand for dollars, the dollar became more valuable—or "stronger"—which raised prices for U.S. exports but generally lowered prices for imports. With more expensive exports and cheaper imports, the trade deficit increased.

A large trade deficit raises two important concerns. First, it creates unemployment. Some things that would otherwise be produced by Americans are produced abroad, and some things the United States might have produced for export are not produced. Second, a large trade deficit indicates that the United States as a whole is living

© 1987 by Herblock in the *Washington Post.*

WORLD AFFAIRS *Some economists worry that the deficits, like the monsters in this cartoon, scare away potential foreign investors from investing in the U.S. economy.* **What two important concerns does a large trade deficit raise?**

beyond its means since U.S. citizens consume more than the United States produces. In the short term, this makes for a higher standard of living. Eventually, however, foreigners will cash in the dollars they have accumulated, and the U.S. standard of living will decline.

SECTION 2 — REVIEW

1. Define the following terms: developed nation, developing nation, comparative advantage, trading bloc, trade deficit.

2. What are some challenges that hamper economic progress in developing nations? How have some developing nations improved their economies?

3. How does international trade promote healthy economies? What are some important trading blocs that promote free trade?

4. How do trade deficits affect the U.S. economy?

5. **Thinking and Writing Critically** Recall the debate over lowering trade barriers under NAFTA. Do you believe that lowering barriers to international trade helps or hurts the economy of the United States?

6. **Applying** **WORLD AFFAIRS** Visit local supermarkets and department stores and examine local newspaper advertisements to compile a list of the kinds of foreign-made products that can be purchased in your community. Write a short paragraph explaining these products' impact on the choices of U.S. consumers.

ENVIRONMENTAL INTERDEPENDENCE

Political Dictionary

global warming
renewable resource
nonrenewable resource
deforestation

Objectives

★ How do air and water pollution challenge the international community?
★ How can population growth and economic development strain the world's resources?

The world's environmental challenges are yet another demonstration of international interdependence. Problems such as air and water pollution and the depletion of natural resources have significant global consequences.

Challenges of Shared Resources

Imagine that increasing temperatures caused polar ice to melt, raising ocean levels and gradually submerging highly populated coastal areas. Imagine also that deadly diseases such as cholera were being spread by contaminated rivers and other polluted water sources. Many people argue that these are potential consequences of air and water pollution and that they could affect people worldwide.

Air Pollution Researchers have warned of the dangers of air pollution for decades. In a 1992 study the United Nations reported that about 1 billion people around the world were breathing unhealthful air. Exhaust from cars and industrial pollution—which are plentiful in large, crowded cities—cause various respiratory ailments and contribute to disease.

Scientists also have warned that the release of certain chemicals into the air is having dangerous climatic and environmental effects. They believe that the chlorofluorocarbons (CFCs) used in air conditioner and refrigerator coolants, as well as in the manufacture of plastic foam products, damage the atmospheric ozone layer. This layer, which surrounds the earth, filters out harmful ultraviolet rays from the sun that can cause skin cancer. In addition, the burning of fossil fuels such as oil, coal, and natural gas adds carbon dioxide to the air. Scientists believe that high levels of carbon dioxide and other so-called greenhouse gases can trap heat and thus cause **global warming**—a gradual rise in the world's average temperature. This warming could melt polar ice caps and thus cause the oceans to rise, flooding coastal areas and submerging tiny island-nations.

Water Pollution Another environmental challenge is water pollution, which threatens people's health by damaging drinking-water supplies and food resources. Industrial waste, pesticides, and

WORLD AFFAIRS *Mexico City, like many of the world's other major metropolitan areas, has an imposing air pollution problem.* **According to UN experts, how many people were breathing unhealthful air in the early 1990s?**

Comparing → Governments

International Cooperation

Cooperation on environmental issues often helps build goodwill between countries. For example, the governments of India and Bangladesh in South Asia have worked to overcome differences regarding management of the Ganges River. The Ganges—which flows through northern India, into Bangladesh, and then to the Bay of Bengal—is a major water source in the region.

In 1977 the Indian and Bangladeshi governments made an agreement fixing the amount of water to flow from the Ganges into Bangladesh. When that agreement expired in 1988, however, India began allowing more water to flow during wet seasons—adding to problems in flood-prone Bangladesh. During the dry season, India used more water to irrigate its farmland. As a result, farmers in Bangladesh did not receive enough water.

In 1996 the leaders of India and Bangladesh signed a new 30-year agreement on management of the Ganges. The two countries will receive equal amounts of water from the river, but Bangladesh will receive more of its water during the dry season.

the scientific community does not agree about the potential consequences. Some experts, for example, have argued that the dangers of greenhouse gases and global warming have been exaggerated. This lack of agreement has sparked debate among world leaders over the best ways to maintain or improve the health of the global environment.

Nevertheless, most countries have begun to work together to reduce pollution. The Montreal Protocol of 1987, the first important international agreement addressing an environmental problem, sought to protect the ozone layer. Environmentalists credit the Montreal Protocol with helping reduce the production of CFCs by more than 75 percent.

In 1992 the United Nations held an "Earth Summit" in Rio de Janeiro, Brazil, to deal with issues including global warming and economic development. As a result of the conference, the United States and other countries agreed to reduce emissions, or discharges, of carbon dioxide. Though some nations have failed to reach the agreed-upon emissions levels, many environmentalists hoped that more countries would meet the new goals agreed to at the second Earth Summit in 1997.

International negotiations about environmental issues raise difficult questions about how to distribute the burdens of pollution reduction. For example, in debates about limiting carbon dioxide emissions, poor countries argue that rich countries

other pollutants sometimes contaminate rivers and other water supplies. Many of these pollutants are suspected of causing various diseases, including cancer. In developing nations a lack of water-treatment facilities forces people to rely on impure water supplies, which often spread disease.

The oceans have long been used as dumping sites. Tons of discarded waste and oil spilled from damaged petroleum tankers have killed ocean life and spoiled large coastal areas. Decommissioned Russian nuclear submarines also threaten to spread radiation in parts of the Arctic Ocean north of Russia where the aging, rusty vessels were dumped.

Seeking Solutions The challenges of global pollution are not easily resolved, particularly since

WORLD AFFAIRS *Trudoya Bay in Russia has become a "cemetery" for nuclear submarines.* ***How does water pollution threaten people's health?***

should bear most of the burden because they cause most of the emissions. Some developing nations also maintain that significantly restricting their emissions would set back their economic development. In turn, some developed nations point out that unless developing nations work to control their own pollution levels now, they will greatly expand emissions in trying to meet the needs of their rapidly growing populations.

Protecting Natural Resources

In addition to combating pollution, countries try to work together on another important environmental issue—protecting the world's natural resources. You are surrounded by examples of how natural resources are put to work—the paper in this book, the cotton or wool fibers in your clothing, and the wood used to construct your school or home. These are **renewable resources**, or natural resources that can be replaced. For example, people can grow trees to replace those used to produce paper and wood. Renewable energy resources are solar and wind power.

Many other important resources, however, are **nonrenewable resources**—natural resources that can be used only once. The gasoline that powered the car or bus that brought you to school this morning is refined from oil, a nonrenewable

World's Most Populous Urban Areas	
City	Population (1994)
1. Tokyo, Japan	26,518,000
2. New York City	16,271,000
3. São Paulo, Brazil	16,110,000
4. Mexico City	15,525,000
5. Shanghai, China	14,709,000
6. Bombay (Mumbai), India	14,496,000
7. Los Angeles	12,232,000
8. Beijing, China	12,030,000
9. Calcutta, India	11,485,000
10. Seoul, South Korea	11,451,000
11. Jakarta, Indonesia	11,017,000
12. Buenos Aires, Argentina	10,914,000
13. Osaka, Japan	10,585,000
14. Tianjin, China	10,376,000
15. Rio de Janeiro, Brazil	9,817,000

Source: *World Almanac: 1997*

These urban areas are the most heavily populated in the world. If population projections are correct, by 2015 there will be 33 cities with populations that are more than 8 million. **Why are experts concerned about population growth?**

PUBLIC GOOD *Many of the world's leaders attend summits, like the one shown in this photograph, to discuss solutions to global environmental problems.* **How are renewable resources different from nonrenewable resources?**

resource. The amounts of oil, coal, precious metals, and other minerals are limited. Once they are used up, they cannot be replaced. However, some nonrenewable resources may be recycled, or processed for reuse. Also, advances in exploration technology have dramatically increased estimated reserves of many nonrenewable resources. As a result of recycling and expanding access to resources, the price of many nonrenewable resources has actually been declining over time, despite increased demand.

Resources are unevenly distributed around the world. For example, many countries in the Middle East are rich in oil while others, such as Japan and most Western European countries, have virtually no oil and must import it. Such uneven distribution of resources sometimes has led to conflict, with countries going to war to take from others what they cannot produce for themselves.

Peace Corps Volunteers

In Costa Rica and other Spanish-speaking countries in the Americas, the Peace Corps is called *Cuerpo de Paz.* In the African tongue of Swahili, the organization is known as *Watu Wa Amani.* People on the frozen plains of the former Soviet republic of Kazakhstan call it *Korpus Mira.* However it is identified, the Peace Corps is one of the key organizations for building ties between the United States and other countries around the world.

More than 140,000 people have served as Peace Corps volunteers since 1961, when Congress and President John F. Kennedy established the agency. Volunteers use their educational and professional experience to teach valuable skills to people in developing countries. Many of these skills are related to farming, business development, technology, and urban planning. Peace Corps volunteers also teach English as a foreign language, help improve health services, and provide aid and information for promoting healthy environments.

In 1997 about 6,500 Peace Corps volunteers were doing such work in more than 90 countries.

Peace Corps volunteers teach many skills to people in developing nations. Here, a volunteer in Ecuador helps local residents plant trees.

Hundreds of such volunteers have worked throughout the former Soviet Union to ease the difficult transition from communism to democracy and capitalism.

Many Peace Corps volunteers discover that people in other countries—particularly in the former Soviet Union—are very curious about the United States. After being interviewed on Kazakh television and radio when she served as a Peace Corps volunteer at the age of 21, Michelle Ostrander found herself receiving phone calls from strangers wanting to talk to "the American."

"After I talked awhile and wanted to go, they'd say 'Don't hang up—you're the first American I've ever talked to,' " Ostrander says. Some Kazakhs, asking for "just a minute with the American," would go to the school where Ostrander taught English classes.

In fact, learning about the United States from these Peace Corps volunteers is helping to break down the barriers between old Cold War enemies. In the days of the Soviet Union, the communist government discouraged contact with foreigners, particularly Americans. Sometimes it was even a crime to make friends with a foreigner, says Kazakh teacher Irina Naumova.

Peace Corps volunteers often must endure difficult living conditions. In developing countries, for example, volunteers must learn to live without conveniences such as air-conditioning and central heating. Even indoor plumbing is an unknown luxury in some locations. Volunteers also must cope with the dangers of various diseases that plague some regions.

In Kazakhstan, Peace Corps volunteers have had to adjust to brutally cold winters, a smothering bureaucracy left over from the communist era, and other difficulties. Many volunteers, however, say that they are thrilled to have had the chance to experience this nation's culture and help its people.

What Do You Think?

1. How are Peace Corps volunteers helping build relations between the United States and other countries?
2. Why do you suppose that many Peace Corps volunteers take assignments in developing nations despite the sometimes difficult conditions?

International trade, on the other hand, is a means of peacefully acquiring needed resources.

A number of factors, such as population growth and economic development, are straining the world's resources. In some regions, drinking water is scarce, and overfishing greatly reduces the number of fish in the oceans. However, predictions made in the early 1970s about certain resources "running out" by the 1990s have proved false.

Population Growth

The demands of the world's rapidly increasing population place a great strain on natural resources. In 1997 there were nearly 6 billion people. Experts say that this number will exceed 8 billion by 2025.

The increase in the number of massive cities and their surrounding areas is evidence of this staggering growth. If population predictions are accurate, by 2015 there will be 33 "megacities," each with a population of more than 8 million. Already, some 27 million people live in the metropolitan area of Tokyo, Japan, while more than 16 million live in São Paulo, Brazil. In the coming years the people in these crowded cities will consume huge supplies of resources, such as gasoline, heating oil, electricity, wood, fresh water, and food.

The most rapid population growth is occurring in developing nations. Where economic growth is slow, it is increasingly difficult to feed growing populations. The World Resources Institute predicts that by 2010 about 300 million Africans will be suffering from malnutrition—a 70 percent increase from today.

Economic Development

Nations need healthy economies to feed, house, educate, and employ their citizens. In some cases, however, unregulated economic development has come at great cost to natural resources.

For example, the rate of **deforestation**—the clearing of forests—has increased as people seek timber and land for economic development. Experts from the World Resources Institute estimate that from 1960 to 1990, one fifth of the world's tropical forest was lost. These forests are home to a wide variety of species of plants, insects, and animals—many of which are now threatened with extinction. Deforestation also contributes to the world's pollution problems by destroying plants, which take in carbon dioxide and give off oxygen, thereby helping to keep the atmosphere's gases balanced.

Economic development also consumes energy resources, increasing demand for the world's nonrenewable supplies of fossil fuels. Because the strains on these resources affect all countries, world leaders are working together to improve resource conservation methods and to promote sustainable development—economic development that does not lead to further resource depletion.

SECTION 3 — REVIEW

1. Define the following terms: global warming, renewable resource, nonrenewable resource, deforestation.

2. What do many scientists say is the cause of global warming? What are some other sources of air pollution?

3. How does deforestation contribute to air pollution? What other resources are threatened by uncontrolled development?

4. **Thinking and Writing Critically**
As you have read, there is some debate over the real causes and consequences of global warming. Nevertheless, some scientists insist that action must be taken now to prevent future catastrophes. How do you think world leaders should address such issues when opinion in the scientific community is divided?

5. Applying **PUBLIC GOOD**
Conduct an Internet search to generate a list of international organizations that work to protect the environment. Then choose one organization and briefly describe the focus of its work and how it helps governments develop policies that promote the public good.

U.S. RELATIONS WITH OTHER COUNTRIES

Objectives

★ How has the end of the Cold War affected the debate over U.S.-Japanese relations?

★ What issues have dominated U.S.-European relations since the end of the Cold War?

★ How have U.S. leaders addressed trade and human rights issues in relations with China?

★ How have a history of intervention and efforts to expand trade marked U.S. relations with Latin American countries?

★ What has been the focus of U.S. policy toward Africa in recent history?

As you have read, nations are interdependent in many ways. As a result, the international relationships of the United States—as one of the world's most powerful countries—are particularly important. As noted in Chapter 10, during the Cold War many U.S. relationships were based on the policy of containment—stopping the spread of communism. With the end of the Cold War, U.S. relations with the rest of the world have undergone significant change.

U.S.-Japanese Relations

The relationship between the United States and Japan has changed a great deal since the end of World War II. After the war, the United States played an important role in the restructuring of Japan's government and economy. Throughout the Cold War, Japan concentrated on economic growth while its defense needs were managed by the United States. When the U.S.-Japan Mutual Security Treaty was signed after World War II, U.S. leaders insisted upon this policy because they wanted Japan to become a strong capitalist and democratic ally rather than to revert to its hostile military practices of the first half of the twentieth century. In addition, the United States wanted to establish a political presence in Asia. Since the end of the Cold War, there has been increased and unresolved debate in both countries over whether this defense policy should continue.

Debate in the United States Supporters of the current relationship note that Japan has a long warrior tradition and was an aggressive military power during the 50 years prior to the end of World War II. They warn that a deterioration of the close U.S.-Japanese relationship could produce a re-armed, militaristic Japan.

Other people argue that Japan has shown for more than 50 years that it no longer supports the warrior tradition. In addition, some say that Japan should pay more for its own military defense now that it is a great economic power. This view that Japan should no longer get a "free ride" from the United States is largely a result of frustration at the growing and longtime U.S. trade deficit with Japan. The first such trade deficit occurred in 1965 but created little tension because few Japanese imports at that time competed with major U.S. industries. The trade deficit has continued to widen since then, and since the late

WORLD AFFAIRS *In 1996 President Clinton, shown here with Japanese prime minister Ryutaro Hashimoto, made a state visit to Japan to discuss trade relations.* **In what year did the United States have its first trade deficit with Japan?**

1970s friction has increased as the quality of Japanese products has improved and U.S. consumption of Japanese goods has grown.

Debate in Japan While many Japanese also wish to maintain their current relationship with the United States, an increasing number believe that Japan cannot remain economically powerful and politically weak. They argue that Japan is a significant economic world power and for this reason must play a more active role in world affairs.

In the early 1990s, Japan moved cautiously—sometimes at the prodding of U.S. leaders—toward a more significant role in world military and political matters. In response to U.S. pressure, for example, Japan contributed $13 billion toward the 1991 Persian Gulf War against Iraq, the largest contribution of any non–Middle Eastern country. Then in 1992–93, Japan sent a limited number of peacekeeping soldiers to supervise elections in Cambodia. Japanese leaders also have formally requested a permanent seat on the UN Security Council. Boutros Boutros-Ghali, UN secretary-general from 1992 to 1996, proposed Japan's membership to the council.

U.S.-European Relations

U.S. relations with European countries also are undergoing change. Some people argue that U.S. relations with Western Europe have significantly decreased in importance since the passing of the Cold War. During the Cold War, Western Europe was vital to U.S. military interests, for it helped balance the Soviet satellite nations. Western Europe remains an important focus of U.S. foreign policy, however, because of close cultural and economic ties.

With the exception of occasional difficulties, trade friction with the European Union has not been as severe as with Japan, mainly because the United States and Europe have had relatively balanced trade. Recently, U.S. leaders have concentrated on building new relationships with the former communist countries of Eastern Europe and in the countries of the former Soviet Union to resolve conflict in the region. As noted in Chapter 10, this has meant enlarging the membership of the North Atlantic Treaty Organization (NATO). In 1997 three new members were proposed—the Czech Republic, Hungary, and Poland.

Promoting Stability In the early 1990s U.S. relations with Eastern Europe focused on helping the region make a stable transition from communism. Some U.S. leaders worried that dramatic changes in Eastern European governments would lead to chaos, particularly in Russia and the other former Soviet republics.

In addition, many people worried about the fate of the former Soviet Union's stockpile of nuclear weapons, which was under the control of various former Soviet republics. Many were afraid that the weapons would not be handled safely or would fall into the hands of terrorists. U.S. foreign-policy advisers strongly recommended that these weapons be removed from some of these newly independent countries—for example, Ukraine and Belarus. These countries have since disposed of the weapons or have transferred them to Russia, where they were dismantled.

Foreign-policy experts also supported sending economic aid to Russia to ease its transition to a market economy. They hoped that economic aid would help stabilize Russia and promote democracy there. Critics of this policy worry about aiding a nation that could potentially move away from

WORLD AFFAIRS *Capitalist reforms in Eastern Europe have enabled the development of privately owned businesses, such as this snack shop in Poland.* **Why do some people believe that U.S. relations with Western Europe are no longer as important as they once were?**

WORLD AFFAIRS *Group of Seven members and Russian president Boris Yeltsin pose for a picture at their 1997 summit in Denver, Colorado.* **In what year did Canada join the group?**

democracy and back toward authoritarianism. Russia has, however, held democratic elections for president and for its national legislature. In 1996 Boris Yeltsin—a strong supporter of democratic and capitalist reforms—was re-elected as the Russian president. Communists and other authoritarians, however, have made strong gains in parliamentary elections. The future of Russia's move to democracy is not yet clear.

Dealing with Conflict Foreign-policy experts are debating how the United States should deal with fighting in some nations in southeastern Europe, where tensions among ethnic groups have erupted in brutal domestic conflicts. Some who believe there are no vital U.S. interests at stake in these conflicts support a minimal U.S. role. Others believe the United States has an interest in maintaining stability and preventing human rights violations anywhere in the world.

One of the greatest challenges for U.S. policy in this region has been how to handle conflicts in the former republics of Yugoslavia. As you read earlier, the United States sent troops to Bosnia and Herzegovina as part of a multinational peacekeeping force. It is not yet clear if efforts to stabilize the region will be successful.

CASE STUDY

The Group of Seven

WORLD AFFAIRS Throughout the Cold War the United States, Japan, and the major Western European countries formed close relationships. To further strengthen these relationships and to address mutual concerns, the leaders of the United States, Japan, Great Britain, Germany, France, and Italy began holding annual meetings in 1975. Canada joined the group in 1976. These industrial democracies are sometimes collectively called the Group of Seven, or G7.

The annual G7 summits are held in a different member country each year. The leaders discuss important economic and political issues that affect their countries and the international community. In 1996, for example, G7 leaders meeting in Lyons, France, adopted a number of measures designed to combat international terrorism. G7 leaders also have addressed ways to promote trade and economic cooperation among their countries.

In 1991 the leader of the Soviet Union first joined G7 leaders at a postsummit meeting. Russia's president is regularly invited to participate with the other seven leaders in what is called the Summit of the 8 after each G7 summit. These meetings often focus on issues related to development in and cooperation among the countries of both Eastern Europe and the former Soviet Union.

U.S.-Chinese Relations

Relations between the United States and China are increasingly important as China's political influence and economic development are on the rise. Since President Richard Nixon visited China in 1972, relations between the two countries have improved. During the 1970s and 1980s the relationship often was intertwined with Cold War politics. Though for different reasons, each country viewed the Soviet Union as a threat to its security. In recent years, however, the relationship between the United States and China began to revolve primarily around two major issues: trade and human rights.

Trade Trade between the United States and China has been growing since Chinese communist leaders embarked on a program of economic change at the beginning of the 1980s. These changes included allowing foreign investment, adopting free-market reforms, and even setting up a stock market. Since then, U.S. businesses have been eager to enter the huge Chinese market. By the early 1990s, China was the United States's sixth-largest trading partner. As with Japan, however, a growing U.S. trade deficit with China has created some tensions between the two countries.

Human Rights The Chinese government's treatment of its citizens also has led to tensions with the United States. While undertaking significant economic reforms, Chinese leaders have refused to allow substantial political change, such as permitting dissent, or criticism of government policies. The government has held thousands of political prisoners who, according to the reports of international organizations as well as the U.S. State Department, are often tortured. The Chinese government has been criticized for the high number of crimes punishable by death and for its use of executed prisoners as a primary source of organ transplants.

In 1989 Chinese leaders ordered troops to crush massive, weeks-long demonstrations by students and other Chinese citizens who were calling for democratic reforms and an end to government corruption. The resulting massacre at Tiananmen Square in the capital, Beijing, left hundreds—possibly thousands—dead and thousands injured. Thousands of Chinese around the country were arrested and imprisoned.

U.S. Debate As a result of the Tiananmen Square Massacre, the U.S. government placed some sanctions on China and canceled most weapons sales to the nation. However, China's relations with the United States—and the rest of the world—are now greatly influenced by economic considerations. The U.S. government has never revoked China's most-favored-nation trading status in spite of the nation's human rights violations.

China's dual policy of economic reform and political authoritarianism has led to great debate among U.S. leaders over U.S.-China relations. Some have demanded trade restrictions to protest the Chinese government's violations of human rights. Others—focusing on the gains from tapping the huge Chinese market—have opposed such measures, also pointing out that isolating the country will only lead to a deterioration of the political situation, while closer ties with the West will strengthen the movement toward democracy in China. Overall, U.S.-Chinese relations are frequently rocky. U.S. officials have pressed China to improve its human rights record, and Chinese leaders have resented such interference with their internal affairs. In addition, efforts to solve trade and economic disputes such as the Chinese piracy of U.S. software and CDs have been difficult, though some agreements have been reached.

WORLD AFFAIRS *Millions of Chinese political protesters march in front of Mao Zedong's tomb in 1989. Chinese troops later crushed the demonstrations in Tiananmen Square.* ***What effect did such actions have on U.S. foreign policy toward China?***

WORLD AFFAIRS *Ships load and unload goods at the Bay of Valparaíso, Chile. Latin American countries have recently opened their markets and expanded trade with the United States.* **Historically, why did the U.S. government intervene in Latin American countries?**

U.S.-Latin American Relations

U.S. relations with Latin American countries have been dominated by the principle of realism. As noted in Chapter 10, realist doctrine stresses placing U.S. interests above all other considerations when dealing with foreign countries. This has often led relations between the United States and Latin American countries to be marked by two things: U.S. intervention in Latin American affairs and efforts to expand trade.

An Interventionist Past Historically, the United States has intervened in Latin American countries when U.S. leaders decided that doing so was necessary to protect U.S. interests. For example, the U.S. government has sent troops to Cuba, Nicaragua, Haiti, Mexico, and the Dominican Republic to protect U.S. citizens and investments during various crises.

Such intervention created considerable resentment among Latin Americans. At times this resentment was reflected in revolutionary movements against U.S.-supported governments in the region. In addition, some Latin American governments pursued economic policies designed to limit U.S. influence.

Expanding Trade Since the late 1980s, Latin American countries have increasingly opened their

markets and expanded trade with the United States. For the first time ever, more or less democratic governments are in power today in every Latin American country besides Cuba. These changes have come as Latin American leaders try to duplicate the success of East Asian governments in developing their economies. As you read earlier, several Latin American countries also have moved to improve their economies by forming a regional trading bloc.

Mexico is a dramatic example of changing attitudes. In the past the Mexican government feared U.S. domination, so it restricted the ability of foreigners to own Mexican companies, kept natural resource industries such as oil under government control, and shielded industry by keeping imports low. In the 1990s, however, Mexico reduced trade barriers under NAFTA and opened industry to foreign investment. After some initial economic difficulties, Mexico's economy improved and trade among the NAFTA countries boomed. U.S. leaders now are debating whether to open NAFTA to include other Latin American countries.

U.S.-African Relations

Compared to its activity in other parts of the world, the United States has been relatively uninvolved in African affairs, particularly in recent years. Some U.S. officials, however, believe the United States

WORLD AFFAIRS *U.S. protesters urge the American government to pressure South Africa into abandoning apartheid. In 1994 South Africa held its first all-race elections.* **Since the early 1990s what has been the focus of U.S. policy toward Africa?**

should increase its efforts to help African nations overcome longtime poverty, political oppression, and other difficulties. This position has generally received strong support among African Americans. For example, in the 1980s African American and civil rights leaders were instrumental in pushing the U.S. government to impose sanctions on South Africa for its racist policy of apartheid.

In 1991 South Africa ended apartheid. Since then, U.S. policy toward Africa has largely focused on humanitarian aid. As you read in Chapter 10, U.S. troops were sent to Somalia in 1992–93 to help feed starving people caught in a chaotic civil war. In 1994 the United States offered assistance in Rwanda, although on a much smaller scale than in Somalia. In addition to humanitarian goals, the U.S. State Department's policy goals concerning Africa include

★ supporting democratic institutions,

★ promoting sustainable economic growth,

★ and gaining greater African participation in dealing with issues such as AIDS and drug trafficking.

The United States has begun to reconsider its longtime support of old Cold War allies in Africa. In 1997, for example, the United States did not support longtime dictator and former ally President Mobutu Sese Seko when rebels ended his rule in Zaire and created the Democratic Republic of Congo.

SECTION 4 — REVIEW

1. Describe the arguments of those who wish to change the relationship between the United States and Japan. Why do some people oppose such change?

2. What two things have U.S. leaders focused on in building relationships in Eastern Europe since the end of the Cold War?

3. How has China's record on human rights complicated U.S.-Chinese relations?

4. How have many Latin American countries changed their economic and trade policies in recent years?

5. What role does humanitarian aid play in U.S.-African relations?

6. **Thinking and Writing Critically**
   With the ending of the Cold War and the decline in Russian military power, the United States is now the world's only military superpower. What responsibilities does such a position place on the United States? For example, should the world's only military superpower take part in peacekeeping efforts around the world? Why or why not?

7. **Applying** WORLD AFFAIRS Do you believe that U.S. relations with China and other countries should focus more on trade than on human rights? Write a short newspaper editorial on your position. You might want to examine newspapers and magazines to read published opinions on the issue.

CHAPTER 23 — SUMMARY

SECTION 1 The struggle for collective security is one example of the interdependence of the world's countries. In today's interdependent world, security is a collective concern because even the regions and countries that are not directly involved in conflicts can be affected.

Nations around the world are constantly challenged to contain conflicts arising from ethnic, religious, and ideological rivalries. Other threats to regional security include the violent change of a nation's government.

An increase in the production and distribution of weapons of mass destruction also imperils collective security. These include nuclear weapons, chemical and biological weapons, and conventional arms.

Through the United Nations, all countries can work together to promote collective security. The UN serves as a forum for settling disputes, protecting human rights, and promoting respect for international law.

SECTION 2 International interdependence also can be seen in economic relationships. Two important factors affect these relationships: the economic development of the world's countries and international trade.

Developed nations share high levels of personal income, relatively low unemployment, wide access to health care, good educational systems, and healthy manufacturing and industrial sectors. These nations strongly influence the economies of other countries around the world, particularly developing nations—the world's poorer countries. Some developing nations have begun to close the economic gap that separates them from developed nations.

International trade fuels the economic interdependence of nations. As trade has become increasingly important for the United States, the country has developed a deepening trade deficit. The trade deficit may contribute to higher unemployment and a lower standard of living over time.

SECTION 3 Global interdependence also is evident in many environmental challenges, such as air and water pollution. International efforts to meet those challenges include the 1992 Earth Summit. Another challenge involves reducing strains on the world's renewable and nonrenewable resources—strains resulting in large part from population growth and uncontrolled economic development.

SECTION 4 U.S. relations with other countries have been changing since the end of the Cold War. Debate over U.S.-Japanese relations revolves around Japan's increasing economic influence in the world and who should bear the burden of Japan's military defense. U.S.-European relations are increasingly focused on promoting stability in the former communist countries of Eastern Europe.

U.S. relations with China have been strained by tensions over trade and human rights issues. On the other hand, after years of resentment over U.S. influence, many Latin American countries—particularly Mexico—have sought closer trade with and economic ties to the United States. Recent U.S. relations with Africa have focused primarily on humanitarian aid, although U.S. policy also supports encouraging economic growth and fostering democratic governments.

Government Notebook

Review in your Government Notebook how you answered the question at the beginning of the chapter about why it is important to understand how events elsewhere in the world affect the United States. Now that you have finished studying this chapter, would you change your answer? Respond in your Notebook.

REVIEW

REVIEWING CONCEPTS

1. How might long-term trade deficits harm the U.S. economy?

2. How do pollution and the scarcity of natural resources challenge the world's countries?

3. How have nations around the world worked together to ease conflict?

4. In what ways does international trade help a country's economy?

5. What has been the focus of U.S. relations with European and with African countries since the end of the Cold War?

6. What is the World Trade Organization? How does it promote international trade?

THINKING AND WRITING CRITICALLY

1. **WORLD AFFAIRS** In what ways do you think that promoting international trade also promotes worldwide collective security?

2. **POLITICAL PROCESSES** Recall that the five permanent members of the UN Security Council have veto power. In some ways, that might be like giving California, Texas, and New York veto power over the actions of Congress. Why do you suppose these five countries have veto power?

3. **WORLD AFFAIRS** What responsibilities do the world's developed countries have to poorer countries? Does the development of the economies of poor countries benefit wealthier countries? If so, how?

4. **PUBLIC GOOD** Some people argue that the U.S. government can best promote the public good by concentrating on solving problems in this country before helping other countries through humanitarian aid and other assistance. Do you agree with this argument? Why or why not?

CITIZENSHIP IN YOUR COMMUNITY

Some U.S. cities have adopted foreign communities as sister cities. Civic leaders, businesspeople, and students in both cities often share ideas about ways of life in their home countries and how to promote international friendship. Working with a group, research possible sister cities for your town or community. You might want to choose a city or town in Canada or Mexico, for example. After you have finished your research, prepare a report for your city's civic leaders, suggesting ways to promote ties between your community and your sister city and the benefits of doing so. You might want to write a letter to high school students in your chosen sister city to solicit ideas about how to build a relationship between your two communities.

COOPERATIVE PORTFOLIO PROJECT

Imagine that your group has been chosen to develop a plan for a United Student World Assembly (USWA). Among the assembly's goals are promoting cooperation and understanding among students around the world. Organizers, however, are open to including other goals. Your group must prepare a draft charter of the USWA. The charter should include a brief preamble explaining the goals of the USWA, the structure of the organization, the location(s) for assembly meetings, and the rules for making decisions. Prepare your draft charter for presentation to other members of your class.

PRACTICING SKILLS: READING MAPS

Using the map and information below, create a special-purpose map that illustrates population growth and population density. Organize your map in whatever way you think is most understandable and effective. Consider the use of color, relative size of countries, and symbols. Include a key to explain the information.

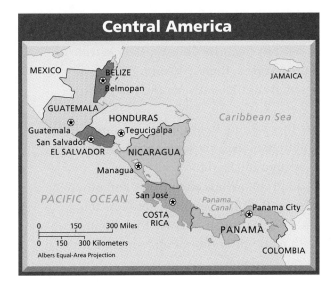

Central America

Population of Central America

Country	Population	Annual Rate of Growth	Pop. Per sq. mile
Belize	219,296	2.4	25
El Salvador	5,828,987	1.8	729
Guatemala	11,277,614	2.5	269
Costa Rica	3,463,083	2.1	177
Honduras	5,605,193	2.7	130
Nicaragua	4,272,352	2.8	92
Panama	2,655,094	1.7	90

THE INTERNET: LEARNING ONLINE

Conduct an Internet search for information about specialized UN agencies and other international organizations. You might try using such search words as *United Nations* and *international organizations.* Choose one and prepare a short report about its purpose, structure, and activities. Add your report to others in the class to create an International Organizations Reference folder that could be placed in your classroom or library.

ANALYZING PRIMARY SOURCES

THE UN SECRETARY-GENERAL'S ANNUAL REPORT

Kofi Annan of Ghana, the secretary-general of the United Nations, is responsible for generating an annual report on the work of the UN. The excerpt below, from the 1997 report, discusses the organization's desire to peacefully resolve conflict between countries. Read the excerpt and answer the questions that follow.

> **"** The prevention of conflict both within and between States requires, first of all, ongoing attention to possible sources of tension and prompt action to ensure that tension does not evolve into conflict. During the past year, the Secretariat, in cooperation with other branches of the United Nations system, has worked to strengthen its global watch, which is designed to detect threats to international peace and security, enabling the Security Council to carry out or to foster preventive action.
>
> Cooperation with regional organizations offers great potential. Close contacts with the Organization of African Unity (OAU) are a case in point. The two secretariats engage in almost daily consultations. . . . There is also increased cooperation between the United Nations and subregional organizations such as the Economic Community of West African States and the Southern African Development Community. **"**

1. According to Annan, what does prevention of conflict within and between states require?

2. What are some regional organizations that cooperate with the United Nations?

United Nations Ambassador for a Day

Imagine that you and other members of your group are ambassadors representing the five permanent member countries of the United Nations Security Council. Decide which country each group member will represent: the United States, Russia, China, France, or Great Britain. Then work together to prevent a potential conflict between the two large neighboring countries of Zelsa and Karnosh.

Growing tensions between the two countries are threatening to erupt into warfare, which could have terrible consequences for them both. War also could impose hardships on neighboring countries as well as other nations around the world.

As a permanent member of the Security Council, you will review documents and other information that council staff members have gathered about the potential conflict. You will find that information on the following pages. After reviewing it, answer the accompanying questions in your Government Notebook. Finally, work with other permanent Security Council members to develop a policy for resolving the situation.

In this case, assume that other, nonpermanent members of the Security Council have agreed to follow the lead of the permanent council members. Remember that any one of the five permanent members may veto any proposed action. Because of this, your proposal must be approved by all five members of your group.

As you know, the Security Council has a variety of options if you decide to take action. The council could, for example, order UN member countries to halt trade with Zelsa, Karnosh, or both. The Security Council also could authorize UN member countries to use force to defend Zelsa or Karnosh if its neighbor appears to be the aggressor in a conflict. You and other Security Council members also could decide to take other actions you believe might be more appropriate.

When your group has reached a decision about the situation, prepare a formal report to the UN secretary-general and the UN General Assembly. The report should briefly explain the circumstances behind the looming conflict. It also should outline the specific steps the Security Council has authorized member countries to take to prevent a conflict.

UNITED NATIONS SECURITY COUNCIL

STAFF REPORT: History of Tensions Between Zelsa and Karnosh

The countries of Zelsa and Karnosh share a common border. Although they historically have been rivals, in the last few decades the two countries have been particularly hostile to each other. In part this is because they have two very different political and economic systems: Zelsa has an authoritarian, communist government, while Karnosh has a democratic government and a capitalist economy.

In addition, the Zelsan government has demanded that Karnosh sacrifice control of the island of Casbah. The island, which lies off the coast of Karnosh near the border with Zelsa, belonged to Zelsa before it was seized by Karnosh following a war between the two nations 90 years ago. Before it lost control of Casbah, Zelsa had ruled the island for almost two centuries. The island still has a large Zelsan minority. Rich oil deposits also are believed to exist in the waters surrounding Casbah.

Over the years, each side has from time to time accused the other of hostile actions toward the other. Zelsan and Karnoshian troops have clashed in minor skirmishes along the border five times over the past quarter of a century. Two of those skirmishes have occurred in the last two years.

The following facts pertaining to each country further clarify the situation:

Karnosh
- Population: 23.2 million
- Political system: democratic
- Economy: capitalist, free-market
- Per capita GDP (in U.S. dollars): $19,200
- Military size: 300,000 (2.2 million reservists)

Zelsa
- Population: 17.9 million
- Political system: communist
- Economy: command economy
- Per capita GDP (in U.S. dollars): $8,800
- Military size: 900,000 (1.9 million reservists)

(1)

★ What are the historic causes of tensions between Zelsa and Karnosh? What do you think is the chance that those tensions will erupt into war between the two countries?

★ How could war between Zelsa and Karnosh affect China, the United States, France, and Great Britain? How does Zelsa's friendship with China and Karnosh's friendship with the other three countries complicate the question of UN intervention?

UNITED NATIONS SECURITY COUNCIL

Zelsan officials claim that the Karnoshian government discriminates against the Zelsan minority on Casbah. In addition, Zelsan officials argue that rich oil deposits in the waters surrounding Casbah should belong to their country instead of to Karnosh.

The Zelsan government, therefore, has intensified its demands that Karnosh hand over the island. Those demands have been matched by increased military activity along the Zelsan-Karnoshian border. Two months ago a border skirmish between the countries' troops caused nearly 50 casualties on each side.

War between the two countries could have serious consequences for other countries. China, for example, has long been an ally of Zelsa and is one of that country's largest trading partners. On the other hand, the United States, France, and the United Kingdom have friendly trade and military relations with Karnosh. War between Karnosh and Zelsa, therefore, could pose economic problems for four members of the UN Security Council, as well as for other countries. In addition, a Zelsan-Karnoshian war could increase tensions between China and the three UN Security Council member countries allied with Karnosh.

The United Nations has a number of options:

1. insisting that Zelsa and Karnosh meet with an impartial body to decide how to protect the rights of Zelsans on Casbah and how to divide the revenue from any oil deposits,
2. sending peacekeeping troops to patrol the Zelsan-Karnoshian border,
3. threatening to cut off trade with Zelsa if its troops either invade Karnosh or try to take Casbah by force, or
4. sending UN forces to fight alongside Karnosh if it is invaded, similar to what happened in South Korea in 1950.

(2)

PUBLIC POLICY LAB

Casbah Residents Brace for Conflict

By Evelyn Washington
Worldwide News Service

CASBAH, Karnosh—People on this Karnoshian island are anxiously waiting as Zelsan troops mass across the border from Karnosh. War, Casbah residents say, would devastate the island and its economy.

"We've spent decades creating a good standard of living for our people, and now war threatens it all," said Lilal Heptat, mayor of Casbah City.

Many members of the Zelsan ethnic minority on Casbah, however, believe that the high standard of living for the majority of the island's residents has been purchased at their expense. In fact, ethnic Zelsans charge that they face discrimination by the Karnoshian majority, particularly in housing and employment.

"If it takes war to change the situation, then we should welcome it," said Metie Sax, a Zelsan community leader. Sax provides various examples of discrimination, such as Zelsans who have been refused jobs or been beaten by Karnoshian gangs.

Not all ethnic Zelsans agree, however. Some, who spoke on the condition that they not be identified, said that discrimination is not a big problem on the island. In fact, said some Zelsan sources, the beatings that Sax mentions are the work of criminal gangs who prey on Karnoshian victims as well as Zelsans.

Some Karnoshian officials say that the government in nearby Zelsa has encouraged ethnic Zelsans on Casbah to exaggerate their claims of discrimination.

"It's all a ploy to force Karnosh to turn over Casbah to the Zelsans," Mayor Heptat said. "Zelsa desperately wants control of the rich oil deposits in the waters that surround our island."

Meanwhile, demonstrations against the Karnoshian rule of Casbah are continuing in the Zelsan capital. An estimated 300,000 people marched through the streets of the capital yesterday, calling on the Zelsan military to seize the island. Zelsan media, all under government control, also have demanded that Casbah be returned to Zelsa. Casbah became a Karnoshian territory following a war between the two countries 90 years ago. Karnoshian officials have announced that military reservists may be called to active duty next week.

◄ WHAT DO YOU THINK?

★ Do you think that Zelsan media coverage might provide important clues about the intentions of the Zelsan government? Why or why not?

★ Because Karnosh took control of Casbah after a war nearly a century ago, do you think Zelsa has a right to demand the return of the island now? Why or why not?

WHAT DO YOU THINK? ►

★ What do Bellany officials fear would happen if war were to break out between Karnosh and Zelsa?

The Republic of Bellany

United Nations Secretary-General
New York, New York

Dear Madame Secretary-General:

As you are aware, troops from Zelsa and Karnosh have been massing along their common border. It appears that war may soon break out between the two countries. In fact, Zelsan officials have been threatening to send their troops to invade Karnosh and seize the island of Casbah.

War would be disastrous, not just for those two countries but also for my own country, Bellany. My people fear that if fighting breaks out, millions of Karnoshian and Zelsan refugees would flee to Bellany. Our country simply does not have the resources to feed and protect so many refugees. In addition, we fear that tensions between the citizens of Bellany and the refugees could erupt into violence.

Therefore, the government of Bellany urges the United Nations to act to prevent a war. Without strong UN action, we believe that war between Karnosh and Zelsa is certain.

Sincerely,

L. Meiibus

Layson Meiibus
Prime Minister
Republic of Bellany

UNITED STATES JOINT CHIEFS OF STAFF

POSSIBILITIES FOR INTERVENTION IN THE KARNOSHIAN-ZELSAN CONFLICT

Below are estimates of the resources needed should the UN Security Council decide to send troops as peacekeepers or to support Karnosh against a Zelsan invasion.

PEACEKEEPING

The United Nations has spent billions of dollars on a variety of peace-keeping missions. It spent $2.8 billion in 1995 on such missions and spent $1.4 billion in 1996. The drop in spending between these two years largely reflects the end of UN peacekeeping operations in Bosnia. In 1996, UN troops were replaced by about 60,000 troops from the North Atlantic Treaty Organization, sent to help maintain peace after years of civil war.

Based on past UN and NATO experiences, a peacekeeping mission along the Karnosh-Zelsa border could be expensive, both financially and in terms of personnel. In fact, UN member countries should be prepared to provide about 50,000 peacekeeping troops. Supporting this force likely would cost about $3–4 billion annually.

Supporting Karnosh

If the Security Council sends troops to Karnosh to stop a Zelsan invasion, costs will increase dramatically. Financial costs are diffi-cult to estimate, but the number of troops needed for such a mis-sion would likely exceed 100,000.

Sources of Support

The United States likely would play an important role in UN peacekeeping efforts in Karnosh. While the United States provided only about 3 percent of UN peacekeeping troops in 1996, it paid a full quarter of UN peacekeeping costs that year. As of mid-1997 the United States also kept a force of 37,000 on the Korean Peninsula, where UN forces went in 1950 to defend South Korea from a North Korean invasion.

The United States also has been an important part of non-UN peace-keeping efforts, such as those in Bosnia. U.S. forces made up nearly a third of the 60,000 NATO peacekeeping troops in Bosnia in 1996.

Nevertheless, since 1945 some 110 countries have contributed personnel to peacekeeping missions around the world. In addition, about three quar-ters of UN peacekeeping costs are paid by countries other than the United States. It is likely, then, that many UN members would be called on to sup-port a peacekeeping mission in Karnosh or to help defend that country from a Zelsan invasion.

◄ WHAT DO YOU THINK?

★ According to the U.S. Joint Chiefs of Staff, how much might a peace-keeping mission to Karnosh cost the United Nations?

★ Why do you suppose that the United States has been an impor-tant source of financial and military support for peacekeeping missions and for the defense of countries such as South Korea?

★ Do you believe the United States should work with other UN mem-bers to prevent a war between Karnosh and Zelsa, or to defend Karnosh if needed? Why or why not?

THINGS TO DO

1. Review with other members of your group the given information and your answers to the accompanying questions.

2. Work with members of your group—the other permanent UN Security Council members—to decide UN policy on the Karnosh-Zelsa issue. Remember that because any one permanent member can veto a proposal, agreement on a policy must be unanimous.

3. Prepare the new UN policy in the form of a report. The report should provide details of the policy and the reasons why the Security Council has adopted it. The report should be typed or neatly handwritten.

4. Share your group's report with other members of the class and compare the proposed solu-tions. Be prepared to explain and defend the policy your group has approved.

H O L T

American Government

REFERENCE SECTION

United States: Political

STRAIT OF JUAN DE FUCA

Seattle
Olympia
WASHINGTON
Spokane
Pend Oreille

45°N
130°W

Portland
Salem
OREGON

PACIFIC OCEAN

Flathead Lake
MONTANA
Helena
Fort Peck Lake
Missouri River

IDAHO
Boise
Yellowstone River
Billings
Yellowstone Lake
Snake River

NORTH DAKOTA
Bismarck
Far

SOUTH DAKOTA
Pierre
Sioux Fa

40°N
Cape Mendocino
Goose Lake
Shasta Lake
Sacramento River

WYOMING
Casper

NEBRASKA
Lince

Pyramid Lake
NEVADA
Carson City
Lake Tahoe

Great Salt Lake
Salt Lake City
Provo
UTAH
Green River

Cheyenne

35°N
125°W

San Francisco
SAN FRANCISCO BAY
Sacramento
MONTEREY BAY
San Joaquin River

Denver
COLORADO
Colorado Springs

KANSAS

Fresno
CALIFORNIA
Bakersfield

Las Vegas

Lake Mead

Santa Fe
Canadian River
Keystone
OKLAHO
Oklahoma City

Los Angeles
Channel Islands
San Diego
Salton Sea

Colorado River

ARIZONA
Phoenix
Gila River
Tucson

Albuquerque
NEW MEXICO

Amarillo

Lubbock

Fort Worth

TEXAS

Aust

30°N
115°W
Gulf of California

El Paso

Pecos River
Amistad Reservoir

San Antonio

Pa Is

To understand the relative locations of Alaska and Hawaii as well as the vast distances separating them from the rest of the United States, see the world map.

Kauai
Niihau
Oahu
Honolulu
Molokai
Lanai
Maui
Kahoolawe
HAWAII
Hawaii
PACIFIC OCEAN

22°N
155°W
160°W
19°N

SCALE
0   75   150 Miles
0   75   150 Kilometers

ARCTIC OCEAN
Arctic Circle
RUSSIA
Bering Strait
Nome
St. Lawrence Island
St. Matthew Island
Nunivak Island

65°N
ALASKA
Fairbanks
CANADA

60°N

Attu Island
Bering Sea
55°N
50°N
170°E
180
170°W

SCALE
0   250   500 Miles
0   250   500 Kilometers
Projection: Albers Equal Area

Anchorage

Kodiak Island
Gulf of Alaska
Juneau
Alexander Archipelago
55°

160°W
150°W
140°W
130°W
120°W

MEXICO

105°W
100°W
25°N

PACIFIC OCEAN

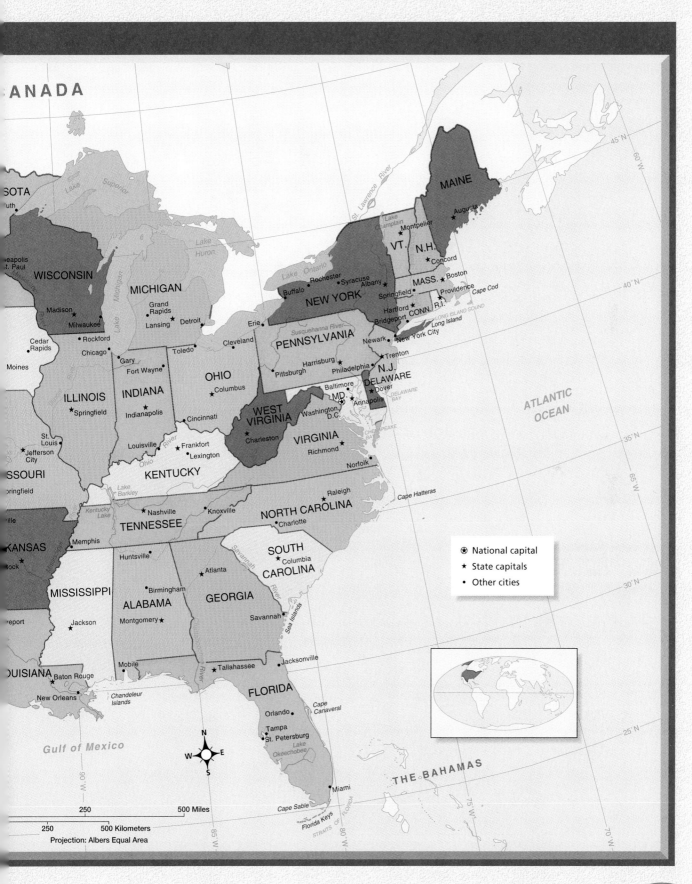

CANADA

MAINE
Augusta ★

VT. Montpelier ★
N.H.
Concord ★

MASS. Boston •
Rochester • Syracuse •
Buffalo • Albany ★ Springfield • Providence ★
NEW YORK Hartford ★ CONN. R.I.
Bridgeport • LONG ISLAND SOUND
Newark • Long Island
Erie • New York City •
PENNSYLVANIA Trenton ★

WISCONSIN
MICHIGAN
Grand Rapids •
Madison ★ Lansing • Detroit •
Milwaukee • Rockford • Cleveland •
Cedar Rapids • Chicago • Toledo •
Moines Gary • Fort Wayne •
ILLINOIS INDIANA OHIO
Springfield ★ Indianapolis ★ Columbus •
Cincinnati •
St. Louis • Louisville • Frankfort ★
Jefferson City ★ Lexington •
SSOURI KENTUCKY

Harrisburg • N.J.
Pittsburgh • Philadelphia •
DELAWARE
Baltimore • Dover ★
WEST MD.
VIRGINIA Washington, Annapolis ★
Charleston ★ D.C. DELAWARE BAY
VIRGINIA
Richmond ★
Norfolk •
CHESAPEAKE BAY

Lake Barkley
Springfield
ville
KANSAS
ock Memphis •
Kentucky Lake
TENNESSEE Nashville • Knoxville •
NORTH CAROLINA Raleigh ★
Charlotte • Cape Hatteras

MISSISSIPPI
ALABAMA
Jackson ★
Huntsville •
Birmingham •
Montgomery ★
GEORGIA
Atlanta ★
Savannah •

SOUTH
Columbia ★
CAROLINA

Sea Islands

report
UISIANA Baton Rouge ★
New Orleans •
Chandeleur Islands
Mobile •
Tallahassee ★
Jacksonville •

FLORIDA
Orlando •
Cape Canaveral
Tampa •
St. Petersburg •
Lake Okeechobee
Miami •

Gulf of Mexico

THE BAHAMAS

Cape Sable
Florida Keys
STRAITS OF FLORIDA

ATLANTIC OCEAN

Lake Superior
Lake Huron
Lake Michigan
Lake Ontario
St. Lawrence River
Lake Champlain
Cape Cod
Susquehanna River
Ohio River
Savannah River
Cape Fear River

45° N
40° N
35° N
30° N
25° N
60° W
65° W
70° W
75° W
80° W
85° W
90° W

⊛ National capital
★ State capitals
• Other cities

250   500 Miles
250   500 Kilometers
Projection: Albers Equal Area

N
W E
S

The World: Political

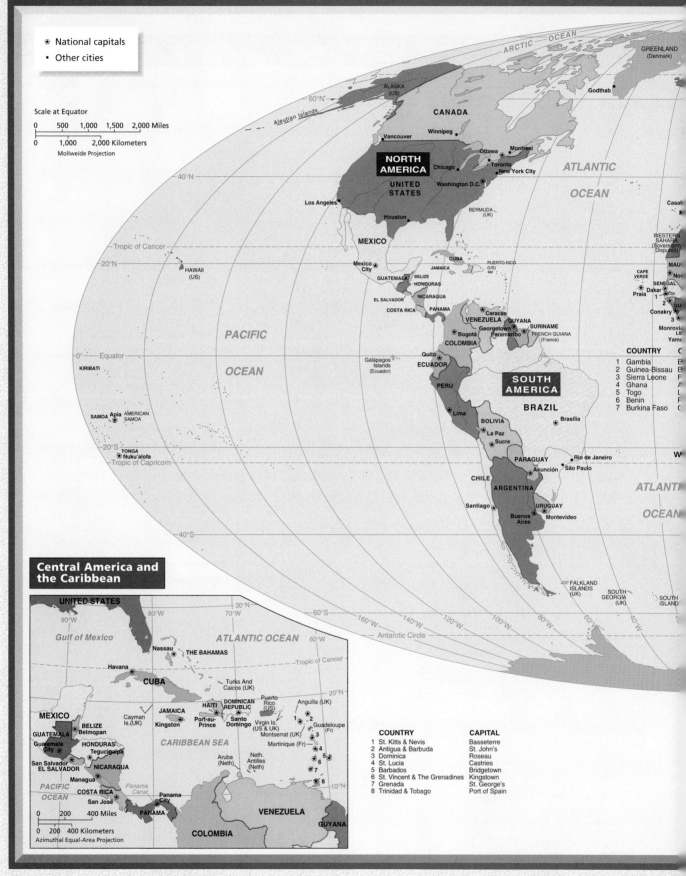

- ⊛ National capitals
- • Other cities

Scale at Equator

0   500   1,000   1,500   2,000 Miles
0   1,000   2,000 Kilometers
Mollweide Projection

ARCTIC OCEAN

GREENLAND
(Denmark)

ALASKA
(US)

60°N

CANADA

Godthab

Vancouver   Winnipeg

Aleutian Islands

NORTH
AMERICA

Ottawa   Montreal
Chicago   Toronto

UNITED
STATES

New York City
Washington D.C.

40°N

ATLANTIC

OCEAN

Los Angeles

BERMUDA
(UK)

Casab

Houston

MEXICO

WESTERN
SAHARA
(Sovereignty
Disputed)

Tropic of Cancer

20°N

CUBA

PUERTO RICO
(US)

CAPE
VERDE

MAU

Mexico
City

JAMAICA

Nou

HAWAII
(US)

SENEGAL

GUATEMALA   BELIZE

Dakar
Praia

HONDURAS

1

EL SALVADOR   NICARAGUA

GU

COSTA RICA   PANAMA

Conakry

3

Caracas

Monrovia

VENEZUELA   GUYANA   SURINAME

Yamo

0°   Equator

Bogotá

Georgetown   Paramaribo

FRENCH GUIANA
(France)

COLOMBIA

KIRIBATI

Galápagos
Islands
(Ecuador)

Quito

ECUADOR

COUNTRY   C

PACIFIC

PERU

SOUTH
AMERICA

1 Gambia   B
2 Guinea-Bissau   B
3 Sierra Leone   F
4 Ghana   A
5 Togo   L
6 Benin   F
7 Burkina Faso   O

OCEAN

Lima

BRAZIL

SAMOA   Apia

AMERICAN
SAMOA

Brasília

BOLIVIA

20°S

TONGA

La Paz

Nuku'alofa

Sucre

Tropic of Capricorn

PARAGUAY

Rio de Janeiro

W

Asunción

São Paulo

CHILE

ATLANTI

ARGENTINA

Santiago

URUGUAY

OCEAN

Buenos
Aires

Montevideo

40°S

FALKLAND
ISLANDS
(UK)

SOUTH
GEORGIA
(UK)

SOUTH
ISLAND

60°S

160°W   140°W   120°W   100°W   80°W   60°   40°W

Antarctic Circle

Central America and the Caribbean

UNITED STATES

30°N
80°W

90°W   70°W

60°S

60°W

Gulf of Mexico

Nassau

ATLANTIC OCEAN

THE BAHAMAS

Havana

Tropic of Cancer

Turks And
Caicos (UK)

CUBA

20°N

Anguilla (UK)

MEXICO

Cayman
Is.(UK)

JAMAICA

HAITI

DOMINICAN
REPUBLIC

Puerto
Rico
(US)

1   2

Guadeloupe
(Fr)

Kingston

Port-au-
Prince

Santo
Domingo

Virgin Is.
(US & UK)

3

GUATEMALA   BELIZE

Montserrat (UK)

Guatemala
City

Belmopan

CARIBBEAN SEA

Martinique (Fr)

4

HONDURAS

Aruba
(Neth)

5

Tegucigalpa

Neth.
Antilles
(Neth)

6

San Salvador
EL SALVADOR

NICARAGUA

7

Managua

8

PACIFIC

OCEAN

COSTA RICA

Panama
Canal

San José

Panama
City

0   200   400 Miles

PANAMA

VENEZUELA

0   200   400 Kilometers

COLOMBIA

GUYANA

Azimuthal Equal-Area Projection

COUNTRY	CAPITAL
1 St. Kitts & Nevis	Basseterre
2 Antigua & Barbuda	St. John's
3 Dominica	Roseau
4 St. Lucia	Castries
5 Barbados	Bridgetown
6 St. Vincent & The Grenadines	Kingstown
7 Grenada	St. George's
8 Trinidad & Tobago	Port of Spain

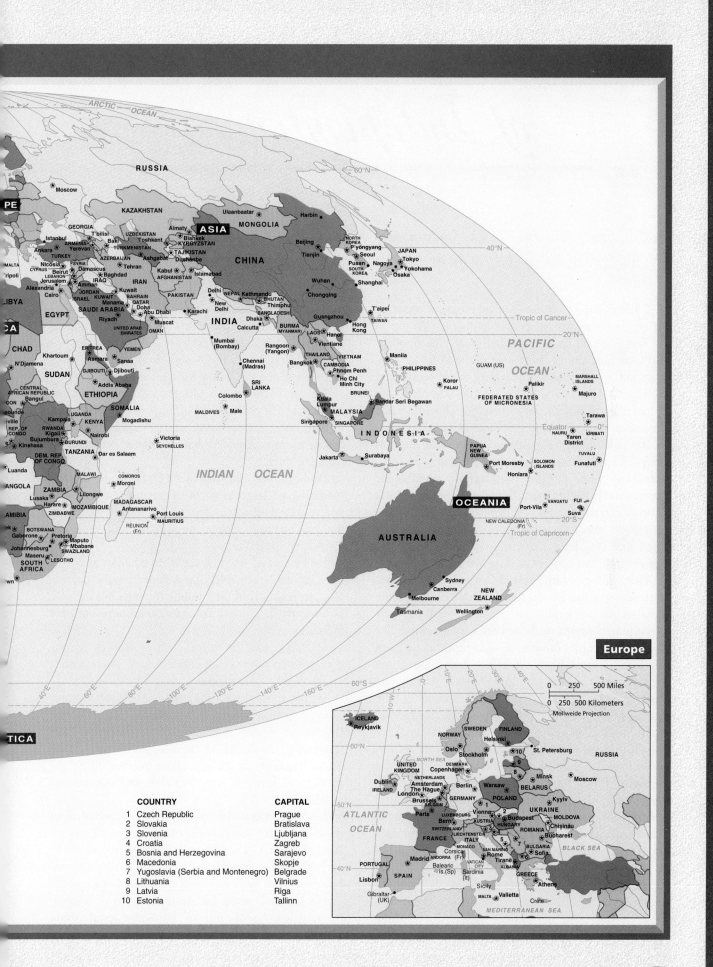

ARCTIC OCEAN

RUSSIA

60°N

KAZAKHSTAN

MONGOLIA

ASIA

Moscow

GEORGIA
Istanbul
T'bilisi
ARMENIA
Ankara
Yerevan
TURKEY
Nicosia
Baki
MALTA
Beirut
SYRIA
Tripoli
Jerusalem
Damascus
LEBANON
ISRAEL
JORDAN
Amman
Cairo

Almaty
Bishkek
KYRGYZSTAN
Toshkent
UZBEKISTAN
TAJIKISTAN
TURKMENISTAN
Ashgabat
Dushanbe
AZERBAIJAN
Tehran
IRAN
Baghdad
IRAQ
Kuwait
KUWAIT
BAHRAIN
Manama
QATAR
Doha
Riyadh
Abu Dhabi
UNITED ARAB
EMIRATES

Ulaanbaatar

Harbin

Beijing
Tianjin

NORTH
KOREA
P'yóngyang
SOUTH
KOREA
Seoul
Pusan

JAPAN
Tokyo
Nagoya
Yokohama
Osaka

40°N

CHINA

Wuhan

Chongqing

Shanghai

Kabul
AFGHANISTAN
Islamabad

PAKISTAN

Delhi
New
Delhi
NEPAL Kathmandu
BHUTAN
Thimphu
BANGLADESH
Dhaka

Guangzhou

T'aipei

TAIWAN

Hong
Kong

Tropic of Cancer

Muscat
OMAN

Karachi

INDIA

Calcutta
BURMA
(MYANMAR)

LAOS
Hanoi

20°N

PACIFIC

OCEAN

SAUDI ARABIA

EGYPT

CHAD

N'Djamena
SUDAN

Khartoum

ERITREA
Asmara
YEMEN
Sanaa
DJIBOUTI Djibouti

ETHIOPIA

Addis Ababa

Mumbai
(Bombay)

Chennai
(Madras)

SRI
LANKA

Colombo

MALDIVES

Rangoon
(Yangon)

Bangkok
THAILAND

CAMBODIA
Phnom Penh
Ho Chi
Minh City

VIETNAM
Vientiane

Manila

PHILIPPINES

BRUNEI

Bandar Seri Begawan

GUAM (US)

MARSHALL
ISLANDS

Koror
PALAU

Palikir

Majuro

FEDERATED STATES
OF MICRONESIA

Male

Equator

Tarawa
KIRIBATI

Yaren
District

NAURU

LIBYA

Alexandria

CENTRAL
AFRICAN REPUBLIC
Bangui

UGANDA
Kampala
RWANDA
Kigali
BURUNDI
Bujumbura

Nairobi
KENYA

Victoria
SEYCHELLES

Kuala
Lumpur
MALAYSIA
Singapore
SINGAPORE

INDONESIA

OCEANIA

PAPUA
NEW
GUINEA

TUVALU

Funafuti

DEM. REP.
OF CONGO

Luanda

TANZANIA
Dar es Salaam

Jakarta
Surabaya

INDIAN OCEAN

Port Moresby

SOLOMON
ISLANDS
Honiara

ANGOLA

MALAWI

ZAMBIA
Lusaka
Harare
ZIMBABWE
MOZAMBIQUE

COMOROS
Moroni

MADAGASCAR
Antananarivo

Port Louis
MAURITIUS

VANUATU FIJI

Port-Vila
NEW CALEDONIA
(Fr)

Suva

20°S

Lilongwe

NAMIBIA

BOTSWANA

Gaborone
Johannesburg
Maseru
SOUTH
AFRICA
Pretoria
Maputo
Mbabane
SWAZILAND
LESOTHO

REUNION
(Fr)

Tropic of Capricorn

AUSTRALIA

Sydney
Canberra
Melbourne
Tasmania

NEW
ZEALAND

Wellington

40°E
60°E
80°E
100°E
120°E
140°E
160°E
60°S

ANTARCTICA

COUNTRY	CAPITAL
1 Czech Republic	Prague
2 Slovakia	Bratislava
3 Slovenia	Ljubljana
4 Croatia	Zagreb
5 Bosnia and Herzegovina	Sarajevo
6 Macedonia	Skopje
7 Yugoslavia (Serbia and Montenegro)	Belgrade
8 Lithuania	Vilnius
9 Latvia	Riga
10 Estonia	Tallinn

Europe

0   250   500 Miles
0 250 500 Kilometers
Mollweide Projection

ICELAND
Reykjavik

NORWAY

SWEDEN

FINLAND

Helsinki

10

St. Petersburg

RUSSIA

Oslo
Stockholm

9

NORTH
SEA

UNITED
KINGDOM

DENMARK
Copenhagen

8

Minsk

Moscow

Dublin
IRELAND

NETHERLANDS
Amsterdam
The Hague
London
Brussels
BELGIUM

Berlin
GERMANY

Warsaw
POLAND

BELARUS

Kyiv

UKRAINE

ATLANTIC

OCEAN

Paris
FRANCE

LUXEMBOURG
Bern
SWITZERLAND
LIECHTENSTEIN
MONACO

Vienna
AUSTRIA
1
2
HUNGARY
Budapest

3
4
5
ITALY
Rome
SAN MARINO
VATICAN
CITY

ROMANIA

MOLDOVA
Chişinău

Bucharest

BLACK SEA

50°N

40°N

PORTUGAL

Lisbon

Madrid
SPAIN

Corsica
(Fr)

Balearic
Is.(Sp)

Sardinia
(It)

7
6
Tiranë
ALBANIA

BULGARIA
Sofia

GREECE

Athens

Gibraltar
(UK)

Sicily

MALTA
Valletta

Crête

MEDITERRANEAN SEA

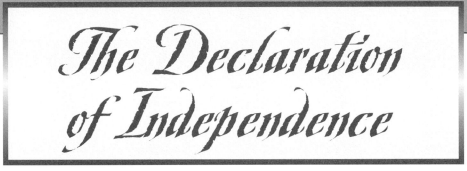

The Declaration of Independence

In Congress, July 4, 1776 The unanimous Declaration of the thirteen united States of America,

When in the Course of human events, it becomes necessary for one people to dissolve the political bands which have connected them with another, and to assume among the powers of the earth, the separate and equal station to which the Laws of Nature and of Nature's God entitle them, a decent respect to the opinions of mankind requires that they should declare the causes which impel [drive] them to the separation.

We hold these truths to be self-evident, that all men are created equal, that they are endowed [provided] by their Creator with certain unalienable [permanent] Rights, that among these are Life, Liberty, and the pursuit of Happiness.

That to secure these rights, Governments are instituted among Men, deriving [obtaining] their just powers from the consent of the governed,

That whenever any Form of Government becomes destructive of these ends, it is the Right of the People to alter or to abolish it, and to institute new Government, laying its foundation on such principles and organizing its powers in such form, as to them shall seem most likely to effect their Safety and Happiness. Prudence [caution], indeed, will dictate that Governments long established should not be changed for light and transient [passing] causes; and accordingly all experience hath shown, that mankind are more disposed to suffer, while evils are sufferable, than to right themselves by abolishing the forms to which they are accustomed. But when a long train of abuses and usurpations [wrongful seizures of power], pursuing invariably the same Object evinces [demonstrates] a design to reduce them under absolute Despotism [unlimited power], it is their right, it is their duty, to throw off such Government, and to provide new Guards for their future security.

Such has been the patient sufferance of these Colonies; and such is now the necessity which constrains [restricts] them to alter their former Systems of Government. The history of the present King of Great Britain is a history of repeated injuries and usurpations, all having in direct object the establishment of an absolute Tyranny [oppressive power] over these States. To prove this, let Facts be submitted to a candid [unbiased] world.

He has refused his Assent to Laws, the most wholesome and necessary for the public good.

He has forbidden his Governors to pass Laws of immediate and pressing importance, unless suspended in their operation till his Assent should be obtained; and when so suspended, he has utterly neglected to attend to them.

He has refused to pass other Laws for the accommodation of large districts of people, unless those people would relinquish the right of Representation in the Legislature, a right inestimable to them and formidable [fearsome] to tyrants only.

He has called together legislative bodies at places unusual, uncomfortable, and distant from the depository [storehouse] of their public Records, for the sole purpose of fatiguing them into compliance with his measures.

He has dissolved Representative Houses repeatedly, for opposing with manly firmness his invasions on the rights of the people.

He has refused for a long time, after such dissolutions, to cause others to be elected; whereby the Legislative powers, incapable of Annihilation, have returned to the People at large for their exercise; the State remaining in the meantime exposed to all the dangers of invasion from without, and convulsions within.

He has endeavored to prevent the population of these States; for that purpose obstructing the Laws for Naturalization of Foreigners; refusing to pass others to encourage their migrations hither, and raising the conditions of new Appropriations [additions] of Lands.

He has obstructed the Administration of Justice, by refusing his Assent to Laws for establishing Judiciary powers.

He has made Judges dependent on his Will alone, for the tenure [term] of their offices, and the amount and payment of their salaries.

He has erected a multitude of New Offices, and sent hither swarms of Officers to harass our people, and eat out their substance.

He has kept among us, in times of peace, Standing Armies without the Consent of our legislatures.

He has affected to render the Military independent of and superior to the Civil power.

He has combined with others to subject us to a jurisdiction foreign to our constitution, and unacknowledged by our laws; giving his Assent to their Acts of pretended Legislation:

For quartering [housing] large bodies of armed troops among us:

For protecting them, by a mock Trial, from punishment for any Murders which they should commit on the Inhabitants of these States:

For cutting off our Trade with all parts of the world:

For imposing Taxes on us without our Consent:

For depriving us in many cases, of the benefits of Trial by Jury:

For transporting us beyond Seas to be tried for pretended offences:

For abolishing the free System of English Laws in a neighboring Province, establishing therein an Arbitrary [unrestrained] government, and enlarging its Boundaries so as to render it at once an example and fit instrument for introducing the same absolute rule into these Colonies:

For taking away our Charters, abolishing our most valuable Laws, and altering fundamentally the Forms of our Governments:

For suspending our own Legislatures, and declaring themselves invested with power to legislate for us in all cases whatsoever.

He has abdicated Government here, by declaring us out of his Protection and waging War against us.

He has plundered our seas, ravaged our Coasts, burnt our towns, and destroyed the Lives of our people.

He is at this time transporting large Armies of foreign Mercenaries to complete the works of death, desolation [ruin] and tyranny, already begun with circumstances of Cruelty & perfidy [treachery] scarcely paralleled in the most barbarous ages, and totally unworthy the Head of a civilized nation.

He has constrained our fellow Citizens taken Captive on the high Seas to bear Arms against their Country, to become the executioners of their friends and Brethren, or to fall themselves by their Hands.

He has excited domestic insurrections among us, and has endeavored to bring on the inhabitants of our frontiers, the merciless Indian Savages, whose known rule of warfare, is an undistinguished destruction of all ages, sexes and conditions.

In every stage of these Oppressions We have Petitioned for Redress [compensation] in the most humble terms: Our repeated Petitions have been answered only by repeated injury. A Prince, whose character is thus marked by every act which may define a Tyrant, is unfit to be the ruler of a free people.

Nor have We been wanting in attentions to our British brethren. We have warned them from time to time of attempts by their legislature to extend an unwarrantable jurisdiction over us. We have reminded them of the circumstances of our emigration and settlement here. We have appealed to their native justice and magnanimity [nobleness], and we have conjured [called upon] them by the ties of our common kindred to disavow [disclaim] these usurpations, which would inevitably interrupt our connections and correspondence. They too have been deaf to the voice of justice and of consanguinity [common ancestry]. We must, therefore, acquiesce [consent to] in the necessity, which denounces our Separation, and hold them, as we hold the rest of mankind, Enemies in War, in Peace Friends.

We, therefore, the Representatives of the united States of America, in General Congress, Assembled, appealing to the Supreme Judge of the world for the rectitude [rightness] of our intentions, do, in the Name, and by Authority of the good People of these Colonies, solemnly publish and declare, That these United Colonies are, and of Right ought to be Free and Independent States; that they are Absolved [set free] from all Allegiance to the British Crown, and that all political connection between them and the State of Great Britain, is and ought to be totally dissolved; and that as Free and Independent States, they have full Power to levy War, conclude Peace, contract Alliances, establish Commerce, and to do all other Acts and Things which Independent States may of right do.

And for the support of this Declaration, with a firm reliance on the protection of divine Providence [guidance], we mutually pledge to each other our Lives, our Fortunes and our sacred Honor.

The Constitution
of the United States
of America

PREAMBLE

The short and dignified Preamble explains the goals of the new government under the Constitution.

PREAMBLE

We the People of the United States, in Order to form a more perfect Union, establish Justice, insure domestic Tranquility, provide for the common defense, promote the general Welfare, and secure the Blessings of Liberty to ourselves and our Posterity, do ordain and establish this Constitution for the United States of America.*

LEGISLATIVE BRANCH

Article I explains how the legislative branch, called Congress, is organized. The chief purpose of the legislative branch is to make the laws. Congress is made up of the Senate and the House of Representatives. The decision to have two bodies of government solved a difficult problem during the Constitutional Convention. The large states wanted the membership of Congress to be based entirely on population. The small states wanted every state to have an equal vote. The solution to the problem of how the states were to be represented in Congress was known as the Great Compromise.

The number of members of the House is based on the population of the individual states. Each state has at least one representative. The current size of the House is 435 members, set by Congress in 1929. If each member of the House represented only 30,000 American people, as the Constitution states, the House would have more than 6,000 members.

ARTICLE I

Section 1. All legislative Powers herein granted shall be vested in a Congress of the United States, which shall consist of a Senate and House of Representatives.

Section 2. The House of Representatives shall be composed of Members chosen every second Year by the People of the several States, and the Electors in each State shall have the Qualifications requisite for Electors of the most numerous Branch of the State Legislature.

No Person shall be a Representative who shall not have attained to the Age of twenty-five Years, and been seven Years a Citizen of the United States, and who shall not, when elected, be an inhabitant of that State in which he shall be chosen.

Representatives and direct Taxes shall be apportioned among the several States which may be included within this Union, according to their respective Numbers, ~~which shall~~

* Parts of the Constitution that have been ruled through are no longer in force or no longer apply.

The Granger Collection, New York.

be determined by adding to the whole Number of free Persons, including those bound to Service for a Term of Years, and excluding Indians not taxed, three fifths of all other Persons. The actual Enumeration shall be made within three Years after the first Meeting of the Congress of the United States, and within every subsequent Term of ten Years, in such Manner as they shall by Law direct. The Number of Representatives shall not exceed one for every thirty Thousand, but each State shall have at Least one Representative; and until such enumeration shall be made, the State of New Hampshire shall be entitled to choose three; Massachusetts eight; Rhode Island and Providence Plantations one; Connecticut five; New York six; New Jersey four; Pennsylvania eight; Delaware one; Maryland six; Virginia ten; North Carolina five; South Carolina five; and Georgia three.

When vacancies happen in the Representation from any State, the Executive Authority thereof shall issue Writs of Election to fill such Vacancies.

The House of Representatives shall choose their Speaker and other Officers; and shall have the sole Power of Impeachment.

Section 3. The Senate of the United States shall be composed of two Senators from each State, chosen by the Legislature thereof, for six Years; and each Senator shall have one Vote.

Immediately after they shall be assembled in Consequence of the first Election, they shall be divided as equally as may be into three Classes. The Seats of the Senators of the first Class shall be vacated at the Expiration of the second Year, of the second Class at the Expiration of the fourth Year, and of the third Class at the Expiration of the sixth Year, so that one third may be chosen every second Year; and if Vacancies happen by Resignation, or otherwise, during the Recess of the Legislature of any State, the Executive thereof may make temporary Appointments until the next Meeting of the Legislature, which shall then fill such Vacancies.

No Person shall be a Senator who shall not have attained to the Age of thirty Years, and been nine Years a Citizen of the United States, and who shall not, when elected, be an Inhabitant of that State for which he shall be chosen.

The Vice President of the United States shall be President of the Senate, but shall have no Vote, unless they be equally divided.

The Senate shall choose their other Officers, and also a President pro tempore, in the Absence of the Vice President, or when he shall exercise the Office of President of the United States.

Every state has two senators. Senators serve a six-year term, but only one third of the senators reach the end of their terms every two years. In any election, at least two thirds of the senators stay in office. This system ensures that there are experienced senators in office at all times.

The only duty that the Constitution assigns to the vice president is to preside over meetings of the Senate. Modern presidents have given their vice presidents more and varied responsibility.

The House charges a government official of wrongdoing, and the Senate acts as a court to decide if the official is guilty.

Congress has decided that elections will be held on the Tuesday following the first Monday in November of even-numbered years. The Twentieth Amendment states that Congress shall meet in regular session on January 3 of each year. The president may call a special session of Congress whenever necessary.

Congress makes most of its own rules of conduct. The Senate and the House each have a code of ethics that members must follow. It is the task of each house of Congress to discipline its own members. Each house keeps a journal, and a publication called the Congressional Quarterly records what happens in congressional sessions. The general public can learn how their representatives voted on bills by reading the Congressional Quarterly.

The framers of the Constitution wanted to protect members of Congress from being arrested on false charges by political enemies who did not want them to attend important meetings. The framers also wanted to protect members of Congress from being taken to court for something they said in a speech or in a debate.

The Granger Collection, New York.

The Senate shall have the sole Power to try all Impeachments. When sitting for that Purpose, they shall be on Oath or Affirmation. When the President of the United States is tried, the Chief Justice shall preside: And no Person shall be convicted without the Concurrence of two thirds of the Members present.

Judgment in Cases of Impeachment shall not extend further than to removal from Office, and disqualification to hold and enjoy any Office of honor, Trust or Profit under the United States: but the Party convicted shall nevertheless be liable and subject to Indictment, Trial, Judgment and Punishment, according to Law.

Section 4. The Times, Places and Manner of holding Elections for Senators and Representatives, shall be prescribed in each State by the Legislature thereof; but the Congress may at any time by Law make or alter such Regulations, except as to the Places of choosing Senators.

The Congress shall assemble at least once in every Year, and such Meeting shall be on the first Monday in December, unless they shall by Law appoint a different Day.

Section 5. Each House shall be the Judge of the Elections, Returns and Qualifications of its own Members, and a Majority of each shall constitute a Quorum to do Business; but a smaller Number may adjourn from day to day, and may be authorized to compel the Attendance of absent Members, in such Manner, and under such Penalties as each House may provide.

Each House may determine the Rules of its Proceedings, punish its Members for disorderly Behavior, and, with the Concurrence of two thirds, expel a Member.

Each House shall keep a Journal of its Proceedings, and from time to time publish the same, excepting such Parts as may in their Judgment require Secrecy; and the Yeas and Nays of the Members of either House on any question shall, at the Desire of one fifth of those Present, be entered on the Journal.

Neither House, during the Session of Congress, shall, without the Consent of the other, adjourn for more than three days, nor to any other Place than that in which the two Houses shall be sitting.

Section 6. The Senators and Representatives shall receive a Compensation for their Services, to be ascertained by Law, and paid out of the Treasury of the United States. They shall in all Cases, except Treason, Felony and Breach of the Peace, be privileged from Arrest during their Attendance at the Session of their respective Houses, and in going to and returning from the same; and for any Speech or Debate in either House, they shall not be questioned in any other Place.

No Senator or Representative shall, during the Time for which he was elected, be appointed to any civil Office under the Authority of the United States, which shall have been created, or the Emoluments whereof shall have been increased during such time; and no Person holding any Office under the United States, shall be a Member of either House during his Continuance in Office.

Section 7. All Bills for raising Revenue shall originate in the House of Representatives; but the Senate may propose or concur with Amendments as on other Bills.

Every Bill which shall have passed the House of Representatives and the Senate, shall, before it become a Law, be presented to the President of the United States; If he approve he shall sign it, but if not he shall return it, with his Objections to that House in which it shall have originated, who shall enter the Objections at large on their Journal, and proceed to reconsider it. If after such Reconsideration two thirds of that House shall agree to pass the Bill, it shall be sent, together with the Objections, to the other House, by which it shall likewise be reconsidered, and if approved by two thirds of that House, it shall become a Law. But in all such Cases the Votes of both Houses shall be determined by Yeas and Nays, and the Names of the Persons voting for and against the Bill shall be entered on the Journal of each House respectively. If any Bill shall not be returned by the President within ten Days (Sundays excepted) after it shall have been presented to him, the Same shall be a Law, in like Manner as if he had signed it, unless the Congress by their Adjournment prevent its Return, in which Case it shall not be a Law.

Every Order, Resolution, or Vote to which the Concurrence of the Senate and House of Representatives may be necessary (except on a question of Adjournment) shall be presented to the President of the United States; and before the Same shall take Effect, shall be approved by him, or being disapproved by him, shall be repassed by two thirds of the Senate and House of Representatives, according to the Rules and Limitations prescribed in the Case of a Bill.

Section 8. The Congress shall have Power To lay and collect Taxes, Duties, Imposts and Excises, to pay the Debts and provide for the common Defense and general Welfare of the United States; but all Duties, Imposts and Excises shall be uniform throughout the United States;

To borrow Money on the credit of the United States;

To regulate Commerce with foreign Nations, and among the several States, and with the Indian Tribes;

To establish an uniform Rule of Naturalization, and uniform Laws on the subject of Bankruptcies throughout the United States;

The power of taxing is the responsibility of the House of Representatives. Because members of the House are elected every two years, the framers felt that representatives would listen to the public and seek its approval before passing taxes.

The veto power of the president and the ability of Congress to override a presidential veto are two of the important checks and balances in the Constitution.

The framers of the Constitution wanted a national government that was strong enough to be effective. This section lists the powers given to Congress. The last sentence in Section 8 (see page 170) contains the famous "elastic clause," which can be stretched (like elastic) to fit many different circumstances. The clause was first disputed when Alexander Hamilton proposed a national bank. Thomas Jefferson said that the Constitution did not give Congress the power to establish a bank. Hamilton argued that the bank was "necessary and proper" in order to carry out other powers of Congress, such as borrowing money and regulating currency. This argument was tested in the court system in 1819 in the case of McCulloch v. Maryland, when Chief Justice Marshall ruled in favor of the federal government. Powers given to the government by the "elastic clause" are called implied powers.

To coin Money, regulate the Value thereof, and of foreign Coin, and fix the Standard of Weights and Measures;

To provide for the Punishment of counterfeiting the Securities and current Coin of the United States;

To establish Post Offices and post Roads;

To promote the Progress of Science and useful Arts, by securing for limited Times to Authors and Inventors the exclusive Right to their respective Writings and Discoveries;

To constitute Tribunals inferior to the supreme Court;

To define and punish Piracies and Felonies committed on the high Seas, and Offenses against the Law of Nations;

To declare War, grant Letters of Marque and Reprisal, and make Rules concerning Captures on Land and Water;

To raise and support Armies, but no Appropriation of Money to that Use shall be for a longer Term than two Years;

To provide and maintain a Navy;

To make Rules for the Government and Regulation of the land and naval Forces;

To provide for calling forth the Militia to execute the Laws of the Union, suppress Insurrections and repel Invasions;

To provide for organizing, arming, and disciplining, the Militia, and for governing such Part of them as may be employed in the Service of the United States, reserving to the States respectively, the Appointment of the Officers, and the Authority of training the Militia according to the discipline prescribed by Congress.

To exercise exclusive Legislation in all Cases whatsoever, over such District (not exceeding ten Miles square) as may, by Cession of particular States, and the Acceptance of Congress, become the Seat of the Government of the United States, and to exercise like Authority over all Places purchased by the Consent of the Legislature of the State in which the Same shall be, for the Erection of Forts, Magazines, Arsenals, dock-Yards, and other needful Buildings;—-And

To make all Laws which shall be necessary and proper for carrying into Execution the foregoing Powers, and all other Powers vested by this Constitution in the Government of the United States, or in any Department or Officer thereof.

Section 9. ~~The Migration or Importation of such Persons as any of the States now existing shall think proper to admit, shall not be prohibited by the Congress prior to the Year one thousand eight hundred and eight, but a Tax or duty may be imposed on such Importation, not exceeding ten dollars for each Person.~~

The Privilege of the Writ of Habeas Corpus shall not be suspended, unless when in Cases of Rebellion or Invasion the public Safety may require it.

If Congress has implied powers, then there also must be limits to its powers. Section 9 lists powers that are denied to the federal government. Several of the clauses protect the people of the United States from unjust treatment. For instance, Section 9 guarantees the writ of habeas corpus and prohibits bills of attainder and ex post facto laws (see page 163).

The Granger Collection, New York.

No Bill of Attainder or ex post facto Law shall be passed.

No Capitation, or other direct, Tax shall be laid, unless in Proportion to the Census or Enumeration herein before directed to be taken.

No Tax or Duty shall be laid on Articles exported from any State.

No Preference shall be given by any Regulation of Commerce or Revenue to the Ports of one State over those of another: nor shall Vessels bound to, or from, one State, be obliged to enter, clear, or pay Duties in another.

No Money shall be drawn from the Treasury, but in Consequence of Appropriations made by Law; and a regular Statement and Account of the Receipts and Expenditures of all public Money shall be published from time to time.

No Title of Nobility shall be granted by the United States: And no Person holding any Office of Profit or Trust under them, shall, without the Consent of the Congress, accept of any present, Emolument, Office, or Title, of any kind whatever, from any King, Prince, or foreign State.

Section 10. No State shall enter into any Treaty, Alliance, or Confederation; grant Letters of Marque and Reprisal; coin Money; emit Bills of Credit; make any Thing but gold and silver Coin a Tender in Payment of Debts; pass any Bill of Attainder, ex post facto Law, or law impairing the Obligation of Contracts, or grant any Title of Nobility.

No State shall, without the Consent of the Congress, lay any Imposts or Duties on Imports or Exports, except what may be absolutely necessary for executing its inspection Laws: and the net Produce of all Duties and Imposts, laid by any State on Imports or Exports, shall be for the Use of the Treasury of the United States; and all such Laws shall be subject to the Revision and Control of the Congress.

No State shall, without the Consent of Congress, lay any Duty of Tonnage, keep Troops, or Ships of War in time of Peace, enter into any Agreement or Compact with another State, or with a foreign Power, or engage in War, unless actually invaded, or in such imminent Danger as will not admit of delay.

Section 10 lists the powers that are denied to the states. In our system of federalism, the state and federal governments have separate powers, share some powers, and are denied other powers. The states may not exercise any of the powers that belong to Congress.

ARTICLE II

Section 1. The executive Power shall be vested in a President of the United States of America. He shall hold his Office during the Term of four Years, and, together with the Vice President, chosen for the same Term, be elected, as follows.

EXECUTIVE BRANCH

The president is the chief of the executive branch. It is the job of the president to enforce the laws. The framers wanted the president and vice president's term of office and manner of selection to be different from those of members of Congress. They decided on four-year terms, but they had a difficult time agreeing on how to select the president and vice president. The framers finally set up an electoral system, which varies greatly from our electoral process today. The Twelfth Amendment changed the process by requiring that separate ballots be cast for president and vice president. The rise of political parties has since changed the process even more.

In 1845 Congress set the first Tuesday after the first Monday in November of every fourth year as the general election date for selecting presidential electors.

The youngest elected president was John F. Kennedy; he was 43 years old when he was inaugurated. (Theodore Roosevelt was 42 when he assumed office after the assassination of McKinley.) The oldest elected president was Ronald Reagan; he was 69 years old when he was inaugurated.

The Granger Collection, New York.

Each State shall appoint, in such Manner as the Legislature thereof may direct, a Number of Electors, equal to the whole Number of Senators and Representatives to which the State may be entitled in the Congress: but no Senator or Representative, or Person holding an Office of Trust or Profit under the United States, shall be appointed an Elector.

The Electors shall meet in their respective States, and vote by Ballot for two Persons, of whom one at least shall not be an Inhabitant of the same State with themselves. And they shall make a List of all the Persons voted for, and of the Number of Votes for each; which List they shall sign and certify, and transmit sealed to the Seat of the Government of the United States, directed to the President of the Senate. The President of the Senate shall, in the Presence of the Senate and House of Representatives, open all the Certificates, and the Votes shall then be counted. The Person having the greatest Number of Votes shall be the President, if such Number be a Majority of the whole Number of Electors appointed; and if there be more than one who have such majority, and have an equal Number of Votes, then the House of Representatives shall immediately choose by Ballot one of them for President; and if no Person have a Majority, then from the five highest on the List the said House shall in like Manner choose the President. But in choosing the President, the Votes shall be taken by States, the Representation from each State having one Vote; A quorum for this Purpose shall consist of a Member or Members from two thirds of the States, and a Majority of all the States shall be necessary to a Choice. In every Case, after the Choice of the President, the Person having the greatest Number of Votes of the Electors shall be the Vice President. But if there should remain two or more who have equal Votes, the Senate shall choose from them by Ballot the Vice President.

The Congress may determine the Time of choosing the Electors, and the Day on which they shall give their Votes; which Day shall be the same throughout the United States.

No Person except a natural born Citizen, or a Citizen of the United States, at the time of the Adoption of this Constitution, shall be eligible to the Office of President; neither shall any Person be eligible to that Office who shall not have attained to the Age of thirty-five Years, and been fourteen Years a Resident within the United States.

In Case of the Removal of the President from Office, or of his Death, Resignation, or Inability to discharge the Powers and Duties of the said Office, the Same shall devolve on the Vice President, and the Congress may by Law provide for the Case of Removal, Death, Resignation or Inability, both of the

President and Vice President, declaring what Officer shall then act as President, and such Officer shall act accordingly, until the Disability be removed, or a President shall be elected.

The President shall, at stated Times, receive for his Services, a Compensation, which shall neither be increased nor diminished during the Period for which he shall have been elected, and he shall not receive within that Period any other Emolument from the United States, or any of them.

Before he enter on the Execution of his Office, he shall take the following Oath or Affirmation:—"I do solemnly swear (or affirm) that I will faithfully execute the Office of President of the United States, and will to the best of my Ability, preserve, protect and defend the Constitution of the United States."

Section 2. The President shall be Commander in Chief of the Army and Navy of the United States, and of the Militia of the several States, when called into the actual Service of the United States; he may require the Opinion, in writing, of the principal Officer in each of the executive Departments, upon any Subject relating to the Duties of their respective Offices, and he shall have Power to grant Reprieves and Pardons for Offenses against the United States, except in Cases of Impeachment.

He shall have Power, by and with the Advice and Consent of the Senate, to make Treaties, provided two thirds of the Senators present concur; and he shall nominate, and by and with the Advice and Consent of the Senate, shall appoint Ambassadors, other public Ministers and Consuls, Judges of the supreme Court, and all other Officers of the United States, whose Appointments are not herein otherwise provided for, and which shall be established by Law: but the Congress may by Law vest the Appointment of such inferior Officers, as they think proper, in the President alone, in the Courts of Law, or in the Heads of Departments.

The President shall have Power to fill up all Vacancies that may happen during the Recess of the Senate, by granting Commissions which shall expire at the End of their next Session.

Section 3. He shall from time to time give to the Congress Information of the State of the Union, and recommend to their Consideration such Measures as he shall judge necessary and expedient; he may, on extraordinary Occasions, convene both Houses, or either of them, and in Case of Disagreement between them, with Respect to the Time of Adjournment, he may adjourn them to such Time as he shall think proper; he shall receive Ambassadors and other public Ministers; he shall take Care that the Laws be faithfully executed, and shall Commission all the Officers of the United States.

Emolument means "salary, or payment." In 1969 Congress set the president's salary at $200,000 per year. The president also receives an expense account of $50,000 per year. The president must pay taxes on both.

The oath of office is administered to the president by the chief justice of the United States. Washington added "So help me, God." All succeeding presidents have followed this practice.

The framers wanted to make sure that an elected representative of the people controlled the nation's military. Today the president is in charge of the army, navy, air force, marines, and coast guard. Only Congress can decide, however, if the United States will declare war. This section also contains the basis for the formation of the president's cabinet. Every president, starting with George Washington, has appointed a cabinet.

Most of the president's appointments to office must be approved by the Senate.

Every year the president presents to Congress a State of the Union message. In this message, the president explains the legislative plans for the coming year. This clause states that one of the president's duties is to enforce the laws.

Section 4.

The President, Vice President and all civil Officers of the United States, shall be removed from Office on Impeachment for, and Conviction of, Treason, Bribery, or other high Crimes and Misdemeanors.

ARTICLE III

Section 1. The judicial Power of the United States, shall be vested in one supreme Court, and in such inferior Courts as the Congress may from time to time ordain and establish. The Judges, both of the supreme and inferior Courts, shall hold their Offices during good Behavior, and shall, at stated Times, receive for their Services, a Compensation, which shall not be diminished during their Continuance in Office.

Section 2. The judicial Power shall extend to all Cases, in Law and Equity, arising under this Constitution, the Laws of the United States, and Treaties made, or which shall be made, under their Authority;—to all Cases affecting Ambassadors, other public Ministers and Consuls;—to all Cases of admiralty and maritime Jurisdiction;—to Controversies to which the United States shall be a Party;— to Controversies between two or more States;— between a State and Citizens of another State; between Citizens of different States;—between Citizens of the same State claiming Lands under Grants of different States, and between a State, or the Citizens thereof, and foreign States, Citizens or Subjects.

In all Cases affecting Ambassadors, other public Ministers and Consuls, and those in which a State shall be Party, the supreme Court shall have original Jurisdiction. In all the other Cases before mentioned, the supreme Court shall have appellate Jurisdiction, both as to Law and fact, with such Exceptions, and under such Regulations as the Congress shall make.

The Trial of all Crimes, except in Cases of Impeachment, shall be by Jury; and such Trial shall be held in the State where the said Crimes shall have been committed; but when not committed within any State, the Trial shall be at such Place or Places as the Congress may by Law have directed.

Section 3. Treason against the United States, shall consist only in levying War against them, or in adhering to their Enemies, giving them Aid and Comfort. No Person shall be convicted of Treason unless on the Testimony of two Witnesses to the same overt Act, or on Confession in open Court.

The Congress shall have Power to declare the Punishment of Treason, but no Attainder of Treason shall work Corruption of Blood, or Forfeiture except during the Life of the Person attainted.

JUDICIAL BRANCH

The Articles of Confederation did not make any provisions for a federal court system. One of the first things that the framers of the Constitution agreed upon was to set up a national judiciary. With all the laws that Congress would be enacting, there would be a great need for a branch of government to interpret the laws. In the Judiciary Act of 1789, Congress provided for the establishment of lower courts, such as district courts, circuit courts of appeals, and various other federal courts. The judicial system provides a check on the legislative branch; it can declare a law unconstitutional.

Congress has the power to decide the punishment for treason, but it can punish only the guilty person. Corruption of blood refers to punishing the family of a person who has committed treason. It is expressly forbidden by the Constitution.

The Granger Collection, New York.

ARTICLE IV

Section 1. Full Faith and Credit shall be given in each State to the public Acts, Records, and judicial Proceedings of every other State. And the Congress may by general Laws prescribe the Manner in which such Acts, Records and Proceedings shall be proved, and the Effect thereof.

Section 2. The Citizens of each State shall be entitled to all Privileges and Immunities of Citizens in the several States.

A Person charged in any State with Treason, Felony, or other Crime, who shall flee from Justice, and be found in another State, shall on Demand of the executive Authority of the State from which he fled, be delivered up, to be removed to the State having Jurisdiction of the Crime.

~~No Person held to Service of Labor in one State, under the Laws thereof, escaping into another, shall, in Consequence of any Law or Regulation therein, be discharged from such Service or Labor, but shall be delivered up on Claim of the Party to whom such Service or Labor may be due.~~

Section 3. New States may be admitted by the Congress into this Union; but no new State shall be formed or erected within the Jurisdiction of any other State; nor any State be formed by the Junction of two or more States, or Parts of States, without the Consent of the Legislatures of the States concerned as well as of the Congress.

The Congress shall have Power to dispose of and make all needful Rules and Regulations respecting the Territory or other Property belonging to the United States; and nothing in this Constitution shall be so construed as to Prejudice any Claims of the United States, or of any particular State.

Section 4. The United States shall guarantee to every State in this Union a Republican Form of Government, and shall protect each of them against Invasion; and on Application of the Legislature, or of the Executive (when the Legislature cannot be convened) against domestic Violence.

ARTICLE V

The Congress, whenever two thirds of both Houses shall deem it necessary, shall propose Amendments to this Constitution, or, on the Application of the Legislatures of two thirds of the several States, shall call a Convention for proposing Amendments, which, in either Case, shall be valid to all Intents and Purposes, as Part of this Constitution, when ratified by the Legislatures of three fourths of the several

THE STATES

States must honor the laws, records, and court decisions of other states. A person cannot escape a legal obligation by moving from one state to another.

Section 3 permits Congress to admit new states to the Union. When a group of people living in an area that is not part of an existing state wishes to form a new state, it asks Congress for permission to do so. The people then write a state constitution and offer it to Congress for approval. The state constitution must set up a representative form of government and must not in any way contradict the federal Constitution. If a majority of Congress approves of the state constitution, the state is admitted as a member of the United States of America.

THE AMENDMENT PROCESS

America's founders may not have realized just how enduring the Constitution would be, but they did make provisions for changing or adding to the Constitution. They did not want to make it easy to change the Constitution. There are two different ways in which changes can be proposed to the states and two different ways in which states can approve the changes and make them part of the Constitution (see the chart on page 163).

States, or by Conventions in three fourths thereof, as the one or the other Mode of Ratification may be proposed by the Congress; Provided that ~~no Amendment which may be made prior to the Year One thousand eight hundred and eight shall in any Manner affect the first and fourth Clauses in the Ninth Section of the first Article; and that~~ no State, without its Consent, shall be deprived of its equal Suffrage in the Senate.

ARTICLE VII

All Debts contracted and Engagements entered into, before the Adoption of this Constitution, shall be as valid against the United States under this Constitution, as under the Confederation.

This Constitution, and the Laws of the United States which shall be made in Pursuance thereof; and all Treaties made, or which shall be made, under the Authority of the United States, shall be the supreme Law of the Land; and the Judges in every State shall be bound thereby, any Thing in the Constitution or Laws of any State to the Contrary notwithstanding.

The Senators and Representatives before mentioned, and the Members of the several State Legislatures, and all executive and judicial Officers, both of the United States and of the several States, shall be bound by Oath or Affirmation, to support this Constitution; but no religious Test shall ever be required as a Qualification to any Office or public Trust under the United States.

ARTICLE VI

The Ratification of the Conventions of nine States, shall be sufficient for the Establishment of this Constitution between the States so ratifying the Same.

DONE in Convention by the Unanimous Consent of the States present the Seventeenth Day of September in the Year of our Lord one thousand seven hundred and Eighty seven and of the Independence of the United States of America the Twelfth. IN WITNESS whereof We have hereunto subscribed our Names.

George Washington—President and deputy from Virginia

New Hampshire
John Langdon
Nicholas Gilman

NATIONAL SUPREMACY

One of the biggest problems facing the delegates to the Constitutional Convention was the question of what would happen if a state law and a national law conflicted. Which law would be followed? Who decided? The second clause of Article VI answers those questions. When a national and state law disagree, the national law overrides the state law. The Constitution is the supreme law of the land. This clause is often called the "supremacy clause."

RATIFICATION

The Articles of Confederation called for all 13 states to approve any revision to the Articles. The Constitution required that the vote of 9 out of the 13 states would be needed to ratify the Constitution. The first state to ratify was Delaware, on December 7, 1787. The last state to ratify the Constitution was Rhode Island, which finally did so on May 29, 1790, almost two and a half years later.

The Granger Collection, New York.

Massachusetts	**Delaware**
Nathaniel Gorham	*George Read*
Rufus King	*Gunning Bedford, Jr.*
	John Dickinson
Connecticut	*Richard Bassett*
William Samuel	*Jacob Broom*
Johnson	
Roger Sherman	**Maryland**
	James McHenry
New York	*Daniel of St. Thomas Jenifer*
Alexander Hamilton	*Daniel Carroll*
New Jersey	**Virginia**
William Livingston	*John Blair*
David Brearley	*James Madison, Jr.*
William Paterson	
Jonathan Dayton	**North Carolina**
	William Blount
Pennsylvania	*Richard Dobbs Spaight*
Benjamin Franklin	*Hugh Williamson*
Thomas Mifflin	
Robert Morris	**South Carolina**
George Clymer	*John Rutledge*
Thomas FitzSimons	*Charles Cotesworth Pinckney*
Jared Ingersoll	*Charles Pinckney*
James Wilson	*Pierce Buttler*
Gouverneur Morris	
Georgia	
William Few	
Abraham Baldwin	

Attest: *William Jackson*, Secretary

THE AMENDMENTS

ARTICLES in addition to, and Amendment of the Constitution of the United States of America, proposed by Congress, and ratified by the Legislatures of the several states, pursuant to the fifth Article of the original Constitution.
[The First through Tenth amendments, now known as the Bill of Rights, were proposed on September 25, 1789, and declared in force on December 15, 1791.]

First Amendment
Congress shall make no law respecting an establishment of religion, or prohibiting the free exercise thereof; or

BILL OF RIGHTS

One of the conditions set by several states for ratifying the Constitution was the inclusion of a Bill of Rights. Many people feared that a stronger central government might take away basic rights of the people that had been guaranteed in state constitutions. If the three words that begin the preamble, We the people—were truly meant, then the rights of the people needed to be protected.

The First Amendment protects freedom of speech and thought, and forbids Congress to make any law "respecting an establishment of religion" or restraining the freedom to practice religion as one chooses.

abridging the freedom of speech, or of the press; or the right of the people peaceably to assemble, and to petition the Government for a redress of grievances.

Second Amendment

A well regulated Militia, being necessary to the security of a free State, the right of the people to keep and bear Arms, shall not be infringed.

Third Amendment

No Soldier shall, in time of peace, be quartered in any house, without the consent of the Owner, nor in time of war, but in a manner to be prescribed by law.

A police officer or sheriff may enter a person's home with a search warrant, which allows the law officer to look for evidence that could convict someone of committing a crime.

Fourth Amendment

The right of the people to be secure in their persons, houses, papers, and effects, against unreasonable searches and seizures, shall not be violated, and no Warrants shall issue, but upon probable cause, supported by Oath or affirmation, and particularly describing the place to be searched, and the persons or things to be seized.

The Fifth, Sixth, and Seventh amendments describe the procedures that courts must follow when trying people accused of crimes. The Fifth Amendment guarantees that no one can be put on trial for a serious crime unless a grand jury agrees that the evidence justifies doing so. It also says that a person cannot be tried twice for the same crime.

Fifth Amendment

No person shall be held to answer for a capital, or otherwise infamous crime, unless on a presentment or indictment of a Grand Jury, except in cases arising in the land or naval forces, or in the Militia, when in actual service in time of War or public danger; nor shall any person be subject for the same offense to be twice put in jeopardy of life or limb; nor shall be compelled in any criminal case to be a witness against himself, nor be deprived of life, liberty, or property, without due process of law; nor shall private property be taken for public use, without just compensation.

The Sixth Amendment makes several promises, including a prompt trial and a trial by a jury chosen from the state and district in which the crime was committed. The Sixth Amendment also states that an accused person must be told why he or she is being tried and promises that an accused person has the right to be defended by a lawyer.

Sixth Amendment

In all criminal prosecutions, the accused shall enjoy the right to a speedy and public trial, by an impartial jury of the State and district wherein the crime shall have been committed, which district shall have been previously ascertained by law, and to be informed of the nature and cause of the accusation; to be confronted with the witnesses against him; to have compulsory process for obtaining witnesses in his favor, and to have the Assistance of Counsel for his defense.

The Granger Collection, New York.

Seventh Amendment

In Suits at common law, where the value in controversy shall exceed twenty dollars, the right of trial by jury shall be preserved, and no fact tried by a jury shall be otherwise reexamined in any Court of the United States, than according to the rules of the common law.

The Seventh Amendment guarantees a trial by jury in cases that involve more than $20, but in modern times, usually much more money is at stake before a case is heard in federal court.

Eighth Amendment

Excessive bail shall not be required, nor excessive fines imposed, nor cruel and unusual punishments inflicted.

Ninth Amendment

The enumeration in the Constitution, of certain rights, shall not be construed to deny or disparage others retained by the people.

The Ninth and Tenth amendments were added because not every right of the people or of the states could be listed in the Constitution.

Tenth Amendment

The powers not delegated to the United States by the Constitution, nor prohibited by it to the States, are reserved to the States respectively, or to the people.

Eleventh Amendment

[Proposed March 4, 1794; declared ratified January 8, 1798]

The Judicial power of the United States shall not be construed to extend to any suit in law or equity, commenced or prosecuted against one of the United States by Citizens of another State, or by Citizens or Subjects of any Foreign State.

Twelfth Amendment

[Proposed December 9, 1803; declared ratified September 25, 1804]

The Electors shall meet in their respective states and vote by ballot for President and Vice President, one of whom, at least, shall not be an inhabitant of the same state with themselves; they shall name in their ballots the person voted for as President, and in distinct ballots the person voted for as Vice President, and they shall make distinct lists of all persons voted for as President, and of all persons voted for as Vice President, and of the number of votes for each, which lists they shall sign and certify, and transmit sealed to the seat of the government of the United States, directed to the President of the Senate;—The President of the

The Twelfth Amendment changed the election procedure for president and vice president. This amendment became necessary because of the growth of political parties. Before this amendment, electors voted without distinguishing between president and vice president. Whoever received the most votes became president, and whoever received the next highest number of votes became vice president. A confusing election in 1800, which resulted in Thomas Jefferson's becoming president, caused this amendment to be proposed.

Senate shall, in the presence of the Senate and House of Representatives, open all the certificates and the votes shall then be counted;—The person having the greatest number of votes for President, shall be the President, if such number be a majority of the whole number of Electors appointed; and if no person have such majority, then from the persons having the highest numbers not exceeding three on the list of those voted for as President, the House of Representatives shall choose immediately, by ballot, the President. But in choosing the President, the votes shall be taken by states, the representation from each state having one vote; a quorum for this purpose shall consist of a member or members from two thirds of the states, and a majority of all the states shall be necessary to a choice. And if the House of Representatives shall not choose a President whenever the right of choice shall devolve upon them, before the fourth day of March next following, then the Vice-President shall act as President, as in the case of the death or other constitutional disability of the President;— The person having the greatest number of votes as Vice President, shall be the Vice President, if such number be a majority of the whole number of Electors appointed, and if no person have a majority, then from the two highest numbers on the list, the Senate shall choose the Vice President; a quorum for the purpose shall consist of two thirds of the whole number of Senators, and a majority of the whole number shall be necessary to a choice. But no person constitutionally ineligible to the office of President shall be eligible to that of Vice President of the United States.

Thirteenth Amendment

[Proposed January 31, 1865; declared ratified December 18, 1865]

Section 1. Neither slavery nor involuntary servitude, except as a punishment for crime whereof the party shall have been duly convicted, shall exist within the United States, or any place subject to their jurisdiction.

Section 2. Congress shall have power to enforce this article by appropriate legislation.

Fourteenth Amendment

[Proposed June 13, 1866; declared ratified July 28, 1868]

Section 1. All persons born or naturalized in the United States and subject to the jurisdiction thereof, are citizens of the United States and of the State wherein they reside. No State shall make or enforce any law which shall abridge

Although some slaves had been freed during the Civil War, slavery was not abolished until the Thirteenth Amendment took effect.

The Granger Collection, New York.

In 1833 Chief Justice John Marshall ruled that the Bill of Rights limited the national government but not the state governments. This ruling meant that states were able to keep African Americans from becoming state citizens. If African Americans were not citizens, they were not protected by the

the privileges or immunities of citizens of the United States; nor shall any State deprive any person of life, liberty, or property, without due process of law; nor deny to any person within its jurisdiction the equal protection of the laws.

Section 2. Representatives shall be apportioned among the several States according to their respective numbers, counting the whole number of persons in each State, ~~excluding Indians not taxed.~~ But when the right to vote at any election for the choice of electors for President and Vice President of the United States, Representatives in Congress, the Executive and Judicial officers of a State, or the members of the Legislature thereof, is denied to any of the ~~male~~ inhabitants of such State, being ~~twenty-one years of age, and~~ citizens of the United States, or in any way abridged, except for participation in rebellion, or other crime, the basis of representation therein shall be reduced in the proportion which the number of such ~~male~~ citizens shall bear to the whole number of male citizens ~~twenty-one years of age~~ in such State.

Section 3. No person shall be a Senator or Representative in Congress, or elector of President and Vice President, or hold any office, civil or military, under the United States, or under any State, who, having previously taken an oath, as a member of Congress, or as an officer of the United States, or as a member of any State legislature, or as an executive or judicial officer of any State, to support the Constitution of the United States, shall have engaged in insurrection or rebellion against the same, or given aid or comfort to the enemies thereof. But Congress may by a vote of two thirds of each House, remove such disability.

Section 4. The validity of the public debt of the United States, authorized by law, including debts incurred for payment of pensions and bounties for services in suppressing insurrection or rebellion, shall not be questioned. But neither the United States nor any State shall assume or pay any debt or obligation incurred in aid of insurrection or rebellion against the United States, or ~~any claim for the loss or emancipation of any slave;~~ but all such debts, obligations and claims shall be held illegal and void.

Section 5. The Congress shall have power to enforce, by appropriate legislation, the provisions of this article.

Fifteenth Amendment
[Proposed February 26, 1869; declared ratified March 30, 1870]

Section 1. The right of citizens of the United States to vote shall not be denied or abridged by the United States

Bill of Rights. The Fourteenth Amendment defines citizenship and prevents states from interfering in the rights of citizens of the United States.

The Fifteenth Amendment extended the right to vote to African American males.

or by any State on account of race, color, or previous condition of servitude.

Section 2. The Congress shall have power to enforce this article by appropriate legislation.

Sixteenth Amendment

The Sixteenth Amendment made legal the income tax described in Article I.

[Proposed July 12, 1909; declared ratified February 25, 1913]

The Congress shall have power to lay and collect taxes on incomes, from whatever source derived, without apportionment among the several States, and without regard to any census or enumeration.

Seventeenth Amendment

The Seventeenth Amendment required that senators be elected directly by the people instead of by the state legislature.

[Proposed May 13, 1912; declared ratified May 31, 1913]

The Senate of the United States shall be composed of two Senators from each State, elected by the people thereof, for six years; and each Senator shall have one vote. The electors in each State shall have the qualifications requisite for electors of the most numerous branch of the State legislatures.

When vacancies happen in the representation of any State in the Senate, the executive authority of such State shall issue writs of election to fill such vacancies: Provided, That the legislature of any State may empower the executive thereof to make temporary appointments until the people fill the vacancies by election as the legislature may direct.

This amendment shall not be so construed as to affect the election or term of any Senator chosen before it becomes valid as part of the Constitution.

Eighteenth Amendment

Although many people felt that Prohibition was good for the health and welfare of the American people, the amendment was repealed 14 years later.

[Proposed December 18, 1917; declared ratified January 29, 1919; repealed by the Twenty-first Amendment December 5, 1933]

Section 1. After one year from the ratification of this article the manufacture, sale, or transportation of intoxicating liquors within, the importation thereof into, or the exportation thereof from the United States and all territory subject to the jurisdiction thereof for beverage purposes is hereby prohibited.

Section 2. The Congress and the several States shall have concurrent power to enforce this article by appropriate legislation.

Section 3. This article shall be inoperative unless it shall have been ratified as an amendment to the Constitution

The Granger Collection, New York.

by the legislatures of the several States, as provided in the Constitution, within seven years from the date of the submission hereof to the States by the Congress.

Nineteenth Amendment

[Proposed June 4, 1919; declared ratified August 26, 1920]

The right of citizens of the United States to vote shall not be denied or abridged by the United States or by any State on account of sex.

Congress shall have power to enforce this article by appropriate legislation.

Twentieth Amendment

[Proposed March 2, 1932; declared ratified February 6, 1933]

Section 1. The terms of the President and Vice President shall end at noon on the 20th day of January, and the terms of Senators and Representatives at noon on the 3rd day of January, of the years in which such terms would have ended if this article had not been ratified; and the terms of their successors shall then begin.

Section 2. The Congress shall assemble at least once in every year, and such meeting shall begin at noon on the 3rd day of January, unless they shall by law appoint a different day.

Section 3. If, at the time fixed for the beginning of the term of the President, the President elect shall have died, the Vice President elect shall become President. If a President shall not have been chosen before the time fixed for the beginning of his term, or if the President elect shall have failed to qualify, then the Vice President elect shall act as President until a President shall have qualified; and the Congress may by law provide for the case wherein neither a President elect nor a Vice President elect shall have qualified, declaring who shall then act as President, or the manner in which one who is to act shall be selected, and such persons shall act accordingly until a President or Vice President shall have qualified.

Section 4. The Congress may by law provide for the case of the death of any of the persons from whom the House of Representatives may choose a President whenever the right of choice shall have devolved upon them, and for the case of the death of any of the persons from whom the Senate may choose a Vice President whenever the right of choice shall have devolved upon them.

Section 5. Sections 1 and 2 shall take effect on the 15th day of October following the ratification of this article.

Section 6. This article shall be inoperative unless it shall have been ratified as an amendment to the Constitution

Abigail Adams was disappointed that the Declaration of Independence and the Constitution did not specifically include women. It took almost 150 years and much campaigning by women's suffrage groups for women to finally achieve voting privileges.

In the original Constitution, a newly elected president and Congress did not take office until March 4, which was four months after the November election. The officials who were leaving office were called "lame ducks" because they had little influence during those four months. The Twentieth Amendment changed the date that the new president and Congress take office. Members of Congress now take office on January 3, and the president takes office on January 20.

by the legislatures of three fourths of the several States within seven years from the date of its submission.

Twenty-first Amendment

[Proposed February 20, 1933; declared ratified December 5, 1933]

Section 1.   The eighteenth article of amendment to the Constitution of the United States is hereby repealed.

Section 2.   The transportation or importation into any State, Territory, or possession of the United States for delivery or use therein of intoxicating liquors, in violation of the laws thereof, is hereby prohibited.

Section 3.   This article shall be inoperative unless it shall have been ratified as an amendment to the Constitution by conventions in the several States, as provided in the Constitution, within seven years from the date of the submission hereof to the States by the Congress.

Twenty-second Amendment

[Proposed March 24, 1947; declared ratified March 1, 1951]

Section 1.   No person shall be elected to the office of the President more than twice, and no person who has held the office of President, or acted as President, for more than two years of a term to which some other person was elected President shall be elected to the office of the President more than once. But this Article shall not apply to any person holding the office of President when this Article was proposed by the Congress, and shall not prevent any person who may be holding the office of President, or acting as President, during the term within which this Article becomes operative from holding the office of President or acting as President during the remainder of such term.

Section 2.   This Article shall be inoperative unless it shall have been ratified as an amendment to the Constitution by the legislatures of three fourths of the several States within seven years from the date of its submission to the States by the Congress.

Twenty-third Amendment

[Proposed June 16, 1960; declared ratified April 3, 1961]

Section 1.   The District constituting the seat of Government of the United States shall appoint in such manner as the Congress may direct:

A number of electors of President and Vice President equal to the whole number of Senators and Representatives in

The Twenty-first Amendment is the only amendment that has been ratified by state conventions rather than by state legislatures.

From the time of President Washington's administration, it was a custom for presidents to serve no more than two terms of office. Franklin D. Roosevelt, however, was elected to four terms. The Twenty-second Amendment made into law the old custom of a two-term limit for each president, if reelected.

Until the Twenty-third Amendment, the people of Washington, D.C., could not vote in presidential elections.

The Granger Collection, New York.

Congress to which the District would be entitled if it were a State, but in no event more than the least populous State; they shall be in addition to those appointed by the States, but they shall be considered, for the purposes of the election of President and Vice President, to be electors appointed by a State; and they shall meet in the District and perform such duties as provided by the twelfth article of amendment.

Section 2. The Congress shall have power to enforce this article by appropriate legislation.

Twenty-fourth Amendment

[Proposed August 27, 1962; declared ratified February 4, 1964]

Section 1. The right of citizens of the United States to vote in any primary or other election for President or Vice President, for electors for President or Vice President, or for Senator or Representative in Congress, shall not be denied or abridged by the United States or any State by reason of failure to pay any poll tax or other tax.

Section 2. The Congress shall have power to enforce this article by appropriate legislation.

Twenty-fifth Amendment

[Proposed July 6, 1965; declared ratified February 23, 1967]

Section 1. In case of removal of the President from office or of his death or resignation, the Vice President shall become President.

Section 2. Whenever there is a vacancy in the office of the Vice President, the President shall nominate a Vice President who shall take office upon confirmation by a majority vote of both Houses of Congress.

Section 3. Whenever the President transmits to the President pro tempore of the Senate and the Speaker of the House of Representatives his written declaration that he is unable to discharge the powers and duties of his office, and until he transmits to them a written declaration to the contrary, such powers and duties shall be discharged by the Vice President as Acting President.

Section 4. Whenever the Vice President and a majority of either the principal officers of the executive departments or of such other body as Congress may by law provide, transmit to the President pro tempore of the Senate and the Speaker of the House of Representatives their written declaration that the President is unable to discharge the powers and duties of his office, the Vice President shall immediately assume the powers and duties of the office as Acting President.

The illness of President Eisenhower in the 1950s and the assassination of President Kennedy in 1963 were the events behind the Twenty-fifth Amendment. The Constitution did not provide a clear-cut method for a vice president to take over for a disabled president or for the death of a president. This amendment provides for filling the office of the vice president if a vacancy occurs, and it provides a way for the vice president to take over if the president is unable to perform the duties of that office.

Thereafter, when the President transmits to the President pro tempore of the Senate and the Speaker of the House of Representatives his written declaration that no inability exists, he shall resume the powers and duties of his office unless the Vice President and a majority of either the principal officers of the executive department or of such other body as Congress may by law provide, transmit within four days to the President pro tempore of the Senate and the Speaker of the House of Representatives their written declaration that the President is unable to discharge the powers and duties of his office. Thereupon Congress shall decide the issue, assembling within forty-eight hours for that purpose if not in session. If the Congress, within twenty-one days after receipt of the latter written declaration, or, if Congress is not in session, within twenty-one days after Congress is required to assemble, determines by two-thirds vote of both Houses that the President is unable to discharge the powers and duties of his office, the Vice President shall continue to discharge the same as Acting President; otherwise, the President shall resume the powers and duties of his office.

Twenty-sixth Amendment
[Proposed March 23, 1971; declared ratified July 5, 1971]
Section 1. The right of citizens of the United States, who are eighteen years of age or older, to vote shall not be denied or abridged by the United States or by any State on account of age.

Section 2. The Congress shall have power to enforce this article by appropriate legislation.

Twenty-seventh Amendment
[Proposed September 25, 1789; declared ratified May 7, 1992]
No law, varying the compensation for the services of the Senators and Representatives, shall take effect, until an election of Representatives shall have intervened.

The Voting Act of 1970 tried to set the voting age at 18 years old. But the Supreme Court ruled that the act set the voting age for national elections only, not state or local elections. This ruling would make necessary several different ballots at elections. The Twenty-sixth Amendment gave 18-year-old citizens the right to vote in all elections.

The Granger Collection, New York.

GLOSSARY

This glossary contains terms you need to understand as you study government. After each term there is a brief definition or explanation of the term as it is used in *Holt American Government*. The page number refers to the page on which the term is introduced in the textbook.

Phonetic Respelling and Pronunciation Guide
Many of the key terms in this textbook have been respelled to help you pronounce them. The letter combinations used in the respellings throughout the narrative are explained in the following phonetic respelling and pronunciation guide. The guide is adapted from *Webster's Tenth New Collegiate Dictionary*, *Webster's New Geographical Dictionary*, and *Webster's New Biographical Dictionary*.

MARK	AS IN	RESPELLING	EXAMPLE
a	alphabet	a	*AL-fuh-bet
ā	Asia	ay	AY-zhuh
ä	cart, top	ah	KAHRT, TAHP
e	let, ten	e	LET, TEN
ē	even, leaf	ee	EE-vuhn, LEEF
i	it, tip, British	i	IT, TIP, BRIT-ish
ī	site, buy, Ohio	y	SYT, BY, oh-HY-oh
	iris	eye	EYE-ris
k	card	k	KAHRD
ō	over, rainbow	oh	oh-vuhr, RAYN-boh
u̇	book, wood	ooh	BOOHK, WOOHD
ȯ	all, orchid	aw	AWL, AWR-kid
ȯi	foil, coin	oy	FOYL, KOYN
au̇	out	ow	OWT
ə	cup, butter	uh	KUHP, BUHT-uhr
ü	rule, food	oo	ROOL, FOOD
yü	few	yoo	FYOO
zh	vision	zh	VIZH-uhn

*A syllable printed in small capital letters receives heavier emphasis than the other syllable(s) in a word.

A

absentee ballot   a ballot that a voter who will be unable to appear at his or her polling place on the day of an election can use to vote in advance by mail.   **441**

act of admission   an act of Congress that, when signed by the president, makes a territory a state.   **76**

administrative law   1) the rules and regulations that government agencies use to carry out statutory law, and the procedures through which those rules and regulations are created and practiced.   2) the body of laws that create government agencies and govern judicial review of actions taken by government agencies.   **272**

affirmative action   a program, supported by law, requiring American employers, labor unions, and other institutions to actively seek to eliminate discrimination against women and minorities and to increase the hiring, promotion, wage, training, and other opportunities for such persons.   **355**

agribusiness   the industry that is involved in producing, processing, or distributing agricultural products.   **386**

Albany Plan of Union   a plan to unite the thirteen colonies in 1754. Proposed by Benjamin Franklin, the Albany Plan of Union called for a council of representatives from each colony to levy taxes, handle military matters, and regulate affairs with American Indians. A president-general with veto power was head of the council, whose acts would be law throughout the colonies unless vetoed by the British monarch. Never approved by the British and colonial governments, the plan was never put into effect. **26**

alien a citizen of one nation who is temporarily or permanently living in another nation. **298**

alliance an agreement between two or more nations to work together toward some common (typically military or economic) goal. **151**

ambassador The highest-ranking diplomat who represents a nation to the government of another nation. An ambassador is the personal representative of his or her nation's head of state. **224**

amendment **1)** an addition to an already adopted constitution. **51** **2)** an addition to a bill that is under consideration by a legislature. **126–27**

amicus curiae brief a formal brief that reflects a group's concerns regarding a court decision. **260**

amnesty an act of forgiveness by a government for persons who have committed a crime, usually a political offense. Amnesty is granted to a group of people, in contrast to a pardon, which is granted to individuals. **344**

anarchy the absence of any legitimate governmental authority, resulting in political disorder and sometimes chaos and mob rule. **14**

Antifederalist someone who opposed the adoption of the U.S. Constitution in the late 1780s. Antifederalists feared the creation of a strong national government, preferring that state governments retain the greater share of power. **40**

appellate jurisdiction the requirement that an appeals court must hear cases that are appealed to it if the cases meet certain conditions set by law. **253**

apportion to determine how many legislators should represent a jurisdiction in a legislative body. **99**

appropriations **1)** funds assigned by a legislature to pay for something that has been authorized by law. **2)** congressional legislation authorizing federal agencies to make payments out of the Treasury for specified purposes. **118**

arraignment in a criminal case, a court hearing in which the defendant is formally charged with a crime, informed of his or her rights, and required to enter a plea to the charge. **277**

Articles of Confederation a legal document to form a single national government in the United States. The Articles of Confederation went into effect in 1781 and created a "league of friendship" for the common defense and mutual welfare of the individual states. **31**

attorney general **1)** the head of the U.S. Department of Justice and the chief legal adviser to the president and federal government. The attorney general is a member of the president's cabinet and is appointed by the president, subject to approval by the Senate. **2)** the primary legal official of a state, usually elected by the people. **174**

authoritarian a system of government in which a dictator answers only to him- or herself. **9**

authoritarian socialism *See* communism.

autocracy a government in which one person, a dictator, has unlimited political power. **9**

bail money that is paid to guarantee that a defendant will appear in court if he or she is released from jail while awaiting trial in a criminal case. **276**

bench trial a trial in which a judge, rather than a jury, decides an issue. **331**

bias **1)** a preference or prejudice, particularly one that hinders impartial judgment. **2)** an unfair act or policy resulting from prejudice. **379**

bicameral having two houses or chambers. Bicameral legislatures were originally designed to represent both the elite and the common members of a society. **22**

bilateral alliance an agreement between two countries to help each other in time of war. **233**

bill proposed legislation that has been formally introduced into a legislature for consideration. A bill that is passed by Congress and signed by the president becomes a law. **118**

bill of attainder a law that convicts people of a crime and punishes them without a trial. **108**

Bill of Rights the first 10 amendments to the U.S. Constitution, which guarantee certain individual liberties, including property rights, the right to trial by jury, and freedom of expression and religion. **53**

block grant a payment that the federal government distributes to a state or local government and for which the recipient determines the specific use. **78**

Bolsheviks a revolutionary group that came to power following the Russian Revolution of 1917. *See also* Communist Party. **517**

bond **1)** a certificate that a government or corporation issues to a lender from whom it has borrowed money **2)** bail money that is held as security to ensure that an accused person will not flee from the jurisdiction of the court if released. Bond money is returned when the accused person appears for the trial. *See also* bail. **201, 276**

bond rating a measure of the probability that a bond issuer will or will not pay its obligation to investors in its bonds. **475**

bourgeoisie the people who own the means of production in a capitalist system. **511**

boycott   a refusal to do business with or buy the products of a company, an industry, or a nation in order to pressure it into changing its policies.   **28**

brief   a written statement prepared by each side before a court hearing to summarize that side's view of the facts in the dispute and how the law should be applied.   **253**

bureaucracy   any management structure that carries out policy on a day-to-day basis, that is based on job specialization, uses standardized procedures, and continues its operations regardless of changes in leadership.   **176**

bureaucrat   a worker in a bureaucracy.   **176**

cabinet   an advisory board that is made up of the heads of the government's executive departments and reports to the chief executive.   **58**

capital punishment   the death penalty. Capital punishment can be ordered only for a defendant who has been convicted of a specified, very serious crime such as murder or treason.   **282**

capitalist   **1)** a person who supports or favors capitalism as an economic system.   **2)** a person who has invested money in business, particularly someone who has a major financial interest in an important business venture.   **507**

categorical grant   a payment that the federal government distributes to a state or local government to fund specific activities.   **73**

caucus   a meeting of political party members to seek agreement on a course of action, nominate candidates for political office, or select delegates to a state or national nominating convention.   **159**

censorship   the legal act of determining if information or speech is suitable for the public, or if that information or speech should be banned.   **377**

censure   a legislature's formal expression of disapproval of one of its members.   **117**

census   a periodic, official counting of a population. Article 1, Section 2, of the Constitution requires a U.S. census every 10 years to use in apportioning seats in the House of Representatives among the states.   **98**

change of venue   the movement of a trial to a court in a different geographic location.   **330**

charter   **1)** a document that monarchs use to grant privileges to groups or individuals.   **23**   **2)** a record that defines the purposes and powers of a city government.   **485**

checks and balances   limitations placed on a branch of government's political power by giving the other branches some control over its affairs.   **48**

circuit   a geographic area over which a federal court of appeals has jurisdiction.   **252**

citizen   an officially recognized member of a state.   **3**

city manager   someone hired to run the daily operations of a municipality.   **488–89**

civil law   the body of law that governs relationships among individuals and that defines people's legal rights.   **78**

civil liberty   a basic individual right to which every human being is entitled.   **297**

civil rights   the rights that legally belong to a person because of his or her citizenship in a nation.   **346**

civil rights movement   the ongoing effort of women and minority groups to gain in practice the rights guaranteed to all citizens by the Constitution.   **347**

civil servant   any nonmilitary employee of government, particularly one who was awarded his or her job on the basis of the merit system. *See also* merit system.   **178**

class-action suit   a court action brought against an individual or a company by a person or small group for themselves and for all others who have been affected similarly by a particular wrong.   **394**

class struggle   according to Marxist theory, the ongoing competition between economic groups for resources and power. The idea of class struggle was introduced by German political theorists Karl Marx and Friedrich Engels in their 1848 work *Communist Manifesto.*   **515**

closed primary   a primary election in which only the members of a political party are permitted to vote in selecting the party's candidates. *See also* open primary.   **432**

cloture   a method for ending a filibuster in the U.S. Senate.   **27**

collective security   a multinational diplomatic and military arrangement to maintain peace by taking united action against any hostile and potentially hostile nation that is a threat to peace.   **237**

command economy   an economy in which government authorities control some or all of the major economic processes.   **514**

commission   a board that holds all executive, legislative, and administrative power in a municipality.   **489–90**

common law   a body of law that developed from traditions, customs, and precedents (or earlier judicial decisions).   **271**

communism   **1)** a theoretical economic system in which all land and capital is owned collectively by society.   **2)** an economic system in which the government owns or controls nearly all factors of production; also known as authoritarian socialism.   **512**

Communist Manifesto   a book completed in 1848 by German political theorists Karl Marx (1818–1883) and Friedrich Engels (1820–1895) that presented the basic principles and beliefs of communism.   **515**

Communist Party a political party formed by the Bolsheviks in Russia following the Russian Revolution of 1917. The party was originally led by Vladimir Lenin and was based on his interpretation of the writings of radical political thinkers Friedrich Engels and Karl Marx. **517**

commutation in law, the reduction of a punishment to a less severe one. **153**

comparative advantage the ability of a nation, region, or company to produce a certain good or service more cheaply than any other good or service. **534**

competition effort that sellers of similar goods or services exert in obtaining the business of consumers. Each seller tries to gain a larger share of a market and to increase profits. **508**

concurrent power a power or authority that is held by more than one level of government. **68**

concurring opinion in a court decision, a formal statement by a judge on a judicial panel. The person issuing the concurring opinion agrees with the decision of the majority but for different reasons than those cited in the majority opinion. **261**

confederal system a form of government in which independent states unite to accomplish common goals. **10**

conference committee a meeting of members from both the House and Senate to resolve differences over similar bills passed in both houses. **119**

Congressional Budget Office an agency created by Congress to provide legislators with data and technical assistance on financial policy, issues surrounding government programs, and other spending-related matters. **205**

constituent a resident of a district or state represented by an elected official. **94**

constitution the basic political and legal structures under which a government operates. **21**

constitutional interpretation a judicial function in which judges determine the meaning of a state's or the federal constitution as it relates to a case before the court. **272**

constitutional monarchy a government whose head of state inherits the position and holds it for life but either shares power with elected leaders or merely serves as the nation's symbolic leader, exercising no significant power. **8**

consul an official whose main function is to further his or her nation's business and trade interests in another country. A consul is thus distinct from the nation's ambassador, who furthers its diplomatic and political interests in the other country. **225**

consulate the office of a consul, from which he or she protects his or her nation's commercial interests. **223**

consumer buyer of goods or services for personal use. **508**

containment a basic U.S. foreign and military policy during the Cold War. Through containment, the United States sought to stop the spread of communism into nations that were not under communist control. **229**

convention an assembly of political party members gathered to perform some official duty, such as choosing candidates for elective office, adopting a party platform, or selecting delegates to a higher-level party meeting. **159**

council-manager system a system of municipal government in which an elected city council appoints a professional city manager to run the government's day-to-day affairs. **488**

county the unit of government directly below state government. Counties are generally governed by elected boards or commissions, although some are administered by a single elected or appointed official. **275**

court of appeals 1) a court established to hear appeals of trial court cases. In the court structure of most states, courts of appeals are midway between the trial courts and the state supreme court. **472** 2) one of 13 federal appeals courts, ranking just below the Supreme Court, that hear appeals from cases tried in federal district courts. **252**

criminal law the body of law that regulates the conduct of individuals as members of the state. **78**

customs duty a tax on imports that may be levied by a nation's government to raise revenue or to protect an industry within the nation from foreign competition. A customs duty is sometimes called a tariff. **193**

de facto **segregation** racial separation that exists not because of laws or government action, but because of social and economic factors and conditions. *See also de jure* segregation. **349**

de jure **segregation** racial segregation that is enforced by law. In the past, laws in many states required separate schools, parks, public transportation, and so on for whites and African Americans. *See also de facto* segregation. **348**

deduction in income tax policy, any business or personal expense or loss that reduces taxable income. **191**

defendant the party accused in a civil or criminal court of having committed a wrongful act. **274**

defense alliance an agreement in which countries come to one another's aid if any of them are attacked. **235**

deficit the amount by which a person's, business's, or a government's expenses exceed its income. **202**

deforestation the clearing of forests without replacing them. Deforestation results from the harvesting of timber and the clearing of land for agriculture, industry, or mining. **542**

delegate someone who is authorized to represent and act for others within a voting assembly, convention, or other meeting in which a small group of individuals makes decisions for a larger general group. **28**

democracy a system of government in which political authority is held by the people. Democracies typically feature constitutional governments with majority rules, a belief in individual worth and in equal rights for all people, freedom of expression, political freedom, and freedom of choice. **8**

democratic socialism an economic system in which some means of producing and distributing goods are owned or controlled by the government. The extent of the government's economic role is determined by elections rather than ideology. **511**

denaturalization the act of taking away a person's citizenship. **341**

deportation the act of officially returning an alien to his or her country of origin. **344**

détente a French word meaning "relaxation of tensions" that is used to describe U.S. foreign policy toward the Soviet Union in the early and mid-1970s. **232**

developed nation a nation with a high level of industrial development and technical expertise, as well as various established economic institutions such as banks and stock markets. The citizens of a developed nation enjoy a high standard of living with an average, annual per capita income of at least $2,000. **533**

developing nation a nation with little industry and that has a low standard of living in comparison with developed nations. The annual, average per capita income in a developing nation is less than $2,000. **533**

dictatorship a system of government in which one person or a small group of ruling elite has total political power. **9**

diplomacy 1) the art of negotiating, conducting, and maintaining relationships with other nations. 2) all formal relations and communications that nations maintain with one another. **144**

diplomatic recognition an acknowledgment by one nation's government that another nation's government is legitimate. Diplomatic recognition occurs when the chief executive of the acknowledging nation sends an ambassador or other diplomatic official to the nation being recognized. **151**

direct democracy a system of government in which decisions are made directly by the people rather than by their elected representatives. **15**

direct primary a primary election in which the winner becomes the party's candidate for elective office. **431**

discount rate the interest rate charged by the Federal Reserve for loans to member banks. **201**

discrimination the practice of treating a person or group

differently because of prejudice, such as that based on race, sex, religion, age, or physical characteristics. **345**

disposable income money that remains after taxes have been paid. Personal disposable income is a key factor in determining the level of consumption and savings in an economy. **198**

dissenting opinion in a court decision, a formal statement by a judge on a judicial panel. The person issuing the dissenting opinion disagrees with the decision of the majority and cites the reasons for disagreeing. **261**

district court a federal trial court in which issues involving federal law are heard. Each state has at least one district court. **252**

docket the list of cases to be heard by a court; also called a calendar of cases. **259**

double jeopardy trying someone more than once for the same criminal offense. The Fifth Amendment to the Constitution prohibits double jeopardy, but this protection is not absolute. If a mistrial has occurred because of some procedural error or if a deadlocked jury cannot reach a verdict, the prosecution may retry the accused. **331**

draft the practice of requiring civilians to serve in the military for a specified period of time. **310**

due process a constitutional protection that prevents the government from depriving individuals of their rights and freedoms without following established legal procedures. **319**

Elastic Clause a clause in Article I, Section 8, of the U.S. Constitution. Also called the Necessary and Proper Clause, it grants Congress the authority to enact all laws that are "necessary and proper" to carrying out its other powers. **68**

elector a member of the electoral college. **157**

electoral college a body of representatives from the 50 states and the District of Columbia who officially elect the president and vice president of the United States. **157**

electorate the total number of citizens who are eligible to vote in an election. **405**

embassy a diplomatic center that a nation maintains in a foreign country. **223**

enabling act a federal law that allows the residents of a territory to draft a constitution and take other steps necessary in preparing for statehood. **76**

endorsement official declaration of support for a candidate for political office by a political party, political action committee, newspaper, labor union, or other organization. **391**

English Bill of Rights a law passed by Parliament in

1689 that forms one of the foundations of Britain's unwritten constitution. The bill prohibited the monarchy from suspending laws, levying taxes, or maintaining an army in peacetime without consent of Parliament. **23**

entitlements benefits that federal law requires the government to give to individuals who meet established requirements. **209**

entrepreneur someone who undertakes and develops a new business enterprise at some risk of failure or loss. The entrepreneur typically invests capital and human resources in the hope of earning a profit. **507**

Establishment Clause the part of the First Amendment to the Constitution that prohibits Congress from passing any law that establishes a religion or that favors one religion over others. **300**

estate tax a tax levied on the estate, or property, of a person who has died. **193**

ethnic group a group of people within a nation who share certain characteristics, such as race, language, cultural heritage, religion, or national origin. **345**

ex post facto law a law that illegalizes specific acts that took place before it was passed. **108**

excise tax a tax placed by the federal government and some state governments on the manufacture, sale, or consumption of certain goods, often those considered to be luxury items or socially undesirable products. **193**

exclusionary rule a Supreme Court precedent establishing that illegally obtained evidence may not be used in a criminal trial. **151, 322**

executive agreement an agreement between the president and the heads of other nations. **58**

executive order a rule or regulation issued by the president or another executive branch official on how to carry out and enforce legislation. **148**

executive privilege the principle that the executive branch may withhold information from Congress and the courts to preserve national security. **149**

exemption an amount of income on which the government does not levy a tax. **191**

exit poll a survey of selected voters as they leave polling places to determine how they voted. **373**

expatriation the voluntary giving up of one's citizenship. **341**

expressed power a governmental power that is specifically granted in a constitution; also called an enumerated or a delegated power. **67**

expulsion the removal by a legislature of one of its members for serious or criminal misconduct. Expulsion is the most serious disciplinary action that a legislature may take against a member. **118**

extradition the process by which one state or nation returns a person accused or convicted of a crime to the state or nation where the crime was committed. **79**

F

faction a group of people seeking to advance their own concerns. **60**

factor of production a resource used in the production process. The four factors of production are natural resources, human resources, capital resources, and entrepreneurship. **507**

federal budget the estimate of the revenues and expenses of the federal government for a fiscal year. **204**

federal mandate a federal requirement that state or local governments take a specific action, offer a particular program, or pay for a program the federal government establishes. **73**

Federal Reserve system the Fed; a system of 12 government banks and 25 branches across the United States run by a board that is appointed by the president. **200**

federal system a form of government in which power is shared among central, state, and regional levels. **10**

Federalist 1) someone who supported the proposed U.S. Constitution in the late 1780s and favored a strong national government. **40** 2) a member of the Federalist Party, an early political party in the United States. **409–10**

felony a major violation of criminal law that almost always calls for a minimum scheduled sentence of a year in prison. **273**

filibuster a delaying tactic that legislators sometimes use to prevent a vote on a bill they dislike. **127**

fiscal policy the overall government program that establishes levels of taxing, borrowing, and spending that promote the desired economic goals for the nation. **198**

floor leader a legislator chosen by members of his or her party to advance their political agenda through the legislative process. **116**

forces of production in Marxist terminology, the combination of the means of production and the potential productivity of workers. **516**

foreign aid any assistance granted by a nation's government or private organizations to another nation's government or people. **234**

foreign policy a nation's plans and procedures for dealing with other nations. **145**

foreign service a nation's professional diplomats, who carry out its foreign policy throughout the world. **225**

franking privilege the right of a member of Congress to send mail without paying postage. **101**

free enterprise a system in which private business operates with a minimal government regulation. **196**

Free Exercise Clause a clause in the First Amendment to the Constitution that prohibits government interference with the "free exercise" of religious practices. **302**

G

general election an election in which voters choose from among candidates running for federal, state, or local elective office. **159, 417**

gerrymandering the redrawing of legislative district boundaries in order to strengthen the political power of one group or political party over another. **100**

gift tax a tax by the federal government and some state governments on large transfers of certain goods that are made without something of value being given in return. **193**

glasnost the Russian term for the late 1980s Soviet political reforms which permitted freer expression of political views. The term glasnost means "openness." **233**

global warming the theory that the world's climates are becoming dangerously warmer. **538**

government an institution that determines and enforces a society's laws. The size and nature of a government varies according to the society it governs. **3**

government corporation an independent agency that manages a self-supporting business. **178**

governor the chief executive of a state government who is elected by the state's voters. **468**

Gramm-Rudman-Hollings Act the Balanced Budget and Emergency Deficit Control Act of 1985. This law set maximum limits on yearly budget deficits and required automatic spending cuts whenever those maximums were exceeded. **210**

grand jury a panel of 12 to 23 citizens who review evidence that a prosecutor presents against a person accused of a crime. The grand jury determines if the government has enough evidence to issue an indictment and bring the person to trial. **277**

grant-in-aid a federal payment to a state, or a federal or state payment to a local government, for a specific purpose. **72**

grassroots lobbying a lobbying technique used to encourage large groups of citizens at the local level to try to influence legislators or other government officials. **394**

Great Compromise the agreement to establish a two-house U.S. legislature. The compromise was presented to the Constitutional Convention of 1787 by the Connecticut delegation. It combined elements of two plans. The Virginia Plan called for proportional representation determined by population and the New Jersey Plan proposed that each state have an equal vote in the legislative process. These two plans became the basis for the House of Representatives and Senate. **58**

gross domestic product (GDP) the total value of all goods and services produced within a country in a given year. **208**

H

hate speech words or symbols that can reasonably be expected to cause anger, fear, or resentment in others on the basis of race, color, creed, religion, or gender. **311**

hung jury a jury that is divided over a case and unable to reach a unanimous decision about a defendant's guilt or innocence. **279**

I

idealism in international relations, the belief that a nation's foreign policy should be guided by noble goals such as justice, equality, and world service instead of purely by national interest. **220**

ideological party a political party that forms around a political idea or point of view that is different from the majority of the population's view. Unlike many third parties, ideological parties tend to exist over long periods of time. *See also* splinter party. **415**

ideology an organized set of beliefs that a person or group holds about people, society, and the world. **368**

illegal alien a person from one country who is living or working in another country unlawfully. **344**

immunity a protection for certain government officials from being sued or prosecuted for actions that are part of their elective office. **101**

impeach the bringing of formal charges by a legislature against a public official. Impeachment is the first step in removing an official from office. **106**

implied power a power that is implied, or suggested, by the expressed powers in a constitution. **68**

incumbent a political candidate who currently holds an elected or appointed office. **113**

independent a candidate with no political party affiliations who is running for a political office. **413**

independent agency a federal executive agency not included in a cabinet department. There are three types of independent agencies: regulatory commissions, government corporations, and independent executive agencies. **177**

indictment a formal document issued by a grand jury that names and charges an individual with a violation of criminal law, usually a felony. **277**

inflation an increase in overall prices that results from rising wages, an increased money supply, and increased spending relative to the supply of products. **197**

information a formal document—issued to a court by the state's prosecuting attorney—charging a specific individual with a violation of criminal law. This process is used in states that do not use the grand jury system. **277**

inherent power   a power that is not specifically granted in or implied by a constitution, but that belongs to the governments of all sovereign nations.   **68**

initiative   a process in some states that allows citizens to propose and enact laws.   **463**

interest group   a group whose members hold common political beliefs and work to influence government officials, policies, and practices. Interest groups are also called pressure groups.   **94**

interdependence   mutual reliances between the world's countries. Countries' actions affect one another's economic growth and stability.   **527**

international law   the principles and rules that have been set up to guide the actions of nations in their relations with one another and in their dealings with other countries' citizens.   **532**

internationalist   a person who believes that nations should act as a community and should interact with one another peacefully and cooperatively. *See also* isolationist and neoisolationist.   **219**

interstate compact   a formal agreement approved by Congress between two or more states to jointly operate mutually beneficial programs.   **79**

isolationist   a person who believes that a nation should interact politically as little as possible with other nations so that it can exist peacefully by itself in the world.   **218**

Jim Crow laws   laws passed in the southern United States to require or permit racial segregation. Jim Crow laws are now unconstitutional.   **348**

joint committee   a congressional committee composed of members from both the Senate and the House of Representatives.   **119**

judicial activism   the practice of judges using their court decisions to make new public policy in order to advance what they believe to be desirable social goals. *See also* judicial restraint.   **265**

judicial restraint   the practice of judges narrowly interpreting laws and limiting their decisions in order to avoid making public policy. *See also* judicial activism.   **264**

judicial review   the power of a court to determine whether laws and other government actions are constitutional or otherwise lawful.   **49**

jurisdiction   the power of a court to interpret and administer the law.   **250**

jury pool   a group of people who are summoned to appear in court and from among which the actual jury in a criminal or civil proceeding will be selected. Also called a jury panel.   **471**

jus sanguinis   the legal principle that a person's citizenship is determined by that of his or her parents rather than by his or her place of birth. *See also jus soli.*   **339**

jus soli   the legal principle that a person's citizenship is determined by where he or she was born rather than by the citizenship of his or her parents. *See also jus sanguinis.*   **339**

juvenile delinquent   a young person who is judged guilty of a criminal offense. The age of a juvenile may vary from under 16 to under 21 years of age, depending on the state.   **283**

Keynesianism   a school of thought pioneered in the 1930s by British economist John Maynard Keynes that calls for government to use fiscal policy and monetary policy to influence a nation's economy.   **202**

---

labor union   an organization of workers that negotiates with employers for better wages, improved working conditions, and job security.   **387**

law   a set of rules, issued and enforced by a government, that binds every member of society.   **3**

legitimacy   the legal and recognized right of a government to make decisions for the citizens of a nation, state, or locality.   **4**

libel   deliberately publishing false written or visual statements harming the reputation or business of an individual or group.   **307**

line-item veto   the power of a government's chief executive to reject specific parts of a bill passed by a legislative body, rather than having to veto the entire measure.   **128**

lobbying   the process by which an individual, a group, or an organization seeks to influence government policy makers.   **392**

loose constructionist   a person who believes that a constitution should be interpreted reasonably, but broadly, in order to meet the needs of changing times. *See also* strict constructionist.   **290**

machine politics   *See* party machine.

Magna Carta   a document prepared by English nobles that granted certain rights to English citizens. The charter was signed under the threat of force by King John of England in 1215.   **21–22**

majority opinion a formal statement of the decision of a majority of members of a judicial panel hearing a case, giving the reasons for the decision. The majority opinion is the official opinion of the court. *See also* concurring opinion and dissenting opinion. **261**

majority party a political party whose members make up the majority in a legislative house. **115**

majority rule the principle that the will of the largest portion of a group should prevail in electing leaders and making policies. Majority rule is a basic characteristic of democratic systems of government. **15**

Marshall Plan a massive U.S. foreign-aid program to help Europe recover from World War II. **235**

mayor-council system a system of urban government in which power is shared by an elected chief executive (a mayor) and a separately elected legislature (a city council). **488**

megalopolis a large, densely populated area made up of two or more cities and their suburbs. A megalopolis forms when metropolitan areas grow into one another. **484**

merit system a system for hiring government workers based on demonstrated qualifications and competitive examinations. **180**

metropolitan area an urban area made up of a city whose population is over 50,000 as well as its suburbs and all the surrounding counties dependant on the city. **484**

minority party a political party whose members do not make up the majority in a legislative house. **115**

minority rights political rights that cannot be abolished in a democracy, even though they are held by less than half of the population. **15**

Miranda Rule an arresting officer's requirement to inform criminal suspects of their rights before questioning. **327**

misdemeanor a minor violation of criminal law that is generally punishable by a fine or by a jail term of less than one year. *See also* felony. **273**

mixed economy an economy that combines elements of the traditional, market, and command economic models. Almost all modern economies are mixed economies. **509**

monarchy a system of government in which the head of state, usually a royal figure, is a hereditary position. **8**

monetarism a school of thought pioneered by American economist Milton Friedman. Monetarism is based on the theory that if left alone, a market economy will operate at full employment and low inflation. **202**

monetary policy a government's program for regulating a nation's money supply and the availability of credit in order to accomplish certain economic goals. **198**

Monroe Doctrine a foreign-policy statement made by President James Monroe in 1823. Monroe declared that the United States would not allow European nations to further colonize or take any aggressive actions in the Western Hemisphere. **228**

multilateral treaty a legal agreement among three or more nations to accomplish a common purpose. **237**

multiparty system a political system in which several major and minor political parties compete for political power and government offices. **407**

municipality a city or town with its own level of government. **487**

national debt the total amount of money that a nation owes its creditors. It is the sum of each year's unpaid spending deficits—that is, the money borrowed to finance deficit spending that has not been repaid. **210**

national security the freedom of a nation to protect its citizens from hostile or destructive forces or actions from within or outside its borders. **217**

nationalization the government takeover of specific companies or of a major segment of a nation's private industry, such as manufacturing, agriculture, or transportation. **512**

natural right a right that is considered to belong to all people, regardless of time or place. Being natural to everyone, these rights do not need to be granted by a government and should not be transferred or taken away. Natural rights are also known as inalienable rights. **4**

naturalization the process by which a nation grants citizenship to an immigrant. **340**

neoisolationist an individual opposed to the internationalism that has dominated American foreign policy since the end of World War II. Unlike a traditional isolationist, a neoisolationist does not oppose all U.S. entanglement with other nations. Neoisolationists support alliances and methods of furthering U.S. national interests abroad. **219–20**

New England Confederation the first confederation of English colonies in North America. The confederation was formed in 1643 to unite four New England colonies, largely for defense against American Indians and England's European rivals. **25**

New Jersey Plan a plan for establishing a one-house legislature in which each state would have an equal vote. The proposal was put before the Constitutional Convention in 1787 by William Paterson of New Jersey. **37–38**

no-contest plea a formal answer in court in which a defendant states simply that he or she will not fight the charge, but neither proclaims innocence nor admits guilt. **277**

nominate to name a political party member as a candidate for a particular public office. **157**

nonpartisan primary   a primary election in which candidates from all political parties are on the same ballot and in which all voters can participate, regardless of their political affiliation.   **432**

nonrenewable resources   any limited resource whose supply cannot be replenished in the short term.   **540**

North Atlantic Treaty Organization (NATO)   a collective security organization created by a multilateral treaty in 1949. NATO was originally created to protect the Western European and North American nations in the North Atlantic region against attack by the Soviet Union.   **237**

Northwest Ordinance   an act of Congress under the Articles of Confederation that set procedures for granting statehood to territories. The Northwest Ordinance allowed an area to become a territory once it had a population of at least 5,000 free males. It allowed a territory to apply for statehood once it reached a population of 60,000 free inhabitants.   **32**

nuclear proliferation   the spread of nuclear weapons to nations that did not previously have them.   **529**

objectivity   the ability to judge or present information factually, in a manner that is not influenced by emotions or prejudices, but that is instead based on evidence.   **379**

obscenity   printed or visual material that is not protected by the First Amendment because it is considered to lack serious social value and to be highly offensive.   **307**

Office of Management and Budget (OMB)   an executive branch agency within the Executive Office of the President that is responsible for preparing the president's budget request.   **204**

oligarchy   a system of government in which political power and control is held by a small group of political elite. The leaders of an oligarchy often govern for their own benefit or for the benefit of their social class.   **9**

one-party system   a political system in which one political party controls the government and clearly dominates political activity.   **407**

open primary   a primary election in which a voter may participate in the selection of a political party's candidates regardless of the voter's own political affiliation.   **432**

open-market operations   the purchasing and selling of securities—usually government securities—by the Federal Reserve system on the open market in order to help carry out monetary policy.   **201**

original jurisdiction   the requirement or authority of a court to be the first to hear a case.   **250**

oversight   the power of a legislature to review and monitor the activities of an executive branch agency to determine whether it is properly executing laws under its administration.   **96**

pardon   the official release of a person charged with or convicted of a crime, at the request of a chief executive.   **153**

parliamentary system   a system of government in which power is concentrated in a legislature. The legislature selects one of its members, usually called a prime minister, as the nation's principal leader and other legislative members serve as the leader's cabinet.   **11**

parochial   religious in nature, as in elementary and high schools run by churches and other religious organizations.   **301**

parole   the release of a prisoner before he or she has served a full sentence.   **282**

party machine   an organized group of individuals who dominate a political party within a geographic area and who use the party's resources to further their own power and to fight off challenges from other party members for party control.   **416**

party platform   a statement of a political party's position on issues.   **161**

party whip   a member of the Senate or House of Representatives who is chosen by his or her party colleagues to assist the party's floor leader in managing its legislative program.   **116**

passport   a document that a nation issues to its citizens that allows them travel to other nations, identifies them to government authorities in those nations, and gives them the right to return home.   **225**

patronage   the practice of elected officials rewarding political supporters with government contracts, appointments to office, jobs, and other benefits.   **416**

peremptory challenge   in choosing a jury for a trial, the right of either the defense or the prosecution to reject a possible juror without providing a reason.   **279**

perestroika   a Russian word meaning "restructuring." Perestroika was an effort by the Soviet Union to change its economy from communism to market socialism.   **233**

petit jury   a group of citizens who decide the verdict in a civil or criminal trial.   **278**

Petition of Right   a document drawn up by the English Parliament and signed by King Charles I in 1628. The Petition of Right, like Magna Carta, limited the ability of the monarch to act on his or her sole authority.   **23**

picketing   marching around in a specific area while carrying signs that communicate a message of protest.   **313**

plaintiff   the party who brings a legal action in a court of law.   **274**

plank a political party's specific proposal for legislation or a statement of a short-term goal regarding a single issue. Planks are the components of a party platform. **161**

plea bargain in a criminal court case, an agreement negotiated between the prosecutor and the defendant and his or her attorney to avoid the time, expense, and uncertain outcome of a trial. **280**

plurality the greatest number of popular votes received by a candidate in an election. A plurality can be, but is not necessarily, a majority. **163**

pocket veto a method of preventing a bill from becoming a law. The pocket veto enables the president to dismiss a bill by simply refusing to sign it, without having to state his or her reasons for doing so. **128**

police power the power of a government to use force if necessary to control affairs within its jurisdiction in order to protect the health, safety, and welfare of its citizens. **322**

political action committee (PAC) an organization that is created to raise and distribute campaign money to candidates for elective political office. **94**

political party a formal organization of people who seek to influence government actions and policies by electing its members to public office. **58**

political socialization the process through which individuals obtain their political attitudes and values. **368**

politics the art and science of governing. Through politics, people express opinions about what government should or should not do. **6**

polling the process of systematically surveying the views of individuals within a selected group or groups in order to determine public opinion on an issue. **372**

popular sovereignty governing authority that comes from the people. **47**

popular vote the total votes cast by the general public in an election. **163**

pork-barrel spending legislative funding for unnecessary projects that favor the district of a particular legislator. **129**

precedent the legal principle of a court's ruling in a case serving as a model for future decisions in similar cases, unless for some reason it is specifically overruled by another case. **249**

precinct the smallest political subdivision of a U.S. city, town, or county for voting purposes and for political party organization. **418**

prejudice the holding of an opinion about a person, group, or thing without rational grounds or without having enough information upon which to base it. **345**

presentment a formal statement issued by a grand jury to authorize a trial for someone accused of a crime. **327**

president *pro tempore* the senator who presides over the Senate when its official presiding officer—the vice president of the United States—is absent. **116**

presidential doctrine a presidential statement that guides the nation's foreign policy—for example, the Monroe Doctrine or the Truman Doctrine. **222–23**

presidential succession the order in which the vice president or other designated official becomes president of the United States should the office become vacant. **147**

presidential system a system of government in which the legislative and executive branches operate independently of each other. **11**

primary election an election to choose a political party's candidates for an elective office. **159, 417**

prior restraint an action by a government to prevent the publication of something or to require approval before it can be published. Thus, prior restraint is a form of censorship. **306**

privatization the act of turning functions previously performed by government over to the private sector. **186**

probable cause reasonable grounds to accuse an individual of committing a specific crime. **322**

probation freedom granted to a person convicted of a crime, with the condition that he or she meet certain conditions of good behavior for a specified period of time. **281**

procedural due process the principle that the law must be applied fairly and evenly to all people, using established rules and procedures. *See also* substantive due process. **319**

profit the difference between the revenue received from the sale of a good or service and the costs of providing that good or service. **508**

proletariat the working class, whose members the radical political theorist Karl Marx believed were oppressed by the bourgeoisie. **511**

property tax government tax revenue levied on the value of certain kinds of property. **493**

public comment the opportunity for interested parties to react to a regulation that is proposed by a government agency before the regulation goes into effect. **177**

public good the common interests of the members of a society; also known as the public interest. **6**

public interest group an interest group that supports positions and causes that it believes to be in the general public good, as contrasted with interest groups that work for a particular social or economic interest. **388**

public opinion the collective opinion on a particular issue or group of related issues that is held by a large segment of society. **367**

public policy decisions and laws that a government makes in a particular area of public concern. **4**

quorum the minimum number of legislators who must be present to vote and conduct other formal business when Congress is in session. **113**

quota the minimum number of new hires to be made through an affirmative action program. **355**

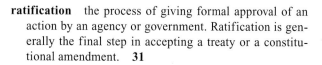

ratification the process of giving formal approval of an action by an agency or government. Ratification is generally the final step in accepting a treaty or a constitutional amendment. **31**

realignment a switching of political loyalties among the electorate or of political parties in a legislature. Realignment generally refers to significant and long-lasting changes in the attitudes of the electorate. **409**

realism in international relations, the belief that a nation's foreign policy should be based on the realities of human nature and history. Realists believes that foreign policy should be directed toward achieving power, maintaining national security, and pursuing other national interests. **219**

recall a procedure that allows the electorate to vote an elected official out of office before his or her term has expired. **464**

recession a substantial and general decline in overall business activity over a significant period of time. **197**

reconciliation a step in the federal budget process in which Congress adjusts the spending requests contained in the president's budget proposal. **207**

referendum a procedure in some states that gives voters the opportunity to approve or reject laws passed by the legislature or a local assembly. **465**

refugee a person who flees from a region, either voluntarily or by force, because of political, military, religious, social, or other conflict. **527**

regulatory commission an independent agency created by Congress with a greater degree of autonomy, or self-rule, than others. **177**

relations of production according to Marxist theory, the way people interconnect in the work process. The relations of production are determined by who owns the means of production, what position workers hold in relation to other groups involved in production, and how production and income are distributed among these groups. **516**

renewable resources resources that can be replenished in the short term through natural means. **540**

repeal to reverse or cancel an existing law or regulation. **52**

representative democracy a system of government in which the people choose political leaders to make policy decisions on their behalf. **16**

reprieve a postponement in the carrying out of a convicted person's sentence. **153**

republic a system of government in which governmental power comes from the people, who elect individuals to represent them in decision making. **8**

reserved power any power that the Constitution does not expressly or by implication give to Congress. The Tenth Amendment to the Constitution specifically reserves such powers to the states or to the people. **68**

reserve requirement a bank's financial reserve held either in its own vaults or in a district Federal Reserve bank. In essence, it is the bank's savings account. **201**

resolution a formal declaration or statement of policy concerning a specific issue or matter. **206**

revenue the total income of a business or a unit of government. **191**

revenue sharing the distribution by a government of a portion of its income to lower levels of government. **72**

roll-call vote a legislative procedure in which each legislator is called on individually to cast his or her vote. **127**

runoff primary a second election that is held in some states if no candidate in the primary election receives a majority of the votes. **432**

rural area a region of low population density where people live on farms or ranches or in small towns and where economic activities center around land-based enterprises such as agriculture or mining. **481**

sales tax a tax on the sale of goods and services. **473**

sampling a procedure for choosing a small portion of a population to represent the population as a whole in a survey. **374**

sampling error an error in polling results caused by choosing a sample of individuals to poll that was not representative of the larger population being studied. **375**

search warrant a written authorization issued by a judge to allow law enforcement authorities to search a person's property for specified items and to seize those items if they are found. **322**

secret ballot the popular name for a voting system that allows voters to choose candidates in private. It originated in Australia and is now universally used in U.S. elections. **441**

secretary the head of a cabinet-level department within the executive branch of the U.S. government—for example, the secretary of defense, the secretary of state, and the secretary of the treasury.   **174**

sedition   language or actions that call for or encourage resistance or rebellion against a lawfully established government. *See also* treason.   **305**

segregation   the separation of people according to any specified identifying characteristic.   **348**

select committee   a House or Senate committee that is generally established for a limited time and for a specific, often investigative, purpose.   **119**

self-interest   the impulse that encourages people to fulfill their needs and wants.   **508**

senatorial courtesy   the practice that allows senators from the same political party as the president to approve or disapprove each potential nominee for certain appointed positions in their state before the official nominations are made.   **254**

seniority system   a system for granting congressional committee positions based on the length of time in service.   **120**

separate-but-equal doctrine   a legal precedent (established by the Supreme Court in the 1896 case *Plessy* v. *Ferguson*) that racial segregation was not a violation of the Equal Protection Clause of the Fourteenth Amendment as long as separate facilities for African Americans and whites were of equal quality. This principle remained in place until 1954, when the Supreme Court overturned it in *Brown* v. *Board of Education*.   **348**

separation of powers   the distribution of political power among the branches of government, giving each branch a particular set of responsibilities.   **48**

sequester   to isolate a jury from the public during a trial.   **279**

shield law   a law that protects reporters from having to reveal confidential sources of information. Shield laws allow people to provide information to the media without fear that they will be revealed as informants.   **307**

sin tax   a tax on products or activities that government authorities consider harmful or otherwise undesirable.   **474**

single-issue voting   a situation in which an individual chooses to support or reject a political candidate on the basis of just one factor, excluding all other issues.   **391**

single-member district   an electoral district in which only one candidate can win election to a particular office.   **440**

slander   deliberately making false spoken statements that might damage the reputation of a business, an individual, or a group. Slander is a criminal offense, but it generally is not prosecuted. However, the victims of slander often seek damages in civil lawsuits.   **307**

social contract   the theory that people give up their individual sovereignty in exchange for peace and order provided by the state.   **4**

socialism   an economic system in which the government owns or controls many of the means of production and directly provides for many of the people's needs. A socialist system may or may not be democratic.   **511**

sovereignty   the absolute authority that a government has over the citizens of a state.   **3**

Speaker   the presiding officer of the U.S. House of Representatives and second (after the vice president) in the line of succession to the presidency. The Speaker is elected by the House and has always been a member of the majority party.   **115**

special district   a unit of government, typically at the local level, that serves a specific function and that sometimes crosses existing political boundaries.   **490**

splinter party   a political party that is created when a group that is unhappy with the candidate, and sometimes the positions, of a major party breaks off from that party (or from both major parties). *See also* ideological party.   **415**

split ticket   the result of an individual voting for persons from different political parties for different political offices.   **417**

spoils system   the practice of government officials awarding public jobs and public contracts to political supporters rather than awarding them on the basis of job qualifications. *See also* merit system.   **178**

Stamp Act   a 1765 law passed by Parliament to raise money by taxing paper goods. However, because of violent protests in the colonies, the tax was repealed the year after it was introduced.   **26**

standard of living   people's economic well-being as determined by the quantity of goods and services they consume in a given time period.   **195**

standing committee   a regular or permanent committee created by a legislature to review bills within a specified subject area.   **119**

stare decisis   the legal principle and judicial practice of following precedents set in earlier legal decision. The Latin term means "let the decision stand."   **261**

state   **1)** a territory whose population maintains an organized governmental body that regulates internal and external affairs. **2)** a political unit in a federal system, such as a state within the United States.   **3**

State of the Union Address   the president's annual message to Congress, in which he or she usually proposes the administration's legislative program.   **143**

statutory interpretation   a judicial function in which a judge decides a law's meaning in regards to a specific court case.   **273**

statutory law   all regulations put forth by a lawmaking government body.   **272**

straight ticket   the result of a voter's selecting only candidates from a particular party for every office on the ballot.   **417**

strict constructionist a person who believes that a constitution should be interpreted rigidly and narrowly based only on what is written in the document. **249**

subcommittee **1)** a smaller, more specialized part of a committee. **2)** a group of committee members selected to work on specific categories of bills or other matters that come before the entire committee. **119**

subpoena a written order requiring a person to testify in court as a witness or to bring certain items to court as evidence. **279**

substantive due process the principle that a law must be fair and reasonable. The right to substantive due process requires a court to consider the fairness of the law itself. **320**

suburb a primarily residential community that is located near a city and whose residents largely depend on the city for jobs and other services. **481**

suffrage the right to vote. **442**

summit conference a meeting between the heads of state of two or more nations in order to discuss and conduct international relations. Summit conferences may involve military, economic, or diplomatic matters. **223**

supply and demand the forces that determine prices in a free market. **508**

suspect classification a potentially illegal basis for making distinctions between individuals or groups. **347**

symbolic speech messages that are communicated nonverbally. Symbolic speech can include articles worn on clothing, hand gestures, and certain types of actions. **310**

tax a required payment to a local, state, or national government, usually made on some regular basis. **191**

term limits legal limits on the number of terms certain elected officials can hold a particular office. **113**

third party a political party outside the dominant parties in a two-party system. **413**

totalitarian a system of government in which a dictator or a small group of leaders exercise tremendous control over citizens' lives. **9–10**

township communities established in states such as New Jersey, New York, and Pennsylvania. Governments of townships served some of the same functions as New England town governments. **487**

trade association an organization formed by companies within an industry that represents the concerns of the industry. **386**

trade deficit a situation in which the total value of a country's imports is higher than the total value of its exports. **537**

trade embargo a government order that forbids trade with a specified nation. **218**

trading bloc a group of nations working together to provide trade benefits to its members. Trading-bloc members set import and export quotas, fix tariffs, and establish other trade controls. **534**

treason an act of disloyalty against one's own country. **304**

Truman Doctrine a 1947 foreign-policy statement made by President Harry Truman that pledged U.S. military and economic aid to nations that were trying to avoid a communist takeover. **229**

two-party system a system in which two political parties dominate the political system and compete for political power. **407**

unconstitutional a law or government action that violates provisions set forth in the U.S. Constitution. **49**

unicameral a legislative body that has one chamber or house. Nebraska is the only American state with a unicameral legislature. **30**

unitary system a system of government in which all legal power is held by the national, or central, government. **10**

urban area a region characterized by cities and other areas of high population density, and in which most of the working residents are involved in manufacturing, commercial, or other nonagricultural economic activities. **481**

U.S. Agency for International Development a U.S. government organization that carries out U.S. foreign-aid programs. The agency concentrates on five areas of foreign policy; promoting economic growth, advancing democracy, delivering humanitarian aid, promoting public health and protecting the environment. **235**

value a basic quality, principle, or standard that is considered important or desirable and by which people live their lives. For example, humility is a value that many people consider important. **6**

vanguard the leading position in a movement, or those who occupy that position. In 1917 the Bolsheviks were the vanguard that led the Russian Revolution. **517**

veto the formal rejection of legislation by a chief executive. **48**

Virginia Plan a plan for establishing a one-house legislature in which each state would have proportional representation based on its population. The plan was submitted to the Constitutional Convention in 1787 by the Virginia delegation. Many of the plan's proposals were included in the U.S. Constitution. **36**

visa the permission that a nation gives to a citizen of another nation who wishes to visit it. **225**

voir dire the questioning of prospective jurors—by the judge and prosecuting and defense attorneys in a court case—to see if they are acceptable—to the judge and the attorneys—to serve on a jury. The phrase *voir dire* means "to speak truth." **278–79**

Ⓦ

---

ward a territorial division of city government that is also often used as a voting subdivision and a unit of political party organization. **418**

writ of *certiorari* a formal order from an appeals court that requires a lower court to provide the record of a case for review. Most cases reaching the Supreme Court are heard because the Court has issued a writ of *certiorari*. **259**

writ of *habeas corpus* a judicial order directing law enforcement authorities to bring any prisoner before a court official and cite the reason for his or her imprisonment, to determine if that person is being held lawfully. **108**

INDEX

absentee ballot, 441

accused persons, rights of, 53, 326–28, *c326*

act of admission, 76

Adams, John: 30, 32, 158, 172, 251, 430, 448; Declaration of Independence and, 29, *p29; Marbury* v. *Madison,* 50

Adams, John Quincy, 106, 159, 163, *c163*

Adams, Samuel, 28

Adelson, Joseph, 369

administrative law, 272–73

admission of states, 76

advertising: freedom of speech and, 308–10

affirmative action, 350, 354, 355–56

AFL-CIO, 199, 387

Africa: relations with United States, 547–48

African Americans: 53; civil rights legislation and, 155; in Congress, 95, 104; discrimination against, 346, *p347,* 350, *p350,* 394; as presidential candidates, 145; redistricting and, *m101;* segregation, 260, *p266,* 347–49, *p348;* separate-but-equal doctrine, 347; voting restrictions for, 30; voting rights of, 53, 442–43. *See also* civil rights; minorities

age: requirement for voting, *p51*

agencies, congressional, 122

Agnew, Spiro, 147

agribusiness, 386

agricultural groups, 386

Air Force, U.S., 152

Air Force One, 146

Alaska, *p68,* 77, *p77*

Alaskan Purchase, the, *p68,* 77

Albany Plan of Union, 26

Albright, Madeleine, *p148,* 189

Alien and Sedition Acts, 305

aliens: civil rights of, 298

alliances, 151

ambassadors, U.S.: 224; appointed by president, 148; congressional approval of, 106

amendment, 51

Amendment, Eighteenth, 52, 54, 55

Amendment, Eighth, 53, *c53,* 329, 332–33, 334

Amendment, Eleventh, 265

Amendment, Fifteenth, 53

Amendment, Fifth, 53, *c53,* 280, 320, 327, 331–32

Amendment, First, 53, *c53,* 299, 300, 304–11

Amendment, Fourteenth, 53, 306, 320, 339–40, 346

Amendment, Fourth, 53, *c53,* 56, 322–24

Amendment, Nineteenth, 53–55, 443

Amendment, Ninth, 53, *c53,* 68

Amendment, Second, 53, *c53,* 323

Amendment, Seventeenth, 53–55, 102

Amendment, Seventh, 53, *c53,* 330

Amendment, Sixteenth, 55, 68, 265

Amendment, Sixth, 53, *c53,* 329–31

Amendment, Tenth, 53, *c53,* 68, 108

Amendment, Third, 53, *c53*

Amendment, Thirteenth, 53

Amendment, Twelfth, *c157,* 158

Amendment, Twentieth, 113

Amendment, Twenty-fifth, 147

Amendment, Twenty-first, 52

Amendment, Twenty-second, 59, 114, 146

Amendment, Twenty-seventh, 54, *p54,* 55, 101

Amendment, Twenty-sixth, *p51,* 265

amendments, constitutional: proposed by Congress, 52, 55

American Association of Retired Persons (AARP), 387

American Bar Association (ABA), 387

American Federation of Labor–Congress of Industrial Organizations. *See* AFL–CIO

American Indians: and American colonists, 26; civil rights of, 352–53; in Congress, 104, *p104;* voting restrictions for, 30

American Medical Association (AMA), 387

Americans with Disabilities Act (ADA), 353, *p353*

amicus curiae **brief,** 260

amnesty, 344

Amnesty International, 236

anarchy, 14

Annan, Kofi, 551

Annapolis Convention, 34

Anthony, Susan B., 443

Antifederalists, 40–41, *p40*

appellate jurisdiction, 253

appointing powers: *p148,* 227, 254, 257; of president, 148–49

appointments, presidential: approval of Congress, 106, 227

apportionment: 99; gerrymandering and, 100–101, *m101*

appropriations, 118

Appropriations Committee, House, *p119,* 121, 206

Appropriations Committee, Senate, *p119,* 206

archivist, 57

Arctic National Wildlife Refuge, 77

Aristotle: influence on U.S. federal court system, 251

armed forces, U.S.: 152, *p152, p153;* branches of military, 152; commander in chief of, 143, *p143;* women in, 152

Armey, Dick, *p115*

Canada: census counting in, 174; government of, 29; independence from Great Britain, 29; NAFTA, 535

capitalism: 507–10; characteristics of, *c509;* economic competition, 508, *c509;* profit, 508, *c509;* factors of production, 507, *c507;* market economy, 508, *c509;* mixed economy, 509; origins of, 508–509; private ownership, 507, *c509;* self-interest in, 508–509; in the United States, 509–10

capitalist, 507

capital punishment, 282–83, 333–34, *m333*

Carter, Jimmy, *c163,* 197

Carter, Rosalyn, 173

Castro, Fidel, 230–31

caucus: 160; political nominations, 429–30

caucus, party: role in choosing delegates to national convention, 160

categorical grants, 73

censorship, 377

censure, 117

census, 98

Census, Bureau of, 174

Center for Auto Safety, 390

Central Intelligence Agency (CIA): 170, 177; role in U.S. foreign policy, 226

change of venue, 330

Chaplinsky v. *New Hampshire,* 311

charter, 23–24, *p23*

checks and balances, 48–50, *c48, c49,* 61

chief executive, 143

chief justice, 256, *p256*

China, People's Republic of: 232, *p233;* communism in, 230, 233; and Hong Kong, 522; interest groups in, 397; relations with United States, 545–46

Chisolm, Shirley, 95

"Choose or Lose" campaign, 378

Christian Coalition: 388, 393

circuit, 252, *c252*

Cisneros, Henry, 499

citizens: definition of, 3

citizenship: acquiring, 339–41, *c340;* by birth, 339–40; *jus sanguinis,* 339; *jus soli,* 339; loss of, 341; by naturalization, 340–41, *c340;* requirements for, 340

city council, 488–89

city government: commission form of, *c489,* 490–91; council-manager form of, *c488,* 489–90; city manager, 489–90; mayor-council form of, 488

city manager, 489–90

civil laws: 274; states and, 78

civil liberties, 297–99

civil rights: 155; definition of, 346; discrimination, 350–52; equality before the law, 346–49; history of, 350–52; of the mentally ill, 258

Civil Rights Acts: of 1866, 350; of 1964, 52, 298, 351–52, 356; of 1968, 352; of 1991, 352

civil rights lawyer, 298

civil rights movement, 347

civil servants, 178

civil service, 178–81, *c180;* as nonelected officials, 183–84

Civil War, 72, 76, 412

class-action suits, 394

class struggle, 515

Clay, Kirk, 393, *p393*

Clean Air Act, 74, 394

Clean Water Act, 394

clear-and-present-danger test, 305–306

Cleveland, Grover, *c163*

Clinton, Bill, *p58,* 62, 73, *p143, p144, p145,* 150, 151, *p154, p159, p171,* 172, *p175,* 199, *p205,* 212, 378, 414

Clinton, Hillary Rodham, *p145,* 173–74

closed primary, 432

cloture, 127

Coast Guard, U.S., 152

Code Napoleon, 321

Cold War, 229–32

collective security, 237, 527–32

colonies, American: *p23, p24;* Albany Plan of Union and, 26; boycott of British goods, 28, 29; British policies concerning, 26–28; charters of, 23–24; economic differences among, 25; geographic differences among, 27; government in, 24; independence of, 29–30; influence of British political ideals on, 21–23; New England Confederation and, 25–26; protests in, 28–29; Stamp Act, 26; types of, 24; unification of, 25–30

Colorado: congressional term limits set by, 114

commander in chief, 48, 143, 151, 223

commerce: interstate, 105; regulation of, 105

Commerce, Department of, *c173,* 174

commission: type of municipal government, *c488,* 490–91

committees, congressional: 118–22, 123–27; appropriations, 118; authorizing, 118; chairs, 120–21; conference, 119; joint, 119; membership of, 121; resources of, 121–22; select, 119; seniority system in, 120; staff of, 122; standing, 119, *c119. See also* names of committees

Committees of Correspondence, 28

common law, 271–72, 321

communism: 515–22; collapse of, 520–21; concepts of production in, 516; Marxian theory of, 515–17; proletarian dictatorship, 516–17; revolutionary ideology, 516; in Russia, 517–21; socialism and, 512

Communist Manifesto, 515, 525

Communist Party: 518; failure of, 520–21

commutation, 153

comparative advantage, 534

competition, 508

concurrent powers, 68, *c69*

concurring opinion, 261

confederal system: *c10;* definition of, 10

Confederate States of America, 158

corporate tax, 192

Corpus Christi, Texas, 483

corrections system, 281–86

Council of Economic Advisers, 172

council-manager system, *c488,* 489

counties: 275; government of, 486

court of appeals, 252–53, *c252*

court reporter, 332

courts: and the public good, 263–66; Russian, 253. *See also* federal court system; specific courts by name; state court system

criminal justice system: 275–80; capital punishment, 282–83; court procedures, 276–80, *c276;* imprisonment, 281–82, *c282;* juvenile crime, 283–86, *c285;* parole, 282; police, 275–76; probation, 281

criminal laws: 273–74; states and, 78

crown colony, 24

cruel and unusual punishment, 333

Cuba: 229, 230–31, 233; freedom of the press in, 378

Cuban missile crisis, 230–31

Curia Julia, *p103*

currency, national, 67, *p67*

customs duties, *c191,* 193–94

D

Davis, Jefferson, 158, *p158*

Davis v. *Bandemer,* 100

death penalty. *See* capital punishment

Declaration of Independence: 29–30, *p29;* natural rights in, 4

deductions, 191

Dees, Morris, 298, *p298*

de facto segregation, 349

defendant, 274

Defense, U.S. Department of (DOD): 170; joint chiefs of staff, 226; organization of, 225–26; role in U.S. foreign policy, 225–26

defense alliance, 235

defense policy: agencies concerned with, 225–27. *See also* foreign policy

deficit: 202, reduction, 208–12

deficit spending, 208–12

deforestation, 542

de jure segregation, 347–49

delegate, 28

delegated powers, 67–70, *c69*

delegates to national conventions: 159–60; women as, *c167*

democracy: *c9;* basic concepts of, 12, 14–15; definition of, 8–9; direct, 15; five basic principles of, 12, 14–15; freedom of choice in, 12–14; majority rule in, 15; minority rights in, 14–15; origins of, 15–16, *p15;* public good and, 15; representative, 16; taking part in, 433; types of, 15–16; worth of individual in, 14

Democratic Party: 411–13; domination of government from 1932 to 1968, 413; formation of, 411; and tax policy, 194

Democratic-Republicans, 409–11

democratic socialism: characteristics of, 512–14; definition of, 511

demonstrations. *See* protests

denaturalization, 341

deportation, 344

détente, 232

developed nation, 533

developing nation, 533

dictatorship: *c9;* definition of, 9–10

diplomacy, 144

diplomatic powers: of president, 149–51

diplomatic recognition, 151

direct democracy, 15

direct primary, 431

discount rate, 201

discrimination: 345; racial, 100–101, 394; rational basis test for, 346–47; reasonable distinction, 346; strict scrutiny test, 347; suspect classifications, 347

disposable income, 198

distributing power, 80–81

dissenting opinion, 261

district court, 252

District of Columbia, 92, 98

diversity: of U.S. population, *c344,* 345

division of powers. *See* separation of powers

docket, 259, 329

Dole, Bob, *p154,* 436

double jeopardy, 331–32

downsizing: of federal government, *c180,* 181

draft, 310

drinking laws, 74

due process: 319–22; definition of, 319; police power and, 322–23; procedural and substantive, 319–20; rights to security and privacy, 322–25

Due Process Clause, 306, 319–22

Durenberger, David, *p117*

Durkheim, Emil, 389

E

Earth Summit, 539

Eastern Europe: 229, 230; collapse of communism in, 521

East Germany: fall of the Berlin Wall, 233

economic deregulation, 197

economic systems: capitalism, 507–10; communism, 515–22; market economy, 508, *c509;* mixed economy, 509; socialism, 511–14

economist, 206

economy, U.S.: deficit spending, 208–12; federal budget and, 204–207; fiscal policy, 198, *c198;* inflation, 197;

Constitution, 69; powers of, *c69;* privatization of, 186; public good and, 131–32; raising revenue, 191–95; responsibilities to states, 69–70; states' responsibilities to, 70; taxing powers of, 105, 191,193. *See also* federalism; specific branches and departments

Federal Insurance Contributions Act (FICA), 193

federalism: *c48,* 50, *c81;* central authority of, 80; checking power, 81; concurrent powers in, 68, *c69;* constitutional principle of, *c48,* 50; cooperative, 76–79; delegated powers in, 67–71, *c69;* distribution of power and, 80–81; expressed powers in, 67, *c69;* implied powers in, 68; individual rights and, 78–79, 80, 82; inherent powers in, 68; local governments and, 81, *c81;* obligations to states under, 69–70; powers denied to federal government under, 69; powers denied to states, 69; powers reserved to states, 68; problems of, 81–82; public good and, 80–82; reserved powers in, 68, *c69;* revenue sharing, 72; Supreme Court and, 70–71

Federalist Papers, 41, 45, 81, 251, 256, 265

Federalists, 40, 41, 409–11

Federal Judiciary Act of 1789, 50

federal mandates, 73–75

Federal Open Market Committee (FOMC), 200

Federal Reserve Act of 1913, 200

Federal Reserve System: 200–201, *m200, c201;* reserve requirements, 201

federal system: *c10;* definition of, 10

federal tax, 191–95, *c191*

Federal Trade Commission (FTC), 178

felony, 273

Ferraro, Geraldine, 145, 427

filibuster, 127

Fillmore, Millard, 257

First Continental Congress, 28–29

first lady: Constitution and, 173; role of 173–74

fiscal policy: 198, *c198;* versus monetary policy, 201–202

Five-Year Plans, 518, 520

flag: burning of, 93–94, 310; saluting the, 303

floor leaders, congressional, 116,

Food and Drug Administration (FDA), 168

forces of production, 516

Ford, Gerald R., 147, *c163*

foreign aid, 234–35, *c234*

foreign commerce: regulation of, 105

foreign policy, U.S: constitutional oath of president, 145; foreign aid and alliances, 234–38; goals of, 217–18; history of, 228–33; isolationist policies, 228; major events of Cold War, 229–30, *c230;* National Security Council, 226; principles of, 218–21; and the public good, 221; rise to world power, 228–29; role of Central Intelligence Agency, 226; role of Congress, 227; role of president, 145, 222–23; role of U.S. Department of Defense, 225–26; role of U.S. Department of State, 223–25

Foreign Service, 224, 225

foreign-service officer (FSO), 224

France: 155, 235; parliamentary system in, 144; president of, 144; prime minister of, 144; right to speedy trial in, 330

Franco, Francisco, 520

franking privilege, 101

Franklin, Benjamin: 32; Albany Plan of Union proposal, 26, *p26;* Declaration of Independence and, 29, *p29;* delegate at Constitutional Convention, 35, 39

freedom of assembly: 312–14; peaceful association, 314; picketing, 313–14; on private property, 313–14; on public property, 312–13; time, place, manner regulations, 312–13

freedom of religion: 53, 300–303; Establishment Clause, 300; Free Exercise Clause, 302–303; schools and, 300–301; separation of church and state, 301–303

freedom of speech: 53, 304–11; advertising and, 308–10; Bill of Rights and, 299; flag burning and, 94; individual behavior and, 310–11; mass media and, 306–10; national security and, 304–306; prior restraint, 306; symbolic speech, 310, *c311*

freedom of the press: 53,150, 306–10; obscenity laws and, 307–308; prior restraint, 306

Freedom Riders, the, 351

free-enterprise system, 196–97

Free Exercise Clause, 302–303

free trade, 218

French and Indian War, 26

Friedman, Milton, 202

Full Faith and Credit Clause, 76–78, *p76*

Furman v. *Georgia,* 334

Gallatin, Judith, 369

Gallup, George, 372, 383

Gallup poll, 372, 383

General Accounting Office (GAO), 122

General Agreement on Tariffs and Trade (GATT), 223, 537

general election, 159, 440, 417

George III: American colonies and, 26, 29

Georgia: colonial, 24, *p24,* 25

Gephardt, Richard, *p93*

Germany: 229, 235; federalism in, 70; judicial review in, 273

Gerry, Elbridge, 100

gerrymandering, 100–101, *m101*

Gideon v. *Wainwright,* 276, 331

gift tax, 193

Gingrich, Newt, *p115, 116, 117, p154*

Gitlow v. *New York,* 320

glasnost, 233, 521

global warming, 538

Glorious Revolution of 1688, 23

Gooding, George, 130

Gorbachev, Mikhail, 233, 521

incumbents, 113–14, *c114*

independent, 413–14, *c414*

independent agencies, 176

India: judicial review in, 273; legislature of, *c98*

indictment, 277

individual rights: and English monarchy, 23; Declaration of Independence and, 29; federalism and, 78–79, 80, 82; fair trial and punishment, 329–34; free speech and, 310–11; protected by Bill of Rights, 53, *c53,* 297–99; protection of, 319–25; rights of the accused, 326–28; student rights, 324. *See also* civil rights

individual tax, 191–92, *c191*

industrial policy, 203

inflation, 197

information (in criminal court), 277

inherent powers, 68

initiatives process, 463–64; *c463*

Inquiry into the Nature and Causes of the Wealth of Nations, An, 508

In re Kemmler, 334

interdependence, 527

interest group directors, 393

interest groups: 94, 95; agricultural, 386; benefits of, 396–97; business, 386–87; cause-based, 387–90; criticism of, 397–99; in the electoral process, 391–92; employing the legal system, 394; environmental, 388, *p390;* functions of, 385–86; labor, 387; influence on congressional legislation, 124, 129; limitations of, 399–400; lobbying by, 392–94; media and, 395; minority, 396–97; professional, 387; public interest, 388, 390; public opinion and, 394–95; public policy and, 391–95; societal, 387; that promote causes, 387–90; types of, 386–90; women and, 387, 391, 403

Internal Revenue Service (IRS), 68, 130

International Broadcasting Bureau, 513

International Court of Justice, 531; judges of, *c531*

internationalist, 219

international law, 531–32

international relations, U.S.: with Africa, 547–48; with China, 545–46; collective security, 527–32; economic interdependence, 533–37; environmental interdependence, 538–42; with Europe, 544–45; with Japan, 543–44; with Latin America, 546–47; United Nations, 531–32, *c531;* weapons proliferation, 529–31, *c530*

international trade, 534–37

International Trade Commission (ITC), 193

interstate commerce: regulation of, 105

interstate compacts, 79

Intolerable Acts, 28

investigatory powers, congressional, 96

Iraq, 152

isolationism, 218–19

isolationist, 218

isolationist policies, 228

Italy: 235; multiparty system of, 408

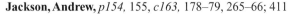

J

Jackson, Andrew, *p154,* 155, *c163,* 178–79, 265–66; 411

Jackson, Jesse, 145, 354

Jamestown, 23, *p23*

Japan: 229, 235; budget deficit, 209; as a constitutional monarchy, 9; judicial review in, 273; U.S. pact with, 238; relations with United States, 543–44

Jay, John: *Federalist Papers,* 41, 256; first chief justice, *p256*

Jefferson, Thomas: 35, 106, 107, 155, 158, *p158,* 305, 317, 410–11; Declaration of Independence and, 29, *p29;* Louisiana Purchase and, 77; *Marbury* v. *Madison,* 50

Jehovah's Witnesses, 303

Jim Crow laws, 348

Johnson, Andrew: 106; Alaska and, 77

Johnson, Lady Bird, 173

Johnson, Lyndon B., 146, 154, 156, *p156,* 170, 232

Johnson, Richard M., 106

Joint Chiefs of Staff, 226

joint committees, congressional, 119

judges: appointment of, 253–54, 257; appointment versus election of, 263–64; congressional approval of Supreme Court nominees, 106; federal, 253–54, 257, *c257, p258;* impeachment of, 106; judicial restraint versus judicial activism, 264–65; state, 472; terms of, 253–54, 256–57

judicial activism, 265

judicial branch: 48, 49–50, *c49;* appointment versus election, 263–64; creation of, 36–38, *c36;* expressed powers of, 67; federal court system, 249–66; federalism and, 70–71; judicial restraint versus judicial activism, 264–65. *See also* federal court system; state court system

judicial powers: of Congress, 265; of president, 152–53, 265; of federal courts, 250

judicial restraint, 264

judicial review, 49–50, *p56,* 108, 273

Judiciary Act of 1789, 250, 255–56

jurisdiction, 250

jurisdiction, court: appellate, 253; of federal courts, 250, *c250,* 253; original, 250; of Supreme Court, 256, 258

jury: grand, 277, *c326,* 327; hung, 279; petit, 278; selection of, 278–79; sequestration of, 279; trial by, 330–31

jury pool, 471–72

jus sanguinis, 339

jus soli, 339

justices of Supreme Court, 256–57, *p258*

juvenile crime: 283–86; boot camps, 285–86; corrections, 285; court, 285, *c285;*

juvenile delinquent, 283

K

Kellogg, Frank, *p218*

Kellogg-Briand Pact, *p218*

majority party, congressional, 115

majority rule, 15

Management and Budget, Office of (OMB), 172

Mapp v. *Ohio,* 322

Marbury v. *Madison,* 50, 56, 256, 273

Marbury, William, 50

March on Washington, 351

Marine Corps, U.S., 152

market economy, 508, *c509*

Marshall, John, *p56,* 256

Marshall Plan, 234–35

Marshall, Thurgood, 256

Maryland: as proprietary colony, 24

Marx, Karl, 511–12, *p512,* 515–17, 525

Massachusetts: charter, 23; colonial, 25

mass media: bias in, 379; censorship in, 377; checks on, 380; criticisms of, 378–80; freedom of speech and, 306–10; as gatekeeper, 378; "horse-race" coverage, 380; impact on politics, 150, 182–83; interest groups and the, 395, *p395;* objectivity of, 379; political campaigns and, 436–37, 447–48; public good and, 377–80; public trials and, 329–30; role of, 377–78; use by president, 155; watchdog function of, 378

mayor, 488

mayor-council system, 488, *c488*

McCollum v. *Board of Education,* 300

McCullough v. *Maryland,* 71, 107

McKinley, William, 180, 305

Medicare, 193

megalopolis, 484

merit system, 179–80

metropolitan area, 484

metropolitan government, 491–92

Mexican-American Legal Defense Fund (MALDEF), 387

Mexico: 151; federalism and, 70; and NAFTA, 535

military academies, U.S., 152

military powers: of Congress, 105, 107; of president, 151–52;

Miller v. *California,* 307

Minersville School District v. *Gobitis,* 303

minimum wage, 199

minorities: in Congress, 104, *p104;* interest groups of, 396–97; as presidential candidates, 145–46; racial discrimination, 100–01; segregation, 260, 269

minority factions, 60–61

minority party, congressional, 115

minority rights, 14–15, 57

mint, U.S., *p67*

Miranda rights, 328, *c328*

Miranda rule, 327–28

Miranda v. *Arizona,* 276, 327–28

misdemeanor, 273

mixed economy, 509

monarchy: *c9;* definition of, 8

monarchy, British: Magna Carta and, 21, *p21;* limited powers of, 21–22

monetarism, 202–03

monetary policy: 198–202; discount rate, 201; open-market operations, 201; reserve requirements, 201; versus fiscal policy, 201–02

money: power to coin, 105

Monroe, James, 154, 163

Monroe Doctrine, 228

Montesquieu, Baron Charles de, 251, *p251*

Montgomery, Alabama, 350

Morrill Act, 72, *p73*

Moseley-Braun, Carol, 104

Mothers Against Drunk Driving (MADD), 388

Motor Voter Law, 444–45

Muir, John, 390

multilateral treaty, 237

multiparty system, 408

municipal government: commission, 490, *c488;* council-manager system of, 489–90, *c488;* federalism and, *c81;* mayor-council system of, 488, *c488*

municipality, 487

Mussolini, Benito, 520

Nader, Ralph, 390

National Aeronautics and Space Administration, 177, *p185*

National Association for the Advancement of Colored People (NAACP), 314, 387, 394

National Association for the Advancement of Colored People (NAACP) v. *Alabama,* 314

National Archives, 57

National Atlantic Treaty Organization (NATO), 528

national conventions. *See* conventions, national

national debt, 210, *c211, p212*

national defense: 105; Department of Defense, 225–26. *See also* national security

National Economic Council, 172

National Endowment for the Arts (NEA), 125

National Guard, 70, *p71,* 72

nationalization, 512

National Labor Relations Board (NLRB), 178

National Organization for Women (NOW), 387

National Rifle Association (NRA), 388

national security: 105, 217; freedom of speech and, 304–06

National Security Council (NSC), 170–72, 226

national sovereignty, 105

Native Americans. *See* American Indians

naturalization: regulation of, 340–41, *c340*

natural rights, 4

Navy, U.S., 152

Near v. *Minnesota,* 306

Nebraska, 52

"necessary and proper" clause, 68, 107

neoisolationist, 220

New Deal, 215, 413

New England Confederation, 25–26

"New Freedom" reform, 153

New Hampshire: first female governor in, 479

New Jersey Plan, *c36,* 37–38

New Jersey v. *T.L.O.,* 324

newspapers: 150; freedom of speech, 306–308

New York Times v. *Sullivan,* 307

Nixon, Richard M., 106, 147, 149, *p149,* 150, *p151,* 156, *c163,* 232, *p233,* 266, 413

no-contest plea, 277

nominate, 157

nomination, political: 407, 429–34; of president, 157–62, *c157. See also* conventions, national

nonpartisan primary, 432

nonrenewable resource, 540

nontax revenue, 194

nonvoting, 448–49

North America: international trade, 535

North American Trade Agreement (NAFTA), 535

North Atlantic Treaty Organization (NATO), 237

North Korea: communism in, 233

Northwest Ordinance, 32

Northwest Territory, *m32*

nuclear proliferation, 529

Nuclear Regulatory Commission, 178

O

objectivity, 379

obscenity, 307–308

O'Connor, Sandra Day, 263, *p263,* 289

Office of Management and Budget (OMB), 204

oligarchy, 9

Olmstead v. *United States,* 324

one-party system, 407

"one-person, one-vote," 99

open-market operations, 201

open primary, 432

Organization of American States (OAS), 238

original jurisdiction, 250

Ortiz, Solomon, *p122*

oversight, congressional, 96

P

Packwood, Bob, 117

Pan American Conference (1933), *p219*

pardon, 153

park ranger, 37

Parks, Rosa, 350

Parliament, British: 22–23, *p22,* 118

Parliament, French, 144

parliamentary system, 11

parole, 282

Parr, John, 499

parties, political. *See* political parties

party activist, 419

party machine, 416

party platform: at national conventions, 161

party whip, 116, *c116*

passport, 194, 225

patronage, 416

Peace Corps, *p176,* 541

Pearl Harbor, 229

Pendleton Act, 180

Pennsylvania: as proprietary colony, 24

Pentagon, 225, *p225*

Pentagon Papers, 306

People for the American Way, 393

peremptory challenge, 279

Peres, Shimon, *p58*

perestroika, 233, 521

"permanent Congress," 114

Perot, Ross, 414–15, 438

Persian Gulf, 152

petition: nomination by, 430–31

Petition of Right, 22

petit jury, 278

Philippines: American control of, 229; bilateral treaty with U.S., 238

picketing, 313

plaintiff, 274

plank: at national conventions, 161

Planned Parenthood: as a cause-based interest group, 388

plea bargain, 280

Pledge of Allegiance: and freedom of religion, 303

Plessy v. *Ferguson,* 348

plurality, 163

pocket veto, 128

Poland: interest groups in, 397

police powers: 275–76; due process and, 322–23; Miranda Rule, 327–28, *c328*

political action committees (PACs), 94, 391–92, *c392, c400* political campaigns: 160, 435–39; benefits of, 450; criticisms of, 447–48; financing of, 437–38, *c437;* mass media in, 436–37; negative campaigning, 447–48; and the public good, 447–50; role of media, 447–48

political gridlock, 62

political parties: *c410;* criticisms of, 421–22; definition of, 58; function of, 405–407, *c406;* history of, 409–13; loyalty toward, 95; in multiparty system,408; national machinery of, 419–20; nominating function of, 407; in one-party system, 407; organization of, 416–20, *c418;* organizing function of, 406; president as leader of, 145; and the public good, 421–24; state and local machinery, 416–20; in two-party system, 407, 422–24; types of, 407–15

political psychology, 369

political scientist, 5

political socialization, 368

politics, 6

polling, 372, 437

pollster, 374

Pomeroy, Earl, 135

popular sovereignty, 47, *c48*

popular vote, 163, *c163*

pork-barrel spending, 129–31, *p131*

Postal Service, U.S., 178

Powell, Colin, *p161*

precedent, 249

precinct, 418

prejudice, 345

presentment, 327

president, U.S.: background of, 145–46; as chief agenda setter, 143; as chief executive, 143; as chief of state, 144; as commander in chief, 48,143, 151, 223; election by House of Representatives, 106, 158; election process of, 39, 157–64, *c157, c163;* Executive Office of the, 169–74, *c173;* executive privilege of, 149; financing campaign of, 437–39, *c437;* as foreign policy leader, 145; formal titles of, 143; impeachment of, 106; lawmaking process and, 128; lobbying for legislation, 153–54; the media and, 150, 155, 182–83; nomination and election of, 429–34; as party leader, 145; and the public good, 182–83; qualifications for, 145; as representative of the nation, 143–44; role in federal budget, 205, *c207;* role in U.S. foreign policy, 222–23; roles of, 143–45; salary and benefits of, 146; speechwriting for, 169–70; and State of the Union Address, 143, 153; succession of, 146–47, *c147;* terms of office of, 146

presidential aide, 183, *p183*

presidential awards, 171, *p171*

presidential doctrines, 222–23

presidential electors. *See* electoral college

presidential powers: appointing, 148–49, *p148,* 254, 257; criticism of, 156, *p156;* diplomatic, 149–51; executing the law, 148; executive, 148–49; executive agreements, 58, *p58;* 151, 223; foreign relations, 149–52, 222–23; growth of, 154–56, 182; how presidents have viewed, 148; judicial, 152–53, 265–66; legislative, 128, 153–54;

military, 151–52, 223; and the public good, 182–83; treaty making, 149–51, *p151,* 223; veto, 48, 128, 153; war, 151, 227

presidential primaries, 159–60

president *pro tempore,* 116, *c116*

president of the Senate, 116, *c116*

presidential succession, 146–47, *c147*

presidential system, 11

press. *See* freedom of press; mass media; newspapers

primaries: closed, 432; direct, 431; nonpartisan, 434; open, 432; presidential, 159–60; runoff, 434; voter turnout in, 434

primary election, 159, 417

prime minister, French, 144,

prior restraint, 306

privacy: right to, 324–25

private property: demonstrations on, 313–14

privatization, 186

privileges and immunity clause, 78–79

probable cause, 322

probation, 281

procedural due process, 319–20

profit, 508

Progressive Party, 415

prohibition, 55

Prohibition Party, 415

proletariat, 511

property tax: by local government, 493–94, *c493*

proprietary colony, 24

protests: freedom of assembly and petition, 312–14; interest groups and, 395

Public Citizen, 390

public comment, 176–77

public funding: of political campaigns, 438

public good: 15, 60–62; Aristotle's writings on the, 251; boot camps, 285–86; civil liberties and the, 298–99; congressional committees and, 131; definition of, 6–7; economic policy and, 202–03; federal court system and the, 263–66; federal government and, 131–32, 183–86; federalism and, 80–83; interest groups and the, 396–400; local government and the, 492; mass media and the, 377–80; political campaigns and the, 447–50; political parties and the, 421–24; pork-barrel spending and, 129–31; and the presidency, 182–83; state governments and the, 465; tax policy and, 195; U.S. foreign policy and, 221

public interest groups, 388, *c390*

public opinion: 366–80; definition of, 367; forms of, 367–68; interest groups and, 394–95; mass media and, 370, *c371,* 377–78, *p377;* measuring, 372–76; nature of, 371; role of, 367; role of schools in, 370

public opinion poll: 372–76, *c376;* conducting, 373–76; origins of, 372–73; types of, 373

public policy: 4, 61; interest groups and, 391–95

public property: demonstrations on, 312–13

public trial, 329–30

Puerto Rico: 98; U.S. control of, 229

Q

Quayle, Dan, 102
quorum, 113
quotas, 355

R

radio: freedom of speech and, 308; influence on public opin-
     ion, 370; Roosevelt's "fireside chats," 155
ratification, 31
rational basis test, 346–47
Reagan, Nancy, 173, *p182*
Reagan, Ronald, *p150,* 154, *p182,* 198, 208, *p263,* 289
realignment, 409
realism, 219
realpolitik, 219
reasonable distinction, 346
recall, 464–65, *c464*
recession, 197
reconciliation, 207
redistricting: 99; racial gerrymandering and, 100–01, *m101*
referendum, 464, *c464*
Reform Party, 414–15
refugee, 527
Regents of the University of California v. *Bakke,* 356
regulatory commissions, 177–78
relations of production, 516
religion. *See* freedom of religion
renewable resource, 540
repeal, 52
reprieve, 153
representation: population and, 99
representative democracy, 16
representative government, 22–23
republic: *c9;* definition of, 8
republican, 69–70
Republican Party: 409; domination of the government from
     1860 to 1932, 412; rise of, 411; and tax policy, 194
reserve requirements, 201
reserved powers, 68, *c69*
resolution, 206
revenue: 191; nontax, 194. *See also* Taxes
revenue sharing, 72
Revolutionary War, 31, 72
Reynolds v. *United States,* 302–03
Rhode Island: as crown colony, 24
Richard, Henry Lee, 41
Rio Pact, 237
Rockefeller, Nelson, 147

"Rock the Vote" campaign, 377–78
Roe v. *Wade,* 262, 325
roll-call vote, 127
Roman Empire, 103
Roosevelt, Eleanor, 173
Roosevelt, Franklin D., 58, *p59,* 146, *p146,* 150, 155, 173,
     215, 229, 257–58, 413
Roosevelt, Theodore, 155, *p155,* 414
Roth v. *United States,* 307
royal colony, 24
rule of law: concept of, 22
runoff primary, 432
rural area, 481
Russia: communism in, 517–21; media and elections, 448;
     U.S. purchase of Alaska territory from, 77
Russian Revolution, 517–18

S

sales tax: 473–74; by local government, 494, *c493*
SALT treaty. *See* Strategic Arms Limitation Treaty
sampling, 374–75
sampling error, 375
Schenck v. *United States,* 305
schools: federal government aid issue, 302; Pledge of Alle-
     giance debate and, 303; prayer in, 301; religious activities
     in, 301; student religious groups in, 301
search and seizure, *c53,* 322–24, *p322, p324*
search warrant, 322
Second Continental Congress, 29, 31
secretaries: 174. *See also* cabinet, U.S., government depart-
     ments by name
secret ballot, 441
Securities and Exchange Commission (SEC), 178
security of home and person, 322–24
sedition, 305
segregation: 269, 347–49; *de facto,* 349; definition of, 349;
     de jure, 347–49
select committees, congressional, 119
self-incrimination, 327–28
self-interest, 508–09
Senate Ethics Committee, *p117*
Senate, Roman, 103, *p103*
Senate, U.S.: *c102;* appropriations committee of, 118; cloture
     in, 127; committee system in, 118–22, *c119;* comparison
     with House of Representatives, 101–02, *c102;* conference
     committees, 119; confirmation of cabinet members, 106;
     confirmation of federal judges, 106, 254, 257; confirma-
     tion of presidential appointments, 106, 149; expulsion of
     members of, 117; filibusters in, 127; joint committees of,
     119; lawmaking process in, 93–95, 123–28; leadership in,
     115–16, *c116;* minority members of, 104, *p104;* powers
     granted in Constitution, 48; president *pro tempore,* 116,
     c116; privileges of members, 101; profiles of members,

Voice of America (VOA), 513

voir dire, 278–79

volunteerism, 13

voter registration, 74, 368, *c368*

voting behavior: factors influencing, 445–46; nonvoting, 448–49

voting rights: 442–45; of African Americans, 30, 53, 442–43; age and, *p51,* 443–44; of American Indians, 30; citizenship and residence requirements, 444; property qualifications for in 1780s, 30; property and tax requirements, 30, 442; psychological factors in, 369; registration requirements, 444; restrictions in early America, 30; of women, 30, 53–55, 443, *p443*

Voting Rights Act Amendments: of 1970, *p51*

Voting Rights Act of 1965: 352; racial gerrymandering and, 100–101, *m101*

Wallace, George C., *c163*

Walz v. *Tax Commission,* 302

ward, 418

war powers: of Congress, 151, 227; of president, 151, 227; undeclared war, 151

War Powers Act, 151–52

Washington, D.C. *See* District of Columbia

Washington, George, 31, 34, 35, 42, 58, 143, 146, 154, 158, 169

Watergate, 147, 149, *p149,* 150, 156, 266

Weems v. *United States,* 333

welfare state, 512

Wesberry v. *Sanders,* 99, 111

West Germany: fall of the Berlin Wall, 233

West Virginia, 130

West Virginia State Board of Education v. *Barnette,* 303

Whigs, 411

Whiskey Rebellion, 154–55

White House, *p141,* 146

White House Office, 169–70, *c170*

Whitewater, 150

Wilson, Woodrow: 144, 153, 155, 162, 229, 443

women: in armed forces, 152; in cabinet, *p148,* 189; civil rights, 353–56; in Congress, 95, *p95,* 104; as delegates at national conventions, *c167;* Equal Rights Amendment and, 52–53, *p52;* as governors, 479; interest groups and, 387, 388, 403; in military academies, 152; in presidential campaigns, 145; on Supreme Court, *c257, p258,* 263, *p263,* 289; as vice presidential candidates, 427; voting rights of, 53–54, 443, *p443,* 453; voting restrictions against, 30

World Health Organization (WHO), 532

World Trade Organization (WTO), 536–37

World War I, 229, 305

World War II, 229

writ of *certiorari,* 259

Yeltsin, Boris, *p145,* 233

Young-sam, Kim, *p172*

Zedong, Mao, 230

ACKNOWLEDGMENTS

For permission to reprint copyrighted material, grateful acknowledgment is made to the following sources:

Antonietta Barbieri: Quote by Antonietta Barbieri from "The Barn-Raising Spirit Still Thrives" by Alan Bunce from *The Christian Science Monitor,* April 26, 1996. Copyright © 1996 by Antonietta Barbieri.

Democratic National Committee: From Geraldine Ferraro's closing statement in "The Bush-Ferraro Debate: October 11, 1984," Online, World Wide Web, September 5, 1997. Copyright © 1984 by the Democratic National Committee. Available online http://wwwnetcapitol.com/Debates/vp84-1st.htm.

Dennis-Yarmouth Regional High School: Adapted from "Constitution of the Dennis-Yarmouth Regional High School Student Council" from World Wide Web, January 22, 1997. Copyright © 1995 by Dennis-Yarmouth Regional High School. Available at http://www.capecod.net/dystuco/const/constidx.html.

The Gallup Organization, Inc.: From speech by George Gallup on July 19, 1990, Online, September 8, 1997. Copyright © 1990 by The Gallup Organization, Inc. Available http://policy.gmu.edu/cif/gallop.html.

National Civic League: From "Reinvigorating Democratic Values: Challenge and Necessity," by Henry G. Cisneros and John Parr from *National Civic Review,* September/October 1990. Copyright © 1990 by National Civic League Press, Denver, Colorado.

The New York Times Company: From John Maynard Keynes's recorded thoughts on Roosevelt's plan, the New Deal, from *The New York Times,* June 10, 1934. Copyright © 1934 by The New York Times Company.

People Weekly: Quote by Gregory Watson from "The Man Who Would Not Quit" from *People Weekly,* June 1, 1992. Copyright © 1992 by People Weekly.

Governor Jeanne Shaheen: From the inaugural address of Governor Jeanne Shaheen of New Hampshire, January 9, 1997, Online, World Wide Web, August 12, 1997. Copyright © 1997 by Jeanne Shaheen. Available http://www.state.nh.us/governor/iaddress.html.

The Heirs to the Estate of Martin Luther King, Jr., c/o Writers House, Inc. as agent for the proprietor: From "Letter from Birmingham Jail" by Martin Luther King, Jr. Copyright © 1963 by Martin Luther King, Jr.; copyright renewed © 1991 by Coretta Scott King.

SOURCES CITED

Quote by an observer from *The Ring of Power: The White House Staff & Its Expanding Role in Government* by Bradley H. Patterson, Jr. Published by Basic Books, 1988.

Quote by a member of Congress from *Legislating Together: The White House and Capitol Hill from Eisenhower to Reagan* by Mark A. Peterson. Published by Harvard University Press, 1990.

Quote by anti-pork spokesman from "Congress" from *American Democracy and the Public Good.*

From *Showdown at Gucci Gulch* by Jeffrey H. Birnbaum and Alan S. Murray. Published by Random House, Inc., 1987.

Quotes by John Culver and George Smathers from *House and Senate* by Ross K. Baker. Published by W. W. Norton & Company, 1989.

From "The Casework Burden" from *To Serve the People: Congress and Constituency Service* by John R. Johannes. Published by University of Nebraska Press, 1984.

Quotes by Marc Glenn and Jo Ann Strickler from "Meet Two Student Delegates to the 1992 Presidential Conventions" from *American Democracy and the Public Good* by Steven Kelman. Published by Harcourt Brace College, 1996.

Quote by political consultant, Frank I. Luntz, about a hypothetical election in Florida from *Candidates, Consultants, and Campaigns* by Frank I. Luntz. Published by Basil Blackwell, 1988.

Quote by Sandra Murphy, owner of S. Buck Pizza, from "Getting by on minimum wage: What a little bit extra means," Online, World Wide Web, March 9, 1997. Published by The Associated Press, 1996. Available http://www2.nando .net/newsroom/ntn/nation/042596/nation5_19151_s1html.

From "The Supreme Court from Early Burger to Early Rehnquist" by Martin Shapiro from *The New American Political System,* 2nd version, edited by Anthony King. Published by AEI Press, 1990.

PHOTO CREDITS

Abbreviations used: (t) top, (c) center, (l) left, (r) right, (bckgd) background, (bdr) border.

Front Cover: Chromosohm-Sohm/The Stock Market. **Reviewers' Page:** Page ii (all), Peter Poulides/Tony Stone Images. **Title Page:** Page iii, Chromosohm-Sohm/The Stock Market. **Author and Copyright Page:** Page iv (all), Peter Poulides/Tony Stone Images. **Table of Contents:** Page v, Andy Sacks/Tony Stone Images; vi(t), Superstock; (b), The Granger Collection, New York; vii(r), M. Theiler/Washington Stock Photo, Inc.; (l), Drew Harmon/Folio, Inc.; viii(t), Luc Novovitch/AP/Wide World Photos; (b), Pamela Price/The Picture Cube;

ix, Collection, The Supreme Court Historical Society; x(t), Alan Klehr/Tony Stone Images; (b), from Page One, © 1987 by The New York Times Corporation, all rights reserved; xi(t), David Woo/Stock, Boston; (b), Bob Daemmrich/Stock, Boston; xii(t), Susan Sterner/AP/Wide World Photos; (b), © 1995 John Skowronski; xiii(l), Steve Helber/AP/Wide World Photos; (r), © Mark C. Burnett/Stock, Boston; xiv(l), AKG Photo; (r), Earth Base/Gamma Liaison; xv(t), © Bob Daemmrich/ The Image Works;(b), R. Rainford/Robert Harding Picture Library; xvi(l), Phoebe Bell/Folio, Inc.; (r), Amnesty International; xvii, Catherine Smith/Impact Visuals. **Critical Thinking:** Page xxi(bdr), Peter Poulides/Tony Stone Images; (other), Ed Honowitz/Tony Stone Images; xxii(bdr), Peter Poulides/Tony Stone Images; (other), Christie's Images; xxiii(bdr), Jay Mallin Photos; (other), Peter Poulides/ Tony Stone Images. **Skills Handbook**: Page xxiv (bdr), Peter Poulides/Tony Stone Images; (other), The Granger Collection, New York; xxv-xxviii (bdr), Peter Poulides/Tony Stone Images; xxviii(other), Steve Skjold/PhotoEdit; xxix-xxxi (bdr), Peter Poulides/Tony Stone Images; xxxi(other), GAMBLE reprinted with special permission of King Features Syndicate, Inc.; xxxii-xxxvii (bdr), Peter Poulides/Tony Stone Images; xxxvii(other), Gary A. Conner/PhotoEdit; xxxviii(bdr), Peter Poulides/Tony Stone Images.

Unit 1: Page 0-1, © Matthew Borkoski/Stock, Boston. **Chapter 1**: Page 2, Telegraph Colour Library/FPG International Corp.; 3, Bernard Boutrit/Woodfin Camp & Associates; 4, Aaron Haupt/Stock, Boston; 5, Chip Henderson/Tony Stone Images; 6, Jose L. Pelaez/The Stock Market; 7, Photo 20-20; 8, Martin Keene/"PA" Photo Library/The Image Works; 11, Robert Trippett/Sipa Press; 12, ©Richard Pasely/Stock, Boston; 13(bdr), Brian Stablyk/Tony Stone Images, (other), Mark Richards/PhotoEdit; 14, David Young-Wolff/Tony Stone Images; 15, R. Rainford/Robert Harding Picture Library;16, Andy Sacks/Tony Stone Images; 18-19(bdr), Image Copyright © 1996 Photodisc, Inc. **Chapter 2**: Page 20, Superstock; 21, The Granger Collection, New York; 22(both), North Wind Picture Archives; 23, Colonial Williamsburg Foundation; 24, Courtesy, Winterthur Museum; 25, The Metropolitan Museum of Art, Bequest of Jacob Ruppert, 1939. (39.65.53); 26, Reproduced Courtesy of the Library and Information Centre, Royal Society of Chemistry; 27(bdr), Peter Poulides/Tony Stone Images; 28, HRW Photo Research Library; 29, Superstock; 31, From *The National Archives of The United States* by Herman J. Viola, courtesy Harry N. Abrams, Inc., New York; 33, Louis Schwartz; 37, David Young-Wolff/PhotoEdit; 38, Library of Congress; 40, The Granger Collection, New York; 42, The Granger Collection, New York; 44-45(bdr), Image Copyright c 1996 Photodisc, Inc.; 45, Superstock. **Chapter 3**: Page 46, The Granger Collection, New York; 51, Bob Daemmrich/Stock, Boston; 52, Arthur Grace/SYGMA; 54(bdr), Brian Stablyk/Tony Stone Images, (other), Zigy Kaluzny; 55, Cartoon by Grover Page, Louisville *Courier-Journal*/Brown Brothers; 56, The Granger Collection, New York; 57, Rick Buettner/Folio, Inc.; 58, Robert Trippett/Sipa Press; 59, UPI/Corbis-Bettmann; 60, National Portrait Gallery,Smithsonian Institution/Art Resource, NY; 61, Dennis Cook/AP/Wide World Photos; 64-65(bdr), Image Copyright c 1996 Photodisc, Inc. **Chapter 4**: Page 66, Randy Foulds/Washington Stock Photo, Inc.; 67, F. Figall/Washington Stock Photo, Inc.; 68, Peter Newark's American Pictures; 71, Todd Buchanan/Black Star; 73, Steve Leonard/Black Star; 74, Sam C. Pierson, Jr/The National Audobon Society Collection/Photo Researchers, Inc.; 75, © David Frazier Photolibrary; 76, Mary Kate Denny-Bim/PhotoEdit; 77(bdr), Peter Poulides/Tony Stone Images; (other), © Mark Kelley/Alaska Stock Images; 78, Ken Hawkins/SYGMA; 79, © Atlan/ SYGMA; 80, David Muench Photography; 84-85(bdr), Image Copyright © 1996 Photodisc, Inc.; 86, Tony Freeman/PhotoEdit; 87, Larry Kolvoord.

Unit 2: Page 90-91, John Lawrence/Tony Stone Images. **Chapter 5**: Page 92, Jay Mallin Photos; 93, Tobias Everke/Gamma Liaison; 94, © 1984, Berke Breathed. Reprinted by permission; 95, Uniphoto Picture Agency; 96, Mark Richards/PhotoEdit; 97, Paul Conklin/PhotoEdit; 99, M. Theiler/Washington Stock Photo, Inc.; 103(bdr), Peter Poulides/Tony Stone Images; (other), Alexandra Avakian/Woodfin Camp & Associates; 104, Dennis Brack/Black Star; 106, Al Stephenson/Woodfin Camp & Associates; 107, Superstock; 110-111(bdr), Image Copyright © 1996 Photodisc, Inc. **Chapter 6**: Page 112, Paul Conklin; 114, Mark Richards/PhotoEdit; 115, Drew Harmon/Folio, Inc.; 117, Greg Gibson/AP/Wide World Photos; 120, Jay Mallin Photos; 121, Dennis Cook/AP/Wide World Photos; 122, Paul Conklin/PhotoEdit; 123, Jay Mallin Photos; 124, Ashe/Folio, Inc.; 125(bdr), Brian Stablyk/ Tony Stone Images; (other), Dennis Cook/AP/Wide World Photos; 126, National Cable Satellite Corporation; 127, UPI/Corbis-Bettmann; 128, Paul Conklin; 129, R. Bouchard/Washington Stock Photo, Inc.; 130, Dirck Halstead/Gamma Liaison; 131, Bob Galbraith/AP/Wide World Photos; 132, Jay Mallin Photos; 134-135(bdr), Image Copyright © 1996 Photodisc, Inc.; 136, Dallas & John Heaton/WestLight.

Unit 3: Page 140-141, M. Win/Washington Stock Photo, Inc. **Chapter 7**: Page 142, Dirck Halstead/Gamma Liaison; 143, ©1994 Robert A. Cumins/Black Star; 144, Greg Gibson /AP/Wide World Photos; 145, John Harrington/Black Star; 146,

National Portrait Gallery, Smithsonian Institution/Art Resource, NY; 148, Diana Walker/Gamma Liaison; 150(bdr), Peter Poulides/Tony Stone Images; (other), Dennis Brack/Black Star; 151, Goksin Sipahioglu /Gamma Liaison; 152, Karl Gehring/Gamma Liaison; 153, Diana Walker/Gamma Liaison; 154(l), J. Scott Applewhite/AP/Wide World Photos; 154(r), The Granger Collection, New York; 155, Brown Brothers; 156, Cartoon by Bob Holland /Chicago Tribune, courtesy of Random House and the Foreign Policy Association; 158(l), The Granger Collection, New York; 158(r), The Bettmann Archive; 159, Luc Novovitch/AP/Wide World Photos; 160, ©Corbin M. Harris /AP/Wide World Photos; 161, Joe Traver/Gamma Liaison; 162, Joseph Sohm/ChromoSohm; 166-167(bdr), Image Copyright © 1996 Photodisc, Inc. **Chapter 8**: Page 168, ©Jeffery Markowitz /SYGMA; 169, Dirck Halstead/Gamma Liaison; 171(other), © RobertTrippett/Sipa Press; 171(bdr), Brian Stablyk/Tony Stone Images; 172, Yun Jai-Hyuoung/ AP/Wide World Photos; 175, Dirck Halstead/Gamma Liaison; 176, Cleo Photography/The Picture Cube; 177, Chris Chapman/Gamma Liaison; 178, J. Blaustein/Woodfin Camp & Associates; 179(t), North Wind Picture Archives; 179(b), Benelux Press/WestLight; 181, Richard T. Nowitz/The National Audobon Society Collection/Photo Researchers, Inc.; 182, Pamela Price/The Picture Cube; 183, Tomas Muscionico/Contact Press Images; 184(t), © Tribune Media Services, Inc. All rights reserved. Reprinted with permission; 184(b), Gary Braasch/Woodfin Camp & Associates; 185, T. Campion/SYGMA; 186, Phil McCarten/PhotoEdit; 188-189(bdr), Image Copyright © 1996 Photodisc, Inc. **Chapter 9**: Page 190, G. Petrov/Washington Stock Photo, Inc.; 192(t), Kindra Clineff/The Picture Cube, Inc.; 192(b), Art Montes de Oca/FPG International Corp.; 193, R. Frasier/Folio, Inc.; 194, Paul Conklin/PhotoEdit; 195, Courtesy of David Horsey, Seattle *Post-Intelligencer*; 196, Mary Kate Denny-Bim/PhotoEdit; 199(bdr), Peter Poulides/Tony Stone Images; (other), W. B. Spunbarg/The Picture Cube; 202, courtesy Museum of American Financial History; 205, Denis Paquin/AP/Wide World Photos; 206, Dennis Brack/Black Star; 210, David Young-Wolff/PhotoEdit; 212, Jack Kustron/AP/Wide World Photos; 214-215(bdr), Image Copyright © 1996 Photodisc, Inc. **Chapter 10**: Page 216, Joseph Sohm /ChromoSohm; 217, Renault/Rieger/Gamma Liaison; 218, Brown Brothers; 219, UPI/Corbis-Bettmann; 220, Dennis Brack/Black Star; 222, John Ficara/SYGMA; 223, Peter Aaron/Esto Photographics; 224, Photo courtesy of the U.S. Department of State; 225(l), R. Foulds/Washington Stock Photo, Inc.; 225(r), Dennis Cook/AP/Wide World Photos; 226, ©Wilfredo Lee/AP/Wide World Photos; 227, Brown Brothers; 228, Nawrocki Stock Photo; 231, Photo # AR7522B, John F. Kennedy Library; 232, Sandra Baker/Liaison International; 233, UPI/Corbis-Bettmann; 235, Les Stone/SYGMA236(bdr), Brian Stablyk/Tony Stone Images;(other), Amnesty International; 238, UPI/Corbis-Bettmann; 240-241(bdr), Image Copyright © 1996 Photodisc, Inc.; 242(t), © 1990 David J. Sams/Stock, Boston; (b) The White House.

Unit 4: Page 246-247, ©Jeff Greenberg/The Picture Cube. **Chapter 11**: Page 248, Jane Rosenberg/AP/Wide World Photos; 251(bdr), Peter Poulides/Tony Stone Images; (other), The Granger Collection, New York; 254, UPI/Corbis-Bettmann; 255, Library of Congress/Theodore Horydczak Collection; 256, National Portrait Gallery, Smithsonian Institution/Art Resource, NY; 258, Collection, The Supreme Court Historical Society; 259, Michael Newman/PhotoEdit; 260, (c) 1997 John Skowronksi; 261, 262, Franz Jantzen/Collection of the Supreme Court of the United States; 263, © 1981 Fred Ward/Black Star; 264, Bob Daemmrich/Stock, Boston; 265, Don Smetzer/Tony Stone Images; 266, UPI/Corbis-Bettmann; 268-269(bdr), Image Copyright © 1996 Photodisc, Inc. **Chapter 12**: Page 270, Bob Daemmrich/Stock, Boston; 271, Topham Picturepoint/The Image Works; 272, HRW photo by Sam Dudgeon; 273, ©Danny Johnston/AP/Wide World Photos; 275, J.B. Boykin/PhotoEdit; 277, Alan Klehr/Tony Stone Images; 278, Los Angeles Times Photo by Bob Chamberlin; 279, © Fred Prouser/Sipa Press; 281, Michael Newman/PhotoEdit; 283, ©Mary Ann Chastain/AP/Wide World Photos; 284(bdr), Brian Stablyk/Tony Stone Images; (other), Copyright (c) Larry Kolvoord; 286, ©David Bundy/AP/Wide World Photos; 288-289(bdr), Image Copyright © 1996 Photodisc, Inc.; 290, H. Armstrong Roberts; 292, Corel Corporation.

Unit 5: Page 294-295, ©Joe Sohm, 1990 /ChromoSohm. **Chapter 13**: Page 296, The Granger Collection, New York; 297, The Bettmann Archive; 298, Paul Robertson Photography, photo courtesy the Southern Poverty Law Center, Birmingham, AL; 300, ©Camerique/The Picture Cube; 302, Gay Shackelford/*Texas Highways* Magazine; 304, ©1991 Stephen Shames/Matrix; 306, from *Page One*, © 1987 by The New York Times Corporation, all rights reserved; 307, Bob Daemmrich/Stock, Boston; 309(bdr), Brian Stablyk/Tony Stone Images; (other), UPI/Corbis-Bettmann; 310, ©1968 Dennis Brack/Black Star; 312, Jacques Chenet/Woodfin Camp & Associates; 313, ©Jeff Lowenthal/Woodfin Camp & Associates; 314, Gary Tramontina/AP/Wide World Photos; 316-317(bdr), Image Copyright © 1996 Photodisc, Inc. **Chapter 14**: Page 318, © Dave Bartruff/Stock, Boston; 319, ©Reinstein/The Image Works; 320, Alan Solomon/AP/Wide World Photos; 321(bdr), Peter Poulides/Tony Stone Images; (other), Gilles Bassignac/Gamma Liaison; 323, ©Bob Daemmrich/The Image Works; 324, David R. Frazier Photolibrary; 325, UPI/Corbis Bettmann; 329, David Woo/Stock, Boston; 330, © Jonathan Nourok/PhotoEdit; 331, ©Frank Fournier, Contact Press Images/Woodfin Camp & Associates; 332, © Jeff Robbins/AP/Wide World Photos; 334, UPI/Corbis-Bettmann; 336-337 (bdr), Image Copyright © 1996 Photodisc, Inc. **Chapter 15**: Page 338, © 1978 Matt Herron/Take Stock; 339, Randy Duchaine/The Stock Market; 341, Betty Press/Woodfin Camp & Associates; 342, Levick/Archive Photos; 343, Michael Grecco/Stock, Boston; 346, © Michelle Bridwell/Frontera Fotos; 347, Hank Walker/LIFE Magazine © TIME Inc.; 348, Bern Keating/Black Star; 349, © Michelle Bridwell/Frontera Fotos; 350, AP/Wide World Photos; 351, Archive Photos; 353, Bob Daemmrich/Stock, Boston; 354(bdr), Brian Stablyk/ Tony Stone Images; (other), ©Denis Poroy/AP/Wide World Photos; 355, Brown Brothers; 356, Tom Stewart/The Stock Market; 358-359(bdr), Image Copyright © 1996 Photodisc, Inc.; 360, © Troy Maben/David R. Frazier Photolibrary.

Unit 6: Page 364-365, AP/Wide World Photos. **Chapter 16**: Page 366, Deborah Davis/PhotoEdit; 367, Louise Gubb/The Image Works; 369(bdr), Peter Poulides/Tony Stone Images; (other), Catherine Smith/Impact Visuals; 370, Mark Richards/PhotoEdit; 372, Bob Daemmrich/Stock, Boston; 373, Frank Siteman/The Picture Cube, Inc.; 374, Bob Daemmrich/Tony Stone Images; 377, Superstock; 379, © 1999 by Sidney Harris; 382-383(bdr), Image Copyright © 1996 Photodisc, Inc. **Chapter 17**: Page 384, Kenneth Jarecke/Contact Press Images; 385, Carlos Chavez/AP/Wide World Photos; 386, L.G. Patterson/AP/Wide World Photos; 388, © Larry Ulrich/Larry Ulrich Photography; 389(bdr), Peter Poulides/Tony Stone Images; (other) , © M. Antman/The Image Works; 393, Jay Mallin Photos; 394, ©Randy Squires/AP/Wide World Photos; 395, Goddard-Claussen/First Tuesday; 396, ©E.J. Flynn/AP/Wide World Photos; 398, Andy Hayt/NBA/Allsport; 402-403(bdr), Image Copyright © 1996 Photodisc, Inc.; 403, © 1995 John Skowronski. **Chapter 18**: Page 404, Dennis Brack/Black Star; 405, The Granger Collection, New York; 407, Forrest Anderson/Gamma Liaison; 408, Patrick Piel/Gamma Liaison; 409, 411, The Granger Collection, New York; 412, Brown Brothers; 416, The Granger Collection, New York; 417, Jonathan Nourok/PhotoEdit; 419, Jay Mallin Photos; 420, Photo courtesy GOP-TV; 421, Rick Friedman/Black Star; 422, ©1995 John Harrington/Black Star; 423(bdr), Brian Stablyk/Tony Stone Images; 423(other), Jay Mallin Photos; 424, John Jonik © 1997 from The Cartoon Bank. All rights reserved; 426-427(bdr), Image Copyright © 1996 Photodisc, Inc. **Chapter 19**: Page 428, Art by Mark Hess/The Image Bank, Inc.; 429, Bob Daemmrich Photography; 431, Phoebe Bell/Folio, Inc.; 433(bdr), Brian Stablyk/Tony Stone Images; (other), Allan Tannenbaum/SYGMA; 435, Peter Newark's American Pictures; 436, Brown Brothers; 439, Matthew McVay/Folio, Inc.; 440, Spencer Tirey/Liaison International; 441(l), Reed Saxon/AP/Wide World Photos; 441(r), Susan Sterner/ AP/Wide World Photos; 442, The Granger Collection, New York; 443, Archive Photos; 444, Gary Gardiner/AP/Wide World Photos; 446, L. Dematteis/The Image Works; 449, Tom Pantages; 450, AP/Wide World Photos; 452-453(bdr), Image Copyright © 1996 Photodisc, Inc.; 454, HRW photos by Lance Schriner; 456, 457 (all), HRW Photo by Sam Dudgeon.

Unit 7: 458-459, © 1990, Joseph Sohm/ChromoSohm. **Chapter 20**: Page 460, Joseph Sohm/ChromoSohm; 461, ©Dennis MacDonald/PhotoEdit; 463, Rhoda Sidney/PhotoEdit; 465, © 1987 Rick Browne/The Stock Shop/Medichrome; 466, Steve Helber/AP/Wide World Photos;469(bdr), Peter Poulides/Tony Stone Images; (other), The Granger Collection, New York; 472, Bob Bird/AP/Wide World Photos; 475, © Brian Yarvin ©1990/The Image Works; 476, Jim McKnight/AP/Wide World Photos; 478-479(bdr), Image Copyright © 1996 Photodisc, Inc. **Chapter 21**: Page 480, Don & Pat Valenti/Tony Stone Images; 481, Donovan Reese/Tony Stone Images; 482, Dick Durrance II/Woodfin Camp & Associates; 483(bdr), Brian Stablyk/Tony Stone Images; (other), David Robeau; 484, Photri; 485, © Mark C. Burnett/Stock, Boston; 486, David R. Frazier Photolibrary; 487(t), © Paula Lerner/Woodfin Camp & Associates; 487(b), Mark E. Gibson; 489, © Bob Daemmrich/Tony Stone Images; 491, © Ian Shaw/Tony Stone Images; 494, © Charles Gupton/Stock, Boston; 495(t), Michelle Bridwell/Frontera Fotos; 495(b), © Kevin Horan/Stock, Boston; 496, ©Pedrick/The Image Works; 498-499(bdr), 500, Image Copyright © 1996 PhotoDisc, Inc.; 502, HRW Photo by Russell Dian.

Unit 8: Page 504-505, UN/Sygma. **Chapter 22**: Page 506, Eric Bouvet/Gamma Liaison; 508, © William Campbell/SYGMA; 509, The Granger Collection, New York; 510, © Alan Schein/The Stock Market; 511, Tomas Sodergen/MIRA/Impact Visuals; 512(t), E.T. Archive; 512(b), © '95 Josef Polleross/The Stock Market; 513, Voice of America/U.S. Information Agency; 514, © Andrei Iliescu/AP/Wide World Photos; 515, Giraudon/Art Resource, NY; 516, Sovfoto/Eastfoto; 517(both), AKG Photo;518, Ria-Novosti/Sovfoto; 519(bdr), Peter Poulides/Tony Stone Images; 519(other), Peggy Plummer/Black Star; 520, Sovfoto/Eastfoto; 521, © Alain Keller/SYGMA; 524-525(bdr), Image Copyright © 1996 Photodisc, Inc. **Chapter 23**: 526, Luc Novovitch/Gamma Liaison; 527, Betty Press/Woodfin Camp & Associates; 528, Nathan Benn/Woodfin Camp & Associates; 529, © 1997 Alex S. MacLean/Landslides; 532, © P. Robert/SYGMA; 533, Superstock; 534, © Stephen Ferry/Gamma Liaison; 535, Paul Howell/Gamma Liaison; 536, Diego Giudice/AP/Wide World Photos; 537, © 1987 by Herblock in *The Washington Post;* 538, Photri; 539, © Laski Diffusion/Gamma Liaison; 540, Earth Base/Gamma Liaison; 541(bdr), Brian Stablyk/Tony Stone Images; (other), Steve Maines/Stock, Boston; 543, FPIJ Pool/Sipa Press; 544, Peter Wilson/Sylvia Cordaiy Photo Library Ltd.; 545, Cynthia Johnson/The Gamma Liaison Network; 546, Jeffrey Aaronson/Network Aspen; 547, Mark Harvey/Network Aspen; 548, Wally McNamee/Woodfin Camp & Associates; 550-551(bdr), Image Copyright © 1996 Photodisc, Inc.; 552, Sandra Baker/Gamma Liaison; 553, Image Copyright © 1996 Photodisc, Inc.

Reference Section: Pages 556-557, Uniphoto, Inc.